GUSTAVUS ADOLPHUS

VOLUME ONE

THE SOUTH AFRICAN OPPOSITION 1939-1945
An Essay in Contemporary History
by MICHAEL ROBERTS and A. E. G. TROLLIP

GUSTAVUS ADOLPHUS

A History of Sweden
1611–1632

by

MICHAEL ROBERTS

Professor of History, Rhodes University
Grahamstown, South Africa

VOLUME ONE

1611-1626

LONGMANS, GREEN AND CO
LONDON □ NEW YORK □ TORONTO

LONGMANS, GREEN AND CO LTD
6 & 7 CLIFFORD STREET LONDON W 1
ALSO AT MELBOURNE AND CAPE TOWN

LONGMANS, GREEN AND CO INC
55 FIFTH AVENUE NEW YORK 3

LONGMANS, GREEN AND CO
215 VICTORIA STREET TORONTO 1

ORIENT LONGMANS LTD
BOMBAY CALCUTTA MADRAS

First published 1953

Edinburgh : Printed in Great Britain by T. and A. CONSTABLE LTD.

To
my friends in Sweden

Gud glädje och styrke de män, som där bo
Vid älvom, på berg och i dalom !

PREFACE

EVERYBODY who has tried to teach the history of Europe in the seventeenth century must at some time or other have felt the want of an up-to-date account of Sweden's 'Age of Greatness'. No such account, as far as I am aware, exists in English; and a glance at the very meagre sections devoted to Scandinavian affairs in such otherwise reliable modern series as *Peuples et Civilisations* or *Clio* would seem to suggest that the position is no better in France. In Germany, indeed, there appeared in 1932 the third and final volume of Johannes Paul's *Gustaf Adolf*; but this was a work devoted mainly to diplomatic and military history, with the emphasis upon the period from 1630 to 1632, and in any case it appears to be less well known in England than it ought to be.

This book, then, is an attempt to fill a portion of the gap. It makes no pretension to archival research (for which, indeed, a lifetime would be needed); but it is based as far as possible on the printed sources (which are abundant), and it attempts to synthesize the large body of research which has appeared since the corresponding chapters in *The Cambridge Modern History* were written, nearly half a century ago. It differs, perhaps, from many books on the subject in treating the reign as a portion of the history of Sweden, rather than as an episode in the history of Germany; but it has no other claim to originality. To any Swedish readers I can but plead that the book is written for an English public; and add, in the words of the author of *The Swedish Discipline*, that

I doe it not upon any vaine thoughts or presumption, to teach you *new wayes*: a many of you, and your *Leaders* especially, are so curious, I know, and so skilful . . . that you need not my Booke for a Maister in this kinde. 'Tis meant for your *Recreation*, to put you in a *Discourse* now and then: and to testifie withall, mine owne *private respects* both to your *Persons*, and of your *Practise*; thats the purpose of it.

I take this opportunity to return thanks to the Council of Rhodes University, for their generosity in awarding me a Travelling Fellowship to enable me to spend some months in Swedish libraries. Nor can I omit to express my gratitude to the staff of Kungliga Biblioteket in Stockholm for their kindness and courtesy while I was working there. I am most grateful to those of my colleagues who found time to read all or part of the MS.; and especially to Mrs. W. A. Maxwell, Mr. Godfrey Le May and Mr. Alan Hall, whose criticisms have, I hope, been attended to.

The spelling of proper names in foreign languages is a perennial problem. Since many Swedish and Danish names have no English equivalent, I have thought it better to make it a rule to spell all Scandinavian names as they are spelt in their own languages, including that of Gustavus Adolphus himself, who henceforward will be 'Gustav Adolf'. There is, however, one Scandinavian name which it would be pedantic not to write in its English form; and accordingly I write 'Copenhagen' rather than 'København'. Non-Scandinavian proper names are, where possible, given in their English form.

M. R.

CONTENTS

CONTENTS

PLATES

The photograph of the statue of Johannes Rudbeckius is
by Lena Böklin. All other photographs are copyright
Svenska Porträttarkivet, Nationalmuseum, Stockholm.

MAPS

The publishers are indebted to Försvarsstaben, Krighis-torika Avdelningen for permission to use maps in *Gustaf II Adolf* in preparing the maps in this book.

ARGUMENT

THE reign of Gustav Adolf changed the course of Swedish history, and in doing so changed the course of European history too. The contrast between the position in 1611, when a beaten, impoverished and insignificant Sweden lay almost unregarded on the periphery of the Protestant world, and the position in 1632, when Sweden gave the law to Germany, bullied Richelieu, dominated the Baltic, and stood unchallenged at the head of evangelical Europe—this is a contrast that needs no pointing. Historians in England and on the Continent have been understandably apt to concentrate their attention upon the brilliant and crowded period which lies between the landing at Peenemünde and the tragic apotheosis of Lützen, and to interest themselves in Gustav Adolf only when, with the intervention at Stralsund, he begins to impinge directly upon the main stream of European history. But the saving of Stralsund and the glory of Breitenfeld are not adequately to be explained or understood unless the painful efforts of the first decade and a half of the reign are understood too. The key to the deliverance of German Protestantism is not to be found in the general course of European affairs, still less in the bloody confusion of Germany: it lies in the story of Sweden's recovery from the humiliation of 1613, in her stubborn struggle against encircling enemies, in the great constructive reforms which were the work of her King and ministers. And it is with that story that this volume will be concerned.

The history of the reign divides clearly at the beginning of the year 1626, when Gustav Adolf, fresh from his first important victory over the Poles at Wallhof, decides to transfer the seat of war from Livonia to Prussia. The period from 1611 to 1626 has a logical unity of its own. It is the record of Sweden's battle, in the first instance for survival, and afterwards for security. It begins at a moment when it seemed at least possible that Kristian IV of Denmark would conquer the country; and it continues through precarious years of strain, in which the intrigues of the Polish Vasas to recover the throne they had lost in 1600 are a recurrent menace. For the first ten years of the reign Sweden appears almost as a fortress beset by foes. She makes sorties now and then (as in 1617); she

A

fights on bastions pushed far out from the centre of defence (as in Russia); she is haunted always by the fear of the traitor within the gates. Outside, Denmark and Poland await her collapse with greedy expectancy; inside, the antiquated administration can barely cope with an alarming breakdown of law and order, and more than once the country hovers on the brink of bankruptcy. Little by little, after infinite efforts and some mistakes, the King and his ministers bring the situation under control; the work of reform begins to gather momentum; the outside world which had treated Karl IX so coldly begins to warm towards his son, and an ally appears here and there. Peace with Russia succeeds peace with Denmark; against all probability Älvsborg is recovered; the agents of Poland are kept in check by the savage penalties of the Ordinance of Örebro; the King is crowned at last, and by his marriage with a Princess of Brandenburg inflicts a diplomatic defeat upon his cousin of Poland. By 1620 it appears reasonably certain that Sweden is to survive, and that the younger line of Vasas is to rule her.

It was a question of more than local interest. The stakes for which Gustaf Adolf had been playing were high; and the issue involved all Europe. The restoration of Sigismund of Poland to the Swedish throne would have meant the triumph of Catholicism in northern Europe. It might have meant the passing of the control of the Sound into Catholic hands; the destruction of Dutch trade to the Baltic; and hence, perhaps, the subjection of the Netherlands to the Spanish Crown. And with the Netherlands once crushed, the power of the Habsburg family alliance might have been restored to something like its condition sixty or seventy years before, and Germany and France (the France of Marie de Medicis) might have seen the nightmare of Habsburg domination of Europe become a reality. If, on the other hand, Sweden had become politically dependent upon Denmark—if Älvsborg had not been recovered—then the mercantile states of the west must certainly have felt the effects of Denmark's stranglehold upon the Baltic trade, and the Hanse towns must have been gravely weakened in their efforts to resist Danish dynastic imperialism in north Germany. Thus, though the story of Sweden in these years may seem obscure and parochial, it is not really so: something important is happening, just as it was in England in the years between 1558 and 1588. The period is a period of preparation: preparation for a dramatic and decisive entry upon the stage of world history.

With 1621 comes a slight change of emphasis. Survival has now been assured; but the problem of security remains. Yet it is still essentially a Scandinavian and dynastic problem. It is true that the troubles of Bohemia are spreading confusion in ever-widening circles over Germany, and the Protestant powers make efforts to organize a united front of resistance to the progress of Emperor and League. It is true that from time to time appeals are directed to Gustav Adolf to join in a general coalition. But these appeals are all in the end without result; for before 1626 the threat to Sweden—the main threat, the immediate threat—does not come from Germany at all. It comes, as it had come in the years from 1611 to 1620, from the old enemies Poland and Denmark: from Poland, because Sigismund III declines to abandon his attempt to make good by force of arms his pretensions upon the Swedish throne; from Denmark, because the restless ambition of Kristian IV is not to be trusted, because the ancient matters of dispute between the kingdoms (and some new ones too) keep their relations in a state of latent hostility which on occasion comes very near to issuing in an open breach. Hence Gustav Adolf, with the possibility of war on two fronts always before him, finds it impossible to embark upon enterprises on behalf of the Protestant cause in Germany without full security against attack from Warsaw and Copenhagen; and such security (at least as regards Poland) the western powers are never able even to promise, and still less to make good. Consequently, Gustav Adolf is forced to continue his war with Sigismund, and with respect to Kristian to be *toujours en vedette*. In 1624, indeed, a great crisis in Sweden's relations with Denmark ends in a settlement which marks a real turning-point: Sweden carries all her demands, Denmark gives way, and there is virtually an end of real danger from that side, at least for the present. But no peace nor lasting truce is to be had from Poland. It is in an effort to extort peace quickly that Gustav Adolf in the summer of 1626 abandons the Livonian theatre of operations and seeks to strangle Polish resistance by getting a grip upon the Vistula.

From this moment the political climate begins to show a rapid change for the worse. Denmark goes down to disaster at Lutter; the Imperialist armies appear on the Baltic shore; the attempt to force a quick decision in Poland proves a failure. The Danish collapse throws Gustav Adolf's time-table out of reckoning: the danger from Germany, which had seemed inferior in importance to the need for finishing with Poland, becomes acute much earlier than might have been expected. Gustav Adolf has scarcely landed in Prussia before he is driven to take the situation in Germany into account. He is drawn swiftly into participation in the German struggle, into collaboration with Denmark, into the expedition to Stralsund; and Poland, from being the prime consideration, becomes a nuisance to be abated with the aid of Richelieu's diplomacy. The period which began in 1611, the period of essentially Scandinavian concerns, is over for ever, and a wider prospect is opening. That security which hitherto had been sought by thwarting the designs of Kristian and defeating the pretensions of Sigismund is obviously no longer attainable by so modest a programme; and the King is drawn on step by step to seek it in the defence of north Germany, the conquest of central Germany, the occupation of south Germany, and even in the invasion of Alsace. The quest for security, in fact, has ceased to be a Baltic, and has become a European affair.

This fateful extension of Sweden's interests could hardly have been undertaken at all had Sweden in 1626 been still the country she was in 1611. But the years between the King's accession and the transference of the war to Prussia were not merely years in which the external foe was repelled, the bastions held, the strength of the garrison built up for the eventual sortie; they were years of intense creative activity in every sphere of national life, years of reforms, developments, innovations, experiments, in all civil and military matters. Before it is possible to understand how it was that a country so small in population was able to play the part in Europe that Sweden played, from Breitenfeld to Pultava, before any consideration of the political and military history of the period which begins in 1626, it is essential to obtain some idea of the moral and material resources which were the preconditions of the Swedish military triumphs. The narrative of events therefore pauses at the year 1626, and we proceed to an examination of the progress made in various departments of national life since 1611: to the development of the constitution, the part played by the Church, the great efforts in the field of education, the new spirit of resurgent Gothicism in thought and literature. It is plain, too, that we must know something of the social structure and economic development of the country; of the administrative and tactical reforms which shaped the new Swedish armies; of the great efforts which laid the foundations for a powerful Swedish navy. All these things contributed, in greater or lesser degree, to the Swedish victories. But the provision of the sinews of war, the reorganization of the army and the evolution of a new system of tactics, the securing of the command of the seas—all obviously of prime importance as providing the basis for Sweden's emergence as a great power—can best be appreciated when they are considered in relation to the campaigns in Germany with which they are so closely connected. It seemed better, therefore, to defer the treatment of them to a second volume; and in the present volume we deal only with those aspects of national regeneration which exercised a less direct influence upon the course of events in Germany. It is possible that to some readers it may appear that they have been allotted a disproportionate share of space in comparison with that devoted to the political narrative. Yet, after all, Sweden's brief career as a great military power ended more than two hundred years ago: the martial glories of the seventeenth century were but a brilliant episode. No doubt it was an episode of high importance; but it was out of line with the main course of Swedish history. The effect of these military triumphs upon the future of the country, great as it was, was less enduring than some other influences that have made less noise in the world; and though Breitenfeld may have been a turning-point in the history of Germany, this book is designed to be a history of Sweden. The strength of Swedish Lutheranism, the survival of a free peasantry, the expansion of the country's economic resources, the unrelaxing grip on the idea of liberty and the rule of law—these, when all is said and done, are the real stuff of Swedish history; and in the long run the foundation of the *gymnasia* and the endowment of Uppsala University have probably meant more to Sweden than all the captured standards of Tilly and Wallenstein.

Such, then, is the scope of this volume. But to read the history of Sweden in the seventeenth century without knowing at least something of what came before is as misleading as it would be to consider the reign of Elizabeth in ignorance of that of Henry VIII, or to omit any notice of the work of Ferdinand and Isabella from an account of sixteenth-century Spain. If we are to grasp the nature of the crisis which confronted Gustav Adolf upon his accession, we must have some knowledge of the factors which went to produce it: some knowledge, therefore, of the history of Sweden in the preceding fifty or sixty years. Chapter I, then, endeavours to provide the bare minimum of information necessary to make what follows intelligible.

CHAPTER I

INTRODUCTORY

(i) *The Struggle for Baltic predominance, 1560-95*

ABOUT the middle of the sixteenth century the long-drawn struggle for the mastery of the Baltic entered upon a new and critical phase. The days when the Hanse had held a dominant position in these waters were now long gone by. Since the middle of the fourteenth century Denmark had been struggling to break that domination, and since the beginning of the fifteenth she had herself been a strong competitor for the sovereignty of the sea. The rise of Denmark was naturally repugnant to the Hanse, who fought hard to maintain themselves in something like their former position. From time to time favourable circumstances gave them an opportunity to reassert themselves; and thus it was that in the first quarter of the sixteenth century Lübeck was able to use the internal troubles of the Scandinavian kingdoms to regain some of her former political influence: in 1524 she arbitrated between Denmark and Sweden, and both Gustav Vasa and Fredrik I of Denmark could fairly be said to owe their thrones to her support, and to reign by her favour. But the ill-advised adventure of the Counts' War in the early 'thirties brought this brilliant period of her history to a disastrous close; and the great naval defeat of 16 June 1535, at the hands of the combined fleets of Denmark and Sweden, really eliminated Lübeck and the Hanse from the political race. Economically, they had already been hard hit by the tolls which Denmark imposed upon ships passing through the Sound, and their efforts to develop an alternative route by portage across the neck of the Slesvig isthmus were not very successful. To the eastward, their interests had been prejudiced by the consolidation and expansion of the Muscovite realm. The great Hanseatic emporium for the eastern trade had been Novgorod; but in the 'seventies of the fifteenth century Novgorod lost its independence and became subject to Moscow; and in 1494 Ivan III closed the Hanse's establishment there and revoked their trading privileges. The purpose of this measure was to cut out the Hanseatic middlemen and open up direct trade be-

tween Muscovy and the West; its effect was to transfer the activities
of the middlemen to coastal towns such as Narva, Reval and Riga,
and to the great inland city of Pskov, whose water communications
through Lake Peipus made it easily accessible. This in its turn
spurred on the rulers of Muscovy to press on their advance against
Pskov and the Baltic littoral, that they might get these towns into
their hands. By the opening of the sixteenth century the struggle
for the control of the trade-routes to Russia had begun; and so too
had the long drama of Russia's attempts to obtain an outlet to the
sea. It was a situation which had political as well as economic
implications. The foreign policy of the Tsars, henceforward directed
to the 'recovery' of what they were pleased to consider their patri-
mony, pressed uncomfortably upon their neighbours. It must
necessarily alarm Sweden, whose eastern frontier in Finland marched
with Russian territory for hundreds of miles of unmapped and un-
beaconed wilderness, and whose foreign policy by long tradition
looked towards the east. Already in the later fifteenth century
Sweden's rulers had been made sensible of the danger of Russian
aggression in this quarter, and of the possibility of the revival of
ancient claims which would, if conceded, have given Russia access
to the Gulf of Bothnia. Equally threatened by Russian expansion
were Poland and Lithuania, then at the height of their power and
prosperity, and themselves just awakening to the consciousness
of the need for a better stretch of coastline.

The ambitions of the Baltic powers must probably in any case
have come into violent conflict, but an occasion was provided by
the collapse, at the close of the 1550's, of the political power of the
old crusading Order of the Knights of the Sword. In the Middle
Ages this Order had done effective work in extirpating or forcibly
converting the heathen of the Düna region; and when this task
was completed it had maintained a long intermittent struggle with
the Poles. Latterly, however, it had fallen upon evil days. Its
brothers-in-arms, the Teutonic Knights of East Prussia, had been
turned into a secular principality by a Hohenzollern Grand Master
in 1525, and the Knights of Estonia and Livonia had gradually
settled into a peaceful and unenterprising existence in which all
trace of their former martial qualities had been lost. Their helpless
condition had now become apparent to their covetous neighbours,
and not least to the Tsar Ivan IV. It was not difficult for him to
fabricate claims to the lands he desired, nor was it a hard matter to

terrorize the Grand Master of the Order. It was more difficult, and indeed it was to prove impossible, to exclude Poland from a share of the plunder; for when the blow fell upon the Knights they naturally turned to their southern neighbour for assistance, and that assistance was promptly given. But Poland was not the only Baltic state to intervene. The King of Denmark was interested in the fate of Livonia, for he had inherited some antiquated claims to the island of Ösel, which he now took the opportunity to acquire by purchase. Russia meanwhile had occupied Dorpat and Narva, and Poland was beginning the conquest of such portions of the country as lay most conveniently adjacent to her own territory. It was at this juncture that the great trading city of Reval appealed to Gustav Vasa for aid. At first the appeal went unanswered, for as recently as 1557 Sweden had concluded hostilities on the Finnish border by a forty-years' truce with Russia, and Gustav had no wish to reopen that question. The accession of Erik XIV in 1560, however, put a different face on the matter. Erik perceived the opportunity and seized it. The invitation from Reval was accepted, and an expeditionary force was sent to Estonia. With its despatch Sweden entered upon a new and momentous period of her history, which was not to terminate until 1721.

Erik's intervention was a sign that Sweden was no longer prepared to stand aside and see the great questions of Baltic politics decided without her participation. Even before his accession he had interested himself in these problems: his attempt to win the hand of Elizabeth of England was part of a plan for an English-Swedish-Russian *entente* which should dominate the Baltic trade-routes and eliminate the Sound Tolls by moving goods across Sweden by a canal which was to link the North Sea and the Baltic. The end-ports and staple-towns for this trade must however be under Swedish control. One such staple-town Sweden possessed already, in Viborg; but Erik could not suffer the whole of the south coast of the Gulf of Finland to pass into other hands; and above all he disliked the Russian attempt to force trade to Narva. The appeal from Reval was therefore peculiarly timely. If Erik could conquer the Estonian coastline, he would control both shores of the Gulf of Finland, and would then be in a position to claim that the Gulf was a Swedish 'stream', flowing through Swedish territory, and able to be closed or opened by him at his choice. It was in accordance with this theory that Erik in 1562 declared Narva blockaded, and prohibited all trade to that port; and so opened a controversy which was not settled until Sweden captured Narva in 1581.

The doctrine of *mare clausum*, thus applied by Erik to the Gulf of Finland, was the basis of Denmark's political position in the Baltic, for it was in virtue of this doctrine that she imposed tolls upon the shipping passing through the Sound. Sweden was not herself dependent for her contacts with western Europe upon traffic going this way, for she had an outlet to the open sea at the mouth of the Göta river; and here Swedish Kings strove hard to build up a port around the fortress of Älvsborg. But this was an outlet so narrow as to be highly precarious. From the north the Danish-Norwegian province of Bohuslän ran down almost to the river; and equally close at hand to the south was the Danish province of Halland. In any war with Denmark it would need great efforts to prevent the jaws of these pincers from closing and severing Sweden's line of communications westwards. In other respects too Sweden's geopolitical position in regard to Denmark was highly unsatisfactory. It was perhaps no great matter that the provinces of Jämtland and Härjedalen, which by geography were clearly Swedish, should be in Norwegian hands, for Sweden's communications northward were secured in any case by sea, and the danger from Jämtland was small; but it was something more than an inconvenience that Halland, Skåne and Blekinge should be separated from Sweden; for these were rich agricultural provinces whose towns and ports were the natural markets of the Swedish upland, and they formed the ideal base from which Danish armies could invade Sweden. And above all they were so many links in a chain of possessions which ran from the Danish islands through Skåne, Bornholm and Gotland, and was now reaching out to the Livonian coast by the new acquisition of Ösel. The effect was that more and more of the Baltic could be plausibly represented to be Danish territorial waters, and that Sweden's communications with north Germany became more and more vulnerable to attack. Apart, therefore, from Erik's ambitious economic schemes, apart from the well-established Swedish nervousness at any advance on the part of Russia, there was good reason for intervention in Estonia, if only to scotch the threat of Danish 'encirclement'.

The collapse of the states of the Order of the Sword, in fact, constituted a critical point in the history of all the states of north-eastern Europe. The great question of supremacy in the Baltic was suddenly posed, and the countries of the littoral were plunged into a struggle which was to last for more than a century and a half. Opening as a contest between Poland and Russia, it set in motion forces which were eventually to lead to the Swedish attempt to establish a hegemony in the Baltic. The whole extraordinary development of the Swedish empire has its roots in the reign of Erik XIV, and Breitenfeld and Klissow are in a sense implicit in the insignificant expedition to Reval. For, once possessed of a thin strip of territory in Estonia, once established in Reval, Sweden could not afford to abandon her acquisitions to any greedy or powerful neighbour, and must therefore seek the best means to defend them. The safest means—perhaps the only means in the long run—was by pushing back the frontier to a defensible line, by securing the land-bridge round the head of the Gulf of Finland (to link Finland with Estonia), and thus incidentally by excluding Russia from the Baltic Sea.

For the moment, however, these considerations had to take second place to the more immediate danger from Denmark. Fredrik II of Denmark felt that Erik had stolen a march on him in Estonia; he undoubtedly wished to restore the old Union of the three Scandinavian countries; and considerations of internal politics made it desirable for him to force on a war. He determined therefore to pick a quarrel. This was not very difficult, since there was a stock of petty disputes and 'questions of honour' between the two countries which could always be relied upon to provide the pretext for a war. Erik was thus forced to concentrate on repelling a Danish invasion, and found it expedient for the moment to court the friendship of the Tsar; while Denmark found allies in Poland, who hoped to use the occasion to evict Sweden from Estonia, and in Lübeck, who resented Erik's stopping of the trade to Narva. Erik for his part entered upon the war not unwillingly, for he had been carrying out remarkable experiments in military organization and tactical dispositions, and he was disposed to seize an opportunity to test them. But the Seven Years' War of the North (1563-70) was less successful for Sweden than he had hoped, and proved indeed a sufficiently costly experiment. Before it had ended, Erik had been deposed (1568), and his successor Johan III hastened to make peace. The Treaty of Stettin, which concluded the war, threatened to be extremely onerous to Sweden (among other things, it would have deprived her of all her conquests in Estonia), but by persistent procrastination she was able to avoid fulfilling any of its provisions except one. That one concerned the ransoming of Älvsborg, which the Danes had captured in the course of the war; and here the most urgent considerations of national security impelled her to pay the prescribed amount as soon as possible. The heavy financial burden involved in redeeming this vital position brought home to Sweden once again the reality of the danger of a Danish *dominium* in the Baltic.

The conclusion of the Danish war left Johan III free to turn his attention to the struggle for Livonia. Here Poland and Russia continued their efforts to overrun the country, and even Denmark did not relinquish her claims until 1578. Johan realized, as Erik had realized, that Sweden could not hope to fight Poland and Russia simultaneously; but unlike Erik he chose to cooperate not with Russia but with Poland. For several years before his accession his relations with Poland had been cordial; he had married a Jagiełłon wife; and he regarded Ivan IV as his personal enemy. But apart from these considerations it was plain that for the moment Sweden's interests accorded with Poland's better than with Russia's. Both Poland and Sweden desired to exclude Russia from the sea. Each desired to prevent the establishment of Narva as the great staple for trade with Russia. Each was anxious to deter the Muscovite from importing armaments and 'strategic raw materials'. And each was suspicious of the designs of Denmark. At this point, however, their interests diverged. Poland would have liked to overrun the whole littoral up to the Neva; failing that, she wished at least to secure Riga and Pernau on the coast, and Dorpat and Pskov inland. Her King, Stefan Batory, dreamed of a conquest of Russia and the establishment of a great Slav empire to be ruled from Warsaw. Johan III, on his side, already coveted Pernau and Dorpat, and was shortly to define his war-aims as the cession to Sweden of Novgorod and Pskov. In the long run, therefore, the clash of interests would probably prevent any firm friendship between the two countries; but for the moment, at all events, a certain measure of military collaboration was possible.

Thus Poland and Sweden fought side by side in Livonia, where the war dragged on throughout the 'seventies without decisive advantage to either party. But with the beginning of the 'eighties the tide of fortune took a sudden turn. In 1580 the Swedish commander, Pontus de la Gardie, captured Kexholm, and in the following year, aided by Batory's memorable but fruitless siege of

Pskov, the Swedes conquered almost the whole of Estonia, and rounded off their successes by the taking of Narva. Johan no doubt hoped that the possession of Narva would give Sweden the control of the Russia trade, which in the past twenty years had flowed in great volume through that port; and to the indignation of Reval he hastened to transfer the Swedish staple thither. But the hope proved illusory. The trade filtered away by other channels: through Pskov to Dorpat, Riga and Pernau; or to Königsberg, Elbing and Danzig; or—worst of all—by a new route, opened or reopened by English navigators in 1553: the route by the White Sea and St. Nicholas. Already in 1555 the Muscovy Company had been founded; already by the 'seventies the new route was used by the Dutch; and the Swedish capture of Narva had the effect of driving more and more shipping round the North Cape. In 1584 the town of Archangel was founded. Johan III observed these developments with chagrin. If skippers were to be forced to sail to Narva, the way by Archangel must be blocked up. For the first time, therefore, the question of the Russian trade-routes was linked with that of Sweden's peaceful penetration of the Arctic. It was a development which was to have important consequences a quarter of a century later.

Meanwhile Batory had abandoned his ambitions in Russia, and in 1582 had concluded a ten-years' truce at Jam Zapolsky, leaving Sweden to continue the struggle alone. His death in 1586 created a vacancy on the Polish throne; and after many hesitations and deliberations Johan III at last allowed his son Sigismund to be put forward as a candidate—mainly, it appears, because he hoped that a dynastic union would ensure a common effort against the Russians. Sigismund, at his mother's desire, had been brought up a Roman Catholic, and as he grew older he became an ardent devotee. His religion, his Jagiełłon mother, his youth, and the fact that he was not a German, all commended his cause to that section of the Polish nobility which disliked the Habsburgs, and aimed in foreign policy at continuing the great traditions of Batory. Led by Zamoyski, this party succeeded in carrying the election, and the heir-apparent of Sweden became Sigismund III of Poland.

The event was greeted with satisfaction on both sides of the Baltic. Sweden and Poland, firmly bound by the dynastic link, seemed likely to become joint lords of the North. The Russian menace would be definitively removed; the united weight of the

Swedish and Polish navies would make short work of any remaining Danish dreams of *dominium maris*. The prospect, so fair in appearance, proved false in reality. From the moment of Sigismund's accession it became clear that the union would be an uneasy one, for neither country was prepared to give way to the other in the matter of their rival claims to the possession of Estonia. It did not need much foresight to perceive that the ruler of two countries whose institutions and political interests were so widely at variance would soon find himself in a delicate situation. A Polish-Swedish alliance served a natural and intelligible purpose—the presentation of a common front against Danish domination and Russian encroachment; but to convert that alliance into a union was, as a recent Polish historian has remarked, 'nonsense'[1]: it raised needless difficulties, and did not, as the event proved from the very beginning, lead to any closer cooperation between the two states.

Meanwhile Sweden had been left to carry on her war with Russia unaided, and she had not found the task easy. The gains of 1581 could not all be permanently held, and she was glad at last to make a two-years' truce in 1593, which was converted in 1595 into the peace of Täysinä. This treaty, which stabilized for the moment the position in the eastern Baltic, registered a marked Swedish advance. Though Sweden retroceded the fortress and fief of Kexholm to the Russians, her right to Estonia and Narva was now admitted; and though she renounced her claims (such as they were) upon the Kola Peninsula, she secured an agreed rectification of her eastern frontier in Finland which gave her an undisputed right of access to the Arctic Ocean, and, incidentally, shut out for good the old Russian claims to a position on the Gulf of Bothnia. The Russian window to the west was not yet blocked up, but it was becoming dangerously narrowed.[2]

[1] Wł. Konopczyński: *Dzieje Polski Nowożytnej*, I. 179.

[2] For the question of *dominium maris Baltici* and the Russian trade-routes, see especially: A. Attman, *Den ryska marknaden i 1500-talets baltiska politik; id. Till det Östersjöväldets problematik* (in *Studier tillägn. Curt Weibull*); I. Andersson, *Erik XIV:s engelska underhandlingar*; A. G. Hassø, *Den danske Regering og Kofferdifarten Nord om Norge i det 16. Aarhundrede*; S. Arnell, *Die Auflösung des Livländischen Ordensstaates*; W. Sobieski, *Der Kampf um die Ostsee*; E. Hornborg, *Kampen om Östersjön*; C. E. Hill, *The Danish Sound Dues and the command of the Baltic*; A. Szelągowski, *Der Kampf um die Ostsee, 1544-1621*; G. Jenš, *Rivalry between Riga and Tartu for the trade with Pskov* (*Baltic and Scandinavian Countries*, 1938); S. Kutrzeba, *Danzig and Poland in History* (*Baltic and Scandinavian Countries*, 1938); I. Lubimenko, *The Struggle of the Dutch with the English for the Russian Market in the Seventeenth Century* (*Trans. Royal Hist. Soc.* 4th Series, vol. vii.).

(ii) *The Swedish Revolution, 1593-1600*

Before the war with Russia had reached its provisional ending at
the peace of Täysinä, Sigismund III of Poland had succeeded his
father as King of Sweden. This event, which took place in 1592,
opened a new chapter in Swedish history, and was to lead to
consequences pregnant with importance for the whole Baltic area.
For Sigismund contrived very soon after his accession to involve
himself in difficulties with his Swedish subjects; those difficulties
in the end led to his eviction from Sweden; and this in turn to a war
between Sweden and Poland which lasted, with long intermissions,
for more than half a century.

In the prolonged crisis which led up to Sigismund's deposition
two main issues were at stake: the one constitutional, the other
religious. Both took their rise in the reign of Gustav Vasa. Gustav
Vasa had been the liberator of Sweden from the Danish yoke, the
architect of her independence; and as the only visible bulwark
against anarchy, or (what was worse) a Danish reconquest, he had
been in an exceptionally strong position. He was the only nucleus
around which a new and healthy national life could crystallize, and
he had therefore usually been able to silence opposition or complaint
by a simple threat to abdicate. The nobility's ranks had been thinned
in the troubles which preceded liberation, and some of them were
discredited by association with the party which had wished to maintain the Union with Denmark. The old Council of the Realm
(*riksråd*), which in mediaeval times had formed the main check upon
the monarchy, was no longer able to discharge that constitutional
function. The relatively new institution of the Diet (*riksdag*) was
carefully cultivated by the King, who had as a rule little difficulty
in associating it with his policies. By the end of Gustav Vasa's
reign there was really no body or order in the state which was able
to exercise an effective check upon his actions (though it is true that
as far as possible he avoided proceedings which ran counter to the
wishes of the mass of his subjects); and he had in consequence
secured for himself an authority such as no King in Sweden had
enjoyed before him. A decisive step was taken in 1544, when by
the Succession Pact (*arvförening*) of Västerås the Crown was
recognized by the *riksdag* as hereditary and not elective. Thus
already in Gustav Vasa's time the monarchy was evolving in the

direction of a parliamentary despotism of the Tudor type; and in the time of his successor, Erik XIV, the evolution was pushed a good deal further.

These developments ran contrary to a long-established constitutional tradition. There had long lain upon every King a general obligation to govern his kingdom with the advice of his *riksråd*; and since the middle of the fourteenth century the great magnates who comprised that body had often appeared as the champions of the rule of law, as the guardians and interpreters of the constitution, almost as umpires between King and people. Under the early Vasas they wholly lost this position. The *råd* as a body now met but rarely; its members were scattered and politically unimportant; and the economic basis of its power no longer appeared formidable in comparison with the wealth of a monarchy gorged with the spoils of the Church. Government was paternal, personal and primitive; the King's eye was upon everything, the King's hand was set to an immense diversity of business, from the high concerns of foreign politics to the pettiest details of the marketing and consumption of these perishable foodstuffs which formed so large a proportion of the royal income; and his ministers were his clerks and bailiffs. The concentration of manors in the King's hand afforded a solid basis for his power, and his creation of duchies for his younger sons was designed to provide a similarly solid basis for the claims of the junior members of his House against the contingency of a failure of the senior line. In the 'forties Gustav Vasa did indeed experiment with Burgundian administrative methods, introduced into Sweden by his German minister Konrad von Pyhy; but the experiment was short and unsuccessful, and the close of his reign saw the central government still as rudimentary as it had been in the years immediately after his accession. But already by the middle of the century the burden of personal supervision was proving too great; the old manorial methods of administration were beginning to break down; and under Erik XIV the monarchy began to cast about for further assistance. In Gustav Vasa's time the old *råd*-families had been incapable, for lack of education, of providing such assistance; indeed, it had been difficult to find, among his unlettered subjects, even the handful of indispensable clerks which he required. But in the 'sixties a new generation was growing up, a generation educated at the north German universities, able to conduct correspondence in German and Latin, skilled in theological subtleties, and well versed in contemporary trends of political thought. Erik found his ministers among such men; but he chose them, on good Machiavellian principles, from the non-noble classes. Government remained still largely the King's personal government; the new 'secretaries' were his agents, mere extensions of his sovereignty, the projections of the royal will.

The accession of Johan III in 1568 did not really change the situation. Johan, like his brother, attempted to rule the country by methods which were no more than a modification of the *ad hoc* devices of Gustav Vasa. Like Erik, he relied on base-born secretaries; and when he died the central government was as unorganized, and almost as patriarchal, as ever. By thus failing to provide an administration suited to the changed times, the monarchy was forfeiting the position of authority which the creative energy of Gustav Vasa had won for it. It was precisely this creative energy which had formed the real justification for its emancipation from those constitutional checks which had been devised during the mediaeval period. The younger generation of nobles—more cultured, more travelled, more learned than their fathers—perceived this. They began to take the initiative in proposing administrative reforms; the *råd* began to emerge once more as a political factor to be reckoned with; and a real constitutional opposition began to appear. Of this opposition Erik Sparre was the most talented and articulate leader. The programme of Sparre and his party was as much a demand for better governance (which, they contended, only the new educated nobility could supply) as the assertion of abstract principles of politics, though these last were certainly of great importance. Against the exercise of royal absolutism *de facto*, and the pretension to absolutism *de jure*, they advanced a body of doctrine which was compounded of old and new elements. On the one hand was the appeal to the fourteenth-century *landslag* (land-law), the assertion of the traditional Swedish respect for law, the revival of the claims of the *råd* to act as the watchdog of the nation's liberties; on the other was a contractualist theory borrowed from Hotman in France and Huitfeldt in Denmark, with an infusion of Polish notions of *aurea libertas*. Sparre's legal antiquarianism, his appeal to the *landslag*, recall Coke's brandishing of Magna Carta; and he is indeed a sort of constitutional Janus, linking the traditions of the Middle Ages with the 'Form of Government' of 1634 and the 'Age of Liberty' in the eighteenth century. He preferred an elective to a hereditary monarchy, and probably an aristocratic republic to either, though he professed himself an adherent of the idea of a 'mixed' constitution. The institution of a hereditary monarchy by the Succession Pact of 1544 seemed to him to be big with possibilities for constitutional aggression from the side of the Crown. The Swedish constitution, in his view, was based upon the reciprocal obligations of King and Estates, and if either party failed to do its duty, or overstepped the boundaries of its rights, the other would be justified in interfering. The Succession Pact, he held, had in fact been a contract between the King and his people. The nature of the practical programme which Sparre and his friends based upon their abstract theorizings appeared in 1594, when a scheme was put forward which would have given a monopoly of the great offices of state to the high nobility, and which outlined a plan of government strikingly anticipatory of the 'Collegial' organization which was to be consummated in the 'Form of Government' forty years later. But the 'Form of Government' of 1634 came at the end of a reign in which the Crown had reconciled itself with the aristocracy: in 1594 their relations were almost openly hostile; and if Sparre's ideas had prevailed at that date the Swedish råd might well have developed into something resembling the Danish Council half a century later, with results which would have been as unfortunate in the one case as in the other.

Sparre and his friends looked with suspicion upon every element in government which might seem to strengthen the hands of the King; and their disfavour fell therefore not only upon the 'rule of secretaries' but also upon the riksdag, which since 1523 had been steadily assuming an increasing importance. Gustav Vasa had found it an effective weapon against his adversaries, and the råd-party was well aware of the danger that a popular monarch might override the nobility if sustained by the approval of 'Herr Omnes'. Their nervousness on this head was thoroughly justified, for experience was to show that the King could use the Estates to destroy the råd; and in Johan III's brother, Duke Karl of Södermanland, the råd had a ruthless and unsleeping opponent. Karl, the youngest of Gustav Vasa's sons, had little of the mental agility of Erik XIV, or the enlightened cultural interests of Johan. His nature was stern, his temper short, his language rough even to grossness. The morbid suspiciousness hereditary in his family, which in Erik had issued in actual insanity, in him took the form of a sour and

complaining misanthropy.[1] He found his main intellectual interest
and exercise in theology; and unfortunately for his peace of mind in
later years his theology appeared to the more orthodox of his subjects
to be tinged with Calvinism. Always a good hater, he hated the Pope
with a perfect hatred, and held that all true Protestants should sink
their differences in the face of the common enemy. He made no
bones about avowing that his own creed was based 'on God's word,
and not on Doctor Luther's polemics'; and remarks of this sort
(which were not infrequent) were sufficient to render him suspect
to the straiter Lutherans. When in 1592 he married Kristina of
Holstein, who came of irreproachable Lutheran antecedents, his
orthodoxy was considered so dubious that the Holstein chancellor
found it expedient to deliver a solemn warning to the bride on the
dangers of being led away from the true faith.[2] Unlike Sparre and
his friends, Karl was a man of action; but that is not to imply that
he lacked command of words. On the contrary, he had inherited
much of his father's gift for stirring demagogic oratory, and could
hurl a pungent phrase at the head of an opponent with damaging
effect. Like his father, he had the knack of being popular, particularly with the commonalty; though this useful quality wore very
thin towards the end of his life. To the peasantry he could develop
a rough geniality which, skilfully used as he used it, became a
political asset. His undeniable ambition and self-interest did not
prevent him from being a patriot. His physical bravery was matched,
fortunately for Sweden, by great moral and political courage; for
he was not afraid to take risks in order to pursue the course which
he believed to be the best for the country. In a crisis or an
emergency he seemed to shed all scruples and all respect for persons
and conventions, driving straight to his goal with a recklessness of
consequences which earned him irreconcilable enemies. And it was
Karl's personality that dominated the constitutional and religious
crisis that followed the accession of his nephew Sigismund.

Sigismund himself was a monarch who yielded to none of his
predecessors in the matter of high notions of the prerogative, and
who was not disposed to be tolerant of institutions or individuals
who might seek to limit it. From the beginning, therefore, it was

---

[1] He had his lighter moments. He enjoyed a game of rackets, and in congenial
company could even 'dance and be merry': *Abraham Brahes Tidebok*, pp. 8, 9.
[2] On the question of Karl's religious position, see O. S. Holmdahl, *Karl IX:s
förmenta Kalvinism* (K.Å. 1919); and H. Block, *Karl IX som teolog och religiös
personlighet.*

probable that he would come into conflict with the resurgent constitutionalism of the aristocrats of the *råd*; and so far he and Duke Karl were at one. But on the other hand he differed sharply from Karl in feeling no less dislike for the *riksdag*; and in this the *råd*, as we have seen, were inclined to agree with him. His experiences of the Polish *sejm* had not predisposed him in favour of representative institutions, and the idea that the Commonalty (*allmogen*) might play a part in politics was wholly alien to him. He suspected Karl (with justice) of harbouring ambitious designs to become Regent, and feared that he might use the *riksdag* as a political tool. Thus the new reign produced a triangular constitutional struggle between the *råd*-party of Erik Sparre, the absolutism of the King, and the political ambitions of Duke Karl as self-constituted champion of the *riksdag*.

Side by side with this conflict, and by no means inferior to it in importance, was the religious issue. The Swedish Reformation was the work of Gustav Vasa. It had been prompted, in the first instance, by political and financial, rather than by religious considerations; and neither the doctrinal innovations nor the despoiling of the monasteries had at first been popular. Nevertheless, the Lutheran doctrines gradually conquered the country, and by the time of Erik XIV they had become firmly rooted. The Protestants of the second generation proved more zealous for the faith than their fathers had been. Proximity to Germany made resort to the Protestant universities of Rostock and Wittenberg easy; and the former, especially, became the nursery of a pugnacious school of Swedish Lutheranism, whose representatives jealously guarded the purity of their creed from contamination either by Rome or Geneva. They formed a party of action strong among the clergy, and growing stronger as the century drew to its close; for they could point across the narrow waters of the Baltic to the danger of the new-built stronghold of the Counter-Reformation in Poland. They were increasingly alarmed, moreover, at the trend of ecclesiastical affairs at home during the 'seventies and 'eighties. If Karl was suspected by his adversaries of Calvinism, Johan III's religious policy was thought by many to smell of Popery. Johan, like Karl, was an advocate of reconciliation between the Churches; but whereas Karl wished to move the Swedish Lutherans to the Left, Johan desired to edge them to the Right, with the result that he drew down upon himself much of the same kind of odium as later attached to Laud. And indeed, his religious position was considerably affected by the example of the Anglican Church. He was, moreover, an assiduous liturgiologist, and he insisted on forcing upon Sweden a service-book of his own devising which gave great offence. The Lutheran zealots had thus every reason, from their own point of view, for taking advantage of any opportunity for a clear definition of their position and for placing Sweden's religious alignment beyond all doubt.

That opportunity came with the death of Johan III. The accession of Sigismund at once confronted the Church (in appearance, at least) with a situation more dangerous than any they had yet encountered. For Sigismund's education in the Roman Catholic faith had inspired him with the crusading zeal of the Counter-Reformation. His favourite advisers were Jesuits: he dreamed of reconquering Sweden for Rome. The Papacy had early recognized his quality and potentialities, and had fixed on him as the destined champion of the Catholic cause in northern Europe. His marriage into the House of Habsburg, his friendship with Spain, were parts of a long-distance policy whose inspiration was neither Polish nor Swedish but Roman. In Poland itself, the suppression of dissent was making progress under his leadership: it was to be followed (or so Clement VIII hoped) by the destruction of the Protestant Churches of Scandinavia, and this in its turn by a crusade against the Turks. The Habsburgs, as the coadjutors in this work, would naturally not go unrewarded: already in the time of Maximilian II the Emperor had begun to dream of reasserting his imperial rights over the Baltic, and already there was vague talk of handing over Älvsborg to Spain. And if Spain were to acquire a naval base at Älvsborg, she would be able to threaten the Dutch trade-route to Danzig and Riga, and would thus be in a position to deal a crippling blow at the insurgents. The *dominium maris Baltici* would pass into the hands of the Catholic group of powers.[1]

The Swedish Church, egged on by Duke Karl, lost no time in meeting the danger by resolute measures. At a great national Convention at Uppsala early in 1593 the trimming policy in religion which Johan III had pursued was condemned, and the most stringent resolutions were taken against the toleration of any deviation from the narrow path of Lutheran orthodoxy. The final resolution of the meeting, circulated round the country for signature, attained a

---

[1] See J. Paul, *Die nordische Politik der Habsburger vor dem dreissigjährigen Kriege (H.Z.* 1925-6).

significance analogous to that of the National Covenant in the history of Scotland. And that there might be no misunderstanding of the nation's attitude, the Estates now insisted that the Uppsala resolution should form a part of the Charter which they proposed to extort from Sigismund as a condition precedent to his coronation. Sigismund had no option but to comply with these demands; and the Charter was accepted. Its exaction, in addition to the usual coronation oath, was something new in post-mediaeval Swedish history, and it was eloquent of the distrust with which Sigismund was regarded.

The coronation had no sooner taken place than Sigismund, by openly countenancing Roman Catholic services in Stockholm, showed that he did not mean to abide by the pledges he had given. At the same time he went out of his way to cross the constitutional pretensions of the *råd*, and to disappoint the ambitions of Karl. To the demands of the *råd* that he should appoint some permanent form of central government in Sweden, in view of his impending return to Poland, he paid no attention; and he showed no disposition to make his uncle Regent. Karl was indeed recognized by the King as the 'leading personage' of the realm, but he was expressly prohibited from calling a *riksdag*; and it soon became obvious that Sigismund placed more reliance upon his own agents than upon the official government in Stockholm. Klas Fleming in Finland, and the brothers Stenbock in Sweden, looked to the King alone for orders, and paid no particular attention to the instructions of Karl and the *råd*. It soon became clear that Karl, *råd* and *riksdag* were all to be ignored, and that Sweden was to be ruled from Poland by a King whose only Swedish advisers on the spot were to be a couple of secretaries. It was to meet this danger and to extort if possible a properly defined and constituted government for the country that the *råd* agreed to connive at Karl's summoning a *riksdag* to Söderköping in 1595.

The Söderköping *riksdag* confirmed Karl in his position at the head of the government; it reiterated the decisions and demands of the Uppsala Convention in still sharper form (all Roman Catholic priests were now to leave the country within six weeks); and, on Karl's instigation, it made demands which would have given to the central government a fair measure of independence, and to Karl himself considerable discretionary power. Finally, it resolved that all who would not concur in these resolutions should be considered as 'unruly and lopped-off members' of the body politic. Sigismund immediately made it clear that he had no intention of accepting these demands. To him the meeting at Söderköping had been simply an unlawful assembly, and he promised his protection to all loyal subjects who should resist its decisions. This intransigence came as a shock to the members of the *råd*, who had persuaded themselves that their actions and resolutions at Söderköping had not been incompatible with their duty and loyalty towards their legal sovereign. In this awkward situation the *råd*-party came at last to a determination which was ultimately to cost them dear. In their anxiety to keep on the right side of the law they dissociated themselves from Karl, and abandoned the movement of resistance to Sigismund. Karl, thus deserted by the *råd*, was driven back more and more upon the lower orders in the *riksdag*; and like his father before him appealed from the nervous hesitations of the nobility to the rude vigour of the Swedish yeoman. But for such supporters as these the controversy between King and people had to be reduced to elementary and unambiguous terms. It was therefore convenient to represent the struggle as a purely religious one, and Karl's propaganda took this line with marked success. The next generation, as represented by Axel Oxenstierna, firmly believed that this view of the case was the correct one.[1] But in fact the quarrel was political, no less than religious; and in this it presents a close analogy to the English revolution a century later.

Despite Sigismund's veto, one at least of the resolutions of Söderköping took effect. The handful of Roman Catholic clergy resident in Sweden made all haste to cross the frontiers within the appointed time; and the great monastery of Vadstena—the last remaining religious house in Sweden—closed its doors for ever to the adherents of the old faith. It was not so easy to execute the resolution directed against 'unruly and lopped-off members'; for the *råd* refused to countenance the sending of an expedition against Fleming in Finland, and Karl was reduced to giving underhand encouragement to the infuriated Finnish peasantry who had risen in revolt at Fleming's severities. The difference of opinion with the *råd* on this point led Karl to refuse any further participation in the government; but at the same time he announced his intention of summoning a *riksdag* to Arboga early in 1597. This was in fact to appeal to the nation at large to take his part against the *råd* as well as against the King. The appeal was successful. The Arboga *riksdag*, carefully primed by

[1] W. Tham, *Axel Oxenstierna*, pp. 127-30.

Karl's propaganda, gave him its full support. The members of the *råd*, feeling themselves isolated, fled to Sigismund, to whom the *riksdag* now sent a pressing invitation to return to Sweden. In thus holding a Diet in defiance of both King and *råd*, Karl had crossed the dividing-line which separated constitutional opposition from open rebellion.

The decisive phase was now rapidly approaching. In 1598 Sigismund set out a second time for his hereditary kingdom, and both sides prepared for battle. The two armies met at Stångebro, and an engagement followed which left matters much as they had been, except that both parties were now ready to attempt a negotiated settlement. The result was the treaty of Linköping. It was much more favourable to Karl than the course of military operations warranted. Sigismund bound himself to summon a 'free *riksdag*' to Stockholm; to publish an amnesty; to rule according to his oath and the law of the land; to dismiss his foreign soldiery; and to hand over to Karl five of those members of the *råd* (headed by Erik Sparre) who had taken the lead in opposing the Duke's actions.[1] They were, however, to be tried by impartial, non-Swedish judges. Lastly, the King bound himself to go at once to Stockholm to take over the government. It was perhaps too much to expect that Sigismund should reconcile himself to these humiliating conditions; but in any case affairs in Poland urgently demanded his attention, and he used this as a pretext for evading his promise to go to Stockholm.

It was the cardinal error of his career. Even those Swedes who had been most reluctant to take any overt steps against the legal sovereign were now convinced that no reliance was to be placed upon his word. On the first day of 1599 a *riksdag* met at Jönköping to consider the position. It appointed Karl 'ruling prince', and gave Sigismund a time-limit of four months within which to summon a *riksdag*; failing which the Estates would proceed to further action. Since to this ultimatum Sigismund vouchsafed no reply, another meeting of the *riksdag* in Stockholm six months later formally renounced allegiance and declared the King deposed. They did not, however, exclude Sigismund's line from the throne altogether: on the contrary, they announced that they were prepared to recognize his son Władysław, provided he were brought up as a Lutheran under Karl's guardianship. Sigismund was given six months to

---

[1] The five were Erik Sparre, Gustav and Sten Banér, Göran Posse and Ture Bielke.

accept this offer, after which the Estates would proceed to choose a King 'in accordance with the Succession Pact'. It was not to be expected that these terms would be acceptable to Sigismund; and in the absence of a reply from him the Estates in the following year declared that they would have Karl for their King, and that the throne should descend to his son Gustav Adolf. But in this they were certainly not adhering to the Succession Pact; for if Sigismund and Władysław were excluded, the proper heir by primogeniture was the son of Johan III by his second marriage with Gunilla Bielke. This was a lad of eleven named Johan, a person who fortunately for Karl was to grow up a man of colourless disposition and apathetic temper. The Estates probably felt that a stronger hand than his would be needed if the dynastic revolution were to be upheld. Karl, however, was keenly sensible of the superiority of Johan's claims, and even up to the time of his coronation in 1607 he was in the habit of reminding the *riksaug* that Johan's rights must be safeguarded. He contrived indeed to keep the question so regularly before them that it seems just possible that Johan could have taken the throne for himself in 1611 if he had been prepared to act with energy and promptitude.

Meanwhile Karl had come to a reckoning with his old adversaries the *råd*-members, whom Sigismund had so weakly handed over to his mercies. Sigismund's breach of the treaty of Linköping could be adduced by Karl as good reason for his refusal to implement the clause in that treaty which had assured to Sparre and his colleagues an impartial tribunal; and Karl proceeded to set up an extraordinary court of 155 members, drawn from each of the four Estates. He himself acted almost as public prosecutor, and this fact more than outweighed his release (for this occasion) of the members of the court from their oath of allegiance to himself. The verdict was not really in doubt. Karl had taken the opportunity to accuse four other members of the *råd* at the same time[1]; but three of these, and one of the original five, confessed their guilt, implored mercy, and were spared. Hogenskild Bielke's case was reserved, though he too was fated ultimately to perish on the scaffold. The other four—Erik Sparre, Ture Bielke, Gustav and Sten Banér—were condemned to death, and on 17 March 1600 they were executed in the market-place of Linköping.

The 'blood-bath of Linköping' made a deep impression on

[1] Hogenskild and Klas Bielke, Erik Leijonhufvud, Krister Horn.

contemporaries, and is a good example of how ruthless Karl could be when he felt that the occasion demanded severity. It was political justice, to be excused only by arguments of expediency. No doubt it is true that the action of these men in the years after 1595 brought them within the scope of the resolution of Söderköping against 'unruly and lopped-off members'; but in reality, as Sparre himself remarked, their only fault had been a too scrupulously conscientious effort to serve two masters; and, as Gustav Banér observed, they had always opposed Sigismund on the purely religious question. It was their misfortune to cling to constitutional forms and counsels of moderation at a time when neither of the two parties between whom they vacillated was much concerned either with the one or the other. And when they finally made their choice, the party they selected failed to stand by them at the crisis. Their execution is of great importance; for it marks a violent check to that movement towards increasing the control of the state by the nobility which had been steadily gaining ground for the last two decades. The principle of personal kingship had been savagely reasserted; and for as long as Karl lived, the constitutional theories of Erik Sparre were driven underground.

(iii) *The rule of Karl IX, 1600-11*

Although Karl's rule over Sweden dates from 1600, his reign did not begin for another four years. The cause of this anomaly was Karl himself. Whether from genuine scruples, or from a desire to bring home to the country his indispensability as a bulwark against counter-revolution, Karl for four years steadfastly refused to take the crown which the *riksdag* pressed upon him. Having driven events along a path which could lead to but one conclusion, he balked at the moment when that conclusion must be drawn, and thus left the *riksdag* somewhat in the air. It was not until the Norrköping *riksdag* of 1604, and then only after heavy pressure and as part of the terms of a new Succession Pact, that his real or feigned reluctance was overcome. Until that date he had been, in his own view at all events, no more than Regent.

The resolution of the Norrköping *riksdag* of 1604 settled the crown on Karl and his descendants, being Lutherans, including descendants in the female line. Duke Johan voluntarily renounced his claims, so that the young Gustav Adolf became heir-apparent. Important provisions were made as to the age at which he would attain his majority, and also in regard to a possible regency in the event of Karl's dying while his son was still a minor. The dynastic revolution was completed at the *riksdag* of Stockholm in 1605, when the Estates drew up and subscribed a solemn renunciation of Sigismund and his line.

Karl was still uncrowned, and until the coronation had been performed he could scarcely be considered to be securely established. It was not merely that he lacked the unction of an anointed King: the difficulty from the point of view of the *riksdag* was that he still had a loophole left whereby he could wriggle out of the responsibilities of royalty; he could still vex them by proposing to retire in favour of Johan. This might be merely political tactics, but in any event it would be to the advantage of the nation to put a stop to it, and hence they felt it expedient to press on the coronation. It took place at last in 1607, not without considerable friction with the Clergy, who endeavoured to extort an oath of fidelity to the Uppsala resolutions of 1593. This Karl refused to take without qualification; but it required a threat of abdication before the Clergy gave way. However, Karl was crowned at last, and upon the occasion of his coronation gave a Charter based solely upon the principles contained in the Scriptures, and on the law of the land. Two years later, he performed that ceremonial progress round the kingdom (the so-called *Eriksgata*) customary at the beginning of a new reign; and thus, a bare two years before his death, he was King indeed. To the Estates it must have been a great relief: on no less than five occasions he had threatened to lay down the government; and he had used the threat, as his father had used it, as an instrument to force his will on a reluctant *riksdag*.

Nevertheless, Karl's crown sat far from comfortably on his head. The nobility was disaffected, and resentful of his brutal methods; the emissaries and propaganda of Sigismund were both able and effective; and Karl lived in an atmosphere thick with conspiracy and poisoned by delations. Karl, it is now clear, was by no means the 'peasant-king' of his enemies' propaganda, and of subsequent historians' imagining.[1] Whatever his previous practice, there was little that was revolutionary in his theory. It might suit his book to pose to the outside world as a King elected by his people, but at heart he was conservative, legitimist and legalistic. To the nobility as such he had no objection, and he was not in the least inclined to

---

[1] On this see S. U. Palme, *Karl IX—Bondekonung?* (*Svensk Tidskrift*, 1943).

exclude them from a share in the government, provided their loyalty was to be relied on. He was conscious of the deficiencies in the machinery of state, and aware that the aristocracy could help to make them good. So far was he from excluding them, that of the six ministers (*hovråd*) whom he appointed in 1602, no less than five were taken from the old *råd*-families. Yet he was perfectly well aware that the majority of the nobility disliked him and his methods, and at the beginning of his reign he treated them with a mixture of bullying and cajolery which scarcely achieved the intended result. On the contrary, the Bielkes, the Horns and the Posses, to name no more, undoubtedly indulged in secret plots against the King. In 1605 Karl struck at his enemies in the persons of Hogenskild Bielke, Klas Bielke and Klas Kristersson Horn—all three men who could count themselves fortunate to have escaped the massacre of 1600. Hogenskild Bielke was executed, and his rotting skull remained for years over the Söderport of Stockholm, until, it is said, Ebba Brahe begged Gustav Adolf to permit its removal.[1] Horn was condemned to death, but pardoned; and Klas Bielke was dismissed into exile, with the characteristic exhortation to 'pack yourself off to the Pope in Rome or the Devil in Hell'. It is perhaps significant that one of the charges against Horn was that he had said that Karl was a Calvinist; and that one of the charges against Hogenskild was that he had urged that fewer peasants be summoned to the next *riksdag*, since 'peasants cannot properly weigh any matter, nor is it usual in other lands that peasants should be called to the Diet'.[2]

The prosecutions of 1605 inaugurated a miniature Terror; and although no one else suffered death, the whole aristocracy felt itself menaced. Consequently as the reign progressed Karl's relations with the nobility showed a tendency to deteriorate rather than to improve. Quarrels about noble privileges, and attempts by the Crown to resume lands which had been alienated for services rendered, embittered feelings still further. The King could still count on the support of the common people—his *jabröder*, as Sigismund's friends contemptuously phrased it[3]—but even they seem to have been severely tried by the failures and miseries of the Polish war, the King's stiff intractability in religious matters, and his project for revising the

---

[1] The authenticity of the anecdote seems more than doubtful: see B. Steckzén, *Johan Banér*, p. 29.

[2] *Rikskansleren Axel Oxenstiernas Skrifter och Brefvexling*, I. 1. 10 (cited hereafter as *AOSB*).

[3] *Jabröder* may be translated 'yes-men'.

Common Law. It was no wonder if Karl grew more misanthropic than ever. He complained continually of the ingratitude of his people; was heard to remark that 'rather than live among such folk, who cared neither for oath nor troth, he would go live among wolves and bears'; and fell at times into undignified outbursts of almost childish peevishness.[1] No doubt the passing away of the immediate danger of a Catholic restoration did something to weaken the ties which bound the mass of the people to the King. Certainly a Norwegian spy in Värmland in the last year of the reign could report that he had heard peasants whispering the old story of Holy Brother Staffan and the stone in the green valley, and of how Staffan's prophecy was now coming to pass: for it had been foretold that there should come a ruler in Sweden whose name should be Karl; he should smuggle himself in like a fox; in his life he should be as a lion; and at last he should be driven out like a dog.[2] The first two branches of the prophecy had been so strikingly fulfilled that it was not surprising that some wishful thinkers should have looked forward confidently to the fulfilment of the third.

Karl came to the throne with half a lifetime of experience in practical administration, acquired in the management of his semi-independent Duchy of Södermanland. As King, he simply applied on a more extended scale those methods of estate-management which had served him as Duke. Swedish administration was still simple to the point of being rudimentary. The annihilation of Erik Sparre and his party had meant the postponement of any major adminis-trative reform. Yet Karl, if he made no important innovations, at least infused a certain vigour, and his officials were made to feel that no dereliction of duty would escape his observation. In this, as in so much else, he is reminiscent of Gustav Vasa. Like him, he used the *riksdag* as a support or a smoke-screen in moments of crisis and as an instrument in the ordinary business of government. With no idea of developing its competence or regulating its forms of procedure, he nevertheless did much by his incessant calling together of the Estates—six meetings of the Diet in eleven years—to increase their political self-consciousness; though the individual members felt such frequent attendance to be a great inconvenience and complained bitterly of the time and expense involved. But at difficult moments,

[1] See his deplorable letter to Archbishop Olaus Martini, in *Handlingar rörande Skandinaviens Historia*, VIII. 9-11.
[2] N. Ahnlund, *Oljoberget och Ladugårdsgärde*, p. 166.

or on contentious questions, it was always the King's endeavour to get the Estates to shoulder the responsibility—as they did, for instance, for the Linköping massacre, and for the alteration in the order of succession.

The *råd*, shattered and harried in 1600, was first reconstituted two years later, its members now being recruited mainly from among Karl's partisans, and a resolution of the *riksdag* explicitly condemned Sparre's pretensions by declaring that 'the Council shall give counsel, and shall *not* direct'. For some years thereafter the *råd* was in semi-eclipse. Yet something of the claims of the old body lived on in the new; and they were to emerge into the daylight when Karl was dead. Meanwhile the King placed his main reliance upon non-noble advisers such as Dr. Nils Chesnecopherus; and by the end of the reign there had developed something like that old 'rule of secretaries' which had been so obnoxious to the *råd* under the earlier monarchs of the Vasa line. It was clear that when the King died the whole question of the constitutional relations of the monarchy to the *råd*, the nobility, and the *riksdag* would come up for revision. There were many nobles in Sweden who were by this time prepared to fight to the bitter end to keep out Sigismund and Roman Catholicism, but were not prepared to tolerate such another monarch as Karl IX. The divine-right absolutism of Sigismund was scarcely more repugnant to them than the parliamentary despotism of Karl. A change of ruler, particularly if the next King should be a minor, might well lead to a constitutional revolution in the spirit of Erik Sparre. An anonymous writer was only echoing the sentiments of many Swedes when shortly after Karl's death he wrote: 'God in Heaven preserve us here in Sweden from so many *herredagar* and from another such bloody and plaguy reign as this last has been.'[1]

(iv) *The international consequences of the Swedish Revolution*

The dynastic revolution in Sweden had important international consequences. The possibility of Sweden's and Poland's proceeding hand in hand to an attack upon Russia was now ruled out. In future, it was clear, the ill-concealed rivalry of these two powers would be open and bitter. For the secular struggle between them, in which both the personal quarrel between Karl and Sigismund

---

[1] *Svenska Riksdagsakter*, I$_2$. 1. 143-4 (cited hereafter thus: *SRDA*, I. 143). *Herredag* was the older name for *riksdag*.

and the constitutional question in Sweden had now become blended, was itself only part of a much greater issue. The battle of the creeds which was being fought out in France, the Netherlands and on the English seas had opened a new front in the far north. The great ideological issues of the day had transcended and submerged the purely local strife. Sigismund's cause was now the cause of Rome, and of all who supported Rome.[1] And it was the aim of Karl—it was to be Gustav Adolf's aim too—to persuade the Protestant princes of Europe that their fate was bound up with his, that they could not afford to allow him to be crushed, and that he must not be suffered to continue the contest in isolation. But the Protestant world, influenced, perhaps, by the attitude of Sweden's old enemy Denmark, showed itself unmistakably cool. The great Catholic sovereigns, for their part, affected to treat Karl with the contumely due to an upstart usurper, and more than one Protestant power tended to follow their example. No one wished to prejudice relations with Poland for the sake of an adventurer whose future seemed at best uncertain. Karl's efforts to arrange a marriage for the young Gustav Adolf, either in England or France, met with little response beyond the usual courtesies of diplomacy. Henri IV politely evaded his suggestions for a political alliance in 1608, and showed no disposition to include Sweden in his league of 1609 with England and the Dutch. Even James I would go no further than to recognize Karl as King in virtue of the choice of the Estates.[2] When in 1609 Karl raised an alarm that a Spanish attack on the North was impending, and begged the Dutch to send him aid, Their High Mightinesses found it inexpedient to jeopardize their negotiations for a truce with Spain, which were then pending. Nor were they willing to include Sweden in that truce. Karl, however, had the importunity of the *parvenu*, and in 1610 he despatched two great embassies to the Netherlands and England, whose main object was to be the securing of Sweden's inclusion in any Anglo-French-Dutch alliance. But both England and the Dutch took exception to Karl's hostility to Denmark, and the mercantile interests of both

[1] Sigismund made efforts to obscure the connection. In 1597, for instance, Paul Działyński was sent on a mission to England and the Netherlands to persuade them to 'leave Sweden to her fate': see A. Szelągowski, *Dzieje współzawodnictwa Anglii i Niemiec, Rosyi i Polski* (Lwów, 1910). I was unable to secure a copy of this work: the reference is taken from Małowist, p. 424.

[2] James also presented Karl with a copy of his theological works; but this was only as a *quid pro quo* for some falcons: J. Hallenberg, *Svea Rikes Historia under Konung Gustaf Adolf den Stores Regering*, I. 84.

were offended by his attempt to force them to suspend their trade with Riga, then blockaded by the Swedish navy. Holland imported grain from Poland, and England had important interests in Elbing, where the Eastland Company was settled, and neither was anxious to give umbrage to Sigismund.

Hence Karl's attempt to form a Protestant front with the western powers proved a failure. It remained to be seen whether he would have any better success with the evangelical princes of Germany. The prospects here should have been more promising, for Karl was connected by marriage with the ruling families of Hesse and the Palatinate,[1] and those states were always accounted as among the more active and forward section in the Protestant camp. The omens for a religious war were gloomy, for the tide of triumphant Catholicism was pounding at the rickety structure of the religious peace. The Emperor had at last freed himself from the Turkish danger by the treaty of Zsitva-Török, and he had thus full leisure to turn his attention to the *Reich*. The Donauwörth troubles of 1607 provided an indication of the temper of the Catholic party too clear to be ignored. In 1608 the Protestant princes of north-west Germany drew together for self-defence and formed the Evangelical Union. The lead was taken by the Palatinate, and within two years the Union had been joined by Baden, Württemberg, Hesse and Brandenburg, as well as by several smaller states and imperial towns. Apart from Brandenburg, the Union was wholly Calvinist. The Lutheran powers, headed by their leader the Elector of Saxony, viewed the proceedings of the party of action with disfavour, as threatening that imperial constitution which all good Lutherans respected. The division in the ranks of Protestantism went so deep that in a crisis the Lutherans would probably be found on the Catholic rather than on the Calvinist side. It is no matter for surprise, therefore, that the Evangelical Union at first made no attempt to secure the adhesion of Lutheran Sweden. Hesse and the Palatinate were well-disposed to Karl personally, and they had some idea of the identity of Karl's struggle with their own; but they could not forget that Sweden herself was as fanatically Lutheran as their enemy Saxony. The Lutheran states, on the other hand, with their essential conservatism, their respect for law and order, their reverence for constituted authority, and their abhorrence of revolutionary violence, naturally

---

[1] Karl's first wife was a member of the Palatine House; his second, Kristina of Holstein, was descended on her mother's side from Philip of Hesse.

saw in Karl an enthroned rebel, to ally with whom would be to
compromise the principle of legitimacy. Only the north German
towns, with Baltic interests similar to Sweden's, were prepared to
be friendly; and even of these Lübeck had shown a disposition to
side with Sigismund, and was for the first few years after 1600 on
bad terms with Karl.[1]

Karl had therefore to face the struggle with Sigismund alone.
The attitude of the Polish Republic to the new situation was not
altogether clear. The country was torn by factions, and for years
there had been a strong party in more or less permanent opposition
to the King. Many Poles had viewed the connection with Sweden
with distrust, and even Zamoyski, whose support had been mainly
instrumental in securing Sigismund's election, had thrown obstacles
in the way of his journey to Sweden in 1592. In the Swedish crisis
that followed, the Polish nobles and *sejm* had observed a cautious
neutrality: it was no part of their policy to oppose a movement
which, in limiting the authority of the monarch, had some points of
resemblance to their own political programme. Moreover, in the
last few years of the century Poland began an attempt to extend her
political influence to the south; and this attempt, premature, ill-
organized and ill-supported as it was, engaged for the time being
the main attention of her statesmen. It was in order to have his
hands free in the south that Zamoyski had encouraged Sigismund
to make his disastrous second journey to Sweden. The deposition
of Sigismund, however, confronted the Poles with a new situation,
or rather, it revived an old one. Sweden and Poland became once
more open enemies. Sigismund had not as yet redeemed the promise
to hand over Estonia to Poland which he had made at the time of
his election; and since the garrisons and commanders there declared
for Karl, it became plain that Poland must fight in her King's cause
if this object of her ambition were to be realized. Men like Zamoyski
and Lew Sapieha were in favour of accepting the logical consequences
of the new situation, and of supporting Sigismund in his attempt to
reconquer his fatherland; holding that—to a certain extent, at all
events—dynastic and national interests were now coincident. But
it is doubtful whether the *sejm* could ever have been brought to
cooperate wholeheartedly in such an enterprise if Karl had not carried
the war into the enemy's country by attacking Livonia in 1600.

[1] Lübeck had been injured by the treaty of Täysinä, which reserved the
Narva trade as a Swedish monopoly.

GUSTAV ADOLF
as a young man

KARL IX

Estonia had never been Polish, and the Polish magnates were not prepared to sacrifice much to make it so, especially since the Republic was involved in complications in the Ukraine. Karl's attack on Livonia, therefore, bears all the appearance of a political blunder as well as of an act of aggression. Yet in reality it was necessary and even politic. Necessary, since the acquisition of at least a part of Livonia was needed to make Estonia secure, and since the conquest of Pernau and Riga was essential if Sweden were really to control the Russia trade; politic, since fresh annexations might be retro-ceded at a general peace in return for a renunciation by Sigismund of his claims on Sweden. Nevertheless, it gave Sigismund a convenient text for a sermon on the danger to Poland of Swedish aggression; it led the *sejm* to rally to the King's cause; and it drove Sigismund himself into still closer relations with Austria and Spain.

Thus was begun a war which was to last long after the original protagonists were dead. It was a war of desultory frontier campaigns, waged under severe climatic conditions and leading to little positive result. In Karl's time the Swedish armies were ill-trained and undisciplined, with a faulty organization and a marked lack of any maturely considered strategy. None the less, they were far more numerous than their opponents, whose internal dissensions and political distractions compelled them to trust to the valour of small but brilliantly handled forces, mainly composed of the unsurpassed Polish cavalry. It was this cavalry, combined with the inefficiency of the Swedish armies, that produced the astonishing victory of Kirkholm in 1605, when a small Polish force overwhelmed and annihilated a Swedish army many times as numerous as itself.[1]

The victory of Kirkholm encouraged the highest hopes in Sigis-mund and his supporters. He confidently looked forward to the recovery of Sweden, and planned to leave his son to rule Poland under the regency of his stepmother, Constantia of Austria. These dreams, however, were soon dissipated by the severe internal crisis which occurred in Poland in the following year. The discontent of the Dissidents at the vigorously catholicizing policy of the King and his advisers, the new enthusiasm of the nobles for their *aurea libertas*, reinforced by a liberal dose of unassimilated monarcho-machist theory, combined to produce the great *rokosz* (insurrection)

[1] The best accounts of Kirkholm are in B. C:son Barkman, *Kungl. Svea Livgardes Historia*, II.; and (from the Polish side) T. Korzon, *Dzieje wojen i wojskowości w Polsce*, II.

of Zebrzydowski, which paralysed Poland's conduct of the war, and
was to have a permanently damaging effect on the prestige and power
of the monarchy. Sweden was given time to recover from the
disaster, and was able to consolidate her footing in Estonia, and
even to make considerable progress in Livonia. The feebleness of
Poland's resistance, and the apathy of her selfish nobility, gradually
loosened her grip on the country. As a contemporary Polish poet
mournfully observed:

> Truly these lands have slipped from our grasp
> As foam is borne away by the waters.[1]

By 1610, however, both sides were deeply engaged elsewhere,
and both were anxious for a truce. There had been several fruitless
attempts at mediation by foreign powers in the previous decade.
Brandenburg, for instance, had offered good offices, and so also had
Henri IV. It was characteristic of Karl that upon the latter occasion
he had submitted the terms suggested to the University of Uppsala,
in order that the onus of rejecting them (for they were obviously
unacceptable), and thus also the odium of continuing the war, might
be shifted to other shoulders than his own. But in 1610 he was
ready to treat; and in the last year of his life he was able to arrange
the prolongation of a local armistice for some months: successive
extensions were to carry it on for several years. Meanwhile both
Poland and Sweden transferred their attention to the affairs of
Muscovy; and, while hostilities were suspended in Livonia, continued
their struggle with no less bitterness in the confused arena of Russian
politics.

In 1598 the old dynasty of Rurik became extinct upon the death
of the Tsar Feodor, and Russia was left, for the first time for centuries,
without any obvious candidate for the throne. The results were
disastrous. The Russians had come to look upon their Tsars with
peculiar veneration; but it was a veneration which extended only
to princes of the old blood-royal. The old Tsars had formed the
keystone to the social arch: when that keystone was withdrawn the
fabric of society collapsed into anarchy. No elected candidate, however wide the support he might command, could attain to the semi-
sacrosanct prestige of even the feeblest or most vicious representative
of the old royal house; no modernizing ruler, however able or enlightened, could compensate by his progressive measures for his

---

[1] Szymon Szymonowicz; quoted in W. Sobieski, *Historja Polski*, p. 177.

lack of the essential quality of birth.   The indispensable binding-force that had held the state together was suddenly removed, and Russia was left to grope her way through a series of unhappy experiments before finding a solution which depended for such success as it enjoyed on the fact that it represented itself to be a return to the old ways.

Such was the origin of the period of the Troublous Times. The domestic upheavals that followed offered obvious opportunities for the intervention of Russia's envious or fearful neighbours; and Sigismund III was not likely to let the chance slip.   His Ukrainian subjects were showing disquieting signs of falling under Russian cultural and ecclesiastical influences, and the idea was taking shape in his mind that this difficulty, as well as others, might be solved by a resumption of Batory's plans (never wholly abandoned) for incorporating Moscow into the Polish state.   There were many Polish nobles who shared his opinion, and even the more cautious of them considered that the moment should be seized to make good Polish ambitions upon Smoleńsk and the surrounding districts.   The new Tsar, Boris Godunov, in spite of good intentions, energy and ability, had soon exhausted his early popularity, and towards the end of his life lived in constant terror of treason.   While lacking the enterprise to make common cause with Karl against Sigismund, he naturally tended to sympathize with the new dynasty in Sweden, and had rejected, curtly enough, Sigismund's request to be recognized as King.

The prospects from the Polish point of view seemed not unfavourable; yet Sigismund for the moment refrained from direct intervention.   Instead, he gave unofficial assistance to a pretender who alleged himself to be Dmitrij, the son of Ivan IV, whom all the world supposed to have been murdered at Uglič in 1591.   Backed by Polish money, aided by Polish adventurers, and encouraged by a Polish wife, Dmitrij succeeded in toppling the Godunov dynasty from the throne in 1605.   From the point of view of the Russian boyars who had supported him, Dmitrij had now fulfilled his function: he had eliminated the family of the usurper, and left the way clear for one of their own number.   Within a fortnight of his coronation, therefore, an aristocratic conspiracy had removed him, and in his place put a typical representative of the high nobility, Vasilij Šuijskij.   Sigismund had hoped much from his protégé: a Polish embassy which was in Moscow when Dmitrij was murdered had been pressing a project for a union between the two countries, on lines which Sigismund had suggested as early as 1600. From Šuijskij, on the other hand, little was to be expected; and Sigismund might perhaps have intervened more actively at this point, if his energies had not been paralysed by the Zebrzydowski *rokosz*.

The removal of the first Dmitrij inaugurated a period of political chaos and social upheaval, in which the whole structure of Russian life was shaken to its depths. The inarticulate and oppressed masses found their first leader in Bolotnikov; the Cossacks began a course of systematic support of any forces making for disorder; and new pretenders appeared in considerable numbers. The first Dmitrij was scarcely dead before supporters were rallying to a claimant who as yet had no existence; a second and a third Dmitrij were in due course put forward by this or that group of interested politicians; and apart from these at least eleven other pretenders attracted adherents at one time or another. The setting up of a pretender, indeed, became little more than a gesture of dissatisfaction with the existing state of affairs; and it was not required of any of the later candidates that there should be even a shadow of plausibility about their persons or pretensions. None of them, however, proved as apt to Polish designs as the first Dmitrij. The second pseudo-Dmitrij was indeed supported by Poles—by Lisowski, Rozyński, Sapieha—but they were the aristocratic wreckage of Zebrzydowski's *rokosz*, adventurers seeking to retrieve their fortunes in the turmoil of Russian affairs, and not at all willing to do the errands of the King whose disciplinary measures had driven them across the border. Sigismund therefore remained for the present on good terms with Šuijskij; made a treaty of neutrality with him in 1607; and promised to recall Lisowski and his associates—a promise which was, to be sure, easier to make than to carry out.

It was not until 1608 that the confusion in Russia began seriously to affect the position of Karl IX. In that year the success of Dmitrij's Polish supporters began to give him some cause for alarm; for they obtained possession of a series of important fortresses in the north-west—Pskov, Ivangorod, Nöteborg, Kexholm—which threatened the Swedish positions in Estonia, and which had long been the object of Swedish ambitions. It was true that Lisowski and his friends were almost in the position of rebels against Sigismund's authority; but the characteristic instability of Polish politics might at any time lead to a reconciliation with their sovereign which would put these important outposts in Sigismund's hands. Karl determined therefore to seek an understanding with Šuijskij; and Šuijskij, who was much in need of external aid, was well disposed to listen to his overtures. The result was the Treaty of Viborg, in February 1608,[1] whereby in return for an auxiliary force of 5000 Swedish troops under Jakob de la Gardie the Tsar promised to confirm the Peace of Täysinä and in addition to cede to Sweden the fortress and fief of Kexholm, which Sweden had handed back to Russia in 1595. Unfortunately for Šuijskij, the Treaty of Viborg was considered by Sigismund to be a breach of the neutrality to which Šuijskij had pledged himself in the previous year; and Sigismund accordingly determined upon personal intervention in Russia. He ordered all those Polish subjects who were gathered round the second Dmitrij at his stronghold at Tušino to abandon the pretender and return to their allegiance, and himself proceeded to form the siege of Smoleńsk. Dmitrij, feeling himself now insecure, deserted his followers and fled to Kaluga at the beginning of 1610; and in February most of his Russian supporters agreed to accept Sigismund's son Władysław as Tsar. They imposed stringent conditions: full guarantees for the Orthodox religion; a pledge that no improvement in the condition of the serfs would be attempted; and an undertaking that Russia and Poland should remain separate states. Thus Karl's support of Šuijskij had brought about a situation even more dangerous than that which it had been designed to avert. A dynastic union between Poland and Russia would give the elder line of Vasas an excellent jumping-off place for the reconquest of Sweden. It would encircle the Swedish bastion in Estonia, bring Sigismund's agents to the Finnish frontier, hand over to Poland the long-disputed Russian trade-routes, and threaten the whole Baltic area with subjection to the Counter-Reformation. Hence Karl must struggle to the last against the establishment of Polish influence in Russia, and above all against the election of a Polish Tsar; and for the present his best means lay in support of Šuijskij. If Šuijskij were to fail him, it would not be easy to pitch upon another ally. But just at this moment the fortunes of Šuijskij began to droop; his supporters began to drift off to Władysław; his able brother Skopin met an untimely death; and to crown all the cosmopolitan mercenary army of de la Gardie turned mutinous for lack of pay. Catastrophe came on 24 June 1610, when the combined forces of Šuijskij and de la Gardie were crushed by

---

[1] Text in *Sverges Traktater*, V$_2$. 158-76.

Żółkiewski at Klušino. De la Gardie himself, with a bare 400 men, managed to regain his base in Estonia; but for the Tsar the disaster was irreparable. Żółkiewski advanced with his Polish army upon Moscow; and on 17 July Šuijskij was forced to abdicate, and was relegated to a monastery. The Treaty of Viborg was now worthless; the triumph of Poland seemed assured. The position could be retrieved only if Karl made a vigorous military effort, and (even more important) if a candidate could be found for the Russian throne capable of challenging the pretensions of Władysław. The last year of Karl's life saw Sweden fumbling desperately for a policy in Russia; and when Gustav Adolf came to the throne it was not yet certain that she had found one.[1]

(v) *The drift to war with Denmark, 1595-1611*

The attitude of Denmark to the dynastic revolution in Sweden was at first reserved and non-committal. Kristian IV undoubtedly hoped to be able to extract concessions as the price of his mediation; but Karl, at all events, was not prepared to give him a chance to meddle in Swedish affairs. Kristian was not sorry, perhaps, to see the personal union between Sweden and Poland dissolved; but he sympathized with Sigismund as the representative of the cause of legitimacy, he gave temporary shelter to those members of the *råd* expelled by Karl, and he stretched the concept of neutrality very far in order to provide facilities for Sigismund's abortive naval expedition against Älvsborg in 1599. But he was not entirely immune to Karl's Protestant propaganda; and his Council was emphatic in discountenancing any attempt to use the occasion for a policy of adventure or aggression.

None the less, it seems certain that for a full decade before the outbreak of hostilities in 1611 Kristian was planning a war against Sweden. In 1600, for instance, he was thinking of launching a surprise attack; and he recurred repeatedly to the idea in the years that followed. His motive was a double one: on the one hand he shared the desire of all Kings of Denmark since 1523 to restore the Union—an enterprise for which the confused dynastic situation in Sweden seemed to offer an excellent opportunity; on the other hand

---

[1] The closing stages of the Troublous Times will be dealt with in Chapter II. There is a reproduction of a good contemporary sketch of Klušino in Korzon, II. 164.

he looked upon a forward foreign policy as necessary to emancipate the monarchy from the control of the Council. Since the Peace of Stettin in 1570 the Council had established a virtual supervision over Denmark's relations with Sweden. The terms of that treaty had provided a machinery of conciliation to settle disputes between the two countries: all cases of difficulty were to be submitted to a joint meeting, to be held on the frontier, of members of the Danish Council and the Swedish *råd*, who were to be released for the occasion from their oaths of allegiance; and if either King refused to accept the findings of such a meeting, his subjects were to be freed from the obligation of obedience to him. These arrangements, naturally enough, were galling to Kristian; but to Karl they offered certain compensating advantages. Karl was well aware of the reluctance of the Danish Council to engage in a war which might strengthen the monarchy. His own *råd* (after 1602) was firmly under his control. The machinery provided by the Peace of Stettin was therefore in some sort a guarantee that peace would be preserved at all costs, and that Swedish aggression, unless it were exceptionally gross, would not lead to war, and could be prosecuted with impunity provided it were prosecuted discreetly. Kristian on his side was resolved that a situation must be created in which the machinery would no longer function; the points in dispute between the two countries must be so exacerbated, the Swedes put so clearly in the wrong, that even the Council would be unable to withstand his demand for a declaration of war.

There was certainly no lack of controversies to exacerbate; and the most prominent of them was the very complex problem of the Arctic, where the whole coastline, from Titisfjord in the west to the Kola Peninsula in the east, had for some years been the object of conflicting ambitions. Norway-Denmark, Sweden and Russia all had more or less colourable claims to some or all of these districts, and each of them had at one time or another claimed the right to tax the wandering Lapps and Finns who formed (with the exception of a handful of traders and officials) the only population of these wastes. The Danish government had since 1523 made the castle of Vardøhus the centre of an administrative district of Finnmark, linked with the administration at Bergen; and from 1571 there had been a permanent official, resident at Vardøhus, in charge of it. The area under his jurisdiction extended from Varanger in the east to Loppen Island in the west (about half-way between Hammerfest and

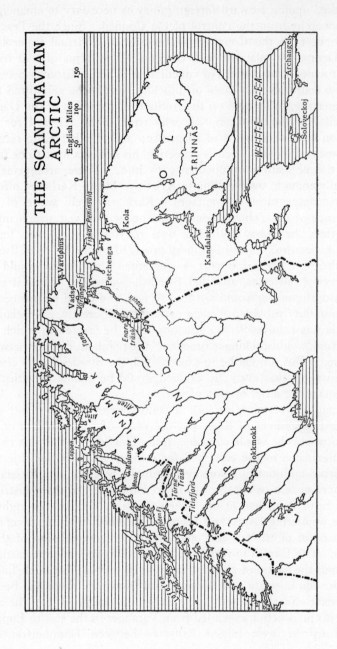

Tromsø). In the third quarter of the century there was a thin trickle of Norwegian settlers into this region; and the government at Copenhagen began to regard it as definitely a part of the dominions of the Norwegian Crown. Simultaneously, they made an attempt to extract taxes from the Lapps living as far east as the Murmansk coast and the Kola Peninsula. Here, however, they came into conflict with the Russians. The first Russian settlement in these parts had occurred as recently as the 'twenties of the sixteenth century, when a certain hermit named Trifon had founded the great monastery of Petchenga. In 1556 this monastery was by Ivan IV given a large grant of land in Kola and further west; a grant which, besides annexing much territory that was of disputable ownership, incorporated some that was considered (in Norway) as indubitably Norwegian. As to Kola, while the Russians had a tiny settlement there, the Danes had nothing at all, so that on this point at least Moscow had the better of the argument. At all events, after a number of frontier disputes, Ivan IV in 1573 offered, not ungenerously, to make the Pasvik river the boundary. Denmark refused to accept this compromise, and persisted in maintaining her claims on Kola. Twice in the 'eighties Fredrik II sent expeditions north to assert his 'rights', and in 1586 he formally laid claim to the whole of Lappland. This claim Denmark maintained at a frontier-parley in 1595. But in spite of this Denmark had really little or no influence in the eastern districts, especially in those lying to the east of Vardøhus.

A much more serious competitor from the Russian point of view was Sweden. Ever since the reign of Gustav Vasa Sweden had been trying to obtain a treaty which would define the boundaries of Finland in such a way as to give her access to the Arctic Ocean. The frontiers of Finland in relation to Russia had last been defined by the Treaty of Nöteborg in 1323, but the precise significance of the lines then laid down was by this time lost in the mists of antiquity. It was at all events certain that from the 1530's Swedish penetration began to be effective in this region. A Swedish map published in 1539 even showed the Murmansk coast as Swedish territory. The importance attached to the control of the north by Swedish statesmen can be seen from the terms of the Treaty of Täysinä, when Sweden deliberately sacrificed her gains in Kexholm in return for concessions beyond the Arctic Circle. A new frontier was drawn by this treaty, passing through the Enare Träsk and reaching the sea just east of

Varanger. The Russians abandoned to Sweden their claims to tax the Lapps west of this line, and the Swedes made a similar renunciation in regard to lands lying to the east of it. This arrangement, however, completely ignored the claims of Denmark-Norway; for the Danish government had certainly taxed the Lapps west of this line in the past. Moreover, Sweden herself had not really given up all hope of obtaining the Kola region. In Karl IX's time there were attempts at settlement to the east of the new frontier; efforts to delimit a new boundary further to the east; and even (taking advantage of Russia's internal troubles) abortive military expeditions to seize the land by force. The Troublous Times, indeed, put Russia more or less out of the hunt in the north.

The field then remained clear for Denmark and Sweden. Sweden had for some time been following a policy of stealthy encroachment on the Danish preserves. The trade with the Lapps had for many years been in the hands of the merchant gild of the 'Birkarlar', who, in return for a contribution to the Swedish exchequer, had been given the right to collect taxes. This right had been withdrawn in 1550, and the Crown had taken the fiscal administration into its own hands. But not content with taxing the 'fell-Finns' of the mountains, it now pushed its agents across the watershed and began to tax the 'sea-Finns' too. In the early 'sixties it succeeded for a brief moment in exacting taxes from the inhabitants of the Titisfjord region. Denmark for long failed to perceive the danger; failed to realize that the object of this taxation was to establish a title to political sovereignty. Sweden, indeed, had pursued a consistent policy to this end ever since the time of Gustav Vasa, and this policy received open expression at the Kongsback conference of 1591, when Sweden demanded of Denmark the right to tax the Titisfjord, and even Lofoten. In Swedish eyes the position was much strengthened by the Treaty of Täysinä. For on the assumption that Sweden, Denmark and Russia had each enjoyed the right to one-third of the taxes of the Lapps west of the Pasvik, Sweden (now in possession of the Russian share in this region) could henceforth claim two-thirds of the taxes. But the new King of Denmark, Kristian IV, who had recently attained his majority, was not the man to allow the Danish claims to go by default. In 1590 he made an expedition to the North Cape, Vardøhus and the Fiskar Peninsula. The experience of actual conditions which he then obtained determined his policy for the future: henceforth Denmark adopted a much stiffer attitude to Swedish pretensions. She now boldly claimed the whole northern ocean as her territorial waters; the Swedish argument from the treaty of Täysinä was dismissed as worthless, since it was contended by Denmark that Russia had no claims to cede west of the Pasvik; and in order to be ready for any emergency, a policy of rearmament was vigorously pushed on. Karl's reply was to instruct his agents to pursue an actively colonizing policy, to build a church and a parsonage at Varanger, and to see that no taxes were paid to Denmark.

Such was the position in 1600. In the years that followed, all attempts to solve the problem by negotiation broke down. Frontier meetings in the approved form were held in 1601 and 1603, but no real agreement was reached, and Karl vigorously maintained his colonizing activities. A Swedish fleet was sent from Göteborg to collect taxes from the coastal Finns; but Kristian had it stopped at Bergen. However, permanent fiscal agents were stationed on the rivers Tana, Alten and Maals; prospecting for precious metals was begun; trade regulations were issued; churches were built; and in 1607 Karl appointed a special lord-lieutenant (*ståthållare*) for Lappmark, with instructions to build a fort at Vadsø big enough to take a hundred men. At his coronation in 1607 Karl took the serious step of including among his titles that of 'King of the Lapps of Nordland'. To his new town of Göteborg he gave in 1608 the right to fish off the Finnmark coast; and in 1610 he granted this right to Lübeck too, on condition that the burghers paid him a proportion of their profits. This steady persistence in aggression infuriated Kristian. As early as 1603 he demanded of his Council that they should agree to a declaration of war against Sweden. He repeated the demand in 1604; but his ministers were pacifically inclined, and tried to damp his ardour by pointing out that Sweden was a country where large armies starve and small ones are beaten.[1] But by 1609 even the Danish Council was beginning to admit that the situation was becoming intolerable.

Meanwhile the government in Stockholm was gradually awakening to the fact that they were not going to be allowed to carry out their policy of pin-pricks unscathed. Sweden had made no serious effort to accept the mediation of benevolent neutrals,

---

[1] G. Petri, *Kungl. första Livgrenadjärregementets Historia*, I. 411; *Kampen om Østersjøen*, p. 127.

although Brandenburg, Hesse and Mecklenburg had at one time or another been suggested as intermediaries; but by 1609 even Karl was showing signs that he might be ready for some compromise. The *råd*, while fully sharing Karl's view of Sweden's rights in the Arctic, was alarmed at the prospect of a war with Denmark, at a time when it appeared certain that Sweden would inevitably be deeply committed in Russia. Three times in 1609 the *råd* wrote to the Council in Copenhagen with proposals intended to be conciliatory; but when at last they received a reply it was anything but encouraging. At this juncture—on 11 August 1609—Karl was prostrated by an apoplectic stroke; and though he mended a little in November he was not fit for transacting business until well into 1610, and he never really recovered. His removal from the control of affairs was a change in favour of peace; but unfortunately it came too late to make much difference.

The Arctic controversy was by this time no longer the only nor perhaps the main topic of dispute between the two countries. In the course of years it had attracted to itself a whole litter of other problems. Prominent among these was the legitimate Danish grievance about the activities of Swedish privateers in the Baltic. In the course of her war with Poland, Sweden had been trying to block up the lucrative trade of Riga, to the great annoyance of the maritime powers; and Swedish privateers were using this as a pretext for committing depredations from one end of the sea to the other. This involved the Danish mercantile community in loss, or else entailed upon the Danish government the expense of providing convoys. Further, Denmark complained that the privileges which Karl had conferred upon Göteborg infringed Denmark's fishing preserves in northern waters. On the other hand, Sweden complained that though by treaty she was exempt from the Sound Tolls, the exemption was being infringed: in 1606 Kristian had levied toll on wine consigned to the King of Sweden; he was high-handedly arresting skippers of ships alleged to carry goods of suspicious origin; he was kidnapping sailors from passing vessels to man his fleet. To this Kristian could retort by pointing to the tax which Karl had imposed upon all purchasers of Danish goods, which (he contended) was equally a violation of the free-trade agreement between the two countries. Then there were the 'questions of honour'. Karl's assumption of the style of 'King of the Lapps of Nordland' had no doubt a very practical significance; but so much could hardly be said of the matter of the royal arms. Since Denmark had never formally renounced her claims on Sweden, Danish Kings felt justified in displaying the three crowns of Sweden in their royal coat of arms, though they usually refrained from doing so except in times of political tension. As recently as 1593 Kristian IV and Sigismund had agreed that the matter should be allowed to remain in abeyance for both their lifetimes; but Denmark had raised the point again in 1603.

Of all these controversies, that of the Riga blockade and that of the control of Finnmark were the two that were of most importance. It is not easy to see why Karl should have attached so much weight to either of them. Poland had other ports than Riga; the Russia trade would easily take to other channels; the gain from the blockade scarcely offset the loss of good-will which it entailed, and certainly did not justify running the risk of war. The same is perhaps true of the Arctic question. Even if Karl had been wholly successful here, the advantage would not have been impressive. Three possible objects could be imagined for such a policy: it might aim at a port; it might aim at revenue; it might aim at control of the trade-route to Archangel. Kristian undoubtedly feared that Karl was seeking a warm-water outlet at Narvik as a way round the obstacle of the Sound —a window to the Atlantic which Denmark could not block up in war-time. It is possible; but it would have been a port most difficult of access from Stockholm—more difficult, probably, than Archangel was from Moscow. As to revenue, that was a bagatelle not worth consideration. The control of the Russian trade-route would require a fleet stationed in northern waters, and it is clear that Karl did seriously contemplate the construction of a naval base and ship-building yards on the Alten: ships were to be built of local timber— a provision which sheds a certain light on Karl's information about the Arctic, or argues unexpected modesty in the dimensions of his intended men-of-war. And if the building of a fleet was mere fantasy, it was not likely that the establishment of a settlement on, say, the Pasvik, would seriously deter English and Dutch shipping, any more than Kristian's fort at Vardøhus had deterred it. The final possibility was to prepare the way for a conquest of Kola and later of Archangel. This was a more rational programme; but there appears to be no valid reason why it should not have been attempted without offering provocation to Denmark. In short, Kristian involved himself in war for fear of a bogy, and Karl provoked it in pursuit of a shadow. It was to be another half century before Swedes were cured of the Arctic delusion.[1]

By January 1611 Kristian had made up his mind for war. The Council was informed that if he could not begin it as King of Denmark with their consent, he would begin it as Duke of Slesvig-Holstein without it. In the spring the Danes arrested on Swedish soil the English agent James Spens, who was on his way to Scotland to recruit mercenaries for the Swedish army. Swedish protests at this outrage were answered at the beginning of April by a declaration of war. And now, when it was too late, Karl made great efforts to undo what could no longer be undone. But it was useless to urge the need for solidarity among all Protestants in the face of the menace of the Counter-Reformation when he had himself in the past decade shown so small a regard for it in his dealings with Kristian. The hesitations of the Danish Council, indeed, had in the end been overcome by nothing but the obvious aggressiveness of Swedish policy. Kristian might loudly proclaim to Protestant Europe that he would be compelled to conquer Sweden in order to prevent its falling into the hands of Sigismund; and Sigismund on his side might formally protest against Kristian's invasion of his hereditary dominions; but these were conventional gestures, and the Protestant powers of Europe, at least for the present, went on with their affairs without paying much attention to either of them.

Karl was personally in no state to conduct a war. His health was broken past recovery, his nerves had been shaken by the untimely appearance of a comet, and it was known that his death could not long be delayed. The misfortunes of the campaign of 1611 kindled a flash of his old fighting spirit, and he sent a personal challenge to his adversary to meet him in single combat; but Kristian's only reply was a rude jest at Karl's bodily infirmities. For Karl this was the last rally: the campaign was hardly over before he collapsed, and on 30 October 1611 he died at Nyköping in his sixty-second year.

---

[1] The last word on the antecedents of the War of Kalmar has been said (at least for the present) in S. U. Palme's *Sverige och Danmark, 1596-1611*, a monumental monograph. Nevertheless, two earlier studies are worth reading: O. A. Johnsen, *Finmarkens politiske Historie, aktmaessig fremstillet*, and N. Enewald, *Sverige och Finnmarken.* See too N. Ahnlund, *Oljoberget och Ladugårdsgärde,* pp. 103-9. J. Nordlander, *Om Birkarlarne* (*H.T.* 1906-7), is valuable. A. Zettersten, *Svenska Flottans Historia,* I. 320-1, has the detail about shipbuilding on the Altenfjord; B. Boëthius, *Skogen och Bygden,* p. 213, for a proposal for a Swedish colony in this area in 1672: *Kong Christian den fjerdes egenhændige Breve,* I. 49-54, for his decisive message to his Council on 30 January 1611.

Throughout December the body lay in state in the great hall of the castle, until in January 1612 it was transferred to Norrköping: the funeral proper did not take place till 21 April, at Strängnäs. Among those who made orations on the occasion were Axel Oxenstierna, who spoke, '*per longam circuitionem verborum*', of the inevitability of death; and the Bishop of Strängnäs, who proved by historical examples from Adam to the sixteenth century that no man born into the world had hitherto escaped mortality, and on the strength of this circumstantial evidence '*concludit hic omnes esse morti subjectos*'. This point disposed of, the Bishop proceeded to a comparison of Karl with Josiah—largely, it seems, because of the disasters which followed the latter's death.[1] It was not a very cheering auspice for the new reign.

(vi) *Sweden in 1611*

And indeed the situation at the moment of Gustav Adolf's accession could hardly have been more critical. He found himself committed to a conflict with Denmark from which he had no means of withdrawing, and upon whose outcome the whole future of the country seemed to hang. If Kristian were as successful as he hoped to be, the work of Gustav Vasa might be undone, and the Union of Scandinavia restored. And even if Sweden were able to preserve her independence, she might emerge from the struggle so crippled as to be unable henceforth to offer effective resistance to a real *dominium maris Baltici* in Danish hands. The great question which had agitated the North throughout the preceding century might be settled for good in Denmark's favour, and the Baltic might become a Danish 'stream'; the Russia trade might pass effectively under Danish control, Sweden's immunities in the Sound be abrogated, and Sweden herself be cut off from access to the open sea. It was a struggle for existence to which Karl had committed his successor. Yet at this grave crisis, when every man was required at home, it was impossible to contemplate the withdrawal of any Swedish troops from Russia, for there too the position seemed critical. And in Russia lay the key to the great dynastic feud which had been raging since 1600: once abandon Ivangorod and Kexholm to the control of a Polish Tsar, then farewell Narva and Viborg; and should they be lost, the road to Stockholm might not prove a long one. And with

_____
[1] *SRDA*, I. 139, 142.

Sigismund restored to the throne of his father, the Counter-Reformation would have its entry-port into the Protestant fortress of Scandinavia. Upon the ability of Jakob de la Gardie to maintain himself in Ingria hung not merely the future of the younger Vasa line but the fate of Lutheranism in the Baltic region.

At this perilous moment Sweden was really in no state to wage war. She could barely defend herself at home; she could not possibly reinforce her armies in Russia. Her navy was inefficient, her military organization in confusion, her administration lax and profoundly unpopular, her exchequer almost empty. The personal monarchy of Gustav Vasa had broken down under the weight of business which was thrust upon it; the 'rule of secretaries' had proved inadequate to redress the situation; and this lent additional urgency to the demands of the nobility for constitutional reform. For half a century rival constitutional principles had struggled for mastery, and now the hour for the triumph of oligarchical theories seemed at hand. The discontent of all classes with the government, the determination of the Lutheran zealots to impose their religious views upon any future sovereign, the uncertainty of the succession, the resentments and rancours of an aristocracy who for ten years had suffered the rigour of a harsh and suspicious ruler, the desire for vengeance on the part of many of the relatives of those who had perished at Linköping: all these things might seem to presage an oligarchical *coup d'état* which should put fetters on the monarchy and ensure the triumph of the principles of Erik Sparre.

Thus on the death of Karl IX the struggle for mercantile and political supremacy in the Baltic, the dynastic issue between the elder and younger Vasa lines, the clash of Protestantism and Catholicism in the North, and the constitutional conflict between monarchy and aristocracy, were all concentrated into one appalling crisis which summed up and brought to a point the history of the last four reigns. The prospect must have appeared daunting to the most experienced and sagacious of statesmen: at the time of Karl's death Gustav Adolf had not yet attained the age of seventeen.

CHAPTER II

THE LEGACY OF KARL IX

(i) *Accession Crisis*

GUSTAV ADOLF, the eldest son of Karl IX's second marriage with Kristina of Holstein, was born on 9 December 1594. Two months later, as Abraham Brahe informs us, his christening feast was held; and by an irony of history one of the child's godfathers was that same Erik Sparre with whom Karl was to come into such desperate conflict, while among the guests upon the occasion was Kristian Friis, then upon an embassy to Stockholm from the court of Denmark. But Sigismund's envoy, Lindorm Bonde, with more prophetic insight, declined an invitation to attend. The child was given two names in baptism: Gustav, in honour of the founder of the Vasa dynasty, and Adolf, after his maternal grandfather, the first Duke of Holstein-Gottorp. Duke Adolf's wife, Kristina of Hesse, was the daughter of the Protestant hero Philip of Hesse, and had once vainly been sought in marriage by Erik XIV: the link between Sweden and the leading Protestant state of western Germany, which Erik then had failed to forge, was now achieved in the person of the young Gustav Adolf.

Although the deposition of Sigismund was not immediately followed by Karl's assumption of the royal style, and although, as we have seen, he was always scrupulously careful to leave an opening for the claims of his nephew, Johan of Östergötland, Karl undoubtedly hoped that his son would succeed him on the throne of Sweden. The boy's education was designed to equip him for the responsibilities of royalty, and was carefully supervised by his father with this end in view. The child early showed unusual promise, and in after years a small mythology surrounded his infancy and childhood. The folk-traditions of his precocious courage and belligerency are numerous and picturesque, and some of them may have a basis in reality; but in the main they are valuable only as illustrating the effect of Gustav Adolf's personality and achievements upon the popular imagination. More solidly attested are the details

D

of his training for kingship. This was both academic and practical.
As his principal instructor the King selected Johan Schroderus, who
upon being raised to the nobility took the name of Skytte: a man of
middle-class origin with an encyclopaedic knowledge reinforced by
practical acquaintance with some sides of the business of government. Skytte grounded his pupil thoroughly in the Latin classics,
and even familiarized him to some extent with Greek, adding to
this an extensive reading in history, politics, theology and law. His
teaching seems to have been successful, for Gustav Adolf retained
his familiarity with the Latin classics throughout his life, and is
said to have carried a copy of Grotius with him on his campaigns.
History, too, had an enduring attraction for him; and, like his father,
he tried his hand at writing a history of his own times. He was
well versed in the heroic exploits of the half-legendary kings of
Swedish antiquity, and the notions then prevalent concerning
Sweden's achievements in past ages sank deeply into his mind, so
that he never forgot that he was the heir to a long line of great
monarchs who in the past had sallied out from the north to conquer
Europe and overthrow the old Empire of the Caesars. Runic studies
were just beginning to be cultivated in Sweden, and in Johannes
Bureus, their leading Swedish exponent, Gustav Adolf found a
friend who inspired him with his own taste for archaeology and his
own misconceptions of Sweden's historic past.[1]

Gustav Adolf early showed a special aptitude for the acquisition
of foreign languages. From his childhood he was bilingual in German
and Swedish, and by the time he had reached maturity he was more
or less conversant with seven other languages (or eight, if we count
Scots). This was to prove an important asset to him in the future.
With the study of mathematics, optics and mechanics, his purely
academic education began to shade off into practical preparation for
his profession, since these subjects were pursued mainly in their
military implications. In after-life he held strong views upon the
necessity of mathematics to the practical soldier, and it was not
the least of the causes of his military success that he had acquired a
thorough mastery of the theoretical and technical side of the art of
war. The versatile Skytte, indeed, studied all branches of military
science with his pupil, and surveyed the literature of war from Roman
times down to the latest innovations of Maurice of Orange; but
Gustav Adolf probably learned more from conversation with foreign

[1] For further discussion of this point, see below, Chapter IX.

soldiers of fortune who might be visiting the court of Stockholm, and above all from Jakob de la Gardie, who had succeeded John of Orange in the command of the Swedish armies in Livonia, and had probably picked up some of the new Dutch tactics which his predecessor had tried to introduce during his period of command. Rhetoric, too, he learned from Skytte; and here the seed fell on good soil, for Gustav Adolf had inherited that gift for vivid and pungent oratory which had been so conspicuous in his father and his grandfather.

His apprenticeship to the practical business of government began before he was out of his childhood. At the age of ten he was attending council-meetings; at the age of twelve hearing complaints from his future subjects. He was employed to receive and respond to ambassadors, and at the period of Karl's illness was commissioned to address the assembled *riksdag* on his behalf. At the age of fifteen, he asked to be given an independent military command; and though this was refused, he was able to press his claims successfully a year later, upon the outbreak of war with Denmark. Before his father's death he had seen most sides of the work that lay before him, and had been in many parts of the dominions that he was to rule.

This rigorous and purposeful preparation had been put to its first trial in 1610, when the old King's illness had led to a virtual Regency by the Queen and her eldest son. The assumption of full charge of the government, which was to follow his father's death, was a severer test; and it is a tribute to Skytte and Karl IX that it should have been so easily surmounted. Sweden had good cause to thank them for the care they had lavished on the heir to the throne; for besides the book-learning that they crammed into him, they succeeded in inculcating a sense of duty, a consciousness of responsibility, and a salutary touch of Christian humility, which saved him from his innately despotic temper, kept his learning free from pedantry, robbed his ambition of vainglory, and preserved his valour from wantonness. His mind and body were well armed at all points for the work that awaited him. It was a triumph of sound pedagogy.[1]

[1] For Gustav Adolf's birth and education see, in general, Hallenberg, I. 3 *seqq.* (all the favourite anecdotes); N. Ahnlund, *Gustav Adolf den Store*, Ch. I; G. Wittrock, *Gustav II Adolf*, pp. 5-19; Generalstaben, *Gustav II Adolf* (cited henceforth as Generalstaben, *G II A*), pp. 1-2, 39-44; *Anteckningar af Johannes Thomae Agrivillensis Bureus*, p. 23.

The death of Karl IX on 30 October 1611 inaugurated a political crisis which was not finally resolved until nearly two months later. In the days that immediately followed, the government was assumed provisionally by Queen Kristina and Duke Johan. It was they who made the necessary arrangements for calling the *råd* to Nyköping, and it was in their name that writs went out early in November summoning the *riksdag* to meet at the beginning of the following month—a *riksdag* which they took care should be as fully representative as possible.[1] It was clear to them that the support of the Estates would be necessary. The treasury was almost empty; a new onslaught by Kristian IV faced them next year; the temper of the country was uncertain. In more than one district Karl's death was made the occasion for popular outbursts indicative of the general dislike of the government of the late King, and these showed an alarming tendency to concentrate hatred upon Kristina herself. There were pamphlets in circulation championing the cause of Sigismund. The situation in Estonia was so dubious that the government deferred notifying that province of the demise of the Crown. But the main problem to be faced was the blunt question: Who was to succeed Karl IX? A Regency? Gustav Adolf? Johan? This question should have been settled beyond cavil by the decision of the Norrköping *riksdag* of 1604, and the Succession Pact of that year. It had then been laid down that Gustav Adolf should succeed his father, but that until he reached the age of eighteen the government should be in the hands of a Regency consisting of the hereditary Princes, with one other member to be named in Karl's will. At the age of eighteen he should enter into a half share of the government, and was not to obtain full control until he had completed his twenty-fourth year. Unfortunately, there were only two hereditary Princes of full age in Sweden—the Queen-Mother and Duke Johan; and Karl had neglected to nominate another Regent in his will. Instead, he had complicated the issue by reserving the rights of Johan and urging the Estates to recognize him as King, if he should show any inclination for the crown. But the will had never been accepted by the Estates, and thus (in the matter of the succession) lacked legal validity. Furthermore, it seems very probable that Karl in the last year of his life left behind him more specific instructions about a Regency; but as these had never been committed to paper they could not now be taken as a guide.

[1] *AOSB*, I. i. 47, I. ii. 28-9; *SRDA*, I. 21.

There can be no doubt that the main purpose for which the *riksdag* was now summoned to Nyköping was to obtain its opinion upon this delicate matter. In the meantime Kristina and Johan carried on the government on Gustav Adolf's behalf, assisted and counselled by Karl IX's old *råd*, and supported by the waning influence of his former secretary, Dr. Chesnecopherus. The strongest man in this circle of counsellors was Axel Oxenstierna, and this in spite of the fact that he was one of its youngest members. Oxenstierna was born in 1583 of an ancient noble house intimately connected by marriage with the leading families of the kingdom: his mother was a Bielke, his maternal grandmother a Posse, his own wife a Bååt. The Oxenstiernas had steered a careful course through the political breakers of the last two decades of the century, and had emerged on the winning side, having saved their heads, their lands, and, on the whole, their honour—no inconsiderable feat. Axel and his brother were sent overseas to study at German universities, perhaps with a view to keeping them safely out of the way in case of political accidents at home. Axel proved himself in all things the model student, and won some reputation among his tutors and companions for his theological attainments. It is said that his mother intended him for the Church; and Oxenstierna himself was conscious that he might have made a successful ecclesiastical career for himself, and was occasionally inclined to regret that pressure of business left him no time for the pure scholarship in which he delighted. Yet his education was not thrown away; for the logic, politics and history which he imbibed were useful to him in later life, and he acquired in his student days the habit of working long hours, without which he could scarcely have got through the multitudinous duties that Gustav Adolf was to place upon his shoulders. He returned home from Germany to find his family the object of Karl's suspicion, thanks to the connection kept up by his mother with her relatives the Bielkes; and thus it came about that his academic ambitions were sacrificed to political necessity, and he was put to work in the Chancery for free clothes and small and irregular wages, as a sort of family hostage to the Crown.[1] Taken on the permanent staff in 1605, he was given as one of his earliest duties the task of assisting at the trial of his relative Hogen-

---

[1] This was not the only example of Karl's securing the fidelity of his nobles by these tactics: *cf.* the case of Henrik Fleming: [S. Loenbom], *Historiskt Archivum*, I. 48.

skild Bielke, by whose traitorous activities his own mother was gravely compromised. It is hardly surprising that he should have disapproved of Karl IX's treatment of the nobility. Subsequently he was employed upon business of steadily increasing importance— including an embassy to Mecklenburg in 1607—and at last, in May 1609, at the exceptionally early age of twenty-six, he was appointed a member of Karl's *råd*. His seriousness and serenity of temper, his high sense of public duty, together with an aptitude for affairs surprising in view of his education, soon gave him a leading position among his fellow counsellors. Head of a great family, backed by great wealth, he had gifts of leadership and a stock of political courage which had nothing to do with birth or position, and which were to leave permanent marks on Swedish history. And now Oxenstierna had a policy framed, a plan of campaign thought out; he had formulated views on the most desirable form of government for his country, and these views he was prepared to back by action.[1]

The uncertain position in November 1611 offered him precisely the opportunity for which he was waiting. Oxenstierna was too good a Lutheran to have any doubts about adhering to the younger Vasa line; but he was far from averse to seizing the opportunity to set right what he, in common with most of the nobility, considered had been done amiss by Karl. The rule of secretaries, the conception of a popular or parliamentary despotism, were alike repugnant to him. The weakness of the monarchy at this moment, therefore, must be used to bring the government of the country back to its old legal basis; the *råd* and the nobility must resume their rightful place in public affairs. A Regency, or the immediate rule of Gustav Adolf, would suit Oxenstierna and his friends better than the accession of Johan; for if Johan, who had attained his majority, obtained the throne, he might be less easy to deal with than a minor, or a Council of Regency upon which the nobility might hope to be represented. From Gustav Adolf constitutional guarantees might be extracted as the price of his immediate investiture with full powers, particularly as he had already shown signs of being more favourably disposed towards the aristocracy than his father had been.[2]

---

[1] For Oxenstierna's early years, see N. Ahnlund, *Axel Oxenstierna*, pp. 7-101; W. Tham, *Axel Oxenstierna, 1583-1612, passim*.
[2] Tham, p. 217.

From the point of view of the Queen-Mother, too, the recognition of Gustav Adolf was the most desirable solution; for she must have felt that a Regency upon which Johan would be one of the leading personages might offer temptations to him to effect a *coup d'état*. Despite her talent for business—especially for finance—she does not herself seem to have been anxious to assume the responsibilities of government, and she cannot have been unaffected by her obvious unpopularity in the weeks after her husband's death. Kristina, then, might well be willing to purchase by constitutional concessions the support of Oxenstierna and his associates for the immediate succession of her son.

There remained Duke Johan. Johan at this time was twenty-two years old, and had recently been showing signs of emancipating himself from the tutelage in which Karl had always been careful to keep him. He had been brought up at his uncle's court, a sickly, rather apathetic child, and from his boyhood until the hour of his death remained more or less in subjection to Karl and his family. In 1604 he had meekly renounced his claims to the throne, and when the Estates offered him the duchy of Finland (which was indeed rightly his, since Johan III had given it to him) he declined it under pressure from Karl, and contented himself with the much less important province of Östergötland instead. Karl, with his outward vacillations and inward qualms, was always nervous about Johan. He had headed him off the dangerous Finnish frontier; but who could tell what plots might not be brewing at Bråborg, the Östergötland manor where the Duke kept his court and his council? Johan was therefore kept under supervision; he was not allowed to acquire military experience or given much share in the government. Naturally he felt aggrieved; and it would not have been very surprising if he had participated in the intrigues of his half-brother Sigismund. But Johan, though sulky, was loyal. It is unlikely that he ever had serious thoughts of a usurpation. He commanded no following in the country, had little ambition, and no great taste for work. As long as he could obtain an addition to his estates—as long as his Duchy could be 'improved', as the phrase went—he would probably be content: content even to abandon the idea of a Regency.[1]

None of the three persons, therefore, in whose hands the fate

---

[1] Tham, pp. 157-60, 168, 205, 208, 229, 245, 271; *SRDA*, I. 551; Wittrock, p. 15.

of the King and the kingdom really rested, was prepared to make much of a fight for the resolution of Norrköping, and two of them were very willing to upset it. This was not the view of the nation at large. The assurances of fidelity which came in from various parts of the country upon the news of Karl's death almost all tacitly took it for granted that the arrangements of 1604 would stand.[1] But the decision scarcely lay in the hands of the nation and its representatives. With the *riksdag* the line taken by the *råd* would probably be decisive, for it was to the *råd* that the Estates would look for a lead. And the *råd* was solidly behind Axel Oxenstierna.

When the *riksdag* met at Nyköping, therefore, on 6 December 1611, it is likely that the issue had been virtually decided, and that the 'Proposition' which the *råd* submitted to them for their consideration—they were to consider how the government was to be carried on, and what measures were to be taken in regard to the Danish war—was, as to its former part at least, of a mainly academic nature.[2] Gustav Adolf celebrated his seventeenth birthday on the 9th, and on the 10th Duke Johan addressed the Estates on behalf of himself and the Queen. He asked them whether they desired to adhere to the Norrköping resolution, or 'adopt any other method'— a form of words which certainly left it open to anybody to suggest that Johan should take the crown himself.[3] But nobody seems to have taken this hint, and the replies which the Estates returned to his question showed remarkable unanimity in favour of the arrangement of 1604, only the Burghers venturing to suggest that Gustav Adolf had now entered upon his eighteenth year.[4] It was now clear to Johan that he had no chance of the crown, and he accordingly reformulated on the 14th his demands for an 'improvement' of his Duchy.[5] Two days later he made a formal renunciation of his claims and professed his unwillingness to participate in a Regency. At the same time Oxenstierna made a similar statement on behalf of the Queen-Mother. The Estates, somewhat disconcerted, were now invited to consider altering the resolution of Norrköping so as to permit Gustav Adolf to assume the crown at once, and to suggest

---

[1] *SRDA*, I. 8-15.
[2] *SRDA*, I. 28-30, 36-7; Tham, pp. 270-9.
[3] *SRDA*, I. 37-8; C. A. Hessler, *Gustaf II Adolfs konungaförsäkran*, pp. 178-9.
[4] *SRDA*, I. 38-42.
[5] *ibid*, I. 45; I. Wadén, *Berättande källor till Calmarkrigets historia*, p. 103 note 1.

'in what manner he may best carry on the government'. The Estates rightly interpreted this as an invitation to formulate their grievances, and in the course of the next few days all of them, except the Peasantry, produced miscellaneous and somewhat incongruous schedules of abuses or demands for privileges, upon the acceptance or redress of which the immediate recognition of Gustav Adolf was to be made dependent. The demands of the Nobility, which seem to have been drafted by Oxenstierna himself, were particularly significant. They asked that their goods and lands be not taken from them contrary to law without previous lawful judgment, and that all who had suffered deprivation in this fashion might have their property restored to them; they asked that the King in future entertain no irresponsible accusations against his nobles, nor visit them with his displeasure, nor imprison them, nor ransack their houses, without proper preliminary investigation of the charge; they protested against the threats and accusations from the Commonalty to which they were exposed, and which purported to display the nobility as the bloodsuckers of the country and the origin of all misfortunes and disorder; they asked for large extensions of their economic and social privileges; and they demanded that no war be begun without the consent of råd and Estates, and that no foreigner be given an official position in the country. It was an indictment of the rule of the late King.[1]

It was left to the råd to coordinate the replies of the Estates into an orderly programme of constitutional reform. The råd had its own grievances, as Oxenstierna's notes show. Letters and mandates had been sent out bearing the words 'with the advice and consent of the råd', when in fact no such advice had been asked or consent given; members had been visited with the King's displeasure because they gave unpalatable advice, and their counsel had been judged '*ex eventu*'; their wages had apparently not been regularly paid; the working of the Chancery had been interfered with; and members had been compelled to attend *riksdagar* at great cost to themselves.[2] It is obvious that the råd desired to get a firmer grip on the business of state, for one clause in Oxenstierna's draft read: 'that *no* matter be dealt with which concerns the Kingdom without the advice, counsel and participation of the råd'.[3]

[1] *SRDA*, I. 29, 31, 47-8, 52-4, 57, 110, 143-6; *AOSB*, I. 1. 610; Hessler, *op. cit.*, pp. 180-3.
[2] *SRDA*, I. 69.
[3] *ibid.*, *loc. cit.*; Hessler, p. 184.

This was indeed dropped as too extreme; but it shows how far the *råd* would have liked to push their advantage. For the rest, most of their demands, and the principal demands of the Estates, were in substance incorporated into the document of thirteen clauses which was presented to Gustav Adolf on 19 December. The draughtsmen of this document made their attitude perfectly plain in their final paragraph:

in return [for the Crown's making these concessions] and *when* we have received guarantees for the fulfilment of these demands, as well as those which each Estate severally has put forward, the *råd* and Estates of the kingdom promise . . . that they will not only firmly and constantly adhere to their . . . pledges . . . but will after that day have and hold His Royal Highness for their . . . ruling Lord and King,

and, despite the resolution of Norrköping,

will, of the authority which thus far in them lies, acknowledge His Royal Highness as of full age, seeing that God . . . has made up in understanding what is lacking in years.[1]

It was an ultimatum; and it was scarcely possible for Gustav Adolf to reject it. By 23 December it had been embodied as a draft Charter, which was duly submitted to the approval of the Estates, and accepted by them; and three days later Gustav Adolf signified his willingness to assume the government on these terms.[2] It only remained now to give formal sanction to those extensions of his Duchy which Johan desired, and to draw up a fair copy of the Charter. This was ready on 31 December; but it was then so late in the afternoon that Oxenstierna asked the Estates (who had been waiting above three hours to hear it read) whether they would not defer the reading till the following day.

Fit conclamatio: placet, placet; unus vero e medio turbae extulit vocem ac alte dixit: 'We humbly ask that no foreigners may be put to rule over us in the provinces, as has been done in the past', et dixerunt omnes, Amen, fiat, fiat.[3]

Oxenstierna was able to pacify this bold spirit (with whose sentiments he was himself in cordial agreement) and the assembly dispersed amicably enough. They had already passed a resolution formally

---

[1] *SRDA*, I. 64-5. [2] *ibid.*, I. 29. [3] *ibid.*, I. 33.

setting aside the resolution of 1604 and accepting Gustav Adolf as their King. The Charter, when finally read on 1 January 1612, conformed closely to the previous draft, though the monarchy avoided the appearance of complete capitulation by making a few alterations and omissions. On 4 January the *råd* took the oath of fidelity to the new ruler, and two days later Oxenstierna was appointed Chancellor in terms which seemed to promise him unusual latitude and discretion.[1] It was the first sign of the coming reconciliation between the Crown and the aristocracy; and it was the beginning of one of the great political partnerships of history.

Gustav Adolf was King at last. The misrule of Karl IX had goaded the *råd* to hold the monarchy to ransom, and his foolish havering about the succession had provided them with their opportunity. The reaction which he had provoked had fallen upon his successor, and Gustav Adolf's reign began with a major constitutional crisis. The significance of the Charter, in the minds of its framers, and in the light of what was to come after it, is discussed elsewhere [2]: here it is sufficient to notice that the settlement of January 1612 proved a stable one. Duke Johan never revived any pretensions to the crown; the *råd* and the aristocracy made no further attempt in Gustav Adolf's lifetime to press their political theories on the monarchy. For the present, at all events, the long controversy between Erik Sparre and the Vasas seemed to have reached an amicable conclusion, and King and nobles were free to turn their attention from clashing theories of government to the urgent problems of war and foreign policy. The old wounds, it appeared, were not to be kept open; the signature of new privileges for the Nobility sealed the reconciliation of the Crown and the first Estate [3]; the process of 'healing and settling' had begun. It was time to think of the danger from Denmark. And on the day upon which he put his signature to the privileges of the Nobility, Gustav Adolf took his departure from Nyköping, 'in a sleigh all draped in black', and set his course for the battlefront in the south.

---

[1] *AOSB*, II. 1. 1. The commission appointing him ran: '. . . it being impossible precisely to prescribe what he is to order and do in such an office and calling, We leave it to his discretion and understanding, as he may deem best, and as he shall answer for it to God, to Us, and to every honourable Swedish man'.

[2] See below, Chapter VI, section (i).

[3] *SRDA*, I. 111-24: compare their original demands, *ibid.*, 103-11. This question will be dealt with in Vol. II, Chapter XI.

(ii) *The War of Kalmar*[1]

He found a military situation which was anything but encouraging. The campaign of 1611 had gone very badly for Sweden, and the prospects for 1612 were dark. The fall of Kalmar in May 1611, followed two months later by the capitulation of the strong castle which guarded it, had put the leading harbour in the south-east into Kristian IV's hands, and had opened the way to the conquest of Öland, and a Danish advance against Östergötland, and perhaps beyond. The Swedish navy had lost twenty ships, scuttled by their commanders in Kalmar harbour to save them from the Danes. Finnmark, for whose sake Karl had risked a war, had already been overrun by a Norwegian force. Such successes as the Swedes had obtained—at Kristianopel, in Jämtland, and on the island of Ösel—by no means countervailed these serious reverses; and though Öland had indeed been recovered before Karl's death, the event was to show that the Swedes were unable to hold it. The plain truth was that Karl IX had provoked a war which he had not the means to wage, and had drawn down upon himself an adversary whose forces were more numerous, better equipped, more professional than his own. The main Swedish army was fighting in Russia, and Karl had refused to recall it; and he had delayed too long to be able to obtain mercenary assistance from overseas in time. Sweden therefore began the war with a home army which was probably weaker than at any time previously in Karl's reign, and which in training and armament was unfitted to meet the Danish mercenaries in pitched battle. Nor did the prospects appear much better for a purely defensive strategy; for though the peculiarly Swedish type of ambush (*bråte*) could be, and was, employed with effect in forest country, any serious resistance must be based on fortresses, and these as a rule were in an unsatisfactory state. Göteborg had no defences, and was dependent for safety upon the neighbouring strongholds of

[1] Short accounts of the war are to be found in Wittrock, *op. cit.*, and J. A. Fridericia, *Danmarks Riges Historie 1588-1699*. An old-fashioned standard history is A. Larsen, *Kalmarkrigen. Et Bidrag til de nordiske Rigers Krigshistorie*. General-staben, *G II A*, is full and non-technical. The best account, however, is in *Sveriges Krig*, I. (for land operations), and *Sveriges Krig*, App. Vol. I. (naval operations): the latter may be supplemented by *Svenska Flottans Historia*, I. To these may be added F. Baehrendtz, *Striden om Kalmar 1611*; T. Michell, *History of the Scottish Expedition to Norway in 1612*; G. Petri, *Kungl. Första Livgrenadjärregementets Historia*; B. Broomé, *Nils Stiernsköld*; I. Wadén, *Berättande källor till Calmarkrigets historia*, and the review of this book by I. Andersson in *Scandia* for 1936.

Älvsborg and Gullberg; Jönköping, the strategic key to central
Sweden, was inadequately protected by defensive works which were
still under construction; Stegeborg, which guarded Söderköping,
was weaker still. Stockholm, Vaxholm and Nyköping, though they
had recently been repaired, were hardly likely to make prolonged
resistance if seriously attacked. Only Kalmar was really strong;
and Kalmar had been lost almost at the outset of the war. Moreover, the Danish superiority on land was matched by an even
greater superiority at sea. The Swedish navy was indeed numerous,
thanks to Karl's unremitting efforts; but it was inferior in tonnage,
and still more so in weight of metal; and it was hopelessly emas-
culated by a dilatory, unenterprising and corrupt administration.
Consequently Kristian was able from the outset to gain command of
the sea, and to retain it throughout the war. He was able to institute
an immediate blockade of his enemy: the north German ports
could no longer send to Sweden the goods of which she stood in
need. The Swedish fleet was never in sufficient strength to meet
the Danes in battle. Denmark was able to transport her troops
round the Swedish coasts unhindered, and to raid them with
impunity. She was able to cut off Sweden from the mercenary
market of western Europe. She could undertake the successful
siege of a maritime fortress such as Kalmar. In a war in which the
strategy of the armies was rarely successful, her naval preponderance
was of very great importance.

Kristian IV seems from the beginning to have aimed not merely
at victory but at conquest: the Union, broken in 1523, was at last
to be restored. His strategy was consequently directed not so much
at the annihilation of the Swedish armies as at a victorious advance
upon Stockholm. Such a plan, however, was made difficult by the
facts of geography. Geography admittedly gave him certain advantages: from his bases in Blekinge, Halland and Norway he could
strike simultaneously and unexpectedly at widely separated points,
and thus distract and confuse the enemy. But on the other hand
geography severely limited his possible lines of advance. Assuming
that a serious offensive through Värmland or Jämtland was out
of the question, he must first take Jönköping, and then advance
northward over the rugged and thickly forested defiles of the
Tiveden or the Holaveden (*i.e.* west or east of Lake Vätter);
and even when he had passed these he would find himself confronted
by the great water-barrier which stretches through the Hjälmaren

and Mälaren to Södertälje and protects Stockholm from the south. Sweden, indeed, was a very difficult country for an invader. Roads were few and bad, population and means of subsistence scanty, the opportunities for ambushes and guerilla fighting almost unlimited. The moving of a large force tended to be a matter of extreme difficulty, while the moving of small bodies exposed them to great danger. Moreover, it was impossible to advance even against Jönköping

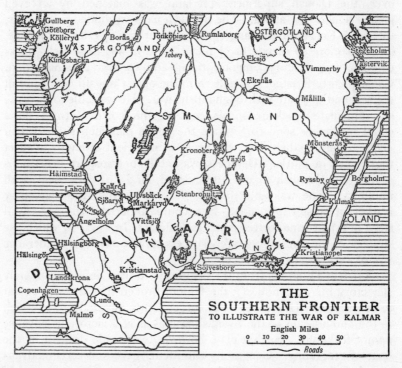

THE
SOUTHERN FRONTIER
TO ILLUSTRATE THE WAR OF KALMAR
English Miles
0   10   20   30   40   50
Roads

without protection for the inner flank of the Danish army—the right flank for a force advancing from Halland, the left, for a force advancing from Blekinge; and such advances would therefore entail subsidiary operations either in Västergötland or Småland. The capture of Kalmar had been an element in such a subsidiary operation; and it must inevitably be followed by an attack on Älvsborg. In the meantime it would probably prove impossible to prevent Swedish detachments from penetrating into Danish territory and laying waste the frontier provinces, and though the military importance of such raids might be small, they could be a considerable annoyance. The strategic problem was thus not an easy one; and the most important single fact about the military operations of the War of Kalmar is that Kristian IV never came within measurable distance of solving it. Indeed, he was never able to begin his grand advance north from Jönköping at all. His forces were never at any time large enough for combined operations on the necessary scale, and such numerical superiority as he did enjoy was not great enough to outweigh the disadvantage of campaigning in a hostile and inhospitable country. The preliminary operations on the flanks were all that he was able to achieve.

Nevertheless, at the beginning of 1612 it was by no means apparent that this would be the case; and Kristian's preliminary operations had already inflicted very serious damage. The Swedish army on the east coast, which had retreated from Kalmar, was observing the Danes from its entrenched camp at Ryssby and looking out for a chance to recover the town; but the best chance that was ever likely to present itself had already been bungled by Karl IX. And unless Kalmar could be recovered by arms, it was likely to prove a costly business to buy it back at a peace conference.

The short winter campaign upon which Gustav Adolf was now to embark had no aim so definite or so ambitious as the recovery of Kalmar. Its object was simply to molest the enemy by harassing raids at a time of the year when frost made movement easy. It was conceived in the true spirit of border warfare, and sought to inflict damage by plunder, arson and massacre, rather than by serious military operations. The Danes on their side had planned a precisely similar enterprise on another part of the front; for this was a war long and evilly remembered for the atrocities committed by both sides. No major clash between the armies resulted. Gustav Adolf ravaged Blekinge, Kristian devastated Västergötland. Neither expedition presented any points of serious military interest, and each achieved its object, as the smoke of the burning villages testified. The Swedish raid is remembered for a mishap to Gustav Adolf which might well have had fatal consequences: as he was returning with his small force from his expedition he was overtaken by Danish cavalry near Vittsjö; his rearguard was taken by surprise and scattered; the King fled with his men across the ice of a small lake, and of the streams that fed it. He was crossing one of these streams when the ice cracked under the weight of man and horse, and he was rescued only with difficulty. The episode made some stir a the time; but the only circumstance about it of any real significance was that the King's rescuer was Per Banér—son to that Gustav Banér whom Karl IX had executed. Thus the water of Vittsjö helped to wash away the bloodstains of Linköping.[1]

Less than a month later Kristian IV was also in personal danger. After completing his raid into Västergötland he had returned to Bohus; and there he received intelligence that the Swedish army of the west, under Jesper Matsson Cruus, was making a foray into Halland, and had burnt the port of Varberg to the ground. He moved out from Bohus in an effort to intercept Cruus' retreat, and at the end of a long day's ride came up with him on 20 February at Kölleryd, just north of the Danish frontier. Here a battle was fought which resulted in the only real success won by the Swedes in the whole course of the war. Kristian's exhausted force came up against considerably superior numbers, and was completely defeated: Kristian himself escaped with great difficulty from the battlefield. The strategic effect was *nil*.

Thereupon this sporadic winter campaign of raids and counter-raids came to an end; and both sides began to collect their resources for the summer. The Swedish *råd* did not look forward with much confidence to the campaigning season. A survey of the situation drawn up in their name towards the end of March by Axel Oxenstierna painted the condition of the country in the darkest colours. Surrounded by open or concealed enemies, without a reliable friend in Europe, Sweden could not feel that any part of her territory was safe from the invader. For over half a century the country had been engaged in almost continuous warfare. Its resources were now exhausted. Its stores of guns, ammunition and powder were running out; it had neither food nor clothes for its soldiers, nor fodder for its horses; the best sailors were deserting because the government could no longer pay their wages with regularity, and many of them had actually entered the Danish service. There seemed no prospect of any change for the better: taxes were already as heavy as the country could bear; and to attempt any further exactions would be 'intolerable and unwise'.[2] Yet, had the *råd* but known it, the future was not so sombre as it seemed. Kristian too was feeling the strain of the war. His mercenary soldiers were ruinously expensive, and

[1] For an example of the interest aroused abroad by the affair at Vittsjö, see the circumstantial account of it in Hist. MSS. Comm. *Rutland*, I. 434.

[2] *AOSB*, I. ii. 42-7, Oxenstierna to Kristina, 25 March 1612. A summary is printed in *Register öfver Rådslag i Konung Gustaf II Adolfs tid*, pp. 249-51.

he was finding it increasingly difficult to pay them. Shortage of food and fodder, the ravages of epidemic disease, were taking heavy toll of the Danish armies; and the ruthless devastation on either side of the frontier must certainly increase his difficulties in the forthcoming campaign.

And in fact the Danish attack in 1612 was never as formidable as it had seemed likely to be. The plan of campaign was essentially the same as in 1611. The primary strategic object, as before, was an advance into the Mälar region over the Holaveden, preceded by the capture of Jönköping; and the preliminary advance on Jönköping was to be prepared and protected by diversionary attacks on either flank. The capture of Kalmar in 1611 gave Kristian a strong base in the east; and it was now his object to take Älvsborg and Gullberg, and so provide himself with a similar advanced base in the west. At the worst, the capture of Älvsborg would give him a powerful weapon in any peace negotiations; for the experience of 1570 had proved how highly the Swedes were willing to pay for its redemption. Once Älvsborg was in his hand, and his left flank thus secured, he would move on Jönköping. In the meantime he hoped that his eastern army would have cleared Småland of the enemy and have made some effect upon the defences of Östergötland; it would then be in a position to join him either at Jönköping or on the march northward from that town over the Holaveden.

In May, therefore, Kristian began the long-expected attack on Älvsborg. Älvsborg was a fortress strongly sited on a high rock rising steeply from the southern bank of the Göta river; and, with its twin fortress of Gullberg, a little to the east,[1] it barred the passage of the estuary, and protected Karl IX's new town of Göteborg (which lay on the north bank) from attack. Älvsborg at this time had a garrison of some 600 men, and was by contemporary standards a formidable obstacle. Under the shadow of its guns lay the Swedish west-coast fleet. This unfortunate squadron had at the beginning of the war been even more backward in its preparations than the Baltic fleet at Stockholm; and in spite of repeated exhortations from Karl IX and Gustav Adolf it had not yet put to sea. It was not now ever likely to do so, since a Danish detachment was watching the entrance to the harbour as long as the channel remained ice-free,

---

[1] Kristian had made a demonstration against Gullberg at the beginning of the year: Wadén has shown that the tradition of its heroic defence upon that occasion by Emmerentia Pauli is largely legend: Wadén, pp. 60-77.

E

and had already made an unsuccessful attempt to burn the Swedish ships as they lay at anchor. The Danish blockade of Älvsborg had the further inconvenience that it barred the way to much-needed reinforcements: Sweden had been raising mercenaries in Holland and England, and Älvsborg was their only possible port of disembarkation.

The Swedish commander in Älvsborg, Olof Stråle, seems to have done the best he could in the circumstances. The attack apparently took Gustav Adolf by surprise: at all events, a relieving army was hardly to be expected. The besiegers had heavy artillery and trained sappers; and both were used with effect. The attack began on 5 May; by 17 May Kristian was summoning Stråle to surrender; by 22 May a complete breach had been made in the defences; and two days later Stråle, who had been wounded in the fighting, accepted terms and marched out with flying colours, followed by what was left of the garrison. The warships lying in the harbour had been scuttled, in accordance with Gustav Adolf's instructions; but the Danes had no difficulty in raising them. A few days later Gullberg capitulated too.[1]

The moment had now come, it would seem, for Kristian to advance against Jönköping. Instead, he attempted a forward move to Lake Väner—possibly with a view to probing the Tiveden route northward. He ran into such difficulties that he was unable to get further than Lidköping; and after what amounted to little more than an excentric raid was forced to fall back on the Göta. About the same time, in the latter half of June, the Danish eastern army under Rantzau, which had already recovered Öland, began to push northwards into Östergötland, and met with little organized opposition until it came to the neighbourhood of Vimmerby. Rantzau, like Kristian, found great difficulty in feeding his army, and hoped to overcome it by sending the Danish fleet in advance up the coast to capture Västervik, which could then, it was supposed, be used as a supply base. Unluckily for him the road between Västervik and Vimmerby proved impassable for anything but pack-horses. Nevertheless, an isolated Danish force was able to capture Söderköping, and to maintain its hold on it until August.

---

[1] Stråle was imprisoned by Gustav Adolf for surrendering; was later released for lack of evidence against him; was employed in 1614 in the new Supreme Court (*Svea Hovrätt*); and in 1619, after Gustav Adolf had paid a personal visit to Älvsborg, was again prosecuted, and heavily fined. Hallenberg, II. 422-3, 633-4. There is an account of the reduction of Älvsborg by one of the English soldiers in the Danish army in Hist. MSS. Comm. *Various Collections*, VII. 265-8.

At the time when this two-pronged advance on either flank was developing, Gustav Adolf was at Jönköping. Had Kristian, after capturing Älvsborg, moved at once against him, he would have immobilized Gustav Adolf, and so have left Rantzau a free hand on the east coast. As it was, Gustav Adolf was able to deal with each Danish army in succession, and effectually to parry the designs of both. He struck first at Rantzau; and though he failed to cut off his retreat, as he had hoped to do, he compelled the Danish eastern army to fall back on Kalmar, which it reached in such a condition as to make it incapable of serious operations for some time to come. Meanwhile the news had reached him that Kristian was at last advancing on Jönköping. He calculated, however, that the defenders could be relied upon to hold out until he came to their assistance; for he knew that Cruus was blocking the only road from Älvsborg— that by Alingsås—over which guns could be transported. Kristian would therefore take the more southerly route, and would arrive before Jönköping without his siege-train. These calculations proved correct. Kristian could do nothing with Jönköping; Cruus was threatening his left and rear; Gustav Adolf was hurrying back from Småland to attack his right flank. The attack on Jönköping was therefore abandoned, and Kristian retired somewhat ignominiously to Skåne.

This really marks the end of military operations on land; but before Kristian would abandon his hope of conquest he was resolved to see what could be effected by sea. Collecting a considerable squadron at Copenhagen, he set sail for Kalmar, and thence cut across to Danzig, in the hope of catching the elusive Swedish fleet in the open seas and annihilating it. But the Swedish fleet, which had indeed recently been out on a somewhat aimless cruise to the Vistula, was now back at its base at Älvsnabben, in the Stockholm archipelago. Kristian decided to seek it out there. On his way he took on board a small contingent of Rantzau's troops; and this gave the Swedish government the impression that he intended to attempt a landing in force in the neighbourhood of Stockholm and carry the capital by assault. This, however, was probably not his intention. At the southern end of the Stockholm skerries Kristian made contact with the Swedish fleet under Admiral Gyllenstierna. Gyllenstierna, being heavily outnumbered, deemed it prudent to withdraw through the labyrinth of islands and channels to the protection of the fort of Vaxholm, some miles to the east of Stockholm. With great

daring, Kristian followed him in; came up with him at Vaxholm;
and began to cannonade the castle and the Swedish men-of-war
under its walls. Fortunately, Vaxholm had at that moment received
a garrison of fresh Flemish mercenaries under the command of one
Mönnichhofen. These men had had an adventurous journey to
Stockholm. Sailing from Amsterdam early in July, twelve hundred
strong, they had been compelled by the loss of Älvsborg to seek some
other landing-place, and had eventually disembarked at the extreme
inner end of the Trondheim fjord. Thence they had marched
across Norway into Jämtland, and so reached Stockholm at a moment
when their arrival was extremely opportune. A party of Scots
mercenaries under Alexander Ramsay, which had landed in the
Moldefjord about the same time, and with similar intentions, had
been less fortunate: they were ambushed by Norwegian peasants as
they were marching up the Gudbrandsdal, and massacred almost to
a man.[1]

It was Mönnichhofen's vigorous defence that turned the scale
at Vaxholm. By 4 September Kristian was no nearer destroying the
fleet or taking the castle; autumn was drawing on; the Baltic would
soon be stormy. It was better to give it up and make for home.
The Danish fleet accordingly withdrew; and Kristian's final effort
had been made in vain. Its main effect had been on the nerves of
the government at Stockholm, who in their alarm had fetched
Gustav Adolf home post-haste from Jönköping.

The failure at Vaxholm was immediately followed by an offer to
negotiate. Already in January Gustav Adolf had attempted to parley,
and as an earnest of good will had abandoned the use of the style
'King of the Lapps of Nordland'; but the Swedish trumpeter had
been turned back by the Danes without an answer, and Kristian
when negotiating about exchange of prisoners continued to refer
to Gustav Adolf merely as 'duke'. But on 18 September Kristian
suggested a meeting on the frontier, and his suggestion was at once
accepted. Since the Danes refused an armistice, both sides made
ostentatious preparations for the next campaign. Troops were
concentrated on the border in the hope of influencing the negotiations by a show of force; the work on the fortifications at Jönköping
was speeded up; and Gustav Adolf made arrangements to hire
warships from the Dutch. But to all intents and purposes the war
was over. Both sides were weary of it, and Europe was weary of it

[1] Michell, pp. 22, 34 *seqq.*

too. Ever since the outbreak of hostilities, interested powers had been trying to restore peace. The war had interfered seriously with commerce, and Lübeck, in particular, had been severely affected by the Danish blockade of Sweden and the activities of Danish privateers. The Hanse in general feared the possible aggrandizement of Denmark, and cordially hoped that Sweden would win. The Dutch were of the same mind. Ever since 1609 Oldenbarnevelt had pursued a policy directed towards closer political contact with the Protestant states of the north; and the outbreak of war had thrown his plans out of gear. The Dutch were from the beginning anxious to mediate. But Kristian's behaviour to them was anything but conciliatory. In February 1611 he had forbidden all trade to Sweden for the duration of the war; in April he had raised the Sound Tolls by one-third; and the Dutch skippers complained bitterly to their government of the 'barbaric' proceedings of Danish privateers. In August 1611 the States General had sent an embassy to the belligerents, headed by Jakob Obdam, which was charged to expatiate on the injury being done to the common cause of Protestantism. From Karl IX they had obtained a sympathetic hearing; but Kristian, flushed with his victory at Kalmar, had candidly told them that this was a war 'non de religione, sed de regione'. He had replied to their complaints by remarking that as far as he knew no merchant had ever died of high tolls; and had added that he was ignorant of the existence of any such state as the United Netherlands, though he would be quite prepared to treat with the King of Spain. The Dutch were deeply incensed, and it was said that in all the Netherlands there was not one soldier, from Prince Maurice downwards, who did not hope for a Swedish victory. From this moment Dutch foreign policy took a new orientation; the friendship and alliance of the Hanse towns was assiduously cultivated; and for some years relations with Denmark were cool.[1]

It was left therefore to James I to take upon himself the part of peacemaker. He was fortunate in having two able representatives

---

[1] For the above paragraph, see E. Wiese, *Die Politik der Niederländer während des Kalmarkrieges* [etc.], pp. 32-72; B. Thyresson, *Sverige och den protestantiska Europa från Knäredfreden till Rigas erövring*, pp. 40, 43, 59; D. Schäfer, *Der Kampf um die Ostsee im 16. und 17. Jahrhundert* (*Sybels H. Z.* 1899), p. 437; M. G. Schybergson, *Sveriges och Hollands diplomatiska förbindelser 1621-30*, pp. v-vi. For an example of Swedish counter-blockade, see A. A. von Stiernman, *Samling utaf Kongl. Bref, Stadgar och Förordningar etc. angående Sveriges Rikes Commerce, Politie och Oeconomie uti Gemen, ifrån Åhr 1523 in til närwarande tid* (cited henceforward as Stiernman, *CPO*), I. 566. For the political repercussions, see also Chapter IV, below.

in Scandinavia—Robert Anstruther at Copenhagen and James
Spens at Stockholm. Spens was a Scottish soldier who first came to
Sweden in 1610, and was employed by Karl IX and Gustav Adolf
to raise mercenary troops in Scotland for the Swedish service. He
rose rapidly in Gustav Adolf's favour, and eventually became as
much the Swedish agent in Britain as the British representative in
Stockholm. He grew gradually to be more of a Swede than a Scot,
though as late as 1624 he was still receiving letters of credence from
James I. He died in 1632.[1] It was through Spens that James in
June 1612 made his offer of mediation to Gustav Adolf, while
Anstruther was simultaneously sent to Copenhagen; and when in
September Kristian decided that nothing was to be gained from
further fighting, it was natural that the negotiations should be
conducted through the two British emissaries. James' offer, incidentally, was a blow to Sigismund's pretensions, for it implicitly
recognized Gustav Adolf as *de jure* King of Sweden—which was
more than James had cared to do for Karl.

The diplomats met at the end of November at the frontier bridge
of Sjöaryd, not far from the Danish village of Knäred. The
negotiations proved difficult, and it was not until 21 January 1613
that a settlement was reached.[2] Gustav Adolf, however, was determined on peace at almost any price, and he was prepared to make
very substantial concessions to obtain it: when at one point Oxenstierna suggested that it would be well to consult the *råd* before
giving way on the grave question of the Three Crowns, the King
agreed in principle, but announced that as the matter was urgent he
was determined to act on his own responsibility.[3] The Swedish
negotiators showed some resource and ingenuity in their endeavours
to soften the final terms, but the Danes declined to be diverted, and
in the end had matters very much their own way.

The main provisions of the Treaty of Knäred were as follows.
On the Finnmark question Sweden was decisively defeated: she
renounced all claims to sovereignty over the sea-Finns between
Titisfjord and Varanger, and also such rights of taxation as she had
enjoyed there in previous times, or in virtue of alleged cessions

---

[1] *Den Svenska Utrikesförvaltningens Historia*, pp. 73-4.
[2] For the negotiations, see *AOSB*, I. 1. 49-85; I. 11. 89-134; II. 1. 9-18. The
text of the treaty is in *Sverges Traktater med främmande magter*, V$_2$. 211-23;
James I's guarantee, *ibid.*, pp. 223-4. See too L. Stavenow, *Freden i Knäred år
1613.*
[3] *AOSB*, II. 1. 18: this was strictly speaking a breach of the Charter.

by Russia in the peace of Täysinä; though she retained her rights over the fell-Finns. If Swedish Kings in future made use of a title which included mention of the Lapps of Nordland, that was to be understood as applying only to those Lapps over whom their authority was recognized by the present treaty.[1] As to the Riga tolls, it was agreed that Sweden had the right to levy them only when Swedish forces were actually besieging Riga. Sweden abandoned her claims to Sonnenburg on the island of Ösel. Each King was to be entitled to display the Three Crowns, but under the condition that no right or title to the territories of the other was thereby implied or acknowledged. The Norwegian province of Jämtland, which Sweden had occupied, was handed back to Kristian IV. The free trade formerly existing between the two countries was confirmed, and it was expressly provided that Swedes were to be exempt from the Sound Tolls. Denmark restored all her conquests except Älvsborg, Göteborg, Gamla- and Nya-Lödöse, which, with seven adjacent hundreds in Västergötland, were to be retained by her as a pledge for the payment by Sweden of a war-indemnity of 10 *tunnor* of gold (equivalent to a million *riksdaler*) in four equal annual instalments, beginning on 20 January 1616. Some minor points upon which no agreement could be reached were omitted by common consent.

The War of Kalmar was over; and on the face of it the result seemed to be the definitive defeat of Sweden's pretensions in the North, the definitive establishment of the *dominium maris Baltici* in the hands of Denmark. Sweden was now cut off from the Atlantic Ocean; her solitary west-coast port was in Danish hands, and Kristian confidently counted on Gustav Adolf's being unable to raise the ransom for Älvsborg within the stipulated time. Sweden herself appeared to be utterly exhausted. The devastation of her southern provinces had been terribly thorough.[2] She had a war in progress in Russia, and a war in suspense with Poland, to weaken her still further. Her navy had proved unable to keep the seas; her armies incapable of risking a pitched battle against equal numbers. Yet at least Sweden had escaped reconquest. The attempt to undo the

---

[1] The Arctic question still bred controversy and local clashes even in the 'twenties, and no firm frontier between Sweden and Norway was drawn here till 1751: see *Samling af Instructioner för Landt-Regeringen* (cited henceforward as *SILR*), pp. 160-1; *Peder Galts Depescher*, pp. 43-4, 81, 83-4; Enewald, pp. 206-14; *Kong Christian den fjerdes egenhændige Breve*, I. 273.

[2] See, *e.g.*, *AOSB*, II. III. 4; II. XII. 161, 232-3, 348, etc.

work of Gustav Vasa had clearly failed; and to that extent the Peace of Knäred was a check to Kristian's ambitions.

Sweden entered the war without a reliable friend. Her defeat and humiliation at Knäred at once improved her diplomatic position. Kristian's triumph alarmed the Dutch with visions of a Danish monopoly of the Baltic; and Dutch statesmen turned almost at once to seek for a counterpoise, and soon drew closer to Sweden. Within a few years they had formed alliances with Sweden and the Hanse; and with their help the Älvsborg ransom was eventually paid.[1] But though the very venom of the Peace of Knäred thus produced its own antidote, this was an effect which at the beginning of 1613 was hidden from Gustav Adolf and Oxenstierna, or at least was only dimly perceived by them. What they did perceive very clearly was that having thus disposed of one item of Karl IX's disastrous political legacy, they must without delay deal with another, less censurable in its origin, but not a whit less imperative in its demands upon their statesmanship. The war with Denmark was no sooner over than Sweden's attention shifted to the east, and she proceeded to plunge heavily into the barbarous turmoil of Muscovy.

(iii) *The Russian Imbroglio* [2]

In the interval of two-and-a-half years which had intervened between the battle of Klušino and the Peace of Knäred, the situation in Russia had undergone many vicissitudes. The abdication of Šuijskij and the defeat of de la Gardie had seemed, in the summer of 1610, to ensure the triumph of Sigismund's policy; and it had appeared certain that Sweden would be faced with the threat of a great Polish-Russian state stretching right up to the Finnish

---

[1] For this, see Chapter IV, below.

[2] For the Troublous Times in general, H. Fleischhacker, *Russland zwischen zwei Dynastien*; V. O. Kluchevsky, *A History of Russia*, III.; K. Waliszewski, *Les Origines de la Russie moderne*, II.-III.; I. Lubimenko, *Les relations commerciales et politiques de l'Angleterre avec la Russie avant Pierre le Grand*; H. Hjärne, *Det Moskovitiska Rikets Uppväxt*; V. Gitermann, *Geschichte Russlands*, I. For the Polish side, K. Tyszkowski, *Gustav Adolf wobec Polski i Moskwy*; W. Sobieski, *Żółkiewski na Kremlu*; Wł. Konopczyński, *Dzieje Polski Nowożytnej*; Korzon, *op. cit.* For the Swedish side, H. Almquist, *Sverge och Ryssland*, and his two articles, *Tsarvalet år 1613. Karl Filip och Michael Romanov* (in *Hist. Studier tillägn. H. Hjärne*) and *Die Carenwahl des Jahres 1613* (*Zeitschr. für osteurop. Geschichte* 1913); E. Grill, *Jakob de la Gardie*. H. Hjärne, *Utdrag ur ryska krönikor, hufvudsakligen angående Jakob de la Gardies fälttåg* is a collection of sources. Hallenberg is very full on this episode, at least in its later stages.

border and encircling her outwork in Estonia. The dissident
boyars had abandoned the second pseudo-Dmitrij to support a
Polish candidate; the Polish adventurers for once had made common
cause with their King; and on 17 August 1610 the Polish commander
in Russia, Żółkiewski, had reached an agreement with the boyars,
as a result of which Władysław had been proclaimed Tsar.

In the sequel, however, events took an unexpected course. The
Polish victory proved ephemeral; the Polish party turned out to
have no solid backing. It was composed of heterogeneous elements
which agreed ill with one another; and it was weakened from the
beginning by the divergent aims of Sigismund and Żółkiewski.
Żółkiewski was the champion of Władysław's candidature, and to
ensure its success he was prepared to make considerable concessions
to Russian susceptibilities; while Sigismund's attitude was rigid
and bigoted, and from the beginning he intended the crown for
himself rather than for his son. He took no trouble to disguise
Poland's territorial ambitions upon Russia; he pushed on with the
siege of Smoleńsk; and he outraged Russian feelings by imprisoning
a solemn embassy which had been sent to him in the hope of
modifying his attitude. By the close of the year 1610 the Poles, who
six months earlier had seemed to have the game in their hands, had
thrown away almost all their advantages, and their little army could
with difficulty maintain itself in Moscow. The murder of the second
pseudo-Dmitrij, on 11 December 1610, deprived them of one of the
best arguments in Władysław's favour; for many moderate men had
embraced his cause because they preferred even a Polish Tsar to the
anarchy, social upheaval and Cossack terror which the rule of
Dmitrij would have brought with it. The Polish candidature now
appeared in all its odiousness; and in March 1611 a wave of patriotic
emotion produced the first National Rising, under the leadership of
Prokopij Ljapunov. It was joined by all those who hated the
foreigner and loved the Orthodox religion, by those who distrusted
the feeble and treacherous rule of the Moscow boyars, by middle-
class men of substance in the towns: by all, in short, who had the
interests of Russia at heart, as well as by some who had not. By
Eastertide 1611 Ljapunov and his following had reached Moscow,
and the Polish garrison was closely besieged in the Kremlin.

The declining fortunes of the Polish cause in their turn produced
modifications of Swedish policy in Russia. After the catastrophe at
Klušino, when the prospects had seemed desperate, Sweden had

concentrated her efforts on preventing Polish sympathizers from getting possession of Kexholm and Ingria; and even when it became plain that Sigismund's plan for a union of Russia and Poland would break down, Karl IX confined himself to seizing such portions of Russian territory as could most conveniently be conquered. Karl IX, indeed, never seems to have grasped the intricacies of the internal situation in Russia; and apart from some hazy notions of collaboration with the second pseudo-Dmitrij he never faced the problem of devising a policy to take the place of that which had broken down at Klušino. Jakob de la Gardie, however, was better informed, more enterprising, and less pessimistic than his master; and by the close of 1610 he had produced a policy of his own. De la Gardie proposed to fight the Poles with their own weapons: the best reply to a Polish candidate, he considered, was to pit a Swedish candidate against him.

In the existing circumstances the idea was not so fantastic as it might appear to be: Władysław and Sigismund had made themselves hateful to every patriotic Russian; and there was no obvious native candidate. Gustav Adolf's younger brother, Karl Filip, was sufficiently youthful to reassure the leading boyars, and sufficiently old for his candidature not to be an absurdity; and there might conceivably be less difficulty about his conversion to the Orthodox faith than in the case of Władysław. De la Gardie accordingly began to form a party in support of Karl Filip, and after some persuasion he succeeded in inducing Novgorod to join it. Novgorod may well have been influenced in her attitude by the recent emergence of a third pseudo-Dmitrij in the neighbouring town of Pskov; for the third pseudo-Dmitrij, like his predecessor, stood for anarchy and social war, and the wealthy citizens of Novgorod were alarmed at his proceedings. The adhesion of Novgorod undoubtedly gave both prestige and solid advantage to any pretender to the throne; for though it was no longer the great city it had been in the Middle Ages, it was still the trading centre of the north-west, it was massively fortified, and it was still animated by something of its old independent spirit, and not indisposed to take the lead in Russian affairs in opposition to Moscow. 'Who can stand', ran the Russian proverb, 'against God and Great Novgorod?' For de la Gardie, however, it was not enough merely to have Novgorod's support: he desired also to have the control of the city in his hands. On 17 July, therefore, he carried out a plan he had long meditated, and captured Novgorod by a *coup de main*. He proceeded to impose upon it a treaty [1] whereby the city recognized the validity of the treaties of Täysinä and Viborg, accepted one of the sons of Karl IX as Tsar, and agreed to send an embassy to Sweden to discuss terms.

Meanwhile the cause of Karl Filip had received an even more important accession. Ljapunov, alarmed by the advance towards Moscow of a Polish relieving army under Sapieha, opened conversations with de la Gardie, and soon afterwards publicly declared himself in favour of a Swedish Tsar. With the National Rising on his side, with Novgorod in his hands, de la Gardie might well feel sanguine of Karl Filip's chances. At this point, however, his plans suffered an unexpected check. Ljapunov had been forced, in order to maintain himself, to come to terms with the Cossack leader Zaruckij, and also with Trubeckoj and the boyars who had formerly supported the second pseudo-Dmitrij. It was a triumvirate of one honest man and two rogues; and from the beginning relations between them had been strained. Zaruckij and his Cossacks resented Ljapunov's efforts to convert them into respectable citizens; Trubeckoj was playing for his own hand. The latent quarrel between them now came to a sudden crisis; and on 22 July Zaruckij murdered Ljapunov. The National Rising at once disintegrated, and Karl Filip lost his most important supporter.

Nevertheless Novgorod remained; and the example of Novgorod had considerable effect, as the long list of Russian towns which declared for Karl Filip testified. At the moment of Karl IX's death the prospects for the Swedish candidature were not unhopeful, while the outlook for Sigismund was distinctly gloomy.

The accession of Gustav Adolf coincided with the arrival in Sweden of an embassy from Novgorod, which had been sent (in accordance with the city's treaty with de la Gardie) to ask for Karl Filip as Tsar. Gustav Adolf's reception of this embassy at once made it plain that he would take a more positive attitude than his father to the Russian problem. Indeed, his attitude was if anything too positive. To the consternation of the Novgorod envoys, he announced that he intended to accept their offer, not for Karl Filip, but for himself. This was not what Novgorod wanted at all. It was one thing to take a Swedish prince, convert him to Orthodoxy, and set him up as Tsar in default of anyone better; it was quite another

---

[1] Text in *Sverges Traktater*, V₂. 200-11.

to accept the reigning monarch of a foreign country. De la Gardie had no illusions about Russian sentiment on this point. The more plainly Gustav Adolf declared his intention of standing as the Swedish candidate, the more anxiously did de la Gardie explain away his words and assure the friends of Sweden that Gustav Adolf would really send them Karl Filip.[1] In the first half of 1612 Sweden's chances in Russia were being jeopardized by a clash of policies between the King and his commander, reminiscent of that clash of policies between Sigismund and Żółkiewski which had been so fatal to the cause of Poland. It is not very likely that Gustaf Adolf seriously contemplated uniting the crowns of Russia and Sweden upon his own head, least of all at a time when all his attention was taken up by the War of Kalmar.[2] He intended his candidature to be a weapon against Poland, or an instrument for obtaining concessions from the Russians which might safeguard Sweden against a Polish attack. But whatever his motive, it seems that his attempt to push his own pretensions was a mistake; and events were to prove de la Gardie right in his contention that only Karl Filip had any real chance of being elected.

This was made plain by the attitude of the second National Rising. This movement, under the leadership of Minin and Požarskij, had developed in the autumn of 1611 as a reaction to the murder of Ljapunov. It inherited the political principles of its predecessor; but it was more formidable and had less need to compromise with dubious allies. Nevertheless Požarskij, like Ljapunov, needed a Tsar to play off against the third pseudo-Dmitrij; and he needed help against Zaruckij's Cossacks and Trubeckoj's adventurers. Necessity drove him, as it had driven Ljapunov, to look for aid from outside[3]; and he accordingly sent to Novgorod to enquire about the details of the city's treaty with Sweden. The information he received was apparently reassuring; for soon afterwards he made a formal offer to de la Gardie. Požarskij intimated that he was ready to adopt Karl Filip as the candidate of the National Rising; but he made it equally plain that he was not prepared to consider the candidature of Gustav Adolf. It was an offer

[1] *AOSB*, I. ii. 56-7; II. v. 6-7.
[2] In May, nevertheless, he would have gone to Finland to be near the Russian frontier, if the news of the fall of Älvsborg had not stopped him: J. E. Waaranen, *Samling af urkunder rörande Finlands Historia*, IV. 50.
[3] He made attempts, for instance, to come to an arrangement with James I: see I. Lubimenko, *A Project for the Acquisition of Russia by James I* (*E.H.R.*, XXIX), *passim*.

too important to be rejected; and from this moment Karl Filip
becomes the official candidate of Sweden.

By the autumn of 1612 his prospects seemed to be bright: the
National Rising was triumphant; the third pseudo-Dmitrij was
dead; Zaruckij was a fugitive in the steppes; and Trubeckoj was
finally reconciled with Požarskij. On 25 October the Polish garrison
in the Kremlin, after a heroic defence, capitulated. The partisans
of Karl Filip were everywhere victorious; and Gustav Adolf could
boast that over two hundred Russian cities had acknowledged his
brother as their Tsar.[1]

Everything now depended upon Karl Filip's early arrival in
Russia; and since August 1612 de la Gardie had been insisting that
he must be sent off without delay, if only as far as Viborg. But
Gustav Adolf hesitated. The Queen-Mother, Kristina, was very
reluctant to commit her son to the hazards of Russian politics, and
Gustav Adolf was equally reluctant to overrule her. In November
the *riksdag* was consulted, in an obvious attempt to shift the burden
of responsibility to the Estates. The Estates, however, showed no
anxiety to shoulder it. The Clergy were especially uneasy at the
prospect of Karl Filip's being required to renounce the Lutheran
religion, and were pacified only when Gustav Adolf assured them
that there could be no question of his doing so—a reply which was
certainly disingenuous, and probably a direct falsehood. Kristina
insisted on guarantees that Karl Filip should be accompanied to
Viborg by an escort sufficient to ensure his safety; Duke Johan, in
spite of peremptory demands from Gustav Adolf that he should give
his opinion *absque ambagibus*, refused to commit himself. In short,
though everybody was prepared to agree that Karl Filip's candidature should be persisted in, nobody was altogether without misgivings about it.[2] And one result of this state of affairs was that his
departure for Viborg was once again deferred.

In January 1613 the Russian National Assembly met to elect a
Tsar. Požarskij was still in favour of Karl Filip, as the only hope
against Poland and the only candidate who could unite Russia; but
he was understandably anxious for his arrival in Russia without
further delay. At last de la Gardie was able to inform him that it
had been decided in Stockholm that he should reach Viborg some
time in February. Encouraged by this news, the Assembly on

---

[1] *SRDA*, I. 211.
[2] For these debates, see *SRDA*, I. 180-219.

7 February agreed in principle to choose Karl Filip; but the formal
ceremony of election was postponed until the end of the month, by
which time it was expected that the Prince would be on Russian
soil. But as the days passed without any news of Karl Filip's coming,
de la Gardie grew alarmed; and on 17 February he wrote that if the
Prince did not arrive soon there was a danger that a Russian candidate
might be chosen.[1] These forebodings were justified by the event.
The postponement of the election, the dilatoriness of the government in Stockholm, proved fatal to Karl Filip's chances. The
Cossack party was given time to recover and reassert itself. They
had always been opposed to a foreign Tsar; and in Michael Romanov
they had now found a candidate who, they believed, would be a
puppet in their hands, and who had the additional advantage of
relationship by marriage with the old dynasty of Rurik. On 21
February, after a period of growing disorder, the Cossacks forced
their way into the Kremlin and insisted on Michael's election. A
month later, after many hesitations, Michael accepted the crown;
and in July 1613 his coronation took place. Sweden had lost the game
by procrastination at the critical moment. The Troublous Times
were virtually over; and the new dynasty of the Romanovs was to
succeed, as Šuijskij had never been able to do, in winning for itself
the political support of all Russia, and also some measure of that
mystic religious reverence which had hedged about the old line, and
which for a time seemed to have perished with it.

De la Gardie at first refused to admit defeat. He informed
Oxenstierna that Michael was not likely to hold his ground in face
of the hostility of the leading boyars; and he pleaded more urgently
than ever that Karl Filip be sent at once to Viborg. This time,
when it was too late, his advice was taken; but Karl Filip did not
reach Viborg until the middle of July, and by that time the case was
hopeless. Even de la Gardie now recognized that a new situation had
arisen, and that a radical reconsideration of Swedish policy in
Russia had become necessary. There were several possibilities:
Karl Filip's candidature might be maintained—partly to conciliate
Novgorod, partly as a means of harassing Michael; Gustav Adolf
might prosecute hostilities against Russia with the idea of extracting
the concessions already promised by Šuijskij in the Treaty of Viborg,
and perhaps something in addition; the whole Russian venture
might be abandoned and peace concluded with the new Tsar; or,

---

[1] *AOSB*, II. v. 27.

as de la Gardie for a moment suggested, Sweden might unite with Poland in a campaign of plunder and partition. Gustav Adolf at once ruled out the possibility of collaboration with Poland; but he agreed with de la Gardie that the moment had not yet come to make peace. The Swedish armies had not yet a sufficiently commanding position in Ingria to ensure that a peace would bring advantages proportionate to the effort already made, or sufficient to establish Sweden's position on the southern shore of the Gulf of Finland. It was accordingly decided to carry on the war; but at the same time to use Karl Filip's candidature as a diplomatic weapon, and to keep up those negotiations with the Russians which had already been opened at Viborg.

The Swedish representatives at the Viborg conference were therefore provided with alternative sets of instructions, one for use in the unlikely event of Karl Filip's acceptance, the other to apply in case of his final rejection. Both sets included demands which can only be called exorbitant. Sweden claimed not merely the inner ring of fortresses which guarded the Ingrian coast and the land-bridge to Finland (Ivangorod, Jama, Kopore, Nöteborg and Kexholm) but in addition Pskov, Gdov, Ladoga and Tichvin, together with the Arctic ports of Kolahus, Sumskoj, Soloveckoj and Archangel. If Karl Filip were rejected, the Swedish negotiators were to try to induce Novgorod and Pskov to put themselves under Swedish protection, or even to allow themselves to be incorporated into the Swedish realm, *salvo jure et privilegio*; and should these terms be refused, an indemnity of a million *riksdaler* was to be demanded as the price of evacuation.

Of these terms it was only the indemnity which had even a faint chance of acceptance. Novgorod had little positive enthusiasm for Karl Filip, and was strongly averse to incorporation into Sweden. Yet Gustav Adolf certainly contemplated the possibility of creating a kind of buffer-state in north-west Russia, based on Novgorod, Pskov and Gdov, with Karl Filip for its ruler. He took care to treat Novgorod with great leniency, at least in the first years after its capture; he referred to the Metropolitan as 'our Metropolitan'; he made grants of lands and privileges within the city's territories; and in general he acted as though Swedish sovereignty were settled and permanent.[1] But whatever the attitude of Novgorod, there was

---

[1] On relations with Novgorod, see Waaranen, *Samling*, IV. 16-20, 48-52, 86; Hallenberg, *Handlingar*, p. 73; Hallenberg, *Svea Rikes Historia*, III. 174-6, 383-4; Hjärne, *Moskovitiska Rikets Uppväxt*, p. 242.

by this time no hope whatever that Moscow would be willing to buy Sweden off by concessions which would put the virtual control of her Baltic trade into Swedish hands. The Viborg conference dragged on through the autumn of 1613, and even into the following year; but its failure had long been beyond doubt, and on the Swedish side it had been protracted mainly with the idea of gaining

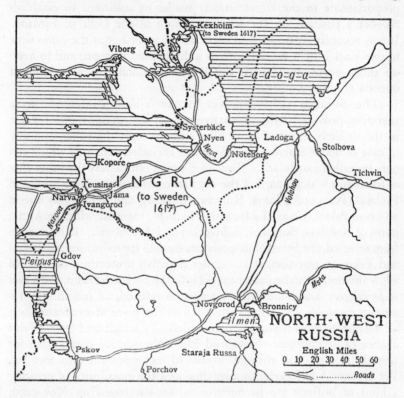

time to prepare for the serious war with Moscow which, it was clear, was now inevitable.[1]

. . . . . .

At the opening of the campaigning season of 1613 Sweden had in her possession a number of the most important strongholds in north-west Russia.[2] Since 1611 Kexholm, Novgorod, Ladoga,

---

[1] Waaranen, *Samling*, IV. 214-15.
[2] For the military operations, *Sveriges Krig*, I.; Petri, I.

Tichvin, Staraja Russa, Jama, Kopoŕe and Gdov had successively fallen into her hands; and though Staraja Russa had been recently lost, sufficient remained to put de la Gardie and Horn in a strong position. In 1613, however, things went badly. The Russians recaptured Gdov and Tichvin, and so dealt a hard blow at either flank of the Swedish position; and all attempts to retake these places proved unsuccessful. The exhaustion of Sweden at the end of the War of Kalmar threw the commanders in Russia largely upon their own resources, and often they were at their wits' end to pay and clothe their troops. Both de la Gardie and Evert Horn were driven to make great loans out of their own pockets, and to pledge their own credit, in order to pay their soldiers enough of the arrears due to them to keep them to the colours.[1] The Russian war was unpopular with the army, and reinforcements on their way to the front mutinied in Finland. By the spring of 1614 the condition of the Swedish troops in Russia was so bad that the military initiative was largely abandoned to the Russians, who made damaging raids in the direction of Novgorod, on the one hand, and Ladoga and Nöteborg, on the other; while a Russian army under Trubeckoj threatened the centre of the Swedish front at Bronnicy. In June 1614, however, Gustav Adolf arrived at Narva with 2000 men, and the situation began to improve. In July de la Gardie defeated Trubeckoj at Bronnicy in a considerable engagement; and soon afterwards the Swedes settled down to the siege of Gdov. The recapture of Gdov was a necessary preliminary to any move against Pskov, for Gdov barred the road running south from Narva along the eastern shore of Lake Peipus. Gdov itself was no very formidable fortress; but the Swedes were as yet unskilled in siege-warfare, and their foreign expert, Mönnichhofen, was killed in the course of an assault upon the walls. It was not until 10 September that Gdov capitulated; and by that time it was too late in the year for any other major

---

[1] *AOSB*, II. v. 55, 71; E. Grill, *Jakob de la Gardie*, pp. 23-4. De la Gardie had turned his command into a highly remunerative investment by trading in sables—in which commodity, indeed, the armies were sometimes paid. By May 1614 his loans to the Crown totalled nearly 60,000 *daler*. This was an even better investment, for he got interest at the rate of about 16 per cent., together with honours, revenue-grants, and (in 1617) 3000 roubles out of the indemnity of 20,000 roubles paid by the Russians under the Treaty of Stolbova, and a further 1500 roubles at the same time as a gift. Not surprisingly, he made further loans (45,000 *daler* by December 1617): these were eventually repaid in copper. Small loans were not despised: when Oxenstierna paid a visit to the King at Narva in 1614, Gustav Adolf took the opportunity to borrow 500 *daler*: Ahnlund, *Oxenstierna*, p. 180.

operation. The attack upon Pskov was accordingly postponed until 1615.[1]

By this time it was clear to everybody that Karl Filip's candidature had lost any reality it might once have possessed. Sweden was not going to be able to thrust a Vasa upon the throne of the Tsars; and it was becoming extremely improbable that Poland would be able to do so either. The war in Russia was being fought partly for compensation; partly, perhaps, with some idea of reviving the old policy of controlling the Russian trade-routes (hence the importance attached to the capture of Pskov); partly because it would be unwise to lose an opportunity to build up defences against any possible revival of Polish influence in Muscovy. But by the end of 1614 it was already a question whether Sweden could afford to continue hostilities for ends such as these. The financial pressure entailed by the payment of the ransom for Älvsborg was crippling the country. It was doubtful whether the armistice—or succession of armistices—which had interrupted the course of the war with Poland could be renewed for much longer. If serious fighting broke out again in Livonia, would it be possible for Sweden to continue the struggle in Ingria at the same time? Would it not be wise, in view of all these things, to seek the mediation of some benevolent neutral, and try to patch up a peace in Russia while the military situation was still in Sweden's favour? The råd certainly thought so: in May 1614 they replied to an enquiry of the King on these points by formally advising him to approach England, the Dutch and the Landgrave of Hesse with a request for mediation.[2] As a matter of fact, James Spens had already been sent to England at the close of 1613 on just such an errand. He found James I nursing imaginary slights, and somewhat hostile to Sweden; but he succeeded in persuading him to undertake the task, and to promise that England would give no assistance to the Tsar in the meantime—an important point, since England's trading interests led her to court Michael's favour, and the Tsar's father Filaret was known to be English in sympathy. It was the suspicion entertained in Sweden that England's impartiality could not be relied upon that led to the search for another mediator who could be trusted to watch over Swedish interests. After some persuasion the Dutch were at last

---

[1] In Finland Hans Munck had won a victory at Ristilahti (north of Ladoga) which did much to consolidate Sweden's grip on Kexholm; but a plan put forward by Hans Georg von Arnim for an attack on Kola had come to nothing.

[2] SRDA, I. 512-18.

induced to volunteer their good offices, and ultimately mediation was undertaken by the States-General and England jointly. The arrangement did not prove a very happy one: it gave rise to a number of awkward diplomatic difficulties, and it probably rather deferred than hastened the conclusion of peace.

And, indeed, more than two years were to pass in fruitless and tedious negotiations before a settlement could be obtained. In the meantime, military operations perforce continued, and the terms demanded on each side varied according to the fortunes of war. The Swedish military programme was simple, and was in fact a continuation of the plan of 1614: Sweden was to hold her position along the Volchov and the Narva, and to concentrate her efforts upon the capture of Pskov. It was with Pskov, therefore, that the campaigns of 1615 and 1616 were mainly concerned.

Pskov was a town of some 14,000 inhabitants, situated in a wide open plain but strongly defended by walls and water. It covered a considerable area,[1] contained forty-six monasteries (besides another twenty outside the walls) and by its position at the southern end of Lake Peipus commanded one of the main routes from Lithuania to northern Russia at the point where it intersected an important road leading southwards from Narva to Smoleńsk. It had become famous for its triumphant resistance to Stefan Batory in 1581; and though the garrison in 1615 numbered only 400, the town was strongly Russian in feeling, and could be counted upon to offer stubborn resistance to the foreigner. But by now Sweden had considerable forces in Ingria, and with the fresh troops that Gustav Adolf brought with him in June 1615 he could dispose of an army of nearly 14,000 men. Very careful preparations were made to secure satisfactory commissariat and transport services, and to provide the heavy guns and equipment needed for a regular siege; and Gustav Adolf had even caused small boats of shallow draught to be built in Sweden and transhipped to Narva, that they might operate upon the waters of Lake Peipus. It seemed not improbable, therefore, that Gustav Adolf might succeed where Batory had failed.[2]

---

[1] A generation before its area was said to equal that of Paris: *Etienne Batory*, p. 402.

[2] *Sveriges Krig*, I. 522, for a description of Pskov by Rudbeckius; and see Hallenberg, III. 404 *seqq.* An interesting comparison of Gustav Adolf's siege of Pskov with Stefan Batory's is H. Sepp, *Stephan Báthorys och Gustav II Adolfs krigståg mot Pskov* (*Svio-Estonica* 1937).

The best defence of Pskov against these elaborate preparations lay in the diplomatic activity of the mediating powers, and especially of the English agent, Sir John Merrick. Merrick was an important personage in the Muscovy Company, and he used his position as mediator to establish a credit of goodwill with the Moscow government upon which his Company might draw in the future. He played with skill upon Gustav Adolf's obvious desire for an early settlement, and succeeded in staving off any serious attack upon Pskov until the early autumn, first by representing that the Russians were upon the point of concluding peace upon favourable terms, and then by threatening that if Gustav Adolf pressed the siege he would consider it a contempt of the King of England, and would abandon his mediation.[1] By these means Pskov was given a valuable breathing-space; and as it was able, despite the Swedish shallops, to revictual itself by water, it was in a good posture to repel an attack when Gustav Adolf at last grew impatient of Merrick's manœuvres and in September launched a determined assault. But Sweden had no luck with sieges in this war. Gustav Adolf's best commander, Evert Horn, was killed in a casual skirmish; and once again he was unfortunate in losing his chief sapper. The Swedish camp was harried by epidemics. The attack itself was mismanaged. The ring of besiegers was not drawn tight. The Swedish guns made a practicable breach in the walls, but the defenders were given time to build an inner rampart. There was a shortage of ammunition for the heavier guns. And when at last the ravages of sickness induced the King to make up his mind to retreat, a lucky hit from the town's batteries blew up the Swedish powder-magazine. In mid-October the siege was abandoned. In June of the following year another attempt was made, under the command of Gustav Adolf's half-brother Karl Karlsson Gyllenhielm. But this time the preparations were far less careful, and the attack itself was not vigorously pressed. After little more than a month before the town, the Swedes were forced to retire owing to failure of supplies, leaving a fortified camp behind them. Towards the end of the year this camp was itself hard pressed by the Russians, and on 11 December its defenders were driven by hunger to capitulate. The attack on Pskov, it must be confessed, had proved a somewhat ignominious failure.

Meanwhile the diplomats had begun their thankless labours. An abortive conference opened at Novgorod in September 1615, under

[1] Hallenberg, III. 410, 412.

Merrick's auspices, but the real bargaining began at Diderina in October. By this time the Swedes had been heartened by the arrival of the Dutch mediators; and de la Gardie was also inclined to hope something from a Mr. Bitzer, an English merchant who had been extruded from Russia on account of his Swedish sympathies.[1] But before serious business could begin, the solemn farces of diplomacy had to be played out. Should the Swedish or the Russian delegates enter Merrick's tent first? Was the Tsar to be styled 'Autocrat'? Ought his title to Livonia to be admitted? Would the Swedish delegates have to walk further to the meeting-place than the Russians? Was it Sweden or Russia that had asked for mediation? Was it admissible to avoid disputes by using shortened titles in referring to the two sovereigns? These, and other delicate questions of a like nature, vexed the delegates, and severely tried the patience of Sir John Merrick, who was suffering much from rheumatism in the prevailing wintry weather.[2] The negotiations took place in singularly uninviting circumstances: the country was devastated in all directions, and food for diplomats had to be fetched from long distances, while for those who were not diplomats cannibalism is said to have been the universal resource, and the horses ate each other's manes and tails. The cold was so intense that the beards and moustaches of the cooks froze as they bent over the fire, and roasted joints were found to be still frozen inside. To escape the cold, both sides at last agreed to meet in Merrick's quarters rather than in a tent pitched in the open air; but here the garlic-eating habits of the Russians added a new disagreeable to diplomacy. But the soldiers on the watch might freeze at their posts: the diplomats fought grimly on. It was felt on the Swedish side that nothing should be done to encourage, by a show of weakness, tne 'barbaric insolence' of the enemy. At last the inevitable compromises were reached on these questions of prestige, and on 11 January 1616 the negotiations proper could begin. De la Gardie, representing Sweden, was inclined to moderation; but both Gustav Adolf and Oxenstierna felt that Russia must be crushed while she was weak. It was the old, historic fear of Russia that now came to the surface; the fear of

---

[1] *AOSB.* II. v. 82. On Merrick's Russian sympathies, see Hallenberg, III. 388; S. F. Hammarstrand, *Försök till en historisk framställning af förhandlingarne om Sveriges deltagande i trettioåriga kriget* (cited as Hammarstrand, *HF*), p. 19.
[2] For a good description of the complications of diplomatic etiquette, and for the negotiations generally, see *SRDA,* II. 113 *seqq.*; *En holländsk beskicknings resor i Ryssland Finland och Sverige 1615-1616*, pp. 95-120; G. W. Vreede, *Nederland en Zweden in staatkundige Betrekking*, I. 152.

a neighbour barbarous, aggressive and formidable, against whom precautions must be taken in good time. The newer lines of Swedish policy—those economic ambitions to control the Russian trade-routes which successive Swedish Kings had cherished, from Erik's time to Karl IX's—dropped into the background. What mattered now was to exploit to the full a unique opportunity to give Sweden security on her eastern frontier, and at the same time build up a barrier against a Polish attack upon Sweden's back-door. The negotiators might appear to pitch their demands absurdly high; they might seem to be animated by an aggressive spirit; but to the King and his Chancellor their policy seemed essentially defensive, and they felt that they would be culpable in the eyes of posterity if they abated their claims in the smallest particular without doing their best to force them through.[1] The Swedish delegates, therefore, were instructed to fight their hardest to obtain the maximum concessions from the Tsar. Sweden, it was pointed out, could claim an indemnity (under the Treaty of Viborg); she could claim the Russian throne (by election); and she could claim the country actually occupied by her troops (*jure belli*). In respect of all these claims she was prepared to be bought off; but she must insist on the Ingrian fortresses, with Gdov and the region to the south of Ivangorod. These modest requirements were not seriously entertained either by the Russians or by the mediators; but the Russian offers of compensation were equally preposterous. By February 1616 the mediators had succeeded only in arranging a three-months' truce. The horses were by this time eating shirt-buttons.[2] In March, a new difficulty appeared, in the shape of a copper door

---

[1] Oxenstierna wrote on 15 November to the Swedish delegates: 'It is undoubtedly true that we have in the Russian a false and at the same time a mighty neighbour; in whom, by reason of the guile and treachery which he has (as it were) drunk in with his mother's milk, no faith is to be reposed; but who by reason of his power is terrible not to us only, but to many of his neighbours, as will still readily be remembered. He is now so far brought to his knees, that the greatest and best parts of his land are either in the hands of his enemies or harried and waste; besides that his best men have in these past times been killed, and little remaining but a collection of bandits. That we should now not only let go, but ourselves help him to his legs again, before his feathers be somewhat plucked and his condition a little embarrassed (but we on the other hand somewhat strengthened and improved) is what seems not only to be unsafe and prejudicial, but despicable and censurable, and on its heels will follow a tardy and ineffectual repentance.': *AOSB*, I. II. 246. Compare his comment to John Casimir on 4 February 1620: '[The Russian] Est bestia unius et plurium capitum, vivere sueta suo more, lest sich niecht leichtlich merken undt handelt niemals sincere, gehett mitt ihren tractaten ob insolentiam langsamb umb . . .': *AOSB*, I. II. 371. And see Hallenberg, III. 448.
[2] *En holländsk beskicknings resor*, p. 119.

located in the city of Novgorod: Gustav Adolf had got it
into his head that this door was of Swedish workmanship, and
demanded that it be handed over as a trophy of war. The
Russians, who were well aware that it was in fact of Greek origin,
not unnaturally refused.[1] The Dutch and English negotiators
now began to squabble seriously among themselves; and by
midsummer 1616 no noticeable progress had been made towards
a solution.

By this time Gustav Adolf, and, still more, the *råd*, were genuinely
anxious for peace. In January the King had addressed a meeting of
the Estates in Helsingfors on the subject of the Russian negotiations,
and in a brilliant but tendentious survey of recent Russian and
Polish history had tried to show them that this war was not of
Sweden's making, and that the obstacles to its termination did not
come from the Swedish side. But both he and the *råd* felt that if
hostilities were prolonged into 1617 it might not be altogether
pleasant to face another *riksdag* with a demand for further sacrifices.
In May, and again in August, the *råd* offered a formal advice to the
King, recommending him if necessary to sacrifice gains of territory,
and even the money indemnity, provided he could retain the Ingrian
fortresses.[2] Karl Karlsson Gyllenhielm, in command of the army
in Russia, wrote to Oxenstierna in July: 'As for those who want
war, I wish them joy of it. God give us peace here, for the country
can bear war no longer.'[3] And so in the autumn the indefatigable
negotiators foregathered once again at Diderina, somewhat handicapped on this occasion by the garrulity of a habitually intoxicated
interpreter.[4] The Russians fought hard to keep Nöteborg, and the
Swedish delegates had to pay a formal visit of leave-taking to Merrick
before they could be brought to abandon it.[5] It took four days'
continuous haggling to agree on the indemnity. At last the final
hindrances were removed, the last procrastinations of the Muscovite
circumvented. On 20 November a preliminary agreement was
signed; on 3 December it was made definitive; and after further
infuriating delays it was embodied on 27 February 1617 as
the Treaty of Stolbova. The titles of both sovereigns were

---

[1] *AOSB*, II. v. 94.
[2] *SRDA*, I. 523-33, 546-50; II. 8-9; Styffe, *Konung Gustaf II Adolfs Skrifter*,
pp. 124-38.
[3] *AOSB*, II. ix. 17.
[4] Hallenberg, III. 464.
[5] The Swedes knew that the thaw would prevent their going for a day or two
in any case: *Sveriges Krig*, I. 561.

much abbreviated, and only England's mediation was mentioned.[1]

By the Treaty of Stolbova the Tsar renounced his rights on Ivangorod, Jama, Kopoŕe and Nöteborg, with their districts, and paid an indemnity of 20,000 roubles; he confirmed the cession of Kexholm, and the Treaties of Täysinä and Viborg in so far as they were not superseded by the present treaty; and he abandoned his claim to Livonia. Sweden dropped her pretensions to the Russian throne and her claims to Novgorod, and restored Novgorod, Ladoga, Staraja Russa and Porchov on payment of the indemnity. Gdov was to remain in Swedish hands as a pledge until the ratification of the treaty, which was to take place only after a boundary commission had made a new delimitation of the frontier. The upper classes in the towns ceded to Sweden were to have the option of emigrating to Russia within fourteen days. Finally, each party agreed not to assist Poland against the other.

Sir John Merrick was given a triumphant reception in Moscow upon the conclusion of these long and trying negotiations. But the signature of the treaty was not quite the end of the business. Russo-Swedish relations remained for some time very delicate. There were long delays and a good deal of bickering, and suspicion of bad faith on both sides, about the boundary commission; and until that commission had concluded its labours, Gdov remained in Swedish hands.[2] Throughout 1617 Karl Karlsson Gyllenhielm was pessimistic as to the chances of keeping the peace, and sent in alarming reports of the destitution and penury of the Swedish armies.[3] Gradually relations improved. Each side was anxious to cultivate the other's friendship, and though Gustav Adolf's attempt to conclude an offensive alliance with Russia in 1620 failed, he was able to obtain free access to the Russian grain-market (a matter of importance to him later), and in return he sent Swedish officers and equipment to improve the Russian army.

[1] Text in *Sverges Traktater*, V₂. 242-66, with annexure to the treaty pp. 266-9. The successive boundary conventions in *ibid.*, pp. 270-303. See the general survey of the progress of the negotiations in Gustav Adolf's speech to the Estates on 28 January 1617, in *SRDA*, II. 102-10.

[2] It was not evacuated until 1621, after further tedious wrangles: see Hallenberg, IV. 748-83, 785-7. In August 1620 Oxenstierna wrote to John Casimir: 'Ich durffte wohl sagen, were Augdow in I.K.M:tzen meines allergnedigsten herren henden nicht gelassen, die grentzen würden so baldhe keine richtigkeit erlangen': *AOSB*, I. II. 364; and when Henrik Fleming brought Gustav Adolf the news that a final settlement had been reached, he is said to have leapt from his chair and cried, 'You have the tidings of an honest man', and to have rewarded him with several choice manors: [S. Loenbom] *Historiskt Archivum*, I. 77.

[3] *AOSB*, II. IX. 21, 23, 29, 37.

From Sweden's point of view, the Treaty of Stolbova was the first victory of the reign. In spite of very dubious military advantages, Sweden had obtained everything she could really hope for; and there was little prospect that a continuance of hostilities would have given her more. The Gulf of Finland was now Swedish from shore to shore. Russia was cut off from the Baltic. The Finnish frontier had been strengthened by the acquisition of Kexholm and Nöteborg, and was now established virtually on the line of the Finnish-Russian frontier between 1919 and 1939. To the southeast, the newly won areas were protected by the interposition of Lake Ladoga and its marshes between Swedish territory and any attacking force; and here, in a wilderness well to the east of the site of Peter's future capital, Gustav Adolf caused a stone to be erected, bearing the Three Crowns of Sweden, and the inscription

> Huc regni posuit fines Gustavus Adolphus
> Rex Sveonum, fausto Numine duret opus.

Gustav Adolf, in common with most of his predecessors and successors on the Swedish throne, had an ingrained fear of Russia. He realized in 1617 that the period of her impotence and anarchy was over; he foresaw the day when she would be a menace to all the Baltic states. He had seized the fleeting opportunity which the Troublous Times provided, and utilized it to the limit of his resources. He had pushed Russia back towards Asia; he had undone and reversed the achievements of a hundred years of Muscovite effort; he had excluded Moscow from Europe for nearly a century. For this reason, Stolbova has importance not merely in Swedish but also in European history. And it is this feeling above all which animates the King's triumphant oration to the Estates at the Örebro *riksdag* of 1617. In comparison with these advantages, it was of minor importance that Sweden should now have abandoned the attempt to monopolize the trade of Russia. The design had been largely chimerical from the beginning. The Treaty of Stolbova gave the project a silent burial. For by that treaty Sweden did indeed obtain the Ingrian ports; but she did not obtain the great staple-towns of Novgorod and Pskov, nor did she improve her position in the Arctic. Narva and Ivangorod might squabble about the trade as much as they chose; the Swedish government might issue regulations to its heart's content; but the obstinate fact

remained that it was easy for the Russia merchants to get round the
Swedish barrier, either by way of Pernau and Riga, or by way of
Archangel. Gustav Adolf was not indifferent to those considerations of commercial policy which had moved his predecessors, as
his instructions to his negotiators make plain; but it is very
unlikely that they occupied as large a place in his calculations as—
for instance—in those of Erik XIV; and it is a one-sided view of
history which calls Stolbova a 'defeat' for Sweden and sees in
Gustav Adolf's subsequent attack on Poland mainly an attempt to
stop the chinks in Sweden's monopoly-system by seizing Riga and
Pernau.[1]

Apart from the satisfactory nature of the settlement with Russia,
the Peace of Stolbova registered a victory over Poland. Karl IX had
not in the first instance been concerned to safeguard the Baltic
against the advance of Russia when he began his intervention in
Muscovite affairs. His object had been rather to prevent Poland
from obtaining an aggrandizement of her power that would be
dangerous to Sweden. By 1617 this object had been in part attained.
Sweden had extracted concessions from Russia which interposed
serious obstacles to any Polish attack on Finland from the south.
Even if Sigismund still succeeded in obtaining the throne for
Władysław, or for himself, Sweden might now hope to meet the
danger with confidence. But Sigismund's hopes were waning fast:
in January 1619 they became virtually extinct. They were defeated
mainly by the revival of Russian patriotism, assisted by the disorder
in Poland itself; but they could hardly have been defeated so easily
without Swedish intervention. First by the support of Šuijskij,
and subsequently by cooperation with Ljapunov and Požarskij,
Sweden had given the Russians invaluable help in their struggle
against the dynastic ambitions of the Polish King and the Panslav
dreams of his advisers. The Treaty of Stolbova, then, was a defeat
for Poland; it marked a check not only to her designs upon Russia
but also to the hope of the elder Vasa line to use Russia as a jumping-
off ground for the reconquest of Sweden. The battle between
Sweden and Poland had been fought mainly with diplomatic
weapons; the engagement had taken place in a subsidiary theatre
of war; but the result affected the whole course of the Swedo-

---

[1] For this view, see A. Attman, *Freden i Stolbova 1617. En aspekt* (*Scandia* 1949),
and also A. Soom, *De ingermanländska städerna och freden i Stolbova 1617* (*Svio-
Estonica* 1936). For a typical Swedish trade-regulation, Waaranen, *Samling*, V.
234.

Polish conflict. Sweden, secure in Ingria and Estonia, was able to give her undivided attention to the main sphere of operations in Livonia and Lithuania. The resolution of the discords in Russia meant that the war with Poland, hitherto so desultory, would soon be taken up in earnest.

CHAPTER III

DOMESTIC AFFAIRS, 1611-17

(i) *Introductory*

FOR the first few years after Gustav Adolf's accession, Sigismund III had had little time to spare for Scandinavian affairs. Such portion of his energies as was not devoted to forwarding his ambitions in Russia was fully occupied by the internal troubles which harassed the Republic. But though for the moment he might allow his attention to wander, he had not the least idea of abandoning his claims to the throne of Sweden. And never, perhaps, were his prospects better, never was the future for the dynasty of Karl IX more dark, than in the years during which Gustav Adolf was engaged in war with Denmark and Russia. It is possible, no doubt, that Sigismund missed his best opportunity during the War of Kalmar; but even when that war was over and the soil of Sweden cleared of the invader, his chances remained good. A succession of truces, punctuated by futile negotiations for peace, prevented any overt hostilities until 1617; but if there was no fighting, there was equally no peace. Until 1617, and even until 1621, the throne of Gustav Adolf appeared anything but secure; and it seemed that a resolute and well-directed effort to deprive him of it could hardly fail to be successful. Sigismund spared no pains to undermine his cousin's position; his propaganda was widely disseminated; his agents were constantly at work underground. Around him gathered a hopeful and rancorous band of Swedish exiles.

These attempts to seduce Gustav Adolf's subjects from their loyalty, these constant threats of a legitimist invasion, were the more formidable because of the extremely critical condition of affairs in Sweden during this period. The country was exhausted and impoverished; the administration weak and disorganized; and there was at least one revolt with which the King was forced to come to terms. Gustav Adolf's effective control of the country was jeopardized by the existence of great appanages, made over to members of the royal family, and largely withdrawn from the supervision of the central government. The burden of taxation, already felt to be crushing, was increased to an unprecedented degree by the necessity of raising the stipulated indemnity for Älvsborg; and there were many who believed that the fortress would not be regained without another war with Denmark. Lastly, the future of the dynasty remained uncertain for so long as the King's coronation was postponed, and for so long as he should remain without heirs. Until 1617, then, Sweden was struggling for bare survival. Unless Gustav Adolf and Oxenstierna could beat down the threat of internal treason; unless they could grapple successfully with the deficiencies of the administration; unless they could redeem Älvsborg from the Danes; all the annexations in Russia, all the tedious labours of the diplomats of Diderina, would be utterly in vain. It is with the efforts of the government to extricate the country from the desperate state in which she found herself on the morrow of the peace of Knäred that this chapter will be concerned.

(ii) *Polish Intrigues in Sweden: the émigrés*

In his attempts to recover the throne of his father Sigismund was fortunate in having at his disposal a devoted group of Swedish *émigrés* ready to risk anything for revenge upon Karl IX and upon Karl's usurping son, and at least as anxious as Sigismund himself for a triumphant return to their native land. The number of Swedes residing in Poland in 1611 was about 400. They were persons of every station of life, and of a wide variety of professions, ranging from trumpeters and common soldiers to academics and former members of the *riksråd*. Some had accompanied the King upon his first going to Poland; others were the political wreckage of the 'nineties; others again had fled from the wrath of Karl IX. There was a concentration of them in Danzig, which consequently became a centre for *émigré* intrigues. Some of them helped to staff a special Swedish Chancery which Sigismund took care to maintain in token of his legitimate claims. Many found their way sooner or later to the little court of Sigismund's sister, the Princess Anna. Anna, though a Lutheran, had found herself unable to live upon satisfactory terms with Karl IX, and had in 1598 retired permanently to Poland. There she made it her business to befriend the unfortunate exiles, caring little what religion they professed; and among those to whom she gave her protection were the unhappy son of Erik XIV by Karin

Månsdotter,[1] and Karl IX's illegitimate son, Karl Karlsson Gyllenhielm, who from 1601 to 1613 was a prisoner in Polish hands. It was
among the exiles—and notably in such men as Georg Larsson and
Gregor Borastus—that Sigismund found his ablest propagandists.
Their lot was not an easy one, for Sigismund could not afford to be
over-generous with pensions.[2]

No less than 105 of the exiles are counted as nobles; and among
them could be found representatives of most of the great families
of Sweden. Thus Count Abraham Brahe had two brothers Gustav
and Erik across the water; there were three sons of Erik Sparre;
three brothers Stenbock, two Banérs, and two Bielkes. The Leijon-
hufvuds were well represented, and so were the Gyllenstiernas.
Indeed, there was hardly a noble house but could reckon a member
in either camp, and probably not one which was not related by
marriage to an exile. The Bielkes and Posses, for instance, were
linked by marriage to the Oxenstiernas, Natt och Dags, Soops and
Bååts; and Erik Gyllenstierna and Göran Posse were both cousins
of Axel Oxenstierna. When the second generation of exiles grew
up, in ignorance of Sweden, and unknown save by report to their
Swedish relations, it became possible for a bold man to practise
imposture on both sides of the water. It was this which allowed
Lars Wivallius to pass himself off in Poland as a Swedish, and in
Sweden as a Polish, Gyllenstierna.[3] But the soul of the emigration
was the Posse family. Göran Knutsson Posse had been condemned
to death at Linköping in 1600, and subsequently pardoned. In 1603
he had fled to Poland, where he became one of Sigismund's most
trusted advisers. He was the author of *Hertig Karls Slaktarebänck*
(*Duke Karl's Slaughter-block*), the most famous, as it is the most
venomous, of all the exiles' pamphlets; and was the inspiration of
most of the intrigues against Gustav Adolf in the early years of the
reign.[4] He died in 1616, at a moment when his hopes were high;
but he bequeathed his vendetta to his eldest son Gabriel, who rose

[1] J. Anderson, *Historia om svenska kronprinsen Gustaf* . . ., p. 14.
[2] For the *émigrés*, see J. Trypucko, *Svenskarna i Polen under Sigismund IIIs
tid, passim*; E. Anthoni, *Kring en förteckning över politiska flyktingar i polsk tjänst*
(*H.T. för Finland* 1933) *passim*; E. Anthoni, *En förteckning över flyktingar i Polen
i början av 1620-talet* (*H.T. för Finland* 1942) *passim*; Ahnlund, *Kring Gustav
Adolf*, pp. 21-2, 44-51; *id.*, *Oxenstierna*, pp. 153-5; *id.*, *Storhetstidens Gryning*,
p. 45; *Abraham Brahes Tidebok*, pp. 88-9; Belfrage, *Erik Soop*, p. 15.
[3] For Wivallius, H. Schück, *Svenska Bilder*, III. 61-233; and *infra.*, p. 501.
[4] The best edition of this famous pamphlet is by Tor Berg (1915), who established the authorship of Göran Knutsson Posse, as against his kinsman Göran
Nilsson Posse.

rapidly in Sigismund's favour, and was in 1626 established in Danzig as his 'naval commissioner'.[1] Gabriel's younger brother Knut was given command of the Polish fleet in 1623, but was reconciled to Gustav Adolf in the following year, and returned to Sweden.

The spirit of the emigration was at least as much negative as positive. It was not really that the exiles felt themselves bound by strong ties of loyalty and devotion to Sigismund; but rather that they cherished an intelligible animus against Karl. Many of them had fathers or uncles who had been among Karl's victims, or had themselves barely escaped his executioner. It was hatred, not loyalty, which supplied the driving-force for their intrigues and enabled them to keep in good heart; and when Karl IX died they were deprived of one of their main moral supports. It was not easy to transfer their attacks from the father to the son, and the difficulty is plainly to be seen in their pamphleteering. Against Gustav Adolf they can find little more to say than that he is a usurper, and the son of his father. For the rest, they find it simplest to fall back on the old charges against Karl IX. Thus the poem *Konung Sigismund till Sveriges Rike* (*King Sigismund to the Swedish Realm*), which dates from 1617, is really no advance upon *Grafskrift öfver Hertig Karl* (*Epitaph on Duke Karl*), which dates from 1611: there is the same bitterness, the same accusations, but for the rest the only difference is that the later verses are more lengthy and less effective.[2] In short, it was one of the weaknesses of Sigismund's position that he was compelled to try to keep alive rancours which were losing their point, to blow always upon the embers of a dying wrath, to ignore the present and concentrate upon historic grievances which most men were glad to allow to fall into oblivion.

There was thus an obvious opening for Gustav Adolf to detach the less embittered and less dangerous of the exiles. The process of reconciliation between the Crown and the nobility, to which the Charter had been the preliminary, might be extended to some of those nobles who had fled the kingdom. Gustav Adolf was certainly not unaware of his opportunity; and in any case there were many

---

[1] His commission is printed in *Handlingar rörande Skandinaviens Historia*, XVI. 135-7.

[2] For these verses, see G. S. Hyltén-Cavallius and G. Stephens, *Sveriges Historiska och Politiska Visor*, I. 228, 234. The *Epitaph* is strikingly reminiscent of Skelton's *Epitaph upon John Jayberd of Diss*, both in matter and in metre.

to remind him of it.[1] Oxenstierna was anxious for the repatriation of the more presentable of his relatives, and many of the nobility cherished similar hopes. The Queen-Mother, and Johan of Öster-götland, too, were prepared to intercede on behalf of individuals. But the King was not ready to grant pardons indiscriminately. He had been brought up to hate the enemies of his father; and though candour might compel him to the tacit admission that there was much in Karl's reign that was indefensible, he was not prepared to censure his father's memory by too ready a lenity. Some obvious injustices he did indeed redress: the plunder which Karl's servants had taken from innocent relatives of condemned persons was restored to them, and some victims of odious delations were compensated. But in general he insisted that no exile should venture to return home without a safe-conduct from himself; and a safe-conduct entitled him to no more than a fair investigation of his case. He was extremely angry when his mother, or Duke Johan, gave asylum within their duchies to émigrés who had no right to be in Sweden. He dealt trenchantly with the attempt of an impudent ruffian such as Axel Leijonhufvud to force his way into the country. No doubt he felt justly sceptical of the political trustworthiness of many of those who now professed contrition: there was always the possibility that they might use a feigned submission to establish themselves in Sweden as secret agents of Sigismund. But in all save a few cases he eventually allowed himself to be persuaded, either by his mother or by Oxenstierna, to receive those who expressed a desire to return. Göran Posse and Axel Leijonhufvud, however, he excluded absolutely: no plea by interested friends could move him here; and there is no doubt that in this instance he judged aright. On the other hand, the victims of Karl's confiscations in many cases recovered their property; the Banérs, Bielkes, Stenbocks and Posses had their estates restored to them; and the special administrative arrangements for forfeited lands quickly became superfluous, and were discontinued. But though penitent émigrés might, if they behaved themselves, be tolerably sure of obtaining his grace at last, they scarcely ever enjoyed his trust. There is hardly an instance of

[1] For Gustav Adolf's policy to the exiles, see *AOSB*, I. II. 165-6; II. III. 14-17; Hallenberg, I. 238-9; III. 91-7, 105-10; Styffe, p. 345; Ahnlund, *Oxenstierna*, pp. 147-53, 160; *Den Sv. Utrikesförvaltningens Historia*, p. 49 (for the case of Larsson); Ahnlund, *Kring Gustav Adolf*, p. 22; B. Steckzén, *Johan Banér*, pp. 42-3; T. Berg, *De särskilda fögderierna för förbrutna gods under Karl IX:s och Gustav II Adolfs regeringar*, pp. 180-203 ; *RRP*, I. 21 (for Karl Banér).

a former exile's rising to a position of importance in Gustav Adolf's service. His suspicions long remained awake. When in 1625 Karl Banér was in Paris on a diplomatic mission, a report became current that he had published a pamphlet in defence of the men executed by Karl in 1605. The report was, as it happened, false; but it was taken seriously enough for the *råd* to debate what steps were to be taken. And as late as 1627 an otherwise unexceptionable civil servant was dismissed from his post in the Chancery only because he had a brother in Sigismund's employ. Only rarely, as in the case of the young Gyllenstiernas in 1626, did the King take the initiative in seeking a reconciliation.

There remained, however, many exiles in Poland: some sought pardon and were refused; more had linked their fortunes with Sigismund's for too long to separate from him now. From this hard core of resistance came the intrigues and conspiracies which, for the next decade, threatened Gustav Adolf with domestic plots and kept hanging over him the menace of a Polish invasion. At any time between 1613 and 1617 there seemed a chance that the machinations of these *émigrés* might lead to a reversal of the verdict of Stångebro, with, maybe, another Linköping to follow. They kept the Swedish government in a constant state of nervous tension; they filled the air with dark and fearful rumour; and they did in fact make persistent efforts to tamper with the loyalty of Gustav Adolf's subjects. The situation bore an obvious resemblance to that in which Elizabeth had found herself in the decade before the Armada; and it is not surprising that Gustav Adolf's reaction should have resembled hers. In each instance the authorities struck out in blind panic at manifestations which were trivial in themselves but which were suspected of being the indications of more serious danger. The very intangibility of the threat made it at times the more alarming.

The legitimist invasion, if it came, might be expected either by way of Finland, or as a direct descent on the south-east coast of Sweden. At first the former alternative seemed the more probable; and in 1612 Gustav Adolf was prepared for an attack on Viborg.[1] Sigismund was especially active in disseminating propaganda in Finland, and he had some ground for supposing that there was no part of the Swedish realm where he would meet with less opposition. Finland had been the last stronghold of his adherents in the years

---

[1] Waaranen, *Samling*, IV. 60-1; *Sveriges Krig*, II. 7.

after Stångebro. Lutheranism had not taken root so deeply there as in Sweden proper: the Bishop of Åbo, Eric Erici Sorolainen, had been remarkably complaisant to the Romish tendencies of Johan III, and his son actually apostatized to Rome and established himself in Poland.[1] The Swedish government, therefore, kept a particularly sharp eye for any possible Polish agents in Finland; and one reason why Gustav Adolf held a provincial Diet at Helsingfors in 1616 was to stimulate the loyalty of his Finnish subjects and to counteract the plots of Sigismund's emissaries.[2]

The threat of invasion through Finland, however, never really developed; and in the years after 1613 the main danger appeared rather to be that of a landing in force somewhere in the neighbourhood of Kalmar. This danger reached a climax in the years 1615-1617. It was a time when the King was much absent from Sweden, for the Russian campaign was demanding his personal attention; and in the spring of 1616 the alarm in Sweden was so great that some members of the *råd* pressed for his return home.[3] In 1615 information reached Gustav Adolf that Göran Posse had planned a descent on Kalmar and was confident of success; and troops were accordingly concentrated there on the pretext of working on the fortifications, while the forces of Johan's duchy were similarly assembled at Norrköping and the levies of Västergötland at Jönköping.[4] In the following year the rumours of an attack were even stronger: Sigismund was said to have 16,000 men in Danzig awaiting embarkation; and there is no doubt that Danzig, Elbing and Königsberg were asked to fit out ships for use against Sweden.[5] The exiles were reported to be of the opinion that the supreme moment had arrived, and they were said to be confident that within a twelvemonth the King would enjoy his own again. At the Örebro *riksdag* of 1617 Gustav Adolf was predicting an invasion for the following summer; while the Estates were urging that the navy should be reinforced to the utmost, and that Kristian IV should be requested to stop all ships of war and warlike stores coming eastward through the Sound for Polish ports.[6] And Kristian himself was debating whether he

---

[1] Trypucko, p. 48.
[2] Ahnlund, *Ståndsriksdagens Utdaning*, p. 135.
[3] *ibid.*, p. 135. There were also other reasons why his return was desirable: see below, p. 264.
[4] Hallenberg, III. 381-2; *Sveriges Krig*, II. 19; *AOSB*, II. 1. 83.
[5] *Samling af Instructioner för Landt-Regeringen*, pp. 103-4; Thyresson, p. 76; Hammarstrand, *op. cit.*, pp. 44-5.
[6] *SRDA*, II. 121-3, 131-2, 135, 150.

ought not to give Gustav Adolf a friendly warning of impending danger.[1]

Nothing came of these alarms; but it is obvious that the fears of the government had ample foundation. And even had the information from abroad been less explicit than it was, they had more than enough evidence of Sigismund's activities to justify their nervousness. From the very outset of the reign Sigismund had been actively attempting to create a party in Sweden and to win over prominent persons to lead it. In 1612 and 1613, for instance, he had made attempts to debauch Jakob de la Gardie, baiting the hook with judicious flattery and the prospect of a joint campaign against the Russians.[2] At the same time he had begun an attempt, which was long persisted in, to undermine the loyalty of Johan of Östergötland.[3] Both Johan and de la Gardie lost no time in communicating these offers to Gustav Adolf. But the government in Stockholm felt uneasy. They had a suspicion amounting almost to certainty that Polish spies and agitators were coming into the country, and that correspondence which would not bear inspection was passing between the exiles and their connections at home. Public opinion was in an uncertain state, and there was some ground for thinking that Sigismund might be waging a 'war of nerves': strange stories of ghosts and apparitions came from Småland and from Kalmar, and Gustav Adolf was inclined to think that they were disseminated by evilly disposed persons with a view to upsetting the public mind.[4] Manifestos written by *émigré* hands began to make their appearance in the country; and though patriots might affect to despise them,[5] they had a disturbing effect. There were reports that Sigismund's agents were smuggling such writings over the Norwegian border into Dalarna, and a certain Long Måns was said to be the organizer of this traffic.[6] In 1615 Sigismund himself addressed an open letter to his Swedish subjects, in which he reaffirmed his rights to the throne, denied current rumours that he was in treaty with 'Duke Gustav

---

[1] Kristian IV to his *Raad*, 1 December 1616: *Kong Christian den fjerdes egenhændige Breve*, I. 107-8.

[2] *AOSB*, II. v. 33; Waaranen, *Samling*, IV. 48-52; *Sveriges Krig*, I. 392.

[3] Hallenberg, II. 552-5; *Sveriges Krig*, II. 7.

[4] *AOSB*, I. ii. 175; II. i. 35, 48.

[5] *e.g.* Karl Karlsson Gyllenhielm, who perhaps felt that some show of patriotic zeal was called for: he had wavered in his loyalty while in prison in Poland, and Posse was trying to seduce him just at this time. *AOSB*, II. x. 6; E. Granstedt, *Karl Karlsson Gyllenhielms fångenskap i Polen* (*Svio-Polonica* 1944-5), and *id.*, *Carl Carlsson Gyllenhielm och Vasahuset* (*PHT* 1943-5).

[6] S. Clason, *Förhållandet till Polen . . .*, p. 190.

Adolf' for their renunciation, promised a free pardon to all who should return to their allegiance, and denounced vengeance upon those who persisted in adherence to the usurper.[1] A letter written in Sigismund's interest was delivered to the Bishop of Strängnäs; another appeared mysteriously on the Archbishop's table; a third was actually read from the pulpit in certain parishes in the hundreds in pawn to Denmark.[2] In the following year, 1616, appeared Göran Posse's famous pamphlet, *Hertig Karls Slaktarebänck*, as the climax of this literary campaign. Even in remote Norrland a peasant was heard by his neighbours to utter 'gross, evil and witless words', ascribable by the nervous or imaginative to Polish propaganda.[3] It was no wonder that at *riksdag* after *riksdag* royal messages should invite the Estates to take into consideration suitable counter-measures.[4]

The tension reached its height, despite the death of Göran Posse in 1616, in the years 1616 and 1617. It was in 1616 that there was founded an odd sort of crusading Order, with a regular hierarchy of degrees, circles, priories and commanderies, whose prime object was the recovery of Sweden for the Roman faith. The founder of this Order was the Austrian Field-Marshal Michael Adolf von Altheim (or Althann). By the beginning of 1617 he had his plans all ready and a contract prepared for Sigismund's signature. Altheim proposed to raise an army of 14,000 men, ship it to Sweden, and conquer the country for Sigismund. Leading Swedish exiles were thought to be concerned in the scheme; and one of them, Erik Gyllenstierna, is said to have attempted to raise a loan from the Fuggers to finance the project. The troubles in the Habsburg lands soon gave Altheim other employment, and the project for the moment went no further. Yet it is a mistake to say that the whole affair was no more than a bluff.[5] The Swedish government had good reason to take it seriously, and from Holland Oldenbarnevelt sent earnest warnings that mischief was afoot. It was perhaps fortunate that the waters of the Baltic divided Sweden from the enterprising Field-Marshal.[6]

---

[1] S. Clason, *op. cit.*, pp. 192-4; *Sveriges Krig*, II. 19.
[2] Hallenberg, IV. 531-4.
[3] R. Gothe, *Medelpads Finnmarker*, p. 53.
[4] *SRDA*, I. 236-43, 331-2; Hallenberg, III. 376.
[5] As J. Paul does: *Gustaf Adolf*, I. 123 *note* 1; and also Cronholm, I. 314-15.
[6] For the Altheim Order, see: Ahnlund, *Kring Gustav Adolf*, pp. 51-2; Hammarstrand, *op. cit.*, pp. 46-7; *AOSB*, II. x. 187; Thyresson, p. 154; Szelągowski, p. 236; and *infra.*, p. 189.

Even more alarming, because closer at hand, was the sensational case of Messenius, which came up for trial in this same year 1616.[1] Messenius was the son of a miller (hence his *cognomen*, from Latin *messis*); was born at Motala about 1580; and had been put to school at Vadstena, where he came much under Jesuit influence. After the Söderköping *riksdag* of 1595 he had been sent abroad for safety at the expense of his Roman Catholic master, and in 1596 had been enrolled among the papal scholarship-boys at the seminarium of Braunsberg in Prussia. Braunsberg was at this time one of the great outposts of the Counter-Reformation in northern Europe. The Jesuit Fathers who directed it provided an education more modern, more intelligent, and more attractive than that which any Protestant academy in the North could offer. They made it their especial care to try to attract youths from Scandinavia, and particularly from Sweden; and they hoped to train there a body of zealous converts, to be used eventually for the winning back of their native countries to the true faith. By lavish awards of papal *stipendia* they were able to provide a university education at a considerably cheaper rate than was possible in, for instance, Rostock, which was the university to which most Swedes then resorted.[2] Thus Braunsberg became for some decades a Swedish Catholic university, and stood in the same relation to Sweden as Douai did to Elizabethan England.

Messenius had a distinguished academic career at Braunsberg, where he remained until 1603. He had already attracted the favourable notice of Bishop Tylicki of Kraków, and was now attached to his household; and with Tylicki he visited Rome in 1604. In the following year he was at Ingolstadt, where he obtained his Doctorate; and soon afterwards his literary gifts, which were already considerable, gained for him the title of *Poeta Caesarea* at the hands of Rudolf II. It was now his object to get a powerful patron, and in an attempt to commend himself to the Bishop of Ermeland, he composed a scurrilous attack upon Karl IX, which was to prove damaging to him later. He managed somehow to maintain himself by teaching, and by the sale of occasional verses; and in 1607 he married Lucia Grothusen. Lucia was a Roman Catholic like himself: her father, Arnold Grothusen, had at one time been

---

[1] For Messenius, see: H. Schück, *Messenius, passim*; S. Ljung, *Erik Jöransson Tegel*, pp. 84-110; Trypucko, pp. 27 *seqq.*; N. G. Ohlson, *Hertig Sigismunds tukto- och läremästare, passim*.

[2] This point was strongly made during the discussions on the Statute of Örebro in February 1617: *SRDA*, II. 59; and see below, p. 461.

tutor to Sigismund III, and she herself had been one of the Princess Anna's Ladies. Messenius did his best to win the favour of Sigismund with a *Genealogica Sigismundi*, which he published in 1606; but Sigismund remained indifferent: he may well have had other matters than genealogy to think of, for this was the year of Zebrzydowski's *rokosz*. Messenius consequently came to the conclusion that Poland held no prospects for him, and being a man of limitless ambition, inordinate vanity, and singularly few scruples, he decided to turn his coat. He intimated to Karl IX that he was prepared to give him important information in return for employment; and Karl, who was much in need of literary talent, accepted his offer. In 1609, therefore, Messenius returned home, and entered Karl's service for an annual wage of 150 *dalers* and 150 *tunnor* of wheat, at the same time binding himself by his oath of office to maintain the Succession Pact of 1604, and to abjure the Church of Rome. Messenius' sharp pen and varied talents soon recommended him to his new master; but the favour he enjoyed drew upon him the hatred of two other of Karl's servants, who found themselves outshone as pamphleteers. These were Nils Chesnecopherus, the most important of Karl's 'secretaries', and Erik Göransson Tegel, the son of that Göran Persson who had been the hated minister of Erik XIV. Within a year of Messenius' return, however, Karl had decided to make use of him in other fields, and appointed him to the vacant Chair of Politics in the University of Uppsala. Messenius' stormy career at Uppsala is dealt with elsewhere[1]: here it is sufficient to say that by 1613 he had made the university too hot to hold him, and in the interests of academic peace Gustav Adolf found it necessary to provide him with other employment. The Chancery's archives were in urgent need of care and arrangement, and Messenius appeared a very suitable person to undertake the work. He was accordingly appointed to the Chancery as archivist, a position in which it might have been hoped that his quarrelsome and captious temper would have less scope than at Uppsala. Messenius showed great enthusiasm for his new task, and displayed laudable zeal in the collection and publication of documents. His labours between 1613 and 1616 paved the way for his important work as a historian later in life.

In 1614 his industry and talents were rewarded with a further appointment, when he became one of the non-noble Assessors in

---

[1] See below, Chapter VII.

the new Supreme Court (*Svea Hovrätt*). It was this appointment,
however, which ultimately led to his downfall. When the Grothusens
retired to Poland at the end of the previous century, the family
property had been appropriated, in a more or less shady fashion,
by none other than Chesnecopherus; and Messenius now caused a
suit to be instituted for its recovery. The case went badly for
Chesnecopherus from the beginning, and he cast about for means
to compass Messenius' ruin. He soon found an ally in Tegel, who
resented the aspersions which Messenius, in one of his historical
works, had cast upon the character of Göran Persson.[1] Tegel began
the attack by raking up the old pamphlet against Karl IX which
Messenius had written in his Polish days. This, though it certainly
prejudiced the King against him, might not in itself have entailed
his fall; but Tegel now succeeded in unearthing a scandal which was
of a much more serious character. He discovered that Messenius
kept up a correspondence with Poland, and he succeeded in laying
hands upon the intermediary by whom it was sent. The tables were
now turned with a vengeance; and Chesnecopherus might make
himself easy about the Grothusen property, since his prosecutor
was himself accused of something not far removed from high
treason.

Messenius did not make the situation any better by the equi-
vocations and prevarications with which he sought to maintain his
innocence. The facts of the case seem clear enough. In his zeal
to collect material for the Archives he had undoubtedly entered into
correspondence with the monastery of Oliva in Poland; had begun
negotiations for a possible exchange of archival material; and, in
order to gain the good graces of Oliva, had been willing to allow his
correspondent to suppose that he was still a Roman Catholic at heart
—a supposition, incidentally, which later turned out to have been
perfectly correct. But this was not all. Not only had he corresponded (as he alleged in his defence) on purely personal and
private matters with his brother-in-law in Danzig, but he had also
asked his intermediary to intercede for him with Sigismund. All
this was certainly a violation of the decisions of the Norrköping
riksdag of 1604, which had forbidden any correspondence with the
exiles in Poland. But Messenius' shifty behaviour in the dock;

[1] Ljung (*op. cit.*, pp. 84-110) contends that there was no conspiracy between
Chesnecopherus and Tegel; suggests that Messenius himself was mainly responsible for his own downfall; and in general takes a more favourable view of Tegel's
character than has been usual in the past.

the progressively more compromising revelations, under torture, of the intermediary; the apparent ease with which such communication had been established and maintained; and, not least, the suspicion, still hanging over Messenius from his Uppsala days, that he was a crypto-Papist, and perhaps a secret agent—these things gave to the whole affair a very sinister aspect. Was Messenius the only culprit? Was there not perhaps a plot, the other threads of which still remained to be disentangled? It is no matter for surprise if the Swedish government, in this dark year 1616, with Altheim raising his banner and an invasion hourly expected, should have used harsh measures.

In reality, there was no plot at all; but Messenius' case was probably not unique, even though no others like it were unearthed at the time. Messenius had merely succumbed to the temptation to reinsure himself against any change in the political weather. It was a temptation which the generation after Stångebro must have felt as strongly as did the generation after the Boyne, though apparently their political virtue was more usually proof against it. Messenius, a careerist and an academic, an intriguer by nature and a Catholic by conviction, was not the man to resist it.

Gustav Adolf may not have been wholly convinced of Messenius' guilt, but he could not afford to take chances. Messenius, unable to comply with the absurd requirement that he should bring twelve compurgators to swear that *all* his letters were innocent of treason, was condemned to death. His sentence was, however, immediately commuted to imprisonment for life. The place chosen for his incarceration was Kajaneborg, a remote castle in the wildest and most inhospitable part of Arctic Finland. Here for the next twenty years he lived a life of heart-rending hardship, and was treated by his gaolers with revolting brutality.[1] The government connived at their excesses, even if it did not tacitly encourage them. His wife accompanied him to Kajaneborg, and shared all the rigours of his captivity. The sole concession made to him was the permission to take with him his books; for the government was aware that he was a historian of whom great things might be expected, and was prepared to allow him to write, if he still cared for it. And so, in conditions of infinite misery, and under every sort of handicap,

---

[1] Various documents concerning this part of Messenius' career are printed in *Handlingar rörande Sveriges äldre, nyare och nyaste Historia*, VI. lx-lxxx; and see Ahnlund, *Kring Gustav Adolf*, pp. 197-204.

Messenius wore away the rest of his life in the pursuit of authorship, labouring upon his great work *Scondia Illustrata*, which he vainly hoped would win him the pardon of Gustav Adolf.[1] But though he failed in this, he succeeded in establishing a secure reputation as one of the best of Sweden's earlier historians; and so conscious were his contemporaries of his merit that after Gustav Adolf's death the Regency provided him with a secretary to make a fair copy of his work. In 1636 they even set him free; but by this time he was a broken man. On 8 November 1636 he died, professing his Catholicism; and by a final act of cruelty was buried, in defiance of his wishes, in the Protestant church of Uleåborg, the victim of Sigismund's intrigues and Gustav Adolf's fears, and a standing warning against excessive zeal in archivists.[2]

It was under the influence of the impression produced by the Messenius case that the *riksdag* met at Örebro towards the end of January 1617. Gustav Adolf opened the proceedings with an address to the assembled Estates.[3] It was a speech of remarkable eloquence and power—the first, perhaps, in which he displayed that talent for vivid and stirring oratory which was not the least notable of his kingly qualities. It was at once a cry of alarm, an appeal for aid, and a defiance of the nation's enemies. Patriotic fervour and Protestant zeal were commingled in characteristic and inseparable confusion. He was lavish in denunciation of the popish religion ('if I may so call it') and harped effectively on the theme '*de haereticis non est servanda fides*', illustrating the application of the maxim from the career of Sigismund himself. Taking then a wider view, he surveyed recent European history, touched on the Inquisition, the massacre of St. Bartholomew, the defeat of the Armada, and the unhappy fate of Don Carlos, whom he supposed (as did most Protestants at that time) to have been done to death by Philip II because of his leanings towards heresy. The aid of the Estates was invoked to meet the threat from Polish agents, and to ward off the expected invasion; and he ended by reminding them that no foreign monarch had ever succeeded in conquering a united Sweden. It was a speech which Cromwell would have applauded.

The Propositions which were subsequently made to the Estates

---

[1] For Messenius' literary activities, see Chapter IX, below.
[2] His 'contrefait in natura' was still visible when Linnaeus visited Uleå church in 1732: Linné, *Ungdomsresor*, I. 202.
[3] *SRDA*, II. 102-10; or Hallendorf, pp. 39-44.

included the great reform in *riksdag* procedure which was eventually accepted as the *Riksdag* Ordinance and which will be more fully treated in another place.[1] But it had importance not merely in a constitutional aspect but as a measure of defence against Sigismund's intrigues. For it appeared that the Estate of Peasants, being unable to find among their own members persons capable of discharging the secretarial work which the *riksdag*-meeting made necessary, were in the habit of coopting any suitable outsider who presented himself. Polish agents took advantage of this state of affairs; and it had actually happened that such agents had been employed to draw up the answers to the King's Propositions. Sigismund had thereby been able to inform himself of *riksdag* proceedings from the most authentic source. The *Riksdag* Ordinance, by providing official clerks for the lower Estates, made this dangerous abuse impossible for the future.[2]

The Estates were now given a further illustration of just how active and how daring Sigismund's adherents had become. A certain Henrik Hammerus, who had been a pupil of Messenius, had lapsed to Roman Catholicism, studied in a Jesuit seminary, and enlisted in Sigismund's service. Towards the end of 1616 he made his appearance in Sweden, bearing letters (one of which was concealed in the haft of a large knife) from Sigismund and from Gabriel Posse. These letters were addressed to Johan of Östergötland, and were duly delivered to him. But once again Johan disappointed Sigismund's expectations. He arrested Hammerus, handed him over to Gustav Adolf, and discreetly left the letters unopened. They were now read, in the presence of the assembled Estates; and Johan took the opportunity to make a solemn declaration of loyalty.[3]

The arrest of Hammerus may possibly have added to the rigour of Messenius' captivity: it undoubtedly came at an appropriate moment for the government. For it disposed the Estates to acquiesce in the drastic legislation against traitors and Roman Catholics which Gustav Adolf now submitted to it. On 1 February the King invited

---

[1] See below, Chapter VI.

[2] *SRDA*, II. 24. Curiously enough the Polish *sejm* had in 1616 resolved that henceforward sessions should be secret, because of the presence of Russian spies among the general public: H. Almquist, *Polskt författningslif under Sigismund III*, pp. 192-3.

[3] For the Hammerus episode, see *SRDA*, II. 32, 42, 52; Styffe, p. 224; Holmquist, *Sv. Kyrkans Hist.*, IV. 1. 128, 130; F. Lindberg, *Johan av Östergötland* (*H.T.* 1941), pp. 135-7.

the *riksdag* to take into consideration the draft of a Statute. The propositions contained in this draft provided that any person who should visit Sigismund, Anna, Prince Władysław, or any of their servants, was to be esteemed a traitor; any person who should visit any other of the Swedish exiles in Poland, or enter into conspiracy with them by correspondence, or send them news, was to be deprived of life and estate; any person who should engage in purely private correspondence with such exiles was to be banished for life; any person receiving letters from prohibited persons was to escape punishment only if he notified the authorities in time for the emissary to be caught, while if such letters were 'planted' on him by an unknown hand he must bring twelve compurgators to swear to his loyalty, or failing that suffer the penalties of treason; and any bearer of such letters, as well as all who carried or disseminated Sigismund's propaganda, or spread 'a pack of lies', were to be punished with death. Sigismund's Polish subjects, if they were caught at such work in Sweden, would be deemed traitors, and dealt with accordingly. Fathers, guardians or relatives, who should send their sons to Polish academies, or advise the sending of them to Jesuit institutions, were to be exiled, and their property forfeit to the next-of-kin; and any young man resorting to such places on his own initiative was to be declared an outlaw. Finally, any Swede lapsing to Roman Catholicism was to be deprived of all civil rights as though he were naturally dead; any attempt to seduce another to such a defection by a person entering Sweden from abroad was to be accounted sedition; and all Papists living in the country were to quit it within three months: recalcitrants suspected of harbouring evil designs to be punished as traitors.[1]

This ferocious programme was, in the main, endorsed by the Estates. It is clear, however, that they regarded it as being excessively rigorous in some of its provisions [2]; and in the course of the discussions that followed they succeeded in obtaining a softening of a few of the more oppressive clauses. Thus on Johan's suggestion the application of the Statute was limited to the duration of hostilities with Poland; the clause requiring twelve compurgators, which had been generally disliked, was struck out [3]; and various minor altera-

---

[1] *SRDA*, II. 143 *seqq.*
[2] For discussion of the Statute by the Estates, *SRDA*, II. 122, 130, 136-7, 139, 151, 155-7, 160-3, 184 *seqq.*
[3] The Clergy had remarked that if it were adopted 'there would be no end of oaths and swearing'.

tions were conceded, all of which tended to secure that no really innocent person should be punished. Even so, the Statute of Örebro in its final form remained a most formidable weapon in the hands of the government. Its point, as can be seen, was directed primarily against *political* enemies: in so far as it also threatened religious persecution, it did so only because in the political context of the moment Catholics, or at least Swedish Catholics, were inevitably politically suspect. Gustav Adolf was not by temperament a persecutor: he was quite prepared to allow Roman Catholic merchants and military experts exemption from the provisions of the Statute, as long as they were not Poles or Swedes. When the Clergy—who had been most earnest in their efforts to safeguard the innocent and moderate the sharpness of the law—suggested making the final clause apply also to Calvinists, the King at once refused. The Örebro Statute was, after all, only an extension and reinforcement of the Norrköping decisions of 1604. It was, in fact, essentially a measure of defence, of national security: it was emergency legislation for abnormal times; and in this respect it was analogous to the penal laws of Elizabeth, or to the similar legislation introduced between 1604 and 1624 in Denmark.[1] But undeniably it was not a law which a nation would wish to see for long upon its statute-book.

With the acceptance of the Statute of Örebro the government was now effectively armed, and it at once proceeded to abuse its new powers by executing the unfortunate Hammerus, although at the time of his arrest the offence with which he was charged was not yet a capital crime. Tegel was sent on a mission to Småland, to track down suspects there; and three days of intercession lent spiritual strength to the secular arm.[2] And in fact, from this moment the situation improved, at all events for a time. Sigismund did indeed promulgate another manifesto in the summer of this year, with the idea of blasting the usurper's coronation; but it seems to have fallen rather flat. Moreover, Gustav Adolf had already begun to turn the tables by the establishment of a counter-espionage system in Poland.[3] There were still isolated cases to engage the government's attention, as when in 1618 a man was delated for boasting, in the presence of *certe honorifica et fide dignissima matrona*, that he

---

[1] For Danish legislation, see J. A. Fridericia, *Danmarks Riges Historia*, IV. 115.
[2] Styffe, p. 227; Ljung, p. 55.
[3] Trypucko, p. 50.

had friends at court who would take care of him in the event of Sigismund's restoration.[1] The hopes of the exiles were still buoyant in 1619. In 1621 a *riksdag* was again called upon to give the problem its serious attention; and Sweden celebrated the centenary of the Reformation with an earnestness and ardour which were not free from nervous anxiety. But in reality the protective machinery had its effect; and for five or six years after 1617 the authorities had the situation comfortably in hand.

But in 1623-24 there was a revival of agitation, and for a moment it seemed as though the dark days of 1616 had come round again. The conversion to Catholicism of Jakob Hunterus in 1623 caused a considerable stir, for Hunterus had been a pupil of Johannes Bureus.[2] In 1624 matters took a more serious turn. Polish spies were discovered in various parts of the country. The Supreme Court was called upon to investigate the suspicious case of one Sven Didriksson, who had been wandering round Östergötland giving vent to 'provocative speeches and rumours' of Sigismund's imminent return.[3] In Småland there was a little rebellion, led by one Jöns Stind, who turned out (and this made it the more sinister) to be a collateral descendant of that Nils Dacke who had given such trouble to Gustav Vasa in the same province eighty years before. And it was generally supposed that his movement was inspired by Sigismund.[4] The Resolution of the *riksdag* of this year mentioned the danger of Popish plots, for the first time since the Örebro *riksdag* of 1617.[5] Finally, the government's agents at last unearthed what looked to be a genuine plot. The leading personages involved were two crypto-Catholics, Göran Bähr and Zakarias Anthelius, both of whom had in their time frequented Jesuit seminaries. Bähr was employed in the Chancery, and Anthelius, after having been *Konrektor* in the school at Gävle, had become burgomaster of Södertälje. Between them they had contrived to secure the introduction into Sweden of a German Jesuit named Schacht, who had entered the country disguised as a wine-merchant and seller of rat-traps, a combination of professions which, one would have thought, might have excited suspicion in the

---

[1] *AOSB*, II. xii. 239; and see *Samling af Instructioner för Landt-Regeringen*, p. 115.
[2] Holmquist, *op. cit.*, IV. 1. 402.
[3] *ibid.*, pp. 404-6.
[4] *AOSB*, II. xii. 222; Ahnlund, *Kring Gustav Adolf*, p. 54; S. Arnoldsson. *Krigspropagandan i Sverige före trettioåriga kriget*, p. 5; Hallenberg, V. 139 *seqq.*
[5] A. A. von Stiernman, *Alla riksdagars och mötens Besluth*, I. 760-6 (cited henceforward as Stiernman).

most credulous. However, Schacht escaped detection, and all might have gone well had not Bähr seduced the wife of an Italian court-musician whose aid the conspirators were trying to enlist. The musician thereupon betrayed them to the government.[1] They were arrested and condemned to death; though Schacht, as a foreigner, was merely expelled the country. But in the course of their trial they had compromised the *Rektor* of the school at Enköping, Nicolaus Campanius, who, it appeared, had been influenced by Messenius' pupil Hammerus, and had also studied at Braunsberg. Campanius denied that he was a Catholic, and was examined in doctrine by a committee of theologians headed by the Archbishop. Though his answers were not deemed wholly satisfactory, the committee recommended only that he be suspended. By this time, however, the authorities had scented a plot whose ramifications might extend in all directions. They executed Campanius; and they put Bähr and Anthelius to the torture, in the hope of extracting from them some confession of treasonable designs. No such confession was forthcoming, for in fact their 'plot' had been purely religious. They both at this stage turned Lutheran; but this did not save them from execution. In the meantime, two further persons had become involved. One was the *Rektor* of Gävle school, Erik Niurenius, who, like the rest, had fallen away to Catholicism while studying abroad, and had spent some time both at Braunsberg and at Olmütz. He had been compromised already by the confessions extracted from Hammerus, under torture, in 1617; and like Hammerus he was probably a pupil of Messenius. No proceedings had been taken against him then; and he had already confessed his errors to his brother Olof, and to the Archbishop, both of whom had assumed that his confession betokened contrition and a change of heart. It now appeared, however, from Anthelius' evidence, that he was a Roman Catholic still. Powerful interest was made on his behalf by the Archbishop, by Oxenstierna, and by his congregation (who were much attached to him), and in the end he was lucky to escape with a sentence of three years' exile in the antiseptic atmosphere of Rostock University. The final victim was none other than Messenius' son Arnold Johan. Arnold had been sent to Uppsala to ensure that he had a proper Lutheran education, but he had soon made off to Braunsberg, entered Sigismund's service, and in 1624

---

[1] It is not absolutely clear that his motive was a desire for revenge: see L. A. Anjou, *Svenska Kyrkans Historia*, p. 165 *note* 3.

had returned to Sweden as a Polish spy. His presence had nothing
to do with Bähr and Anthelius, but upon his arrest (which took
place soon after his arrival) his case became mixed up with
theirs. He was condemned to death; but on his promising
to reveal important information (some of it damaging to his
father) his sentence was commuted to imprisonment in the fortress
of Kexholm; and in Kexholm he remained for the next fourteen
years.[1]

The Bähr-Anthelius 'plot' could only have been treated as a
plot by a government that was frightened. Yet the sentences,
drastic though they were, were justified by the Statute of Örebro;
and the victims must have known what would happen to them if
they were caught. Happily, the episode proved to be unique of its
kind. We hear very little more of such alarms for the rest of Gustav
Adolf's reign. A Jesuit was caught in 1630, but he was let off with
a caution; and an undergraduate excited suspicion in 1631, but
nothing was proved against him.[2] Bloodthirsty as the Statute of
Örebro was, it was not the occasion of much bloodshed, and the
only martyrs the Roman Church could claim as the result of its
provisions were the three luckless victims of 1624.

The conclusion of the Truce of Altmark in 1629 really brought
the state of emergency to an end. It also spelt the final shipwreck of
the hopes of such exiles as remained.[3] Gabriel Posse, irreconcilable
to the last, continued the feud by raising a regiment to serve with
Wallenstein against Gustav Adolf, and a few other stalwarts preferred
to live out their lives in Poland: the last of the Polish Gyllenstiernas
did not die till after the Treaty of Oliva—the treaty by which Sigismund's line at last formally renounced all pretensions to the
Swedish throne. But Altmark took the heart out of the emigration;
and the Swedish colony in Poland, whose spirit had been so
optimistic in 1616, dwindled into a melancholy handful of ageing
and embittered outcasts, without roots, without future, without
resources and without hope.

[1] For the Bähr-Anthelius episode, see Schück, *Messenius*, pp. 253-4; Ahnlund,
Kring Gustav Adolf, pp. 54, 69; Holmquist, *op. cit.*, IV. 1. 402-7; *AOSB*, I. 1.
518-19; *Peder Galts Depescher*, p. 113; V. Söderberg, *Högförräderimålet emot
Arnold Johan Messenius 1624* (*H.T.* 1901), pp. 1-24; Hallenberg, V. 174 *seqq.*

[2] For traces of these later alarms, see *Svenska Riksrådets Protokoll* (cited henceforward as *RRP*), I. 37; II. 29, 48, 52, 114; *AOSB*, I. v. 673; II. III. 230. For
Polish intrigues in 1633 and 1635, B. Lövgren, *Ståndsstridens Uppkomst*, p. 11.

[3] Already by 1623 their number had shrunk to 64: E. Anthoni (1942), pp.
62-71.

(iii) *The Breakdown of Law and Order*

In many respects, as we have seen, the situation in which Gustav Adolf found himself in regard to Sigismund bears a resemblance to that in which Elizabeth had found herself in regard to Philip II. But in one important particular the comparison does not hold good. The Babington Plot was not hatched in a country exhausted and prostrate; nor were the plans of Philip aimed at a land where the authority of the law was precarious. Sweden in 1613 was in far more danger of internal collapse than was England under Elizabeth. If ever a nation offered a favourable field for subversive activity, it was Sweden on the conclusion of the War of Kalmar. The wonder is not that Sigismund should have found adherents here and there, but rather that he should have found so extraordinarily few of them. But Lutheranism was now so deeply ingrained in the national character that not even the extremity of distress could seduce more than an insignificant handful to do the errands of a catholicizing King.

The war had left much of the south of Sweden in a devastated condition. From Kalmar and Jönköping, from Växjö and Skara, and even as far north as Linköping, came the same story of burned farmsteads, untilled acres, roofless buildings and plundered cathedrals.[1] It had been a war of atrocities, on both sides of the border; and it left very bitter memories behind it. To the wasted farms relief had perforce to be given, by remission of taxation for a shorter or longer period; and this at a time when the exchequer was in the greatest straits for revenue. Nor was the damage confined to Sweden proper. The barbarities of the Russian war left a trail of desolation behind them in Estonia and Karelia, and nowhere in the Swedish realm were more farms lying derelict than in Finland.[2] And if the King's bailiffs could not collect the rents and taxes, the clergy could not get in their tithe, and were themselves thus prevented from paying what was due from them to the state. The poverty of the government meant that it was impossible to raise money to pay off the foreign mercenaries, with the result that they wandered at large, robbing, plundering and murdering, in spite of all efforts to prevent them. When Per Brahe came in later years to write down his

[1] *AOSB*, II. xii. 161, 232-3, 348.
[2] Hallenberg, I. 339, 347-8; II. 573, 775.

reminiscences, one of his earliest memories was of his home's being barricaded to resist an attack from a band of a hundred Scots who were roaming the countryside, ravaging as they went.[1] Nor were the native levies much better; for discipline was lax, and the Norr-länning cared little for the feelings of the Västgöta *knalle*.[2] At the meetings of the *riksdag* the lower Estates complained bitterly and repeatedly of such excesses. Only very gradually did things improve: in 1614 the King was still nervous of the mischief which the foreign troops might do, should they combine in a military revolt.[3]

The danger from the troops was only one aspect of a more general problem—the alarming increase of a lawless and violent temper throughout the community. We hear of arbitrary eviction of Crown tenants from their holdings; of violent interference with the due process of law; of the protection of guilty parties by persons of consequence.[4] The King's own servants—his bailiffs out in the country and his trusted officials in the central or local government— were themselves among the chief culprits: the conduct of Erik Göransson Tegel on occasion showed an outrageous contempt for legality.[5] The misdeeds of the nobility, who treated royal officials and their own peasantry with almost equal contempt, were a constant source of complaint, and Sweden lacked the machinery for bringing the over-mighty subject speedily to book. In Finland, especially, disorders of this kind reached such a height that the whole frame-work of law and order was shaken. A powerful noble such as Sten Axel Leijonhufvud, for instance, did exactly as he thought proper, without paying the slightest attention to the hail of entreaties, exhortations, warnings, reprimands and summonses which was showered on him by the central government. He tortured his peasants, and abused the king's bailiffs, with every circumstance of barbarity; and all that happened to him was that in 1616 he was compelled to 'reconcile himself' with his peasants, in order to avoid investigation and punitive action by the Crown. Two years later, his conduct was as bad as ever. He was by no means the only one. Henrik Fleming, Erik Bertilsson Ljuster, and above all Joachim Berndes and his wife, Gertrud Ungern von Sternberg, all dismally

---

[1] *Svea Rikes Drotset Grefve Per Brahes Tänkebok* (ed. D. Krutmeyer), p. 2, sub anno 1613.
[2] *AOSB*, I. II. 217; II. XII. 355-7.
[3] *SRDA*, I. 145-6, 252; cf. Cronholm, III. 128-32.
[4] *AOSB*, II. XII. 154-6.
[5] *AOSB*, II. XII. 197-200; Hallenberg, III. 274-5; Ljung, pp. 61-2.

H

distinguished themselves by their cruelty. Nor were the servants
of the government in Finland any better: the bailiffs made the
peasants pay their taxes twice over, and their nominal superiors the
ståthållare not only did not effectively control them, but were themselves guilty of the grossest outrages. An investigation in 1618, for
instance, revealed a terrible story of atrocities perpetrated or connived at by the authorities in Kexholm: one *ståthållare* had driven a
regular trade by selling letters of protection to criminals—in one
particular case to two men who had been guilty of roasting a man to
death and chopping off his son's right arm. As late as 1624 Nils
Bielke, the new Governor-General of Finland, was appealing to the
government to take stronger measures against the bailiffs. It was no
wonder that the peasants were fleeing across the frontier to the
comparative security of barbarous Russia. The government did
indeed attempt to check these outrages. It issued letters of protection to those who applied for them, which theoretically ought to
have safeguarded them from oppression. Many did apply for them,
both in Sweden and in Finland: in 1612 the city of Stockholm sought
and obtained such a guarantee against 'violence and injustice'; in
1613, in a desperate effort to check the horrors in Finland, the
government issued a general letter of protection for all peasants
living on estates in Finland whose revenues had been alienated by
the Crown to private persons; and the ridiculous situation frequently
arose that special letters of protection had to be issued for the
Crown's own servants. The authority of the common law had in
fact broken down; but it was not to be restored by devices of this
sort: men like Berndes and Leijonhufvud laughed at the government's letters of protection, and Gertrud Ungern von Sternberg
impudently contended that she did not owe obedience to any royal
official. It was necessary to take more positive action; and a beginning was made with the appointment of special commissions of
enquiry. One such was appointed for Norrland in 1614, another
for certain parts of Finland in 1616; special instructions to *ståthållare* in Åbo, Kexholm and Kalmar were issued in 1615 and 1616;
and a very strong commission was sent to Kexholm in 1618. The
King himself spent a considerable period in Finland between 1614
and 1616, in an effort to come to grips with the evil. But the
government was short of money, short of staff, and overburdened
with work; and though its commissions brought much lawlessness
to light, and made one or two salutary examples, the work was not

done thoroughly. The great offenders were not brought to book. Sten Axel Leijonhufvud was left untouched; and not until 1636 did retribution finally overtake him. Even worse, Gustav Adolf went out of his way to promote some of the most odious offenders. Berndes, who had stolen the King's revenues, was in 1618 made a member of the Exchequer Council (*kammarråd*), presumably on the poacher-gamekeeper principle, and in 1619 was sent to investigate administrative abuses in the area where he had committed his own illegalities; Henrik Fleming was in 1617 made *ståthållare* of Viborg; Ljuster became a Lieutenant-Colonel, and in 1638 was called to ornament the judicial bench as Assessor in the Supreme Court at Åbo; and a certain Örneram, who had whipped and cropped the ears of a woman who had letters of protection from the Supreme Court, remained *ståthållare* of Åbo in the full sun of royal favour. In Sweden proper the rule of law does seem to have been effectively restored by the end of the second decade of the century; but in Finland the government seems to have resigned itself to a policy of making friends with the evil-doers, as the only hope of controlling them.[1]

There was one abuse, in particular, which provoked the loudest complaints, and which was so glaring that the government was forced to persist in fruitless attempts to find a remedy. There had long lain upon all peasants an obligation to provide transport (in the form of pack- or saddle-horses) for the King, the members of the royal family, and all who travelled upon the King's business: this obligation was known as *skjutsning*. Together with it, as was inevitable in a sparsely populated country, went the obligation to

---

[1] For a general picture of the prevalence of lawlessness, see Hallenberg, II. 687-94; III. 117-51. For Sten Axel Leijonhufvud, Waaranen, *Samling*, IV. 129, 131-2, 138, 162, 168, 248; V. 324; Waaranen, *Landtdagen i Helsingfors 1616 och Finlands dåvarande tillstånd*, pp. 8-10; Melander, *Drag ur Åbo Hovrätts äldre Historia*, pp. 12-17; for the other noble offenders, *ibid.*, pp. 17-24; for the iniquities of the government's servants in Finland, Waaranen, *Landtdagen i Helsingfors*, p. 16; Waaranen, *Samling*, IV. 245; V. 116-18; Melander, pp. 41-5. For the *ståthållare* who sold letters of protection, Waaranen, *Samling*, V. 256-312, and *ibid.*, 313-20, for his very lame 'explanation'; and *ibid.*, 330, 378, for further proceedings in the matter. K. K. Tigerstedt, *Bref från General-guvernörer*, I. 1-3, for Bielke's letter to Oxenstierna, Aug. 1624; Waaranen, *Samling*, IV. 197, 258-60, for flight of peasants to Russia in 1613 and 1614; *Stockholms Stads Privilegiebrev*, pp. 154-5, for letters of protection to the town, Jan. 1612; other examples of these letters in Waaranen, *Samling*, IV. 75-6, 128; the general letter of protection for Finnish peasants, May 1613, in *ibid.*, IV. 148-51. Instructions to *ståthållare* in *SILR*, pp. 94, 107. It is only fair to point out that Gustav Adolf inherited the problem: see Waaranen, *Öfversigt af Finlands tillstånd i början af sjuttonde seklet*, passim. Conditions continued bad until Karl X Gustav's reign: Melander, pp. 120-1.

provide food and lodging for such travellers: this obligation was known as *gästning*.[1] Of recent years all sorts of abuses and mal-practices had aggravated what was already a heavy burden, and at the Norrköping *riksdag* of 1604 Karl IX had attempted to cure the evil by commuting both obligations for cash payments: a new tax was imposed, the so-called *skjutsfärdspenningar*, at the rate of two marks for each whole *hemman*,[2] and a fixed tariff established for horse-hire and food. At the same time the nobility were forbidden to exempt their peasants from payment.[3] This solution did not prove successful. So bad were the abuses of *skjutsning* in Karl IX's time that the King expressly permitted the peasants to resist by force those who attempted to extract food, lodging or transport from them by violent means.[4] By about 1613 the situation had apparently become intolerable. Numbers of stray soldiers were roving at large, living on the peasantry on the pretext that they were in the King's service, or falling on them 'with hacks and blows' ('*med hugg och slag*'—the standard formula for complaints against violence) until they were given what they required; special royal commissioners were scouring the country in all directions for deserters; the nobility was increasingly demanding free *skjutsning* for itself and its servants,[5] and was refusing to allow its peasantry to contribute their proper share; all sorts of travellers were fraudulently re-presenting themselves to be on royal errands; and even merchants were attempting to extort the services which were due only to those with the King's commission.[6] A time of war, especially when hostilities are actually raging in the country, inevitably imposes a severe strain upon such a system; but even in peace-time, and when no improper persons intruded themselves, it was sufficiently onerous. It provided the only postal service in existence at that time in Sweden; upon it the connection of local and central government essentially depended. When a member of the *råd* travelled on the King's business, he needed some 40 to 60 horses for each stage. A foreign ambassador might require up to 200. The burden did not

---

[1] The question had a long history. For a general account, see P. Jacobson, *Gästgifveri- och skjutsningsbesvärens uppkomst och äldsta utveckling* (*Ekon. Tidskr.* 1919). And see N. Staf, *Marknad och möte*, pp. 29, 134-5, 161-2, 187.

[2] The *hemman* was the homestead considered as a fiscal unit of account.

[3] S. Clason, *Till reduktionens förhistoria*, pp. 16-17; Hallenberg III. 157-9.

[4] N. Forssell, *Svenska Postverkets Historia*, p. 16.

[5] This may have been a consequence of the fact that most court officials were noble: see C. Öhlander, *Bidrag till de adliga privilegiernas historia*, p. 55.

[6] *AOSB*, II. XII. 160; Hallenberg, I. 330-1; II. 700-9.

affect the peasantry only: clergy who lived near the great roads were often at heavy expense to entertain distinguished travellers, who resorted to their parsonages because they offered better accommodation than could be found elsewhere.[1] No wonder that Gustav Adolf considered that 'of all the burdens which lie upon a subject, there is none greater, none more irritating, and none more troublesome.'[2] In May 1612 the King put out a stern rebuke to those who took free *skjutsning* to which they were not entitled, or committed acts of violence upon the peasantry[3]; but it had no effect, and in 1613 the complaints were more general than ever. At last, at the Örebro *riksdag* of 1614, the government attempted a remedy. The peasants were offered the following alternatives: either the commutation-system of 1604 might be retained, with an increase of the *skjutsfärdspenningar* from 2 marks to 1 *daler* on the *hemman*; or they might revert to *skjutsning* and *gästning* as they had existed before 1604. In either event the King promised to take effective steps to see that the law was observed. For the peasantry this was Hobson's choice: they could not possibly contemplate any increase in their fiscal burdens, with taxes already intolerable and the ransom for Älvsborg still to be raised in addition. They opted therefore for the second alternative, and Gustav Adolf accordingly issued orders for stricter control of the issue of passes in the name of the King or of the royal dukes. In addition, he instructed bailiffs and sheriffs (*häradshövdingar*)[4] to arrange for the appointment of taverners at regular intervals, so that those who were not entitled to *skjutsning* might be assured of refreshment, and would not be tempted to resort to force to extract their requirements from the peasantry along the road. For these inns a special tariff was prescribed, and rates were fixed for horse- and boat-hire for those who had no pass.[5]

Had the government been able to fulfil its promise to the Estates,

---

[1] The pressure on peasants living near the great highways was so severe that they took to not keeping horses at all, preferring ox-traction. In 1610 the men of Uleå and the neighbouring parishes lost 270 horses dead: sometimes they were forced to drive them for 22 (Swedish) miles (=220 kilometres). K. R. Melander, *Drag ur Åbo hovrätts äldre historia*, pp. 171-2. For examples of the complaints of the clergy, and the relief which was sometimes given them, see K. R. Leinberg, *Finska prästerskapets besvär och Kongl. Majestäts därpå gifvna resolutioner*, p. 3; *Handlingar rörande finska kyrkan och prästerskapet*, I. 357.

[2] A. Bratt, *Svenska Allmogen*, p. 21; N. Forssell, p. 15; C. Annerstedt, *Om Samhällsklasser . . .*, p. 31; Hallenberg, III. 204.

[3] Hallenberg, I. 331.

[4] For explanation of this term, see Chapter VII, below.

[5] *SRDA*, I. 440-1, 432, 455-7, 464-5; Hallenberg, III. 157-9.

and enforce the observation of this Ordinance, little more might have been heard of the matter. But unfortunately it was not. It had too many other preoccupations, and its local officials were too weak, or too untrustworthy, to prevail against the obstinate refusal of interested parties to conform to the law. This was particularly true of Finland, where lawlessness was endemic. A Dutch embassy, travelling from Russia to Stockholm by way of Österbotten in 1615, was appalled at the treatment of those responsible for the organization of *skjutsning*, and of the peasants who supplied the animals:

one takes their food, their hay and rye; one takes their horses from the stall, harnesses them to one's waggons and drives them away, without the owners' venturing to say a word; they are glad if they get them again after having had to run five or six *mil* after them; if they dare to make any objection, they get a good beating.

A constable (*länsman*) who would not or could not obtain horses was beaten till his back was bloody, 'so that it was a shame to see the old man in tears'. And the embassy heard stories of a *länsman* who in similar circumstances had been stripped naked in mid-winter, soused with water, and left to freeze. But in Finland conditions were perhaps exceptional: the Dutchmen found that this 'Finnish game' could not be played with impunity in Estonia.[1]

In the meantime supplementary Ordinances had been promulgated in February 1615, reinforcing and extending the legislation of the previous year.[2] The complaints continued, however, and at the Örebro *riksdag* of 1617 the whole question was thrashed out afresh.[3] But the case was really plain enough. There was nothing wrong with the policy of the government: all that was required was that it should be enforced.[4] This, however, continued to be beyond the power of the authorities. Another Ordinance of 1624 traversed the old ground, and repeated the old provisions; but its effect was not noticeably greater than that of its predecessors.[5] Some progress was indeed made with the institution of taverns, but for many years to come they remained inadequate to the needs of travellers, who continued, only too often, to take what they needed by force. A

---

[1] *En holländsk beskicknings resa . . .*, pp. 221, 232-3, 239; cf. *SRDA*, I. 485.
[2] *SRDA*, II. 236-40; Hallenberg III. 358-61; A. A. von Stiernman, *Samling utaf Kongl. Bref, Stadgar och Förordningar etc angående Sweriges Rikes Commerce, Politie och Oeconomie* (cited henceforward as Stiernman, *CPO*), I. 635-44, 645-54.
[3] *SRDA*, II. 44, 51.
[4] See *SILR*, pp. 95, 101, 121, 129, 153, etc.; *AOSB*, I. ii. 365-6.
[5] Stiernman, *Alla Riksdagars . . . Besluth*, I. 765.

riksdag resolution of 1627, and an Ordinance of 1630, made little difference; at the end of 1632 the Nobility were still debating the question; at the beginning of 1633 the *råd* was consulting Oxenstierna about it; and conditions in the 'thirties showed little improvement upon the state of affairs twenty years earlier. It continued to plague the peasant, and baffle the government, for another century.[1]

The general predisposition to lawlessness, of which the abuse of *skjutsning* was only the most notorious example, was encouraged by the ineffectiveness of the state's legal machinery. Gustav Adolf and Oxenstierna were both alive to the need for amendment, and they took early measures to provide a remedy. The Judicial Procedure Ordinance (*Rättegångsordinantian*) of 1614 undoubtedly did much to make the operation of the law more certain and to enhance the prestige of the highest tribunal; but its effects were not felt in a moment, nor could it remove more than a limited number of the grievances under which the country was labouring.[2] The quality of the King's servants was in many cases highly unsatisfactory, and their proceedings at times goaded the faithful Commons to desperate reprisals. Thus in January 1617 tension reached such a pitch in northern Småland as to make advisable the presence of Gustav Adolf in person, and the King accordingly deferred the opening of the Örebro *riksdag*, and went down to Jönköping to investigate. It appeared that the oppressions of the royal bailiff in Västbo hundred had become so intolerable that the infuriated peasantry had murdered the clerk of the local assembly in the presence of the sheriff (*häradshövding*) himself. The leaders were now summoned to meet the King at Jönköping, and from all over Småland the peasantry were ordered to attend, that they might see the strength of the arm of the law and refrain from following the evil example of Västbo. The sentence which the King pronounced was clearly intended to discourage any repetition of these incidents: all the

---

[1] Stiernman, I. 795; *Sveriges Ridderskaps och Adels Riksdagsprotokoll* (henceforward cited as *SRARP*), I. 206-8; Stiernman, *CPO*, I. 986-7; S. Loenbom, *Uplysningar i Swenska Historien*, III. 90-1. And see, among innumerable other examples that could be cited, *SRARP*, I. 76, 123, 185; *RRP*, II. 135, 139, 222; K. K. Tigerstedt, *Bref från Generalguvernörer och Landshövdingar i Finland, förnämligast under Drottning Kristinas tid*, I. 6-7; Melander, pp. 114-15; N. Forssell, pp. 35-6; Ogier, pp. 20, 22, 57-8; B. Whitelocke, *Journal of the Swedish Embassy*, I. 169, 180, for a description of the system in 1653. The matter of *skjutsning* and *gästning* was of such burning topical interest to the men of Gustav Adolf's time that it appears even in the otherwise not very topical drama: cf. the highly illuminating speech of *Pålwel* in J. Rondeletius' *Judas Redivivus, Thet är: En christeligh Tragicomoedia*, pp. 34-5.

[2] For *Rättegångsordinantian*, see below, Chapter VI.

leaders were condemned to death by wheel and stake, and every male in Västbo hundred between the ages of 15 and 60 was mulcted of a fine. But justice, if terrible, was even-handed: the bailiff whose misdeeds had provoked the disturbance was himself condemned to death. And the sentences do in fact seem to have had the deterrent effect intended: at all events there was no further trouble in Småland for some years.[1]

The tumult in Västbo, however, was a bagatelle compared with the disturbances in Dalarna three years earlier. The Dalesmen had for centuries been notoriously difficult to handle. No part of Sweden, perhaps, had so strong a provincial feeling, and certainly none had played a more conspicuous part in Swedish history. If Småland corresponded to the English Border counties, Dalarna was, in many ways, the Swedish Kent. From Dalarna traditionally came revolts, protests against misgovernment, resistance to excessive burdens. Nowhere in Sweden were the nobility of less account, or more suspect.[2] The Dalesmen were notorious for a sturdy independence, which to an unfriendly critic might pass for arrogance; and though Gustav Vasa had dealt hardly with them, they had not forgotten that once they had made and unmade Kings, and that the Vasa dynasty had owed the throne largely to their aid. It was an old tradition that no King might enter their province without their permission. They had their special arrangements with the government about providing recruits for the army. In short, as Ogier justly observed, they were men who 'do not willingly submit themselves to any other ruler than one who does right by them'.[3]

Just at this moment they were feeling very strongly that their ruler was not doing right by them. As one grievance was piled on another, as the burdens laid upon them mounted to intolerable proportions, the men of Dalarna began to murmur, then to take the law into their own hands, until finally they came to open defiance of authority.[4] The most substantial of their complaints concerned

---

[1] For the Västbo disturbances, see *Handl. rörande Skandinaviens Historia*, XXV. 17-22; *SRDA*, II. 11; Ahnlund, *Oxenstierna*, p. 217. Hallenberg, IV. 524-7; R. Björkman, *Jönköpings Historia*, II. 59-67. For similar complaints of misgovernment, *AOSB*, II. ix. 3; II. xii. 154, 187-8.
[2] There is a Swedish saying that north of the Dalälv there are no nobles and no crayfish (*kräftor*).
[3] Ogier, p. 66.
[4] For the troubles in Dalarna, see Hallenberg, II. 715-28; III. 324-31, 341-2; Ahnlund, *Oxenstierna*, pp. 143-4; R. Holm, *Terserus*, pp. 6-7; *AOSB*, I. ii. 153-4; *SRDA*, I. 477-9, 495-504, 507-11; B. Boëthius, art. *Karl Bonde*, in *Sv. Biogr. Lex.*, p. 327; A. Pihlström, *Kungl. Dalregementets Historia*, I. 15-16.

recruiting for the army (*utskrivning*).[1] There seems little doubt that the government had employed violent means to beat up men for the campaign in Russia. Dalarna, by its special agreement, was privileged to contribute a contingent of fixed size, and should thus have been exempt from the ordinary *utskrivning*; but apparently the province had failed to fill the gaps in the ranks of its contingent, and the recruiting authorities had taken their own measures to make good the deficiency. The Dalesmen responded to this treatment as might have been expected of them. The recruits deserted in hundreds and their countrymen gave them shelter and asylum. No less than six hundred were eventually run to earth in Dalarna. The King was known to be severe upon deserters, and the rumour began to run about the Dales that all the six hundred were to be executed. At this, Elaus Terserus, the Vicar of Leksand, who was a man of great influence among his flock, advised them to petition the King. They did so; but before an answer could arrive the military authorities on the spot made a beginning with the executions, and this came near to provoking immediate rebellion. However, the King in his answer mitigated the punishment so far that only one deserter in ten was to suffer death; and with that Terserus advised them to be content. Nevertheless there were attacks upon the prisons, and in some instances the prisoners were liberated; and, in general, Dalarna was inclined to be defiant.

In this disturbed state of public opinion a new and alarming idea began to gain ground. Long ago in 1598 the Dalesmen had been forward in supporting the cause of Duke Karl against Sigismund III, and had done to death a certain Jacob Näf (said to be a Scotsman) who was one of Sigismund's adherents. Now it so happened that Johan Skytte, who was known to be high in Gustav Adolf's favour, had married Näf's daughter. The Dalesmen now leapt to the conclusion that the present troubles had been contrived by Skytte in order that he might find a pretext for avenging his father-in-law. It was in vain that Skytte protested that such an idea had never entered his head: the Dalesmen stuck to their opinion. Indeed, they went further. Skytte was not the only person in high places, they reflected, who might bear them a grudge: the whole nobility disliked the independent spirit of Dalarna. What more likely than that the whole affair was a noble plot against their liberties? Had not the Dalesmen latterly been urging the resump-

[1] For explanation of *utskrivning*, see Vol. II, Chapter XII, below.

tion of those extensive revenue-grants (*förläningar*) whose giving-away had impoverished the Crown, enriched the nobles, degraded the peasantry, and increased the burden of taxation? Their defiance of the government now blended with fear and hatred of the nobility; the cry was raised that all nobles should be slain. A miniature social war appeared quite possible.

In the late autumn of 1613 Gustav Adolf paid a personal visit to Dalarna in an endeavour to allay the fears of his subjects. He was ably seconded by Terserus, who did his best to persuade his congregation to be reasonable, and even embarked upon a defence of the nobility as a necessary element in every well-ordered society. But neither the King nor the parson was wholly successful in quieting these turbulent spirits; and it was thought well to summon a deputation of Dalesmen to discuss matters with the King at the Örebro *riksdag* of 1614. Terserus came with them, partly to explain the Dalesmen's grievances to the government, partly to put his influence at the government's disposal. And at last a settlement was reached which was more or less satisfactory to all concerned. The King pardoned his disobedient subjects, and promised to lighten their burdens; but in return all deserters were to return to the colours, and Dalarna was to keep its contingent up to strength in future. To make assurance doubly sure, the King took occasion to pay another visit to the province on his way to Finland; but even this did not altogether put an end to unrest, and early in 1615 he found it wise to go and talk to them once again. This time he appears to have been successful, though for some time Dalarna continued to require delicate handling.[1]

(iv) *Financial Difficulties: Älvsborg's ransom*

These disturbances, and the manner in which they were ended, give a good idea of how really weak Gustav Adolf's position was in the opening years of the reign. The plain fact was that he had not the resources to suppress the rebellion of a single province. He was forced to parley with his subjects; to beg the influence of the clergy in restoring order; and finally to accept a compromise upon the points in dispute. Fundamentally, the weakness was financial. The monarchy lacked authority, the government wanted efficiency,

[1] Pihlström, I. 17; II. 1-13.

because the state was trembling perilously on the verge of bankruptcy. As Gustav Adolf told the *råd* in 1615:

for many years now there have been no reserves in the Treasury; our subjects are exhausted by the taxes and impositions which have continued for several reigns; the last Danish war has exhausted them still further.[1]

About the same time he was lamenting that he could find nothing in his Treasure Chamber to give to Johan of Östergötland, except two cannon captured at Gdov. There was the greatest difficulty in finding money for ordinary current expenses: the King's tailor had to wait for the payment of so small an account as 30 *daler*; the official courier to Finland could not be provided with sufficient money to feed him on the road; and in 1616 the government was at its wits' end to pay for the return to Germany of John Casimir of the Palatinate. Short-term loans which had been contracted during the Kalmar war in order to hire mercenaries began to fall due, and the state was unable to meet these obligations. The revenue was inelastic, and had indeed declined as a result of the war; taxes had to be remitted to war-victims; and there were great arrears of taxes which it was hopeless to look for, and which must therefore be written off. There was bad money in circulation, and the government was unable to track down the false coiners. The administration —or at least the local administration—was not always honest; and any attempt at accurate book-keeping was made difficult by the system of issuing to the more pressing creditors of the state notes of appropriation (*invisningar*) whereby local officials were authorized to pay certain revenues from local sources direct to the creditor. The abuses to which this gave rise forced the King to cancel all *invisningar* in 1614; but the characteristic inconsequence of the financial administration, and the necessity for hand-to-mouth measures, offered no guarantee that this decision would be adhered to.[2]

One of the most serious causes of the diminution of the royal revenues was the extent to which the monarchy had made over its sources of income, in perpetuity or during good pleasure, to private persons. The soldier who distinguished himself, the civil servant whose wages were in arrear, the noble to whom the Crown turned in a hurry for a loan—all these would obtain a grant of the revenues

[1] Styffe, *Konung Gustaf II Adolfs Skrifter*, p. 116.
[2] *SRDA*, II. 4; I. 228-30; Hallenberg, II. 519 *note*, 526-7, 533, 658-9, 684, 696-8; III. 169-70; Ahnlund, *Oxenstierna*, pp. 184-6.

from this or that portion of the royal domain. The number of such grants (*förläningar*) was steadily increasing, as was the number of service-fiefs (*län*) assigned to Crown servants for their normal maintenance; and thus to some extent a vicious circle was set up.[1]

Yet in the prevailing financial stringency the King was driven to take money where he could get it. The Russian war, for instance, could hardly have been carried on had it not been for loans from Jakob de la Gardie, the Commander-in-Chief. But the great financial standby of the government in these early years was undoubtedly Kristina, the Queen-Mother. Kristina was a very wealthy woman; and, being possessed not only of great force of character but also of marked business ability, she soon occupied the position of a sort of bank, to which the state turned for aid in an emergency, and did not turn in vain. Her loans on occasion were very substantial; and without her aid the government would more than once have found itself in great straits. As the state was prepared to pay up to 8 per cent. for the accommodation, and gave good security in the form of that very marketable commodity, copper, the Queen-Mother had no reason to be dissatisfied with her investment.[2]

But these were, after all, only expedients. The relentless pressure of necessity made it imperative to increase the contribution of the ordinary subject; and taxation was in consequence screwed as high as the country could bear, if not higher. As if this were not enough, the terms of the peace of Knäred had imposed upon Sweden a gigantic war indemnity as the ransom for Älvsborg.[3] Sweden was bound to pay to Denmark one million *riksdaler* in four equal instalments, the first payment falling due on 20 January 1616, the remaining three at yearly intervals thereafter. For a country as poor as Sweden then was, the sum was absolutely crushing; and there is little doubt that Kristian IV was confident that the terms could not be complied with, and that Älvsborg and its dependent hundreds (*härader*) would eventually pass permanently into Danish hands. Six months after the conclusion of peace, a special meeting of the Estates was summoned to consider ways and means of raising the money. To this meeting, which was in reality a meeting of a select

[1] *SRDA*, I. 228-30, 243-4, 267-75; II. 81, 141, 179; *AOSB*, II. x. 30. For further discussion of this question, see Vol. II, Chapters X and XI, below.

[2] *AOSB*, I. II. 197, 219, 225; II. I. 98; II. v. 69, 121; Styffe, p. 474; Waaranen, *Samling*, IV. 225.

[3] For Älvsborg's ransom, see E. Heckscher, *Ett svenskt Krigskadestånd för 300 år sedan*; G. Lindstén, *När Elfsborgs lösen betalades*; E. W. Dahlgren, *Louis de Geer*, I. 31-92.

committee of the *riksdag*, no representative of the Peasantry was summoned, in order, as the King afterwards explained, that they might not be burdened with those 'over-many *herredagar*' of which they had latterly been complaining.[1] It is likely, however, that the King was afraid of the opposition which his propositions would arouse. For the meeting was called upon to sanction a special tax of unheard-of universality of incidence, and of extreme severity: with the solitary exception of the Queen-Mother, whose contribution was to be according to her 'will, ability and inclination', every adult Swede was to pay his or her share. The King and Duke Johan promised 32 per cent. of their incomes; the nobility forwent their privilege of exemption, and were rated according to the number of armed men they owed in knight-service; and a special rate was fixed for every class of society, even down to the unattached mechanic, the chambermaid and the farmer's boy.[2] Not even foreign merchants resident in the country escaped. It was explicitly stated that the tax was to be paid in *riksdaler*, and not in *daler*. Now the *riksdaler*, or *Reichsthaler*, was the coin of the Empire, and it was doubtful whether all taxpayers would be able to obtain it. It was precisely for this reason that Kristian IV had stipulated for *riksdaler*. The government was well aware of the difficulty, and accordingly provided an alternative. If the taxpayer could not pay in *riksdaler*, he might pay in silver, or copper, or iron, or grain, which would be assessed at fixed rates.[3] These commodities (except silver, which could be minted into *riksdaler*) were selected as being the most certain to find a market abroad, and thus to obtain for Sweden the foreign exchange she needed. None of the usual exemptions—for war-damage, fire, etc.—were to be allowed. The yield from the tax was to be paid into a separate account, housed in a separate treasure-chamber, and kept distinct from the normal revenue; and four commissioners (of whom Johan Skytte was one) were appointed to manage it. All classes were assured that these measures would not constitute a precedent, nor prejudice rights or immunities.

These arrangements ought to have been adequate to the payment of the ransom within the stipulated time. Unfortunately they were

---

[1] *SRDA*, I. 305, 307-8.
[2] *SRDA*, I. 310-14; Hallenberg, II. 667-76. There had been an impost almost as severe, and on much the same principles, in 1605: H. L. Rydin, *PM angående det svenska skatteväsendets utveckling*, pp. 66-7.
[3] *SRDA*, I. 313-14.

not; and this for a variety of reasons. In the first place, the tax was evaded, despite all efforts of the government. The King himself was not able to contribute his share; the Queen-Mother was apparently not willing to contribute hers; and the royal duchies in general escaped. The nobility did not, when it came to the touch, live up to the spirit of self-denial which had led them to waive their privileges: they soon contrived to get exemption for such of their estates as had suffered war-damage, and even for the remainder they seem to have been backward in making payments. The burghers were not much better, if Gustav Adolf is to be credited. The clergy sent in incomplete lists of their parishioners, deliberately omitting those whom they considered too poor to pay. Disbanded soldiers offset their liability against arrears of wages. Tax-collectors were, as usual, dishonest; and investigation of their defalcations was in some cases not concluded until 1622. Foreign merchants soon obtained exemption, for fear of international complications; and so too did the wives of soldiers on active service.[1]

There was very real difficulty in collecting *riksdaler* in sufficient quantity. At an early stage the government was forced to accept payment in *daler*, which were subsequently employed by Crown agents to purchase *riksdaler*; but this method did not yield important results. Nor did the coinage of *riksdaler* from silver mined in Sweden or from silver plate melted down, or the recoinage of *daler* into *riksdaler*, do much to fill the gap. The best way of getting *riksdaler* was soon found to be from the sale of copper. The copper was obtained partly in lieu of cash from the taxpayer, partly by purchase with *daler*. Some of this copper was sold at home in exchange for *riksdaler*, and this was the most satisfactory method; for if it were sold abroad, and paid for, as it often was, in bills instead of coin, it was not always a simple matter to arrange that the bills should be encashed at the right time and in the right place. Another and very serious difficulty was that the Crown was not punctual in paying the copper-miners, who retaliated by threatening to suspend deliveries. One of the great internal purchasers of copper was the Queen-Mother, and among her chief customers, by an irony familiar from recent experience, was none other than Kristian IV himself. Kristian, however, was not prepared to offset his owings against the

---

[1] *AOSB*, I. ii. 158, 243; II. x. 170; *SRDA*, II. 199, 202, 212; Hallenberg, III. 172, 319; IV. 806-7; *Kammarkollegiets Protokoll*, I. 194-216, 218-22; G. Wittrock, *Svenska Handelskompaniet och Kopparhandeln*, p. 3; S. Lundqvist, *Finlands folkmängd*, pp. 16, 23, 29, 34.

next instalment of the ransom: the coin in which he paid was carefully escorted over the border into Sweden, and in due time escorted back again into Denmark. Thus in the end the amount of coin which actually left Sweden was not very large, and the bulk of the ransom was really paid by exports of copper.[1] Another difficulty—and indeed it was the chief difficulty—lay in the administration of the ransom-fund. In the first place, the expenses of collection appear to have been unnecessarily high. In the second, the commissioners were not able to maintain the distinction between the ransom-money and the ordinary revenue. And finally, and most important, the King repeatedly raided the fund and applied the moneys lying in it to the defraying of current expenses. There is an instance of this as early as May 1614,[2] and from henceforward he made no real effort to avoid treating it as ordinary revenue. As a result, it was only with the greatest difficulty that Sweden made her payments upon time; and the oppressiveness of the ransom was made to appear vastly heavier than was really the case. It has been calculated that nearly half the amount raised to redeem Älvsborg was applied to other purposes; that Gustav Adolf over the whole period sold more than 8 per cent. more copper than would have served to pay the whole indemnity; and that the total amount of money raised probably exceeded the amount demanded by no less than 85 per cent.[3]

The result of the King's misappropriation of the fund was seen as early as 1616, when the first instalment fell due. In the autumn of 1615 Gustav Adolf began to take measures to melt down his silver plate. This did not carry him very far, and he was driven to seek a loan from abroad. The obvious place to apply was in Amsterdam; for it by no means suited Dutch commercial interests that Sweden should lose Älvsborg for ever, and the position of Denmark in the Baltic be thus strengthened. For the moment, he had no success; and the first instalment of the ransom was paid in January 1616 without external aid. But there was a strong demand for Swedish copper in the Netherlands, and the Dutch were generally willing to make an advance against the promise of deliveries of copper at an

[1] Wittrock, *op. cit.*, pp. 3-7; *AOSB*, II. x. 192; I. ii. 264; Heckscher, *Sveriges Ekonomiska Historia*, II. 272-5.

[2] *AOSB*, II. i. 43. Other examples in Waaranen, *Samling*, V. 33-4; F. Wernstedt, *Ståthållaren Christoffer Wernstedt*, p. 68; Hallenberg, IV. 747.

[3] *SRDA*, II. 192; Heckscher, *Sv. Ek. Hist.*, II. 443-4; *id. Sv. Krigsskadestånd*, pp. 8, 34-5.

agreed time and price. In 1616, therefore, Gustav Adolf renewed his application for a loan. This time he was successful, in spite of the fact that it had become a party question in the United Provinces; and a loan of 150,000 *riksdaler* enabled him to meet his obligations for this year. But it was already apparent that the grant made by the Estates in 1613 would no longer suffice. It had then been decided that the tax should be levied four times, and each levy, it was hoped, would pay one instalment of the ransom. But the yield from the tax had been steadily declining; and in 1617 it produced scarcely more than half the estimated amount. The King was therefore forced to seek the approval of the Estates for its collection for a fifth year, and, later, for a sixth. Even so, the situation did not improve. On the contrary, as the time for the payment of the third instalment drew near (it fell due in January 1618) the position seemed desperate. Skytte had been despatched on a diplomatic tour of the Protestant Courts, and had been instructed to try to raise another loan in the Netherlands. In this he had, indeed, failed; but the situation could be saved if a large consignment of copper could be disposed of in Amsterdam for cash without delay. Unluckily, most of the copper failed to arrive in time. Frantic appeals for a postponement were now made to Kristian IV; but, as was to be expected, they had no success. Kristian looked forward eagerly to a Swedish default and the incoporation of Älvsborg into the Danish realm. But, once again, the situation was saved. The bulk of the copper arrived in the Netherlands on 26 December; and now that it was actually in the country the Dutch were prepared to be accommodating. They advanced 16,000 *riksdaler*, and the instalment was paid with a fortnight to spare. The final payment did not cause such anxiety, for on this occasion Dutch aid came in good time; and with another 150,000 *riksdaler* of Dutch money the ransom was at last paid in full. At the very last moment there was a good deal of anxiety in Sweden in case Kristian should refuse to fulfil his part of the bargain; but in the end everything went smoothly, and on 31 January 1619 Älvsborg was Swedish once more.[1] The strain on the nation had been terrible, and much of the subsequent animus against Denmark, which was felt by nearly all Swedes, is to be attributed to the memory of the years between 1613 and 1619, when Kristian had so ruthlessly

[1] *SRDA*, II. 35, 43, 187-8, 210-12; *AOSB*, I. II. 305, 327; II. IX. 9, 13; II. X. 12; Styffe, pp. 232, 476-80; *Abraham Brahes Tidebok*, pp. 122-9; Thyresson, pp. 87, 145, 167-75; Dahlgren, I. 42-62.

applied the thumbscrews.[1] Yet, in the long run, Älvsborg was cheap at the price, and Denmark sacrificed advantages for which a million *riksdaler* were no sort of compensation. But, if it was a good bargain, it was still much dearer bought than it need have been. And the debt to the Netherlands—totalling more than a quarter of a million *riksdaler*—continued to hang around the nation's neck. When Gustav Adolf was killed, even though interest to the amount of 188,000 *riksdaler* had already been paid, Sweden's indebtedness still stood at nearly 200,000 *riksdaler*.[2]

(v) *The Problem of the Duchies*

The difficulties in enforcing the payment of the taxes voted to redeem Älvsborg are a reminder of the peculiar position occupied by the royal duchies in the first decade of Gustav Adolf's reign. It was a position which caused the King and his advisers very grave concern, and which on at least one occasion came near to provoking an open quarrel within the royal family. The royal dukes—the King's cousin, Johan of Östergötland, and his brother, Karl Filip—held a situation of great independence.[3] In themselves they constituted an 'Estate'; and they dealt with their sovereign in a way which no other Estate would have dared to attempt. At *riksdagar* they were represented, if they were not present in person, by their 'ambassadors'—as though they had been Princes of the Empire attending a Diet by proxy. The King habitually treated them with the greatest consideration, making no move of importance unless he had consulted them. In their dealings with the Crown they negotiated and argued in a tone not much lower than that which they might have adopted if they had been independent Princes indeed.

This anomaly dated back to the reign of Gustav Vasa. It was he who by the creation of special principalities for his younger sons

[1] It is said that when Torstensson's troops invaded Jutland in 1643 the common soldiers jested among themselves saying, 'Now let's have a look where Älvsborg's ransom went.'

[2] Heckscher, *Sveriges Ekonomiska Historia*, II. 276; Dahlgren, I. 63-92.

[3] For the problem of the duchies, see, in general, Lundqvist, *Om hertigdömenas statsrättsliga ställning till kronan i Sverige, passim*; J. A. Almquist, *Den civila lokalförvaltningen i Sverige*, I. 19-45, 101-7; F. Lindberg, *Hertig Johan av Östergötland och hans furstendöme (H.T.* 1941), *passim*; S. Loenbom, *Svenska Archivum* (cited as Loenbom, *SA*), I. 159-253; S. Loenbom, *Berättelse om Swea Rikes Arf-Furstes Samt Hertigens til Södermanland, Nerike och Wermeland, Carl Philips Lefwerne och Utländske Resor* (cited as Loenbom, *CP*), *passim*.

had established a system which had continued since that time without an interruption. His design had been, in the first place, to care for the provision of his family, and in the second, to use the duchies as extensions of the power and authority of the dynasty and the central government, whose interests, he imagined, would in all major points coincide with theirs.[1] And hence he had not hesitated to confer very extensive rights upon the royal dukes—so extensive that it was only in military matters and in foreign policy that any real limitation upon their sovereignty remained. Erik XIV, who was not on good terms with his brothers, perceived the threat to the authority of the Crown in this arrangement; and the Arboga Articles of 1561 curtailed the dukes' franchises by insisting upon conformity to the economic and judicial arrangements in the kingdom, by prohibiting the dukes from granting immunity from taxation, and by subjecting the duchy accounts to periodical royal audits. The fall of Erik and the accession of Johan III, however, gave Duke Karl an opportunity to free himself from the restrictions imposed at Arboga. Karl claimed for his duchy the full rights laid down in Gustav Vasa's testament, and successfully asserted his right to hold his lands 'as freely as His Majesty holds his kingdom'. He was able, for instance, to pursue an independent religious policy, and in economic matters showed a determined particularism. Moreover, even when he became King, Karl continued to interpret the rights of the royal dukes in the most liberal spirit: after 1604, for instance, they were permitted to grant assignments of revenue (förläningar) or donations on the same terms as they were granted by the King within the Kingdom.[2]

The second generation of royal dukes, as it existed in Karl IX's time, comprised Karl's own sons, Gustav Adolf and Karl Filip, and their cousin Johan, the son of Johan III by Gunilla Bielke. Gustav Adolf's duchy was intended only as a provision for him during his father's lifetime; but the other two were considered to be permanent arrangements. Johan had originally been given Finland by his father in 1590—the same duchy, that is, which Johan III had held in Erik's time; but in 1600, at the diet of Linköping, Karl had deprived him of Finland and conferred upon him Östergötland and Dalsland instead: experience perhaps suggested that a Duke of

---

[1] E. Heckscher, *Ekonomi och Historia*, p. 91.
[2] E. Heckscher, *Den äldre Vasatidens ekonomiska politik*, pp. 75-7; J. A. Almquist, *op. cit.*, I. 19-27; E. Brännman, *Frälseköpen under Gustav II Adolfs Regering*, pp. 41, 53.

Finland was dangerously liable to succumb to the temptation to pursue a private foreign policy of his own. Yet Johan received Östergötland on the same terms as Karl had held his duchy from Johan III—the terms of Gustav Vasa's testament. From 1606 he had his own court, his own chancery, his own mint, his own *råd* established at his ducal capital of Bråborg: from 1607 to 1610 no accounts from the duchy were submitted to the exchequer in Stockholm.[1] He had the right to appoint bishops and local government officials. He had, in short, the right to 'rule, order and command . . . as the Kings of Sweden had it aforetime'; and he was so nearly a sovereign prince that the limitations upon him went no further than to secure the state from absolute fragmentation. In Karl's lifetime, however, the letter of these privileges did not quite correspond with the reality. Karl interfered in appointments; he gave orders direct to Johan's servants.[2] It was moreover undeniable that Östergötland was not equivalent to Johan's former duchy of Finland; and on the accession of Gustav Adolf Johan insisted, as the price of his renunciation of the throne, upon an 'improvement' of his duchy by the addition of four hundreds in Västergötland. On the other hand, Gustav Adolf stipulated for uniformity between the duchy and the kingdom in all questions of law, tolls, *utskrivning*, aids, and the weight and fineness of the coinage.[3]

In the meantime Karl Filip had in 1609 been given an extensive duchy comprising Södermanland, Västmanland and Närke, for himself and his legitimate heirs male, upon conditions similar to those formerly enjoyed by his father: he had the right to strike coin and to make religious and civil appointments; and no appeal was to lie from his courts to the courts of the kingdom except in the most serious cases. These arrangements were confirmed by Gustav Adolf in 1613; but since Karl Filip was still a minor, the Queen-Mother acted for him, and in maintaining what she conceived to be the rights of her younger son showed a truculence which was often a sore trial to her first-born.[4]

As if these vast duchies were not danger enough, still further areas were withdrawn from the direct control of the Crown by reason of their having been assigned as dower-lands to the two surviving Queens-Mother—Katarina Stenbock, the widow of Gustav Vasa,

---

[1] J. A. Almquist, I. 27-30; Tham, *Oxenstierna*, pp. 157-60, 168, 205, 229, 245.
[2] Lindberg, *op. cit.*, pp. 128, 132.
[3] *SRDA*, I. 45, 99, 551; *cf.* Hallenberg, II. 793.
[4] J. A. Almquist, I. 31-3.

who did not die until 1621; and Gustav Adolf's mother, Kristina, who survived until 1625. After Karl Filip's death in 1622 Kristina succeeded in appropriating some of his lands, and she was as vigilant in repelling any attempt to infringe her own rights as she had ever been in resisting curtailment of her son's. Gustav Adolf, on his marriage to Maria Eleonora, made similar provision of dower-lands for her; and these were not surrendered to the Crown until 1648.[1]

It was almost inevitable that the existence of these islands of ducal power, planted down in the middle of the country, and almost cutting off the central government from the southern provinces, should give trouble. The probability was turned into a certainty by the characters of the persons concerned. On the one hand Gustav Adolf, hot, impulsive and impatient, unwilling to be thwarted by a strict insistence on privileges at a time when the state was struggling for mere survival; on the other Johan, sulky, depressed, resentful and often ill; or Kristina, able, ruthless, grasping and devoted to Karl Filip. Until death removed the dukes and swept away their duchies, relations with the King were increasingly strained, and sometimes they came near to breaking-point. The worst danger of all was, indeed, averted: neither of the dukes tried to pursue an independent foreign policy. But apart from this, the royal family was at loggerheads on all sorts of issues, and in many important respects the dukes showed an inclination to insist on concessions prejudicial to the interests of the monarchy and of the nation.

They quarrelled, first of all, about their respective shares of the family property of the Vasas. Karl Filip, indeed, had had his fair share; but Johan had been rather shabbily treated by Karl IX. The offers made to him by Gustav Adolf were equally unsatisfactory; and the matter was still unsettled at the time of Johan's death.[2] But this was a mere family quarrel without wider significance. More serious was the claim of the dukes to withdraw their subjects (the word is inescapable) from liability to the taxes and aids (*gärder*) payable in the kingdom. Kristina was especially opposed to allowing them to contribute aids; and when a new aid was imposed (which happened pretty frequently) had usually to be negotiated with before she would consent to it. So too with regard to the attitude of the

---

[1] J. A. Almquist, I. 33-43.
[2] J. A. Almquist, I. 105-7; S. Loenbom, *SA*, I. 159-76, 177-83.

dukes to the Älvsborg ransom. Kristina was equally intransigent
in questions of economic policy, seeking always for special exemptions, concessions or privileges for the duchy. She made a strong
resistance, for instance, to the Trade Ordinance of 1614, because
she thought that it might prejudice the prosperity of Karl Filip's
port of Södertälje.[1] There are also occasional signs of attempts by
the dukes to develop religious policies of their own: thus Johan
imposed the death sentence for adultery, while Gustav Adolf did
not; and Karl Filip towards the end of his life was intriguing for
the appointment of a separate archpriest for his duchy.[2]

Another subject of controversy concerned jurisdiction. The
dukes from time to time advanced a half-hearted claim to the right
to give asylum in their duchies to certain classes of offenders who
might cross the border from the kingdom.[3] Some of the exiles in
Poland, who found that their return was somewhat premature, took
refuge in the duchies from the King's displeasure. Karl IX, when
he was duke, had certainly given asylum to victims of Johan III's
religious policy. But whatever precedents might be adduced, this
was obviously a most dangerous pretension. Gustav Adolf resisted
it from the first; and Johan never really succeeded in making it
good. On the other hand the Queen-Mother fought an obstinate
rearguard action over another legal question which arose in 1614.
The Judicial Procedure Ordinance of that year set up a new
Supreme Court, the *Svea Hovrätt*, partly with the purpose of
relieving the King of the burden of hearing appeals. Kristina was
very reluctant to permit appeals from Karl Filip's duchy to this new
court. She explained that she was quite prepared to admit that an
appeal lay from the duke to the King in person; but she was not
willing to permit an appeal to a court which, in her view, was only
a mediate instance. But though her protests were listened to with
politeness, they did not turn Gustav Adolf from his purpose, and the
Judicial Procedure Ordinance duly became law.[4]

[1] Hallenberg, III. 310, 340-1; IV. 612 *seqq.* Kristina's commercial activities
were on occasion directly prejudicial to the interest of the country. Thus in October
1617, Skytte, on his way to the Netherlands to raise money for payment of
Älvsborg's ransom, arrived in Lübeck to find that the market for the sale of copper
had been ruined by Kristina's heavy exports from her ports of Hudiksvall and
Gävle: Hallenberg, IV. 690.
[2] *AOSB*, II. xii. 518; Holmquist, *Sv. Kyrkans Hist.*, IV. i, 49; Hallenberg,
V. 205.
[3] Ahnlund, *Oxenstierna*, pp. 204-5.
[4] Hallenberg, III. 301-14; K. G. Westman, in *Minneskrift ägnad 1734 års
Lag*, I. 42.

The irritation produced by these anomalous relations reached a climax in 1617. At the Örebro *riksdag* in January and February interests clashed on point after point. To begin with, the dukes protested at the new rules for procedure laid down in the *Riksdag* Ordinance, since the dukes, as an 'Estate', were apparently expected (like the other Estates) to engage in impromptu debate with the King upon the text of their written answers to his Propositions, and this they considered degrading. Next, they made an ill-judged attempt to secure special precedence under the new arrangements for the members of their Councils, and for other of their servants also. And lastly, Johan took this opportunity to ventilate an old grievance, and objected to Karl Filip's being given precedence of himself in the new seating regulations for the *riksdag*.[1]

But this was a mere skirmish compared with the battles over the draft for the Statute of Örebro. Johan and Kristina demanded that any partisans or spies of Sigismund arrested in terms of the Statute within their duchies should be tried by the ducal courts, even though they might be charged with high treason. The Queen-Mother, in a lengthy written statement, and subsequently in debate through her representative Dr. Nils Chesnecopherus, contended that in terms of their donations and of Gustav Vasa's testament the ducal courts were courts of first instance for all cases, and that the King had only appellate jurisdiction; and she added (rather rashly) that in any case no modern state, if it were well-run, would permit appeals in straightforward criminal cases.[2] On the following day (12 February) Gustav Adolf replied in person to these contentions in a speech which showed his irritation: '*haec Rex verbis ponderosis et aculeis*' (noted an eyewitness) '*praeferabat versa facie ad Principem Johannem*. Duke Johan answered with few words, which nobody at the back of the hall could hear.'[3] The King clearly felt that it was time to make a stand against the pretensions of the dukes, for he followed this up next day with another speech in which, while protesting that he had no wish to infringe the privileges granted in their donations, he made it quite clear that he would not hesitate to override them if he considered that the national interest demanded it, or if it appeared that those privileges were curtailing his sovereign authority; 'for H.M. is not conscious of having read in the text of any donation that the hereditary princes shall obtain the cession in

[1] *SRDA*, II. 22, 25, 89, 91-3.
[2] *SRDA*, II. 189-91, 194.
[3] *SRDA*, II. 51.

their duchies of all regalian rights without exception'. Gustav Adolf therefore insisted; and the dukes gave way, though with a very bad grace.[1]

The line here adopted by the King marks an important change of policy. From the time of Karl IX's accession, all the trends had been in the direction of wider and wider franchises for the duchies. The dukes, and especially Karl Filip acting through his mother, had resisted, on the whole successfully, any attempt to modify their status in favour of the central authority. Hitherto the Crown had, as often as not, given way. But the experiences at Örebro in January and February 1617 seem to have convinced the King that matters had reached a pitch humiliating to himself and dangerous to the country. From this moment he was openly hostile to the liberties of the dukes; and he found it increasingly difficult to keep his temper in face of the provocations offered by the Queen-Mother.

This emerges from the history of the dispute concerning knight-service (*rusttjänst*), which began at this *riksdag* and which eventually led to a violent quarrel between the dukes and the King. Nowhere, perhaps, were the inconveniences and possible dangers of the position of the duchies more apparent than in regard to military matters. The dukes had their own special recruiting systems, and jealously attempted to control all levies raised in their territory.[2] They had some success in fostering a sense of personal allegiance among such troops: when in September 1610 the Östgöta levies mutinied outside Ivangorod, the men complained that they were being used outside the limits of the duchy, and pleaded that their oath of fidelity was not to the King but to the duke.[3] During the War of Kalmar Johan's conduct had not been wholly satisfactory; and it is probable that on occasion he failed to cooperate effectively with the royal army because he was too concerned for the safety of his lands. Kristina, too, had grudged a proper contribution of soldiers from Karl Filip's duchy. In November 1612 Gustav Adolf had bitterly reproached his mother on this score.[4] There was thus already a good deal of friction over military matters, and by 1617 it had generated sufficient heat to precipitate an explosion. The issue at Örebro was a quite simple one: were those of the nobility who resided in the duchies to remain as a separate military unit under the command of the dukes, or were they to form part of the royal

---

[1] *SRDA*, II. 203-8, 227-9. [2] Petri, I. 356, 423; *Sveriges Krig*, I. 108.
[3] *Sveriges Krig*, I. 340. [4] *SRDA*, I. 199-201.

army and to be incorporated into the special cavalry-corps raised from the nobles of the kingdom? Or, more simply still, had the King the right to dispose as he thought fit of troops raised in the duchies? Kristina and Johan insisted not only that the *rusttjänst* of their nobles should be kept distinct but also that no troops should be removed from the duchies (in view of Sigismund's threatened invasion) until it became clear that the duchies were not likely to be attacked. They had some basis for their contention in the terms of an agreement between Karl IX and Johan, concluded in 1608; whereby Johan was recognized as Commander-in-Chief of all troops raised in his duchy, but bound himself to place 600 foot at the King's disposal: if ducal troops were used outside the duchy, their pay was to be paid by the King after the first fortnight.[1] The dukes now developed their point of view with great hardihood; and Chesnecopherus, in a memorandum on Kristina's behalf, used language so extreme, and so offensive to the King, that he was immediately placed under arrest.[2] He was not released for four months, and then only after he had made a most abject apology. When the diet at Örebro ended, the question was still undecided: each side obstinately stuck to its guns. The battle was renewed at the coronation *riksdag* in Stockholm, in August of the same year. The King was exasperated by the objections of his mother to the terms of the oath to be taken by the hereditary princes at the coronation. His patience was at an end. When she proposed a compromise on the *rusttjänst* question, he refused to consider it. Karl Filip, intervening personally in politics for the first time, continued to press his brother to accept it. The King, infuriated by this importunity, took the paper from him, and wrathfully threw it into the fire.[3]

A situation had now been reached which Gustav Vasa had fore-seen, and for which he had made provision in his will. In the event of irreconcilable division within the royal family, he had prescribed an appeal to an impartial tribunal. Kristina now demanded that this procedure be followed, and asked that the whole question of military service should be referred to a jury of arbitrators. The King reluctantly assented; and a committee of the Estates was to

---

[1] Lindberg, *op. cit.*, p. 123.

[2] It seems that Chesnecopherus' written argument came to light by in-advertence rather than design: Hallenberg, IV. 567; Loenbom, *CP*, pp. 21-3.

[3] *SRDA*, II. 45, 78, 168, 215-16, 230-1; *A. Brahes Tidebok*, p. 96; Loenbom, *CP*, pp. 21-3; Loenbom, *SA*, I. 208-10; Hallenberg, IV. 594-606.

have been constituted to undertake this delicate and invidious task. Fortunately, its services were never required. Before proceedings could be begun Johan of Östergötland had ended his unhappy and ineffective existence[1]; and the Queen-Mother, deprived of her ally, allowed the matter to drop.[2] But the whole affair had cast revealing light upon the weakness of the monarchy. Upon a point which touched directly the sovereign authority of the King, Gustav Adolf had felt himself bound to submit his case for judgment by his own subjects. He had been dragged by Kristina into the scandal of a public quarrel, and he had been unable to constate a clear-cut victory. The damnable inheritance of Gustav Vasa was threatening to poison his reign, as it had poisoned the reigns of his uncles.

It is difficult to believe that in these circumstances he did not feel the death of Johan as a relief. Now that the royal dukes were reduced to a single representative it would be less easy for claims against the Crown to be presented as the rights of an Estate. Johan had died without lawful heirs, and his duchy fell in to the Crown; and this considerably strengthened the King's position. In 1620 he was able to extract from Karl Filip an undertaking which safe-guarded the King's effective control in all military matters; and the controversy was thus at last terminated in his favour.[3] Two years later Karl Filip himself succumbed to camp-fever at Narva; his domains reverted to the Crown, apart from those portions which his mother succeeded in retaining until her death in 1625; and with that the institution of royal duchies came to an end. It was high time. As long as they existed, the effective exercise of the royal sovereignty over the whole country was impossible. To all progress, military, financial and administrative, the duchies opposed at least a potential obstacle. Had Johan and Karl survived, they might have acted as the foci of discontent. They would very probably have retarded that national advance over all fields of endeavour which was characteristic of the reign. Years afterwards Oxenstierna is reported to have said: 'You know well what bad blood existed between King Gustav Adolf and the two princes, Duke Karl Filip and Duke Johan of Östergötland. Had not God called them both to Himself so early,

[1] Johan died on 5 March 1618; his wife Maria Elisabeth died a few months later.
[2] For the later stages of the quarrel, see Loenbom, *SA*, I. 213-17; Loenbom, *CP*, pp. 21-33; Hallenberg, IV. 632-6.
[3] Lundqvist, p. 76; Hallenberg, IV. 709-10. There had been considerable friction in the years between 1618 and 1620: *ibid.*, IV. 872-3; *SILR*, p. 116; and Kristina continued troublesome even afterwards: Hallenberg, IV. 915.

there had certainly been bloodshed in the land.'[1] When in 1650 Queen Kristina obtained the recognition of Karl Gustav as hereditary prince, she was careful to insert, in the undertaking which she made him sign, a clause debarring him and his heirs from asking for a royal appanage; and she laid it down as a condition that the country was never to be split up as it had been in her father's time.[2] And Gustav Adolf himself is reported as saying, 'that if God gave him many children, they should never be given principalities'.[3]

(vi) The Position in 1617

Among the representations made by the Estates at Örebro in 1617, none had been so earnestly and unanimously put forward as the request that the King should proceed as soon as possible to his coronation.[4] He had now sat on the throne for nearly six years, and he still lacked the unction of royalty. Men remembered the long delay in Karl IX's coronation, and the feeling of unsettlement and insecurity which it had caused. The hallowing of the King had been deferred long enough. The war with Russia was ended; hostilities with Poland were in abeyance. The time was apt: who could tell how long it might be before so good an opportunity would recur? The King, if less eager than his subjects, was alive to the necessity. Already in 1615 there had been talk of it, but the expense had compelled postponement.[5] Coronation would strengthen him against internal enemies; it would be a blow to Sigismund's pretensions; it would regularize his position in international relations. And so, in October 1617, the Court moved to Uppsala; and there on the twelfth of that month Gustav Adolf was crowned by the Archbishop, proclaimed by the heralds, and given the insignia of royalty.[6] The country fetched a sigh of relief. And, indeed, the coronation may fitly be taken as the point at which it is possible to say that the worst of the danger was over. The government was warming to its work, the King sat more securely on his throne, the treaty of Stolbova was made; and though some of the problems

[1] Hallenberg, IV. 999.
[2] C. Weibull, *Drottning Christina*, p. 77.
[3] S. Clason, *Till Reduktionens Förhistoria*, p. 23.
[4] *SRDA*, II. 122, 128, 132, 135, 139, 140, 170.
[5] Hallenberg, III. 343.
[6] *Abraham Brahes Tidebok*, pp. 98-109, has a full account of the ceremony; Holmquist, *Sv. Kyrkans Hist.*, IV. 1. 142.

of this opening period still awaited solution, the first great crisis was passing, if it had not passed already.

The coronation naturally turned men's minds to the future of the dynasty and the question of the succession. Karl IX left behind him four unmarried children: Gustav Adolf, Karl Filip and Maria Elisabeth, his children by Kristina; and Katarina, his daughter by his first wife, Anna Maria of the Palatinate. In addition, Johan of Östergötland had claims to the throne which might easily be revived, in spite of his renunciation in 1612, if Gustav Adolf should die childless. Kristina, whose matriarchal instincts were highly developed, had foreseen the possibility of trouble, and had tried to prevent it in good time. In 1612 she had forced the reluctant Johan to marry her daughter Maria Elisabeth, in spite of the opposition of the Clergy to a union which fell within the prohibited degrees.[1] The results were disastrous. The marriage was unhappy; both parties were sickly; there were no children; and Maria Elisabeth soon showed unmistakable signs of insanity. In March 1618 Johan died; and five months later his wife died also.

In the meantime, Karl's other daughter, Katarina, had made a match which was to have great importance in the future. In 1615 she married John Casimir of Pfalz-Zweibrücken-Kleeburg, a very distant cousin of the Elector Palatine, and like him a Calvinist. As such, he was suspect to many Swedes, and most notably to Axel Oxenstierna : they were to be political enemies, more or less avowed, for the rest of the reign. The first child of this marriage was a daughter; and it was not until 1622 that there was born a son, Karl Gustav, who was one day to reign in Sweden as Karl X. In the meantime John Casimir and his wife had retired to Germany; so that after 1618 there remained in Sweden, of the line of Karl IX, only the King and his brother, who was still a mere youth.

The marriage of the King, from about the end of 1618 onwards, was therefore a matter of real urgency, if the Protestant revolution in Sweden were to be safe. Gustav Adolf had fallen in love, early in the reign, with Ebba Brahe, and had wished to marry her; but Kristina had exerted her maternal authority to the utmost, and had succeeded in breaking off the match. The King had since formed a casual connection with a certain Margareta Slots, by whom he had a bastard son; and for this irregularity he had been publicly rebuked by his Chaplain, Johannes Rudbeckius. In 1619 he had come within

[1] *SRDA*, I. 264-6; Hallenberg, II. 586.

an ace of losing his life when his horse went through the ice on Bråviken. Thus considerations of national interest and Christian morality combined to make a speedy marriage essential.[1] But Gustav Adolf, having been prevented from marrying for love, was now resolved to marry for political advantage. His marriage, therefore, and the negotiations which led up to it, were a part of his foreign policy; and they are accordingly most conveniently treated in the next chapter.

[1] For the Ebba Brahe episode, Ahnlund, *Gustav Adolf den Store*, pp. 57-71; C. Hallendorf, *Gustav II Adolf, Tal och Skrifter*, pp. 1-9, gives their correspondence; *AOSB*, II. 1. 81. For Margareta Slots, Holmquist, *Sv. K. Hist.*, IV. 1. 148-50. For the Bråviken accident, *Abraham Brahes Tidebok*, p. 121.

CHAPTER IV

FOREIGN AFFAIRS, 1611-20

(i) *The Period 1611-20*

FOR the first half of Gustav Adolf's reign—until the moment, that is, when the triumphant Imperialists began to menace the security of north Germany and the Baltic—Sweden's foreign policy was controlled by her relations with Poland.[1] The Danish war, desperate and dangerous as it was, was nevertheless excentric to the main issue: it was an unwelcome complication, to be disposed of as quickly as possible, once the threat to the nation's independence had been beaten off. So too with the enterprise in Russia: despite the dynastic ambitions which the younger line of Vasa for a moment permitted itself to indulge, Sweden's intervention in the Troublous Times was at all stages determined by considerations of its effect upon the perennial quarrel with Poland. For some years after Gustav Adolf's accession it was a nice question whether this indirect approach was in fact the best method of checkmating the plans of Sigismund III. There were moments when the internal troubles of the Republic seemed to offer to an attacker an opportunity so tempting that it appeared to be the part of wisdom to patch up peace with Moscow upon any reasonable terms and proceed at once to a direct onslaught upon Livonia or Lithuania. At other times, again, Sweden fell back on defensive tactics, and sought, by pushing her advantage in Russia to the uttermost, to extract from the National

[1] For this Chapter, see, in general, Hallenberg; Cronholm; B. Thyresson, *Sverige och det Protestantiska Europa*; S. F. Hammarstrand, *Historisk Framställning af förhandlingarne om Sveriges deltagande i trettioåriga kriget* (cited as Hammarstrand, *HF*); Szelagowski; Konopczyński; Korzon; *Sveriges Krig*, II.; J. A. Fridericia, *Danmarks Riges Historie* (cited as Fridericia, *DRH*); Hill; P. J. Blok, *Geschiedenis van het Nederlandsche Volk*, IV.; E. Wiese, *Die Politik der Niederländer während des Kalmarkrieges* [etc.]; G. W. Vreede, *Nederland en Zweden*, I; J. H. Hora Siccama, *Schets van de diplomatieke Betrekkinge tusschen Nederland en Brandenburg 1596-1678*; J.-H. Mariéjol, *Henri IV et Louis XIII*; M. Ritter, *Deutsche Geschichte im Zeitalter der Gegenreformation und des dreissigjährigen Krieges*, III.; Droysen; R. Koser, *Geschichte der brandenburgischen Politik bis zum Westfälischen Frieden von 1648*; J. Janssen, *History of the German People*, X.; S. R. Gardiner, *History of England from the accession of James I to the outbreak of the Civil War*, II.-IV.; A. Ballesteros y Beretta, *Historia de España y su influencia en la historia universal*, IV. 1; R. Quazza, *Preponderanze straniere*.

Rising cessions of territory which would bar any Polish attempt to reach the Gulf of Finland. Between these two lines of policy Gustav Adolf vacillated for some time; and if in the end he decided for the latter, that was mainly because the incorrigible dilatoriness of the Russian diplomats deprived him of any hope of an early end of the war.

Similarly, in the wider sphere of European diplomacy, Sweden's line was marked out for her by Gustav Adolf's hostility to Sigismund III. Herein lies one of the explanations of his attitude to Kristian IV in the years after 1613. No doubt anxiety for the fate of Älvsborg, fear of a renewed Danish attack, played their part in shaping his conduct; but essentially his first requirement of Denmark was that she should not hinder (if she would not help) his fight against his cousin. He looked for allies, therefore, who might insure him against Danish interference, just as he looked for allies whose interests, either in the Baltic or in the general context of European affairs, put them in opposition to Sigismund. Karl IX had tried to persuade Protestant Europe that his struggle against Poland was the struggle of evangelical religion everywhere. His success had been small; and at the end of his reign Sweden was still without an ally, though not, perhaps, quite without a friend. Gustav Adolf must follow the same line; must seek to end his country's diplomatic isolation; must prove the relevancy of obscure frontier fights in Livonia to the grand controversy which was moving to its climax in Germany. And finally, when the time should come for his marriage, he must so contrive matters as to draw from it advantages which should be of service against Poland. Swedish foreign policy, in the nine years to be covered in this Chapter, may seem at times confused and tentative. In reality it was not so; for throughout it was dominated by the unceasing, unappeasable feud between the two branches of the House of Vasa.

(ii) *Relations with Poland, 1611-16*

At the time of Karl IX's death the war with Poland was in a state of suspended animation. In the disputed areas of Livonia neither side had been able to make any lasting impression on the other. The great Polish triumph at Kirkholm had been barren of results, for it had been immediately succeeded by the Zebrzydowski *rokosz*. There had been moments when Swedish invasions from

Estonia, driving southward along the coast, had seemed to threaten Riga; but on the whole the fighting had been evenly balanced: a war of small numbers, ill-supplied (and on the Swedish side ill-led too); an affair of raids and sieges, skirmishes and devastation. By 1611 Sweden had succeeded in clearing Estonia of Polish troops; but she had lost Pernau, her most important conquest, in 1609; and of her earlier gains now retained only the coastal town of Salis. At the beginning of 1611 Chodkiewicz had arranged an armistice with Anders Larsson, the *ståthållare* in Reval, and this armistice was still in force when Gustav Adolf succeeded his father. Both Poland and Sweden were well content that it should continue. Poland was deeply committed in Russia, and Gustav Adolf needed every man he could spare from Ingria, to fight the Danes. The Poles had even for a time shown an inclination to convert the armistice into a formal truce of some duration[1]; but Karl's death had revived Sigismund's hopes of the Swedish throne, and, perhaps, the *sejm's* hopes of obtaining Estonia. The Polish Senate in April 1612 wrote to the *råd* in provocative terms, recommending submission to Sigismund as the lawful sovereign; and in these circumstances it was useless to enter into serious negotiation. Nevertheless, the local armistice, which was to expire on 1 June 1612, was renewed for successive terms, and hostilities remained suspended throughout the whole time of the War of Kalmar.

Yet for Gustav Adolf, as for Karl, no durable compromise with Sigismund seemed possible. Despite the obvious desire of the Estates for an interval of quiet on the Livonian front,[2] he refused to agree to any proposals which would tie his hands for any length of time. He was quite prepared to use negotiation to lull the enemy into a sense of false security. He was even willing for some sort of settlement, if the opening of negotiations were preceded by Sigismund's recognition of him as lawful king of Sweden; but this was a concession which Sigismund would never make until he had been defeated in the field, and perhaps not even then. Gustav Adolf, therefore, proceeded on the assumption that a war in Livonia was sooner or later inevitable; that only by victory could his throne be secured from attack; and that the only question to be decided was whether to begin hostilities now or later. The armistices, the truces, were for him (as he was convinced they were for Sigismund)

[1] Hallenberg, *Handlingar*, pp. 1-21.
[2] *SRDA*, I. 189-90, 196-9, 216-18.

convenient instruments of policy, whereby the outbreak of war was postponed to the right moment. All his efforts were directed to securing that his commissioners should not be lured into an agreement which might leave him pledged to peace at the very moment which would be most propitious for war. That moment would come when the Russian venture was successfully concluded; and until at least the spring of 1614, Gustav Adolf, ever sanguine, hoped that it might be concluded very shortly. Until that date, therefore, he showed little anxiety to arrange anything more binding than a succession of armistices; while the Poles, on their side, tried hard to secure a long truce, which would tide them over the serious military revolts which began towards the end of 1612.

From time to time proposals were made for mediation. Thus in May 1612 the Elector John Sigismund of Brandenburg, acting under Polish pressure, offered his good offices[1]; a year later, in May 1613, Sigismund proposed mediation by England and France; while the Polish Senate added the suggestion that the sovereigns of these countries should arbitrate upon the whole dispute. A few months afterwards (November 1613) James I and the Dutch, at John Sigismund's instigation, themselves offered to mediate; and though Gustav Adolf was entirely sceptical of the outcome, he felt that it would be wise not to offend his friends in western Europe by refusing. But nothing came of these suggestions. In December 1613 the commissioners on both sides arranged an exchange of prisoners, which liberated, among others, Karl Karlsson Gyllenhielm, who had been captive since 1601, and whose loyalty had latterly been decidedly compromised.[2] And in January 1614 an agreement was signed at Weltz to protract the armistice to 1 May 1614, or until a congress should meet to negotiate a truce.[3]

Despite these appearances, and despite the obvious desire of the Örebro *riksdag* for a settlement, Gustav Adolf's intentions in the spring of 1614 were not pacific. He confidently counted on the conclusion of peace in Russia within a very few weeks; and the reports which reached him of the confusion in Poland led him to

---

[1] Cronholm, I. 300.　　　　　　　　　[2] Cronholm, I. 294-5 *note.*
[3] Text in *Sveriges Traktater*, V₂. 225-8. For the diplomatic activity which preceded it, *AOSB*, I. ii. 147; Hallenberg, *Handlingar*, pp. 59, 61-7; Hallenberg, *Svea Rikes Historia*, III. 79-80, 83, 90, 224-6; Hammarstrand, *HF*, p. 22 and *notes.* John Sigismund was anxious for a definitive peace, and persisted after the conclusion of the truce in his attempts to persuade England and Holland to join in mediation: Hist. MSS. Comm., *Buccleuch*, I. 151 (Wm. Colwall to Winwood, from The Hague, 23 Feb. 1614).

believe that the moment had come to renew the war in Livonia with all the forces at his disposal. But Muscovite diplomacy was not to be hurried: more than two-and-a-half years of patient negotiation would still be needed before Gustav Adolf obtained the peace he desired. In these discouraging circumstances he was willing for the first time for a relatively stable arrangement in Livonia. On 20 June 1614 he ratified the Weltz agreement, limiting its duration, however, to two years; and on 29 September this was supplemented by a regular truce, to last until 29 September 1616.[1] Sweden ceded the town of Salis, which was in any case an isolated outpost difficult to maintain. But the hints from the Polish side as to the possibility of peace met with no response; the issue between the countries was not even touched upon; and both Gustav Adolf and Sigismund hoped that by the time the truce expired their affairs might have taken so favourable a turn as to make an extension of it unnecessary.

(iii) *Sweden, Denmark and Europe, 1611-17*

Between the beginning and the end of the War of Kalmar, the general political situation in Europe underwent important modifications which were to affect the future course of Swedish policy. The first, and perhaps the most important, of these changes was that produced by the murder of Henri IV of France in 1610. It cannot be said that Henri, for the greater part of his reign, had pursued a consistent or resolute foreign policy: in Italy, in Germany, and in his relations with Spain, he had too often displayed a half-heartedness which was in part the result of his desire to prove himself the faithful son of the Church to which he had been converted. But at least in the last year of his life these ambiguities had been resolved, and Henri, from whatever motives, had emerged as the enemy of Habsburg and as the head of a coalition of Protestant powers. The regency of Marie de Medicis brought the gradual liquidation of this policy. She perceived well enough that her task would be sufficiently difficult without the added embarrassment of foreign complications; she feared possible Spanish intervention in French affairs if the Huguenots were allowed too much licence; and she wished by a *rapprochement* with Spain to avert this danger. The Regent, therefore, though she honoured the commitments of her husband up to a point, and though she did not abandon France's

---

[1] Text in *Sverges Traktater*, V₂. 229.

friendship with England and the Dutch, drew nearer to the Catholic powers. The anti-Habsburg crusade of Henri's imagining fell to pieces; France for a decade became an almost passive spectator of the European scene; and the hopes which Karl IX had once entertained of French friendship, and perhaps of French aid, vanished for half a generation.

For Germany, on the other hand, Henri's death meant a respite from civil war. The Calvinist party of action, which in 1608 had formed the Evangelical Union,[1] had only reluctantly leagued itself with France. Its Roman Catholic analogue, the League, was no friend to Habsburg pretensions. The disputed succession to Cleves-Jülich did not, therefore, as had at one time seemed likely, produce a general war. The 'Possessioners' (as the two principal claimants were called) received sufficient aid from the Union, from England, from Maurice of Hesse-Cassel and from the Dutch to enable them to conquer most of the duchies; the Imperial attempt at sequestration was defeated; and it remained only to adjust the rival pretensions of Brandenburg and Pfalz-Neuburg. The family quarrel among the Austrian Habsburgs drove Matthias to expensive concessions in order to win his victory over Rudolf; the hereditary dominions were in a state of alarming unrest; and, in short, the power of the Emperor was at a low ebb. It required an imagination nurtured on memories of St. Bartholomew to build up a nightmare of Habsburg aggression from the policy of expedients pursued by Matthias and Khlesl.

In so far as danger really existed, it came not from Vienna but from Madrid. Spain was still to outward seeming the Spain of Philip II, though already a more apathetic ruler, coerced by virtual bankruptcy, had swallowed his pride to accord in 1609 a twelve-years' truce to the rebellious Dutch. Spanish statesmen still saw the key to Spain's European position in the possession of Belgium; and Spanish policy, now and for another generation, would be directed essentially to keeping open the overland route to the Netherlands through north Italy and the Franco-German borderlands. To safeguard this route Spain was prepared to take risks, and even to assume the offensive: Henri IV's clashes with

---

[1] The members of the Union were: the Elector Palatine, the Margraves of Ansbach and Baden-Durlach, the Count Palatine of Neuburg, and the Duke of Württemberg. The cities of Strassburg, Ulm, Nuremberg, Worms, Frankfurt a. M. and Speyer, with the Elector of Brandenburg, joined it in 1609; the Landgrave of Hesse-Cassel in 1610.

Spain—over Savoy, the Grisons and Switzerland—had been provoked by Spanish sensitiveness in this all-important region. But apart from this vital interest, Spain's policy was cautious and defensive. She desired French friendship; and in 1608 she had vainly proposed an alliance. In 1611 she obtained it: the Regent bound France to Spain for the next ten years (*i.e.* until the Dutch truce should expire) and arranged that Louis XIII should marry the Infanta Anne of Austria. The treaty did not, indeed, remove all differences, as appeared when the Mantuan question first troubled the diplomats in 1612; but it secured tranquillity to Spain for a decade, and to Philip III and Lerma that was much.

Spanish statesmanship had already begun to speculate upon the possibility of repeating this diplomatic success in England; but here the auspices for the moment were unfavourable. In 1610 Salisbury was working for a foreign policy based on religious considerations. England was linked to the Dutch by an alliance concluded in 1608; she warmly espoused the cause of the 'Possessioners'; she concluded a treaty with the Union at Wesel, early in 1612; and she followed this up, in May of the same year, by negotiating a marriage between the Princess Elizabeth and the young Elector Palatine, Frederick V. The circle of alliances was completed by the treaty of Heilbronn in 1613, which bound the United Provinces to the Evangelical Union. Despite the defection of France, therefore, something like a Protestant front existed in the west. But as yet it was anything but solid: James I's chronic lack of money diminished the value of his promises; there was much ill-feeling between England and the Dutch upon commercial and colonial matters; and once Salisbury and Prince Henry were dead there was little guarantee that England would remain deaf to the eager solicitations of Spain.

Spanish interest in the Baltic was for the moment dormant, and would not become active until the Dutch truce should expire; but Spain could not forget how great a proportion of Dutch commerce went through the Sound. In the previous century the Baltic policy of the Habsburgs had been mainly directed to winning the friendship of Sweden, for under Johan III Sweden had appeared (to foreign eyes at least) as a possible field of action for the Counter-Reformation[1]; but when Spain renewed her diplomatic offensive in this area it

---

[1] See J. Paul, *Die nordische Politik der Habsburger vor dem 30-jährigen Krieg* passim.

would be to Denmark that she would direct her attention—to Denmark and to Poland. The hope of obtaining, from one or other of these countries, a Baltic base from which to strike at Dutch commerce was still cherished at Madrid; and in the 'twenties it was to be an important element in the foreign policy of Olivares. Any such development must obviously be resisted by Sweden. A Danish alliance with Spain would menace every Protestant power in the North, and might prevent Gustav Adolf from settling accounts with Sigismund. A Spanish alliance with Poland would give Sigismund that advantage of confessional solidarity which Sweden had hitherto sought in vain from the Protestant West. Sweden's task in the Baltic, in the period after the peace of Knäred, was the double task of denying suitable invasion-bases to Poland and resisting any Danish attempt at a real *dominium* over that sea.

In the carrying out of this programme it was clear that the attitude of Brandenburg would be of extreme importance. The Elector John Sigismund of Brandenburg was personally well-disposed to Sweden, but his political position in 1611 was such that he was not able to translate his good-will into action. Upon the secularization of the states of the Teutonic Order in 1525, its Grand Master, a member of the cadet line of Hohenzollern, had seized the lands of the Order in East Prussia for himself, turned them into a lay principality, and acknowledged the King of Poland as his feudal lord. His successor, Albert Frederick, was an imbecile, and for most of his long reign the duchy was administered by his relative, George Frederick of Jägerndorf. George Frederick had died in 1603; and Sigismund III, with considerable reluctance, had transferred the administration to the head of the House of Hohenzollern, the Elector Joachim Frederick, as a bribe to secure his neutrality in the struggle with Karl IX. Upon Joachim Frederick's death in 1609 it became the object of his successor John Sigismund to obtain the administration of the duchy for himself. Albert Frederick had no male heirs, and by an arrangement concluded in 1563 it had been agreed that the electoral line might inherit the duchy; but this arrangement had never been ratified by the *sejm*; it was repugnant to the Estates of East Prussia; and John Sigismund feared that upon Albert Frederick's death the King of Poland, as feudal superior, might attempt to treat Prussia as a lapsed fief. If before this event the Elector could obtain the administration, the Hohenzollerns would be in a better position to discourage any such attempt. In 1611, after long negotiations, John Sigismund got what he wanted, thanks to the prevailing distraction in Polish affairs; and Sigismund III proceeded to demand political services in return.[1] Hence Brandenburg's attempted mediation between Poland and Sweden in 1612, which, as the Elector was careful to explain in private, was forced upon him by Sigismund III. Once John Sigismund had got a firm grip on East Prussia he was able to follow a more independent policy; his claims on Cleves-Jülich led him to draw closer to the extreme Protestant party in Germany; and eventually (in 1613) he turned Calvinist. These developments resulted in improved relations with Sweden. John Sigismund's sister had married a member of the Radziwiłł family,[2] and the Elector was thus in touch with the Lithuanian opposition to Sigismund III. Nevertheless, however benevolently the Elector might view Gustav Adolf's cause, it was not to be expected of him that he should take any overt steps against Poland until the Prussian inheritance had been safely secured. The feudal relationship between the Crown of Poland and the Hohenzollern family gave to Sigismund III a lever which he might hope to use to ensure at least the neutrality of Brandenburg.

Of even greater importance was the attitude of the Dutch. For the Dutch, as for the Hanse, freedom of the seas within the Baltic was of vital importance. The attempts of Karl IX to prohibit trade to Riga had aroused very general resentment, and had undoubtedly contributed to the diplomatic isolation of Sweden. But the high-handed proceedings of Kristian IV during the War of Kalmar, his exaggerated pretensions to *dominium maris*, and his obvious desire to apply to those waters the doctrine of *mare clausum*, effaced the memory of Karl's offences. Skytte's embassy to the Netherlands in 1610 had indeed failed to obtain an alliance; but Oldenbarnevelt had shown himself decidedly friendly. During the War of Kalmar Kristian had raised the Sound Tolls; he had endeavoured to enforce a blockade of Swedish ports; he had attacked a fleet of Lübeck merchantmen. His resentment at the influx of Dutch colonists to Göteborg had betrayed him into insulting behaviour to a Dutch

---

[1] For all this, see Konopczyński, I. 205, 210, 237; Szelągowski, pp. 58-60, 164-7; R. Koser, *Geschichte der brandenburgischen Politik bis zum Westfälischen Frieden von 1648.* The Elector was bound to assist in the defence of Prussia, to provide four ships for coastal defence, to pay a cash subsidy, and to maintain one church for the use of Catholics in Königsberg. Appeals were to lie to Polish courts.

[2] *AOSB*, I. ii. 139.

embassy which attempted mediation. All these things led Olden-barnevelt to draw closer his friendly relations with Lübeck. There was talk of reviving the old Hanseatic portage-route from Hamburg to Lübeck, or even of cutting a canal through the Kiel isthmus, in order to avoid the burden of the Sound Tolls; and though these projects came to nothing, the peace of Knäred saw both Lübeck and the Dutch very well-disposed to Gustav Adolf.[1]

This good-will extended also, as far as the Dutch were concerned, to Sweden's difficulties with Poland. The Dutch early showed some realization of the importance to Europe of the struggle in Livonia; and in the sequel they were the first Protestant power to lend Sweden assistance in this quarter. It was even asserted in the Netherlands that the War of Kalmar had been fomented by Sigismund as part of a Catholic conspiracy designed to paralyse the Protestant powers in the North by setting them at each other's throats[2]; and though there was in reality no foundation for this belief, it helped to make the Dutch suspicious of Poland.

Thus by 1613 the general aspect of European affairs had altered considerably since the outbreak of the War of Kalmar. On the whole the alteration was in Sweden's favour. If the Protestant front in the West had suffered by the removal of Henri IV, the evangelical party had been strengthened in Germany as a result of the successful resistance to the Emperor in the Cleves-Jülich dispute; Brandenburg had passed the most critical point in her relations with Poland; and Holland, England and the Hanse were all more ready than hitherto to look to Sweden as the best support of their mercantile interests in the Baltic. And though in January 1613 not one of these powers was as yet bound to come to Sweden's aid in an emergency, they all, to a greater or less degree, recognized that their common interest forbade them to permit her to be overwhelmed.

The first clear indication of the changed condition of affairs was provided by the Swedish-Dutch alliance of 1614. The United Provinces had not been appeased by Kristian IV's reduction of the Sound Tolls at the conclusion of peace. In 1613 their resentment was again aroused by the news of the despatch of a Danish embassy

---

[1] Hallenberg, I. 357-61; Fridericia, *DRH*, p. 156; Thyresson, pp. 36-9; Hill, pp. 79-80; *Sv. Krig*, App. Vol. I. 109; Schybergson, pp. v-vi; T. Berg, *Skytte*, pp. 191, 214-16; Blok, IV. 68; Hammarstrand, *HF*, pp. 4-5; E. Wiese, *Die Politik der Niederländer während des Kalmarkrieges* . . ., pp. 3, 5-7, 55, 82; J. A. Fridericia, *Danmarks ydre politiske Historie*, pp. 19-20; F. B. van Veen, *Louis de Geer*, pp. 46-8.

[2] Hallenberg, I. 95.

to Spain. Dutch suspicion of Danish designs was strengthened, and Kristian IV was thought in Amsterdam to be anxious to revive the old Burgundian alliance.[1] Dutch diplomacy aimed in the first place at building up a barrier against Danish threats to freedom of commerce, and they would have liked a general alliance with the Hanse. Failing to secure this, they contented themselves for the moment with a treaty with Lübeck; and in April 1613 an alliance was concluded which bound the contracting parties to mutual aid. The object was declared to be the maintenance of freedom of navigation; the treaty was strictly defensive; and its duration was fixed at fifteen years.[2] In the following month the United Provinces signed the Treaty of Heilbronn with the Evangelical Union, which was at this time somewhat resentful of Kristian IV's refusal to become a member. Both these treaties might be considered as having a point against Denmark. But there was no doubt whatever that this was the correct interpretation of the treaty which was concluded between Gustav Adolf and the Dutch in April 1614.[3] By this treaty, Sweden joined the Netherlands-Lübeck alliance. The King of Sweden and the States-General pledged themselves to render aid, each to the other, in case of attack; to give early information to their ally when an attack was expected; to give no aid of any sort to their respective enemies. Sweden promised freedom of navigation to all Dutch ships sailing to Baltic ports, even to those which might lie in the dominions of the King of Poland, provided that such ports were not actually being besieged by Swedish forces.[4] The allies were to permit recruiting for each other in their respective territories. The old privileges of the Dutch in trading to Sweden were renewed. A special clause bound the States-General to respect the 'hocheitt, regalien, rechten, dominio maris Balthici etc' of the Swedish Crown, which nothing in the treaty was to prejudice. The aim of the alliance was stated to be purely defensive, and it was not to invalidate existing international engagements: in particular, it was stated that it was not intended in any way to infringe the Treaty of Knäred. Should the allies become involved in war as a result of the treaty, neither was to conclude peace without the other. Provision was

---

[1] G. W. Vreede, *Nederland en Zweden*, I. 126.

[2] For the antecedents of this treaty, see Wiese, pp. 50-3, 66-7, 71-2, 79-81, 83; *Christian den fjerdes Breve*, I. 57 *note* 1.

[3] *Sverges Traktater*, V₂. 230-41.

[4] Hammarstrand (*HF*, p. 16) makes the treaty read '*even* if such ports were actually besieged . . . [etc.]'. But the original Dutch has 'ten waere'—*i.e. unless*, and the sense is clear.

made for the exchange of permanent resident ambassadors; and the duration of the treaty was to be fifteen years. By a separate act the amount of assistance to be rendered by each ally to the other in time of war was fixed at 4000 men, to be supplied within three months, the cost being to be borne by the ally who was giving aid, and not by the ally asking it. Either party had the option of taking money or armaments in lieu of soldiers. The obligation to give assistance was cancelled if the party appealed to were already attacked on his own territory; while the amount of aid that could be claimed was to be halved if the party bound to give help were already committed by treaty to aid a third power.

The Dutch alliance thus concluded was the first diplomatic success of Gustav Adolf's reign. The isolation of the country was now broken; and the initiative, it was satisfactory to note, had come from the side of the Dutch. By making this advance they had declared to all the world their conviction that the interests of the Baltic trade would not suffer Sweden to fall victim either to Denmark or to Poland. The balance of advantage in the treaty was heavily on the side of Sweden. The only power from which the Dutch were likely to suffer attack was Spain; and for another seven years this danger was removed by the truce of 1609. Sweden was not likely, therefore, before 1621 to be called upon for the stipulated assistance; while on the other hand she gained a most valuable guarantee of aid in the not impossible event of attack from Denmark and in the highly probable event of attack from Poland. If Kristian IV should be tempted to try to improve the verdict of Knäred, if Sigismund should venture to renew the war, each would find that it was no longer Sweden only with whom he had to deal. Moreover, it was in this year 1614 that the first Russian ambassador made his appearance at The Hague; and the consequent improvement in relations with Russia made possible Dutch mediation in the negotiations that led up to Stolbova; and that mediation served once again to make it clear that the United Provinces had espoused the Swedish cause.[1]

Less than two years later, on 5 January 1616 (N.S.), Oldenbarnevelt was able to extend his alliance with Lübeck to include many of the most important of the Hanse towns. This was the result of a long struggle between the city of Brunswick and Duke Frederick Ulric of Brunswick-Wolfenbüttel. Frederick Ulric had been making

[1] Blok, IV. 69.

determined attempts to force Brunswick to acknowledge his feudal overlordship; and in this he had been seconded by his uncle, Kristian IV. It came at last to open war between the city and the duke. Brunswick appealed to her sister towns of the Hanse; and the Hanse in turn appealed to the Dutch. The Dutch responded by despatching an army of 7000 men under Frederick Henry of Orange, and in December 1615 Frederick Henry forced the duke to raise the siege of Brunswick and compelled him to a reconciliation with the burghers. The upshot was a personal humiliation for Kristian IV, a further deterioration of Dutch relations with Denmark, and the accession to the Dutch-Lübeck alliance of Hamburg, Brunswick, Lüneburg, Magdeburg, Bremen, Wismar, Rostock, Greifswald and Stralsund.[1] The Hanse did not yet venture to provoke Kristian by entering into a direct alliance with Sweden; but it was sufficiently obvious where for the moment their sympathies lay.

The intervention of Kristian IV in the affairs of Brunswick was only one aspect of a new policy of meddling in north German questions which was one day to cost Kristian, and Denmark, very dear. In the second decade of the century Kristian began to develop dynastic ambitions in the Lower Saxon Circle; he began to aspire to control the mouths of the Elbe and the Weser; and he began to seek to establish his family in secularized German bishoprics. His brother Ulrik was already bishop of Schwerin; and about 1615 Kristian launched an attempt, which was long persisted in, to obtain for his younger son Fredrik a whole series of sees: Halberstadt, Osnabrück, Bremen, Verden, Paderborn—all these at one time or another engaged his attention. In 1616 he founded a new town, Glückstadt, on the estuary of the Elbe, in the hope of stealing the trade of Hamburg[2]; for Hamburg had steadily refused to admit his claims, as Duke of Holstein, to be considered as her overlord. This

---

[1] Blok, IV. 66-7; Fridericia, *DRH*, p. 159; Szelągowski, p. 199-200; Paul, I. 114; Wiese, pp. 87, 109-43. A project for a Dutch-Hanse alliance in 1614 had been stopped only by an Imperial prohibition: Wiese, p. 99. Relations between Kristian and Lübeck continued to be very strained. Kristian was especially incensed at reports that the Lübeckers had called one of his best ships an 'eel-trap', and is said to have retorted 'er werde ihnen Aale braten, sofern er anders Christian heisse'. In March 1615 he prohibited all trade with Lübeck, whereat the Lübeckers protested to the Emperor, and pointed out to Kristian that even worms will turn, and 'formicae sua bilis inest': D. Schäfer, *Der Kampf um die Ostsee im 16. und 17. Jahrhundert*, p. 439.
[2] And also to scotch any scheme for evading Sound Tolls by an Elbe-Oder or Elbe-Havel canal.

system of petty aggression had as its natural consequence the alienation, to a greater or lesser degree, of most of the Protestant states of north Germany; and this in its turn had the double effect of leading Kristian to toy with the Catholic powers, and of causing the evangelical party in the Empire to cultivate good relations with Gustav Adolf.[1]

In the years after 1611 Sweden, as Karl IX had always desired, drew gradually nearer to her natural friends in Germany. In Karl IX's time any close relationship had been difficult. The natural legitimism of the Lutherans caused them to look askance at Karl as a usurper; while the Calvinists could not altogether forget that Sweden was not of their faith. The Palatinate and Hesse-Cassel, the two states to which Sweden was most closely linked by dynastic ties, had been afraid to espouse her cause openly. They had wished to keep on good terms with Sigismund III, for they had hoped to induce Brandenburg to join the Union—a step which would have compromised the Elector's chances of obtaining the administrator-ship of East Prussia if the Union had appeared to Sigismund as the supporter of Karl.[2]   But since 1611 the situation had altered. Brandenburg was now a member of the Union, and East Prussia for the moment was safe. Maurice of Hesse-Cassel had done his best for Sweden during the war with Denmark.[3] He was anxious to persuade England and the Dutch to come forward as mediators in the Russian affair; for Maurice, the wisest and most level-headed of the advanced party in Germany, had already seen the importance of relieving Sweden of the Russian commitment, so that her hands might be set free for enterprises of more immediate interest to Germany. In 1613 Maurice sent an embassy to Sweden to sound Gustav Adolf as to the possibility of cooperation; and this was followed, in February 1614, by an envoy from Frederick V and the other members of the Union. There was even talk of inviting Sweden to become a member. But though for the moment nothing came of this, Gustav Adolf's relations with the Union were drawn closer by the marriage of his sister Katarina to John Casimir of Pfalz-Zwei-brücken-Kleeburg, in June 1615; for John Casimir made it his business to champion Gustav Adolf's cause in Germany and to promote good relations between Sweden and the Palatinate party.

---

[1] Fridericia, DRH, pp. 141, 161-2.
[2] Thyresson, pp. 3, 15.
[3] Hammarstrand, HF, p. 6. A useful short study of Maurice is M. Lenz, Landgraf Moritz von Hessen.

And it is clear that the evangelical princes had done everything in their power to promote the match.[1]

There was thus evidence that a great part of Protestant Germany was interested in the fate of Sweden, and looked already to Gustav Adolf as a possible auxiliary in the hour of danger. Gustav Adolf's own attitude, as revealed in his response to these various overtures, was simple and straightforward. He could not fail to be pleased that the Princes had abandoned the attitude of reserve or indifference which they had adopted in his father's time. He was gratified by the suggestion that he should join the Union, and might possibly have accepted the invitation if it had been made. He was prepared to give assurances that he would aid the Union in an emergency. He fully admitted their moral right to call for that aid in the name of the great cause of Protestantism. But he pointed out repeatedly that at the moment he was fully occupied with Poland, and that the struggle in Russia or Livonia must for Sweden be the first consideration. Indeed, if his assistance were called for in Germany he conceived that it could be most usefully given—and perhaps for the moment it was the only way in which it could be given—in the form of a diversionary attack on Poland.[2] Here, then, full ten years before the matter reached the stage of practical politics, begins the long history of Gustav Adolf's cherished plan of a diversion through Poland. It was a plan which always rested upon the contention that the Polish war could not be separated, in idea or in fact, from the struggles of Protestantism in other areas. Gustav Adolf from the very beginning of the reign sought to identify the dynastic feud, the inherited battle for the old lands of the Knights of the Sword, the rivalry for the Baltic littoral, with the great defensive action against the forces of the Counter-Reformation, which was developing all over central Europe. There was great justice in his contention. And therefore, while freely owning that the cause of Hesse and the Palatinate was his cause, Gustav Adolf strove always to persuade his German friends that the cause of the younger Vasa line was also their cause—a cause in which they could not, dared not, disinterest themselves. His success was for the present but small. There was scarcely a Protestant prince in Germany, of those who were friendly to Sweden, who would not at this time have preferred him to patch

[1] Hallenberg, III. 246-9; *AOSB*, I. ii. 194; I. i. 85 *seqq.*; *A. Brahes Tidebok*, p. 89; Hammarstrand, *HF*, pp. 8-12, 14-15; Thyresson, pp. 66-9, 90-1; Hammarstrand, *Historisk Öfversigt*, p. 6; Koser, p. 379.
[2] Hammarstrand, *HF*, p. 13; Hallenberg, III. 250; Paul, I. 116-17.

up a peace with Poland. They conceded the necessity of the Polish war, from Sweden's point of view; they were ready even to recognize its confessional character; but as an effective 'diversion' they found it hard to take it seriously.

Since this was how the land lay, it is not surprising that Gustav Adolf should have taken little more than a benevolent interest in the loose notions of a general Protestant League which were current between 1613 and 1615. The Cleves-Jülich affair had left both Protestants and Catholics nervous. Dutch and Spanish troops had appeared in the duchies, as auxiliaries for one side or the other, and in such circumstances the Twelve Years' Truce seemed to be wearing dangerously thin. Oldenbarnevelt was haunted by nightmares of a great Popish League; while Sarmiento, the Spanish ambassador in England, was equally convinced that a monstrous Protestant combination was preparing.[1] Both were equally mistaken. Any effective Protestant League must be based on England and the States-General; and experience seemed to prove that no permanent co-operation between them was to be looked for. England's policy continued to speak with two voices, as James I laboured by contradictory expedients to keep the peace. In 1613 she was fearing a Spanish invasion; in 1614 the strong Protestant Winwood became Secretary; and in the Cleves-Jülich affair England and the Dutch worked hand in hand. Yet it was in 1614 that James first began serious negotiations for the Spanish marriage; it was in 1614 that he became involved in quarrels with the Dutch over the Greenland fisheries and the East India Company, which the retrocession of the Cautionary Towns in 1616 did little to allay. The dissolution of the Addled Parliament, moreover, deprived him of the resources for conducting a resolute foreign policy. Yet he could still (1616) release Raleigh; and he could still, even with no parliament to give him supplies, find £15,000 to send to the Duke of Savoy, to aid him in his struggle against Spain. The Savoy affair, incidentally, served to demonstrate to any interested Protestant power the feebleness of France: from the Protestant viewpoint the country of Henri IV was now a political nullity, or worse.

The Protestant League, therefore, remained an unrealized dream; and Gustav Adolf was quite right to take no account of it in his calculations. Kristian IV had already come to the same conclusion. Kristian felt that he was perfectly able to take care of himself, and

[1] Blok, IV. 76; Gardiner, II. 252-3.

he expected other Protestant princes to do the same. He did not share the general suspicion of a Catholic conspiracy. He regarded the Dutch and the Hanse, justifiably enough, as no friends to Denmark; and he was deaf to the appeals of his brother-in-law of England. He feared, perhaps, that if he entered a Protestant League of which Sweden was also a member he might find his hands inconveniently tied in his relations with Gustav Adolf. For Kristian had by no means been satisfied by the outcome of the War of Kalmar. The decisive victory which he had sought had undoubtedly eluded him. He might indeed hope that Sweden would default on the war indemnity, and that Älvsborg would fall to him in the end, but he felt that he had missed his best chance. Sweden's relations with Denmark, therefore, in the years after 1613, were uneasy and somewhat variable. Both sides developed grievances about the interpretation and execution of the terms of the treaty of Knäred; and a plan to send Oxenstierna to Copenhagen in 1614 to clear up these differences had to be dropped owing to more pressing calls on the Chancellor's time. Kristian was undoubtedly angry and suspicious at the Swedish-Dutch alliance of 1614. He did indeed offer his mediation in Russia; but his recognition of Michael as Tsar did not encourage Gustav Adolf to accept it.[1] When Skytte was sent on a special mission to Denmark in March 1615, he was cordially received; but his efforts to induce Kristian to agree to easier terms for the payment of Älvsborg's ransom were met by an absolute refusal.[2] Sweden's attempts to mollify Danish displeasure with Lübeck had no success; and when the Danish Chancellor was despatched to the Russian front he was turned back by the Swedish commander.[3] Kristian's feelings towards Gustav Adolf remained cool, and his policy continued non-committal: he declined to depart from a strict neutrality to the Polish war; and if he was prepared to allow mercenaries and armaments for Sweden to come through the Sound from western Europe, he was equally prepared to grant the same facilities to Poland. At the time when the war in Livonia was renewed in 1617 [4] there had been no real clarification of Denmark's attitude. Gustav Adolf was already seriously uneasy about Älvsborg; and though he had little positive evidence to go on, rumours reached

---

[1] Hallenberg, III. 235-43; *AOSB*, I. II. 207-8; II. I. 61-7.
[2] Hallenberg, III. 364-5; *AOSB*, II. x. 178 *note*.
[3] *AOSB*, I. II. 235. James I made similar efforts with respect to Lübeck: Hammarstrand, *HF*, p. 57.
[4] See below, p. 158.

him from time to time of secret Danish armaments.[1] The danger of a stab in the back from across the Sound, should the Polish war once more become active, was not, perhaps, very imminent; but it was always present in the calculations of Swedish statesmen. Kristian had probably not made up his mind. Possibly he hoped that Gustav Adolf's difficulties in Russia and Poland might make him complaisant. Certainly he looked upon the Polish war primarily as a useful means of keeping Sweden occupied; secondarily as a nuisance to trade[2]; and hardly at all as a struggle in which the sympathies of all Protestant powers must necessarily be engaged.

(iv) *The Renewal of the War in Poland, 1617-18*

Neither Sweden nor Poland ventured to violate the two-years' truce which began in September 1614. Gustav Adolf was still doggedly pursuing a peace through the morasses of Muscovite diplomacy, while Sigismund and Władysław were straining every nerve to raise the siege of Smoleńsk, and thus in some degree to retrieve the fortunes of a struggle which latterly had turned against them. The *sejm*, on the one hand, the *riksdag*, on the other, consistently expressed a desire for peace, and as consistently resigned themselves to the impossibility of obtaining it. John Sigismund of Brandenburg, presciently apprehensive of embarrassments for himself once the attention of the protagonists ceased to be distracted to Russia, maintained his hopeless efforts to arrange a compromise where no compromise was possible, and in September 1615 launched an abortive congress at Stettin, to which Sweden did not even trouble to send a delegate.[3]

Sigismund, like Gustav Adolf, had never regarded the truce as more than a convenient breathing-space. He had not felt himself precluded from pursuing his attempts to seduce the subjects of his cousin; his propaganda continued to be poured out; his agents did not cease to hatch their plots. Indeed, the threat from the exiles was never more alarming than during the period when hostilities were suspended. In the summer of 1615 Gustav Adolf deemed it necessary to send Gyllenstierna with a small squadron upon a

---

[1] *AOSB*, II. x. 13.

[2] See the memorandum drawn up for Oxenstierna's projected embassy, 27 June 1614: *AOSB*, II. 1. 61-6.

[3] Thyresson, p. 77; *AOSB*, I. 11. 221, 286.

reconnaissance to the Polish coast, with instructions to report upon any signs of naval activity.[1] No such signs could be discerned: there was, it appeared, no immediate danger of invasion. Nevertheless Gustav Adolf was anxious. In order to obtain more specific and detailed information as to what was going forward on the other side of the water, he also sent Petrus Petrejus on a special mission to Danzig; ostensibly to buy ammunition and cultivate the good-will of the burghers, but really to spy out the land. His report was, for the moment, entirely reassuring. The dispositions of Danzig, it seemed, were not unfavourable to Sweden; Lithuania was discontented at having to bear the main burden of Sigismund's Russian war; a Tatar invasion was reported from the south; and there were virtually no signs of hostile preparations. Sigismund had indeed caused one great ship to be built; but the expense had been so heavy that he had been forced to try to sell it as soon as it was ready; no purchaser had come forward; and the vessel had rotted where it lay.[2]

All this was satisfactory enough; and in 1616 Gustav Adolf, taking a leaf out of Sigismund's book, made some attempt to sow dissension among his enemies. In February he sent an agent, Jost Clodt, charged with messages to Chodkiewicz and Radziwiłł.[3] He was to complain that Sigismund by his propaganda had broken the truce; and he was to try to win the confidence of the two Polish leaders. For Chodkiewicz, the old bait of an alliance against Russia was once more to be extended; while Radziwiłł was to be assured of Gustav Adolf's sympathy in his differences with Sigismund. These differences were mainly of a religious nature; and it seemed possible that his grievances, if properly managed, might be used to distract Sigismund's attention from any designs upon Sweden. As it turned out, neither Radziwiłł nor Chodkiewicz could be found, for both were away at Warsaw attending a Diet; and this part of Clodt's mission came to nothing. But Clodt had other instructions beside these. He was to offer Gustav Adolf's assistance to Duke Frederick of Kurland, who had just at this moment become involved in a serious quarrel with his feudal overlord the King of Poland.

Upon the death of Gotthard Ketteler, the last Grand Master of the Livonian Knights, his duchy of Kurland had passed to his two

[1] Cronholm, I. 316.
[2] S. Clason, *Förhållandet till Polen* . . . *1615*, pp. 186-92.
[3] *AOSB*, I. II. 252, 254; Cronholm, I. 318; Hallenberg, IV. 541.

sons, Frederick and William. Between the dukes and their nobility subsisted a more or less perennial feud; and the last episode in this struggle had occurred in 1615, when Duke William had arrested, and subsequently executed, two brothers of the noble house of Nolde. Unluckily for the dukes, one the Noldes was at the time of his arrest acting upon Sigismund's instructions, and was the bearer of his commission. Sigismund took Duke William's action extremely ill, and both dukes were threatened with deprivation. Here, then, was a situation which Gustav Adolf might hope to turn to his advantage. If the Kurland dukes could be incited to rebel, if judicious aid were sent to them—sufficient to keep their cause alive, but not so much as to tax Sweden's overburdened resources—then Sigismund might find his attention fully occupied by domestic affairs. It would in any case be most undesirable to permit Poland to annex the duchy of Kurland to the Crown, for though the Kurland ports were of no great size, they might well serve as supplementary bases from which to launch an invasion. Clodt, then, was to make offers of assistance to Duke Frederick. But here again his mission proved unfortunate. Duke Frederick had prudently dissociated himself from the proceedings of his brother, and had succeeded in reconciling himself with his sovereign. Duke William, no doubt, was still to be reckoned with; but Duke William judged it wiser to flee the country, and was shortly to appear in Sweden, where he became a pensioner on Gustav Adolf's bounty. The prospect of a profitable intervention in Kurland seemed to vanish as suddenly as it had appeared.

At this point, however, there came a most unexpected offer. Among Duke William's adherents was a certain Wolmar Farensbach, the feudal Lord of Karkus. Farensbach was a person of restless and turbulent humour, and was decidedly not to be trusted by any man. He was a braggart and a brute, he had an immense conceit of himself, he was utterly devoid of scruples or honour; but he was a man with a knack of extricating himself from situations which would have embarrassed the less thick-skinned; he was a military leader of vigour and dash; and in general he had abilities considerably in excess of those normal in the boorish Livonian nobility.[1] He had already, in December 1615, made contact with Gustaf Adolf, for he was one of those who desired an alliance of Sweden with Poland and a joint campaign against Russia. Now, in the spring of 1616, he came forward with a more original proposal. He intimated to Gustav

[1] For Farensbach, see Ahnlund, *Storhetstidens Gryning*, pp. 92-143.

Adolf that he would be willing to betray to the Swedes the fort of Dünamünde, which guarded the mouth of the Düna river, and would further assist in every way any expeditionary force which Sweden might care to send over to Kurland to restore Duke William. Sweden could not fail to be interested in this proposition.[1] There were already disquieting rumours that Danish ships had been seen off the Kurland coast, and it would never do to allow Kristian to get a footing in that quarter.[2] Indeed, there seemed only two possible objections to the scheme. One was the character of its originator. 'Der Farensbach', Wallenstein was later to remark, 'ist gut zu einer desperierten diversion oder impresa',[3] and as such might be suited for the kind of enterprise he was proposing; but Oxenstierna could not help reflecting that he was a person of little consideration, encumbered by debts, and inheriting from his father a tradition of treachery to allies.[4] It was a matter for serious consideration whether Sweden should adventure her resources upon so unsound a bottom. The second objection consisted in the argument that, if only the existing truce could be prolonged upon some solid basis, Sweden would gain the security she needed, without being at the expense of an expedition to Kurland, and without risking her troops in the dubious company of Farensbach. This was an argument which made a very strong appeal to the råd. When Gustav Adolf consulted them in August 1616, he found that the general opinion was in favour of prolonging the truce if reasonable terms were to be had. It was felt that Sweden should keep her hands free, at any rate until the ransom for Älvsborg was paid; since there was no knowing when a crisis in her relations with Denmark might not arise. In effect, then, the råd was recommending peace on the Polish front until 1620.[5]

On the other hand there were strong reasons to suggest that Sweden could not afford to give Poland so long a respite for recovery from her internal troubles. In the summer of 1616 Sigismund was known to be making military preparations on a very large scale. It might well be that they portended an attack on Estonia or Finland in the spring of 1617. As a matter of fact, though Gustav Adolf did not know this, they were intended for a great effort in Russia: the sejm had made a special grant in order to relieve Smoleńsk.[6]

[1] *AOSB*, II. i. 93-5; Hallenberg, IV. 652.   [2] *AOSB*, II. x. 17.
[3] Ahnlund, *Storhetstidens Gryning*, p. 108.   [4] *AOSB*, I. ii. 278.
[5] *SRDA*, II. 3-7, 12. De la Gardie was of the same opinion: Grill, p. 77.
[6] *Sv. Krig*, I. 559.

But even if the Polish effort were directed to Russia in the first instance, its success would spell danger: Gustav Adolf was nervous of a Polish attack upon Pskov, with an invasion of Estonia from the south-east to follow. The Kurland troubles offered an opportunity, which might not recur, to throw Sigismund's plans in Russia out of gear. The duchy had been largely stripped of troops. The cause

could be represented as a blow for Protestantism. Disaffected elements in Lithuania might be blown into flame. There might even be a prospect of assistance from England or from the Dutch.

Despite these considerations, Gustav Adolf temporized. The truce with Poland was to expire on 29 September 1616; but it might perhaps be possible to renew it on a more solid basis. At all events, the attempt was made; and from the early autumn of 1616 desultory and intermittent negotiations took place with that end in view, culminating in May 1617 in a meeting of negotiators near Weissenstein. It proved a fruitless endeavour. On 6 June the Swedish negotiators notified the King that the conference had broken up; and three days later the first Swedish detachment disembarked at Dünamünde.[1] It seems probable that Gustav Adolf never had much expectation of any positive result from these negotiations. As early as December he had reached an agreement with Farensbach; in January the conclusion of the Treaty of Stolbova relieved him of any apprehensions on that side; and by the time the Örebro *riksdag* dispersed he had probably already resolved on war. His speech to the Estates on 28 January was a clear indication that he expected the outbreak of hostilities.[2] Already in January his ambassador at The Hague had been instructed to ask the Dutch for naval aid.[3] The negotiations, however, would occupy Poland's attention until the Baltic should be open to navigation; and there was always the faint possibility that the diplomats might arrive at some acceptable compromise. But in the meantime he pressed on his preparations; and it was no accident that he was able to strike a blow within a week of the failure of the conference.

The objects of the campaign which now opened were limited, and indeed modest. In the first place it was hoped to deny the use of possible invasion-ports to the enemy; in the second it was hoped to establish a secure lodgment at selected strong-points in Kurland and Livonia. The restoration of Duke William to his duchy, while providing a pretext for intervention, would also give Sweden a friend from whose territories she could later launch attacks either on Livonia or Lithuania; for Gustav Adolf seems to have intended that William should give him the right to garrison certain Kurland fortresses, by way of compensation for his expenses. The positions which Farensbach already controlled included (besides Dünamünde) Goldingen, Windau and Treiden; but the main effort was to be made in the Düna estuary. With Dünamünde in their hands, the Swedes would have a useful advanced base for a stroke at Riga. If they could take Riga, they would be in a position to levy tolls upon navigation up or down the river: already, therefore, we catch an anticipatory glimpse of a policy which was to be of the greatest importance in the future—the attempt to control the mouths of the

---

[1] *Sv. Krig*, II. 25-9. See the curious exculpatory letter to the Polish Senate, dated 30 June 1617, in *AOSB*, I. II. 302.
[2] *SRDA*, II. 75-6, for Skytte's memorandum in favour of peace; *ibid.*, III *seqq.*, for Gustav Adolf's speech.
[3] Thyresson, pp. 102-3; Hallenberg, IV. 646-7.

great rivers, in order to use the revenue from tolls to supplement the inadequate resources of Sweden herself. Finally, the expedition aimed at the recovery of Pernau; partly because Pernau was a useful port for Sigismund's purposes, but also because it commanded the easiest route for any invasion of Estonia from the south. No great forces were to be committed to the enterprise: the maximum aid promised to Farensbach did not exceed 8000 men; and there are some signs that the King was willing to throw the burden of the dangerous initial period as far as possible upon his ally. If the venture turned out badly, it would be convenient to represent it as a spontaneous move by Farensbach on behalf of Duke William.

On 9 June 1617, then, a small advance party of 400 men arrived off the mouth of the Düna, and two days later, after a show of parleying, were admitted by Farensbach into Dünamünde.[1] Had Gustav Adolf been ready to follow up the initial surprise in force, the subsequent history of the expedition might have been very different. For Livonia and Lithuania were almost bare of Polish troops; Chodkiewicz, with the main armies of the Republic, was far away in Russia; while other important detachments were busy on the southern frontier, where Stanislaw Żółkiewski was endeavouring to meet the attacks of Skinder Pasha.[2] The available forces to oppose to the Swedish invasion were mostly scattered in widely separated garrisons; and, as the event showed, it took Christopher Radziwiłł, the commander on the spot, fully two months to collect a couple of thousand men. The reinforcements from Sweden, however, upon which Farensbach was counting, dallied unaccountably, to his great discontent; and when they did arrive, they totalled no more than 2000 foot. Their commander, Nils Stiernsköld, was an unenterprising and discontented person, suffering from the effects of an old wound: by no means a good choice for a venture where everything depended upon making the best use of the advantage secured by surprise.[3] Nevertheless, the army at once marched upstream against the Düna Redoubt, which really formed the outermost of the defences of Riga. On 23 July the Redoubt capitulated. Had Stiern-

---

[1] For details of the campaigns of 1617 and 1618, see *Sv. Krig*, II.; and B. Broomé, *Nils Stiernsköld*, pp. 86-132.

[2] Szelągowski, p. 229.

[3] In the middle of the campaign he asked to be relieved of the command, and drew upon himself a rebuke from Gustav Adolf couched in terms of unusual severity: Broomé, pp. 108-12; Hallenberg, IV. 661-2. He was to redeem his reputation later, as a naval commander.

sköld now pressed on to Riga, there was just a chance that the town might have fallen.[1] Its defences were not fully in order; its morale was somewhat shaken; and its garrison, though recently reinforced, was not numerous. Stiernsköld, however, was unaware of his opportunity, and unwilling to risk his small force upon an object which might probably prove beyond its strength. Riga was therefore left undisturbed. But Stiernsköld was apparently equally unwilling to attempt any other objective. The road to Kurland lay open; but he declined to take it. It was only after much persuasion from Farensbach that he was prevailed upon to make an attempt on Pernau. Thanks to superior forces and a number of guns (badly handled, but still useful), the attempt was successful. After little more than a week's investment, Pernau capitulated on 8 August.

And with that Stiernsköld's initiative was exhausted. He was, perhaps, mistrustful of Farensbach. He was certainly short of money to pay his troops; some of his regiments were fresh levies; his lack of cavalry made him naturally reluctant to risk an engagement; and he was losing many men by desertion. At all events, it is plain that Stiernsköld considered that the capture of Pernau marked the conclusion of the main part of his task: henceforward he confined himself to taking measures for the defence of what had already been won. This rather tame passivity cannot have been very encouraging to Farensbach. Already in August Christopher Radziwiłł had collected an army equal or superior in numbers to that of the Swedes. At the beginning of September the burghers of Riga made a sally and retook the Düna Redoubt, whose garrison had been decimated by disease. The initiative was plainly passing into the hands of the Poles. All this did not escape Farensbach's observation. The Swedish alliance, as represented by Stiernsköld, no longer appeared to him to offer any very alluring prospects. Appeals to his patriotism by members of his family reinforced doubts which had already been provoked by the calculations of self-interest. By the middle of September he had decided to change sides. On 15 September he made a beginning by surrendering Goldingen to Radziwiłł; on 25 September he formally abjured his compact with Gustav Adolf; and by the beginning of October he was once more a loyal member of the Polish Republic. His fate was destined to be involved in

---

[1] Such at any rate was the opinion current in Denmark at the time: *AOSB*, II. x. 184-5 and *note*.

Sweden's history more than once in the future; but his part in the Kurland affair was over.[1]

It was some time before Stiernsköld realized what had happened, and much longer before the situation was grasped in Stockholm. The recovery by the Poles of Dünamünde and Windau, however, at last opened Stiernsköld's eyes to the true state of the case. Sweden had now lost the advantage of Farensbach's treason; she had lost the very necessary aid of Farensbach's troops; and there remained only Pernau to show for the speculation. Pernau, to be sure, was a valuable prize; but it was now a question whether even it could be retained. Had Christopher Radziwiłł attacked resolutely in the autumn of 1617, he could scarcely have failed to drive the enfeebled Swedish forces to the shelter of the strong places of Estonia. Fortunately Radziwiłł had difficulties with his own army; and the severity of an early winter put a stop to campaigning for the time being.

Gustav Adolf had by now ceased to expect any major gains from his Kurland venture; and the desultory campaigning of the early months of 1618 proved only that neither side was strong enough to inflict any serious damage on the other. In June 1618 an armistice was arranged in order to facilitate negotiations for a resumption of the truce, and this armistice was subsequently extended to 5 August. There was more trouble on Poland's Ukrainian frontier; Władysław was making a last supreme effort to wrest a solid gain from the dreary struggle in Russia[2]; while in Bohemia a situation was developing which Sigismund could not but view with disquiet. Once again, therefore, both sides were willing to parley; and once again the negotiations were protracted. At last, on 28 November 1618, the Truce of Tolsburg was concluded.[3] It was to run till 11 November 1620; and should either party be unwilling to extend it thereafter, three months' notice was to be given. As to Pernau, which had been the main difficulty during the negotiations, it was agreed that Gustav Adolf should declare his intentions in regard to it within a year and a day of the signing of the treaty—the tacit assumption being that Sweden would then retrocede the town. Sigismund, however, according to his custom, declined to ratify the truce; and though the absence of this formality did not prevent

---

[1] For later details of Farensbach's career, see Ahnlund, *op. cit.*, *loc. cit.*
[2] Korzon, II. 193.
[3] *Sverges Traktater*, V₂. 308-12.

its being observed by both parties, it gave Gustav Adolf sufficient pretext to keep Pernau in his hands.[1] Five weeks later, on 3 January 1619, Poland abandoned the struggle in Russia. The Truce of Deulinie shelved for fourteen years Władysław's claim to the Russian throne—an arrangement which was tantamount to a confession of defeat; but in return Moscow ceded Smoleńsk, Dorogobuzh and a number of other towns in White Russia.[2]

The Truce of Deulinie was of great importance to Sweden. Although it freed Poland from a commitment which had become a serious drain upon her, and gave her leisure to devote her attention to other problems, the existence of the Truce of Tolsburg, and the serious crisis which was soon to develop on her south-east frontier, prevented her from using the opportunity for an intensification of her effort against Gustav Adolf. On the other hand, by abandoning the game in Russia, Sigismund had lost his easiest line of attack upon Sweden. It was no longer possible for him to strike at her—as Gustav Adolf had latterly feared that he might—by way of Pskov, Gdov, Narva, and so to Finland, either round the head of the Gulf, or even, in winter, by a direct march across the ice. He must now make a frontal attack upon the comparatively short southern frontier of Estonia; or he must boldly commit himself to an element which was strange to him, and steel himself to the hazards of an invasion, trusting that no Protestant wind would bring his transports within range of the guns of a superior Swedish fleet. This last proved a task beyond his powers, and perhaps beyond his courage, even at that moment of high promise when Wallenstein, as 'Admiral of the Baltic and Oceanic Seas', stood ready to give him aid. Thus in the long struggle between Sweden and Poland the Truce of Deulinie marks something of a turning-point. From this moment the initiative really passes out of Sigismund's hands.

The Truce of Tolsburg was in comparison of minor importance: another breathing-space between bouts, no more. Nothing was settled; no solution was in sight. Gustav Adolf had seized the opportunity presented by Sigismund's preoccupations; but the weakness of Sweden, the inertness of Stiernsköld, the treachery of

[1] Since Sigismund did not ratify the treaty, he was not bound by the provision which laid it down that ' nulla bellica impressio seu hostilitas, vel aperta *vel clandestina* [my italics] contra regnum Sueciae . . . suscipi', which would have debarred his propaganda.

[2] Konopczyński, I. 248-9; Sobieski, p. 182; Waliszewski, *Le Berceau d'une Dynastie*, p. 14. There is a sketch-map showing the territory ceded by Russia in C. Stählin, *La Russie des Origines à la Naissance de Pierre le Grand*, p. 109.

Farensbach, and the threat of complications with Denmark, had prevented his making full use of his chance. Had Dünamünde, or, still better, Riga, then passed permanently into Swedish hands, the speculation must have appeared a highly profitable one. In the event, it was open to doubt whether the recovery of Pernau could be held to justify the expenditure upon the expedition. The chance, in fact, had been a little bungled. But at least Gustav Adolf had gained two years: two years in which to get clear of Älvsborg's ransom; two years in which to translate into measures of reform the military lessons learned since 1611. When the next opportunity arose, when next Poland's misfortunes should give him an opening, Gustav Adolf would have begun that reorganization of the Swedish army which was ultimately to astonish Europe on the battlefields of Germany.

And the campaigns in Kurland had produced one other effect which might be considered encouraging for the future: for the first time in Gustav Adolf's reign other Protestant powers had shown themselves ready to look upon these distant skirmishes as things not irrelevant to the evangelical cause. With James I, indeed, a good deal of careful explanation had been required before that captious Scottish intelligence professed itself convinced[1]; but as early as February 1617 the Elector Palatine had shown his interest, and had written to the States-General advising them to keep an eye on the situation. This friendly hint had been seconded by Skytte's embassy, soon to be described; and in the end the Dutch (though with some reluctance in view of their mercantile interests in Poland) admitted Gustav Adolf's contention that the *casus foederis* had arisen, since Sigismund was demonstrably the aggressor, in virtue of his intrigues in Sweden. They accordingly fulfilled their engagements under the treaty of 1614 and promised the stipulated aid in money. The virtual suspension of hostilities in Kurland in the summer of 1618 made it unnecessary, in the event, to send these succours; but it was a diplomatic success for Gustaf Adolf to have induced Oldenbarnevelt to admit that the struggle with Sigismund came within the scope of the alliance.[2]

The Protestant powers made the less difficulty about identifying Sweden's cause with their own because in recent years Polish policy had given good ground for the idea that Sigismund would be an

---

[1] Hammarstrand, *HF*, p. 98.
[2] *ibid.*, pp. 49-50; Dahlgren, I, 50 *seqq.*

active member of any Catholic *bloc*. In 1613 Sigismund had concluded an important alliance with the Emperor Matthias. The Papal Nuncio had played a leading part in these negotiations; and one of the secret articles in the treaty was clearly directed to a possible reconquest of Sweden. Panslav politicians of the stamp of Chodkiewicz and Żółkiewski, who had spent their lives fighting German influences in Polish affairs, looked on the new alliance with distaste; but henceforward Sigismund might be reckoned as the most easterly member of the Habsburg ring. In 1615 the Emperor made great efforts to mediate between Poland and Russia; and in the following year Sigismund repaid these services by intervening against Matthias' rebellious subjects in Silesia.[1] Thus to Protestant statesmen there seemed good evidence to prove that Sigismund had linked his quarrel to the great religious controversy in Germany and the west, and their attitude to the Polish war began to be modified accordingly.

(v) *The Détente with Denmark, 1619*

Kristian IV, less ready than the Elector Palatine or the Landgrave of Hesse-Cassel to look on foreign politics in terms of religion, remained obstinately sceptical. He had no wish to see the dynastic feud of the Vasas turned into a Protestant crusade, for a victory of Gustav Adolf and his Dutch allies would compromise Denmark's control of the Baltic; but neither did he desire the triumph of Sigismund, for a legitimist restoration in Sweden would invalidate the peace of Knäred and put an end to his hopes of retaining Älvsborg. On the whole, the wisest policy for Denmark appeared to be neutrality. But it probably occurred to Kristian in the course of 1617 that if Sweden could be tempted into a Danish alliance, a provision might be inserted guaranteeing him compensation for any expenses incurred on his ally's behalf; and he was sufficiently aware of Sweden's financial difficulties to realize that any such arrangement might offer him a chance of further acquisitions of territory in lieu of payment. At all events, in the summer of 1617 a vague project for an alliance was in the air, and it seems to have originated in Copenhagen. Gustav Adolf, always anxious for security on the side of Denmark, if security were to be had on reasonable terms, sent

---

[1] Konopczyński, I. 242-3, 253-6; Szelągowski, pp. 202-3; Hammarstrand, *HF*, pp. 7 *note* 1, 25 *note* 2.

Skytte in September to make enquiries on the spot. Skytte had a reassuring conversation with the Danish Chancellor, who emphatically disclaimed any intention of assisting Poland; but he was not able to get any precise information as to Kristian's intentions; he appears to have been somewhat disgruntled by his inability to keep pace with Danish potations; and after only a short stay he proceeded, according to his instructions, to Holland, to consult Oldenbarnevelt and Maurice as to how Sweden should receive any Danish advances.[1]

Sigismund, meanwhile, had been alarmed at the rumours of a Danish-Swedish reconciliation; and in October 1617 he too sent an embassy to Copenhagen. His envoy, John Weiher, was instructed to offer Älvsborg in exchange for Denmark's benevolent neutrality and to ask for a free pass through the Sound for ships shortly expected from Dunkirk. Hard on the heels of this embassy came Don Francisco de Medina from Spain, bearing an invitation to Kristian to join the Catholic League, and to conclude an alliance with Spain against the Dutch, and with Poland against Sweden.[2] Kristian had no real intention of allying with either of these powers, and still less of joining the League; but he received the ambassadors courteously, being well aware that their solicitations strengthened his hand. And by way of a hint to Gustav Adolf, he began for the first time to accord to Sigismund the title of King of Sweden. He was careful to keep open the frontier disputes arising from the treaty of Knäred, which Skytte had tried to clear up; he evaded Gustav Adolf's proposal for a conference on the border in January 1618; and he offered his mediation in the Kurland war, explaining that until these matters had been disposed of the project of an alliance must be suspended.[3]

Skytte had by this time arrived in the Netherlands. His mission had a triple object: he was to ask the advice of the Dutch upon the proposed alliance with Denmark; he was to try to raise a loan for the third instalment of Älvsborg's ransom, and to obtain an extension of time for the repayment of the previous loan; and he was to demand aid against Poland in terms of the treaty of 1614. He came to the Netherlands at an unfortunate moment. The provinces were torn

---

[1] *AOSB*, II. x. 190-2; Thyresson, pp. 113-23; Hallenberg, IV. 666-82; Broomé, p. 89.

[2] Fridericia, *DRH*, p. 160; Szelągowski, p. 219; Hammarstrand, *HF*, p. 63; Hallenberg, IV. 683.

[3] Hammarstrand, *HF*, pp. 64-5.

by dissension; Oldenbarnevelt's authority was declining; and the Dutch appeared to be drifting to a civil war in which Gomarist would be ranged against Arminian, Remonstrant against Counter-Remonstrant, Oldenbarnevelt against Maurice. 'Here is seen such a hubbub about predestination' (wrote Skytte) 'that all the skippers argue *pro et contra.*' [1] Skytte contrived to keep on friendly terms with both sides, and gave to each good advice which they did not take, but he found it difficult to obtain any decision. The Dutch suspected that Kristian intended the alliance only as a means of getting from Sweden another pledge which she would be unable to redeem. They preferred that Kristian should be 'grouped' in a general Protestant League; and they urged Skytte to talk the matter over, as a preliminary step, with James I. Skytte, therefore, fortified by a tun of English ale (a present from the English ambassador at The Hague),[2] braved the wintry Channel, landed at Margate, and by Canterbury made his way to London. He and James were kindred spirits, and each admired the other, but even so the mission was not really a success; and it would probably have been even less so if Skytte had obeyed his instructions to warn the King against the Spanish marriage. He did indeed persuade James of the justice and necessity of the war in Kurland; but he failed to raise a loan from the Exchequer, and when he approached the London merchants they frankly told him that James' name was not good enough security for an advance. As to the idea of a general Protestant alliance, James was not encouraging. The news had just reached England of the capture of Puloway by the Dutch, and feeling was too bitter for any Englishman to welcome the idea of collaboration with the States-General, at any rate for the present. James's advice to Skytte was to enter into direct negotiations with Denmark.[3]

Skytte accordingly returned to Holland in the New Year, having got little out of his trip to England except a Knighthood for himself.[4] His second visit to the Netherlands was mainly taken up with fruitless attempts to induce the States-General to make another loan

---

[1] *ibid.*, pp. 69 *note* 1, 66-80; *AOSB*, II. x. 200-3, 209 *note*, 214-15 *note*; Thyresson, pp. 129-31.
[2] *AOSB*, II. x. 212 *note*.
[3] For Skytte's mission to England, *AOSB*, II. x. 222-42; Hammarstrand, *HF*, pp. 81-100; Thyresson, pp. 133-8; Gardiner, III. 167.
[4] In the meantime Sigismund had offered the Dutch ambassador in Brandenburg an alliance, with valuable trading privileges; but it does not seem that the Dutch took the suggestion seriously. Blok, IV. 70; Vreede, *Nederland en Zweden*, p. 133.

for Älvsborg, and an uphill struggle (in which he was eventually successful) to persuade them that they were bound, in terms of the alliance of 1614, to give assistance to the Kurland expedition. No progress was made towards a decision on the relative merits of a Swedish alliance with Denmark, or a general Protestant League.[1] Already, indeed, Dutch statesmen were veering round to a *rapprochement* with Kristian IV. The Netherlands had heard with concern of the arrival of Spanish and Polish embassies in Copenhagen. With barely three years of the truce with Spain still to run, they were beginning to reflect on the extreme danger to their commerce of a Denmark on terms of friendship with Philip III. Kristian, on his side, was coming to see that he had little chance of making good his designs upon north Germany as long as the Dutch stood in his way; and in any case he was very anxious to wean the States-General from their alliance with Sweden. In January 1618, therefore, Kristian sent Jonas Charisius to The Hague on a mission of good-will; and the Dutch lost no time in returning the compliment by sending the Heer van Culemborg to Copenhagen, with instructions to discuss plans for the foundation of a Danish East India Company. There was talk of a general Protestant League, or a separate Danish-Dutch alliance; but the plan of a general league stranded upon Kristian's refusal to join it unless he were given the direction; and the Dutch, out of consideration for Swedish feelings, rejected the proposal for a separate alliance.[2]

Meanwhile the idea of an alliance between Gustav Adolf and Kristian was still in being; but its chances of crystallizing into something definite appeared to be diminishing. Kristian was remarkably fertile of 'grievances', and equally ready with reasons for postponing the long-expected conference on the border, which was to settle them.[3] As the year 1618 wore on, Gustav Adolf, alarmed by Kristian's negotiations with the Netherlands and the perceptible cooling of Dutch friendship, began to fear that Sweden might once more find herself friendless. If then, upon the payment of the

[1] For Skytte's later negotiations with the Dutch, Hammarstrand, *HF*, pp. 100-110; Thyresson, pp. 141, 145, 156-7; M. G. Schybergson, *Sveriges och Hollands diplomatiska förbindelser*, p. xiii.

[2] Blok, IV. 69; Thyresson, pp. 150-1, 162; Hammarstrand, *HF*, pp. 117-19.

[3] Kristian's 'grievances' included: political libels; non-return of prisoners of war; stoppage of legitimated Danish travellers in Sweden; deeds of violence on the frontier; imposition of tolls on Danish subjects; prohibition of their trading to upland towns; fraudulent declaration of foreign goods as Swedish, to evade the Sound Tolls (Thyresson, pp. 162-5). Sweden's grievances were very similar: see the list in *AOSB*, I. II. 357-9.

final instalment of the indemnity in January 1619, Denmark refused
to fulfil her engagements and restore Älvsborg, what would be his
position, if he could not count on Dutch aid? Throughout the
second half of 1618 his agents were urgently canvassing the
Protestant courts for moral support. The Dutch were asked to use
their influence with James I to persuade him to write to his brother-
in-law of Denmark. Christopher von Dohna, sent to England just
at this time by Frederick V on the business of Bohemia, was charged
with a similar mission. The envoys of Savoy and Venice added
their entreaties: James after all was a guarantor of the peace of
Knäred. It did not need much persuasion to induce James to assume
the part of peace-maker; and he did in fact address a serious warning
to Kristian, which may not have been without its effect. At the
same time Gustav Adolf sent Filip Scheding to north Germany to
ask financial aid of Duke Frederick of Holstein and the Archbishop
of Bremen; he endeavoured, through John Casimir, to obtain the
intervention of the Evangelical Union; and he made efforts to
arrange an alliance with Lübeck, by way of a second line of defence,
should Kristian succeed in seducing the Dutch.[1]

Whether as a result of these measures, or upon the advice of the
pacifically inclined Danish Council, or under the influence of the
Bohemian crisis, Kristian, when the moment arrived for handing
back Älvsborg, agreeably disappointed Gustav Adolf's expectations
and made no sort of difficulty. On the contrary, he agreed at last to
the conference on the border, and invited Gustav Adolf to visit him
in Halmstad when the conference should be concluded. Early in
February 1619, therefore, the negotiators met at Sjöaryd. The
instructions of the Swedish delegation were obviously designed to
test how far Kristian's newly discovered complaisance could be
construed into an expression of Protestant solidarity. Avoiding all
discussion of tedious and petty 'grievances', which might waste the
time and destroy the harmony of the meeting, they came forward
with a clear-cut proposal for an alliance against Sigismund; or, if
this were unacceptable, for an alliance to be directed against all
enemies of Protestantism—it being understood that the arrangement was to be without prejudice to Sweden's existing alliance with
the Dutch. It is possible that Gustav Adolf genuinely hoped to
obtain Kristian's assent to one or other of these propositions; but

[1] Hammarstrand, *HF*, pp. 122-4, 140, 143-4; Thyresson, pp. 167-8, 171,
174-5, 177; Ljung, *Tegel*, p. 57.

it seems more likely that they were put forward as a touchstone of his good faith. At all events, the negotiators were not long in discovering irreconcilable differences, and the conference separated without reaching any decision. At the end of the month Gustav Adolf accepted Kristian's invitation and visited him in Halmstad. At the interviews which followed in the next few days a good deal of superficial cordiality was developed, and each came away with a certain admiration for the other; but the meeting was as barren of solid political results as the Sjöaryd conference which had preceded it.[1]

Nevertheless, the spring of 1619 saw the first real relaxation of tension in Sweden's relations with Denmark since the close of the War of Kalmar. The reconciliation did not go very far; the interminable 'grievances' remained, ready to be disinterred when occasion served; but if there was no real friendship, there was less covert ill-will. The two countries were already rivals for Dutch friendship, and were soon to be so for the friendship of German Protestantism, but these things were not yet matters of serious dispute. Älvsborg had been recovered without another war, and from Gustav Adolf's point of view that was a great gain. The danger of complications with Denmark while Sweden was still weak was now behind him: when next that danger should become acute he would be better able to meet it with confidence. The *détente* with Denmark in 1619, coming after the Truce of Tolsburg and the Peace of Stolbova, marks the end of the triple problem with which the King had been faced on his accession. For the moment he had leisure for the works of peace; and among those which his subjects accounted not least important were the negotiations for a satisfactory marriage.

(vi) *Gustav Adolf's Marriage*

In the summer of 1615 a certain Hieronymus von Birckholtz, a Brandenburger in the pay of Sweden, who was employed on counter-espionage work against Sigismund, contrived a quasi-accidental meeting with Dr. Saffius, physician-in-ordinary to the

---

[1] *AOSB*, II. i. 122, 128, 129; *ibid.*, I. ii. 341, 343-8; Thyresson, pp. 183-4, 186, 189, 191; Ahnlund, *Oxenstierna*, pp. 221-4. There is a good description of the meeting at Halmstad in *Abraham Brahes Tidebok*, pp. 122-9.

Elector of Brandenburg.[1] Through Saffius he was introduced to John Sigismund himself, who asked him many questions about Gustav Adolf, mentioned how much he hoped for Sweden's friendship, but added that his delicate situation in East Prussia unfortunately made it impossible for him to take any overt step for the time being. Not very long afterwards various members of the Elector's court remarked 'casually' to Birckholtz that a marriage between Gustav Adolf and the Elector's eldest unmarried daughter, Maria Eleonora, had much to commend it. It is uncertain whence this idea originated, but it appears at least that Dr. Saffius had predicted that Maria Eleonora would marry a king; that he was anxious to make his prediction good; and that he was from the outset one of the strongest supporters of the match.

When Birckholtz returned to Sweden, he reported his conversations to the government, upon whom they seem to have made some impression. The Queen-Mother was at this time hoping for a marriage between Gustav Adolf and a daughter of Maurice of Hesse-Cassel; but on purely political grounds Gustav Adolf was anxious to draw closer to Brandenburg. Birckholtz was therefore sent back to Germany in 1616 to take further soundings, though with instructions to avoid anything which might give the appearance that Sweden was angling for a Hohenzollern princess. In reality, the King was already interested in the suggestion. Birckholtz did not succeed in meeting John Sigismund until August, and he then found him in very low spirits. The sentence of deprivation recently passed upon William of Kurland—accused, among other things, of intriguing with Sweden—had frightened him. He was disturbed, too, at the state of public opinion in East Prussia, where the Lutheran population had been much upset by the Elector's conversion to Calvinism. He did not wish to lose East Prussia, which had cost him so much effort to gain; and he felt that he had better be careful not to provoke Sigismund by engaging in negotiations with Gustav Adolf. In the privacy of his chamber he could speak brave words of defiance; in his cups he even committed the indiscretion of toasting Maria Eleonora as 'Queen of Sweden'; but extravagances

---

[1] For Gustav Adolf's marriage, and the negotiations that preceded it, see: Hammarstrand, *HF*, pp. 29-42, 130-8, 194-217; Thyresson, pp. 78, 91, 97-8, 200, 226-9, 270; *AOSB*, I. II. 260, 315, 391-3, 399; II. I. 135-46, 149, 152; II. IX. 15; II. X. 211 *note*, 405; Styffe, pp. 336, 473, 485-6; Koser, pp. 381-9; Droysen, I. 102; Vreede, *Nederland en Zweden*, pp. 137-9; G. Irmer, *Hans Georg von Arnim*, pp. 13-18, 21-5, 28-32; Szelągowski, pp. 249-53, 256; Ahnlund, *Gustav Adolf den Store*, pp. 55-104; Wedgwood, p. 115.

such as these brought immediate retribution. The Electress Anna (to quote the Elector himself) 'had a Polish heart'; she feared above all the loss of her native Prussia; and she exercised a merciless marital tyranny over her unfortunate husband. John George of Saxony on one occasion remarked to John Sigismund, in an outburst of what was probably intended for good advice: 'Herr Schwager, Ew. Liebden und ich, wir wollen uns vergleichen, wenn Ew. Liebden Gemahlin nicht wäre. Ich habe auch eine; wenn sie mich aber so tribulierte, wie sie Ew. Liebden zu Zeiten thut, es würden gewiss Maulschellen fallen!' And even Maurice of Hesse-Cassel considered that 'Das muss ein stutzig Weib sein.'

For the present then, the strong-minded Electress interposed an apparently insurmountable obstacle to any progress in the affair; for as the Elector's health deteriorated her influence grew stronger in political matters, and in the autumn of 1617 the Elector was disabled by an apoplectic stroke. He rallied after an interval, and he did not die till Christmastide 1619, but henceforward he counted for little or nothing in the direction of the policy of the Electorate. The heir-apparent, George William, was anxious above all not to prejudice his position with Sigismund, since he must shortly seek investiture for the East Prussian fief. The mad duke, Albert Frederick, was also nearing the end of his long reign (he died in 1618); and it was of the utmost importance to Brandenburg that upon his death the succession of the Electoral line should be acknowledged by Poland. Against these considerations, the personal predilections of John Sigismund—which he now made little attempt to conceal— were of small significance. It was indeed arguable that the hands of the Hohenzollerns might be strengthened at a critical moment by a marriage with Sweden; but to most Brandenburg statesmen—and also to John George of Saxony, whose advice they asked—it seemed rather that Sweden was so weak a power that her support would avail little against Sigismund's anger.[1] Besides, there were other possible suitors: the Prince of Wales was one; young William of Orange was another; while Kristian IV, always anxious to keep Sweden isolated and dependent on Danish good-will, was intriguing

---

[1] John George wrote warningly to John Sigismund in November 1617: 'Wir auch nicht zweifeln, E. L. werde neben dero herzliebsten Gemahlin, wes hierinnen das rathsambste, selbst am beste finden, Insonderheit aber vnd vor allen dingen erwegen, wie gefährlich es itzo vmb das königreich Schweden steht, sowohl wie stark E. L. der Kön. W. inn Polen wegen Preussen verbunden.' A. Fryxell, *Handlingar rörande Sverges Historia*, IV. 12-13.

on behalf of Adolf Frederick of Mecklenburg. There is some reason for thinking that Sigismund III would have been glad of the hand of Maria Eleonora for his son Władysław [1]; and certainly Władysław's name appeared in the list of possible candidates.

Thus the Brandenburg match became another trial of strength between the two branches of the House of Vasa; and though the reign of George William suggests that both Gustav Adolf and Sigismund greatly overrated the political advantages which would accrue from such a marriage, it is intelligible that each should have made strong efforts to thwart the other. Gustav Adolf enlisted the aid of his friends and relations in the Palatinate and Hesse; John Casimir, on his return to Germany from Sweden in 1618, was commissioned to plead his brother-in-law's cause in Berlin; and the Dutch gave diplomatic support. In September 1618, Gustav Adolf, impatient at the slow progress of his agents, toyed with the idea of going to Berlin to plead his cause in person. Under cover of exercising his fleet in naval manœuvres, he sailed across to the Pomeranian coast, and possibly spent a night at Stralsund. He was warned, however, that the moment was not propitious for a visit, and he returned home without having attempted it.

John Casimir, and Gustav Adolf's friends in the Palatinate generally, had by this time abandoned hope of the Hohenzollern marriage. They pressed him to look out for some other suitable princess, and they hinted that the Palatinate House could probably produce a candidate; or failing that, there was the charming (if somewhat youthful) Sibylla Magdalena of Baden-Durlach. To these suggestions Gustav Adolf paid little attention. He had by now decided in his own mind for Maria Eleonora, and he did not mean to confess himself beaten so easily. His visit to Berlin had not been cancelled: it had merely been deferred to a more favourable moment. That moment seemed to have arrived in the summer of 1619. Gustav Horn, who had been sent to the electoral court to urge the alliance, had managed to elicit from John Sigismund (in the absence of his wife) an uncompromising declaration in Gustav Adolf's favour and a recommendation that the marriage should take place as soon as possible. Upon this intimation, Gustav Adolf began making preparations for the wedding. He transferred himself to Kalmar; and he intimated that he hoped in the immediate future to make the journey to Berlin to claim the bride. But he had

[1] Sobieski, *Historja Polski*, pp. 183-4.

M

reckoned without the Electress. Anna considered her husband to be senile, and in a letter to Gustav Adolf's mother she said so; adding that a Swedish marriage would mean the destruction of Brandenburg. And she let it be known that rather than allow Maria Eleonora to marry the King of Sweden she would prefer to see her daughter in the grave. She hoped, however, to avoid the necessity of choosing either of these disagreeable alternatives by accompanying Maria Eleonora upon a visit to her married sister at Wolfenbüttel: there, it was to be presumed, they would both be beyond the reach of the King's importunity.

The death of the old Elector at the end of the year was less of a blow to the friends of Gustav Adolf at Berlin than might have been expected. True, it made it certain that George William, anxious about his investiture, would oppose the match; but on the other hand it freed him from personal responsibility, for the custom in the Hohenzollern family was that the Electress-Dowager, not the new Elector, should have the disposition of her daughters' hands. Now it so happened that Anna and George William were not upon good terms. Anna was a Lutheran; George William was a Calvinist; and Anna, concerned as always for Prussia, would have preferred George William's younger brother Joachim Sigismund (a Lutheran) as Duke of Prussia. George William sought support against his mother from the King of Poland. Anna, in consequence, was less unwilling than before to consider the King of Sweden as a son-in-law. Even Gustav Adolf would be better than Władysław; and it was Władysław that George William seemed now to favour.[1]

In these circumstances Gustav Adolf determined to carry out his intention of visiting Berlin. In the spring of 1620 his confidential agent there, Hans Georg von Arnim, had visited Stockholm to report; and shortly after his return John Casimir also arrived in Sweden. It was quickly decided that Gustav Adolf should accompany his brother-in-law to Germany; that he should travel incognito as one of John Casimir's suite; and that an attempt should be made to arrange an interview with Maria Eleonora.

And so began that romantic journey—'for all the world like a comedy'—which so curiously anticipates the expedition of Charles

---

[1] It was even suggested that Anna engineered the Swedish match in order to compromise George William with Sigismund, so that Prussia could be given to Joachim Sigismund (Koser, p. 388). Poland was trying to create trouble in East Prussia by playing upon the discontent of the Lutherans against the Calvinist Elector.

and Buckingham to Madrid.[1] Maria Eleonora had promised the old
Elector before his death that she would marry no one but the King
of Sweden; and upon Gustav Adolf's appearance in Berlin she
conveniently discovered a violent attachment to him, which he on
his side seems to have reciprocated. The Electress-Dowager was
not so easily gained; and Gustav Adolf received a rebuff which
might have discouraged a less pertinacious suitor. He was probably
aware, however, of Anna's fear that George William might force
Władysław upon her as a son-in-law, and he calculated that, given
time, she might be won over. He therefore left Berlin for a round
tour of the Protestant courts of Germany, with the avowed intention
of looking out for a wife. His departure spurred on his friends in
Berlin—among whom Maria Eleonora herself was now not the least
important—to put pressure on the Electress; and by the time he
had reached Heidelberg she had been definitively converted. All
idea of a marriage with a Palatinate princess was now abandoned;
but Gustav Adolf did not immediately return to Berlin, for he was
finding much to interest him in Germany. He had bribed a priest
at Erfurt to allow him to witness the celebration of the Mass, and
had found his darkest imaginings of Popish mummeries gratifyingly
confirmed. At Heidelberg he held interesting conversations on
tactical questions with John of Nassau. Towards the end of May he
witnessed the crossing of the Rhine at Breisach by the troops of the
League, while the army of the Union lay inactive within striking
distance. It was his intention to attend the meeting of the Union
at Ulm, and to return by way of Bohemia and Lusatia; but the news
from Brandenburg made further delay inadvisable, and by mid-
July he was back at Berlin. The trip had been worth the trouble,
even had the marriage been out of the question. It put Gustav
Adolf personally in touch with some of the statesmen of the
Protestant party of action; it gave him his first view of the German
problem at close range; and it probably left upon his mind a permanent impression of the feebleness, the cross-purposes, the lack of
statesmanship and the military incompetence of the leading
Protestant powers of western Germany. He may well have
reached Berlin with a private resolve to be very certain of his
ground before committing Sweden's slender resources to the
assistance of such feckless and inconsequent champions of the
Protestant cause.

[1] There is a classic first-hand account of the journey in *Johan Hands Dagbok*.

On his return to Berlin he at once interviewed the Electress-Dowager. This time he seems to have captivated her completely. She did, indeed, make some show of resistance; but on the day after his arrival she permitted the formal betrothal to take place; and from that moment she made every effort to hasten on the wedding. When it appeared that there might be difficulty and delay because the corpse of the old Elector was still unburied, she threatened if necessary to bury it on her own responsibility, and 'by force'. George William was fortunately away at Königsberg, and her main concern was to compromise him irrevocably before he could interfere. She succeeded. Maria Eleonora was again sent off to her sister at Wolfenbüttel to be out of the Elector's reach; Anna herself made preparations to accompany her daughter to Sweden, and, when George William refused her money for the journey, plundered the treasury of portable plate to put herself in funds. In September Oxenstierna arrived to fetch the bride; and on 25 November 1620 the wedding was celebrated in Stockholm, the bridegroom manifesting a creditable anxiety to do the thing well.[1] George William was left to make such lame explanations as he could. Sigismund received them badly, and was neither appeased nor convinced; but he had troubles enough on his hands without involving himself in a quarrel with Brandenburg, and to George William's immense relief he abstained from showing his resentment by political reprisals. It seems likely, indeed, that George William had no great objection to the match, provided that he was personally relieved of all responsibility for it; and his expressions of regret may have failed to carry conviction for the very good reason that they were known not to be sincere.[2]

The marriage was not altogether a happy one. Maria Eleonora's devotion to the King was of an almost neurotic vehemence, and her overwhelming possessiveness was a nuisance.[3] Gustav Adolf's long

[1] *AOSB*, II. i. 149, 152, etc.

[2] On the other hand, it is a distortion of the facts to write (as Professor Nowak does): ' Fearing that he would not be permitted to control East Prussia, the new Elector sought to bring pressure on Poland by negotiating with Gustavus Adolphus, who was allowed to marry Mary Eleanor immediately after the Polish defeat at Cecora.' *The Cambridge History of Poland*, I. 472.

[3] For Maria Eleonora, see Ahnlund, *Gustav Adolf den Store*, pp. 93-105; Ogier, pp. 36, 104; *AOSB*, II. i. 669-70; E. Hildebrand, *Kristina*, pp. 8, 113; C. Weibull, *Drottning Christina*, p. 87. Some doubts on the accepted judgment on her are voiced by S. Nilsson in *1634 års regeringsform* (*Scandia*, X. 20). For examples of the problems caused by Gustav Adolf's '*malum domesticum*', see *AOSB*, II. i. 216; II. iii. 115; II. x. 291; *RRP*, II. 88-9; and especially Styffe, p. 546, *AOSB*, II. i. 669-70.

absences on campaign made her miserable, and she grew to hate Sweden because Sweden's interests took her husband away from her. She was in many ways charming, though capricious and inclined to be extravagant; but she was not blessed with brains. She was quite incapable of being of any assistance to her husband. She could not be left as regent during his absences; and Gustav Adolf was so conscious of her incapacity for business or responsibility that he excluded her from the arrangements for a regency after his death, and took care not to leave the education of his daughter to her charge.[1] She failed to give him the son he desired; and her daughter Kristina seems at an early age to have regarded her with a sort of contemptuous pity—in this, as in most things, displaying that odious precocity which was to be so characteristic of her. Upon Gustav Adolf's death Maria Eleonora indulged in the most extravagant and protracted orgies of grief, and conducted herself generally in an unbalanced fashion which culminated in the scandal of her secret flight to Denmark.

If, then, the match left something to be desired in point of domestic felicity, it seemed at first sight to be scarcely more successful as a political speculation. It was not followed, as Gustav Adolf had hoped, by an alliance with Brandenburg: George William was not to be induced to appear openly against his suzerain. Its direct effects on Sweden's position were few and insignificant, and remained so for a decade. Yet in spite of this the marriage was important. It rounded off the first period of the reign. It helped to secure the general recognition of the younger line of Vasa as lawful possessors of the Swedish throne. It marked the entry of Gustav Adolf into German politics. It was, without any doubt, a diplomatic victory over Sigismund III. It was a disappointment to Kristian IV. And it played its part in that drawing together of the German and Polish questions which was to be the main work of Gustav Adolf in the succeeding five or six years, and which was to pave the way for the relief of Stralsund and for the landing at Peenemünde.

[1] Her sister Katherine, who married Bethlen Gabor, was even more unstable in temperament.

CHAPTER V

POLAND AND THE PALATINATE, 1618-26[1]

(i) *The Opening of the Thirty Years' War*

THE Defenestration of Prague (23 May 1618) sent a premonitory shiver down the spines of European statesmen. In itself, the event was not serious enough to have provoked a strong reaction: incidents hardly less grave had jeopardized the peace of Germany, and sometimes broken it, in the half-century since the Peace of Augsburg, without on that account involving all Europe in war. In 1618 there was not one of the greater powers which sought to provoke a conflict, or was particularly anxious to suborn others to fight on its behalf. The Bohemian rebels professed loyalty to Matthias, and probably felt it, despite their rough handling of his ministers; and even after Matthias' death there was more than one occasion upon which it seemed possible that a compromise might be found which would reconcile them to Ferdinand. Yet from Warsaw to London, from Dresden to Madrid, men felt obscurely that they stood at the opening of a tragedy. On the eve of the Defenestration the political atmosphere was already oppressively charged with fear and suspicion: Protestants saw themselves immeshed in Jesuit plots, and scented a design for a Universal Monarchy; Catholics were convinced of the existence of a general Protestant conspiracy to overturn order and good governance, and sweep away monarchy upon a flood of revolutionary and tyrannicide political theory. It mattered little that there was small truth in either belief: the nerves of statesmen were on edge, and when they started at shadows it was no wonder if they reared in violent alarm at the too palpable exploit

---

[1] General Bibliography as for Chapter IV; and add: V.-L. Tapié, *La politique étrangère de la France et le debut de la guerre de trente ans*; G. Hanotaux, *Histoire du Cardinal de Richelieu*, III.-IV.; W. Mommsen, *Kardinal Richelieu. Seine Politik im Elsass und in Lothringen*; A. Rydfors, *De diplomatiska förbindelserna mellan Sverige och England*; G. Ericsson, *Gustav II Adolf och Sigismund, 1621-1623*; J. A. Fridericia, *Danmarks ydre politiske Historie*, I.; C. Wibling, *Sveriges förhållande till Siebenbürgen*; D. Angyal, *Gabriel Bethlen*; H. Hallwich, *Fünf Bücher Geschichte Wallensteins*, I.-III.; H. Wertheim, *Der toller Halberstädter*, I.-II.; G. Pagès, *La Guerre de Trente Ans*; C. V. Wedgwood, *The Thirty Years' War*; A. Szelągowski, *Sprawa północna w wiekach XVI i XVII*, III.: *O Ujście Wisły.*

of Thurn and his confederates. All thinking men feared that the expiry of Spain's truce with the Dutch in 1621 must probably give the signal for a general European war; and many doubted if the peace could last so long.

This was especially true of the German states, for to them the Bohemian affair was really of the first importance. Upon the issue of the quarrel with Habsburg hung the disposal of the crown of St. Wenceslas, and hence the result of the approaching Imperial election, where the Bohemian vote might well be decisive; and upon the election depended the religious, and perhaps the political, future of Germany. If Ferdinand were to recover Prague, were to obtain the Empire, were to abrogate the Letter of Majesty in which Rudolf had guaranteed the peculiar rights of the Protestant majority in Bohemia—then Germany might expect an intensification of Rome's efforts to make good her earlier losses. The Calvinists, excluded as they were from such protection as the Peace of Augsburg was supposed to afford, might look forward to no mercy; and even those north German Lutherans who in more expansive days had blithely secularized one church property after another, without much regard for the true meaning of the Ecclesiastical Reservation—even they might possibly feel the ground hot beneath their feet. Unfortunately for Germany, some at least of the German Calvinists had developed, in the state of religious outlawry in which they stood, the outlaw's contempt for legality, the outlaw's recklessness and violence, the outlaw's desperation. Christian of Anhalt, or the Margrave of Ansbach, had no compunction in overturning a world in which their own footing was anything but secure, and they laid hold of the levers for their enterprise wherever opportunity seemed to offer. The foolish ambitions of Charles Emmanuel I of Savoy, and his desire to avenge his recent defeat by the Habsburgs in Italy, gave them an ally as irresponsible as themselves. Dark compacts were concluded to secure the election of Charles Emmanuel, now to the throne of Bohemia, now to the Empire itself; Savoyard mercenaries under Mansfeld were transferred to the service of the Bohemian rebels; and evangelical agents were set to work in England, in Holland, in Venice, in France—at any court, in fact, which from Protestant connection or hatred of Habsburg seemed likely to offer any sort of assistance.

These diplomatic fumblings, ineffectual at first, became serious as events in Bohemia moved from one climax to another. The death of Matthias, the deposition of Ferdinand by his new Bohemian subjects, the election of Frederick V of the Palatinate to the Bohemian crown—followed, two days later, by the election of Ferdinand to the Empire—these were stages in a crisis which, as it deepened, made it increasingly difficult for any state, however pacific, to maintain a perfect detachment. By the beginning of 1620 it was plain that the European powers were grouping themselves into two camps, Catholic and Protestant, for Habsburg or against. Sigismund III, who had once before helped the Habsburgs to deal with their refractory subjects, stood firm by his alliance with Ferdinand, permitted the recruiting of Cossacks for the Imperial army, and menaced the King of Bohemia in flank and rear.[1] The Catholic League, which since 1616 had been in a state of suspended animation, was revived and reconstituted at the end of 1618 under the leadership of Bavaria on a more strictly confessional basis; and already in October 1619 Maximilian had obtained from Ferdinand a promise of the transference of Frederick's electorate to the younger line of Wittelsbach. In the background, lumbering hesitantly into action, was the soft bulk of Spain. Philip III—or rather Oñate, his arrogant and enterprising ambassador at Vienna—had sought as early as 1617 to turn the succession of Ferdinand to Spain's advantage. In that year the agreements of Graz and Prague had promised Spain the Habsburg lands in Alsace in return for her aid in the forthcoming Imperial election.[2] No acquisition could have been more welcome, and none, to Spain's over-anxious statesmen, more necessary to her safety. The bargain of Prague had not yet been fulfilled, and was destined never to be completed; but in the meantime Spain could not be indifferent to the possibility of warfare in the Rhenish Palatinate. If Frederick were to be extruded from his hereditary dominions, it must be by Spanish forces, not by Bavarian: rather than see Maximilian in Heidelberg, Spanish statesmen were almost prepared for a restoration of Frederick's line. Spain, then, must help her cousins at Vienna, lest Bavaria establish too long a credit and appear too plainly as the Emperor's saviour. Besides, any intervention by Savoy would constitute a threat to Spain's life-line by Genoa and the Valtelline to Franche-Comté. Philip III and Ferdinand had only recently concluded a quad-

---

[1] Ritter, III. 64.
[2] The importance attributed to these Treaties by W. Platzhoff (*Europäisches Staatensystem 1559-1660*, p. 149) seems, however, exaggerated.

rangular struggle against Savoy and Venice; in Italy their interests were complementary, if not identical; to both of them it was a principle of politics to keep open the roads running north and north-east over the Alpine passes from Genoa.

On the other side the Palatinate party was feverishly angling for allies. The Dutch made no difficulty about giving substantial financial support. Alone of all the states of Europe, the United Provinces fervently desired a major war in Germany. Their truce with Spain was to end in 1621, and there was everything to be said for diverting Spinola's armies away from the territories of the Republic and committing them to a struggle on the middle Rhine.[1] Early in 1620 the Dutch prepared the way (as they hoped) for yet another diversion, by an alliance with Venice, who only two years before had terminated her war with Ferdinand by a treaty at Madrid. Frederick V might also expect some help, perhaps, from the turbulence of the Huguenots and from the ambitions of the Duke of Bouillon.[2] At the other end of Europe Bethlen Gabor, the Prince of Transylvania, was prepared to show Protestant solidarity for so long as the weakness of the Habsburgs provided an opportunity for loot. Behind him lay his master the Sultan; and in view of past history the Palatine party would probably not be squeamish in accepting any diversion that might be contrived from that quarter, if the Turks could be induced to violate the peace of Zsitva-Török. In Germany itself the Evangelical Union still existed, though its unity was less evident in practice than Anhalt could have wished; and for the time being it was more forward in its preparations than was the League. But the Union needed a patron, and Frederick needed an ally, more reliable than Bethlen Gabor, and more mobile, in a military point of view, than the Dutch. For the Bohemian cause much would depend on the attitude of England and of France.

James I saw fairly clearly that the crisis was political as well as religious; and though paternal feeling and Protestant zeal might incline him to appear actively on the side of the Palatine, he could not subscribe to the political principles which lay behind the Bohemian revolt or condone the contempt for legality which marked Frederick's conduct throughout the whole affair. An ignorant and obstreperous Parliament, exacerbated by misgovernment and petty

---

[1] Tapié, p. 387; Wedgwood, p. 110; Gardiner, III. 310; van Veen, *Louis de Geer*, p. 22; Hammarstrand, *HF*, p. 220.
[2] Tapié, pp. 396-7.

tyrannies, thought only of a freebooting war in the old style and kept a tight grip on supplies.[1] The King, believing too readily that with good-will and wise guidance the discords of Europe might be composed, perceiving too the mixed feelings with which Spain regarded the fate of the Palatinate, revived a project recently dormant, and sought by a Spanish marriage for the Prince of Wales to enlist the aid of Madrid in imposing peace on the disputants. But his policy was too variable, too incoherent, and too full of irreconcilable means and diametrically opposed ends to be of much assistance to his son-in-law.

Still less could Frederick count on France. Henri IV, of glorious memory, had no doubt in a sense been the patron of the Union; and since the two-facedness of Henri's foreign policy was imperfectly known in Germany, the members of the Union were from their point of view justified in appealing to Louis XIII to return to the tradition of his father. But Richelieu and Villeroy and Puysieulx, who successively managed French foreign policy after 1616, could claim with perfect justice to find very different principles of action in the preceding reign.[2] And apart altogether from any argument about Henri IV, it was the opinion of most French statesmen that the Spanish alliance was necessary to France. It was not wholly agreeable, of course: there were clashes of interest in Mantua and Savoy and Switzerland; but it gave a measure of security at a period when the domestic situation was repeatedly disturbed. This was no time for an adventurous statesmanship. Nor was it a time to encourage religious dissidents and their foreign allies, when at any moment the Huguenots might challenge the authority of the central government.[3] Roman Catholicism in France was just now experiencing a sudden quickening of the spirit,[4] and Louis XIII himself had a piety such as his father would have found an encumbrance. French foreign policy was thus Catholic by conviction, and France's attitude to Frederick's Bohemian adventure was one of cool disapproval. But it was not only Catholic: it was Imperialist.

---

[1] cf. Gardiner, IV. 35: 'To them every Protestant was a model of saintly virtue; every Catholic a dark conspirator against the peace and religion of the world. Of the weakness and rashness of Frederick, of the low intrigues by which his election had been preceded, of the anarchical character of the Bohemian aristocracy, they had simply no conception whatever.'

[2] Tapié, pp. 14-15, 26: 'On gémissait ensemble sur l'abandon de la politique de Henri IV, qu'on disait si nette, si franche (alors qu'elle avait été on ne peut plus souple, ingrate et retorse). . . .' And see ibid., p. 220.

[3] ibid., pp. 171, 233-5, 238-9.

[4] There is a recent popular treatment of this religious movement in A. Huxley, Grey Eminence.

From the beginning France had favoured Ferdinand's candidature for the Empire, if only as a preferable alternative to that of Philip III. To the Union she had given warnings rather than encouragement, and to Ferdinand's appeals she had listened with obvious sympathy. At first, the French ministers had contented themselves with watching the conflict in central Europe from afar; but at Christmas 1619 Louis XIII, in a sudden access of religious enthusiasm, explicitly committed himself to the despatch of armed assistance to the hard-pressed Emperor. It looked for a moment as though France, by prompt succour, might steal a march on Spain and Bavaria alike, and stand forth as the effective leader of the Catholic coalition.[1] This, however, did not happen. Once the fervid moment was past, the King (and still more his ministers) relapsed into expressions of sympathy and offers of mediation. The French troops dallied, and soon were countermanded; and France, like England, confined her exertions to the despatch of embassies impotent to affect the course of events. Nevertheless, French support, for what it was worth, went decidedly to the Imperialists; and though the Valtelline caused friction with Spain in 1621, the old policy of exploiting the discontents of Protestant Germany to weaken the House of Habsburg was quite abandoned. The hour of Richelieu had not yet struck.[2]

Frederick V, if he had been more clear-sighted, might thus early have abandoned hope of rescue by England or France. In Lutheran Germany was no hope from the beginning. John George of Saxony was scandalized by the violence of the Bohemian rebels and shocked at Frederick's acceptance of the crown; and his influential court-chaplain, Hoë von Hoënegg, heard with deep indignation of the iconoclastic orgies of the Calvinist dominies in Prague.[3] By the agreement of Mühlhausen (March 1620), John George ranged himself solidly behind the Emperor in the struggle to maintain the political decencies, and made no bones about joining with Maximilian of Bavaria in executing the Imperial Ban upon Frederick.[4] But Lutheranism was not everywhere so rigid as

---

[1] Hammarstrand, HF, p. 234; Tapié, pp. 430, 455, 459.

[2] Mariéjol, p. 211, G. Hanotaux, Richelieu, II. 509, for the usual condemnation of French foreign policy in this period: contrast Tapié, passim, and see Mommsen, p. 18, and Gardiner, III. 388-9.

[3] Gardiner, IV. 173-4; Tapié, pp. 471, 487-8.

[4] Ferdinand agreed to guarantee that the secularized bishoprics of the Upper Saxon Circle should not be interfered with as long as their holders remained loyal. Thyresson, pp. 219-22; Wedgwood, pp. 107-8.

in Dresden: at Copenhagen and Stockholm a Calvinist, though reprehended, was at least regarded as preferable to a Papist. What hope had Frederick of effectual aid from Scandinavia?

To Gustav Adolf, as to James I, the Bohemian question could not fail to be interesting on purely dynastic grounds. Through his brother-in-law John Casimir he was kept informed of the progress of events in Germany; and in return John Casimir was provided with information for dissemination in that country, so that he became for a time a most valuable member of Sweden's propaganda service.[1] John Casimir kept him in touch not only with Frederick but with members of the Union, and Ludwig Camerarius, one of the most important of Frederick's ministers, was induced to accept a Swedish pension, together with a 'contrefaict' of Gustav Adolf, and the promise of a consignment of furs to follow.[2] As early as November 1619 Gustav Adolf sent Rutgers to Prague with the request that he might be allowed to remain as resident agent.[3] The Swedish government was consequently better informed about the real state of affairs in Bohemia than, for instance, the government of Louis XIII, which had no permanent representative at Frederick's court. But the dynastic link between Gustav Adolf and Frederick was after all a somewhat tenuous one; and Gustav Adolf never felt the strong personal interest in the fortunes of the Palatine House which was natural enough in James I and Charles I. Nevertheless, he early recognized the gravity of the situation in central Europe, and diagnosed it as inaugurating the politico-religious crisis which, in common with many other statesmen, he had been expecting for some years. For Sweden, indeed, the struggle lay as yet only on the periphery of her sphere of interest; and to Gustav Adolf the Bohemian troubles appeared first and foremost as an extension of his struggle with Poland, to be handled according to their probable effect upon that struggle.[4] It is noteworthy that in the instructions for Oxenstierna upon the occasion of the frontier meeting with Denmark at Sjöaryd at the beginning of 1619 the object to be aimed at is defined as a defensive alliance with Denmark against Poland. There is not a word of the troubles in central Europe, and Bohemia is mentioned only as one of a number of countries (including

[1] *AOSB*, II. x. 398-401, 412, 418; Hammarstrand, *HF*, pp. 144-6.
[2] Droysen, I. 130; Hammarstrand, *HF*, p. 162; *AOSB*, I. ii. 373 *note*; II. i. 150.
[3] Styffe, p. 317; Droysen, I. 135-6; Tapié, p. 187.
[4] The Dutch, *mutatis mutandis*, took much the same line.

Russia!) which have recently been menaced by Jesuit 'practices'.[1]

This was no doubt a somewhat narrow and parochial outlook; but it had some justification in the news which came to Sweden of the exploits and projects of the sinister Altheim Order. At the time of the Defenestration Altheim was reported by John Casimir as being busy with recruiting, and the object of his levies was still reputed to be Sweden.[2] A little later the rumour ran round Protestant Germany that the Bohemian rebels had secured proof that the Jesuits had been planning a general massacre of Protestants, and that the execution of this godly work was to have been entrusted to Altheim and his knights.[3] Before the end of 1618 came a development which was not rumour at all but hard fact, and which seemed to justify those who had always contended that the danger from Altheim was anything but chimerical. For some years the pious but unstable Duke of Nevers had been dreaming of a Crusade against the Moslems, and since 1615 he had been in touch with Altheim through Dampierre, a mercenary commander in Habsburg service. Nevers had founded a crusading Order of his own in 1616; and plans for the Holy War, with a Rule for the Order, had been drawn up by no less a person than Father Joseph. Altheim himself had meanwhile made direct approaches to Louis XIII, and early in 1618 had received a non-committal but encouraging reply. Later in the year Nevers, with Louis XIII's approval, set out for Vienna and Warsaw on an exploratory tour; and though for some reason which is obscure he failed to reach Warsaw, his mission was a decided success. In November 1618 he had a meeting with Altheim at Olmütz at which one Petrignani, the head of an Italian analogue of Nevers' Order, was also present. The upshot of their talks was the fusion of all three Orders into one, to be called 'The Order of the Chevaliers of the Soldiers of Christ, under the protection of Our Lady and St. Michael'. On All Saints' Day 1619 the consolidated Order held its first Chapter in Nevers Cathedral, Father Joseph preaching the sermon upon the occasion. Membership was restricted to those who could show four quarters of nobility, but this limitation by no means implied that the forces at the disposal of the Order would be small. Its members were wealthy, and were well able to hire mercenaries. Nevers boasted of being able to raise 6000 foot and

---

[1] *AOSB*, II. i. 121 *seqq*.

[2] *AOSB*, II. x. 401: '. . . die Altheimische werbung fortgehet, undt ausstrück-lich auf Schweden, dahin dann sein angefangenen order gerichtet.'

[3] Tapié, p. 228.

2000 horse in France alone, and hoped eventually to have a total of 50,000; in 1619 the Order handed over 200,000 écus as a donation to the Habsburg war-chest; while Altheim seemed to have no difficulty in levying Cossacks in Poland for the Imperial service.[1] Naturally Ferdinand II, whose position in 1619 more than once seemed desperate, welcomed the foundation of the Order with enthusiasm; and naturally Gustav Adolf saw in this menacing expansion of its activities the confirmation of his worst fears. For a moment, the Order came near to being an international power. And Swedish statesmen could not forget that this power had developed from an organization which had been created with the express purpose of replacing Sigismund III on the throne of Sweden and bringing back that country to the Roman Catholic religion. Thus the Thirty Years' War, in its opening phases, inevitably appeared to Gustav Adolf as an aspect of his war with Poland—an affair in which great religious issues were involved, but also an affair which was linked, in more ways than one, with Sweden's temporal interests.

Such, then, were the general considerations which guided Gustav Adolf and Oxenstierna in their dealings with Frederick V and the Evangelical Union. At first, there can be no doubt, Gustav Adolf would have been glad of an alliance both with the Union and with the King of Bohemia. Like Maurice of Hesse-Cassel, he hoped for a general evangelical league which should include Lutherans and Calvinists, Germans and non-Germans, and link Protestants everywhere in one single struggle.[2] He would have welcomed an embassy from the Union, and an invitation to join in such an alliance.[3] Hitherto, however, he had been disappointed by the caution and indecision of the evangelical party.[4] The Union, formidable as it might appear to its Catholic adversaries, was in reality far from

---

[1] Tapié, pp. 279-85, 305, 401, 408-9, 452 note; AOSB, II. x. 403, 422: '... der von Nevers ... dem hauss Österreich so zu sagen verbunden, auch ahnjezo einer von der principalen des Altheimischen Ordens (welcher orden directe auf recuperation Schweden gerichtet)'; A. Boëthius, Romanus Nicephori och Gustaf Adolf (HT 1912), pp. 298-9; L. Dedouvres, Le Père Joseph de Paris, I. 356-78, 390-5, 400, 417, 418 note 3, 419-23.

[2] Ritter, III. 33-4; Hammarstrand, HF, p. 150; Droysen, I. 129, 131. But it is impossible to endorse Droysen's comment: 'es ist die Idee eines grossen evangelischen Bundes, für die Gustaf Adolf hier zum ersten Mal mit Eifer auftritt.'

[3] Hammarstrand, Historisk Öfversigt af förhandlingarne mellan Konung Gustaf II Adolf af Sverige och Kurfursten Fredrik V af Pfalz, åren 1618-1620 (cited as Hammarstrand, Öfversigt), pp. 11-13, 27-31, 36; Hammarstrand, HF, pp. 140, 146.

[4] Rutgers wrote of the Princes: 'Sunt enim Germani, qui ob nugas longe consultant, ut semel dicant NON': Hammarstrand, Bidrag, p. 8 note.

being a strong and coherent political system. It was deeply divided between a party of adventure, headed by Anhalt and Ansbach, and a more conservative section represented by Württemberg and the Imperial Cities, with Maurice of Hesse-Cassel occupying a middle position between these extremes. Both Maurice and the Cities were anxious to preserve Germany as far as possible from foreign interference; and it was this desire, among other reasons, which made them so impervious to Gustav Adolf's hints that he would not be unwilling to become a member. They sent him no invitation to attend the *Korrespondenztag* appointed to meet at Nuremberg in December 1619, though they took care to ask Kristian IV, as a member of the Lower Saxon Circle.[1] Instead, they sent him a letter expressing their hope that he could be counted on for 'real aid' if it should be required. But already the Union was drifting into a position in which aid, however real, would avail them nothing. The election of Frederick to the crown of Bohemia brought into the open the latent divisions among them; and the Nuremberg *Korrespondenztag* revealed only too plainly the paralysis which was creeping over the former 'party of action'. Frederick was left to sink or swim, as it might happen; and the Union formally washed its hands of Bohemian affairs. In the words of a later historian, 'not action but transaction' seemed now the aim of the assembled princes.[2] The Union was playing for safety.

These developments had at least the effect of stimulating Frederick's interest in Sweden. Hitherto he had appeared somewhat indifferent, and Camerarius had been unable to induce him to undertake the expense of sending an embassy to Stockholm in proper form.[3] Soon after his election, however, he wrote to Gustav Adolf, explaining that he had not sought the Bohemian crown, and asking in general terms for support.[4] Gustav Adolf's reply was cordial, but promised direct assistance only when he should be quit of the war in Poland. In the meantime (in November 1619) Rutgers had been sent on his mission to Prague. The ostensible purpose of this mission was to congratulate Frederick on his election; its real object was to obtain reliable information as to the condition of affairs in Bohemia. Rutgers was ordered to take Dresden in his

---

[1] Hammarstrand, *HF*, pp. 151-2; Thyresson, p. 203; Tapié, pp. 358-61.
[2] 'Ej handla, blott underhandla': Hammarstrand, *HF*, pp. 166-7; Gardiner, III. 316; Ritter, III. 69; Tapié, pp. 421-3.
[3] Hammarstrand, *HF*, pp. 143-5.
[4] Thyresson, p. 206; Droysen, I. 132-3; Hammarstrand, *HF*, pp. 164-5.

road, and there to remonstrate with John George on the impropriety of his collaboration with the Emperor.[1] The Elector, as might have been expected, took this remonstrance badly. It was the beginning of those uneasy and often strained relations with Saxony which were to handicap Gustav Adolf at intervals for the rest of his life.

Thus far, it is clear, Gustav Adolf had been ready to entertain the idea of an alliance with the Union, and even with Frederick. But with the opening of 1620 comes a sharp change in tone. On 25 January he writes to John Casimir in terms of almost petulant complaint. It is all very well (he points out) for John Casimir to talk of striking while the iron is hot. He for his part has been willing enough, but he has had little encouragement from Frederick, except in the vaguest and most general terms. No Protestant hand has been raised to aid him in his own fight against Sigismund, and for years he has been left to fend for himself 'gleichsam als vnther den wolfwen'. The Palatine alliance is not a necessity to him, and he has no intention of making his friendship cheap by soliciting it. Nevertheless, should Frederick propose reasonable terms, he is ready to consider them.[2] Oxenstierna's letter to John Casimir of 4 February, and the simultaneous instructions to Rutgers, show similar unmistakable signs of a revision of policy. Rutgers is directed to confine himself to vague tenders of good offices, and to avoid the question of an alliance. To John Casimir, Oxenstierna makes offers so clogged with conditions as to become almost derisory. If the Poles decline the amended truce which Sweden will propose to them; and if both Frederick *and* the Union send an embassy timeously to Stockholm in due form, charged to solicit an alliance; and if, finally, James I and the Dutch can be got to plead with Gustav Adolf to join such an alliance (and hence make themselves more or less responsible for assisting Sweden if things should go wrong)—if all these conditions are fulfilled, then Sweden will give Frederick active assistance.[3] It is scarcely probable that even an incorrigible optimist like Frederick V can have conceived any very high hopes of penetrating this zareba of preconditions.

Nevertheless, Frederick was not prepared to lose Swedish aid

---

[1] Hammarstrand, *HF*, pp. 168-78; Thyresson, p. 212; Styffe, pp. 317-19: Gustav Adolf wrote to John Casimir: 'ich habe ihm bevolen zu einickeit zue raathen; sorge aber er wirdt nicht wilkummen sein, ich aber thue mein devoyr.'
[2] Styffe, pp. 320-5.
[3] *AOSB*, I. II. 368-73, 375; Thyresson, pp. 213-17; Hammarstrand, *HF*, pp. 179-82, 242, 245. Contrast Droysen's view: *op. cit.*, I. 137-8.

for want of asking; and in the spring of 1620 he sent John Casimir to Stockholm to get what terms he could. John Casimir landed early in March 1620, about the time when a Polish embassy of unusual magnificence was being received in Dresden.[1] He asked of Gustav Adolf an army, money to pay it, and an alliance: he returned to Germany with a promise of 8 guns and 500 rounds apiece—provided that Frederick arranged to have them fetched from Stettin.[2] Not a man, not an *öre*, were to be made available for Frederick to squander. In a letter to Rutgers of 7 May 1620, Oxenstierna explained this tight-fistedness. Sweden, he wrote, was too poor in resources, too exhausted by continual warfare, to lavish men and money on the needs of others. Moreover, before entering into any arrangement of the kind John Casimir had proposed, he would require much fuller information about the present state and future prospects of Bohemia. And thirdly, the approach had been somewhat informal, the proposals lacking in precision: if Frederick wanted assistance and an alliance, let him ask for it in regular form.[3]

It is not difficult to conjecture the motives which prompted this change of front. It was quite true that Sweden needed an interval of repose: the years from 1618 to 1621 proved to be of the utmost importance for her internal development, precisely because the King for the first time since his accession was able to devote himself almost uninterruptedly to domestic affairs. But this consideration might have been waived in the interests of the Protestant cause, and of Sweden's own external position, had circumstances seemed to justify the sacrifice. Gustav Adolf was ready, in certain eventualities, to assist in the defence of evangelical religion by renewing the war in Poland. It had always been his contention that the struggle with Sigismund was part of a wider struggle against Catholicism, and events had clearly proved him right. Therefore he was prepared, if reasonable security could be had, to renew his attack on Livonia: his war with Sigismund would thus be, for the German Protestants, what he had always insisted that it was—a *diversion*. More than this, in a military sense, could not be expected of him: there were plenty of Protestant princes near to the scene of action in Germany who were much better able to offer direct aid. But even so much would be inconvenient, at a moment when a period of peace was needed

---

[1] *AOSB*, II. x. 436; *Abraham Brahes Tidebok*, p. 133.
[2] *AOSB*, II. i. 147; II. x. 439; Hammarstrand, *HF*, pp. 185-93; Hallenberg, IV. 790.
[3] *AOSB*, I. ii. 383.

to develop the first instalment of important reforms. Therefore, before he committed himself to another campaign against Poland, he must have reasonable assurance that he would not be left to bear a disproportionate burden, or even, perhaps, be left in the lurch altogether owing to the weakness or incompetence of his allies. By the spring of 1620 the prospects of getting such an assurance were fading. Britain and France were unlikely to give any effective aid; the Dutch would soon have their own battles to fight. The feebleness of the Union had appeared at the Nuremberg *Korrespondenztag*; and in any case it was fairly obvious that the Union did not want a Swedish alliance. Gustav Adolf would be reduced, then, to an alliance with Frederick V and his Bohemian subjects. It was a prospect which might well give pause to any statesman. The disorganization of Frederick's government, the indiscipline of his mercenary army, the blunders in his treatment of the Moravians, the selfishness and lethargy of the Bohemian nobility, the tangle of petty jealousies which paralysed all military effort[1]—these things must discourage even the most sanguine. Again, a renewal of the war with Poland might have presented less risk if the Tsar could have been induced to enter it on Sweden's side. An approach had been made to him in August 1619[2]; but the interminable epilogues to the Treaty of Stolbova were still dragging on; a final delimitation of the new frontier had not yet been agreed upon; and at the end of May 1620 the Russians rejected the suggestion of an alliance.[3] The spring and summer of this year saw Gustav Adolf increasingly occupied with his pursuit of Maria Eleonora, and the outbreak of war would probably have meant the postponement of a marriage which in the opinion of his subjects was already much overdue. And finally it was undoubtedly true that Frederick, like the Union, had been backward in making serious overtures in proper form, and it is quite possible that Gustav Adolf took umbrage at what he considered to be a slight.

It is at all events clear that there were cogent reasons for avoiding any commitments to Bohemia; and the events of the summer proved that they were well founded. In July French mediation succeeded in arranging the Treaty of Ulm between the Union and the League.[4] From that moment the Union ceased to count in the affairs of

---

[1] Tapié, pp. 260-1, 543-52.
[2] Thyresson, p. 211; Droysen, I. 142.
[3] *AOSB*, I. II. 384; Hallenberg, IV. 744-8, 762-82, 787.
[4] Tapié, pp. 509-12; Gardiner, III. 364; Ritter, III. 95; Pagès, p. 76.

Germany, and its dissolution became a mere question of time. And this occurred at a moment when Spinola was winning victory after victory in the Rhineland. As 'Captain Gars'[1] made his tour through Germany and observed at close quarters the condition of the Palatine party, he can hardly have failed to congratulate himself upon his caution; and it is not to be wondered at that he should have avoided a meeting with Frederick V. In vain did John Casimir pointedly inform Oxenstierna of the monetary aid supplied (at the instance of Anstruther) by Kristian IV: the hint was blandly ignored.[2] As the fortunes of the Palatine House darkened with the coming of autumn, Gustav Adolf renewed, in still more pressing terms, an invitation to John Casimir and his wife to seek asylum in Sweden[3]; while Oxenstierna was full of sympathy in reply to the lamentations which came, ever more clamant, from Kleeburg or Prague; but Sweden had taken her decision, and the catastrophe now plainly imminent in Bohemia was but another reason for not departing from it.[4] When Frederick's throne was tottering—and still more, when the battle of the White Hill had been fought and lost—no diversion in Livonia was going to be of any service to anyone. But if Gustaf Adolf thus resolutely held aloof, neither he nor Oxenstierna was under any illusions as to the nature of the tragedy, or the extent of the danger, that now threatened Germany. When in September 1620 the Chancellor went to Wolfenbüttel to fetch home Maria Eleonora, he was shocked at the pusillanimity and wilful blindness of many of the north German princes; and he wrote to Rutgers that the day might well come when Gustav Adolf would be forced to intervene.[5]

In the meantime, he got little encouragement when he put out feelers about the possibility of a north German league under Swedish leadership. This was an idea which had been in the air

---

[1] 'Captain Gars' was the name assumed by Gustav Adolf on his visit to Germany in 1620. It was derived from the initial letters of his name and title: *Gustav Adolf Rex Sueciae.*

[2] *AOSB*, II. x. 445; Gardiner, III. 386; Hill, p. 89.

[3] *AOSB*, II. x. 448; Styffe, p. 337; and see Styffe, p. 343.

[4] Hammarstrand, *HF*, pp. 246-7. Gustav Adolf's remedy for the state of the evangelical cause was neither helpful nor characteristic: he recommended making a clearance of Roman Catholic priests. 'Vor war es ist itz nicht die zeit civiliter zu procedieren, dan im bürgerliche krige ist kein vnsicherer wegh zu nehmmen als der mittel wegh.' Styffe, p. 332.

[5] *AOSB*, I. II. 401-3: 'Plerique mihi videntur his in locis neutralitatem ut tutissimam colere; quam consulto, ipsi videant. Verum vix est remedio locus, cum in imperio nullum sit imperium, nullum obsequium, nulla vis, nullum denique publicae rei studium.'

since the summer of 1619, when an embassy from Lübeck had come to Stockholm to explore the possibilities of an alliance between Gustav Adolf and the Hanse. The suggestion seems in the first place to have come from Sweden, and though Lübeck was not unwilling, the other Hanse towns—notably Hamburg—had made difficulties, and the project had been abandoned. The scheme was now revived, and was linked up with another project of a similar nature. In 1619 Gustav Adolf had been inciting his maternal uncle, Archbishop John Frederick of Bremen, to form a north German league as a defence against Kristian IV's designs upon the secularized bishoprics of that area, and had declared himself willing to give any such alliance the backing of Sweden. He now suggested to the Hanse the conclusion of a double treaty. On the one hand there was to be commercial agreement between the Hanse towns and Sweden; on the other a general league, to include John Frederick of Bremen and the Dukes of Mecklenburg and Holstein, as well as the Hanseatic members. The league was to be defensive, but with a point against Poland and Denmark, and Gustav Adolf indicated that he was willing to assume a sort of general patronage and *Directorium* over it. Nobody seemed very anxious to conclude upon these terms, for the war with Poland was bad for trade, and the mercantile community did not wish to see it prolonged. Nevertheless the episode has a certain interest; for it marks the first independent attempt by Sweden to form a party of her own among the states of Germany.[1]

On 8 November 1620 was fought the disastrous battle of the White Hill; and in December Frederick, already a fugitive in Silesia, abandoned his subjects to their fate, and made the best of his way, *via* Berlin, to the Netherlands. He lost no time in appealing to Gustav Adolf for succour[2]; and his appeal was seconded by the moribund Union, which in December met at Worms. These belated cries for help were not very likely to produce a positive response from Sweden. In Bohemia the battle was irretrievably lost; and no 'diversion' by way of a Swedish attack on Sigismund III would make any difference here; while to aid Frederick in his hereditary dominions, or give effective assistance to the Union, was made impossible by the hard facts of geography. And in any case

---

[1] Ahnlund, *Gustaf II Adolf och tyska kriget 1620-1625* (*HT* 1917), pp. 252-3; Paul, I. 130-1; Thyresson, pp. 195, 269, 295-6; Styffe, pp. 389-400; V. Schweitzer, *Christian IV von Dänemark und die neiderdeutschen Städte*, p. 117.
[2] Cronholm, I. 369.

Gustav Adolf is not likely to have had any mind to champion lost causes, or buttress crumbling political edifices. The publication of the Imperial Ban against the leaders of the Palatine party, in January 1621, meant that any attempt at intervention would meet with active resistance by John George of Saxony, who, with Maximilian of Bavaria, was entrusted with the Ban's execution. When in February 1621 the Union met at Heilbronn, and invited Gustav Adolf to 'intercede' for them with the Emperor, or failing success in that, to help them in arms,[1] they must have realized that their best chance of aid from this quarter was gone already.

At this moment, when it had become plain that nothing was to be hoped from Sweden, the friends of the Palatine were heartened by the prospect of intervention by Kristian IV. Just as Gustav Adolf looked at the Bohemian question in the light of his struggle with Sigismund III, so Kristian tended to view it in the context of his dynastic ambitions in north Germany. He was indeed connected by marriage with James I, and hence with the Palatine, and Christian of Brunswick was his nephew; but he did not allow these considerations to influence his policy much. There had been a moment, in the spring of 1619, when rumour spoke of him as a possibility for the Bohemian throne[2]; but though Kristian's foreign policy often (in the opinion of his Council) erred on the side of rashness, it nearly always bore a real relation to the solid interests of his dominions. In 1618 and 1619 he was mainly concerned to use the German crisis to enforce his claim of overlordship upon Hamburg; to secure the coadjutorship of Bremen to his son Fredrik; and to wean the Dutch from their dangerous friendship with Sweden. By the close of 1621 he had accomplished all these objects. In the meantime he gave little encouragement to Frederick V. An embassy from Bohemia which reached Copenhagen in January 1620 was coolly received, and in February his Council advised Kristian against any attempt to champion the Protestant cause.[3] He did indeed lend the Palatine money, at the solicitation, and on the somewhat dubious security, of James I; but he did so mainly because he desired English diplomatic aid. James, in return for the loan, was expected to put pressure on the Dutch to acquiesce in Danish

---

[1] Hallenberg, V. 81-2; *cf.* Styffe, pp. 340-1.
[2] *AOSB*, II. x. 419.
[3] *Christian IVs Breve*, I. 158-9; Fridericia, *DRH*, p. 165; Hammarstrand, *HF*, p. 224.

designs in Germany.[1] On the other hand, Kristian's ambitions, especially in Brunswick, made it imperative for him to keep on good terms with the Emperor.[2] Yet he was not wholly devoid of proper evangelical warmth: in March 1620 he declined the suggestion of an alliance with Ferdinand, and in the following month sternly adjured John George to follow his example. But he did almost as little as Gustav Adolf to avert the disaster which overwhelmed Frederick at the end of the year; and when the Union dangled the see of Paderborn before him as the reward for his assistance he refused to swallow the bait.[3]

By the beginning of 1621 the long-awaited moment seemed to have arrived when Kristian, repairing the errors of ten years ago, might obtain a *rapprochement* with the Dutch. The overthrow of Oldenbarneveldt, and the dictatorship of Maurice, had removed Sweden's best support in the Netherlands.[4] As the truce with Spain ran out, it became increasingly important for the Dutch to ensure that Denmark, the mistress of the Sound, should not be drawn (as had more than once seemed probable in the past) into the Spanish sphere of influence.[5] Both parties therefore were anxious for improved relations; and accordingly in January 1621 the Dutch sent Gaspar van Vosbergen to Copenhagen, while Kristian despatched Jacob Ulfeld to The Hague.[6] When Vosbergen arrived in Denmark he was disconcerted to find that Kristian had just rebuffed an envoy from Maurice of Hesse and was advising the Union to reconcile itself with the Emperor. Vosbergen, however, found himself received with flattering cordiality; and Kristian developed, almost overnight, the liveliest concern for the safety of German Protestantism. The first fruits of this new-born confessional zeal appeared in an invitation to the members of the Lower Saxon Circle to meet him at Segeberg at the end of February, there to discuss what measures might be taken in their common interest.

---

[1] For Kristian's relations to the Hanse, England and the Dutch in the period 1618-20, see Schweitzer, pp. 101-20; J. Goll, *Der Konvent von Segeberg*, pp. 9-13; Vreede, I. 127-8; Hallenberg, IV. 713; Droysen, I. 146-7; Hill, p. 89; Gardiner, III. 334, 386; *cf.* Styffe, p. 333.

[2] Hammarstrand, *HF*, p. 223.

[3] *ibid.*, p. 225; Ritter, III. 89; Goll, p. 18.

[4] The Dutch had made overtures of friendship to Kristian, however, as early as the spring of 1618—*i.e.* before the fall of Oldenbarneveldt: Goll, pp. 9-10; and see above, p. 172.

[5] Thyresson, pp. 273-6; Fridericia, *Danmarks ydre politiske Historie* (cited henceforward as *YPH*), I. 27; Schybergson, p. xiv.

[6] Fridericia, *DRH*, p. 165.

Kristian tried to secure the presence of delegates from England and
from Sweden; and a representative of James I did in fact put in an
appearance; but Rutgers did not arrive until the congress was over.[1]
The attendance was not large, and no representatives of the Hanse
were invited; but Kristian appeared in person, Frederick V was there,
and Christian of Lüneburg and Frederick Ulric of Brunswick-
Wolfenbüttel represented their many-branched families. At the
first blush, the results may have appeared encouraging to the King
of Bohemia. It was agreed to raise an army of 30,000 men and to
form a general Protestant league to restore Frederick to his possessions. But in reality this meant nothing, for the implementing of
these plans was contingent upon active assistance from Great
Britain, and the continued resistance of the Union to Spinola; and
in the event neither of these preconditions was fulfilled. Nor is it
at all likely that it was the warning sent to Spinola from Segeberg
which restrained that enterprising commander from attacking
Maurice of Hesse-Cassel. In short, the Segeberg congress, from the
Palatine point of view, turned out to be a fiasco.[2] But not from the
point of view of Kristian. His vigorous diplomatic demonstration
brought him quick political dividends. In April he allied with
James I; in May he reached a preliminary agreement with the
Dutch; in September he converted it into a firm alliance.[3] Maurice
of Orange, lacking the experience of Oldenbarneveldt in foreign
affairs, and anxious above all about the Sound, abandoned Holland's
traditional care for north German independence. In July, Hamburg
submitted to Kristian's terms; in September Bremen accepted
Fredrik as coadjutor; in November Verden followed suit.[4] In spite
of Maurice's rather feeble attempts to persuade Sweden and the
Hanse towns that they were not being thrown over, it was difficult
to find any other interpretation of this conduct.[5] Ever since Oldenbarneveldt's fall Sweden had been pestered by demands for the

---

[1] His instructions in any case enjoined him not to commit Sweden to anything
definite: Schybergson, p. xx.
[2] For the Segeberg meeting and its antecedents, see: Goll, pp. 18-28; Schweitzer,
pp. 110-20, 140; *Christian IVs Breve*, I. 187-8, 196-8; Hallenberg, V. 3, 83;
Fridericia, *DRH*, p. 165; Ritter, III. 126; Schybergson, p. xv; Thyresson, pp.
236-7. It was here that Kristian cried to Frederick: 'Who advised you to drive
out kings and to seize kingdoms? If your counsellors did so, they were scoundrels.'
Gardiner, IV. 180.
[3] Actually, neither treaty was ratified: Thyresson, p. 276; Droysen, I. 151;
Paul, I. 144; Fridericia, *DRH*, p. 166; Goll, pp. 32-3; Schweitzer, pp. 121-2.
[4] Schweitzer, pp. 124-5; Fridericia, *DRH*, p. 166; Hallenberg, IV. 834.
In 1623 Christian of Brunswick resigned Halberstadt in favour of Fredrik also.
[5] Blok, IV. 232, 239-41.

repayment of Dutch loans—demands in themselves not unreasonable, but indicative of the fact that the wind was blowing from a
new quarter.[1] The events of 1621 were a decided political defeat for
Sweden, and a decided success for Denmark. Gustav Adolf's
attempts to form a north German party devoted to himself had
been counterchecked,[2] and Kristian might reasonably hope to have
secured his position as paramount in the Hanseatic littoral.

Meanwhile Protestant affairs in Germany went from bad to worse.
In March the Union began to break up, with the secession of Strassburg and other city members; in April, this example was followed
by some of the leading princes—Maurice of Hesse, John Frederick
of Württemberg, Joachim Ernest of Ansbach; and on 14 May 1621
the Evangelical Union finally expired, without any serious attempt
to prolong it.[3] 'In summa' (wrote John Casimir in March), 'es ist
gantz ein deplorandus status patriae.'[4] Frederick V, from his
retreat at The Hague, continued to importune his numerous royal
and princely relations for aid, and even offered to make over Mansfeld
and his army to Gustav Adolf. But nobody, unless it was James I,
was tempted by this Greek gift; and even James I was wavering.
Buckingham was temporarily possessed with the idea of a war against
the Dutch; and James was disgusted because his son-in-law's
intransigence had spoilt the prospect of a settlement which Digby's
negotiations in Vienna had seemed to make possible. Kristian IV,
busy garnering the fruits of Segeberg, had little time to spare for
the Palatinate. No wonder, then, if Gustav Adolf turned away from
Germany, where single-handed intervention could do no good;
no wonder if he seized a fleeting opportunity—in 1621 as in 1617—
to aim a blow at Sigismund III. But he did not lose sight of German
affairs; and as the Protestant cause dissolved into ruin from negligence, apathy, selfishness and sheer incompetence, he uttered a
prophetic warning to those Lutheran princes who stood aside inactive while the armies of Emperor and League rolled slowly northwards into central Germany. 'Hodie illi,' he wrote to Adolf Frederick
of Mecklenburg, 'cras tibi.'[5] It was a text upon which Oxenstierna
could have dilated at any time up to the eve of Breitenfeld.

---

[1] *AOSB*, I. ii. 407; Hallenberg, IV. 876; Thyresson, p. 277.
[2] Styffe, pp. 333-4, 400; Thyresson, pp. 254, 283-6.
[3] Thyresson, p. 235; Ritter, III. 114-16; Gardiner, IV. 191. Maurice was
anxious to fight, but his subjects would not let him; Lenz, II. 137.
[4] *AOSB*, II. x. 455 (22 March 1621).
[5] Styffe, p. 402 (5 July 1621).

(ii) The Livonian War, 1621-22

About the time when Tilly's army was entering Prague, and Frederick V was retiring discreetly to Silesia, the Truce of Tolsburg expired. It had never been intended to be more than a provisional arrangement; but it had been hoped that during the two years of its course some more permanent and satisfactory agreement might be concluded. And indeed negotiations continued intermittently throughout its duration. Gustav Adolf's terms for a renewal of the truce remained much what they had been before: it must be for a period of at least ten years; Sigismund must stop his propaganda; the truce must extend to all the possessions of both sovereigns. On these terms Sigismund might, if he chose, call himself 'King of Sweden'—provided it were clearly understood that the title conveyed no right to the crown. Any arrangement must be ratified both by Sigismund and the *sejm*. And as the price of *peace* (as distinct from armistice or truce) Gustav Adolf was willing to retrocede Pernau.[1] There is no need to doubt the sincerity of Gustav Adolf in making these propositions. But he knew, none better, that peace on such terms could be extracted from Sigismund only by total victory. In the tentatives of Chodkiewicz and the other Polish negotiators he had no faith at all: 'das feuer des kriges so itz in den aschen der stillestandes begraben liget,'[2] and sooner or later it must flame out once more. And hence it happened that the Truce of Tolsburg ran out in November 1620 without any provisions having been made for its prolongation. Nevertheless, the negotiations went on. Neither side for the moment wanted to renew the fight—Sigismund, because of the crisis on his south-east frontier; Gustav Adolf, because the most favourable season for campaigning was over for that year.

With the approach of the spring of 1621, however, the situation changed. Ever since 1614 there had been desultory warfare on Poland's Turkish border. There was ordinarily no lack of pretext for hostilities in that wild no-man's-land, but just recently the Sultan had received what he considered to be unusual provocation. On the one hand Sigismund had sent Lisowski and his Cossacks

---

[1] Hallenberg, IV. 921-2; Ericsson, p. 16; *AOSB*, II. v. 145.
[2] Styffe, p. 321 (Gustav Adolf to John Casimir, 25 Jan. 1620); *cf.* the resolution of the *riksdag*, 17 March 1620: Stiernman, I. 735-41.

against the Sultan's client, Bethlen Gabor; and on the other, Gratiani, the Hospodar of Moldavia, had intercepted Bethlen's correspondence with Constantinople and forwarded it to Warsaw.[1] Accordingly, the Tatars were incited to attack Moldavia. Sigismund sent Żółkiewski with an inadequate army to Gratiani's assistance. The result was the appalling disaster of Cecora (October 1620). In the retreat which followed, Żółkiewski was killed, Koniecpolski taken, and the Polish army annihilated. In 1621 Poland made tremendous efforts to repair the damage. A great army, with Władysław in nominal command, was collected and hurried to the frontier; the Cossacks were cajoled; the Dissidents placated. The reward was a drawn battle and a peace at Chocim, just a year after Cecora, which restored the *status quo ante bellum* in the Ukraine.[2] In the meantime, however, news of these distant events had reached Stockholm. By the beginning of 1621 it was apparent that Poland would have few troops to spare for Livonia. If the war with Sigismund were to be renewed—and the negotiations of the last two years made it plain that it must be renewed, sooner or later—it could hardly be renewed under more favourable auspices. The opportunity was too good to lose. Gustav Adolf would not, perhaps, have ventured upon war, with resources depleted and internal affairs urgently demanding his attention, had the circumstances been less tempting. But if Sigismund were victorious in Moldavia, he would certainly return with renewed energy to his designs upon Sweden. It was the part of wisdom, therefore, to seize such advantages as were to be had in the meantime.[3] Gustav Adolf would, no doubt, incur some odium by thus stabbing in the back the defender of Christendom against the Moslem onslaught, but that could not be helped.[4] In mid-March 1621, therefore, Gustav Adolf ordered Jakob de la Gardie (in command in Livonia) to serve formal notice upon the Poles that hostilities would recommence in three months'

---

[1] Konopczyński, I. 250-1; Korzon, II. 194-9; Cronholm, I. 363-4; Ericsson, p. 34. The Patriarch, Kyrillos Lukaris, and the Dutch ambassador in Constantinople, Cornelis Haga, are said to have incited the Sultan to attack. Konopczyński, I. 256-7; Sobieski, p. 189; Vreede, *Nederland en Zweden*, p. 141 *note* 2.

[2] Konopczyński, I. 262; Sobieski, p. 190; Korzon, II. 201-17.

[3] *Sv. Kr.*, II. 60; Hjärne, *Gustaf Adolf, Protestantismens förkämpe*, pp. 66-7; contrast Mankell, *passim*.

[4] See, *e.g.*, the comment of Konopczyński (*Dzieje Polski Nowożytnej*, I. 265): 'At a moment when the Republic was sustaining the weight of a Turkish invasion, whose aim was the subjugation of Central Europe, and when German Protestantism was trembling under the blows inflicted by the Habsburgs, Gustav Adolf drew the sword from its scabbard—not to save the "Evangelical Cause", but to deal Poland a stab in the back.'

time; but at the same time he left the door open to a real settlement by ordering negotiations to be continued in the interim. The Poles, for their part, were understandably anxious to prolong the truce, if that could be done without essential sacrifices; but Gustav Adolf was determined not to be cheated of his campaigning weather,[1] and nothing short of Sigismund's renunciation of the Swedish crown was likely to make him change his decision. In effect, the die was cast for war.

Protestant Europe received the news with marked disapprobation. James I wrote urging that it was Gustav Adolf's duty to ally with Sigismund rather than to attack him. George William of Brandenburg, as usual, offered mediation. The Dutch and the Hanse had excellent commercial reasons for desiring that the peace be kept. Only Bethlen Gabor, Mansfeld, and the Margrave of Jägerndorf expressed their satisfaction; and they, perhaps, were persons whose approval most statesmen would prefer to escape.[2] But it was easy for James I to be high-minded at a safe distance; and it was not the first time a Protestant state had utilized a Turkish invasion to strengthen its position against a catholicizing enemy. Nevertheless, Gustav Adolf probably felt a little ashamed of himself.[3]

Early in July the army was assembled in readiness to embark at Älvsnabben; and on 13 July, at a great parade in Årsta Meadows, Oxenstierna read to the troops for the first time Gustav Adolf's new Articles of War.[4] They might be collaborating with the Turk, but no man should say hereafter that they were an ungodly army. Four days later they embarked, and on 24 July the armada, 158 sail strong, with 14,000 men aboard, left Sandhamn for the Gulf of Riga. They made a good passage until the Kurland coast came in sight; but off Domesnäs a violent storm scattered the convoy, sank one ship and drove another ashore. The King's ship was separated from the main body, and made landfall at Pernau on 28 July; the remainder, having rallied under the lee of Runö, reached the mouth of the Düna on 4 August. The navy forced the defences of the river mouth, and the army landed, with little interference, on the Livonian bank. In the next few days they formed camp at Mühlgraben, and thither

[1] Hallenberg, IV. 919-20; Cronholm, I. 370-1; *Sv. Kr.*, II. 59.
[2] Hallenberg, IV. 930-3; Thyresson, pp. 249, 280.
[3] See, *e.g.*, *AOSB*, I. II. 417; Styffe, pp. 344, 348.
[4] Ahnlund, *Oxenstierna*, p. 244; *Sv. Kr.*, II. 63-4. For a discussion of these articles, see Vol. II, Chapter XII, below.

Gustav Adolf hastened to join them.[1] On the evening of 4 August Riga burnt its suburbs and prepared for defence.[2] For it was at Riga that Gustav Adolf's blow was primarily directed. The King gave Oxenstierna the credit of suggesting Riga as the main objective[3]; but it is unlikely that Gustav Adolf needed much persuasion. Riga was, after Danzig, Poland's greatest port, the gateway to the Lithuanian corn-lands, and to all that area of north-west Russia which sent its exports down the Düna and its tributaries. From the point of view of Sweden's defence, Riga was a menace, as being the most convenient base for an invasion. Its capture would be a severer blow to Sigismund than the overrunning of some thousands of square miles of the Livonian countryside; and indeed the control of Riga would put much of Livonia at Sweden's mercy.[4] If it came to negotiation, Riga was a bargaining counter much more valuable than Pernau. And if the war was to continue, no better bridgehead could be imagined for operations in this area. From Riga armies could strike eastward into Livonia, westward into Kurland, or south-ward into Lithuania. Whether for war or peace, defensive or offensive, the possession of the city would give Sweden important advantages.[5]

Riga was at this time a considerable town of some 30,000 souls. Reputed one of the strongest fortresses in the North, it lay on the right bank of the Düna, some six or seven miles from its mouth, at a place where the broad stream was broken up by a number of eyots into two or more channels. It was surrounded by an elaborate system of mediaeval walls, crowned by no less than twenty-five towers or bastions; but these fortifications were by now out of date, and, in at least one critical point, somewhat decayed. Some efforts at modernization had indeed been made, but they had been no more than partially effective. Of guns the town had plenty; of ammunition a good deal less; of trained troops least of all: only 300 hired mercenaries; though these were supplemented by a burgher militia some 3700 strong. Unluckily for the citizens, their dispositions and defences were well known to Gustav Adolf, for a Dutch engineer

---

[1] Gustav Adolf's own vivid description of the crossing is in Styffe, pp. 486-8. See also *Sv. Kr.*, II. 64-6; Ericsson, pp. 69-73; Korzon, II. 227-8. For the naval side, *Sv. Kr.*, App. Vol. I., and Vol. II, Chapter XIII, below.
[2] The attempt to burn the suburbs was, however, partly frustrated: *Sv. Kr.*, II. 74.
[3] *AOSB*, II. 1. 164.
[4] Konopczyński, I. 265.
[5] *Sv. Kr.*, II. 60.

had enlisted with the city as fortifications officer, and had transmitted these useful details to Stockholm, in the hope of a commission in the Swedish service.[1]

The burghers of Riga were not altogether taken by surprise at the Swedish attack. They had foreseen the possibility of such a blow, had tried (in vain) to levy more troops, and had been earnest with Sigismund to provide better for their defence. Sigismund took no notice. Every man that could be spared, or could be induced to turn out, was required for service against the Turks. Sigismund in any case seems to have believed that the threat of a Swedish invasion was not serious. Radziwiłł, left in command in Livonia, warned him of the danger; but Sigismund disliked and distrusted Radziwiłł as a Calvinist, a relation by marriage of the Hohenzollerns, and hence a distant connection of Gustav Adolf himself. Consequently, at the moment when the Swedes disembarked in the Düna, the Polish forces in that area numbered no more than 1500 men, of whom only 650 were infantry. Compared with Gustav Adolf's army of 14,000 this was (as Radziwiłł himself remarked) 'as a fly to an elephant.'[2] It is true that the Poles had grown accustomed to fighting the Swedes at a considerable numerical disadvantage. They placed great faith in the superiority of their reconnaissance, the skill and valour of their cavalry, the fluidity of their organization and tactical formations.[3] They had not forgotten Kirkholm. Radziwiłł considered that 5000 men would have been adequate to defend Livonia.[4] But an army of 5000 was not vouchsafed to him. Hence from the beginning the citizens of Riga had little or no prospect of relief by a field army. And on the other hand the weakness of the Riga garrison, and the imperfect state of the defences, forbade Radziwiłł to hope that the city might hold out until an adequate relieving force could be assembled. In such conditions it was no wonder if Radziwiłł thought that the only hope lay in a speedy peace.[5]

On 11 August 1621 Gustav Adolf made a personal reconnaissance of Riga's defences. On the twelfth he sent a trumpeter to demand surrender. The citizens, protesting that they had no quarrel with the King of Sweden, rejected this demand, and prepared for defence,

---

[1] For these details, see Cronholm, I. 377-80; Hallenberg, IV. 948; Ericsson, pp. 63-7; *Sv. Kr.*, II. 61 *note* 2, 72-5; Steckzén, *Banér*, p. 65.
[2] H. Almquist, *Svenska Folkets Historia*, p. 428; Petri, II. 25; *Sv. Kr.*, II. 69; Ericsson, pp. 12, 26, 40, 54-5; Szelągowski, pp. 258-9; Hjärne, p. 65.
[3] Ericsson, pp. 57-61; *Sv. Kr.*, II. 3; Some attempts at improvement in recruiting had been discussed at recent Diets: Konopczyński, I. 264.
[4] Ericsson, p. 57.   [5] Ericsson, p. 42.

encouraging themselves with the delusive hope of relief. Gustav Adolf accordingly proceeded to a regular siege, though it seems at least possible that if he had attacked at once he might have carried the town with a rush. The besieging army grouped itself into three main camps on the east bank of the Düna, established redoubts upon the islands in the river, and detached small parties to north and south—the one to invest Dünamünde, the other to block Radziwiłł's direct approach from Birże or Kokenhusen. Radziwiłł, meanwhile, was at Birże, scraping together as best he might an army of a couple of thousand men, with which he proposed to embark on the uninviting task of relieving Riga. By the end of August his preparations were complete, and on the 30th his army appeared on the west bank and skirmished with the Swedish outposts on that side. The burghers of Riga, who had discerned his approach, made efforts at sortie by boat, but these were unsuccessful. Radziwiłł for his part soon found that the Swedes were too strong for him. On 31 August he burnt his camp and withdrew, and the spirits of the citizens, which had been elated on the previous day, were now correspondingly depressed. Riga was thus thrown back upon her own resources; and these, as has been seen, were decidedly slender. Nevertheless the defenders made a brave fight of it—'eine galliarde defesa', as Gustav Adolf himself remarked.[1] The Swedish efforts were now intensified: the trenches and traverses approached close to the walls, as Gustav Adolf and Karl Filip dug with enthusiasm alongside their men. On 1 September the water was drained from the moat. On 2 September the first attempt at storm was beaten off; on 9 September it was followed by another, equally unsuccessful, in which Johan Banér first distinguished himself and sustained serious wounds[2]; and on 12 September came a third effort. The King had more than one narrow escape of his life, and the Swedish losses were severe. But the besiegers had overwhelming superiority in guns, and they subjected the town to a bombardment of such intensity that prolonged resistance became impossible.[3] On 13 September the burghers decided to parley rather than risk the sack which Gustav Adolf was now threatening. The King had been much irritated by their tenacious defence, which had cost him some 2000 in killed and wounded; and he was not much mollified by being

[1] Styffe, p. 348.
[2] G. Björlin, *Johan Banér*, I. 49.
[3] The Swedish batteries were said by the Poles to have fired 1000 rounds *per diem*: Korzon, II. 228.

addressed by the burgher delegates as 'Ruling Prince in the Kingdom of Sweden'. Nevertheless, the terms which he imposed upon Riga by the capitulation of 15 September 1621 were moderate enough. Riga retained her privileges and municipal autonomy; her overseas trade was not to be interfered with; and she was allowed to retain her own coinage, provided it conformed to Swedish standards in denomination, weight and fineness. Any Polish officers, or foreigners or Jesuits, who might not wish to remain in the town, were to be free to depart. If peace were concluded with Poland within three years, Riga was to be at liberty then to return to the Polish allegiance. On the other hand, the town recognized Gustav Adolf and his successors as its lords; Sweden was to be permitted to maintain as large a garrison as might be convenient to her; in certain types of case appeal was to lie from the town courts to the *Svea Hovrätt*[1]; and Riga was to send representatives to the *riksdag*. These provisions seem to show that Gustav Adolf was already thinking of the permanent incorporation of Riga into the Swedish realm, and that he had no great faith in the possibility of a peace with Poland within the stipulated three years; and this impression is borne out by the tenderness with which the city was treated in the following months.[2]

The capture of Riga is one of the great landmarks of the reign. It was a feat of arms which arrested the attention of Europe. The monarchs of the west had not greatly concerned themselves when de la Gardie took Novgorod; they had remained indifferent to the failure before Pskov or the acquisition of Gdov. The Kurland episode of 1617-18 had appeared, in the general European context, as of no more than peripheral significance. But the taking of Riga was different; for Riga was a great German city, well known to the maritime powers. Its fall announced a shifting of the balance of power in the Baltic, presaged an extension of the Swedish dominion southward from Estonia to embrace the Gulf of Riga, outflanked the Danish position on Ösel, placed Sweden in command of one of the great riverine trade-routes of eastern Europe. It marked the beginning of a development which, ten years later, would subject every important river flowing into the Baltic to Swedish control. In another aspect, it announced—though as yet in accents only im-

[1] For this, see Chapter VI, below.
[2] Styffe, pp. 261, 645; *AOSB*, II. 1. 165; Cronholm, I. 406. For the siege and capitulation of Riga, see: Ericsson, pp. 75-116; *Sv. Kr.*, I. 534; II. 61-3, 70-93; Styffe, pp. 254-9; Hallenberg, IV. 953-65, 969, 974-6; Cronholm, I. 382 *seqq.*

perfectly intelligible to the outside world—the coming of a new era in the military art. The siege of Riga had in itself presented no new features: the conduct of it might indeed have appeared, to the expert from the Low Countries, either unduly ponderous or unduly rash. But from this moment Gustav Adolf emerges from his apprenticeship. It is possible to criticize his operations against Riga; but at least they present a very different picture from the fumbling and feebleness at Pskov. He has learned the elements of the art; he masses his batteries, puts up a creeping barrage, quite in the manner of Maurice of Orange. And he adds features of his own: he combines musketry with gunfire to make the defenders keep their heads down; he digs, and his ardour makes his men dig too. The new armies which were to finish off the Polish war and startle Germany were not yet fully fashioned, but they were taking shape; and at Riga western and central Europe became conscious of them for the first time. The constrained and grudging congratulations of Kristian IV only imperfectly concealed his grave concern at a development which was certain to prejudice Denmark's position in the North.[1]

It might be true that the master of Riga was the master of Livonia; but it was no less true that Riga could not be firmly held as a solitary outpost in a hostile country. The surrender of the city must necessarily be followed, then, by a systematic effort to expand the bridgehead which its capture afforded. And this was the more urgent because the problem of feeding the army would become insoluble unless the King could obtain effective control of a considerable tract of country. The Düna basin, though less rich than that of the Vistula and liable to occasional failures of the harvest, was yet sufficiently fertile to make its acquisition of great importance. A beginning had been made already by the capture of various small places on or near the route from Pernau to Riga, and on 19 September the capitulation of Dünamünde had secured the estuary of the river; but now it was time to take in hand the work on a more systematic plan. Gustav Adolf decided to strike out in three directions. Westwards he would move on Mitau, the capital of Kurland; south-eastwards up the Düna he would aim at Kokenhusen; while a push to the north-east, designed to culminate in the capture of

---

[1] Kristian had earlier remarked: 'I say nothing of the King's being off to Riga; but God forbid that he should get it into his power; for then were our arsenal barred up as touching tackle and sailcloth, were we (which God defend) ever to have another brush with Sweden.' *Christian IVs Breve*, I. 219.

Dorpat, would establish a solid link with the Swedish possessions in Estonia.

There was at the moment really no military force in the area capable of hindering the realization of this project. Radziwiłł had some 4000 men near Birże and Bauske, but in itself this army was too inconsiderable to be an obstacle. Mitau, Kokenhusen and Dorpat, in common with the other towns of the region, were weakly held and unlikely to offer serious opposition. The real difficulty lay in supply and in the nature of the country. The siege of Riga had depleted the Swedish reserves of powder, and the troops were short of all necessities. The lack of cavalry put blinkers on the higher command and impeded the business of foraging. The possibility of free movement was still further curtailed by the extremely swampy nature of the ground, especially between the Düna and the Kurland Aa, and by the badness of the roads, which (if they existed) became impassable in the autumn rains. Yet speed was highly desirable. Sigismund had made peace with the Turks at Chocim on 29 September,[1] and might be expected by spring to be able to give all his attention to the Livonian front. Now, if ever, was the moment to annihilate Radziwiłł's army and fasten upon the Düna basin a grip so firm that no assault would be able to shake it.[2]

On 24 September, therefore, Gustav Adolf broke up from Riga, and with all his cavalry and 9000 foot crossed the Düna and made for Mitau. He reached the town on 2 October, found it open and undefended, and on the following day forced the castle to surrender. One section of the triple plan was thus completed, and Duke Frederick of Kurland had lost his capital. Frederick, as in 1617, was obstinately Polish in sympathy, and had already shown his colours by confiscating a Swedish ship laden with munitions which had run ashore near Windau. His brother William, Gustav Adolf's former *protégé*, was at this time living quietly in retirement at Schwerin. It would have been convenient to have him on the spot in Kurland, to give some shadow of legitimism to the Swedish occupation. William, however, discreetly preferred the rural peace of Mecklenburg to the stormy airs of his native duchy; and though he protested his devotion to Gustav Adolf, he was

---

[1] To Oxenstierna's indignation: *AOSB*, I. II. 432-3.
[2] For all this, see Styffe, p. 489; *AOSB*, II. I. 164; *Sv. Kr.*, II. 70-1, 94, 96, 98; Ericsson, pp. 119-20, 123-4.

firm in declining invitations to come home and hold Kurland as a Swedish fief.[1]

Radziwiłł had been expecting an attack upon Kokenhusen rather than upon Mitau, and was taken by surprise by the King's movement. He advanced with his small army from Bauske; but being too late to prevent Mitau's fall, contented himself with sitting down in an entrenched camp at Annenburg. It was obviously Gustav Adolf's policy to seek a general engagement, and no less obviously Radziwiłł's to avoid one. In such a contest all the advantages were on the side of the smaller and more mobile army: the Poles slipped away from Annenburg before the King could bring them to battle; and nothing remained to him but to withdraw, after leaving a garrison of 500 men in Mitau, with instructions to defend the castle to the last. The Swedish army was feeling a shortage of provisions; the light Polish cavalry was harrying their communications; and Cossacks were causing anxiety in Livonia. When in the second week of November Cockburn [2] was sent with a small detachment to take Kokenhusen, he was pounced on by Gąsiewski at Kroppenhof, and routed before the King could come to his aid. The advance up the Düna was thus checked, and Kokenhusen—important as a centre of communications and a bridge over the river— remained in Polish hands. And Radziwiłł's little army was still intact.[3]

Having thus failed on his central front to obtain the decisive success which the situation required, Gustav Adolf turned to the last of his three objectives, and on 23 November set out with his army for Dorpat. If Estonia were ever to be secure on that side, if the roads linking Mitau and Riga to Weissenstein and Pernau were ever to be safe, the capture of Dorpat was essential. It was already clear, however, that the citizens of Dorpat had no great cause to disturb themselves, at all events for this year. The Swedish army, chronically short of necessities, was already grievously weakened by epidemics. It lumbered slowly northeastward, taking a full month to reach Wolmar. Wolmar it did indeed capture; but with that its impetus was exhausted, and it settled down to 'starve and freeze and rot' in winter quarters scattered up and down central Livonia; while Gustav Adolf hurried

---

[1] Hallenberg, IV. 984-5; Cronholm, I. 400; Ericsson, pp. 120-1; *Sv. Kr.*, II. 99-100; *AOSB*, II. 1. 166-7.
[2] The Swedes pronounced—and spelled—the name of this officer 'Cobron'.
[3] Ericsson, pp. 123-6, 128, 130-1; *Sv. Kr.*, II. 100, 102-4.

back to Sweden by way of Narva,[1] and Jakob de la Gardie and his officers made the best of a bad situation and hoped for better things next spring. In the meantime, the Livonian peasant was made to feel his obligations in the matter of providing quarters and forage. The situation was too critical to permit of any paltering: 'It must make no difference,' wrote the King, 'that the peasantry complain; for We do not attach so much importance to the well-being of the country as to the need for succouring and providing for the soldiers who by faithful service have assisted to conquer it; which you shall look to by all manner of means, not caring if the peasant squeal. . . .'[2]

On the whole, then, the autumn campaign had been something of a failure. Apart from Mitau and Wolmar, Sweden had taken no town of importance since the fall of Riga; the Düna remained barred to her armies; the puny force of Radziwiłł had not only escaped destruction but had administered at least one jab at Gustav Adolf which was something more than a pinprick.[3] For this result the defects in the Swedish supply system, and the inadequate numbers of the Swedish cavalry, were mainly responsible. And now, while the troops of Gustav Adolf dwindled alarmingly in their swampy and insanitary bivouacs, Radziwiłł had positively seized the initiative and had begun an attempt to recover Mitau. From December 1621 Anders Ericsson Hästehufvud and his little garrison were closely besieged; at the end of the month the Poles recaptured the town, though the castle still held out; on 10 February 1622 a determined attempt at storm was beaten off with great difficulty. Thereafter the spring floods gave a respite. But the relief of Mitau must plainly be among the first tasks for Gustav Adolf in the campaign of 1622.

In the late winter and early spring the war languished, for neither side could move much for snow and mud and bottomless roads. Radziwiłł had planned a surprise attack on Riga, whose garrison was much reduced by sickness; but the weather defeated him, and he gave it up.[4] Only the siege of Mitau dragged on, as both sides collected their forces and mobilized their resources for the summer. Sweden's most urgent need was for reinforcements. By midsummer casualties and epidemics had reduced the field army

---

[1] Where Karl Filip died of camp-fever.
[2] Quoted in Cronholm, I. 403.
[3] Though Bennedich's judgment (*Ur det gamla Gardets öden*, p. 57) seems unduly severe when he writes: 'No difference in principle is to be discerned between Gustav II Adolf's manner of waging war in Livonia, and Karl IX's'.
[4] *Sv. Kr.*, II. 113; Ericsson, p. 130; Cronholm, I. 412-13. For other episodes from this period, see *AOSB*, I. II. 437; II. v. 162; II. IX. 22.

to no more than 6000 men, and the toll of horses had been proportionately not less severe.[1] The new levies that came from home were
mostly raw recruits; and some of them had not received proper
equipment by as late as October.[2] It proved impossible, moreover,
to bring the army up to the strength with which it had begun the
campaign in 1621. Every effort was made to strengthen the cavalry
arm, and Gustav Adolf's commissioners scoured the mercenary-
markets for horsemen; but the results were extremely meagre:
only 350 heavy dragoons could be collected for the opening of
operations.[3] There was a shortage of arms and ammunition too;
but it proved possible to get supplies from the Netherlands, and thus
to ensure a reasonably adequate provision.[4] The root of the difficulty
was an acute shortage of ready money. All the ordinary revenues
had been fully allocated; and Sweden's credit was not such as to
make the raising of external loans an easy matter. John Casimir
was still waiting in vain for the payment of his wife's dowry.[5] At
the *riksdag* which met in the spring it was necessary to impose the
'Little Toll' on top of all the other exactions, and even so the lack
of money remained acute. 'Utinam Deus ille praepotens largiatur
nobis securam pacem,' sighed Skytte, 'ut aliquando ex his difficul-
tatibus eluctemur.'[6]

Fortunately the affairs of the enemy were in even worse case.
The reinforcements expected by Radziwiłł from the armies which
had been fighting the Turks failed to arrive; for the unpaid soldiers
were forming 'Confederations' in the hope of extracting their
arrears from a bankrupt government. The Senate dared not summon
the *sejm* for fear that it should be terrorized by rebellious armies.
Ministers and generals expended their energies in unseemly recriminations. Discontented elements among the nobility, led by
Rafał Leszczyński and Jerzy Zbaraski, dallied with the idea of
placing on the throne Gaston of Orleans (who would certainly have
fitted very well into that environment) or Bethlen Gabor, or even—
Gustav Adolf.[7] It must have appeared sharply ironical to Sigismund,

---

[1] Barkman, *Gustaf II Adolfs regementsorganisation*, pp. 139-42; *AOSB*, II.
IX. 23; *Sv. Kr.*, II. 112, 120; Ericsson, p. 136.
    [2] Wrangel wrote of the garrisons of Narva and Ivangorod that they 'are so
destitute that they have literally no shirt to their backs; their swords are but pitiful,
and the more part lack even these.' *AOSB*, II. IX. 26.
    [3] Styffe, p. 352; *Sv. Kr.*, II. 117-19: the first appearance of dragoons in a
Swedish army.
    [4] *AOSB*, I. II. 474; Petri, II. 35.   [5] *AOSB*, I. II. 442.
    [6] *AOSB*, II. X. 260; Cronholm, I. 409.
    [7] Konopczyński, I. 266-8; Sobieski, p. 191; Cronholm, I. 410; *Sv. Kr.*, II. 116.

at a moment when Poland was paralysed by unprincipled faction, that Sweden should have been seized by one of those alarms of impending Polish invasion which periodically sent reinforcements hurrying down to man the defences of Kalmar.[1]

Since both sides were thus beset with difficulties, it is not surprising that the summer campaign of 1622 should have been both insignificant and short. Gustav Adolf, in spite of all his efforts, did not command the resources for a resumption of the offensive on any considerable scale: it would be sufficient if he could retain his gains of the preceding autumn and consolidate himself in the positions already won. As it turned out, even this modest programme could not be carried out. For some time Hästehufvud had been in desperate straits at Mitau. His men had been hard hit by the prevailing epidemics, and the reinforcements for which he had clamoured from de la Gardie had not arrived. Apparently neither de la Gardie nor the King realized just how critical the position was. At all events, when Gustav Adolf appeared at Riga with reinforcements in mid-June, he proceeded to organize a relief expedition at a pace which can only be called leisurely. On 25 June Hästehufvud capitulated to Radziwiłł after a heroic defence: it was not until two days later that the relieving column started its march from Riga.[2]

The fall of Mitau was undoubtedly a blow. The road to Kurland was now blocked. The prestige of the King had suffered. The campaign, whose prospects had never seemed very brilliant, was already a failure, and Radziwiłł had every reason to congratulate himself. Both parties were now ready to treat, if a truce on terms satisfactory to each could be arranged.[3] An armistice was agreed to on 7 July, and negotiations began; and on 31 July 1622 the Truce of Mitau was signed. It provided for a cessation of hostilities until 21 April 1623, for the exchange of prisoners, and for freedom of trade in the disputed area. The rival claims of Gustav Adolf and Sigismund were passed over in silence, and it was provided that each side should retain its possessions: thus Gustav Adolf kept Riga and Pernau, while Radziwiłł remained in occupation of Mitau. At the same time it was agreed that negotiations should be immediately

[1] *AOSB*, II. ix. 23; Ericsson, p. 147; Hallenberg, V. 31.

[2] Ericsson, pp. 137-44, 153-4; *AOSB*, I. i. 99-103; *Sv. Kr.*, II. 114-16, 122-3.

[3] James I had been urging this. Oxenstierna commented sourly: 'Es scheinett das I. M:tt in Gross Brittanien keine rationes sufficient zum kriege halten wollen, et quidvis pati potius quam bellum velint.' *AOSB*, I. ii. 444.

reopened with a view to reaching a more stable settlement.[1] These hopes (if ever they were seriously entertained) proved illusory, for the standpoints of each party were fundamentally different. Gustav Adolf and Oxenstierna really wished for a long truce, or, better still, a peace. To obtain a peace they were prepared for considerable sacrifices: they were willing, for instance, to surrender Riga and evacuate their gains in Livonia, to allow to Sigismund the title of King of Sweden for his lifetime, to permit his sons to style themselves Princes (but not Hereditary Princes) of Sweden. And it is even possible that Oxenstierna would have been ready to make these concessions as the price of a 60-years' truce.[2] Sweden was anxious about her relations with Denmark, and she could not be wholly indifferent to the disasters to the Protestant cause which followed hard upon one another in Germany. But if no long truce were to be had, if Sigismund by refusing to renounce his propaganda and his pretensions plainly declared his intention to resume hostilities at a later date, then they were determined to hang on to Riga and their other gains, partly for obvious military reasons, partly as counters for a future negotiation. For the moment the military position was not so clearly in Sweden's favour as to coerce Sigismund into those renunciations by which alone he could obtain the retrocession of Riga. Gustav Adolf continued, therefore, to treat the conquered areas as Swedish territory. Meanwhile the Swedish delegates were not above attempting to arrange a separate truce between Sweden and Lithuania; but this manœuvre was based on a misconception of the seriousness of Lithuanian discontent, and though it was tried more than once, it never had any success.

Far different was the attitude of Sigismund, of Radziwiłł, and of the Polish magnates. They did not really desire a stable arrangement. Radziwiłł in July was anxious to make a quick truce which would give him time to reorganize, and secure him in the possession of Mitau. He had conducted a difficult defence with marked ability, in face of heavy odds and disastrous chaos in his rear. He had no powers to agree to any important concessions. An arrangement on

---

[1] For the negotiations leading to the Truce of Mitau, see *Sv. Kr.*, II. 124-8; Cronholm, I. 414-16; Ericsson, pp. 159-88; *AOSB*, I. ii. 476-9, 481; II. i. 184-5; II. v. 180; X. Liske, *Öfversigt af den polska litteraturen med särskild afseende på den svenska historien*, V. 361-8, prints Radziwiłł's diary narrating the progress of the negotiations. Liske takes this and other interesting material from *Ks. Krzysztofa Radziwiłła sprawy wojenne i polityczne* (Paris 1859), which I have not seen. Korzon, II. 233. For the Treaty, *Sv. Trakt.*, V₂. 312-13.
[2] Hallenberg, V. 40-4; Cronholm, I. 417-18; *AOSB*, II. i. 210.

the basis of *uti possidetis* was the best he could hope for. Since the Polish army could not be paid, it must be kept to the colours, for it would be too dangerous to disband it unpaid; and therefore a short truce alone would suit. In any case Radziwiłł counted on Gustav Adolf's being involved in Germany in the comparatively near future; and if that happened it would be well that Poland's hands should be free.[1] As to Sigismund, he was utterly intransigent—encouraged, perhaps, by the death of Karl Filip, and by Maria Eleonora's failure to produce an heir.[2] Gustav Adolf must retrocede Riga and Pernau and the rest of his conquests as a precondition to negotiation of a durable truce; he would not recognize Gustav Adolf as King in any circumstances; and if the truce were to be of the order of 15 or 20 years he demanded an express acknowledgment of his right to 'recover his fatherland by any means in his power'.[3] He used every device of diplomacy to hamper and delay the negotiations which were resumed in mid-August. Weeks and months were consumed in wrangles about verification of powers, about precedence, about questions of prestige and etiquette, or in simple empty verbiage. The Treaty of Mitau remained unratified. The Polish armies alarmed and incommoded the Swedish negotiators by violations of the truce. Again and again it seemed as though the diplomats must disperse without having made any progress. But at last, towards the end of November, common sense, or common weariness, prevailed; and on 27 November 1622 the Truce of Ogra terminated these intolerable negotiations.[4] Its purport was simple: it extended the Truce of Mitau from 21 April 1623 to 1 June 1624.[5] No more than that; for in truth no greater measure of agreement was possible. Yet even that was from Sweden's point of view worth having. Two years, at least,[6] to consolidate her grip on Livonia; two years to press on the work of army reform in the light of experience since 1621; two years in which to face once more the menacing ill-

---

[1] Konopczyński, I. 266; Ericsson, p. 182. In the course of the negotiations Gustav Adolf had had a famous interview with Radziwiłł. The King was most affable and gracious, and obviously sought to win over Radziwiłł by a show of sweet reasonableness. Radziwiłł was captivated, but he did not allow his admiration to affect his policy.

[2] This led Gustav Adolf to summon John Casimir and his wife to Sweden this summer. See Sigismund's angry letter to Radziwiłł, in Liske, V. 377-9.

[3] Ericsson, p. 200; *Sv. Kr.*, II. 130.

[4] For the negotiations, see *AOSB*, I. ii. 510, 512, 520, 539, 553, 555-6; II. i. 195, 200, 210, 219; II. v. 182; Styffe, p. 491; Ahnlund, *Oxenstierna*, pp. 257-61; Ericsson, pp. 194, 199, 201, 216.

[5] Text in *Sv. Trakt.*, V$_2$. 314-16.

[6] As it turned out, more: see below.

humour of Kristian IV, without the distraction of a Polish war.
Sigismund indeed had conceded more than he knew; for before
the armies of Sweden appeared again in the Düna valley Gustav
Adolf would have passed the crucial point in his relations with
Denmark and asserted a superiority which Kristian was never to
succeed in shaking. And Riga would have been lost to Poland—
lost beyond hope of recovery, lost for ever.

(iii) *The Threat of Polish invasion, 1623*

Sigismund III did not ratify the Truce of Ogra. Military
necessity might constrain his commanders in the field to come to an
arrangement; the Polish Estates might even confirm it; but the
King considered his hands to be free.[1] And even if, by the attitude
of his subjects, he might be compelled to observe the truce as
regarded Livonia, he did not conceive that the cessation of hostilities
extended to Sweden proper. Liberated for the moment from
anxiety on the Turkish frontier, he determined that in the spring of
1623 he would strike at the heart of his enemy: this year at last the
long-deferred invasion of Sweden should take place. There were
serious obstacles in the way. In the winter of 1622-23 Poland was
plagued by famine and pestilence. There was a chronic shortage
of money, not easily to be overcome. The naval preparations
required for an invasion must necessarily take time, and be confined
to a very few ports; and though progress was made, the Polish
Armada was consistently behind schedule. The *sejm*, moreover,
viewed these preparations with an unfriendly countenance, Sigismund's enemy Zbaraski remarking with some justice that 'after the
frightful devastation of three-quarters of the lands of the Crown by
the enemy, *post innumerabilia tributa*, after the intolerable plundering
of the armies *varii generis* that for some years had been marching
over the country, after floods and famines and the latest Turkish
invasion, the Republic would prefer to get its breath again.'[2]
Nevertheless, Sigismund went on with his preparations. The
harbour of Danzig began to be thronged with small landing-craft
(*lodjor*). Permission was obtained from James I to recruit troops in
Britain, and a patent to levy soldiers was made out to one Robert

[1] Ericsson, p. 246.
[2] Szelągowski, p. 282; and see Ericsson, p. 230.

Stewart. The shortage of money was somewhat relieved by a subsidy from Philip IV, whose bankrupt exchequer could always, it seemed, find a few thousands to aid a good cause. Efforts were made to enlist pilots and helmsmen familiar with the intricate navigation of the Swedish skerries.[1]

The plan of invasion was on a grandiose scale. There was to be a double attack, from west and east. From Danzig, Altheim himself, with the main body of 10,000 men, would sail straight for the Stockholm archipelago and endeavour to carry the capital by direct assault; while simultaneously another expedition of some 8000 British troops, convoyed by a fleet to be obligingly provided by Spain, would land in the Göta river and possess itself of the vital outlet to the west. Spain would be paid for her trouble by the cession of Älvsborg, from which vantage-point she would be in an excellent position to harry the important Dutch trade with the Baltic; and the bargain would be sealed by a marriage between the Infanta and Władysław, who would be an acceptable alternative to the Prince of Wales. And lastly, diversionary attacks on Estonia and the Swedish positions in Livonia would prevent the withdrawal of troops for the defence of Stockholm.[2] It was, undoubtedly, an admirable plan; but it demanded an accuracy of timing not very usual in this century; it presupposed a naval force far stronger than Sigismund was likely to possess for some years; it much exaggerated the yield of the Scottish mercenary-market; and it assumed that Gustav Adolf had neither an espionage service nor the initiative to act on the reports it sent him. However, it is probable that Sigismund realized comparatively early that the invasion could not be launched in 1623: he had at all events abandoned the project for the time being before the summer of that year.

News of these preparations, and rumours of Sigismund's design, reached Sweden in March and April; and though reports were contradictory and confusing they produced a very intelligible alarm.[3] At a meeting of the råd at Västerås in March discussion had turned on the desirability of purchasing even a short extension of the truce by the offer of Riga [4]; for relations with Denmark were becoming critical,[5] and there was no wish for another war on two fronts; but

[1] Ericsson, pp. 253-4; Hallenberg, *Handlingar*, pp. 138-9.
[2] *Sv. Kr.*, II. 141-3; Ericsson, p. 254.
[3] *AOSB*, II. i. 215; II. iii. 49, 53; II. v. 200, 215, 219; II. ix. 28.
[4] Ericsson, pp. 225-6.
[5] See below, p. 231.

since it seemed clear that no settlement with Sigismund was to be looked for, the government turned all its attention to defence. Fortifications were constructed or improved in the neighbourhood of likely landing-places; but the main reliance was placed upon concentrations of force in the neighbourhood of Stockholm and Kalmar, which should be strong enough to overwhelm an invader before he had a chance to get a firm foothold, and also upon the powerful fleet collected at Älvsnabben, which was designed either to destroy the armada in transit, or, if it slipped past unobserved, to cut Sigismund's communications with his base at Danzig.[1] But Gustav Adolf was not content with a passive defence. With sure strategic insight he saw that the key to the situation lay in Danzig, rather than in Kalmar or the archipelago. Rumour had it that Sigismund was intending to visit Danzig in the early summer. Danzig was the only port (now that Riga was in Swedish hands) big enough to hold an invasion-fleet. Gustav Adolf had had his eye on Danzig for some time: in 1621 he had appointed a special agent resident in the town to keep him informed of its dispositions; and immediately before sailing for Riga he had addressed to the city fathers an enquiry as to whether they would permit Sigismund to prepare an invasion in their harbour. Danzig had professed to know nothing of any such scheme, had pointed out that Sigismund was pledged to maintain a fleet, and had indicated that it was none of their concern where he chose to keep it. Another request—in April 1623—for a definition of Danzig's attitude had elicited an equally non-committal reply. It was no longer possible to be content with these diplomatic evasions.[2] It was essential to find out what was going on in Danzig; to constrain the burghers to neutrality, if that were possible; and, if it proved impossible, to singe the King of Poland's beard in Danzig Roads. Single ships had already been despatched to the Vistula on scouting expeditions: it was now decided to launch a reconnaissance and demonstration in force.[3]

On 20 June 1623, therefore, Gustav Adolf suddenly appeared off Danzig with a considerable armament: 21 vessels of various sizes

---

[1] Barkman, p. 156; *Sv. Kr.*, II. 145-9; *AOSB*, II. I. 215; Ericsson, pp. 255-258.

[2] Ericsson, pp. 241-3, 256; and *cf.* the instructions to the *råd* of 6 June 1622, where they are charged to keep an eye on Danzig: *RRP*, I. vii-ix. Danzig, while remaining a member of the Hanse, recognized the King of Poland as its lord. The town was not, however, part of the Polish Republic, and was represented at Warsaw by an 'Internuncio': Ericsson, pp. 233-7.

[3] Hallenberg, V. 45-58.

and over 4000 men. By a singular coincidence there arrived in Danzig on the following day King Sigismund, Queen Constantia, Prince Władysław, and the Princess Anna. They were welcomed with genuine enthusiasm, for Danzig, like Riga, was strongly loyal to Poland. The visit seems to have been mainly a pleasure trip, but from Sigismund's point of view it was certainly well-timed. Gustav Adolf at once formulated his demands. He asked that the Truce of Ogra be properly observed, and that Danzig give guarantees that her harbour should not be made available to Sigismund for preparations directed against Sweden. The city's representatives were conciliatory, but Gustav Adolf demanded explicit assurances, 'otherwise for lack of fresh water I shall be compelled to land my men, throw up a redoubt, and address myself to this matter with somewhat more of emphasis.' This threat was, however, accompanied by courtesies: Gustav Adolf presented his compliments to the Queen, and invited Władysław to visit him 'as one soldier to another', on board the fleet. The invitation was not accepted; but Queen Constantia reciprocated by suggesting that Gustav Adolf come ashore, and Danzig took care to provide the Swedish ships with supplies. Meanwhile the Swedes had captured two Spanish merchantmen lying in the harbour, and threatened to take them as prize; and shortly afterwards they added six Danzigers to their bag. This coerced Danzig into giving Gustav Adolf some sort of assurance; and with Sigismund's consent the city promised not to permit any violation of the truce, nor to allow her harbour to be used as a base against Sweden—for so long as the truce should continue. By the time this stage had been reached, Gustav Adolf was already on his way home with half the fleet. He had already seen enough to reassure him that no immediate danger was to be apprehended from this quarter, and the ten ships left behind under Nils Stiernsköld were more than adequate to continue the blockade and exert pressure on Danzig. It was Stiernsköld, therefore, who accepted Danzig's offer; and at the end of June he weighed anchor with the remainder of the fleet, and put to sea. He did not meet with a very gracious reception on his return. Gustav Adolf had hoped to extort to a binding engagement to observe strict neutrality whether the truce were in being or not; and he hastened therefore to send back Kristoffer Ludvig Rasche with an agreement ready drawn on these lines. But it was now too late. Danzig refused point-blank to sign a document of this nature, and confined herself to reiterating her previous guarantees.[1]

The expedition was thus no more than a half-success. Yet it had served to dissipate the fear of immediate attack; and it had been a useful naval exercise. And if the alarms and preparations of this summer had thus been proved excessive, the Swedish mobilization (for it really amounted to that) had not been wholly in vain.[2] For the danger of invasion, coupled with the increasingly alarming posture of affairs in Germany, were turning the King's mind once again to the idea of intervention on the Continent; and with such a prospect in view a practice mobilization had a good deal to commend it.

(iv) *Gustav Adolf's first plan for a Protestant League, 1623*

In Germany the years 1622 and 1623 had seen the irretrievable ruin of the cause of Frederick V; and of that ruin he had continued to be himself the chief architect. The smashing victories of Tilly— at Wimpffen in April 1622, at Höchst in June of the same year—the desertion of German allies in the face of defeat, the tardy and in-adequate aid from Protestant powers—all these might have been retrieved had Frederick shown any moderation, any statesmanship, any sense of reality. He threw away the chances which undoubtedly presented themselves for the conclusion of a compromise which might at least have preserved the Lower Palatinate to his heirs. The atrocities of the commanders who fought under his banners disgusted and alienated moderates who might otherwise have been friends.[3] By the end of that summer he was a fugitive once more, the guest of the Duke of Bouillon at Sedan; while Mansfeld, with the army of bandits which called itself Frederick's, was pursuing his lamentable Odyssey from the Rhineland to Lorraine, from Lorraine to Holland (where he came in handily for the relief of Bergen-op-Zoom) and so to East Friesland, an unoffending and unpolitical corner of Europe which he devastated with practised thoroughness. The Duke of East Friesland, Enno III, was Gustav Adolf's uncle by

---

[1] Ericsson, pp. 258-64; Hallenberg, V. 58-65; Cronholm, I. 420-4; *Sv. Kr.*, II. 151-4; Broomé, pp. 234-5; *AOSB*, II. 1. 224; II. iii. 52. Oxenstierna's idea of the terms which it would have been desirable to extract from Danzig is in *AOSB*, I. 1. 510-12.

[2] 'Better too soon than too late', as Gabriel Gustafsson Oxenstierna put it: *AOSB*, II. iii. 53.

[3] See, however, H. Wertheim, *Der tolle Halberstädter*, I.-II., for an attempt to rehabilitate Christian of Brunswick.

marriage, and in despair appealed to Sweden to intervene.   Gustav
Adolf did what he could, which was not much; but he might well
wonder into what sort of hands the Protestant cause was falling.[1]
As the year drew towards autumn, Frederick's pitiful tragedy
marched to its conclusion, touched in its final scenes by the heroism
of the English garrisons of the last Palatinate strongholds.   Heidelberg fell on 6 September, Mannheim on 28 October.   The Palatinate
was lost, Tilly was triumphant, and Maximilian was pressing for his
pound of flesh.   In Bohemia persecution had already begun, and
now the Jesuits arrived, in Tilly's train, to ensconce themselves in
the former fastnesses of the Reformed religion.   In February 1623
came the diet of Ratisbon, when by an act which stretched the
Imperial prerogative to breaking-point Ferdinand transferred the
Palatine Electorate to the Bavarian Wittelsbach.   The protests of
Spain, of Brandenburg, of Saxony, of England, availed nothing
against the Emperor's urgent need to acquit himself of his debt to
Bavaria.   And with that violently unconstitutional act the moral
balance began to tilt once again towards an equipoise.   Hitherto
law, and equity, and international decency, had all been on the
Imperial side; and the cause of Frederick had seemed to many—to
James I, for instance, and to John George—to be the cause of lawlessness, of brigandage, of anarchy.   But Ferdinand had now been
forced to abandon his moral advantage: after Ratisbon he appeared
in the odious light of a tyrannical monarch, as formerly Frederick
had appeared stained with the sin of rebellion.

For the moment, there was no choice but to acquiesce.   The
external allies upon whom the Calvinist party had hitherto reckoned
had proved but weak supports.   The Dutch, grappling with
Spinola's offensives, could not spare a man.   Bethlen Gabor had made
peace in January 1622 and retired to his Carpathian principality.
France still saw no danger to herself in the salvation of legitimate
(and Catholic) monarchy; and though she was beginning to renew
contacts with Bavaria which were to be of importance later, her
only positive move in foreign affairs was concerned with Italy,
when in 1623 she formed the League of Avignon with Venice and
Savoy, to counteract Spanish influence in the Valtelline.   No hope
from France, then, now or for several years to come.   In England,
James I, torn between parliament and minister, swayed now by

---

[1] Kristian IV also made some effort to get Mansfeld out of East Friesland:
Christian IVs Breve, I. 298-305.

affection and now by a misty statesmanship, steered an erratic course which led nowhither, satisfied no one, and achieved nothing. In 1622 he was trying to save his son-in-law by diplomatic action: all that summer his agent conferred with Isabella's ministers in Brussels. The Spanish marriage now seemed to him to offer the best hope of peace and a restoration, and in October Endymion Porter left on his mission to Spain, wafted by Protestant cries of 'Bring us war!' which fell discordantly upon the royal ear. In the following February Charles and Buckingham set out upon their journey to Madrid. In March, British diplomacy negotiated an agreement on the Palatinate which might have had some prospect of success if Frederick had not refused to look at it. James' policy, pruned of its ranker growths (as for instance his readiness to engage in secret machinations against the Dutch), was not without a good deal of solid common sense; but to the Protestant world it inevitably appeared as recreant, heartless and stupid.[1]

There remained Denmark; and Kristian IV, as an important member of the Lower Saxon Circle, was bound to be increasingly drawn into German affairs as the hostilities moved northwards. In February 1623 the Lower Saxon Circle, anxious to preserve its neutrality, decided to forbid the passage of troops through its territory, and to resist any who should try to invade it. Kristian, whose north German interests were reinforced by the election of his son Fredrik as Bishop of Verden early in 1623, and who was now looking forward to the acquisition of Osnabrück, was almost forced by circumstances to consider himself in some degree the patron and protector of the Lower Saxon princes. In July he took a definite step towards war, when he induced his Council to agree to the levy of troops designed to give aid in repelling any attack upon a member of the Circle. It was clear that a new situation was developing in Germany. Tilly's final victory over Christian of Brunswick (at Stadtlohn, on 27 July) rounded off a period which had begun with Frederick's acceptance of the Bohemian crown; and even Frederick was induced so far to admit defeat as to conclude an armistice with the Emperor in August. As to what was to come next, no man on

---

[1] Camerarius wrote about this time: 'mit Heidelberg und der Kurpfalz ist's vorbei. Ursache ist der König in England. Er wird es bei der Nachwelt schwer antworten können'; and again: 'der König in England wird die Wunden nicht heilen und das Gebrochene nicht ganz machen können. Wäre besser, man hätte ihm nie getraut. Gott erbarm's. Es ist unmöglich, derselbe muss päpstlich oder ein Stier sein' (quoted in Droysen, I. 160).

the Protestant side could be certain; but no man, equally, could be otherwise than apprehensive.[1]

To Gustav Adolf, viewing European affairs in the late summer of 1623, the situation appeared fraught with difficulties and dangers. There was, in the first place, the state of Protestantism in Germany, which he characterized in a letter to Adolf Frederick of Mecklenburg as 'wol depleurable'[2]; disunion in counsel, timidity in action, wilful blindness to danger, a cynical indifference to the fate of others —these things, he felt, were laying Protestant Germany at the feet of Emperor and League. In this emergency, Kristian IV was appearing in the deceptive guise of protector and deliverer. However genuine might be Kristian's concern for the fate of the evangelical religion, it was undeniable that he was using his championship of the cause to secure important extensions of his influence. It seemed to Gustav Adolf that the Lower Saxon princes were drifting into the position of Danish clients.[3] The assertion of Imperial and Catholic control over north Germany would be a disaster; but the alternative of Danish domination was only a degree less objectionable. Indeed, from Sweden's point of view it might well be more objectionable, since as yet the threat from Imperial aggression was remote, while the possibility of war with Denmark seemed to grow stronger every month. It would be a grievous misfortune if, in an effort to escape the attentions of Tilly, the north German states submitted meekly to the aggrandizement of the power of Denmark, already too strong. Meanwhile the danger from Poland was in no way diminished. The invasion might have been postponed; but Gustav Adolf did not believe that it had been abandoned.[4] The situation as regarded Danzig remained unsatisfactory. Sigismund,

---

[1] Ritter, III. 235-6, 239-40, 251; Fridericia, *DRH*, pp. 167-8; Hallenberg, V. 94; Gardiner, V. 78; Wedgwood, p. 185; Koser, p. 395; Schweitzer, pp. 745-6. The Imperialists were apprehensive too: it was thought that only the victory at Stadtlohn had prevented a Swedish landing in Germany. Ahnlund, *HT* 1917, p. 265 *note* 2.

[2] Styffe, pp. 411-12: 'da der Nidersexsische kreiss nur dagfaarten helt vnd deliberiret auf was weise sihe stillen sitzen mügen vnd praeda victoris werden können.'

[3] Styffe, p. 412; and *cf. ibid.*, p. 420: '. . . E.L. [*sc.* Adolf Frederick] sagen noch sihe wollen ihn [*sc.* Kristian IV] nicht mehr respectiren als einen hertzogh von Holstein, meinen auch das die sachen mehr ihn halten, als ehr die sachen in seinen mechten habe, meinen daneben ihr sembtlich wollet dar vor sein das man in solchem turbido nicht sollen fischen. Aber ich halts dar vor das die fischen schon gefangen sein. . . .'

[4] *cf. Handl. rörande Skand. Hist.*, XVI. 137-40, which prints three letters from Sigismund urging the fleet to get ready and put to sea as quickly as possible (March-August 1624).

taking a leaf out of Kristian's book, was trying to assert his control over the Bishopric of Cammin—a design which, if it were successful, would tear a hole in the solid bastion of Protestant states which guarded the Baltic littoral between Lübeck and the Vistula.[1] If the Imperialists were to be kept from the North Sea, if Denmark were to be checked in her attempts at a north German hegemony, if the gates of Pomerania were to be slammed in Sigismund's face, one thing was obviously needed: a vigorous effort by the German Protestants themselves. It was a fair question whether such an effort, unaided, would avail. Therefore, its success must be assured by the provision of support from outside. That support could come only from two quarters: one was the Netherlands; the other was Sweden.

In the autumn of 1623, therefore, Gustav Adolf evolved a double plan. On the one hand he encouraged the formation of a league of north German princes, independent of Denmark. In a long letter to Adolf Frederick of Mecklenburg, dated 6 August, he outlined the constitution of such a league (its pretext was to be the rescue of the unfortunate Enno III), suggested the size and nature of the forces which it should aim at maintaining, and made a clear offer of support in arms, if they should need it.[2] On the other hand he tried to enlist the cooperation of the Dutch in a joint campaign. Since the summer of 1623 Rutgers had been in The Hague as permanent Swedish Resident, and here he had renewed contact with Camerarius and other advisers of Frederick V. Rutgers was now instructed to propose to the States General the plan of a diversion, which should draw off the forces of the League from central and northern Germany. The ideal place for such a diversion, he conceded, would be Italy; but the practical difficulties made this impossible. The next best place was Poland. Gustav Adolf proposed, therefore, that he should renew the Polish war, and so prosecute it as to threaten Silesia, Moravia and the Habsburg hereditary lands. All remaining Protestant forces in Germany would also concentrate their efforts in this area; while Bethlen Gabor might attack it from the southeast. Thus the whole burden of the war would be transferred to

---

[1] Paul, I. 156; Styffe, p. 412; cf. AOSB, I. III. 85.
[2] Styffe, pp. 413-14, 419-20, and cf. ibid., pp. 408-9. Gustav Adolf suggested as members of the league the Mecklenburg Dukes, Rostock, the Duke of Holstein, Lübeck, Hamburg, the Counts of Schauenburg and East Friesland. 'Bremen wil ich nicht nennen, weil sihe zu stockfische geworden seindt' (because of their subordination to Denmark): ibid., p. 413; ibid., p. 361, for his judgment on Mansfeld, whom he described, with considerable understatement, as 'leichtfertig'.

SIGISMUND III

GUSTAV ADOLF
about 1626

Polish and Habsburg territory, and the centre of hostilities would be shifted bodily eastward, outside the limits of the Empire. If this were done (as he explained later to Adolf Frederick of Mecklenburg) the Emperor could take no umbrage if the Lower Saxon Circle participated in the campaign.[1] And it was to assist in the carrying out of this plan that the Dutch were now to be asked to conclude an offensive and defensive alliance with Sweden.[2]

A month later (in September) the proposal was made still more precise in a set of instructions for Gustav Horn, who was setting out for the Netherlands on a recruiting mission. It was now suggested that Sweden should supply an army of 21,600 foot and 3000 horse; that the landing-place of this army should be Putzig; that the Dutch should make themselves responsible for the neutrality of Danzig; and that the supreme command and direction of the combined operations should be given to the King of Sweden. And it was clearly stated that Gustav Adolf, although much moved by the sufferings of Germany, was not prepared at this stage to undertake direct intervention on German soil: any effort on behalf of German Protestantism must be combined with a blow at Poland, or it could hardly be justified from Sweden's point of view. The aim was thus a double one: first to finish the Polish war (which, as he ingenuously explained, made it impossible for him to pay his debts to the Dutch) and secondly to carry out a complete restoration of affairs in Germany.[3]

The instructions for Rutgers and Horn, taken in conjunction with the series of letters which Gustav Adolf addressed to Adolf Frederick of Mecklenburg in the course of this autumn and the following spring, make it plain that Swedish policy is moving towards new lines of action. Gustav Adolf has begun to suspect that Sigismund is not to be constrained to good-neighbourliness by the loss of Riga and Pernau, nor even, perhaps, by a Swedish conquest of all Livonia. Already the King's thought is turning towards that transference of the war to Prussia which was to come in 1626, and was to be the real turning-point of the reign. If peace is to be won from Poland, the screw must be tightened; and the most sensible purchase, as he already perceives, is to be obtained on

[1] Styffe, p. 424.
[2] *AOSB*, I. ii. 583-6; Droysen, I. 187-9; Schybergson, pp. xxv-xxix, 18-62; Ahnlund, *Oxenstierna*, pp. 272-5; Ahnlund, *HT* 1917, pp. 259-63.
[3] *AOSB*, I. ii. 591-7, 583; Schybergson, pp. xxxi-xxxii, xxxvii; Ahnlund, *HT* 1917, pp. 263-8.

P

the great artery of Poland, the Vistula. At the same time, the
pressure upon Sigismund is to be increased by transporting the
German war to Polish soil. Gustav Adolf is here dealing in that
strategy of forage and quarters, forced contributions and devastation,
which was soon to be typical of the Thirty Years' War. On the
other hand, he contemplates—even if only for a moment—the
prospect of armed intervention in Germany itself. The idea is
indeed abandoned in favour of a Polish 'diversion'; but it has been
put forward for the first time; and Gustav Adolf was never again
wholly to lose sight of it. If the campaign of 1626 was already
implicit, so too was the relief of Stralsund. The two competing
policies which were to struggle for predominance in the later
'twenties—the policy of a 'diversion', and that of direct intervention
in Germany—are already face to face. Further, it has become plain
that Gustav Adolf is approaching a point, if he has not already
reached it, where he will be unable to sit still and contemplate with
indifference the growing influence of Denmark in German affairs.
The rivalry with Kristian IV, not merely in the Baltic but upon the
Continent, is already declared. Lastly, it is possible to discern, even
at this early stage, one of the principles which was to remain constant
in Gustav Adolf's dealings with other Protestant powers: his determination not to commit himself to any enterprise over which he shall
have no effective control. To Adolf Frederick, to the Dutch, he
suggests already that he shall be 'caput', that he shall have the real
direction of any joint army of which Swedes are to form a considerable part. In his attitude to the German problem it seems that he
determined from the very beginning that he would not be the tool
or catspaw of other powers, nor squander his new army (of which
he was already bragging a little) [1] in ventures for which he was not
to be responsible, and which might possibly be unsound.

The negotiations of the autumn of 1623, despite the efforts of
Camerarius (who paid his first visit to Sweden at this time) [2] proved
in fact abortive. The Dutch refused the bait which was dangled
before them; Adolf Frederick merely reiterated his irritating advice
to make peace quickly with Poland. But though the negotiations
thus remained resultless, they were not insignificant. They marked
a stage in the progress from Riga to Peenemünde, presaged the

---

[1] Barkman, p. 149; Styffe, p. 423.
[2] See Ritter, III. 276, for the favourable impression Camerarius obtained of
Gustav Adolf.

opening of a new phase in Swedish policy, at the same time as they represented one more example of the efforts of Gustav Adolf—as of Karl IX before him—to *conjungieren* the Polish war with the Protestant cause elsewhere. The German princes, as appeared from Adolf Frederick, remained as sceptical as ever of the validity of the King's contention that his quarrel was also theirs; they urged peace upon him, accused him of ambition, or of a youthful folly. He answered them, patiently explaining the impossibility of extracting peace from Sigismund[1]: because he had taken Riga, there was no need to charge him with a desire to control all the great ports and estuaries of the Baltic: 'If I draw a pail of water from the Baltic, am I to be supposed desirous of drinking up the sea?'[2] And indeed, his critics did him less than justice in attributing to him a cynicism, a self-interest, a lack of confessional solidarity equal to their own. Sweden's interest, the Protestant cause—they were in Gustav Adolf's eyes nearly identical: the disasters of Höchst and Stadtlohn were defeats for Sweden, just as (he would have contended) the loss of Mitau was a blow to Protestantism in general. With Sigismund on his hands, any large-scale commitment in Germany appeared impossible. With Denmark as a probable foe next year he must try by diplomacy to put a solid German league in Denmark's place, as a bastion for the Protestant North. But that did not mean that he was not deeply concerned at the catastrophes in Germany. His religious feeling was of a different intensity from—for instance— Queen Elizabeth's: his politics were not of the sort that had permitted her cold exploitation of the Dutch. And, as was to appear, he was capable of a large generosity to Kristian IV, in the name of common religion, once Kristian had been brought to abandon—or even to seem to abandon—his hostile designs upon Sweden. For the rest, as Gustav Adolf truly said, he had no secret plans of Baltic predominance. He followed where his enemies pointed, proceeding from expedient to expedient, governed only by the broadest general principles of Sweden's safety and the upholding of the evangelical religion, led on from conquest to conquest not by the ambition of the warrior, nor even by a conscious economic imperialism (as his uncles had been), but by political logic, hard necessity, and the

---

[1] Styffe, pp. 434, 421-2: 'die erlangungh des fridens so solche mit sich füret ist vnmüglich vnd nicht in meiner gewalt oder wilckür dar in zu disponiren, vnd solte auch der Niedersexische kreitz oder aber die gantze welt mit meinen nachbaren sich conjungiren könte ichs doch nicht besseren'.

[2] Styffe, pp. 439, 433 *seqq.*, 442.

imperious demands of a clear-visioned strategy. There was not any time when he would not have preferred peace, if peace were to be had on reasonable terms. For him at least the perpetuation of the German holocaust was not an end in itself. His reign was no isolated phenomenon in Swedish history: a link, rather, in a long chain which had first been forged by his grandfather, and which was not to break until 1718; but with this difference, that in his time the chain was double—religious as well as political—and was therefore the stronger and the more binding.

(v) *Diplomatic Defeat of Denmark, 1624*

Since the proposal for a Protestant League and a Polish 'diversion' had alike met with so unsatisfactory a response, nothing remained but to resume negotiations with Sigismund's emissaries, in the hope that some more extended truce might even yet be wrested from them. The hope proved vain. In the prolonged negotiations which took place at Wolmar in the autumn of 1623 it became clear that however greatly Radziwiłł, or the Lithuanians, or the Poles in general, might desire a period of repose, there was no reasonable agreement to be had from Sigismund; and however much his subjects might disapprove a continuance of the struggle, they were not prepared to coerce him to terms. The Swedish notion of a Lithuanian separatist movement, headed by Radziwiłł, proved, as before, a mere notion. The negotiators, therefore, could constate no progress; and when they separated, the Truce of Ogra still remained unmodified, and hostilities stood suspended only until 1 June 1624.[1]

Unsatisfactory as this was, it was better than no truce at all; for in the autumn of 1623 it was generally expected that war with Denmark was a question only of months, and (as Gustav Adolf observed) 'ne Hector quidem contra duos'.[2] The crisis with Denmark had been banking up since 1619. The discussions of that year, though they had led to a notable diminution in tension, had not wholly cleared the air.[3] Grievances remained, for either side to

---

[1] Swedish terms in *AOSB*, I. ii. 589. And see Hallenberg, V. 243-59; *AOSB*, II. v. 238, 251; Cronholm, I. 426-32; Ahnlund, *Oxenstierna*, p. 264; Schybergson, p. xxxi.

[2] Styffe, p. 417.

[3] Evidence of the desire of Sweden to maintain good relations (at least for the moment) is (*e.g.*) *SILR*, p. 131; *RRP*, I. v.

exploit at the most opportune moment. Already in 1619 Denmark was formulating the complaint which five years later was to be the main bone of contention between the countries and was to bring them to the verge of war. By the peace of Knäred each party had agreed not to levy toll upon the subjects of the other. The Swedish government, however, did not hold itself precluded by this provision from imposing a toll upon its own subjects, in the form of a sales-tax on exports. The Danes complained, with perfect truth, that the Swedish merchants who paid the toll passed it on to their customers in the form of higher prices, so that in effect Danish purchasers were being tolled, in contravention of the terms of Knäred. The Swedes retorted, no less justly, that the Danes were not obliged to buy, and that it would be an intolerable infringement of national sovereignty if Gustav Adolf were to be debarred from imposing upon his own subjects such imposts as he might think proper.[1] Here then was one nice point of controversy. There was no lack of others. The Swedes, for instance, complained in 1620 of outrages by Danish officials on the Norwegian border.[2] The Danes were concerned at the publication of scurrilous pamphlets; the Swedes retorted with stories of tendentious histories by Danish scholars. The Lappmark question, it appeared, had still not been given decent burial, for Danish officials levied taxes in Swedish territory, while Sweden claimed right of access to the North Sea for her nomadic Lapps and *birkarlar*.[3] Despite the ostensible cordiality at Halmstad in 1619, and notwithstanding an admiration for each other's qualities which did something to soften asperities, there was no doubt that Gustav Adolf and Kristian feared and distrusted each other.[4] Kristian rightly believed that the question of *dominium maris Baltici* was still considered open in Stockholm; and he was irritated and alarmed by the rapid growth and prosperity of Göteborg.[5] His attitude to Gustav Adolf's marriage had been notably lacking in warmth; and Oxenstierna had been genuinely concerned at the

---

[1] Hallenberg, IV. 824-8; C. Danielsson, *1500- och 1600-talens svenska tullpolitik* (*Statsv. T.* 1924), pp. 401-2. Possibly the tolls were imposed in an attempt to keep out Danish merchants from the upland towns, and force trade to Göteborg: H. Almquist, *Göteborgs Historia*, I. 245-6. The Danish agent, Peder Galt, on the other hand, viewed the question astrologically, and inclined to the opinion that the difficulty was bound up with the unfavourable position of the planet Saturn: *Peder Galts Depescher*, p. 80.

[2] Hallenberg, IV. 830.

[3] *AOSB*, I. II. 357; *Christian IVs Breve*, I. 273.

[4] Fridericia, *DRH*, p. 163.

[5] Hallenberg, IV. 895-900; H. Almquist, *Göteborg*, I. 3.

possibility that the Danish fleet might interfere with the Swedish squadron that brought home the bride.[1] Kristian had been annoyed, too, by Sweden's failure to participate in the Segeberg congress. Gustav Adolf's attempt to extend the Swedish exemption from Sound Tolls to the new acquisitions in Livonia was resented in Copenhagen; and Kristian complained that non-Swedish goods were passing through the Sound under cover of falsified certificates of ownership which purported to prove that they were Swedish. This was undoubtedly true. In 1621 Gustav Adolf had appointed a special agent stationed permanently at Helsingör to check these abuses; but the evasions had continued.[2] The establishment, in January 1622, of a permanent Danish Resident in Stockholm, tended to exacerbate rather than to improve relations; for Peder Galt, the new ambassador, was difficult, sharp-tongued, and contemptuous of all things Swedish, and he was suspected by the Swedish government of the most dangerous connections with notorious Polish spies.[3] There was some uneasiness in Stockholm lest Denmark might use her control of the Sound to interfere with the supply of munitions of war; but when in the spring of 1622 Gabriel Gustafsson Oxenstierna went to Copenhagen to try to obtain some understanding on this important point, he was sent back empty-handed.[4] In the summer of 1622 Kristian IV was eliciting from his Council a definition of Denmark's claims to the sovereignty of the seas; and there seemed every chance that he would endeavour to make them good.[5] In August of that year he gave Sweden a time-limit of six months within which to remove the obnoxious sales-tax, failing which he proposed to levy duties on Swedes passing the Sound; and for a time all trade between the two countries was prohibited by both sides. Galt appeared to lose no opportunity of aggravating ill-feeling, and by the beginning of 1623 all the superficial friendliness of 1619 had vanished. In January Abraham Brahe was warning his son not to risk the overland journey through Denmark; while in April his sleep was vexed by political nightmares, in which he dreamed that the King and the entire *råd* were languishing in a Danish prison.[6]

[1] Fridericia, *DRH*, p. 168; *Christian IVs Breve*, I. 180.
[2] Hallenberg, V. 265-7; Hill, p. 104; Grill, *Jakob de la Gardie*, p. 73; T. Söderberg, *Sveriges ekonomiska struktur och utveckling*, p. 81.
[3] Ahnlund, *Oxenstierna*, p. 248; Galt, p. iii.
[4] Hallenberg, V. 9-12.
[5] Hill, p. 93, for the limits of the Danish claims.
[6] *Abraham Brahes Tidebok*, pp. 148, 150.

Five days after this alarming portent Kristian denounced that article of the Treaty of Knäred which guaranteed freedom of trade to subjects of both countries, and began to levy toll at Helsingör upon Swedish ships and merchandise, though Gustav Adolf had provided him in March with full explanations about the true nature of the Swedish sales-tax.[1] A formal rupture now appeared imminent. Already in January there had been a rumour of an impending Danish invasion, which had sent Gustav Adolf galloping to the Småland frontier, and had led to the fortification of Skara, Mariestad, and other small places in Västergötland.[2] Now it was feared that the Polish armada—confidently expected for this summer— might be aided or convoyed by a Danish fleet; while on the other hand Kristian suspected that Swedish naval preparations were directed not against Sigismund but against himself.[3] Sweden most certainly did not desire a war with Denmark in 1623: hence the conciliatory attitude of Gustav Adolf upon such minor matters as the Lappmark controversy [4]; hence the communication which the råd in August sent to the Danish Council, wherein they suggested recurrence to the traditional expedient of a conference on the frontier.[5] But Denmark showed no signs of tractability: Rutgers and Horn were denied free transit through Denmark on their way to The Hague[6]; and Peder Galt warned his master to see that the fleet was ready to put to sea.[7]

By the late autumn of 1623 Sweden was better able to deal with the controversy. The Polish invasion had been proved an illusion; the Truce of Ogra, for what it was worth, had been reaffirmed. In these circumstances relations with Denmark were discussed at an important meeting of the råd held at Strängnäs on 23 November.[8] There the King laid before them an analysis of the international situation, particularly as it affected Scandinavia, and asked their advice as to the expediency of a preventive war with Denmark, declaring himself willing to abide by their decision. Their reply was that, since war seemed sooner or later inevitable, it would be better to decide upon a rupture without more ado. But they added that one final effort should be made to settle the differences by negotiating at

---

1 Thyresson, p. 300; Hallenberg, V. 268, 273; Styffe, p. 417.
2 Sv. Kr., II. 157; Galt, p. 49.
3 Generalstaben, p. 129; Christian IVs Breve, I. 288.
4 Galt, pp. 81-3.   5 Sv. Kr., II. 159.
6 Hallenberg, V. 274.   7 Galt, p. 85 (12 May 1623).
8 Ahnlund, Ståndsriksdagens Utdaning, pp. 156-7; Ahnlund, Oxenstierna, p. 279.

the frontier. Armed with this advice, Gustav Adolf went down early in 1624 to Bohuslän to make a personal inspection of an area where the Danes had recently been reported as committing violations of the frontier (he was shot at by a Danish outpost for his pains); while Oxenstierna devoted the winter evenings to the drafting of a memorandum discussing the respective advantages of an offensive and a defensive strategy.[1] As the spring drew on, Gustav Adolf began to think of enlisting the support, or at least the benevolent neutrality, of the Hanse towns, in the event of a conflict with Denmark.[2] But at the eleventh hour Kristian permitted counsels of moderation to prevail: in March 1624 he announced his readiness to negotiate; a meeting at Sjöaryd was fixed for the month of May; and the tension for the moment was somewhat eased.

The discussions which began at Sjöaryd on 29 May 1624 were prolonged for nearly five weeks.[3] Gustav Adolf regarded them as so important that he arranged for the erection of a private tent abutting on that in which the conferences were to take place, so that he might listen to the proceedings unperceived. Within a few days the negotiations had reached a critical phase. On 4 June Gustav Adolf hastily left the meeting place, apparently fearing that a Danish *coup de main* was intended, and that he and his diplomats might shortly find themselves Kristian's prisoners. He made all haste back to Stockholm, and took measures to strengthen the forces near the frontier. The fleet was got ready; a squadron was fitted out at Älvsborg; and the Småland levies moved south, in order to be within call should Oxenstierna require them. Oxenstierna, thus left in charge of negotiations, and promoted for the time being commander-in-chief on the Danish border, found the steady forward roll of his diplomacy rather incommoded by the King's long-range interference. He feared that Gustav Adolf's military precautions might provoke counter-measures on the Danish side, and that a frontier 'incident' might precipitate the war he was labouring to avoid. The King, on the other hand, always believed in supporting diplomacy by a display of force, and contended that Kristian would be unlikely to give way unless he were convinced

---

[1] *AOSB*, I. I. 514 *seqq.*; and see Galt, p. 108.
[2] *AOSB*, I. I. 520.
[3] For these negotiations, see *AOSB*, I. II. 610, 624, 638-9, 641, 664, 668, 681, 695, 701, 714; II. I. 226-38, 242, 244, 247, 260-2; II. III. 74, 76; *Christian IVs Breve*, I. 374-81; Hallenberg, V. 284-300, 307-8; *Sv. Kr.*, II. 161-4; Ahnlund, *Oxenstierna*, pp. 283-8; Petri, II. 148-150; G. Björlin, *Johan Banér*, I. 56-8.

that Sweden was ready for war, and that Oxenstierna would not shrink from it. Certainly Kristian long kept a high tone in his letters to his negotiators: as late as 15 June he was writing 'I will absolutely not allow him [Gustav Adolf] to become stronger in the Baltic than he is.' But in spite of his brave words he was nervous about the military situation. He had not enough men to garrison his fortresses; his sailors had all been paid off. The fortresses could not be provisioned, for there were hardly supplies enough for the fleet. Conscious of their military weakness, the Danes were driven by Oxenstierna's steady pressure of argument to concession, to evasion, to procrastination; Danish suggestions for mediation or arbitration by a foreign power were firmly rejected; and in the days after 24 June the Chancellor brought matters to an issue by presenting successive ultimata. On 29 June 1624 the Danes gave way on all major issues, and Oxenstierna had won a great diplomatic triumph.

The treaty of 29 June was a resounding victory for Sweden over her old adversary.[1] Gustav Adolf's right to toll his own subjects was fully admitted; the provisions of the Treaty of Knäred regarding reciprocal free trade were reaffirmed; and Kristian promised to revoke his order to levy toll on Swedish ships and merchandise passing through the Sound. The Danish demand for a proper certificate of ownership for such merchandise was dropped—at least as regarded a sworn declaration. Sweden was given a free pass for warlike stores through Danish waters. The peccant Danish frontier officials were to be punished for their excess of zeal. Thus on all important points Sweden enforced her point of view.

It is impossible to mistake the significance of what had happened. The verdict of 1613 had been set aside, if it had not yet been absolutely reversed. The challenge offered by Kristian IV had been taken up; and when it came to the touch, he had declined the contest. And the reasons for this result were essentially military and naval. In 1624 Sweden was no longer the enfeebled state of 1613, nor even of 1619. The simple truth was that Kristian had not dared to risk a war; and even had he dared, his Council would have offered such resistance as to make it difficult for him to insist. The Swedish military reforms had begun to have their effect; the Swedish navy was again formidable. Kristian had hoped, perhaps, to bluster his

[1] Text of the treaty in *Sv. Trakt.*, V₂. 321-9; and see *AOSB*, I. II. 713; Hallenberg, V. 297-300; *Sv. Kr.*, II. 165.

way to a diplomatic victory which should conceal from Europe the renaissance of Sweden's strength; his unexpected capitulation dealt a proportionately heavy blow to his own prestige. The issue of a war at this time would, perhaps, have been still doubtful: Sweden had not as yet established a clear military superiority over her neighbour. But Kristian could never recover the ground he lost in these June days of 1624. He went to Sjöaryd incontestably the leading sovereign in the North; he returned home in bitterness and defeat, already constrained to admit Gustav Adolf as his equal, and probably foreseeing the day when he might be forced to admit him as his superior. Throughout the century which had elapsed since Gustav Vasa liberated his country from the Danish connexion, Sweden had always been obviously inferior to Denmark in military strength and European consideration; and even after 1613 the old Danish dream of a restored Union had not been wholly abandoned. After 1624 even the sanguine Kristian could dream that dream no longer; and the road was already opening ahead which was to lead to Brömsebro, Roskilde and Travendal. The balance of power in the Baltic stood nicely poised; but the beam was tipping—slowly as yet, decisively after Lutter—and it was tipping in Sweden's favour.

(vi) *The Anglo-Brandenburg Project for a Protestant Alliance, 1624-25*

While Sweden and Denmark were thus wrangling about tolls and taxes, developments had been taking place in western Europe which were eventually to have a considerable effect upon the history of each of them. The preceding year, 1623, had been the year of Charles' journey to Madrid, the year when it seemed certain that the Spanish marriage must take place, and that England was as good as lost to the Protestant cause. The new year 1624 opened in a very different atmosphere. Charles and Buckingham were home again, full of rancour against the Spaniard; the light airs of English policy veered, backed, and veered again, strengthened to a Protestant breeze, and rose to a storm of evangelical enthusiasm. King and Parliament were at one for war; and though James might think mainly of the Palatinate to be regained, while Parliament through the mouth of Sir Benjamin Rudyerd hankered after Spanish Plate fleets, this disparity of aim was not for the moment apparent. The exiled Palatines took fresh heart, and Protestants everywhere brisked up at the prospect of a 'League Euangelicall'. When Spens landed in England in February to remonstrate upon the permission lately granted to Robert Stewart to enlist men for Sigismund's service, he found the political climate as benign as could be desired.[1] English envoys were departing to all quarters of the sky to stir up trouble for the Emperor and Philip IV. Negotiations were on foot with the Dutch for a closer league; and not even the news of the Massacre of Amboyna (which arrived in May) could disturb a cordiality which must have appeared miraculous to those who minded how lately James had been plotting the conquest of the Netherlands with Gondomar. Sir Isaac Wake was at Turin, inflaming—in super-erogation, as he himself pointed out—the martial ardours of Charles Emmanuel I. Mansfeld arrived in England in April, was greeted 'as a great prince or a saint', and given large commissions to raise troops, and larger promises of their maintenance. And already in February Lord Kensington had left for Paris upon that confidential mission which was to lead, ten months later, to the betrothal of Charles to Henrietta Maria. So much activity looked like business; but Oxenstierna, retailing the news to John Casimir, had his doubts. It might be very well for the moment, 'ich fürchte aber es sey ein fervor, undt nicht wohl durchgekochtt'.[2]

Nevertheless, it accorded well with the trend of events in France, where the old ministers were disappearing, and where on 29 April 1624 Cardinal Richelieu re-entered the Council of State after seven uncomfortable years in the wilderness. Until October, he was nominally subordinate to La Vieuville, but in fact from this moment his spirit began to direct French foreign policy. In the course of the summer he launched a modest diplomatic offensive: in June a treaty of defensive alliance against Spain with England and the Dutch; in July agreement upon the Valtelline with Savoy and Venice; two embassies despatched to Germany—Marescot to the Protestants, Vaubicourt to the Catholics. True, their success was but slender, and from John George of Saxony Marescot must bear even insult; but it was the beginning of a move away from the passivity of Puysieulx. Richelieu had no intention of fighting the Habsburgs until the monarchy had been securely established at home; the initiative in foreign policy could hardly as yet be said to be in his hands; but at least he could do something to distract Habsburg attention from France's weakness, and if by doing so he

[1] Rydfors, p. 11.   [2] *AOSB*, I. II. 610.

encouraged the notion of a 'third party' in Germany, why, so much
the better. France after all was Catholic, and it was ill to ally with
heretics. But if James I should succeed in building up a European
coalition against Spain and Austria, he would have no scruples about
giving it a discreet support.

In the summer of 1624 James took measures to bring the
Scandinavian states into his intended league. In June Anstruther
left for Copenhagen, where he was to persuade Kristian IV to come
in, and shortly afterwards Spens set out for Stockholm on a like
errand. At Copenhagen Anstruther met with a favourable reception.
Kristian was anxious not to be forestalled by Gustav Adolf; but he
was a little nervous of being left unsupported: some reassurance
about the intentions of the north German princes would be required
before he would consent to venture. His Council was strongly
adverse to meddling with the matter at all; and it was as a result of
their pressure that the King finally gave a temporizing and discouraging answer: let Anstruther take soundings in north Germany,
and when he came back to Copenhagen with his report, he should
have a definite decision.[1]

In the meantime Spens had reached Sweden, and communicated
James' proposals to Gustav Adolf. The European league which
England was now suggesting had much in common with the plan
put forward by Gustav Adolf himself in 1623, and Spens may well
have hoped that it would obtain the King's approval. But Gustav
Adolf showed himself decidedly cautious: the scheme was still
nebulous, and he had a well-grounded doubt of England's consistency
of purpose and ability to discharge her commitments. Spens
accordingly came forward with an alternative proposal; for he was
the bearer not only of the official instructions from James but also
of secret offers from Charles and Frederick. The Prince of Wales
and the Palatine intimated that they would be prepared to support a
diversionary attack on Prussia by Gustav Adolf if he would consent
to terminate his truce with Poland; and for this purpose they were
prepared to promise £20,000 a month in subsidies. This was a
suggestion much more to the King's taste. He had disliked James'
proposals for a general league which should contain Roman Catholic
states, preferring that France and Savoy should be relegated to the

---

[1] Fridericia, *DRH*, pp. 170-2; Schybergson, *Underhandlingar*, pp. 27, 29-30,
35; *Sv. Kr.*, II. 167-8; *Christian IVs Breve*, I. 387; P. Engelstoft, *Christian IVs
Tidsalder*, p. 248; *CSP* (Venetian) 1623-5, pp. 364-5, for the scepticism of the
Venetian ambassador with regard to Anstruther's mission.

status of auxiliaries, and the league kept strictly evangelical; and
he had also disliked the implication that the grand aim of a European
coalition must be simply the recovery of the Palatinate: if he
interfered in Germany, it must be for a general restoration of the
status quo. But here now was a more specific and practical suggestion. At last someone had grasped his arguments for a 'diversion',
and was prepared, apparently, to pay for it. There must of course
be guarantees formulated, and conditions laid down: the £20,000
per month he found somewhat speculative and decidedly inadequate,
and he must have reassurance about this. He must have adequate
security for his flank and rear, if he were to make a thrust through
Silesia to the Habsburg hereditary lands; he must have an alliance
not only with England but with the Dutch; and an allied fleet of
48 sail—or at the very least, of 36 (whereof Sweden would supply
12)—to guard the Baltic and protect him from a possible attack from
Denmark. Above all, a port of disembarkation securely in his hands.
If these essential preconditions were fulfilled, he was very ready to
engage; but not otherwise.[1]

At this point there arrived at Vadstena (where the Court was
staying in this month of September) one Christopher Bellin, an envoy
from Brandenburg, whom George William had sent in July to the
northern courts on a vaguely evangelical mission. Bellin's journey
was the outcome of a change in the political balance at Berlin, where
the Imperialist party in the Council, led by Adam von Schwarzenberg,
had recently suffered eclipse. At Copenhagen Bellin was greeted
somewhat coldly, as being too patently Swedish in sympathy. He
arrived at Vadstena just when the King and Oxenstierna were
formulating their terms for invading Silesia. This was a scheme
which had no attractions for Bellin or for his master. It would
inevitably bring the war to Brandenburg territory, and it seemed to
contemplate a restoration of Bohemia to the Palatinate; and though
George William was evangelical, he was not as evangelical as all
that. It was very necessary, therefore, that Gustav Adolf should
be offered some alternative plan. Bellin accordingly proposed the
formation of a general evangelical league (that was of course), and
military intervention by Sweden in *western* Germany, with a view
to the direct recovery of the Palatinate. This would keep

[1] Rydfors, pp. 19-22; Schybergson, *Underhandlingar*, pp. 32-4; Gardiner, V.
247-8; Droysen, I. 193-7; Ritter, III. 267; Ahnlund, *Oxenstierna*, pp. 292-5;
Sv. Kr., III. 123; W. Carlsson, *Gustav Adolf och Stralsund*, pp. 4-5; *AOSB*,
I. II. 729-35.

hostilities well away from Brandenburg, while commending itself
to James I.

Rather unexpectedly, Gustav Adolf reacted favourably to this
proposal. He declared his readiness to undertake a campaign based
on the Weser rather than on the Vistula. But once again he attached
precise conditions. His allies must provide (and pay for) two-thirds
of the force of 50,000 which he deemed necessary to the enterprise;
they must pay him an agreed sum in subsidies, and they must pay it
four months in advance. Danzig must be coerced into neutrality;
two first-class harbours—one in the Baltic, one in the North Sea—
must be put into his hands, and for this purpose he suggested Wismar
and Bremen as the most convenient; a fleet must be maintained by
the allies in the North Sea under his control, and a joint fleet in the
Baltic, as a protection against Denmark; Mansfeld and Bethlen
Gabor, and perhaps the Tsar, must be invited to join[1]; and finally—
and most important—the absolute *Direktorium* of the whole enterprise must be placed in his hands. When Bellin asked him what he
would do for the cause if this last condition were not complied with,
his answer was clear and short: 'Gar nichts'. This was plain
speaking; but it was well that there should be no ambiguities to
afford a breeding-ground for future recriminations. Bellin himself
was for taking Gustav Adolf's terms; George William was persuaded;
Frederick and the Dutch seemed favourable. All now depended on
James I, who would have to find the money, and on Adolf Frederick
of Mecklenburg, who would have to hand over Wismar.[2]

It must at first sight appear a little surprising that Gustav Adolf
should have entertained Bellin's plan, and indeed thrown over
Charles' idea of an attack on Silesia in its favour. Nothing, one
would have thought, could have been more excentric to the struggle
in Poland than operations on the Weser and in the Palatinate. Yet
there were in fact reasons, and reasons of considerable weight, which
Gustav Adolf could adduce for this abrupt change of attitude. As
he himself pointed out to Bellin, the Protestant powers had shown

---

[1] Relations with Russia since 1623 had been somewhat cool, as the result of
the breakdown of marriage negotiations between Michael and Maria Eleonora's
sister Katherine. Hallenberg, V. 69-70.

[2] Rydfors, pp. 23-8; Schybergson, *Underhandlingar*, pp. 38-51; *AOSB*, I. 1.
523-4; I. 11. 747, 749, 754, 760-73; Styffe, pp. 262-3, 446; Droysen, I. 199-204;
Ahnlund, *Oxenstierna*, pp. 292-5; Schybergson, *Sveriges och Hollands dip. förb.*,
pp. xl-li; *Sv. Kr.*, II. 169-70; Ritter, III. 275; Ahnlund, *HT* 1917, p. 268
seqq.; M. Weibull, *Gustav II Adolf och Kristian IV*, pp. 6-9; Gindely, *Beiträge*,
pp. 121-4; *Letters relating to the mission of Sir Thomas Roe*, p. 85.

very little appreciation of the value of a Prussian diversion, and he had grown weary of urging it. The offers of Charles and Frederick were one degree more dubious than those of James I, which were dubious enough in all conscience: almost any properly guaranteed and soundly conceived plan was to be preferred to them. The argument which he had brought against Charles' scheme—that it would expose him dangerously to Polish attacks in flank and rear— did not apply to Bellin's—provided, of course, that the Swedish terms were accepted; for an army on the Weser would be immune from Sigismund's attentions; and since by definition Danzig would be neutralized, the danger of a Polish invasion would be done away. It was true, no doubt, that by diverting Sweden's effort to western Germany he might be endangering her gains in Livonia; but to this it might be answered that some risk must be taken for the cause of religion, that the triumph of the Imperialists would ulti- mately mean the strengthening of Poland, and that sufficient forces might probably be available to defend Riga and Pernau, if no offensive movement were undertaken. And in any case he would hope to arrange a further extension of the Truce of Ogra.[1] Besides, the terms upon which he was prepared to engage with Bellin did much in fact to secure that conjunction of the German with the Baltic issues which it had always been his study to obtain. And they reduced the risk for Sweden to a minimum. The events of 1624 had seemed to show that danger from Denmark was for the moment more imminent than danger from Poland. Gustav Adolf's stipulations took good care of this. The possession of Bremen and Wismar would be a check upon Denmark's ascendancy in the Lower Saxon Circle, and might even be a salutary threat to her open land-frontiers on the south; the allied fleets would give Sweden supremacy at sea, and thus make any Danish aggression impossibly hazardous; and, not least, the giving up to Gustav Adolf of an effective *Direktorium* would scotch Kristian's attempts to arrogate to himself the leadership of the Protestant cause in the North. If ever the notion of an evangelical league were to become a reality, it seemed that now was the moment: for the first time Brandenburg came forward to take a share in it; and there was a reasonable

---

[1] By the Truce of Dalen (18 May 1624) the Truce of Ogra had been extended to 1 June 1625, or (if neither side denounced it by three months before that date) to 1 June 1626. For the Truce of Dalen, see *Sveriges Traktater*, V_2. 317-20; *AOSB*, II. v. 262, 272, 276, 278, 283; Styffe, pp. 622-3; Hallenberg, V. 259- 261; Cronholm, I. 432-4.

expectation that other German princes might follow the Elector's example. The effort by the Germans themselves, which Gustav Adolf had looked for in vain in 1623, might now at last be forthcoming. When matters had advanced thus far, he was unwilling to see a potential league collapse for lack of his support. It would be enough that Denmark should not hinder, if she would not help. He was, perhaps, more willing than Oxenstierna to sacrifice narrowly Swedish interests for the cause of religion, more ready to identify absolutely the Protestant fortunes with his country's welfare. But he never ceased to be a realist in politics; and he judged—probably correctly—that Sweden could benefit from an expedition such as Bellin proposed, provided that his careful preconditions were punctually complied with. And although, when his terms were rejected, he later returned to the plan of a diversion, there is no reason to suppose that his calculations had been mistaken.

It is clear, at all events, that Gustav Adolf and Oxenstierna looked on Bellin's scheme very much in the light of Sweden's relations with Denmark. There was much justification for this; for despite the diplomatic triumph of the summer of 1624, the autumn and early winter saw the authorities in Stockholm in something like a panic at rumours of impending attack. The two countries seem to have been equally nervous of each other; and rumour on either side of the Sound magnified innocent measures into the preparations for a treacherous onslaught. There were frontier incidents at Skårdal, on the Bohuslän border, insignificant in themselves, but interpreted as straws showing the wind. In October came an explicit story of a secret treaty of alliance between Kristian and Sigismund. The story was believed in Stockholm, and Oxenstierna sent urgent orders to his agents and spies to spare no effort or expense to obtain further information, and even offered 10,000 florins reward for a copy of this imaginary state-paper. On 8 December it was decided to send Gabriel Gustafsson Oxenstierna to Copenhagen to demand full explanations of Denmark's military preparations; and three days later the *råd* agreed that the truce with Poland should not be denounced at the stipulated time—a decision which had reference both to the critical state of affairs with Denmark and to the possibility of intervention in Germany in 1625. The French government, alarmed at the prospect of renewed war in Scandinavia, sent des Hayes de Cormenin to compose these dissensions. But before des Hayes could reach the field of operations, the storm had died down as suddenly as it had arisen. Kristian was genuinely surprised at the suspicions entertained in Stockholm; and he made no difficulty about giving the most explicit assurances. As to the soldiers he was raising, he could tell his brother of Sweden (in the strictest confidence, of course) that they were designed for use in— Germany. Gustav Adolf need be under no apprehensions, for Kristian intended shortly to intervene on behalf of his oppressed fellow-Protestants on the Continent. And with this disconcerting intelligence Gabriel Gustafsson Oxenstierna returned to Stockholm at the end of January 1625. Even the recall of Galt soon after, and his replacement by the more conciliatory Ove Hög, imperfectly sweetened the bitter pill.[1]

The news was certainly somewhat unexpected. At the end of 1624 Bellin had gone to London, where he had joined his efforts to those of Spens and Rusdorf, and pressed Gustav Adolf's conditions upon Conway. James and his ministers had been cordial, but they had felt the danger that an acceptance of the Swedish terms might embarrass their good relations with Denmark. A Swedish *Direktorium* would undoubtedly be taken as a slight by Kristian. They therefore temporized, being anxious to acquaint themselves, before coming to a decision, with Kristian's final determination upon Anstruther's proposals. A general congress of Protestant powers was projected for April 1625, to meet at The Hague, and it would be time enough to consider Sweden's financial demands then. Bellin went to Paris a little discouraged, and got small comfort there from Richelieu's wary half-promises.[2]

In the meantime, Kristian had at length bestirred himself. Anstruther had returned to Copenhagen in December armed with fuller powers to conclude an agreement about subsidies and troops. Despite the warnings of his ministers, Kristian now took the plunge. He offered to form an army at once, and to lead it into Germany as soon as possible, provided England would supply 7000 men to his 5000; and he indicated that he hoped to recruit at least 18,000 men

---

[1] *AOSB*, I. II. 766-83; I. III. 11-13, 15, 18, 58-60; Styffe, pp. 454-5; F. C. von Moser, *Neues Patriotisches Archiv für Deutschland* (cited, Moser, *NPA*), I. 37, 41; S. Loenbom, *Svenska Archivum*, II. 51-122 (G. G. Oxenstierna's Instruction and Narrative); A. Tongas, *L'Ambassadeur Louis Deshayes de Cormenin*, pp. 46-55 (much exaggerates the importance of Richelieu's intervention); *Mémoires et Négociations secrètes de Mr. de Rusdorf*, I. 415; Hallenberg, V. 307-19; *RRP*, I. 4, 6-8; *A. Brahes Tidebok*, p. 157; Ahnlund, *Oxenstierna*, pp. 283, 298-301; *Christian IVs Breve*, I. 387; H. Almquist, *Göteborg*, I. 80; M. Weibull, pp. 11-14.

[2] Gardiner, V. 298; Schybergson, *Underhandlingar*, pp. 56-8; Rusdorf, I. 419-81, 493-8.

in addition. Now this, in comparison with Gustav Adolf's stringent demands, was to England a very attractive offer. No advances in cash; no guaranteed landing-places; no auxiliary allied fleets. And the cost was so much less! Gustav Adolf's requirements would probably cost England £400,000 per annum; Kristian's, at most, £180,000—a very important consideration for a government which was committed to spending £240,000 per annum on Mansfeld, £100,000 on the Dutch, and £300,000 on the fleet, out of a parliamentary grant of at most £300,000.[1] The English government did not hesitate for long. By the middle of February it had decided to throw Gustav Adolf over, and on 20 February 1625 James I accepted Kristian's terms.[2]

Kristian now began his preparations. In March he convened a meeting of the princes of the Lower Saxon Circle at Lauenburg. He succeeded in persuading them to arm for defence, and to recommend his election as Captain-General of the Circle, in succession to the aged and somewhat Imperially-minded Christian of Lüneburg. There was no doubt about it: Kristian meant business. As to the motives which prompted this sudden exchange of apparent indifference for religious ardour there has been more than one opinion. It has been alleged that he was jealous of Gustav Adolf, that he wished to scotch Bellin's plan, that he feared to lose, in James I, his only real friend. Oxenstierna certainly believed that he was moved by personal animus.[3] Yet it seems at least doubtful whether Kristian was aware of the proposals which Bellin bore to London; and the supposition that he was deliberately underbidding Gustav Adolf lacks solid foundation. His actions were based on a sound and consistent appreciation of the realities of the situation. He was no crusader for the faith, and religious idealism was not likely to divert him from national or dynastic interests.[4] He was aware that James

---

[1] James said early in 1625, 'I am not so great or rich a prince as to do so much [as Sweden demanded]. I am only the King of two poor little islands.' Rusdorf, I. 422.

[2] Rusdorf, I. 484-8, 510-32; Fridericia, *DRH*, pp. 170-3; Rydfors, pp. 31-41, 46; Gardiner, V. 295-9; Droysen, I. 212-19; *AOSB*, I. III. 14, 30; Ritter, III. 279.

[3] *AOSB*, I. III. 26: 'If this is not so, then I neither know men nor have any skill in policy.' And compare Salvius' judgment (1646): 'The Dutch, France and England laboured for seven years with the King of Denmark to make him go to war with the Emperor; but no argument weighed so much with him to persuade him thereunto, as jealousy against King Gustav Adolf' (quoted by Hallenberg, V. 333).

[4] Contrast Anstruther's view that he took up arms 'for noe other use as for the good of Christendoom and the Libertie of Germany': (Schybergson, *Under-*

was looking for allies, and particularly for some prince to take the military direction of a league in which the Dutch were also to be included; and he realized that Denmark could not afford to see the lead pass into Gustav Adolf's hands. As at Segeberg, he must appear as the champion of the Protestant cause, lest the Dutch incline to Sweden as their mainstay in the North. He therefore asserted a claim to the *Direktorium* for himself; and as he was less conservative in his estimates and more sanguine in his expectations than Gustav Adolf, it happened that he was able to offer terms which were considerably more attractive, although, as he later found to his cost, they by no means secured him against being left in the lurch. He plunged therefore into the adventure, against the wishes of his advisers, without a proper calculation of forces and money required, supported by the barest majority in the Lower Saxon Circle, and handicapped by the sullen ill-will of the north German cities. The political ends were sound; but the method of attaining them was rightly condemned by the Danish historian of Kristian's foreign policy as 'frivolous'.[1]

Whatever may have been the motives which animated Kristian, the facts of the situation were unambiguous: Denmark had seized the leadership of Protestant Europe, and Sweden was left out in the cold. The western powers were a little shamefaced about it. Dudley Carleton, and Camerarius, and Maurice of Orange, felt that some arrangement ought to be possible which would permit both sovereigns to fight side by side. These well-meant suggestions fell flat, at all events in Stockholm. If Kristian imagined that intervention in Germany could be successful with a smaller army and more exiguous subsidies than Gustav Adolf demanded, let him try it: Sweden would wish him all success, and would refrain from interfering.[2] By the end of March 1625 Gustav Adolf had already made up his mind to renew the Polish war, and the only projects he was now interested in were projects for a diversion upon the Vistula.[3] The absolute refusal of Adolf Frederick of Mecklenburg

handlingar, p. 69 *note* 20) with John Casimir's (Moser, *NPA*, I. 37) and Aitzema's: 'dat de koningh meer socht d'incorporatie van de stiften als de restitutie van de Paltz; want des koninghk meest oogmerk was de stiften aen Holstein te hechten, eerst onder tytel van bischop; daerna erfelyck': Schweitzer, p. 753.

[1] *Christian IVs Breve*, I. 402, 408-13; Fridericia, *YPH*, pp. 24-30; Fridericia, *DRH*, pp. 174-5; Schybergson, *Underhandlingar*, pp. 59-75; Hallenberg, V. 333-4; Ritter, III. 278, 282, 284; Droysen, I. 227-8; Carlsson, p. 5 *note* 2; Paul, I. 164-5; Engelstoft, p. 249; Schweitzer, pp. 748-51.

[2] *AOSB*, I. III. 54; Schybergson, *Underhandlingar*, pp. 77-83.

[3] *AOSB*, I. III. 60 *seqq.*; Schybergson, pp. liii-lvii; Ahnlund, *Oxenstierna*, p. 305; *Sv. Kr.*, II. 238.

to consider allowing the use of Wismar as a landing-place and base for any expedition had in any case made Bellin's scheme chimerical as far as Sweden was concerned.[1] In April Gabriel Gustafsson Oxenstierna was sent on a diplomatic tour to Mecklenburg, Brandenburg, the Hanse towns, and so to Holland and England. The pretext alleged was the offering of condolences upon the deaths of James I and Maurice; but the real purpose was less formal and more important. There is no doubt that Oxenstierna was bidden to sow distrust of Denmark in the north German states, to foment the existing ill-will between Denmark and the Hanse, and by offering guarded promises of assistance (notably to Stralsund) to seek to build up a Swedish party in north Germany.[2]

The promoters of the Protestant League, however, were reluctant to believe that the support of Sweden had been lost. As a result of a meeting between George William of Brandenburg and Kristian IV in April a new offer was made to Gustav Adolf. It was now proposed that Denmark and Sweden should field distinct armies, and be assigned separate theatres of action: there was to be a Swedish landing at Stettin, to be followed by a campaign up the Oder in the direction of Silesia, while Kristian was to operate from Bremen up the Weser. Kristian even professed himself to be ready to hand over to Gustav Adolf the mercenary troops he had already enlisted, provided his expenses were refunded to him. It was a plan more indicative of Brandenburg's anxiety to include Sweden in the coalition than of Kristian's magnanimity, and it was received with scepticism in Stockholm. Cooperation in Kristian's rickety venture had still few attractions for Gustav Adolf. But at least he could put the sincerity of these offers to the test. He therefore declared himself prepared to cooperate with Kristian, provided that the allied contributions in men and money were equally shared between them; he was even willing to accept less than his original terms to Bellin; but he must have from three to four months' pay in advance. He took strong exception, however, to the area of operations to be allotted to him. Of the four possible lines of advance into Germany—up the Weser, the Elbe, the Oder, the Vistula—he liked the Oder least, since it would inevitably transfer the fighting to the friendly territory of Brandenburg, and since it would be

[1] Ahnlund, *Oxenstierna*, p. 302.
[2] Hallenberg, V. 336; Ahnlund, *op. cit.*, p. 307; Carlsson, p. 35. The mission had also commercial objects, notably the securing of the export of Swedish copper to Spain without interference from the maritime powers.

dangerously exposed to attack in flank from Poland. He was ready to take the Weser line—if Bremen were made over to him; or the Elbe—if he could have Wismar; but on the whole he recurred to his former plan of operations up the Vistula. For these he must have security from Danzig; and, once again, he expected the allies to obtain it for him. If they could do that, if they were prepared to offer satisfactory guarantees about finance, then he would begin operations in Polish Prussia. But the allies must make up their minds before the end of June, for he was not disposed to lose the campaigning season by waiting upon their deliberations.[1]

It soon became clear that there was no reality in the talk of co-operation. The allies could give him no satisfaction. The deaths of James and Maurice had caused the indefinite postponement of the Hague Congress; nobody was prepared to grasp the Danzig nettle; there was hardly enough money for Kristian, and certainly not enough to pay Gustav Adolf as well. At the end of May Spinola took Breda, and this blow distracted the attention of Frederick Henry from the Baltic. In England, Charles I at last decided that the command-in-chief of the German expedition should be reserved to 'our dear Unkle' the King of Denmark. On 23 May Kristian himself finally declined the terms proposed by Sweden; on 10 June Gustav Adolf formally notified Denmark of his intention to resume hostilities in Livonia.[2] It remained to be seen what Kristian would make of his enterprise.

(vii) *The Livonian War resumed. The Hague Congress. Wallhof.*

As soon as it became apparent the Kristian was really to commit himself in Germany, Gustav Adolf took steps to terminate the truce with Poland.

The purpose of the campaign which was now to begin was to complete the conquest of Livonia, to recover some grip on the south-eastern portions of Kurland (which had passed out of Swedish

---

[1] Rydfors, pp. 48-52; Schybergson, *Underhandlingar*, pp. 86-93; *AOSB*, I. III. 60-71; Styffe, pp. 370-1; *Sv. Kr.*, III. 125-9; Hallenberg, V. 325-30; Carlsson, pp. 6-7; M. Weibull, pp. 17-20.

[2] *AOSB*, I. III. 81, 89; *Christian IVs Breve*, I. 439; Rydfors, pp. 54-7; Gardiner, V. 323, 335; Wedgwood, p. 201; Schybergson, *Underhandlingar*, pp. 94-8. Charles wrote to Carleton (*ibid.*, p. 96 *note* 40): 'The commaunde of this armie in chiefe wee conceive wilbe given to the King of Denmarke, our dear Unkle, and doubt not but the King of Sweden will be well content thereby and contribute a good proporcion towards the good and common cause.'

control when Radziwiłł retook Mitau) and to establish a strong advanced position from which to launch attacks on Lithuania. Gustav Adolf hoped that the campaign would be a short one, for despite exaggerated rumours to the contrary[1] no great store of supplies or armament was taken with the expedition. The troops were to be mainly mercenaries; for doubts as to Denmark's intentions, and the possibility, even yet, of intervention in Germany, made it expedient to keep the Swedish regiments at home against an emergency. The plan of campaign was designed to distract and confuse the little army of 3000 men which was all that Sigismund could dispose of on the spot. On the one flank Karl Karlsson Gyllenhielm was to make a descent upon the Kurland coast and seize Windau; on the other, Horn was to unite with de la Gardie's forces from Estonia and capture Dorpat; while the main body, operating from the Riga area, would strike south to Kokenhusen and endeavour to make itself master of the line of the Düna.[2] The expedition left Sandhamn on 28 June, and reached Dünemünde two days later. On arrival in Livonia the King found it necessary to modify his original plan of action. The expedition against Windau was abandoned, and the tardiness of the Finnish troops forced Horn to move against Dorpat without waiting for de la Gardie. The main offensive towards Kokenhusen was, however, pushed on with satisfactory speed. By 5 July Banér, with the advance guard, was in possession of the town, and had begun the siege of the castle. For this he needed heavy guns, which the roads of Livonia had not been designed to take. Gustav Adolf therefore transported them up the Düna on special flotillas as far as the rapids at Keggum, from which it was but a moderate haul to Kokenhusen. The King with the main body arrived in the town on 14 July, and on the following morning the garrison of the castle capitulated with the honours of war. Three days later he took Selburg; and with the capture of this position the whole of the line of the Düna, from its mouth up to its confluence with the Ewst, passed into Swedish hands.[3]

The King now hesitated whether to turn against the Kurland fortresses of Mitau and Bauske, or whether to adhere to his original design and make for Birże. In the end, he decided to attempt to surprise Birże. He reached it on 29 July; but the shortage of heavy

[1] e.g. Vosbergen, p. 91.
[2] Sv. Kr., II. 175-7; Hallenberg, V. 360-3, 396; Cronholm, I. 441-3. Gustav Adolf had about 14,000 men in Livonia, of whom 5000 were garrison troops.
[3] AOSB, I. I. 103-5; I. III. 116-21; Sv. Kr., II. 178-86; Björlin, I. 64-5.

guns, consequent upon the lack of water transport, made a quick capture out of the question. He was not prepared for a regular siege; and the operation turned itself therefore into a large-scale reconnaissance in force, which eventually led round in a circle through Radziwiliszki back to Keggum, where for the next few weeks he established his headquarters.[1]

Meanwhile Swedish detachments had been reducing the minor places of Livonia to submission: on 4 August Ronneburg fell to de la Barre, and on the following day Ehrnreiter captured Pebalg. Before that week was out Horn and de la Gardie had formed the siege of Dorpat. Dorpat was the stronghold of Roman Catholicism in those parts; but it was in no condition to offer prolonged resistance, and the Jesuits acted with their usual discretion when they made all haste to quit the town at the Swedish approach. On 16 August Dorpat surrendered, amid great Protestant rejoicing, and the Swedish commanders proceeded to mopping-up operations in eastern Livonia. Gustav Adolf had now virtually completed the main item on his programme: all Livonia north of the Düna and west of the Ewst was in his hands, and he might hope with the aid of these natural frontiers to make his rule effective and keep hostilities at a decent distance. He would have felt more secure, however, had Birże been in his possession; for he entertained a high notion— as it afterwards proved, an exaggeratedly high notion—of the value of that town as an outwork to Livonia's river defences. He determined, therefore, to make a more serious attempt upon it. A siege of five days (20-25 August) sufficed to reduce it to submission. It only remained now to turn his attention to Kurland; and he believed that he had just time to take Mitau and Bauske before shortage of supplies and autumn rains should put an end to the campaign. In mid-September he moved against Bauske, which surrendered on the 17th, and then headed north-west for Mitau. Here he was joined by a detachment under Banér, which had escorted the heavy guns up the Kurland Aa. Mitau was summoned to surrender, and after a short delay admitted the King on 24 September. The summer campaign had thus been a decided success. The great quadrilateral of Livonia, bounded by the Düna, the Gulf of Riga, the Estonian frontier, the Russian frontier, and the Ewst, seemed now to be firmly in Swedish hands, and outside it to the south-west lay a bastion of fortresses—Mitau, Bauske, Birże—

[1] *AOSB*, I. III. 122; *Sv. Kr.*, II. 187-90.

which should protect it from attack from Poland and offer excellent jumping-off places for a future invasion of Lithuania. It was with a good deal of satisfaction that Gustav Adolf put his army into winter quarters in the first half of October and himself left the battle zone for Reval, there to negotiate with the Estonian Estates, and to meet his tiresomely possessive Queen.[1]

The departure of Gustav Adolf for the Livonian front had by no means extinguished the hopes of those men of good-will who still looked to see the Swedish armies in Germany, this summer or next; and the first few weeks of the campaign were diversified by the presence at Keggum of an earnest diplomat who had tracked the King to these remote regions in order to preach Protestant solidarity and cooperation with Denmark. This was the Dutchman Gaspar van Vosbergen, who set out for the North in May in a last endeavour to heal the breach in the evangelical camp, and who hoped to persuade Gustav Adolf and Kristian to accept the plan of a joint command in Germany. He went first to the Danish headquarters, which he reached in June; but he found Kristian surly, and openly sceptical of Swedish sincerity.[2] Thence he travelled to Sweden, where he had the mortification of arriving at Älvsnabben only a day or two after the King's departure for Riga. Members of the *råd* who interviewed him found him a 'discreet' man, and to them he would not open his business. As soon as might be they shipped him over to Livonia; and at the beginning of August he was in Riga, waiting for leave to go on to the King at Keggum, and complaining bitterly of the heat, the stink, the plague, and the want of conversation. When at last he reached the Swedish headquarters his reception was courteous but studiously vague. The King impressed him by dialectical fireworks; Oxenstierna bored him with a lengthy account in Latin of the origins and history of the Polish war, and a comparison of it with the struggle of the Netherlands against Spain which Vosbergen did not much relish. But there was little satisfaction to be had. Oxenstierna seemed to hanker after a congress in Stockholm, rather than at The Hague; while Gustav Adolf appeared to be mainly interested in the possibilities of diverting

---

[1] *AOSB*, I. III. 165, 168; *Sv. Kr.*, II. 193-205; Cronholm, I. 453-4, 456, 459; Bennedich, p. 60.

[2] Kristian complained that Sweden 'niet anders als tergiversatien ... souckende was', and Swedish communications 'soo perplexe was ingestelt, dat geen assertive besluyt daeruyt konde getrocken werden'; and even Vosbergen hoped that if Gustav Adolf came to The Hague he would come 'ad agendum ende niet ad eludendum': Vosbergen, pp. 26-7.

Dutch trade from Archangel to Narva, and the prospects of raising the price of copper. All that Vosbergen could obtain was an unsatisfactory assurance that Sweden intended to be represented at the Hague Congress, if it should ever take place. Vosbergen optimistically reported to Their High Mightinesses that Gustav Adolf would intervene in Germany if he were given satisfactory securities; but this, though no doubt true, was not new. The mission had not altered the position one jot.[1]

While Vosbergen was kicking his heels in Riga, Gabriel Gustafsson Oxenstierna was growing equally impatient in London.[2] His enquiries about the possibility of unhampered export of Swedish copper to Spanish ports could hardly have come at a more inopportune moment. England was preparing the reat expedition to Cadiz, which was to bring back the plunder of the Plate fleet; and Parliament had just declared unequivocally that, whatever James or Charles or the Palatine might have promised, England was not ready to pay for intervention in Germany, whether by Kristian IV or by anybody else, since the only war in which the country was interested was war with Spain.[3] On 8 September 1625 England and the Dutch signed the Treaty of Southampton, which provided for an offensive alliance against Philip IV; and the Dutch encouraged Buckingham to concentrate all his energies upon the naval war. The Treaty of Southampton virtually sealed the fate of Kristian, who from that moment was almost certain to see himself denied those modest succours in men and money for which he had stipulated. It virtually nullified the Hague Congress in advance. Only if Buckingham's sanguine expectations should be realized, only if the Cadiz expedition should return laden to the scuppers with the gold of the Indies, could England's foreign policy escape from the meshes into which her rulers had led it. Buckingham might still put a bold

---

[1] For Vosbergen's mission, see Vosbergen, *Verbaal van de Ambassade* . . ., *passim*; Schybergson, *Underhandlingar*, p. 99; Cronholm, I. 447-9; Hallenberg, V. 406; G. W. Vreede, *Inleiding tot eene Geschiedenis der Nederlandsche Diplomatie*, I. App. pp. 81-9.

[2] For Gabriel Gustafsson Oxenstierna's embassy, *AOSB*, I. III. 129; II. III. 85-8; Rydfors, pp. 59-60.

[3] On 5 August a member said: 'We are not engaged to give for the recovery of the Palatinate. For when it was in the Act of Parliament, as it was first penned, it was struck out by order of the House, as a thing unfit to engage the House for the recovery of the Palatinate, and if possible, yet not without great charge and difficulty.' Upon which Gardiner justly comments: 'The full truth was out at last. The House did not mean to support Mansfeld and the King of Denmark, and Buckingham and the King would have to reconcile themselves to the fact.' Gardiner, V. 412.

front on it, Charles might still protest his intention of making a real effort on the Continent, but both were gambling on success at sea. This was not yet apparent either to the unfortunate Kristian or to Gustav Adolf. But on 16 November, the very day the delegates were assembling for the opening of the Hague Congress, the Cadiz fleet started for home, laden not with treasure but with shame and rancours and wasted opportunities. This fatal news was of course unknown to the delegates at their first meetings; yet the atmosphere must have been depressing enough. The general invitation to Protestants and their friends had been singularly ill replied to: the representatives of England, Denmark and the United Provinces made but a pitiful rump of the great evangelical rally to which Rusdorf and Camerarius had looked forward. Brandenburg had been frightened by the menaces of a special Imperial envoy, sent to Berlin to warn George William that Ferdinand had his eye upon him; and no Brandenburg representative appeared at The Hague. Bethlen Gabor did indeed send an agent, who appeared at The Hague under the wing of the Danish ambassador, but the western powers were not favourably impressed, and Bethlen Gabor for the moment was left out. Louis XIII, whose relations with England were steadily deteriorating, and whose Huguenot subjects were giving much cause for concern, remained aloof, in a neutrality whose benevolence was beginning to be dubious. And Sweden was not represented after all. Rutgers had died in October, and at one time Gustav Adolf thought of sending Per Banér as his representative. Influenced, it appears, by a sudden fear of Imperialist encroachments on Pomerania, Gustav Adolf for a month or two entertained the idea of waiving his former objections and engaging in collaboration with Denmark in a campaign along the line of the Oder. It was however but a momentary divagation. Gustaf Adolf changed his mind; Per Banér's instructions were cancelled; and no special Swedish agent left for The Hague. Camerarius and Gabriel Gustafsson Oxenstierna were both on the spot, but they had no powers to participate. In these circumstances the Congress proceeded to the only possible conclusion; and on 29 November England and Holland made a treaty with Denmark, whereby England covenanted to pay Kristian £30,000 per month, and the Dutch engaged for a further £5000. How Charles' impoverished exchequer was to honour this pledge, nobody—least of all Kristian—seems to have paused to enquire. There was some talk of including Sweden among the beneficiaries of this hypothetical largesse, but Kristian, with strong historic irony, gave it as his opinion that Sweden could most usefully contribute to the common cause by a diversionary campaign in Poland. It was agreed, however, that other powers—and especially Sweden and France—should be invited to accede to the triple alliance. The suggestion gave offence to Louis XIII, who felt it to be beneath his dignity to be tacked on as an appendage to a league he had had no share in making. Gustav Adolf, for his part, was prepared to look at the Hague alliance on its merits, and for a moment was even inclined to adhere to it; but fuller information of the proceedings of the congress convinced him that no good was to be expected from Buckingham's diplomacy, and in the end he drew back. And thus the destined supports of the grand Protestant combination—France, Brandenburg, Bethlen Gabor, Sweden—remained unsecured, and even alienated; and Kristian was left to amble doucely into the pit which Charles and his Parliament had so successfully combined to dig for him.[1]

Meanwhile in the Düna valley other diplomats had occupied the autumn of 1625 in transactions which, if they were less dangerous, were equally vain; but here the negotiations had been linked (as Gustav Adolf preferred negotiations to be linked) to the ebb and flow of military operations, and war and diplomacy had gone hand in hand. By the middle of August the conquest of Livonia had made such rapid progress that both the King and Oxenstierna began to imagine that a truce was to be had for the asking, and upon such terms as they might think fit to impose. This optimism was, as it happened, quite unjustifiable. The military position of the Polish commanders might for the moment be weak, but their spirit was by no means broken. In September Gustav Adolf empowered Arvid Horn and Johan Salvius to enter into negotiations on the basis of a withdrawal by both sides from Lithuania and a cessation of arms till 1 June 1626. Since Gustav Adolf's share of Lithuania was for the moment confined to the town of Birże, and Sigismund had all the rest, these were not very

<hr />

[1] For the above, see Rydfors, pp. 62-71; Schybergson, *Underhandlingar*, pp. 101-13; L. Avenel, *Lettres . . . de . . . Richelieu*, II. 198; Schybergson, *Sv. och Hollands dip. förb.*, pp. li, lxi-lxxi; Gardiner, V. 420-1, 433; VI. 5-8, 21, 25 *note* 1, 27, 36-44, 55; Droysen, I. 236, 241, 243; *AOSB*, I. iii. 41, 177; Styffe, pp. 372-3, 461, 509, 515; Ahnlund, *Gustaf II Adolfs första preussiska fälttåg och den europeiska krisen 1626* (*HT* 1918) (cited as Ahnlund, *HT* 1918), pp. 76-7, 81-6; D. Angyal, *Gabriel Bethlen*, pp. 59-61; Hallenberg, V. 410-15; Blok, IV. 266; Hallwich, *Fünf Bücher Geschichte Wallensteins*, I. 370-1.

attractive terms to the Poles. Negotiations had hardly begun when the Swedish diplomats were captured by Cossacks, handed over to Radziwiłł, and by him kept captive, in violation of all the proprieties, for four weeks. Thereupon discussions, not surprisingly, were broken off.[1]

By the beginning of October the Poles were showing considerable activity. Their energetic and capable commander, Gąsiewski, was patrolling along the Ewst, and was making it very difficult for the Swedes to extend the area from which they could draw fodder and supplies. When Horn tried a sally across the river with this end in view he was caught by Gąsiewski, driven back, and sharply chastised at Listenhoff (2 October), being himself wounded in the engagement. Along the Ewst, indeed, the Poles passed to the offensive, and it became a question whether the river line could long be held. The Swedish army was weakened, as so often before, by bad quarters, short commons, and severe losses from disease. Early in November Gustav Adolf, seeing the danger, reinforced the Ewst position. It was already too late. In the second week of November the Swedes were forced out of their positions behind the Ewst; the flank of their entire position in Livonia was threatened; and Gustav Adolf expected to have to fight hard to resist a Polish invasion of the country, as soon as ice on the rivers should permit free movement: even Riga itself might be endangered. But the Poles were ever incalculable. They made no real effort to recover Livonia, contenting themselves with sending flying columns to harass communications and impede foraging. This cautious strategy had considerable success, for starvation and disease took a heavy toll of horses and men that winter. Gustav Adolf confessed that the misery in the area under Swedish occupation exceeded anything in his experience; and the ravages of epidemics on one occasion forced him to do the work of his clerk and batman.[2]

Throughout that bitter December negotiations dragged feebly on; but with the opening of 1626 the war, which had latterly shown signs of flagging, flared up once more, and Gustav Adolf made an effort to round off the campaign with a palpable success. The Polish army was at this time threatening Birże, and lay to the south

---

[1] *AOSB*, I. III. 138-9, 141, 143, 184, 191, 196; II. x. 81; Hallenberg, V. 391-3, and see Gustav Adolf's indignant description of these negotiations in *Sveriges Ridderskaps och Adels Riksdags Protokoll*, I. 25-6.

[2] *AOSB*, I. III. 218, 230, 240, 242; II. I. 275, 300; II. v. 360, 363; II. x. 84-5; *Sv. Kr.*, II. 207-20; Styffe, pp. 376-8, 496, 499, 511-12, 600; Ahnlund, *Oxenstierna*, p. 320; Hallenberg, V. 420-3.

of the Düna in two main bodies—Radziwiłł around Bauske, and the younger Sapieha near Wallhof. Concentrating his forces at Berson, Gustav Adolf crossed the Düna at Kokenhusen, made a forced march of 35 miles in 36 hours, and hurled himself upon Sapieha at Wallhof before reinforcements could reach him. The result was a small but decisive victory (7 January 1626). There was a heavy slaughter of Poles—some 500-600 killed on the battlefield; while the Swedish casualties are stated (somewhat improbably) to have been one killed and a handful wounded.[1] But the importance of Wallhof did not lie in the numbers engaged, nor in the immediate advantages it brought, nor even in its significance as a stage in the maturing of Gustav Adolf as a tactician. It was rather that Wallhof freed him from the need to concentrate any further upon Livonia. The war continued in the Düna valley—another three dreary years of it and more—but it became of secondary importance. The real reason why Wallhof deserves to be remembered in the roll of Swedish victories is that it convinced Gustav Adolf that he might safely transfer the main seat of war to Prussia. It marks the end, then, of the long period in which the Polish war was fought in isolation. Henceforward it will be linked ever closer with the dreadful march of events in Germany. On 19 January 1626 Gustav Adolf left the Livonian theatre of war for Sweden, by way of Reval. He was not to see Livonia again. When next he should sail southward from Älvsnabben, his course would be set, not to Riga and the Düna, but to Pillau, to the Kurisches Haff, and to the Vistula delta.[2]

We have reached the great turning-point of the reign: one of the great turning-points in the history of Sweden, and perhaps in the history of Europe. The remaining three years of the protracted struggle with Poland are to be considered not only as the provisional winding-up of a contest which had lasted for more than a generation, but also as an introductory period which led with irresistible logic to the intervention of Gustav Adolf in the Thirty Years' War, and all the profound consequences which flowed from that intervention.

[1] A year later Gustav Adolf improved on these figures, stating that he did not lose a single man by enemy action at Wallhof. He expressed the conviction that the victory was a divine judgment upon the Poles for their slippery diplomacy, and for the political libels which they disseminated. *Sveriges Ridderskaps och Adels Riksdags Protokoll* (cited henceforward as *SRARP*), I. 27, 31.
[2] For a discussion of the tactics at Wallhof, see below, Vol. II, Chapter XII. For the battle, *Sv. Kr.*, II. 223-35; Petri, II. 58; N. Belfrage, *Erik Soop och Västgöta Ryttare*, p. 38; *AOSB*, II. 1. 302; Styffe, p. 265; Cronholm, I. 479-81; Korzon, II. 235.

Had Sweden confined her struggle with Poland to Livonia, it would still have been conceivable that the issue should have been fought out, and that Sweden should have emerged victorious from the contest, without any serious alteration in the European balance. It would even have been possible for Sweden, having vanquished Poland, to turn upon Denmark and secure for herself the real mastery of the Baltic, without thereby committing herself to the responsibilities and hazards of a great power. But once the war was transferred to Prussia, and thence, by steps almost inevitable, to Germany, Sweden was launched whether she liked it or not upon a career of greatness; and was committed to an attempt to appear as the equal of France and Spain, of Austria and Britain and the Dutch.

The disproportion, in population and material resources, between herself and those other great powers, must have made any such attempt frightening to a statesman consciously designing it. And it may well be asked how Sweden was able to bear the burden of her efforts even from 1630 to 1648. Upon what secret sources of inner strength could she rely, to carry her through the tremendous task of turning back the tide of history, of arresting the Counter-Reformation just when its triumph seemed assured, of carving out for herself an outwork and a *glacis* beyond the sea? The position which she held in Europe, from Breitenfeld to Pultava, was based in part, no doubt, upon pure military force, upon victories won in the field. But the question immediately presents itself: why and how were the victories won? In what manner was she able to develop this formidable power? It was not merely a question of generalship; for the best general must have adequate tools and sufficient resources to his hand. If we are to understand the fabulous story of Gustav Adolf's progress in Germany, we must understand first the bases upon which his victories were built; the nature of his army, and the tactics it employed; the part played by his fleet; the economic condition of his country, which (to begin with, at all events) bore the financial burden of the war. And behind these things lay others, more intangible but not less important: moral factors such as the religious enthusiasm and confessional solidarity of the nation; the spirit of the age as manifested in its literature and learning. What sort of a society bodied forth this race of resurgent Goths? How was it organized and administered? Was it nerved to its efforts by the crack of a despot's whip, or by the act of will of a (comparatively) free people? It is with these questions that the next group of Chapters will be concerned.

CHAPTER VI

CONSTITUTIONAL DEVELOPMENT

(i) *The Charter, 1612*

THE reign of Gustav Adolf opened, as we have seen, with a major constitutional crisis. The political heirs of Erik Sparre sought to use the uncertainty as to the succession to extract concessions from the Crown in a sense favourable to a more aristocratic type of polity; while all those who had been offended at the government of Karl IX—and they were very many—grasped the opportunity to secure safeguards against a repetition of Karl's methods in the new reign. The result was the Charter of 1612; and its acceptance was strictly a precondition for Gustav Adolf's recognition. It was thus intended to be, and was, the basis upon which the government of the country was to repose in the years that followed; and in very many respects the constitutional history of the reign can be considered as a commentary upon, or a development from, the settlement of 1612. And even the Form of Government of 1634 (which, as we shall see, belongs at least as much to this reign as to the next) has been thought by some to be little more than the completion and rounding-off of a political programme which was only half realized by the statesmen of twenty years before.

The Charter was a moderate-sized document of some ten clauses.[1] After a lengthy preamble follows Clause 1, which promises to maintain the Protestant religion in its primitive purity according to the Confession of Augsburg and the resolution of the Uppsala Meeting of 1593. Clause 2 is complementary to the preceding, and declares that no person of any other religion than that of Luther may receive any official appointment in the country.[2] Clause 3 promises in general terms to respect the privileges and persons of Kristina and Johan, as also of the *riksråd* and Estates. Clause 4 engages that Gustav Adolf will rule according to the coronation oath as prescribed in the *landslag*. Clause 5 contains promises of great importance to the nobility. It is laid down that the five great offices of state—the

---

[1] The text of the Charter is in *SRDA*, I. 69-76, or *Sveriges Regeringsformer samt Konungaförsäkringar* (ed. E. Hildebrand), pp. 195-203.

[2] For a discussion of the clauses affecting the Church, see Chapter VII, below.

High Steward, Marshal, Admiral, Chancellor, Treasurer—besides the members of the *riksråd*, Exchequer Council, and *lagmän*[1] and provincial governors (*ståthållare*), with the commanders of the most important castles, must be of Swedish birth, and must be nobles; while sheriffs (*häradshövdingar*)[1] are to be Swedes, 'and particularly nobles, where they are found to be suited to that service': the original demand had been without this qualification. In any case it is conceded that all are to hold office on good behaviour, and are to be removed only upon a judicial sentence. The sixth clause was perhaps the most important of all. The King promised to make no new law, nor abolish or modify any old one, without the consent and collaboration of Duke Johan, the *råd* and the Estates. No injunction or prohibition was to issue, in connection with aids, services, tolls, taxes or *utskrivningar* (militia-levies), without the knowledge and advice of the *råd*, 'and the consent of those concerned'. The King undertook, moreover, not to burden the people with overmany *herredagar*, and to consult the *råd* and obtain their consent before summoning such meetings. And, lastly, Clause 6 bound the King not to begin a war or make a peace without the knowledge and consent of Duke Johan, the *riksråd* and the Estates. The seventh clause confirmed the Church Ordinance of 1571, promised free election for bishops, and made other concessions to the clergy. The eighth and ninth clauses dealt with necessary reforms in local government, and promised security of tenure to all and sundry, unless their right of ownership were disproved in a court of law. And the tenth and last clause promised that no man should be imprisoned, or punished, or degraded, or mulcted of his property upon mere accusation, until after condemnation by proper process of law.

Such was the Charter of 1612. It has been considered by some Swedish historians as a constitutional document of the highest importance, comparable, for instance, to the Petition of Right of 1628. By others it has been dismissed as no more than a formal restatement of what was law already. To one school it marks the triumph of a revived and aggressive aristocracy, seeking to establish upon the basis of a written contract the predominance of the *råd*; to another, it is the visible manifestation of the reconciliation of the nation with the monarchy.[2] It is in the first place idle to deny that

---

[1] These were judicial and administrative officials: the nature of their duties is discussed below. See p. 315 *seqq.*

[2] For the interpretation of the Charter, see E. Hildebrand, *Svenska statsförfattningens historiska utveckling*, pp. 247-9; N. Herlitz, *Det svenska statsskickets*

the Charter was an extraordinary document. Gustav Adolf's two predecessors had indeed given Charters to the Estates, Karl in 1607, Sigismund in 1594; but in each case they had been drafted mainly with a view to securing the predominance and purity of the Lutheran religion. The Charter of 1612 did indeed include similar guarantees; but it included also constitutional provisions which had been wholly absent on the two preceding occasions. It is equally clear that some of the clauses were prompted by reaction to specific malpractices of Karl IX: for instance, the 'Habeas Corpus' clause (Clause 10); the guarantees against too frequent summoning of the *riksdag*; the condemnation of the 'rule of secretaries' implicit in Clause 5. The provisions of Clauses 5 and 6, which placed so much power in the hands of the *råd* and nobility, are certainly traceable to that movement towards the control of government by these elements in society of which Erik Sparre had been the leading representative: indeed, many of the demands granted in 1612 are to be found in his *Postulata Nobilium* of 1594. Sparre's plan for building the administration around the five great officers of state is implicitly accepted, and so too is his view that office-holders are to be considered not as personal servants of the King but as ministers of the nation, not to be dismissed lightly or without good cause. It is noteworthy, moreover, that although in Clause 6 the consent of Johan, the *råd* and the Estates is required for many acts of high policy, it is not required for all. Taxation, for instance, is to be by consent of Johan, the *råd* and 'those concerned'. By this vague phrase it is not likely that the framers of the Charter meant to indicate the *riksdag*: if they had, they would have said so. Now the *riksdag*, as we shall see, had not at this time won secure acceptance as the only tax-granting body. It was open to the King to conduct negotiations for a grant with the general assembly of each province, or he might treat individually with each Estate; and this was a method which Gustav Adolf was to use on various occasions. The old *råd*-party had viewed with distaste the increasingly preponderant share which the *riksdag* was

historia, pp. 89-91; N. Ahnlund, *Ståndsriksdagens Utdaning*, pp. 111-21, 444; N. Edén, *Den svenska centralregeringens utveckling*, pp. 85-90; N. Edén, *Den svenska riksdagen*, pp. 86-8; E. Hjärne, *Från Vasatiden till Frihetstiden*, pp. 31-41; D. Toijer, *Sveriges riksdag*, pp. 14-22; G. Wittrock, *Gustav II Adolf*, pp. 15-17; F. Lagerroth, *Frihetstidens författning*, p. 114; Hj. Holmquist, *Svenska Kyrkans Historia*, IV. 1. 27; L. Stavenow in *Historisk Tidskrift*, I Series, vol. LV. p. 122; C. A. Hessler, *Gustaf II Adolfs konungaförsäkran* (*Scandia* 1932, pp. 168-203) (cited as Hessler, *KFS*); C. A. Hessler, *Den svenska ståndsriksdagen* (*Scandia* 1935, pp. 247-9).

coming to take in the conduct of state business. Karl's reign, which showed what use the monarchy might make of the Estates, had only sharpened their anxiety. It is probable, then, that the framers of the Charter were desirous that the *riksdag* should not establish its sole control over taxation: they preferred the older methods, the more decentralized methods. And it is clear that the *råd*, no less than the nation, was determined not to be burdened with 'overmany *herredagar*' in future; for in another part of the same clause it is laid down that meetings of the Estates are henceforward to be summoned only with the advice and consent of the *råd*.[1] This provision, coupled with the control by the *råd* of foreign policy (or at least of peace and war), of legislation, of taxation, and the express reservation of all the major offices of government to the nobility, with security of tenure *quamdiu se bene gesserint*, seem indeed to hand over the monarchy in chains to the tender mercies of a single ruling class. On the face of it, it is a revolution, an oligarchial *coup d'état*, the triumph of the opposition which had gone down in 1600— the triumph, to put it at its most sinister, of *aurea libertas*. And modern critics, remembering the Regency in Kristina's time and the Form of Government of 1634; recalling that Oxenstierna was the architect of that document, as of this; emphasizing his disapproval of Karl's methods of government, and his close family connection with Karl's bitterest foes; reach the conclusion that Oxenstierna, identifying himself with the old aristocratic programme of Sparre and his party, deliberately engineered a revolution in 1612, with the set purpose of making the monarchy the subservient instrument of his own class.[2]

Much of this argument is sound and incontrovertible; but it is pushed too far, and it proves too much. To begin with, many of these demands were not revolutionary at all. Their defenders might justly say of them that they were an attempt to redress the constitutional balance, which had in Karl's time swung too markedly in favour of the King; to restore that constitutional equipoise which seems to have been the ideal of Swedish mediaeval political thinkers. Now Clauses 1, 3, 4, 10, together with so much of Clause 5 as relates to the employment of foreigners, and most of the vital Clause 6, are either explicitly or implicitly contained in the *landslag*, though naturally the *landslag* could not envisage the collaboration of the

---

[1] Hessler comments: 'The future fate of the *riksdag* looked . . . extremely dubious': *Den svenska ståndsriksdagen*, p. 28.
[2] This represents more or less Hessler's line of argument.

Estates, since at the time when the *landslag* was compiled the *riksdag* was not a normal or recognized political institution. But the essential principle—that the King should rule according to law, and with the advice of his *råd*, and that any extraordinary impost required the consent of those affected—this principle was already as clearly laid down in the *landslag* as in the Charter.

Yet, when so much has been conceded, it remains true that the Charter of 1612 did register a sharp constitutional change. Ever since 1523, the tendency had been in the direction of a parliamentary despotism. The Charter was designed to put an abrupt stop to that progress. The fact that its terms brought the monarchy in some sort back to the position it had occupied in the Middle Ages did not make the change the less violent or the less profound. It is not possible to dismiss a document which suddenly reversed a historical process which had been in action for nearly a century, as though it were no more than a judicious trimming of the ship of state. But it is not therefore necessary to assume that Oxenstierna was the ringleader in a conspiracy to reduce the monarchy to a Polish subjection. Oxenstierna was no crypto-republican, as Sparre had been. And at a time when some of the bitterest supporters of Sparre's programme were in exile, serving a sovereign with whom Sweden was at war, a certain moderation was the part of a patriot. Oxenstierna and the *råd* desired guarantees: they had no certainty that Gustav Adolf might not grow up to become another Karl—if heredity went for anything the probability was that he would—and they took their guarantees when the chance offered. For this it is hardly possible to blame them. The failure of Karl, whatever his intentions, to devise a better form of government than the rule of secretaries, justified the insertion of a provision which secured to the state the services of the class which was probably (after all) best qualified to serve it. But Gustav Adolf agreeably disappointed their expectations. He did not, as his father had done, ride rough-shod over their opposition; he did not habitually employ demagogic violence to overwhelm them. Yet he became a more truly popular and national King than ever his father had been. He used his father's tactics of collaborating with the *riksdag*. He was a much stronger King than Karl, and certainly an abler one. He was therefore more dangerous to any designs for establishing the domination of the *råd* and its supporters. If there had really been such a design in 1611, if such a domination had really been aimed at, if the intention had in fact been permanently to occlude the monarchy, it is at all events true that the *råd*-party, with Oxenstierna at its head, made no attempt to curtail Gustav Adolf's control of government during his reign. Not only did they make no such attempt, but they actively collaborated with him, and looked on indifferently when he violated the Charter in many important particulars. Legislation occurred without the consent of the *riksdag*; foreign policy returned to the personal control of the King; and it is very unlikely that Gustav Adolf ever felt himself hampered in calling a meeting of the Estates by the necessity for the consent of the *riksråd* to that measure, though in point of fact he did usually ask their advice.[1] In short, the Charter was not a great constitutional landmark; it was not the prize of victory of a greedy and ruthless upper class; but neither was it merely a comfortable adjustment of some minor irks and frets in the Swedish polity. It was a guarantee against what its framers held to have been misrule—an opinion which they could base firmly on the *landslag*. When they found that they had a King whom they could trust not to abuse his power, they made no difficulty about its non-observance. The Charter was an interim settlement, which might mean much or little, according to how events should shape themselves; and as the reign progressed, its significance began to alter. In some respects it proved a foundation upon which the new King was to build—most notably in the organization of the central government, and in the dispensing of justice; in others, development proceeded along different lines, and the Charter became a dead letter. Meanwhile, as a statement of principle, it stood on record, and might yet at a future time be useful: essentially, everything depended on the character of the King. And so, though Gustav Adolf repeated his acceptance of the Charter in his coronation oath of 1617, he was not too literal in his adherence to it, and he never found any new Erik Sparre to cast his former pledges in his teeth. But if he had ruled as Karl IX had ruled, it might have been a very different story.

(ii) *The Central Executive*

Whatever the significance of the Charter from the point of view of constitutional theory, it had been intended by its framers to produce practical results in the conduct of government. By

---

[1] There was an instance in 1628 when the *råd* dissuaded the King from calling a *riksdag*: Ahnlund, *Ståndsriksdagens Utdaning*, p. 444.

stipulating for the filling of the high administrative posts—as well local as central—by men of the nobility, and by demanding for such officials security of tenure and a guaranteed remuneration, Oxenstierna and his associates had bound the monarchy to an alteration in the structure of administration which could not fail to have important effects, if fully carried out. They had forced the Crown to pledge anew that collaboration with the Estates of the Realm which the custom of the constitution demanded, and by this they had meant, above all, collaboration with the *riksråd* and the high aristocracy. Whatever else in the Charter might be thrown overboard, as Gustav Adolf settled himself more securely on his throne, whatever else might be circumvented or blandly ignored, this was now a fundamental fact of politics, in which the monarchy must acquiesce. Upon the King's loyal observance of Clause 5 the whole character and fortune of the reign depended.

Considerations of dynastic policy and political good faith were reinforced by the demands of national interest. The experience of Karl's reign had shown the urgency of reform; but it had shown also how difficult it was for the monarchy to effect improvements without the consent and cooperation of the Estates, and especially of the Nobility. And in the situation in which Sweden found herself in 1612, with three wars on her hands, any one of which might demand the absence of the King from Stockholm for prolonged periods, the desirability of a more ordered administration and more regular forms of business was likely to be increasingly felt. It is probable that this must have occurred to Gustav Adolf, as it certainly occurred to Axel Oxenstierna. It is at all events indisputable that throughout the reign the King adhered to the spirit of the Charter in this particular; and proceeded, in harmonious cooperation with his nobles, to a reform of the central government which by 1634 enabled it to function independently of the monarch. In part, this reform was suggested by the Charter, and by the programme of 1594 from which much of the Charter had sprung; but it was throughout given a new and characteristic stamp by the personality of the sovereign, so that a form of government which had originated in the oligarchical theorizings of Erik Sparre became, while Gustav Adolf lived, the flexible instrument of the royal will.

The five dignified offices of state were at this time those of the

High Steward,[1] Marshal, Admiral, Chancellor and Treasurer, with
precedence in that order. Throughout the sixteenth century they
had been merely honorific, and often they had been left vacant;
but since the 'nineties they had formed the nucleus of more than
one scheme of reform. In Karl IX's time they had not been without
competitors: in a project for a regency dating from 1603, for instance,
the *överste arklimästare* (which may be freely rendered as Lieutenant
of the Tower) had supplanted the Treasurer as one of the five, and
the *jägmästare* (Master of the Buckhounds), *stallmästare* (Master of
the Horse) and *tygmästare* (Master-General of the Ordnance) were
also possible candidates. But from about 1608 the list had become
stabilized in the form in which it appeared in the Charter. The
King now lost no time in appointing men to these posts: the
Chancellor, Treasurer and Admiral received their letters of appointment in January 1612, the Steward and the Marshal soon afterwards.
All were given to members of the high aristocracy, and strictly
reserved henceforward to men of this class.[2] At the coronation in
1617 the five great officers took part, for the first time for many
years, each bearing the emblem of royalty appropriate to his office;
and before the reign was over, from being little more than picturesque
antiquities, they had become the nuclei around which a new system
of administration was formed.[3]

Gustav Adolf took over his father's *riksråd* in its entirety; and
in the first few months of the reign there was little change in the
personnel of government. Karl's trusted old servant, Michil Olofsson, was continued in office with the new title of 'King's Secretary
and Secretary of State', and until his death in 1615 was in effect
Axel Oxenstierna's right-hand man; but he had no successor. His
colleague, Dr. Nils Chesnecopherus, was not so fortunate. He had
been the leading minister of the late King, and had held the office
of *Hovkansler* (Court Chancellor): the office was now abolished, and

[1] The High Steward (*drots*) was an officer of indefinite functions. He was
charged with receiving, at meetings of the Estates, the replies of each Estate to
the royal Proposition; he communicated these views to the *riksråd*, and with them
drew up a general Answer on behalf of the *riksdag* as a whole. He had a traditional
but somewhat tenuous connection with Justice (as the High Steward in England
had), and this Gustav Adolf was to strengthen. Hallenberg, I. 265; Edén, *Den
svenska centralregeringens utveckling till kollegial organisation* (cited henceforward
as Edén, *CU*), p. 36.
[2] In 1622, for instance, on the death of the Treasurer Jesper Matsson (Krus),
the obvious candidate for the office was Johan Skytte; but Skytte was a *novus
homo*, and no appointment was made. Edén, *CU*, p. 221.
[3] For the ceremonial side of the coronation, see *Abraham Brahes Tidebok*,
pp. 98-111.

Chesnecopherus was transferred to the service of young Karl Filip, which meant in effect the service of the Queen-Mother. Kristina could appreciate Chesnecopherus' devotion to her husband; and on more than one occasion he allowed his zeal for her service, and his championship of political ideas which had now gone out of fashion, to involve him and his mistress in unpleasant brushes with the Crown. For the King's service the change in the political climate had made him now unapt.

Another survival from the preceding reign was the title of *hovråd* (Court Councillor). But whereas Karl had conferred it mainly upon his personal ministers at home, and had used those who held it in some sort as an alternative to or substitute for the old *riksråd*, under Gustav Adolf it was given almost exclusively to foreigners, and was revived in the first instance in 1612 for Jakob van Dijk, his agent in the Netherlands. There were indeed rare instances (Skytte, for example, and later Salvius) of the title's being given to native Swedes, and some of those who held it afterwards took Swedish nationality; but on the whole it was used to give dignity to foreigners employed upon diplomatic missions in the Swedish interest: among the more distinguished holders were Rutgers, Rasche, Strassburg, Steinwich, Camerarius and Löffler.[1] The *riksråd* had now nothing to fear from the *hovråd*. The two dignities were not competitive, and the *riksråd* was in any case clearly superior: in October 1613 the precedence of *råd*-members was fixed as following immediately upon that of the five great officers of state.[2]

Although the new reign had thus broken with many of the methods of the old, although the *råd* and the aristocracy were now to be the trusted collaborators of the monarchy, there was no immediately noticeable change in the forms of government. The central administration for some years remained simple, haphazard and improvisatory. The King's servants were detailed for individual tasks as need arose, with *ad hoc* powers made out for a single occasion; and there persisted for some years a lack of continuity in administration, inevitable in such a method. The government was peripatetic: the King moved around his kingdom—to the Bergslag in 1613, to the southern provinces in 1616 and 1617—carrying with him an indispensable minimum of clerks and officials, but leaving no organized government behind him in the capital, so that the

[1] *Svenska Utrikesförvaltningens Historia*, pp. 33, 54; *RRP*, II. 27 *note 2*.
[2] *AOSB*, I. II. 150.

centre of business was located wherever the sovereign happened to be. Formal meetings of the *riksråd* were no more frequent than of old, and the King tended to transact business mainly with individual ministers, and above all with his Chancellor, Oxenstierna; though even Oxenstierna was sometimes left behind on the royal progresses. Special measures had indeed to be taken when the King was absent from the country; but the constitutional devices employed on these occasions varied, and the interim governments which he left behind him were formless and irregular. During his absence in Russia in 1614, for instance, some measure of authority was entrusted to the Exchequer Council (*kammarråd*)—which, it is pertinent to recall, he had pledged himself by the Charter to fill only with nobles—with a general supervisory power to the High Steward. The Steward, however, was little more than a figure-head, and the real control lay in Oxenstierna's hands. But any state-papers were to be signed either by such members of the *riksråd* as should chance to be available, or by *riksråd*-members and *kammarråd* jointly, and both methods were in fact used.[1] When Oxenstierna followed the King overseas, the effective authority devolved upon the *kammarråd*; but for nearly a year there was really no organized central government in Sweden. In 1615 it was no better. Gustav Adolf and his Chancellor were both in Russia; the Steward was occupied with presiding over the new Supreme Court; and any matter of importance had to be referred to the small chancery which Gustav Adolf maintained in the field. It was no wonder if in 1616 the members of the *råd* expressed their concern at the stagnation of business, and intimated a wish that the King should return home soon.

Nevertheless, the first ten years of the reign saw the gradual shaping of a new system. The relations between the King and the members of his *riksråd* grew ever closer and more cordial: in 1617 a great infusion of new blood into the *råd* took place, with the simultaneous admission of seven new members; and it was symptomatic of the confidence now subsisting between the monarchy and the aristocracy that Gustav Adolf should have invited the *råd* to select its new recruits.[2] The occasion was also significant in another way; for among those who were now admitted was Johan Skytte. Skytte had, it is true, been the King's tutor; he had been ennobled; but he was a man of humble origin. His admission to the *råd*

[1] *AOSB*, I. II. 155-6 and *note*.　　　　　　　　　[2] *SRDA*, II. 72.

depended on his talents as an administrator; his acceptance by the old aristocracy (not, however, without some private hard feelings) showed that the *råd*-nobility took the business of government seriously, and looked upon the civil service less from the point of view of class interest than from that of national advantage. With the entry of Skytte into the *råd*, Gustav Adolf may almost be said to have fused the tradition of Erik Sparre with that of Erik XIV. It was another sign of the times when in January 1617 the Nobility asked for special precedence to be given to senior civil servants who were *not* members of the *råd*, in order to encourage youthful ambition, and to mark a distinction between 'those who serve their country, and those who sit at home and do nothing'. This was the spirit which Karl had striven, but striven in vain, to inculcate into the Swedish aristocracy.[1]

Meanwhile, in 1614, had occurred the first of a series of measures which were together to transform the central government. The administration of justice had long been in a state of lamentable chaos and inefficiency, and Karl in his day had revolved various schemes for its improvement. The side of the question which touched Gustav Adolf most immediately was the matter of appeals from the courts to the King, and the habit of litigants of seeking justice from the sovereign in the first instance. The pressure of business (and of campaigning) upon the time of the monarch was now such that he was increasingly unable to discharge this part of his royal duties adequately.[2] Some reform was plainly needed. It was provided by the Judicature Ordinance (*Rättegångsordinantian*) of 1614, complemented by the Procedure Ordinance (*Rättegångsprocess*) of the following year. The Judicature Ordinance was possibly modelled on a scheme put forward by Karl IX in 1604[3]; but it went considerably further. It is fairly certain that it was mainly drafted by Oxenstierna himself.[4] It was discussed in draft at a meeting of the *råd* at Västerås in December 1613, when the King asked members for their advice and assistance; and was submitted to the *riksdag* at Örebro in the following month. There it was slightly modified to meet certain suggestions by the Estates; and on 10 February 1614

---

[1] *SRDA*, II. 94.

[2] For the evils and inadequacies of the legal system before 1614, see the vivid description in Hallenberg, III. 117-51.

[3] K. Melander, *Drag ur Åbo hovrätts äldre historia*, p. 2. Oxenstierna seems also to have had the French *parlements* in mind: H. Haralds, *Konungsdom och konungsnämnd* (*HT* 1927), p. 34.

[4] S. Petrén, *Kring Svea Hovrätts tillblivelse* (*Sv. Jur. Tidn.* 1945), p. 175.

it became law.[1] Its essential provision, from the point of view of the central government, was that setting up a Supreme Court (*Hovrätt*) to act as an appeal court of highest instance. The court was to consist of thirteen members: four were to be members of the *råd*; five members of the nobility; four drawn from the non-noble classes; and the *ex-officio* President was to be the High Steward. Vacancies were to be filled by the King's selection of one name from a list of six presented to him by the court. The court was usually to sit in Stockholm.[2] There were to be two full sessions each year, from May to July and from September to mid-November; and three judges, under the presidency of the Steward, were to sit in vacation.[3]

The institution of *Svea Hovrätt* (to give it the title by which it soon became known) is a landmark not only in legal but also in constitutional history. A new central organ of government was created, more carefully defined in its scope, more fully organized in constitution, times of working, procedure, holidays, and methods of recruitment, than any other that the state could show at that time. It was centred on the office of the Steward, who for the first time is made an efficient and responsible member of the government. To assist him, he is given (among others) four members of the *råd*; and thus there is placed upon the aristocracy (which by the Charter had reserved the *råd* to its own members) a real obligation to function as working civil servants. Not only that: the Judges are bound by the Judicature Ordinance to spend at least five months of the year in Stockholm. Thus the nucleus of a body of counsellors, semi-permanently at hand in the capital, is already provided.[4]

In the sequel, not all the expectations which had been entertained were realized. The *Hovrätt* met with difficulties of various kinds. The salaries of the members (even of the vice-president) were considered to be discouragingly low.[5] It proved very difficult to recruit the quota of non-noble assessors: in 1616 one Carl Christoffersson, who had been appointed to the court (as it seems by mistake), went so far as to declare that sooner than serve in it he would lose

---

[1] *SRDA*, I. 392-8, 417-25; Schmedemann, *Kongl. Stadgar, Förordningar och Resolutioner . . . angående Justitiae och Executions-Åhrende*, I. 133 seqq.

[2] It did on rare occasions meet elsewhere: *e.g.* at Örebro in 1623: *Abraham Brahes Tidebok*, p. 152.

[3] Among the first non-noble assessors were Michil Olofsson, Johannes Messenius, and Lars Bengtsson (Johan Skytte's brother).

[4] The legal aspects and consequences of the reform are discussed on pp. 333-6.

[5] *AOSB*, II. III. 115. At first the judges paid themselves out of the fines they imposed, and were even driven to appropriate the fines levied in inferior courts—a most reprehensible state of affairs: Hallenberg, III. 297.

his head.[1] The court was chronically understaffed and overworked, especially in the latter part of the reign, when the *råd*-members were drafted off to other duties by the King, or preoccupied with the day-to-day administration of the kingdom.[2] Magnus Brahe, the Steward, seems to have been lax and lazy; often there was only one noble member on the bench (usually Gabriel Gustafsson Oxenstierna); and little business was attempted in vacation.[3] Above all, the intention of centralizing the highest justice in the court was not realized. The special needs of Finland led to the erection of another *hovrätt* for that part of the kingdom at Åbo in 1623; a *hovrätt* for the Baltic Provinces, located at Dorpat, followed in 1630; and finally the Form of Government of 1634 split off the south of Sweden into a separate jurisdiction, within which appeals lay to the new *Göta Hovrätt* at Jönköping. The relationship of *Svea Hovrätt* to these new courts was not clearly defined; and thus in effect the idea of unifying the central administration of justice was not carried out. Nevertheless, *Svea Hovrätt* appeared in the Form of Government as one of the five Colleges whose heads formed the Regency, and it was of great importance as being the first experiment of Gustav Adolf and Oxenstierna in this form of administration.

It was not long before the Chancellor's reforming spirit made itself felt in another branch of the administration. Already in the time of Karl IX the initial steps had been taken towards a rationalization of the work of the Exchequer. Since 1543 a clear division had been made between that branch of the office which dealt with receipt and expenditure and that which was responsible for audit and account. The former (*räntekammaren*) was in Karl's time already under the permanent control of the Treasurer; but his authority did not extend to those revenues (a considerable proportion) which were paid in kind rather than in cash, and he had no concern with the auditing and accounting branch (*räknekammaren*): this was managed by a small Exchequer Council (*kammarråd*) which in 1611 numbered no more than two members. Finland had a special Treasurer of its own, though he was in principle subordinate to the Treasurer in Stockholm. Gustav Adolf retained Karl's Treasurer, Seved Ribbing, and the patent of his appointment in 1612 gave him

---

[1] J. E. Almquist, *Mannen, som offentligt förklarade sig hellre vilja mista huvudet än bliva assessor i Svea Hovrätt*, pp. 99-103.

[2] *AOSB*, II. III. 78, 80, 213.

[3] Nordwall, *Om svenska riksrådets utveckling mot centralisation under Gustav II Adolf*, pp. 30-3; Hallenberg, V. 34.

considerably wider powers: he was now authorized to deal with revenue in kind, and given power to negotiate with merchants for purchases or loans. Collaboration between the Treasurer and the Exchequer Council became closer than before, though the Treasurer was still debarred from concerning himself with audit. But the first notable change came in April 1613, when an Instruction was issued to the Exchequer which marks the first attempt towards a more unified control of the national finances.[1] The Instruction informed the Exchequer Council that the Chancery had been forbidden to issue any assignments upon the revenue (förläningsbrev), or make out any deed of gift of Crown estates or revenues, without first ascertaining from the Exchequer that the land (or the revenues from it) could be spared by the Crown, and especially that it was not required for defensive purposes or the maintenance of the mining industry. At the same time the Exchequer Council was given definite powers to employ and dismiss certain types of officials. The significance of these Instructions lay in their strengthening of the position of the Exchequer as a self-contained office of government; in their tacit admission that the King—or the Chancellor—could no longer keep these details clear in his memory, as Gustav Vasa had been able to do; and in the recognition of the fact that, in financial affairs, administration was made needlessly incalculable if the government persisted in not letting its left hand know what its right hand was doing.[2]

No further development of importance occurred until 1618, though a mandate issued in February 1614 shows an intention of centralizing receipt as far as possible, by ordering that all revenues, whether in money or kind, which are not explicitly assigned to expenditures in the provinces, shall be paid into the Exchequer or into the central warehouses in Stockholm; while in the same year the accounts branch made what seems to have been a first tentative effort at framing estimates for the coming year. But in 1618 came a major reform. This was the Exchequer Ordinance of 14 October.[3] The Exchequer Ordinance constituted räknekammaren (the accounting and auditing division) as a Collegium, to be presided over by the Treasurer, assisted by five Exchequer Councillors. They

---

[1] Text in Samling af Instruktioner rörande den civila förvaltningen i Sverige och Finland (cited henceforward as SICF), pp. 23-6.
[2] Kammarkollegiets Historia, pp. 38-44; Edén, CU, pp. 62-72, 100, 198-9, 207.
[3] Text in SICF, pp. 26-46.

were to function as an administrative board, with joint and several responsibility. Three of their number was to be a quorum for the signature of all important documents and the transaction of all important business. They were to keep written minutes, recording if necessary dissentient opinions, and each member of the College was to append his signature to them. Decisions were to be subject to the King's approval, if he were readily available; if not, the view of the majority was to prevail. Regulations were laid down for the presentation of bailiffs' accounts; and it was expressly ordered that *all* accounts, of every branch of state activity, were to be submitted to them (including army accounts), with the exception only that Admiralty and Ordnance accounts were first to be scrutinized by their own experts. They were instructed to compile a terrier of all lands which had been alienated from the Crown since the days of Gustav Vasa; and to consider means for the improvement of the revenues. The division of receipt and expenditure (*räntekammaren*) retained its old organization, except that it lost the Treasurer to the new College; but it was henceforward a subordinate office, controlled by the Exchequer Council. The Ordinance further made careful allocation of the work of the College, dividing it among the staff partly upon a basis of topics, partly upon a geographical basis; and specific posts were assigned to each person. One very important provision ordered that in future *all* financial correspondence was to pass through the Exchequer and be drafted by its staff. A number of provisions regarding hours of work, amount of holidays, oaths to be taken by staff, and internal discipline, rounded off the Ordinance.

It was a careful and comprehensive plan for a government department, built out of existing materials, but imbued with an orderly and logical spirit which had been absent from preceding practice; and it fixed the type of all the later *Collegia*. As in the case of the Judicature Ordinance, but even more certainly, it was the work of Axel Oxenstierna. By the members of the Exchequer Council it was at first met with suspicion and opposition: they disliked the procedure of decision by resolution of a board, contending that it was a needless waste of time, especially in view of the arrears of work that had accumulated in the office; and they resented the general obligation to improve the yield of the revenue, which they contended could in some respects be better attended to by the officers of the local administration. But Oxenstierna was convinced of the importance of preventing incoherent and possibly contradictory actions by individual officials; and by insisting on collegial responsibility he ensured that the Exchequer should speak with only one voice and pursue only one policy at a time. The opposition of the Exchequer Council, however, was possibly responsible for Gustav Adolf's neglect to ratify the Ordinance, and in his time it was not in fact law; but—as happened in more than one similar case—the absence of formal acceptance by the King did not prevent its coming into operation. From 1618 the Exchequer was a College, and more truly a College (in the sense which later became accepted) than the *Hovrätt*. It is true that the Exchequer Ordinance of 1618 was not scrupulously adhered to during the remaining years of the reign. In part this was an inevitable result of the King's prolonged absences overseas and the growing burden and complexity of war-finance. For instance, correspondence on economic affairs was frequently dealt with in Gustav Adolf's 'field-chancery', since a reference to the Exchequer in Stockholm would have wasted valuable time; and the proper auditing of army accounts offered insuperable difficulties. Members of the Exchequer Council were sometimes also members of the *riksråd*, and as such were taken away for employment on other matters of national importance; and thus it happened that the quorum of three could often not be found, and letters would be despatched with only two signatures, or even with only one. Upon the death of Jesper Matsson Krus in 1622, the office of Treasurer was left vacant, and remained so for the remainder of the reign; and an immense burden of work fell upon the most efficient member of the College, Johan Skytte, until his transference to the Governor-Generalship of Livonia in 1629.[1] In these circumstances it is not surprising that no minutes seem to have been kept, and that no trace has survived of that procedure by voting which the Ordinance of 1618 had enjoined.[2] On the other hand, the work of the College was modified by the general financial policy of the government. In part it was made easier, as by the tendency towards the farming of revenues, and by the transference of responsibility for bailiffs' accounts to the provincial governors (*ståthållare*); in part it was complicated, as by the King's employment of great financiers with wide powers to manipulate his revenues to the best advantage, and

---

[1] See his complaints in *RRP*, I. 45, 93; and P. Sondén, *Johan Skytte och Oxenstiernorna* (*HT* 1900), pp. 124-7, for observations on his methods in the Exchequer.

[2] *Kammarkollegiets Historia*, p. 61.

by the semi-independent position of the state-sponsored monopoly companies. From time to time schemes were propounded for a revision of the Exchequer Ordinance, and fresh arrangements for the distribution of work within the College were indeed made.[1] But in spite of all difficulties the Exchequer gained ground during these years. Notable progress was made in bringing order and clarity into the national accounts. The first complete budget that has been preserved dates from 1638; but estimates of revenue and expenditure seem to have been made before that. The first national balance-sheet (*rikshuvudbok*) appeared in 1621, and in 1624 a Dutchman, Abraham Cabeliau, was appointed Auditor-General, with two assistants, especially to do this work. It was Cabeliau who introduced Dutch methods of book-keeping into Sweden.[2] The King's absence overseas increased the Exchequer's independence and self-reliance: it now dealt on its own authority with fiscal causes, even pronouncing the death sentence,[3] and took resolutions upon petitions and complaints from the commonalty in regard to matters of taxation; and at the end of the reign it emerged as an administrative organ of proved worth and reasonable integrity.

The Chancery in 1611 was still much as Gustav Vasa had left it. The broad division between a German and a Swedish secretariat, which he had instituted, still stood; the forms of business were still vague and occasional; and no real distinction was made between foreign and internal correspondence. Until Oxenstierna's appointment, in January 1612, the office of Chancellor had long ceased to be an efficient one—though Karl had for a moment toyed with the idea of placing the Chancellor at the head of a sort of *hovrätt*—and the business of the office had latterly been done by a *hovkansler*, Dr. Nils Chesnecopherus.[4] The revival of the Chancellorship as an efficient office in Oxenstierna's person placed the ablest man in the country in the very centre of affairs. For the Chancery touched the affairs of state on every side, and at all levels.[5] All royal correspondence, deeds of gift, state-papers, whatever their content, had

---

[1] *ibid.*, pp. 55-60; *SICF*, pp. 47-9.

[2] F. Lagerroth, *Statsreglering och finansförvaltning i Sverige*, pp. 45-55; and see *AOSB*, I. 1. 452, for Oxenstierna's interest in the question.

[3] *e.g. Kammarkollegiets Protokoll*, I. 216.

[4] For the earlier history of the Chancery, see O. Wieselgren [etc.], *Kungl. Maj:ts Kanslis Historia*, I.; *Sveriges Utrikesförvaltningens Historia*; Edén, *Om centralregeringens organisation under den äldre Vasatiden*; and Edén, *CU*, pp. 36, 57-62.

[5] See especially Ahnlund, *Axel Oxenstierna*, pp. 128, 346-52.

to be drawn up by the Chancery, and despatched from it; and as a
result the Chancellor had a finger in the business of every department. With the Exchequer his relations were particularly close.
He was solely responsible for conducting the King's foreign policy,
and his duties in this field extended to those ceremonial *minutiae*
which were the bane of contemporary diplomacy. The Chancery,
which was thus the parent of the Foreign Office, was equally responsible for such concerns as are to-day managed by a Home Secretary
or a Minister of Education. It cared for such social services as
existed; it had charge of the national archives; it managed the State's
relations with the Church; it exercised supervision over town-
councils. In short, it was a governmental factotum, to whose care
were assigned all those matters which appeared to be not otherwise
satisfactorily provided for. The civil servants of Gustav Adolf's
day were used to sudden transferences from one type of activity to
another, and their minds retained in consequence an unbureau-
cratic flexibility; but there was no official from whom was demanded
such vast and various resources of information, such simultaneity of
expertise, as from the Chancellor. Much therefore depended on
the mental calibre of the holder of the office. Oxenstierna filled it
to perfection. His retentive memory, his astonishing mastery of
detail, were matched by an ability to select what was important, and
a vision which extended beyond the thickets of diurnal files. Inevitably his proceedings were logical and orderly: if they had not
been so, he could hardly have discharged the tasks which were laid
upon him. But he was not the slave of logic, nor the prisoner of
systems. The imperturbability of his temperament was a strong
asset, whether it were a question of riding easily upon the billows
of paper that beat upon him, or of dealing with a sovereign whose
self-control was not always a match for inherited irritability. For
the first few years of the reign he was in reality the King's sole
minister; and in his long career he mastered most types of statesmanship with success. Whether it were a matter of armaments production, economic policy, naval strategy, diplomatic finesse, theological
disputation, educational principle, or parliamentary tactics, seemed
entirely indifferent. He turned from war to administration, from
administration to diplomacy, with sovereign unconcern; un-
hurried, untiring, precise, acute, copious in Latin and German and
a Swedish grievously bespattered with both. He and his master
were in the habit of referring to the Chancery as *anima regni*; but

AXEL OXENSTIERNA

JOHANNES RUDBECKIUS,
BISHOP OF VÄSTERÅS

in reality it was but an inchoate mass of unborn departments, incapable itself of generating the energy to keep its own business in plausible vibration: the soul of the kingdom lay not in the office but in the man.

Oxenstierna had hardly taken office before a modification in the internal arrangements of the Chancery showed that fresh winds were blowing. In February 1612 he revised the distribution of work between the senior officials,[1] in an Instruction which represents the first real attempt to group the business of the Chancery into clear-cut categories, on a partly geographical basis. It was followed by a similar ordinance in 1614, which provided also for a full-time registrar or filing-clerk.[2] But the real reorganization did not come until 1618. By the Chancery Ordinance of 16 October (only two days after the Exchequer Ordinance), the Chancery was given an establishment of a Chancellor, an archivist, six secretaries, and the requisite clerks.[3] To each of these posts is assigned fixed duties: there is to be a secretary for Russian affairs; a secretary for Denmark, Livonia and Poland; a secretary for France, England and the Netherlands; a secretary for Germany; and so forth. Instead of allotting the work on the basis of available staff, as in 1612 and 1614, it is now divided on the basis of topics, each with its secretary, and the staff is hereafter to be assigned as recruited to a definite post on the establishment. A further ordinance of June 1620 slightly modified these arrangements[4]; but in the main they continued in force until 1626, when the approaching departure of Oxenstierna for Prussia probably precipitated a step which he had apparently been meditating since 1624.

Hitherto the Chancellor had made no attempt to organize the Chancery on a collegial basis. His own relations with his sovereign had become established on a footing of perfect confidence and intimacy, and no doubt he felt that much of this must be lost by the substitution of transactions with a Board for the freer and more informal dealings between two individuals. The collaboration between King and minister was too close, the issues dealt with between them too grave or too delicate, for collegial procedure by debate, resolution, vote, and recorded dissent; and the Chancellor

---

[1] Text in *SICF*, pp. 295-7.
[2] Text in *SICF*, pp. 298-9.
[3] Text in *SICF*, pp. 300-2.
[4] Text in *SICF*, pp. 302-5. In 1625 the number of secretaries was reduced to five: *Svenska Utrikesförvaltningens Historia*, p. 46.

was not likely to relish the prospect of being outvoted by his colleagues. But it was inherent in the nature of the Chancery that its work ranged from the highest issues of policy to the most pedestrian routine. With Oxenstierna established at Elbing, those high matters could be transacted, as before, between himself and Gustav Adolf, and the necessary letters written with his own hand; but there was something to be said for bringing the forms of business in the office at home into line with those of the Exchequer: the Chancellor seems already to have envisaged the structure of five Colleges which was to be made definitive in the Form of Government of 1634. The Chancery Ordinance of June 1626, therefore, ran upon lines familiar from the Exchequer Ordinance eight years earlier.[1] The Chancellor was now to preside over a College composed of himself and two Chancery Councillors (*kansliråd*) who were to be resident in Stockholm. A broad division was made between the archival side of the Chancery's work and the despatching-and-administrative side: each division was to have one *kansliråd*. The number of secretaries was reduced to four, and they were to concern themselves respectively with the archives; internal affairs (including relations with Denmark); Poland, Russia and the Baltic provinces; and other foreign countries. By an interesting innovation the newly organized postal system was placed under the Chancery; and so too were Trading Companies, Education, Hospitals and the Poor. Special quarters in the Castle in Stockholm were assigned to the offices, and others to the archives. Working hours, with a five-and-a-half-day week, were rather longer than in the Exchequer, and it was expressly provided that the staff should attend at 6 a.m. each day 'whether there is any work to do or not'. Provision was made for the publication by the Archivist, at weekly intervals, of a digest of information—the beginning of the history of the Swedish newspaper press. And, lastly, the new Chancery was forbidden to deal with correspondence concerning financial matters or *utskrivning*; such correspondence was to be remitted to the Exchequer Council, or to the War Council (*krigsråd*), as the case might be.[2]

The Chancery Ordinance, like the Exchequer Ordinance, never obtained Gustav Adolf's sanction. In his letter of appointment for Per Banér and Karl Oxenstierna as *kansliråd* he declared that he had

---

[1] Text in *SICF*, pp. 306-18.
[2] The *krigsråd* at this moment existed only in Oxenstierna's imagination: see below, p. 276.

had time only to glance at it; that it had not his approval, since there was much in it that needed clarification; but—with curious inconsequence—that nevertheless for the moment it might stand.[1] Thus from 1626 the Ordinance was in fact valid; but it was not therefore literally obeyed. The absence of the Chancellor overseas made collegial procedure impossible—if indeed it had seriously been contemplated; and the routine business was conducted until 1629 by Per Banér and Karl Oxenstierna jointly, while Axel Oxenstierna reserved matters of high policy to himself. In 1629 Karl Oxenstierna died, and Per Banér thenceforward managed—or mismanaged—the Chancery alone, taking the title of Vice-Chancellor. He was a man who enjoyed poor health, and was in addition of a somewhat indolent habit, so that it was not to be wondered at that his papers should have fallen into some confusion. It is only fair to add, however, that the establishment of the office was rarely kept at the level prescribed in 1626. Secretaries were hard to come by, and good men were only too often sent off on diplomatic missions, or called to serve in the entourage of the King.[2] In June 1630 there was but one secretary in the College; in 1632 only two. It proved impossible to recruit suitably qualified young men from the University; and in 1636 Axel Oxenstierna was considering the institution of a special graduate course of training for aspirants to this branch of the King's service.[3] Thus it was that when Johan Adler Salvius took over the presidency of the *kansliråd* in 1634 he complained of the staff's lack of training, and observed that since 1626 things had proceeded, alas, '*more solito*', whereby 'no small confusion' had been occasioned.[4] And lastly, the attempt to decentralize correspondence, so that the Chancery no longer dealt with military or financial affairs, was not fully carried out in practice: indeed, there were complaints on this score as late as 1641.[5] Thus in Gustav Adolf's time the Chancery Ordinance of 1626 remained very largely in suspense. It did not really begin to be effective until

[1] *SICF*, pp. 319-20.
[2] In 1630 Johan Adler Salvius and Karl Banér were created 'Secretaries of State'; but this did not help, since they were almost wholly employed upon missions abroad. Haralds, *Kansliet—anima regni* (*Statsv. Tidskr.* 1928), p. 247; *Sveriges Utrikesförvaltningens Historia*, pp. 51-2.
[3] *Sveriges Utrikesförvaltningens Historia*, pp. 52, 60.
[4] *Kungl. Maj:ts Kanslis Historia*, pp. 33-4. Among the points upon which the *råd* asked Axel Oxenstierna's opinion in March 1633 was 'By what means the Chancery College may come to its right *esse* and be provided with efficient and well-qualified persons.' Loenbom, *Uplysningar*, III. 88.
[5] E. Hildebrand, *Kristina*, p. 67.

after the Form of Government of 1634, when Salvius assumed the direction of the College, and two new *kansliråd* were appointed. But Axel Oxenstierna's draft proved to have been soundly drawn for more normal times; and it remained in force down to 1661, when it was replaced by an Ordinance based essentially upon the plan of 1626.

Of the five great officers of state, three—the Steward, the Chancellor and the Treasurer—had thus by 1634 been transformed into the efficient heads of government departments, each organized (on paper, at all events) upon the same general principles. There remained the Marshal and the Admiral. The idea of establishing a War Office (*krigsråd*) to control the administrative side of the army first appears to have occurred to Gustav Adolf about 1619, when he addressed a series of enquiries upon these matters to Jakob de la Gardie. For some years, however, nothing came of the project —possibly because the old Marshal, Axel Ryning, was unfit to preside over an office of state; but it is clear that the project was not wholly abandoned, since the Chancery Ordinance of 1626 referred to a *krigsråd* as though it already existed, or was about to be created; and Oxenstierna included it in a list of presidents and assessors of the Colleges which he drew up in (probably) November 1627. There were, perhaps, special difficulties in establishing such a department—they applied also to the project for an Admiralty— for it was not easy to delimit the sphere of action of the proposed War Office from that of the Exchequer, and even from that of the Chancery. The Exchequer, for instance, must control pay, clothing and maintenance, must supervise accounts, and was responsible for the transport and quartering of troops; while the Chancery, through its responsibility for dealing with *riksdag* proceedings, and through its control of local government, could not be excluded from a share in the business of *utskrivning*.[1] Progress was made, therefore, along the less debatable line of military jurisdiction; and the first real central office of government for the army—established in May 1630 —was called simply a Court-Martial (*krigsrätt*). This, however, was a misnomer, for in addition to its judicial powers, it exercised numerous administrative functions, dealing for instance with recruiting, mustering, and the provision of arms and equipment.[2] It had a semi-collegial organization, with Jakob de la Gardie (Ryning's

---

[1] Steckzén, *Krigskollegii Historia*, p. 30; Haralds, *Kansliet—anima regni*, pp. 252-5.

[2] Steckzén, *op. cit.*, pp. 34-9, correcting Edén, *CU*, pp. 156-8, 275-80.

successor as Marshal) as President, aided by five assessors and a large secretarial staff; and it was referred to on occasion as *Krigs-rättens Kollegium*—the College of the Court-Martial. It suffered from the usual shortage of staff, as a result of the employment of its members upon other work, and its competence did not by any means extend over the whole field of military matters; but it did achieve satisfactory results within its limited field, and it paved the way for the full collegial organization which followed in 1634.[1]

The history of the Admiralty is similar, and almost contemporary. Towards the end of the second decade of the century the idea of an 'admiralty' as a permanent office of government begins to emerge (admiralty accounts are referred to in the Exchequer Ordinance of 1618); it acquires a secretary in 1621, and its own book-keeper three years later; develops throughout the 'twenties—thanks mainly to Klas Fleming's energy—and by 1630 is a recognized department with a staff of indeterminate size. In 1630 the Admiralty registers of correspondence begin, and there are moves for setting up an office of naval Court-Martial on the lines of the *krigsrätt*. Nothing further was done, however, in Gustav Adolf's lifetime; but on 13 November 1632 a meeting of the *råd* resolved that the Admiralty should be established as a College of the usual type, and in the Form of Government of 1634 it obtained the collegial organization which it was to retain for a century and a half.[2]

By the close of 1632, therefore, the circle of Colleges was virtually complete. Some years might yet be required before all of them should function smoothly upon the lines which Oxenstierna had contemplated, but the direction of development had been indicated so clearly that henceforward it was to be a question only of pursuing

---

[1] For *Krigskollegiet* generally, see Steckzén, *op. cit.*, pp. 16-51. Opinions differ as to the nature of the activities of the *krigsrätt* between 1630 and 1634. Gustav Adolf's original instruction of 1630 was confined entirely to judicial functions; but it seems clear that the *krigsrätt* did in fact discharge administrative duties also. Steckzén's explanation is that the administrative duties were simply transferred from the Marshal to the *krigsrätt*—which was easy enough, since Jakob de la Gardie, the President of the *krigsrätt*, was himself the Marshal—and that the King, being pressed for time on the eve of his departure for Germany, felt that a special instruction with regard to these matters was unnecessary, and confined himself therefore to the purely judicial side. Though the explanation lacks proof, it does explain what happened: the criticisms directed against it by Wittrock, on the other hand, do not. See B. Steckzén, *Till frågan om krigskollegii uppkomst*, and G. Wittrock, *Krigskollegiets tillkomst. Ett genmäle* (both in *HT* 1931).

[2] Edén, *CU*, pp. 284-95; *Sveriges Krig*, Appendix Vol. I. 9-12, 37; *Svenska Flottans Historia*, I. 311-14; Zettersten, *Svenska Flottans Historia*, I. 16-18; A. Munthe, *Svenska sjöhjältar*, V. 19; and see below, Vol. II, Chapter XIII.

a policy which had already been initiated. The Form of Government, in this respect at all events, was indubitably the logical conclusion of Gustav Adolf's policy. The new system was to be based, for the moment at least, only on the five great officers of state: attempts to bring the Church within its orbit had failed,[1] and a project, entertained for a moment by Oxenstierna, of forming a College to take care of those social services which were the Chancery's responsibility, had come to nothing. The first addition to the original five was to be the College of Mines (*Bergverkskollegium*), the rudiments of which are discernible in 1630. The whole process represented a striking transformation of the central government of the country. When the Colleges were functioning properly, Sweden had at her command one of the best-developed, most efficient, and most modern administrations in Europe. The contrast with the still-primitive apparatus with which Gustav Adolf began his reign was very marked.

The effect of these changes was felt all over the constitutional field. Not least in the relations between the King and the *riksråd*. Oxenstierna's great reforms had resulted in the concentration in Stockholm of a corps of noble administrators—assessors of the *Hovrätt, kansliråd, kammarråd*—many of whom were also members of the *riksråd*. The *riksråd* thus became increasingly a body of civil servants, and less and less a casual assemblage of great nobles whose claim to importance was based mainly on their birth or landed interest or military eminence. The member of the *riksråd* was now a working statesman, and recruitment tended increasingly to be determined by that fact. Membership of the *råd* had indeed, as Gabriel Gustafsson Oxenstierna wrote in 1630, become a burden, a responsibility, which it required some physical toughness to bear.[2] The high nobility, while not abandoning that country life and those rural pleasures which always prevented their degenerating into a caste of courtiers, was coming to spend a good portion of the year in Stockholm upon the King's service—or, alternatively, was losing its parochial outlook by missions abroad, or by following the King's colours across half Europe. Stockholm became a real capital. In Gustav Vasa's time the centre of government had been that particular castle or manor where the King happened to be: now, the King might be

---

[1] See below, pp. 410-12.
[2] Nordwall, p. 47. And Axel Oxenstierna said that it was the nobility's 'highest *jus*, . . . that we are *capaces munerorum publicorum*, which *jus* is *onerosum*': E. Hjärne, p. 41, citing *RRP*, VI. 404.

at Åbo or Augsburg, Mora or Mainz, but the machinery of administration—albeit with audible groanings—ground on in Stockholm.
It became possible to leave behind a real interim government, a
quasi-regency, whenever in the 'twenties the King was absent from
the country for any length of time. It was fortunate that this was
so, for of the twelve years which intervened between his departure for
Riga in 1621 and his death in 1632, he was at home for less than six.
The government could not have been carried on, the wars could not
have been waged, nor the armies and fleets equipped, had he been
forced to rely upon the type of formless improvisation which had
done duty in Stockholm during his absences in the preceding decade.
Without the Exchequer Ordinance, the Judicature Ordinance, the
Chancery Ordinance, Stralsund could hardly have been held, nor
Breitenfeld won.

With 1621, then, begins a succession of governments in the
King's absence which extends beyond his death. Their composition was defined, and their duties and competence prescribed,
in a series of very full Instructions. Between the first Instruction of
1621, and the last, issued on the eve of the King's departure for
Germany in 1630, a certain development is naturally observable.
First, in regard to personnel. The Instruction of 1621[1] nominates
nine members of the *riksråd* who are to stay in Stockholm and
conduct the government in the King's absence; and that of 1622
is similar, save that only seven names appear instead of nine. But
it was the practice from the beginning for these persons to coopt any
other members of the *riksråd* who might happen to be available;
and this practice had such obvious advantages that it is explicitly
sanctioned in the Instruction for 1625: *all* members of the *riksråd*
who were not with the King, or especially detailed for other work,
were now to assemble in Stockholm and conduct the government;
but in particular ten persons were specified whose duties confined
them to the capital, and who might therefore presumably be relied
upon to be present.[2] These specially named persons were,
theoretically, the core of the government; but in fact equally
valuable services were performed by members of the *råd* not so
specified, such as Karl Karlsson Gyllenhielm. It proved difficult,
moreover, to secure a constant attendance at the meetings of the
governing council: on occasion the numbers dropped to as few as four.
Members were taken up with the business of their respective Colleges,

[1] *RRP*, I. iii-vi.   [2] *RRP*, I. ix-xii.

or they might be absent on special missions within the country.[1] Yet, on the whole, the system worked. The men abroad complained bitterly of the indifference, neglect and dilatoriness of the men at home; and the home government grumbled that their efforts and their difficulties were alike unappreciated [2]; but it worked, for all that.

Essentially the home government was designed to carry on the routine of administration, to keep the Estates in as good a temper as possible,[3] to guard against the possibility of a direct attack on Sweden, and to satisfy the needs of the armies overseas. It was not normally to meddle with the business of the various Colleges: if it interfered at all, it was to do so by way of encouragement and support. It had no control over policy, and scarcely any voice in the shaping of it: that was decided between Gustav Adolf and Axel Oxenstierna. Its business was to obey the King's orders. Only in one respect was it to be entrusted with something like a portion of the prerogative: in 1630, after some years of uncertainty, it was authorized to exercise the King's residual judicial power upon petitions from the judgment of the *Hovrätt*.[4] For the rest, its members wrestled with an extraordinary diversity of topics: their minutes deal with the most trivial as well as with the gravest issues.[5] But though they had no easy life of it, bearing much responsibility with little power and less thanks, by the regularity of their meetings and their growing sense of corporate responsibility they were sowing seed which was to ripen to harvest in the years after 1632.[6]

The interim governments were a sign of the trust now felt by the King in his aristocracy (if also of the fact that there were limits to that trust), and the same impression is produced by the record of his dealings with the *riksråd* when he was at home. Until Gustav Adolf's time, the customary procedure when the King wished to take counsel of his *riksråd* was for him to submit a point to them and call upon them to frame a resolution upon it. The *råd* then met

---

[1] See, *e.g.*, *AOSB*, II. III. 136-7, 269; *RRP*, I. 31-2, 42, 57, 63; II. 238.

[2] *AOSB*, II. III. 218; II. x. 292. So great were the difficulties that in 1636 Salvius proposed transferring the seat of government to Hamburg: *Svenska Utrikesförvaltningens Historia*, p. 58.

[3] Axel Oxenstierna said in 1636, 'We are *senatores regni* and ought to be as *mediatores inter regem et subditos*. . . .': E. Hjärne, *Från Vasatiden till Frihetstiden*, p. 217.

[4] Haralds, *Konungsdom och konungsnämnd*, p. 245; and see below, p. 335.

[5] For some trivialities, see *RRP*, I. 120; II. 46, 60, 94, 103; *AOSB*, II. XII. 216.

[6] Tham, *Bidrag till svenska riksdagarnes historia, 1626-1629*, p. 63. Regular meetings were first enjoined in 1625. In July and August 1630 they met on 26, 27, 29, 30 July; 5, 6, 7, 9, 10, 11, 12, 13, 16, 17 and 19 August: *RRP*, II. 24-34.

without the King; debated the matter; and embodied its views in
a formal *rådslag* (resolution) which was drawn up in writing. This
type of meeting continued throughout the reign; but from the
beginning of the 'twenties it began to be supplemented by another
and freer type of procedure.[1] According to the new method, the
King appeared in person and presided at the council; the matter
was debated in his presence; the course of the debate recorded in
the minutes; and the issue embodied in a *rådslag* which really only
gave the upshot of the argument. On these occasions the King
took a very active part in the meetings, intervening personally in
the discussion, and not refraining from the making of purely
debating points. He did not, however, submit to his *råd* a *Proposition*: his introductory speech was usually confined to an exposition
of the factors governing the question, and it was left to the *råd* to
frame definite proposals. The great question of whether to intervene
in Germany was debated in *råd*-meetings of this type. At the
meeting of December 1628, Gabriel Gustafsson Oxenstierna and
Johan Skytte were deputed by the King to argue the case for and
against, very much in the manner of an academic disputation; while
at the meeting of November 1629, the two sides were put by the King
himself in his introductory speech. This new style of council-
meeting, so much more intimate, cordial and informal than the old,
was a good illustration of Gustav Adolf's policy of identifying the
office-holding aristocracy with the actions of the Crown. But it did
not therefore mean that the *råd* was admitted to a share in determining policy, any more than the interim-governments were allowed
to do so. The position was not that the King acted in accordance
with the advice given to him, whether that advice were contained
in the old-style *rådslag* or emerged from the new-style round-table
discussion; it was rather that the King, having resolved beforehand
on the line to be pursued, laid the factors governing the situation
before his *råd*, that they might reach their own conclusion. That
conclusion, when it came to the point, turned out to be identical
with the King's own: there is no case, apparently, of a difference of
opinion between them upon a major issue.[2] The facts—or at least

---

[1] The first example of the new type of meeting is considered to be in January
1617, but it did not become usual until after 1620.
[2] See *AOSB*, II. III. 110, for a sharp brush: the King had his way, but the
råd protested by leaving the *rådslag* (drawn as the King desired) unsigned for fourteen days, 'usque ad indignationem Regis'. And see *Abraham Brahes Tidebok*,
pp. 179-80, for a thundery interlude.

the facts as the King, with his remarkable talent for persuasive oratory, presented them—spoke always overwhelmingly for the line of conduct upon which he had already decided. The real debate had occurred earlier, between the two men who were fully informed of all the circumstances—Gustav Adolf and Axel Oxenstierna.[1] The purpose of the debate in the *råd*, therefore, as the King frankly avowed, was to *identify* that body with a decision which had already been taken, to broaden the base of responsibility, to eliminate the possibility that at a later date the *råd* might dissociate themselves from an enterprise which had turned out unsuccessfully.[2] It was the same political tactics as had once led Karl IX to take the advice of the professors of Uppsala upon a point of foreign policy.[3] In 1611 the *råd* had demanded that their counsel be not judged *ex eventu*: the monarchy was now ensuring that its policy should not so be judged either. Thus the kingship remained in all essentials a personal kingship. It had indeed abandoned the attempt—which even Karl IX had persisted in—to supervise every bailiff, control every account, master every petty detail of national affairs: for these tasks the Colleges had been called into existence. But the nation was not therefore—as yet—handed over to a noble bureaucracy. The authority of the King remained unimpaired; limited, as before, only by the traditional checks and obligations which had been built up in the Middle Ages; by no means a despotism, but still less subject to restraint by the machinery which it had called into being. Above the Colleges, above the *råd*, above the interim government, above even the all-wise Chancellor,[4] the prerogative remained intact within its legal limits; and as long as he lived the King reserved to himself the right to override, by personal intervention, the forms which he had established, or had allowed to be established. Hence,

---

[1] In May 1622 the Danish agent Peder Galt reported: 'he [Oxenstierna] alone rules, at which some are ill pleased, and the High Steward Count Magnus [Brahe] has complained thereat': Galt, p. 24.

[2] Thus on 18 February 1629 Gustav Adolf wrote to Oxenstierna that he proposed to obtain a resolution of his *råd* upon the Polish negotiations, for (he wrote) 'better to proceed *communi errore* than run the risk of being blamed, should Fortune (which for our sins is inconstant) turn against us'. *AOSB*, II. 1. 457. In 1642 Per Brahe remarked that Gustav Adolf 'did nothing without the advice of his *riksråd, eoque amatus et venerabilis*'; to which Axel Oxenstierna retorted, 'the late King consulted often with the *råd* and the Estates, more in order that he might not appear to be the cause of any misfortune that might happen, than from necessity'. Quoted in E. Hjärne, p. 56.

[3] W. Tham, *Axel Oxenstierna*, p. 120; T. Berg, *Johan Skytte*, p. 160.

[4] As early as December 1612 Gustav Adolf was informing Oxenstierna that he proposed to ignore his advice not to act without consulting the *riksråd*, since that would cause delay. *AOSB*, II. 1. 18.

perhaps, the lack of a coping-stone upon so many of the constitutional edifices erected at this time, and the absence of any general statute (such as the Form of Government) which might bind his freedom of action too straitly.[1] The King's own temperament, and the desperate character of the times, forbade such dangerous logic. If the Charter had really contemplated the effective control of the country by the aristocracy in the King's despite; if a ruling oligarchy in Erik Sparre's spirit had then been intended; then Gustav Adolf succeeded in evading his obligations on this point. But if, as seems more likely, the demand had been only for the recognition of the right of the nobility to positions of trust, and a safeguard against a recurrence of the rule of secretaries, then it was Gustav Adolf's achievement to reconcile the fulfilment of that demand with the maintenance of the royal authority, and to fuse the spirit of the Vasas with the pretensions of the aristocracy, to the advantage of each. The *rapprochement* of the monarchy and the nobility—made easier, as it was made necessary, by the country's danger—called forth in them a high sense of public duty,[2] and made available a fund of ability with which Sweden could ill have afforded to dispense.

(iii) *The Legislative*

The Charter, which had been so clear and peremptory upon the political relations between the Crown and the aristocracy, and had thus largely determined the future character of the central executive, had been much less positive in regard to the legislative. The complaints of 'over-many *herredagar*', the fear of the monarchy's abuse of the *riksdag*, natural in a generation which vividly remembered the executions at Linköping, might seem to portend a period in which the *riksdag* would suffer eclipse. In fact, the very opposite occurred. Gustav Adolf's accession found the *riksdag* at a critical point in its development: his death saw it established as part of the normal machinery of the state, with constitution and procedure more definitely determined than ever before.

The Swedish *riksdag* had origins stretching far back into the

---

[1] Lagerroth, *Frihetstidens författning*, pp. 115-16, 121, 123-5.
[2] See Skytte's oration on the qualities required in a member of the *riksråd*, upon the occasion of his own admission to that body (28 January 1617): *SRDA*, II. 74.

Middle Ages.[1] It derived almost equally from those afforced meetings of the *riksråd* to which the name *herredag* had early been applied, and from those electoral assemblies of representatives of the nation which gathered when there was a king to be chosen or deposed. The old tradition that the first *riksdag* met in 1435 is now abandoned by historians: it is clear that a national assembly of representative character met as early as 1319, and it seems likely that similar gatherings took place in 1359, 1364 and 1396. However that may be, the troublous times of the fifteenth century saw numerous meetings, either of the *herredag* type or of the electoral-assembly type, summoned by *riksföreståndare* (regents) as instruments or allies in their struggle with the monarchy and its supporters; and their decisions had often the character of *sammansvärjningar*—swearings in common, unions of ruler and people by the bond of an oath to pursue a definite line of conduct. As yet these gatherings had neither consistency of composition, uniformity of nomenclature, nor the recognition of the law; but the idea was gaining ground that the nation should in times of crisis be consulted more directly and more simultaneously than could be done by the old method (prescribed by the *landslag*) of provincial meetings: as Sten Sture the younger said (in words which have a familiar ring to an English ear) 'what touches all should be approved by all'. Young Herr Sten went further than any of his predecessors as *riksföreståndare* in using such meetings for political ends, and his rule is perhaps the decisive epoch in the *riksdag's* emergence. In his employment of *riksdagar* as an instrument of policy, and in his encouraging of them to collaborate with him, he foreshadows Gustav Vasa, who in this as in so much else reaped where Herr Sten had sown.

The meeting which chose Gustav Vasa king, in 1523, was almost the last electoral assembly of the old type. Four years later, at Västerås, a new period in the history of the *riksdag* began, when the King cozened them into becoming his accomplices in the breach with Rome. In the history of the *riksdag* this meeting of 1527 has an importance which may be compared with that of the Reformation Parliament in the history of the English Commons; and from that

---

[1] For the following paragraphs see, in general, the three first volumes of the collective work *Sveriges Riksdag*: they are, S. Tunberg, *Riksdagen under medeltiden*; T. Berg, *Riksdagens utveckling under den äldre Vasatiden*; N. Ahnlund, *Ståndsriksdagens Utdaning*. Reference may also be made to Edén, *Sveriges Riksdag*; Stavenow, *Sveriges Riksdag* (*HT* 1935); Hessler, *Den svenska ståndsriksdagen* (*Scandia* 1935).

moment no major act of state was conceivable without its endorsement. Gustav Vasa's tactics in this respect were followed by all his sons; and already in Erik XIV's time the Estates were made the judges of the King's enemies, as later they were to judge the enemies of Karl IX. It was during Erik's reign that the term 'Estate' first came into common use in Sweden. It was imported, like so much else, from Germany, to describe any body of men possessing common privileges and duties, common claims upon society and common functions in society. It was, however, not especially suitable to Swedish conditions at the time of its adoption; and for some decades remained a political concept notably lacking in precision. The Nobility, the Clergy, the Burghers, and the Peasantry—these might be supposed to be sufficiently clear-cut groups to warrant the use of the term; but there were other groups which from time to time hovered on the brink of making good their claim to Estatehood—the miners of Bergslagen, for instance, the royal bailiffs, the local justices (*lagläsare*) and—last but most persistent of all—the officers of the army. The four-Estate structure of the *riksdag* was anything but inevitable in the sixteenth century. At about the same time as the term 'Estate' began to come into the common speech, came also (equally from the German) the term '*riksdag*'. It took rather longer to make good its ground: the older name *herredag* long competed with it, and occurs now and then even down to the end of Gustav Adolf's reign.[1] It was at this time, too, that the Estates began the practice of each drawing up a separate resolution, and each presenting its own list of 'burdens' (*besvär*). In 1571 comes the first grant of a tax by the resolutions of the non-noble Estates, for the first Älvsborg ransom. Throughout the reign of Johan III the *riksdag* grew steadily more important; and the reawakening of the *riksråd* to political activity probably encouraged this development; for the *riksråd* acted as the leader and guide of the *riksdag*. The crisis of Sigismund's reign accentuated the process: the *riksdag* found itself in the unprecedented position of demanding (and obtaining) religious guarantees from its sovereign.

In the revolutionary period of the 'nineties the *riksdag* played a central part. Duke Karl was employing all constitutional (and some unconstitutional) means to secure his ends: old-fashioned *herredagar* (as at Jönköping in 1599); the combination of markets with provincial assemblies; but above all the *riksdag*. In many

[1] *RRP*, I. 139 (June 1629); *SRARP*, I. 130 (May 1630).

respects his proceedings looked back to the early days of its existence in the fifteenth century: the Arboga *riksdag* which chose Karl as *riksföreståndare* was in the authentic tradition of Karl Knutsson and the Stures, an electoral meeting born out of time, and its resolution was a typical 'swearing in common'. But the resolution of the *riksdag* at Söderköping in 1595, though old-fashioned in that it was sent round the country for subsequent signature at provincial assemblies, broke new ground, for it was the first general resolution of all the Estates, as against earlier resolutions by each Estate separately. Encouraged, perhaps, by the success of his earlier tactics, Karl after Stångebro used the *riksdag* in unheard-of fashion. It was not only that in 1600 and 1605 he caused them to carry something like a Bill of Attainder against his enemies; he even professed to consult them (that is, he forced upon them a share of the responsibility) in the matter of army appointments, and the selection of his new *råd*. By constant meetings he sought to make them accomplices in every major action; and the strength of the political position which he had built up for himself as the saviour of the nation and the bulwark of Protestantism, backed by his father's trick of threatening abdication if thwarted, ensured as a rule that the Estates would be compliant. But the responsibility which he thrust upon them—as if he designed to drive them towards political maturity—left its mark upon them, bitterly as they sometimes resented it. They grew less dependent upon the leadership of the *råd* than of old; and they positively rejected two proposals, each of which the King had very much at heart—the Poor Law of 1607, and the proposed recodification of the laws in 1609. They began to develop views on foreign policy, and showed disapproval of Karl's provocation of Denmark. From 1599 provision was made for the payment of members; the beginnings of procedure by committees could dimly be discerned; and the several Estates were beginning to think of choosing Speakers.[1]

At the time of Karl's death, therefore, the *riksdag* had made a long stride forward from the position it had occupied in the last year of King Johan. But with all this rapid development there was still much about it that was primitive and indefinite. In the first place, it was by no means clear that the *riksdag* was the only means,

---

[1] Ahnlund, *Ståndsriksdagens Utdaning*, pp. 54, 67, 100-1, 430-1, 438-9, 555; Tham, *Bidrag*, pp. 113, 256; Lilliestråle, *Riksdagarna 1609 och 1610*, pp. 3-10; Carlgren, *Riksdagsutskott före 1680 med särskild hänsyn till sekreta utskottet*, pp. 3-13.

or even the best means, of securing the consent of the country, of committing it to endorsement of a policy, of voicing the nation's feelings. There were alternative methods, some of which were still full of life. It was still doubtful if the *riksdag* could pledge its constituents to a new tax: that 'consent of those concerned' which was required by the *landslag* undoubtedly referred to separate negotiations with provincial assemblies (*landsting* or *häradsting*). Until 1600, at all events, Karl had demonstrated how strong was the tradition which united such local gatherings with the more important markets.[1] The old type of afforced *råd*-meeting, from which the lower Estates might be excluded, was not quite dead; and a new sort of meeting—of a small body of selected representatives from some or all of the Estates—was in process of being born. It was always open for the Crown to deal individually with each Estate, or to deal with one only, if the matter were of no concern to the others. Legislation by King and *riksråd* was still legal in certain cases; and for Church affairs the Reformation had brought with it the possibility of ecclesiastical ordinances promulgated on the basis of agreement between King and synod (*kyrkomöte*), as the famous instance at Uppsala in 1593 had shown.[2] The composition of the *riksdag* was still uncertain: apart from the continuing doubt as to how many Estates there should be, and what groups should comprise them, the number of members varied very considerably: from the King's point of view the ideal was the smallest possible number which would be considered as binding its constituents. The idea of 'constituents' was indeed only imperfectly developed, for as yet there could hardly be said to be any election, at all events for some of the Estates: returns were mostly arranged by the government's agents; while for the Nobility the King tried (in vain) to enforce the attendance of all adult males. Procedure was still rudimentary: as late as the end of the sixteenth century a meeting had been held in the open air, and at meetings of the Estate of Peasants decisions were taken not by the counting of heads but by shouting for or against a proposal.[3] All dealings between King and Estates took place in writing: after 1602 Karl abandoned the practice of personally addressing them; and it was one of the minor grievances in 1611 that the Chancery, when drawing up the formal resolutions

---

[1] For this subject, see N. Staf, *Marknad och möte*.
[2] For the character of the Uppsala meeting the most recent authority is H. Hermerén, *Uppsala möte*, which includes a review of previous literature.
[3] Edén, *Gustaf Adolfs riksdagsordning*, pp. 12, 20.

of the Estates, would alter the text of their draft so as to make it more accordant with the royal will.[1]

In short, the *riksdag* was in that interesting adolescent stage (so dear to English constitutional historians) when it is scarcely safe to make a generalization about anything. It had within it, undoubtedly, the promise of evolution into a real parliament. But it was beset also by twin dangers: it might degenerate into the obedient instrument of a monarchy which should be absolute, within the limits of the law (as happened under Karl XI); or it might suffer eclipse precisely because the men who opposed Karl IX's system were conscious of this danger. In 1611 the latter appeared the more probable speculation; especially since the nation at large felt no great enthusiasm for *riksdagar*, and would have been tolerably satisfied to revert to the older method of separate provincial negotiations. The Charter, in fact, made the future of the *riksdag* problematical: essentially, Gustav Adolf's work in this field was to decide the problem in the *riksdag's* favour.

For the first five years of the reign matters continued much as in King Karl's time: there was the same uncertainty as to what was, and what was not, an Estate, as the summonses to the early *riksdagar* make clear[2]; the same variation in numbers; the same types of procedure. *Riksdagar* were held at Nyköping in December 1611, at Stockholm in November 1612, at Örebro in January 1614, and again in January 1617—that is, with much the same frequency as in the previous reign; and in addition the King had recourse to some of the available alternatives. In 1613, for instance, he held a so-called *handelsdag* (trade-meeting) at Stockholm, where he discussed commercial matters with representatives of the towns and the mines[3]; in the same year a typical 'Committee-Meeting', to which the Peasants were not summoned, decided on the measures to be taken for the ransoming of Älvsborg[4]; provincial meetings were held for Finland at Borgå in 1614 and at Helsingfors in 1616.[5] Local confirmation of the resolution of a *riksdag* was sought from Finland in

---

[1] Hallenberg, *Handlingar till Konung Gustaf II Adolfs Historia*, p. 31.
[2] *SRDA*, I. 21, 25, 522-3; II. 14-15, etc.
[3] *ibid.*, I. 279 *seqq.*; and *cf. Stockholms Stads Privilegiebrev*, p. 156.
[4] *SRDA*, I. 303-6; Hallenberg, II. 673-4.
[5] Waaranen, *Samling af urkunder rörande Finlands Historia*, IV. 320-4; Hallenberg, IV. 488-9; *SRDA*, I. 533-7. The Estates of Småland acknowledged receipt of the resolutions of the Finnish Estates, and promised to transmit their own resolutions. For a separate meeting for Dalarna in January 1617, see Pihlström, *Kungl. Dalregementets Historia*, II. 1.

the spring of 1612.[1] The *riksdag* was used as a court to try sedition—
quite in the manner of Karl IX—in 1614[2]; and Karl's characteristic
tactic of spreading the responsibility appeared in Gustav Adolf's
speech to the hereditary princes and *råd* in June 1615.[3] The country's
dislike of the burden of attendance at *riksdagar* was not at all
diminished, as appears from the remarks of the Peasants at Örebro
in 1617.[4] But in spite of all this, one advance was recorded in these
early years. It occurred in 1614, in connection with the Judicature
Ordinance. The Clergy, in their Answer to the King's Proposition,
had made the point that they could not commit their constituents to
such a change in the law, as established by the *landslag*. In theory
they were right: it was precisely for this reason that the Estates in
1609 had refused to accede to Karl's plans for a recodification.
Gustav Adolf's reactions were significant. He perceived that unless
this objection were firmly dealt with, the *riksdag* could never establish
itself as a national legislative body; and in a reply whose caustic
style recalled Karl IX, he heaped ridicule on the Clergy and forced
them to submit.[5] It was an important development. Henceforward
the King and *riksdag* are admitted to be competent to make the law,
to change the law; and their decision needs no confirmation to be
binding on the country. It may be *politic* to supplement, or to
replace, *riksdag* negotiations by negotiations with provincial gatherings; but no one henceforward will contend that it is *necessary*.

The real turning-point in the history of the *riksdag* under Gustav
Adolf came at the meeting at Örebro in January 1617, when Oxenstierna induced the Estates to accept a far-reaching plan of reform.
This was the *Riksdag* Ordinance, designed primarily to regulate
procedure, but having general constitutional implications of great
importance. In an introductory speech Oxenstierna dwelt on the
disorderliness of the proceedings on earlier occasions. 'It was a
shame that His Majesty and the higher and lower Estates . . .

[1] *SRDA*, I. 157-67.
[2] *SRDA*, I. 475; *Borgareståndets Protokoll*, p. 415.
[3] Styffe, p. 119.
[4] *SRDA*, II. 202.
[5] *SRDA*, I. 419: 'For in view of the fact that *riksdagar* are no new thing in
Sweden, and have always been instituted—not only in this country but in all other
well-conducted governments—in order that counsel could there be taken, and
decisions made *de summa rerum et quod ad Rempublicam pertinet*, among which as
it were the most important is the treating of war and peace, and of the good order-
ings whereby law and justice may be done, the kingdom bettered and made
flourishing, sin punished, the destruction of the country prevented, and so forth;
therefore, if the Clergy is not empowered to do such things on behalf of their
Order, then H.M. cannot conceive what they *are* empowered to do. . . .'

T

should rush together like a lot of beasts or drunken peasants': matters were better managed in the hundred moots and parish councils than in the *riksdag*. When the Estates met in joint session, they were so intermingled that all proper precedence was lost. The Clergy and Burghers, it was conceded, did indeed maintain some sort of order in their respective assemblies; but the Nobility were very lax, indulged in too many social activities, and wasted time; while the Peasants ran about looking for scriveners to draw up their replies, and thus fell into the hands of the agents and spies of Sigismund. Many members went home before the session was over, and then protested that they had never agreed to what had taken place in their absence.[1] The Ordinance now brought forward proposals to correct these and other abuses. In the first place, meetings in the open air are for the future to be prohibited. In the second, the seating at plenary sessions is now carefully prescribed: Karl Filip is to sit on the King's right hand, then the five great officers of state, then the Nobility and the army officers; while on the King's left are to sit Duke Johan, the other *råd*-members, the Clergy and the Burghers. In the middle, at the back of the hall, is the place assigned to the Peasants. No strangers are to be permitted to enter, save the sons of the Nobility, who may stand by the door. The order of business is next laid down. The King will open the Session with a speech, and this is to be answered by the hereditary princes, by one member of the Nobility, and by the Archbishop. The King will then deliver to the Estates his 'Proposition', containing his recommendations for legislation, or requests for assistance; after which the Estates are to separate, that they may discuss it privately in their respective chambers. The Proposition is to be in writing (though the King may motivate it in a speech), and all the Estates are to receive copies of it, which must on no account be removed from the chambers where they hold their debates, and in particular must not be taken to irregular gatherings in taverns. Each Estate will then draw up its Answer in writing (a sworn scrivener being provided for the Peasants), and when all the Answers are ready, a plenary session is to take place in the Hall of State, at which they are to be handed over to the King in due order. If the King approves them, 'well and good'; if not, he may deliver a reply, verbally or in writing. But if the Answers of the Estates are not

---

[1] *SRDA*, II. 23-4, 84-7. The Nobility had been conscious of the need for secrecy as early as 1597: Ahnlund, *Ståndsriksdagens Utdaning*, p. 521.

concordant, then their spokesmen are to explain to the King, by means of a speech in full session, the grounds upon which each is based, so that agreement may be reached if possible. And if no agreement can be reached, 'His Majesty shall take which seems best to him'.[1]

The Estates accepted the Ordinance with little amendment. The hereditary princes were rebuffed in an attempt to secure special precedence for members of their own *råd*; but protested successfully against being bound, like the other Estates, to make a public reply to the Proposition, and, still worse, to defend their Answer in an impromptu speech; and Johan put in his own personal protest at the precedence accorded to Karl Filip. The Burghers and the Peasants, too, jibbed at the prospect of engaging the King in impromptu debate upon their Answers; and on this point it was deemed expedient to give way: the Estates might, as before, confine themselves to transactions in writing. The Clergy asked merely that for them, as for the Peasants, a special chamber might be set aside for their debates. And so, with little difficulty, the Ordinance was agreed upon. By some curious chance it was never formally signed and sealed by the Estates, and in consequence was never promulgated as a statute.[2] But this did not matter, for all the Estates had accepted it as their standing orders, and the new arrangements came immediately into force at the coronation *riksdag* later in the year.

The intention of the Ordinance emerges clearly enough from its tenour. The number of Estates was to be stabilized, the methods of procedure fixed; the *riksdag* was to be given a dignity and seemliness which it had hitherto lacked. The espionage of Sigismund was to be made more difficult. But behind these obvious points lay another consideration. The attempt, which was not wholly successful, to replace at least part of the written proceedings by verbal discussion, indicated a certain impatience with the slowness and circumstantiality of the old methods, and also a desire on Gustav Adolf's part to employ forms which would give greater opportunities for the deployment of his peculiar talents. In public debate his ready eloquence could make its full effect, and that sense of common purpose, that spirit of collaboration between Crown and nation,

[1] Text in *SRDA*, II. 84-7.
[2] Objection was taken on this score when in 1778 Gustav III attempted to revive the *Riksdag* Ordinance of 1617: Lagerroth, *Konung och Adel*, p. 29.

which he wished to foster, would be strengthened. Just as, about the same time, he began to substitute debate with his *riksråd* for the stiff formalism of the earlier style of *rådslag*, so too he attempted the same thing in the larger arena of the *riksdag*. It was not for nothing that he was the son of one demagogic orator and the grandson of another. And so, though out of regard for the embarrassment of the lower Estates and the personal susceptibilities of the hereditary princes the demand for *extempore* orations from their side was remitted, the King for his part preserved the opportunity for the spoken word which his Proposition had afforded him. There remains, however, the question as to whether he did not make a constitutional gain more obvious and tangible than this. The right which he now asserted to take which opinion 'seemed best to him' in case of disagreement between the Estates might at first sight seem to give him the chance to play the arbiter between them, and so, perhaps, override the views of a majority. If this were so, it would imply a state of affairs which robbed the resolutions of the Estates of much of their importance. But in reality the phrase had little significance. It caused no comment when the Proposition was submitted to the Estates, for it did not appear to them either dangerous or novel. If they could not agree among themselves, it was for the King to reconcile them, if necessary by indicating which Estate should give way to the others.[1] The King's right of choice did not disturb his obligations as a constitutional monarch to rule according to the *landslag*, the Charter, and his coronation oath. Since the consent of each Estate was needed before a new burden could be laid upon it, there appeared little possibility that the right would be abused.[2] Gustav Adolf, at all events, did not abuse it.

The purpose of the Ordinance, it is clear, was comparatively restricted; yet in some ways it proved the basis upon which the future development of the *riksdag* was built. For example, it finally fixed the number of Estates at four. On the face of it, the text enumerated six: the Hereditary Princes, Nobility, Army Officers, Clergy, Burghers and Peasants. But two of these were soon eliminated. The Estate of Princes perished with the successive deaths of Johan, Karl Filip and Kristina. The Army Officers never grew into an Estate, for two reasons: first, they were mostly absent

[1] Compare the contemporary obligation of the King of Poland to 'conciliare animos' and 'reducere rationes ad unam sententiam': H. Almquist, *Polskt författningslif under Sigismund III (HT* 1912), p. 180.
[2] Edén, *Gustav Adolfs riksdagsordning*, pp. 22-3. But see below, pp. 303-4.

at the wars; and secondly, the promotion of non-nobles to the rank of officer split the officer-class in two, so that a part belonged naturally to the Estate of Nobility (where after 1626 they were in any case bound to appear) and a part had no obvious *riksdag* associates.[1] Hence only four Estates were left; and those four were to continue as the constituent elements of the *riksdag* until its final reform in 1866. It will be convenient at this point to examine in turn the constitution and characteristics of each of them, as they appeared in the years between 1617 and 1632.

The Estate of the Nobility was considered by the Crown as having a peculiar obligation to attend the meetings of the *riksdag*. Its members had a special duty to assist the King with their advice, and to lend the support of their social and political influence to his measures. In Gustav Adolf's time the Nobility did, on the whole, fulfil these obligations, though they always showed a jealousy for the privileges of their Order, and this sometimes made them difficult to deal with. But there was one respect in which they failed to realize the Crown's expectations: it proved impossible to cajole or coerce them into attendance *en masse*. This was an old dispute with the monarchy: Karl IX in his day had tried to insist on the appearance at *riksdagar* of all adult male members of the Estate, while the nobles, on their side, had contended for the right to send representatives. The question had been raised in the course of the discussions which preceded the Charter, but the Nobility had forborne to press it. In the earlier portion of Gustav Adolf's reign their attendance had been slack, and even at the coronation *riksdag* of 1617 they had numbered only 210 (including the *riksråd* and the five great officers of state)— which was certainly below the real figure.[2] If they had appeared at full strength, the Nobility would probably by the end of the reign have been the most numerous of the Estates.

The controversy about attendance was transferred to rather different ground by the important enactment of 1626 which goes by the name of *Riddarhusordningen* (Ordinance for the House of the Nobility). The idea of a special building for the use of the Nobility had arisen about the year 1620, and had found warm support from

---

[1] In 1664 it was finally decided that army officers attended the Estate of Nobles only in an advisory capacity. They continued, however, to press for recognition as a fifth Estate—most notably in 1719—and throughout the Age of Freedom they attended the Estate of Nobles, though they were not entitled to vote upon resolutions. Ahnlund, *Ståndsriksdagens Utdaning*, pp. 522-3, 525; F. Lagerroth, J. E. Nilsson, R. Olsson, *Frihetstidens maktägande ständer*, I. 51, 52, 104, 223-5.

[2] Ahnlund, *op. cit.*, p. 149. *SRDA*, I. 178, for some typical excuses.

Axel Oxenstierna. Such a building would be designed to serve as a meeting-place for the Estate at *riksdag*-time, as a suitable *locale* for weddings or other ceremonial occasions, as a depository for privileges, and, perhaps, as a school for training the noble youth in polite accomplishments. It is possible that the notion may have been imported from abroad: buildings of this sort existed, it appears, in Austria and Württemberg.[1] However that may be, from about 1621 the Chancellor and his circle were on the look-out for a suitable site; and in March 1625 the Nobility resolved to make contributions to the erection of such a house.[2] It was not until 1626, however, that the project was formally sanctioned by the *Riddarhusordning*. But the provision of a *Riddarhus* was perhaps the least important part of the Ordinance, which went on to make far-reaching alterations in the organization and *riksdag* procedure of the first Estate.[3] Henceforward the Nobility was to be divided into three classes. The first class was to consist of Counts and Barons; the second, of those who were descended from former members of the *riksråd*; the third, of the remainder of the Estate. Precedence in the first class was by date of creation of the title; in the other two it was to be determined by lot. In 1626 the first class had twelve families; the second, twenty-two; the third, ninety-two. Within each class every family was to have one representative elected by its members, who would function as its *caput*; and though all adult males were to be bound to attend the *riksdag*, as before, only the *caput* of each family was to be allowed to sit and speak: the others were condemned to stand and be silent. Every family was to have but one vote, to be cast by its *caput*; a majority of such votes would decide the vote of the class; and a majority of classes would decide the opinion of the Estate. Thus the twelve *capita* of the first class became equipollent with the ninety-two *capita* of the third. The president and speaker of the *Riddarhus* was to be a new official termed the *lantmarskalk* (a word borrowed from Germany): this officer, in theory elected by the Estate, was in fact nominated by the Crown. The Estate was henceforward to keep minutes of its proceedings, and a special sworn secretary was to be appointed to take them.[4]

---

[1] It seems now to be considered doubtful whether there was in fact any direct foreign influence: *Sveriges Riddarhus*, p. 69.

[2] *AOSB*, II. x. 53, 55; Stiernman, *Alla Riksdagars och Mötens Besluth*, I. 779-81.

[3] Some of these changes had been in force since 1625.

[4] *Sveriges Riddarhus*, pp. 70-80; Ahnlund, *Ståndsriksdagens Utdaning*, pp. 166-7, 485, 489; *SRARP*, I. 43.

Such was *Riddarhusordningen*; and its effects were of considerable importance. They were least immediately apparent in the purely architectural field. Contributions towards the *Riddarhus* came in slowly, and even when the King permitted the Nobility to apply to this purpose the fines imposed for neglect to perform knight-service, matters were not much expedited. For the time being they were forced to content themselves with a stone house in Prästgatan, and were grateful enough for a royal donation of tapestries to fit it up. The stately building which stands to-day was not completed until 1660, and was not even begun when Gustav Adolf fell at Lützen.[1]

More immediately perceptible were the constitutional effects of the Ordinance. It settled once and for all who was, and who was not, noble; and thus terminated many fraudulent or dubious claims to tax-exemption. It made it clear that henceforward the qualification of nobility was not to be, as of old, the provision of one or more properly equipped cavalrymen: the old criterion of knight-service (*rusttjänst*) ceased to be valid, and *rusttjänst* itself ceased to be a major issue between the King and the Nobility. The only criterion of nobility was now a patent from the Crown. The *quid pro quo* for the privileges they enjoyed was no longer service on horseback, for the King could now raise better cavalry by other means: the *quid pro quo*, implicit if not explicit, was now state service, if not in the field, then at the desk. The elimination of *rusttjänst* as the gateway to privilege might seem to bar the road to ennoblement, and make of the aristocracy a closed caste to which entry was no longer an automatic consequence of compliance with the *rusttjänst* qualification. But in effect this was not so. Nobility merely on the ground of performance of *rusttjänst* had long since ceased to be recognized; a royal patent had in practice long since become requisite. And in any case the closing to ambition of one path was more than compensated by the opening of another, for in the new Sweden that Gustav Adolf and Oxenstierna were shaping any successful civil servant might hope to close his career with an introduction to the *Riddarhus* and a new, melodious and fanciful surname.

Perhaps the most important constitutional change brought about by the Ordinance was in the relations between the Nobility and the *riksråd*. The close ties which had hitherto existed between them were now much relaxed. The *råd* was given no special seat, formed no separate class, in the new *Riddarhus*. Its members might indeed

[1] *RRP*, I. 20; *SRARP*, I. 20-1, 23, 163; *AOSB*, II. III. 98.

attend, but they would find themselves in the position of *extra-capita*, constrained to remain silent while another member of their family functioned as *caput*. This effect was certainly intentional. It was designed as one further measure in a process which was crystallizing the *råd* into a government—the *King's* government—and cutting it loose from the general body of the Nobility. The *råd* was no longer to be the core and kernel of the *riksdag*, the leader and spokesman of the Estates in their dealings with the King. On the contrary, it was to be the royal agent for dealing with the *riksdag*, preparing business, organizing sentiment, applying judicious persuasions.[1] This did not mean, however, that the *råd* ceased to feel that it had class interests in common with the rest of the Nobility, as became apparent in the years after 1632.[2] Lastly, the Ordinance had a general effect upon the organization of the remaining three Estates. The new procedures of the Nobility, the greater order of their meetings, made them a model for imitation by their unprivileged brothers; and already before the end of the reign the beginnings of this process are discernible.

At first, it must be confessed, the meetings of the Nobility left a good deal to be desired. Attendance continued to be poor: the Estate itself soon began to impose fines upon absentees, but these were so unsuccessful as a deterrent that the government began seriously to think of intervening. It took some time to work out satisfactory forms of business and rules of order: it was uncertain, for instance, how far a *caput* ought to commit his family on a serious matter without express reference to them; there was hard feeling when the fortunes of the lot gave lowly precedence to ancient and honourable families; and it was not clear in what order (if any) the Classes were to deliver their votes.[3] Chaotic methods of procedure drew down a sharp reproof from the *råd* in 1632.[4] The separation of *råd* from Nobility seems at first to have left the Estate short of leadership: on more than one occasion the *lantmarskalk* is to be found seeking counsel of the *råd*; and it is not unusual—especially when the Nobility and the government do not see eye to eye—for the Estate to send a deputation to consult with the *råd*, or for them

---

[1] From the beginning of the reign the *råd* had ceased to give in an Answer to the royal Propositions, as the Estates were bound to do: Ahnlund, *Ståndsriks-dagens Utdaning*, p. 121.
[2] See, *e.g.*, Wittrock, *Regering och allmoge under Kristinas förmyndare*, p. 15.
[3] *SRARP*, I. 8-9, 12, 13, 45-7, 61, 69, 102, 186-7; *RRP*, I. 146.
[4] *RRP*, II. 230.

to ask that some members of the *råd* may come down to the *Riddarhus* to talk the matter over.[1] And on one occasion, at least, the *råd* deputed two of its members to appear before the Estate in order to prevent the carrying of a 'perverse' resolution.[2] No more apt illustration could be found of the way in which the *råd* had been transformed into a body not far removed in type from the Elizabethan Privy Council.

The Estate of Clergy was the most dignified of the three non-noble (*ofrälse*) Estates; and, like the Nobility, was regarded by the King as having special responsibility to assist the government. It was a responsibility which the Clergy, as good Lutherans, could not decline; and in fact they rendered important service as mouthpieces of official news and views, directors of public opinion, intelligence agents, and unpaid civil servants generally. At meetings of the *riksdag* the Sunday sermons delivered by each of the bishops in turn were counted upon to influence men's minds in favour of the King's measures.[3]

The Estate was headed by the archbishop and bishops, who were members *ex officio*: the claims of the superintendents to the same position were not finally recognized until 1634. Besides the bishops and superintendents, there were usually summoned, in Gustav Adolf's time, two members of every Chapter, and one priest from every hundred (*härad*). The method of electing these representatives was not fixed either by law or custom. Sometimes they appear simply to have been nominated by the bishop; sometimes to have been elected by the Chapters. It is at least certain that unruly spirits such as Baazius accused the bishops of packing the Estate with their own supporters[4]; and it is clear that there was nothing like a popular election by a constituency comprising all those in Orders. The full number of the Clergy rarely or never appeared at a *riksdag*: at the meeting of 1640, for instance (where the attendance was about the average), no less than 162 *härader* had no priest to represent them. Of those who did appear, parish priests formed the majority, and rural deans (*prostar*) provided the backbone.[5]

---

[1] *RRP*, I. 154; Tham, *Bidrag*, pp. 26, 28, 64-6, 69.

[2] *RRP*, II. 231.

[3] For the work of the Clergy as civil servants, see below, pp. 413-16.

[4] For Baazius, see below, pp. 389-90.

[5] Ahnlund, *op. cit.*, pp. 402-6. In 1623 the bishops were charged to bring to the approaching *riksdag* 'the most tractable and intelligent priests, who could understand the general danger to the Fatherland, and would be able to give good counsel, and with whom it would be possible to deal in confidence': Hallenberg, V. 135-6. The dons at Uppsala (who were all, of course, priests) had formed a regular and separate group among the Clergy in Karl IX's time; but no constant rule is to be discerned under Gustav Adolf.

A recognized position of dignity was occupied by the incumbent of the Great Church in Stockholm. The Clergy had their obvious president and spokesman in the Archbishop of Uppsala; but it was not until 1632 that a secretariat was provided for them.[1]

The Estate always considered itself as having a dual capacity: in one aspect it was a part of a secular institution, the *riksdag*; in another it was a church-assembly, the kernel of a national synod. It was in virtue of the latter aspect that its leaders strove to make good its claim to act as a *consistorium regni* for ecclesiastical causes.[2] In a more purely political point of view, the Clergy made notable interventions from time to time on behalf of the peasantry. A majority of them was sprung from peasant stock; all were bound by common social and economic ties to their peasant parishioners; and they realized, better than the other two Estates, the real weight of the burdens which the peasant was being called upon to bear. They felt, too, the odium of defending from the pulpit a policy which bore heavily upon their flocks. In particular, they felt called upon to take the Peasants' interests under their protection at meetings of the Estates to which the Peasants had not been summoned; and despite the resentment of the government, they showed on occasion great courage in championing the cause of the common man. It was a political alliance which was to assume a portentous character in the two decades after Gustav Adolf's death.[3]

The Burghers were the smallest of the Estates in numbers, as they certainly were least in political importance. They represented towns which, except for Stockholm and two or three more, were little better than large villages or overgrown fishing-hamlets, with a constituency which comprised only an insignificant proportion of the total population of the country. Their mutual jealousies prevented their even presenting a solid front in the interests of their own narrow class. Thus circumstances unfitted them to play anything like the same part which the M.P.'s for the English boroughs played in English history, and threw upon the Clergy the main task of representing at the *riksdag* the views of a middle class that was neither peasant nor noble. The Crown, which went to considerable lengths

---

[1] Ahnlund, *op. cit.*, p. 497; N. Edén, *Den svenska riksdagen*, p. 98.
[2] For the controversy over the *consistorium regni*, see below, p. 406 *seqq.*
[3] In February 1632, at a meeting to which the Peasants were not summoned, the Clergy were reluctant to make a grant, fearing 'to be reproached by the Commonalty as having promised something on their behalf; against which they wished to guard themselves'. To which the *råd* drily retorted: 'That seems a superfluous precaution.' *RRP*, II. 140.

to foster the growth of the towns, expected from their representatives gratitude and compliance, and was apt to use language of more than ordinary asperity if they appeared not to be forthcoming; and the interim governments, drawn from a nobility whose economic interests clashed with those of the townsmen, were even less inclined to be sympathetic.[1]

The *Riksdag* Ordinance had laid down an order of precedence for the towns, but it had not attempted any regulation of their representation. All places which possessed the privileges of a town were expected (it was not yet a question of being entitled) to send representatives to the *riksdag*; but as to how many each was to send, or how such representatives were to be chosen—on these points existed the greatest diversity of practice and the very minimum of theory. The number of representatives, in general, varied directly as the size of the town; and usually they sent less members than the government requested. Only Stockholm regularly sent four (with another two from the suburb of Norrmalm). A few, such as Uppsala, might on occasion send three, or more usually two; but the commonest figure for the great majority was one. In such a case a burgomaster would normally be the representative; and he would usually be joined (if more than one member were returned) by a member of the town council, or a representative of the ordinary burghers. There was little enthusiasm to serve; and a burgher who had been elected might usually buy himself off by contributing to the *riksdag* expenses of his substitute. It was, indeed, these expenses which made the towns reluctant to send many members.[2] The habit (which long persisted) of calling upon their representatives to account for their conduct, upon their return home, must also have been discouraging to political aspirations. Equal diversity prevailed in the manner of election. In some towns, where the burgomasters and council were strong, they nominated the candidates; in others, the generality of burghers met in Common Hall to choose one of the members, while the magistracy nominated the other; in others again—as in Göteborg in 1633—the burghers took matters out of the hands of the magistracy and returned both. The organization of the Estate was still rudimentary in Gustav Adolf's time; but it was

---

[1] *cf.* the stinging rebuke administered by the *råd* in 1629: B. Lövgren, *Ståndsstridens uppkomst*, p. 4; Tham, *Bidrag*, pp. 59-61.

[2] In the years 1620-23 the town of Jönköping paid the expenses of two members, at an annual cost of between 120 and 139 *daler*—a considerable sum in those days: Björkman, *Jönköpings Historia*, II. 236-7.

usual for the burgomaster from Stockholm to act as president and Speaker, and the Stockholm town-clerk acted as secretary. In the last year of the reign the Estate took the first steps towards drawing up a regular procedure, but no minutes were kept as yet.[1]

The fourth Estate, and the most numerous of all, was the Estate of Peasants. It was referred to with equal frequency under the name of the Commonalty (*Allmogen*), and the term was significant of its place in Swedish political life. Here at last the great mass of the people found reasonable representation, if not a voice. For the Estate of Peasants was not given to political oratory, meddled only reluctantly in matters of high concern, and was accustomed to refer to itself deprecatingly as 'poor and simple men'. Normally douce and acquiescent, it could on occasion raise its voice in complaint; and it stood for so overwhelming a proportion of the Swedish people that its patience was not to be tried too high. Since the main burden of war-finance fell upon its shoulders, the government could not afford to alienate its sympathies: 'tali tempore non licet offendere quam antea', as the King observed in 1627[2]: and in the imposition of taxation, or the raising of recruits, a certain regard had to be paid to its convenience, so that the new levies might be made as little disagreeable as possible. 'For' (as Skytte had taught the King in his *Een kort Vnderwijsning*) 'the common man is unstable, inclined to changes, and sees with pleasure an alteration in the rulers of the country'.[3] The Peasantry had been the motive power behind Karl IX's revolution, and Karl's son was not disposed to ride rough-shod over it. 'Herr Omnes,' he believed, was easier to lead than to drive; and it was the business of his *råd*, his local officials, and his clergy, to lead it, tactfully and unobtrusively. And though he might on occasion permit himself a contemptuous reference to 'der pöbel drauff unser land . . . bestehet',[4] he seems to have cherished the conviction that the people were really a very good sort of people on the whole, loyal, self-sacrificing, and sound at heart, and if they made trouble at times, the blame must probably rest on the shoulders of the King's servants, who had been corrupt or tyrannical; or his ministers, who had been slack; or the clergy, who had neglected to preach the nonsense out of men's heads.

---

[1] Ahnlund, *Ståndsriksdagens Utdaning*, pp. 407-19, 503-7; *Borgareståndets Protokoll*, pp. 326, 355-6; Odhner, *Sveriges inre historia under Drottning Christinas förmyndare*, p. 83 *note* 2; Herdin, *Uppsala på 1600-talet*, III. 9-14; H. Almquist, *Göteborgs Historia*, I. 109.

[2] *RRP*, I. 62.   [3] T. Berg, *Johan Skytte*, p. 102.   [4] Styffe, p. 322.

The Estate of Peasantry at this time comprised two representatives for every *härad* (hundred), or two for every *landskap* (province) in Norrland and Västergötland. The members were chosen at the hundred moot (*häradsting*); and here too was drawn up the list of the grievances of the hundred, which they would present upon their arrival at the *riksdag*. Usually the members were selected from among the standing jury of the hundred (*häradsnämnd*); and on the whole there was a genuine election by a popular constituency—the only truly popular element in the *riksdag*. But even here the government could exert pressure; since the sheriff (*häradshövding*) and the bailiffs were present at the meeting. In 1634 the Regency directed its provincial governors to use all possible local officials to secure a favourable election—'but *caute* and in *secreto*'; and it appears that something of the sort may also have been in agitation in 1623.[1] The voters were all yeomen farmers or crown-tenants (*skatte-* or *kronobönder*): the peasants of the nobility (*frälsebönder*) were voteless, since it was held that they were represented by their noble landlords. All voters had to be in effective occupation of a real farm, and crofters or day-labourers were excluded.[2]

The Peasants had as yet no regular president or Speaker; but they had a secretary, appointed by the King, who to some extent supplied the lack. The secretary was also the government's agent, and the part he was expected to play was indicated clearly enough by Axel Oxenstierna's remark in 1649, that 'in the late King's time the Peasants answered not at all, without his late Majesty caused them to be induced thereto through a secretary'.[3]

When the Estates were all gathered in the Hall of State for a *plenum*, they formed a pretty numerous assemblage. At the coronation *riksdag* in 1617 some 575 members attended; and though this figure may have been higher than usual, the average attendance at a full *riksdag* was probably over 500. But by no means all those who ought to have attended did so: as a rule only some 60 or 70 Clergy appeared, instead of some 300; the number of Burghers varied between 50 and 60, though it ought properly to have been about 130 or 140; while of the 250 or more representatives to which the Peasantry was entitled, it was rare to see more than 200. The absentees would as to a certain proportion of them be members from

---

[1] *AOSB*, II. III. 70.
[2] Ahnlund, *op. cit.*, pp. 419-25, 511; Hedenius, *Anteckningar rörande svenska bondeståndet under Gustaf II Adolfs regering*, p. 19.
[3] Ahnlund, *Ståndsriksdagens Utdaning*, pp. 507-10.

the more distant provinces—such as Västergötland, Norrland, and above all Finland—who found the time spent in travel, even in winter (when most *riksdagar* were held) disproportionate to the fortnight or so which was the usual duration of a session. The absence of representatives from these provinces sometimes necessitated supplementary meetings with provincial assemblies, to whom the decisions of the Estates would be submitted for information and confirmation. Finland was in any case under-represented, in relation to its share of the total population of the kingdom.[1] The new Baltic provinces can hardly be said to have been represented at all. It had been the policy of Karl IX to get them to send members to the *riksdag*: he hoped thereby to ensure a real incorporation of the new territories into Sweden. He had summoned Reval to send representatives in 1594, 1595 and 1602, and had desired the attendance of members from Livonia also. His policy had met with opposition, however; and his attempt to force special members for Estonia into his new *riksråd* in 1602 had provoked united resistance from the other *råd*-members. To some extent Karl's policy was carried on under Gustav Adolf, who on occasion showed anxiety to assimilate the Balts to a more Swedish (and more civilized) way of life: an example of this was the famous ecclesiastical visitation conducted by Rudbeckius in 1627.[2] Representatives were called to attend the *riksdag* from Reval in 1617, and from Riga in 1622 and 1624: in the case of Riga the obligation of attendance had been inserted into the terms upon which the town capitulated. One of the warmest supporters of the policy of full incorporation was Johan Skytte, and during his Governor-Generalship of Livonia from 1629 to 1633 he kept this end steadily in view. By this time, however, neither Gustav Adolf nor Axel Oxenstierna was in favour of it. The Baltic provinces were not anxious to send members, and Riga and Reval evaded the obligation when they could; and they resented attempts to impose Swedish standards and methods. The King felt that he could not risk alienating the population of an area which supplied the chief source of corn for his armies; and he felt too that if these provinces were represented in the *riksdag* they could no longer be treated in the arbitrary and summary manner which, for so long as they

---

[1] *ibid.*, pp. 383-5. Finland had about one-third of the total population of the old kingdom: Sundquist, *Finlands folkmängd och bebyggelse i början av 1600-talet*: at the coronation *riksdag* of 1617 (which was a very full one) Finland sent 20 Nobles, 11 Clergy and the Bishop of Åbo, 17 Burghers and 29 Peasants.

[2] For this, see below, p. 422.

remained an active theatre of war, the situation might on occasion demand. No progress was made, therefore, in the parliamentary representation of the Baltic provinces; and though a general summons to return members went out to them (and to Prussia also) in 1633, the Form of Government settled the question by laying it down that only persons actually resident in Sweden proper, and in Finland, should be entitled to sit. But this did not prevent the decisions of the *riksdag* from applying to the new territories.[1]

The *Riksdag* Ordinance of 1617 had prescribed certain forms for the transaction of business in the *riksdag*, and had in particular sought to regulate the dealings of the Estates and the sovereign in such a manner as to give full scope for the personal influence of Gustav Adolf. For so long as he was in Sweden, the King took full advantage of the possibilities thus afforded him. He made frequent speeches to the Estates, not only when the royal Propositions were delivered to them, but also impromptu, upon receiving their Answers; and he succeeded in winning a personal ascendancy over them which made the task of extracting supplies considerably easier. It is true that on occasion he tactfully absented himself when any very unpleasant demand was to be made; and it is true, too, that the willingness of the Estates to make sacrifices is to be ascribed largely to their realization of the dangers threatening the country. But it was in the King's own speeches that those dangers were most vividly depicted; it was his eloquence that stirred their patriotism, his risking of his life that moved them, his personality that silenced the grumblers. He contrived to establish between his Estates and himself a bond of confidence, a tie of affection, which he well knew how to utilize, and which is reminiscent of the similar bond between Elizabeth and her later parliaments. The Estates, on their side, grew more sure of themselves; and despite the concession of 1617 they had begun before 1630 to venture on occasional verbal discussions with their sovereign, as Gustav Adolf had hoped that they would. The King's right to choose which Answer seemed best to him proved to be of little importance: the Estates made efforts to reach agreement among themselves before their Answers were presented. Of more consequence, in reality, was the government's practice of 'collating' the various Answers, and digesting them into

---

[1] J. Rosén, *Statsledning och provinspolitik under Sveriges stormaktstid* (*Scandia* 1946), pp. 229-46, 250; Ahnlund, *Die Ostseeprovinzen und der Reichstag Schwedens* (*Pirmā Baltijas Vēstūrnieku Konference*), pp. 420-3.

a common Resolution, which was then re-submitted to the Estates for their acceptance and signature.[1]

The interim governments of the *råd* were naturally driven to rather different methods. They were overworked officials, not victorious hero-kings, and their personalities counted for comparatively little, at least with the lower Estates. Lacking the aura of majesty, the prestige of victory—and, it may be added, the touch of genius—they could not use the King's methods with much prospect of success. Their Propositions, therefore, tended to be less a demand for specific action by the Estates than an exposition of the circumstances which left it to the Estates to make a concrete proposal; they avoided public debate on the Estates' Answers, preferring private negotiations with deputations; and they made it almost a rule that no Answer should be read in the *plenum* unless it had first been scrutinized by the *råd*. This habit of dealing with deputations of the individual Estates had a certain value, for it led to the development of a system of *ad hoc* committees within the Estates, and was part of a general process of education in the elements of parliamentarism which was proceeding almost unperceived during the later years of the reign, and which was to show results under the Regency.[2]

The most important innovation during this period was undoubtedly the creation of the Secret Committee. At the close of 1627 the critical position of affairs in north Germany, and the danger of the entire subjection of Denmark, produced a situation in which the King felt the need to 'spread the responsibility' before proceeding with a policy which might probably commit him to an invasion of Germany and war with the Emperor. It was necessary to lay the whole state of the case before the Estates; but since some of the information upon which a decision was to be taken was highly confidential, and since some of the arguments to be adduced were not suitable for public ventilation, he compromised by asking each of the Estates to nominate a small number of members to a joint committee; and it was to this committee that he opened the business. It was composed of 11 members of the *råd*, 29 of the

---

[1] *e.g. SRARP*, I. 63. ('Thereupon the King replied that he would have the Answers collated, and cause a resolution to be made of them, which should later be submitted to [the Estates] that they might pronounce upon it.')

[2] For *riksdag* procedure at this period, see Ahnlund, *Ståndsriksdagens Utdaning*, pp. 445-63; F. Lindberg, *Axel Oxenstierna som riksdagstaktiker (Statsv. Tidskr.* 1931), pp. 251-3; Tham, *Bidrag*, pp. 26, 28, 38, 59, 64-9; Carlgren, p. 4.

Nobility including the *lantmarskalk*, 14 of the Clergy, 10 Burghers and 14 Peasants. Its decisions were accepted by the Estates as binding upon each of them, though the members of the Nobility also took the precaution of obtaining full powers from the remainder of the Estate; and, on the motion of the *lantmarskalk*, voting was to be oral, each member of the committee giving his vote in turn, and motivating it if he thought fit. Such was the first Secret Committee, though that name was not applied to it before 1660. One other committee of the same sort met in Gustav Adolf's lifetime. This was in June 1631, when an incomplete meeting of the Estates was asked to nominate a committee to consider various points of foreign policy transmitted by the King for their opinion. On this occasion the membership was confined to delegates from the two upper Estates. It is clear that before 1632 such committees were considered as extraordinary *ad hoc* bodies, constituted to deal with matters of foreign policy which had never come before the *riksdag*; but from these modest beginnings the Secret Committee was to expand in the sequel into a normal feature of political life, and was to draw to itself more and more of the real business of its parent body.[1] This was a development which no one could have foreseen in 1632. But already the position of the *riksdag* seemed to be in danger from another type of committee.

From 1620 onwards the King fell increasingly into the habit of calling meetings of the Estates which were not full *riksdagar*, since the Estate of Peasants was not summoned to them. There had already been one conspicuous example of this in 1613, when such a meeting had agreed to the crushing taxation required to redeem Älvsborg. After 1620 they became common. Sometimes the meeting would be a full assembly of the three upper Estates (as in 1620 and 1631); sometimes a mere handful, as in 1626, when the *råd*, with 16 of the Nobility, 4 bishops, and 5 priests approved the transference of the seat of war to Prussia; sometimes the membership would be unevenly divided between the Estates participating, as in 1630, when some 50 of the Nobility, with the Bishops and one or two Burghers, heard the King deliver his memorable farewell speech. But whatever their constitution, all such imperfect meetings of the Estates were coming to be called 'Committee Meetings' (*utskottsmöte*), in contradistinction to *riksdagar*, and from all of them the Peasants

---

[1] Stiernman, I. 799-801, 806-10, 827-30; *SRARP*, I. 53-4, 57, 59, 160; Tham, *Bidrag*, pp. 33-4, 39.

were absent.[1] The calling of Committee Meetings was usually justified on grounds of expediency: the matter to be decided was urgent, and could not await a full *riksdag*; or no new principle was being raised, and it was not therefore worth while to trouble so many with the journey to Stockholm; or it was inadvisable to hold another *riksdag* so soon after the last, and so burden the Commonalty with 'over-many *herredagar*'; or, finally, it was inexpedient to have a full meeting of the Estates in the King's absence. Not all of these excuses were without some foundation; but undoubtedly the King and the *råd* found a Committee Meeting easier to manage than a full *riksdag*, and undoubtedly there was a design to avoid the complaints of the Peasants, and their opposition to the granting of additional levies. There was a tendency to use just such meetings for the imposition of burdens which would have raised a storm at a *riksdag*: thus in 1613, for Älvsborg's ransom; in 1620, when the Stock Tax was imposed; in February 1632, when the Stock Tax was extended for a further two years. The Estates who were present were not always easy in their minds about these things, which were indeed illegal, and the Clergy on several occasions protested strongly at the illegality. The constitutional authority of such Committee Meetings was sufficiently questionable for the Nobility to pass a special resolution in 1632 that the Estate as a whole should be responsible for the decisions of its delegates to a Committee Meeting, in order that any odium should not fall exclusively to the delegates' share. There is, in fact, no doubt that the rights of the Peasantry were jeopardized by the recourse to Committee Meetings instead of *riksdagar*, and the position of the *riksdag* itself was compromised by the frequency of meetings which omitted its only really elective and popular element.[2]

What then was the position and status of the *riksdag* in 1632, on the day King Gustav was alive and dead? What powers had it acquired, what privileges had it to cherish, how secure was it from the action of the prerogative?

[1] In March 1625 a meeting was held to which were summoned the provincial governors (*landshövdingar*) with two of the oldest and ablest nobles from each province; the Bishops and Superintendents, with one member of each Chapter and one priest from each diocese; one burgomaster from each town; and six peasants from each *lagsaga* (roughly equivalent to a province). It was thus a committee of the whole *riksdag*, plus the *landshövdingar*; and since the Peasants were present it was not a true Committee Meeting. It is usual to call it a Committee-*riksdag* (*utskottsriksdag*). Hallenberg, V. 345; and *cf. AOSB*, II. 1. 297.

[2] Carlgren, *passim*; Ahnlund, *Ståndsriksdagen Utdaning*, pp. 127, 152-3, 181-4, 557-9; *SRDA*, I. 171, 305-8; Hallenberg, V. 346-52; *RRP*, I. 130; *SRARP*, I. 127 *seqq.*; *AOSB*, II. III. 195-6.

Gustav Adolf's reign at all events decided the question of the validity of legislation by the *riksdag*. The precedent of 1614 was not again seriously brought in question. Henceforward a *riksdag* resolution, duly signed and sealed by all the Estates, was the law of the land, and required no submission to, or confirmation by, provincial meetings. This was explicitly stated in Clause 45 of the Form of Government.[1] But it did not therefore follow that the right of legislation inhered in the *riksdag* alone. And in point of fact it had nothing like a monopoly of law-making. Gustav Adolf had indeed promised by his coronation oath that 'no new law be given to the commonalty without their assent and consent first had and obtained',[2] but this formula left two very wide questions open. It did not define what a new law was; and it did not lay down how consent was to be obtained. For instance, was the prolongation of a tax accorded for a limited period to be considered new law? Or the remodelling of the municipalities? And was not the spirit of the oath sufficiently complied with if the assent of those *concerned* were 'first had and obtained'? Such ambiguities as these left a large debatable area within which the Crown manœuvred at discretion without raising more than an occasional query, not as to the legality, but rather as to the expediency of its action, and without its being felt that the acknowledged right of the *riksdag* to make laws was in any way estopped thereby. When the King in 1614 regulated trade by a Navigation Law (*Handelsordning*) he obtained the assent only of the hereditary princes and of the Estate of Burghers; and though when the law was revised in 1617 it was submitted to the full *riksdag*, the Nobility and Clergy declined to consider the question, since it did not concern them. So too with the projected statute to standardize municipal government in 1619. It was submitted by the King to a meeting of representatives of the towns; and when the meeting did not approve it, he characteristically decided to negotiate with the towns *privatim et seriatim*—'in order that no one should be able to say that it was proposed to make new law without consent and assent'.[3] The same methods were applied to the Church:

---

[1] E. Hildebrand, *Sveriges Regeringsformer*, p. 32. The resolutions of *riksdagar* were still sometimes submitted to provincial meetings, if the members from that particular district had been absent. But by now this was largely a formality. There was an isolated instance in the 1660's of the Clergy's protesting that their decision could not bind their constituents; but it was exceptional and had no significance. N. Herlitz, *Om lagstiftning genom samfällda beslut av konung och riksdag.*

[2] Stiernman, I. 725-6.

[3] F. Lindberg, *1619 års stadga om städernas administration*, p. 9.

the King legislated about tithes, or the position and emoluments of sextons, after consultation with the Church's leaders. When his scheme for a *consistorium generale* was submitted to the Estates in 1624, after its rejection by the Bishops, the lay Estates simply referred it to the Clergy. The whole business of the reform of local government was not submitted to the Estates at all, or indeed to any other body. It might of course be argued that many of these enactments are to be considered as Ordinances, rather than as Statutes; and this is probably true. The Crown in Sweden, like the Crown in England, long retained a general legislative power, designed in theory for the correction of abuses or the supplementing of the law. In virtue of his prerogative the King could issue ordinances and proclamations; but the ordinances were recognized to want the permanent and solemn character of laws; and the proclamations were supposed to confine themselves to declaring what the law was, or reinforcing it by fresh and more terrible penalties.[1] None the less, such ordinances and proclamations did constitute, in Sweden as in England, a threat to normal parliamentary legislation. In Gustav Adolf's time, however, the clash of constitutional principle was not felt at all. There was a free-and-easy, informal quality about legislation which was perhaps the reflection of the unity of purpose which bound the nation together. The King omitted to sanction the Exchequer Ordinance; he positively disapproved the Chancery Ordinance; the Estates unaccountably failed to complete the process of legislation which would have made the *Riksdag* Ordinance a valid law. It did not seem to make much difference. They were all obeyed (or ignored) as well as if the formalities had been entirely in order; and no village Hampden or captious lawyer came forward to pick holes in their legality, or martyr himself in the cause of parliamentary rights. A certain hesitation was indeed felt as to the legislative competence of Committee Meetings, and the view was expressed that they ought not to meddle with matters which were properly the concern of a full *riksdag*; but in the years immediately after 1632 there was also a strong current of opinion setting in the opposite direction, and it appeared for a time not impossible that the bulk of the work of the Estates might be transferred to Committee Meetings, or gatherings of civil servants, and the *riksdag* reduced to mere attendance at royal weddings, coronations and other ceremonial

---

[1] Herlitz, *Om lagstiftning* . . ., pp. 86-7.

occasions.[1] This threat soon passed, once Oxenstierna had settled himself in the saddle at home [2]; but it was indicative of the fact that in 1632 the *riksdag* was far from having established—and had scarcely begun to claim—the sole right to legislate. And even if they had succeeded in making good the superiority of statute to ordinance and proclamation they would have found it impossible to stop up two other channels whereby the Crown made law upon its own authority. One of these lay through *Svea Hovrätt*. In the early years of that institution it was no unusual thing for the members of the court, having run into a difficulty, to turn to the King for guidance; and the King in reply would instruct them as to what the law was.[3] Thus judge-made law might occasionally represent a disguised proclamation at second-hand. The other channel was that of privilege-grant.[4] The King's right to grant privileges was uncontested, though not always perhaps uncontestable, and it was freely used. Privileges to the Counts and Barons, privileges to the Nobility, to Uppsala University, to monopoly companies, to towns, to individual capitalists, artists, craftsmen, apothecaries—there was no end to them. Some of them were of advantage to the public, some of benefit only to the recipients; but all in greater or lesser degree curtailed rights in one quarter to expand them in another, and in fact arbitrarily altered the law.

If then the *riksdag* had no monopoly of legislation, still less had it the right of initiating it. Neither Gustav Adolf nor the statesmen who succeeded him were prepared to admit the Estates to so large a share in the shaping of policy. The conduct of affairs of state was for men better informed than the average member, and for judgments more mature than could be produced by eleven months' isolation in the country, leavened by a brief attendance at a *riksdag*. That the Estates should 'air their whimsies in *arcana status*', as Schering Rosenhane put it in 1650, was intolerable.[5] And four years later the aged Axel Oxenstierna expounded the same constitutional theory to the respectful (but sceptical) Whitelocke. If the initiative were conceded, he contended, there must in so large an assembly be

---

[1] See Clauses 43-45 of the Form of Government: E. Hildebrand, *Sveriges Regeringsformer*, pp. 31-2; Carlgren, pp. 17-20; Odhner, *Sveriges Historia under Drottning Christinas förmyndare*, pp. 83-4.
[2] F. Lindberg, *Axel Oxenstierna som riksdagstaktiker*, pp. 259-60, 269.
[3] Herlitz, *Om lagstiftning*, pp. 84-5.
[4] Holmdahl, *Studier öfver prästeståndets kyrkopolitik under den tidigare frihetstiden*, I. 98, makes this point well.
[5] Quoted in Ahnlund, *Ståndsriksdagens Utdaning*, p. 527.

parties and factions: 'if every one amongst them might move and propound what he pleased according to his own fancy, there would never be an end of proposals and debates'. Moreover, the limits of the royal power were clearly laid down by the law, and motions on constitutional questions were therefore supererogatory. In any case, the Estates had the right to present their grievances, and were therefore in a position to refuse supply until these were redressed. Lastly, and in general, 'there is nothing more prejudicial than multitude of laws . . . nor is there any necessity of new laws where both the public rights and private men's property are provided for by the laws in being'. And when Whitelocke told him that 'a liberty of proposing anything in our Parliament belongs to every member of it', Oxenstierna gravely retorted that 'that hath been a great occasion of your troubles'.[1] The picture of the Swedish constitution thus drawn was not wholly applicable to conditions a quarter of a century earlier. In Gustav Adolf's time the principle of 'no supply without redress' had hardly been enunciated, and though during the Regency men's minds were moving unmistakably towards some such doctrine, decades were to pass before there was any sustained effort to make it good: it was not formally conceded until 1723. The Estates did present schedules of grievances at the beginning of each session. Some of them were purely local or individual, some were presented as the grievances of the Estate as a whole. But the constitutional possibilities were not yet perceived; the grievances were sometimes trivial, were often repeated year after year although they had in fact been redressed, and there was as yet no sign that they were near to taking that great constitutional step forward which consists in proceeding from the presenting of petitions to the framing of a definite plan for redress which will in time become a Bill. The interests of the Estates were widely divergent; and this fact, with their number (as against only two Houses of Parliament), made any common action for redress extremely difficult.[2]

The real test of the relative powers of King and Estates was of course provided by the right to tax. The relevant clause of the coronation oath had run as follows: 'For the sixth, I promise and affirm, that I will live of the crown manors (*Uppsala öd*), the royal estates, and the yearly lawful dues of my lands, and no new burden

---

[1] Whitelocke, *A Journal of the Swedish Embassy*, II. 278-81.
[2] Which makes their comparative unanimity upon the issue of the Charter all the more remarkable.

or impost will I lay upon my land, but for these following causes: first, that foreign armies, heathen or Christian, harry my land, or any subject set himself up against me so that I have no other resource; or also that my children . . . are to be married; or that I am to ride my Eriksgata [1]; or that I have need to build up my house or crown manors. In such case, and when thus required, I will use the law-men (*lagmän*) of every province (*lagsaga*), with Bishops and six of my household and six of the Commonalty, who shall consult among themselves what help the Commonalty may most conveniently give.' [2] As the latter part of the clause makes clear, this was a provision which had descended unaltered from the Middle Ages, and its antique formularies were no longer suited to the times. What was worse, they were far from precise. The King, it is plain, promises to 'live of his own' in normal times; but it is not clear what is included in the phrase 'the yearly lawful dues of my lands'; nor is it apparent just what constitutes a 'new' burden or impost. In the seventeenth century, however, it was generally agreed to make a distinction between 'taxes' and 'aids' (*gärder*). Aids, which were taken only in wartime, could be imposed by the King in mere virtue of his prerogative, and were essentially distinguished from taxes by being wholly payable in goods or services, and not in cash. Similarly, it had grown customary to consider certain taxes and imposts and rents and dues as 'the yearly (or determinate) revenues': it was on these that the King was originally supposed to live, in quiet times. But the times were far from quiet, and a series of additional burdens had been imposed which were called 'the indeterminate revenues'; and these in turn became more or less permanent and fixed, so that the 'determinate' and the 'indeterminate revenues' were together known as the 'ordinary revenues'. But now on top of these came casual taxes, granted by the Estates for one occasion, or for a term of years, and known as the 'extraordinary revenues'. [3] In Gustav Adolf's time one main constitutional issue turned on whether this or that tax was to be considered as part of the ordinary revenues, or as a 'grant' (*bevillning*) by the Estates, and hence part of the extraordinary revenues. In almost all cases the decision went in favour of the King. Special taxes became ordinary taxes, grants

---

[1] The Eriksgata (a word of dubious etymology) was the progress which every King on his accession was bound to make round his kingdom.

[2] Stiernman, I. 725.

[3] A very clear account of these revenues is in R. Swedlund, *Grev- och Friherreskapen i Sverige och Finland*, pp. 202-4.

became dues, occasional imposts turned mysteriously into fixed revenues. Thus the monarchy was not required, as the Stuarts were required, to live of its own on a fixed income in an age of rising prices: the income was stretched so gradually and so firmly that it never reverted to its previous dimensions. And every time this happened, another portion of the royal revenues was withdrawn from the Estates' control.

In other respects, and by other methods, the Crown showed that it was not too anxious for that control to be fully effective. There was a marked tendency to go behind the back of the *riksdag* in dubious cases and negotiate directly with provincial assemblies.[1] On other occasions, as we have seen, grants were made by Committee Meetings instead of *riksdagar*, the absence of Peasants being excused by the argument that if the Nobility, whose privileges exempted them from taxation, were for this occasion willing to forgo that exemption, it must be assumed that the unprivileged classes could have no objection to paying their share.[2] In 1630 an ingenious attempt was made to turn an *utskrivning* (militia-levy) into a tax without *riksdag* approval, taking advantage of the admitted fact that the King could hold an *utskrivning* merely in virtue of his prerogative.[3] And apart altogether from these semi-legal or quasi-legal proceedings, there was always the possibility—in the early years of the reign it was almost a probability—of sheer lawless extortion by the government's agents, of which the King would learn only partially and too late.[4] Yet though all this is true, it does seem that the feeling was growing that the granting of supplies was a constitutional function which only the *riksdag* ought to discharge. At the very beginning of the reign

---

[1] *e.g.* for the Three Marks Aid, in 1628. And see Lagerroth, *Konung och Adel*, p. 77, for a very late attempt (by Gustav III) to negotiate directly with parochial assemblies.

[2] Gustav Adolf said on 14 November 1627: 'The Commonalty is indeed to be shown consideration, since they lose their children [in the wars] and suffer other evils; but si nobilitas consensit, the Commonalty are soon persuaded, cum sine capite nil possint.' *RRP*, I. 61-2; *cf. AOSB*, II. III. III.

[3] Klinckowström and Mankell, *Arkiv till upplysning om svenska krigens och krigsinrättningarnes historia*, I. 155-6; but contrast *AOSB*, II. III. 210; II. v. 504; *RRP*, II. 188. In December 1628 the question was raised in the *råd* whether a *riksdag* should be summoned to sanction a new *utskrivning*. 'Rex interrumpit: Non quaeritur, an ego jus habeam imponendi sine consiliis, et quid nostra privilegia admittebant, sed observanda natura vulgi et necessitas tempori, nec tantum quid debeant, sed quid possint subditi, et lex velit, ut quod faciunt, voluntarie faciant': Ahnlund, *Öfverläggningar i riksrådet om tyska kriget 1628-1629 (HT* 1914), p. 115.

[4] *e.g.*, *Samling af Instructioner för högre och lägre Tjenstemän vid Landt-Regeringen i Sverige och Finland* (cited as *SILR*), p. 156.

the towns had extracted a promise that no new burdens should be laid upon them except through grant by the *riksdag*.[1] Soon after the end of it the principle won general acceptance. There were still plenty of loopholes for evasion; but before Kristina's minority was over, the theory had become clear.[2]

Since the right of the *riksdag* to control the granting of supplies stood on so unsatisfactory a footing, it is not surprising that they should have made slow progress in using it as an instrument to compel redress of grievances. Yet some attempt was made to take advantage of the growing sense of the need for *riksdag* sanction in levying new imposts; for such imposts began in the 'twenties to be granted only for two years, and this forced an impecunious government to hold a *riksdag* at reasonably regular intervals. It was from this beginning that the later rule of triennial *riksdagar* sprang.[3] It is significant in another way also; for it affords an illustration of how the old dislike of 'over-many *herredagar*' was giving way to a realization of their value. The Peasants, who had but lately looked upon attendance as a burden, were rapidly coming to regard their omission as a grievance.

The principle of appropriation of supply lay still in the future. The King was expected to do the best he could with the means provided for him, and no man demanded a reckoning; for, after all, the King's interest was supposed to be the interest of his people. There was indeed a promise in the Charter that the special taxes imposed to provide salaries for local justices (*lagmans-* and *härads-hövdingeräntor*) should not be applied to other purposes; and a similar pledge was made when in 1624 a cash payment to scholars was substituted for gifts in kind.[4] Some justified complaints were made of the diversion of Älvsborg's ransom to current expenses, and in 1629 facilities were offered to those nobles who had made voluntary contributions to the navy to see how their money had been spent; but all these were exceptional occasions, and remained without significance.[5]

---

[1] *Stockholms stads privilegiebref*, p. 156.
[2] Herlitz, *Om lagstiftning*, pp. 95-6. A. Thomson (*Grundskatterna i den politiska discussionen*, p. 33), on the other hand, considers that 'only Gustav Adolf's reign shows to any great extent tendencies towards regard for the people's right to tax themselves'.
[3] S. Clason, *Om uppkomsten af bestämda perioder för den svenska riksdagens sammanträde* (*HT* 1892), pp. 147-55.
[4] See below, p. 451.
[5] Hallenberg, IV. 622; Ahnlund, *Ståndsriksdagens Utdaning*, p. 537; *SRARP*, I. 109-10.

It should now be clear how far the *riksdag* of Gustav Adolf's time lagged behind the parliament of the age of James I. Of the great constitutional questions which agitated the contemporaries of Eliot and Buckingham, it knew little or nothing. There was not one Estate—the Nobility came nearest to it—so developed as to have conceived the idea of its right to punish its own members for their behaviour, still less to commit a member of the general public for a contempt. The right of expulsion, the claim to examine disputed election returns, meant nothing to a body which was mostly either returned *ex officio* or under government supervision. Freedom from arrest for members and their servants was a thing undreamed-of; the privilege of favourable interpretation could hardly yet be claimed by Estates which had Speakers newly born, if indeed they had a Speaker at all. Freedom of speech was an issue which hardly appeared. The Estates did indeed discuss foreign affairs, but under Gustav Adolf they discussed them only when invited to do so; and the criticism which they had directed at Karl IX's dealings with Denmark was not heard under his successor. The development of the Secret Committee and of the Committee Meeting was tending increasingly to take the consideration of such questions out of the hands of the Estates as a whole, and to relegate them to such members as might be supposed competent to discuss them. As to religion, Baazius did no doubt attack the Bishops, but he did so with the tacit encouragement, and under the protection, of the King; and the other Estates were not prone to meddle in matters theological. Upon the delicate question of Gustav Adolf's marriage and the succession they maintained a wise reserve; and no voice was raised in protest against the King's experiments in monopolies. The eloquence of the Peasants within their own Estate might at time be loud, and even rude, and their complaints were now and then put with vigour; the opposition of the Clergy forced the King to abandon one of his favourite schemes; but on the whole the Estates observed a dutiful propriety of language. But had any member ventured upon 'lewd and naughty words', there is little doubt that he would have been punished. The experience of the Burghers in 1629, when they made an indiscriminate attack on the Nobility, was not encouraging to unbridled tongues. In short, the *riksdag* was still an assemblage of Estates: it was not yet a parliament. Between those Estates relations were still largely undefined. No one had as yet considered what the situation would be if they divided two against two, and whether a majority of Estates should prevail. It was their duty to reach agreement, that the King's business (which was also their business) might be carried on; and if they failed to do this, it was for the King to *conciliare animos*, or in the last resort take that counsel 'which seemed best to him'. Within little more than a decade of Gustav Adolf's death some of these questions were to be posed, and in acute form; for the late 'thirties and 'forties moved steadily towards the violent strife of classes which reached its first climax in 1650; and there were times when it seemed likely that the unprivileged Estates might combine behind a common political programme. But for the present the authority of the King sufficed to obscure or defer many difficult questions; and the Regents were to inherit constitutional problems in much the same way as James I inherited them from Elizabeth.

(iv) *Local Government*

The reforms in the central government which culminated in the five Colleges were matched by a reorganization of the local administration not less important and equally enduring. In 1611 Sweden had a system of local government which stood half-way between mediaeval and modern forms. It was to be the work of Gustav Adolf and Oxenstierna, while conserving much that was most popular and characteristically Swedish in the mediaeval heritage, to lay down the foundations of a newer and better system, considerable elements of which still survive.

The Swedish mediaeval kingdom had been formed, much as the Anglo-Saxon kingdom was, by the union of various provinces (*länder*), which had no doubt originally been the territories of distinct tribes, and which long retained their own laws and their own provincial assemblies (*landsting*). This division into provinces, however, though it has continued for some purposes until our own day, was soon overlaid by another, broadly coincident with it, the division into *lagsagor*. The *lagsaga* was the area within which the *lagman* dispensed justice; and the *lagman* was originally an elected official, whose business it was to act as the custodian of the law, which he was to declare to the assembled freemen at the *ting*, or moot. From this duty of saying what the law was (*att lag säga*), was derived the untranslatable word *lagsaga*. The *lagman* presided now over the *landsting*; but from the fourteenth century he began also to go on circuit about his district, holding *lagmansting* in every hundred. This entailed the disappearance of the *landsting* as a local court, though it retained political importance for another century or more.

The province, or the *lagsaga* (territorially they were much the same), was a large unit; a more manageable subdivision was the *härad*, which corresponds to the English hundred. As the *landsting* was presided over by the *lagman*, so the *häradsting* (hundred moot) was presided over by the *häradshövding*; but the *häradshövding*, unlike the *lagman*, possessed executive as well as judicial functions. Originally the hundred moot had been an assembly where all the free men of the hundred could equally participate in such business as was going forward; but in course of time there emerged the hundred jury (*häradsnämnd*), which, beginning as a jury of present- ment, became also a jury pronouncing sentence (and sometimes too a jury of recognitors) and ended as the permanent executive com- mittee of the *härad* for many other purposes than the purely judicial, with its members elected for life. All these organs of self-govern- ment—*landsting, lagmansting, häradsting, häradsnämnd*—were still flourishing in 1611, though the *landsting* was now confined to Norr- land, where the division into *härader* had never been carried out: here the *landsting* occupied the same position as the *häradsting* in the remainder of the country.[1]

This administrative system had begun by being purely popular; but after the time of Magnus Eriksson's *landslag* in the mid- fourteenth century it passed partly under the control of the King, who now took the main share in appointing *lagmän* and *härads- hövdingar*. But side by side with it was another system, which was in origin bound up with the political rivalries of monarchy and aristocracy. This was the system of granting to a magnate the right to administer a district on the King's behalf, and to act as his fiscal agent there. Such a grant was called a *förläning*, and the area so administered, a *län*. The possession of a *län*, particularly if it went with the command of an important castle, put a nobleman in a sound economic and military position against possible aggressions from the side of the monarchy. There were various types of *län*;

---

[1] For the arrangements in Norrland, see Ahnlund, *Landskap och län i Norrland*, pp. 233-52; R. Gothe, *Medelpads Finnmarker*, pp. 21-2, 45-51. Västergötland and Dalsland also retained a *landsting*: its composition and judicial status varied, and in Västergötland it seems to have been called indifferently *landsting* and *lagmansting*. But the position was confused and exceptional. Broomé, *Nils Stiernsköld*, pp. 185-9.

but whatever the type, all differed essentially from the feudal honour or fee, for none was hereditary, all were revocable at the King's caprice, and the holder had no right of private jurisdiction: justice ran always in the King's name and was dispensed in the King's courts. Mediaeval Sweden, in fact, was not a feudal country.[1]

At the close of the fifteenth century the Stures made a determined and largely successful attempt to diminish the number of *förläningar* to the nobility, and to increase the number of *län* in the hands of royal bailiffs (*fataburslän*). Gustav Vasa inherited and prosecuted this policy. Its success involved new problems of administration, since special measures were demanded and additional staff required to cope with the much-increased influx of incomes in kind—butter, iron, livestock and so forth—into the royal storehouses. Nevertheless, in spite of these difficulties the process continued, steadily if not quite uninterruptedly, throughout the sixteenth century. The old type of *förläning* to the nobility was confined by Gustav Vasa mainly to the close relatives of the royal family, and after 1550 it virtually ceased. Throughout the whole of the latter half of the century the Crown discontinued one large *län* after the other; and instead of the old system of granting administrative powers over extensive areas began to use *förläning* simply as a method of paying wages or granting pensions. The very word *förläning* changed its meaning: by Gustav Adolf's time it had come to signify the grant of revenues from a certain source to an individual, either as a pension or reward, or as the normal wage for a definite post (in which case it was more properly called *beställning*).[2] The *län* as an administrative unit had become a thing of the past; the new personal monarchy of the Vasas had dispensed with noble assistance, in local as in central government. Instead, Gustav Vasa and his elder sons essayed to

[1] Which is why it is better to avoid translating *län* as 'fief' and *förläning* as 'enfeoffment'.

[2] Such *förläningar* might be of quite small value: 'side by side with the amply-dimensioned estates allotted to the support of a great man ... there figured in the bailiff's schedules a steadily growing number of smaller deductions [from the royal revenues], each perhaps amounting only to one manor or hamlet or some *tunnor* of grain, but each equally treated as "*förläning*", and rightly so, since its existence required a direct order from the King to the bailiff in order that it should be legal and valid. . . . The disposal of estate-revenues which was granted to them [the nobility] was no different in kind from the exemption from taxation which was conceded to the poor peasant who had seen his farm go up in flames, or from the support in butter which was given to a student on his way to a foreign university, or from the allocation of grain which made possible the building of churches or the maintenance of hospitals.' J. A. Almquist, *Den civila lokalförvaltningen i Sverige*, I. 54, 55. For *beställning*, see, most recently, S. Nilsson, *Krona och frälse*, p. 128.

govern the country by their bailiffs (*fogdar*)—a method strictly accordant with Gustav Vasa's habit of ruling Sweden as though it were a private estate. But the bailiff was something more than a mere collector of rents and taxes (though admittedly that was his prime function): he was a general administrator with police powers as well. His immediate superior was the King, or failing him the King's Exchequer, to which every midsummer he rendered his somewhat questionable accounts. It was not a very satisfactory method of administration, in an age of bad communications, and it easily lent itself to embezzlement and extortion. Nevertheless, unsatisfactory as it was, it was the method which the earlier Vasas preferred. Between 1530 and 1560, as the lands of the Church passed gradually under royal administration, the number of bailiffs rose from about 60 to about 180.[1]

The nobility naturally disapproved of the new monarchy's methods of administering the country. They grumbled at being deprived of their *län*; they resented the pretensions of the thrusting bailiff-class. The Vasas offered compensation for their losses in two ways: in the first place they began to reward or propitiate the generality of the nobility by making outright gifts of land (donations), as a substitute for the granting of *län* (a method which in the sixteenth century caused much less diminution of the royal revenues than the old one); in the second place they created a wholly new type of *län* for the benefit of the very highest classes of the aristocracy. This was the countship or barony, which made its appearance under Erik XIV and Johan III. The Count or Baron received a grant of the effective control of a considerable (but usually not compact) area, within which he exercised almost sovereign rights. His position was strictly comparable to that of the royal dukes in their duchies; and since these countships or baronies were hereditary, and since they carried with them a private control of justice, they were in fact more like a feudal fee than anything Sweden had known in the Middle Ages. But they were very few in number; and they by no means satisfied the appetite of the nobility at large. The nobility, however, was not wholly actuated by a desire for the spoils of local government. They were genuinely concerned to provide a better and more developed system of administration than the monarchy seemed prepared to offer. Just as Erik Sparre and his circle had contended for a more modern and less personal central

[1] N. Herlitz, *Grunddragen av det svenska statsskickets historia*, p. 71.

government, so they contended for a more modern and less personal local government. One effort in this direction had indeed been made already under the monarchy's auspices: between 1540 and 1542 Konrad von Pyhy had introduced a special type of administration into Västergötland, whereby a local lord-lieutenant (*ståthållare*), assisted by something like a foreshadowing of the Collegial system, was to supervise the bailiffs and act as a mediate instance between them and the King. But Pyhy's fall involved the abandonment of his experiment, and no more was heard of it. The term *ståthållare* was not forgotten, however: Erik made various unsystematic uses of men with that title; and in the last decade of the century the *ståthållare* (or, as he was sometimes called, the *landshövding*) appeared in the programme of the *råd* as the key to a better administration of the provinces.

The evils of the existing system were not difficult to diagnose, nor the remedies to prescribe. What was needed was that the local government areas should be fixed and definite[1]; that the agents of the central government in the provinces should be permanent and not *ad hoc* appointments; that there should be a regular hierarchy of such officials, with greater division of labour and differentiation of function; and that the executive side of government should be kept rigorously separate from the judicial. In 1593, indeed, a Judicature Ordinance had regulated the legal side by making the *lagman* a superior instance to the *häradshövding*; but on the executive side everything remained to be done. It was reforms of this nature which the *råd* demanded in 1594, and particularly the division of the country into fixed *ståthållaredömen*, with a permanent *ståthållare* in each, in full control of the bailiffs of his area. This was essentially the programme which Gustav Adolf was to make his own; but the times were unpropitious for it in 1594. It would probably have been difficult to find enough competent administrators of high social standing to act as *ståthållare*; and in any case the monarchy was suspicious of a scheme that emanated from its political opponents. Karl was sceptical of innovations, and believed that he could manage well enough with bailiffs, as his father had managed before him. After 1600, he was not so sure. In spite of himself he was driven to appoint *ståthållare* to supplement his administration. But he failed —perhaps he did not intend—to define their position and functions clearly. It was not always easy to distinguish a *ståthållare* from a

[1] J. A. Almquist, *op. cit.*, I. 11, 117.

bailiff; and at least one man was *ståthållare* and bailiff at the same time.[1] And Karl had the habit of appointing several *ståthållare* at once to the same post—there might be half a dozen of them in a single castle [2]—with a view, no doubt, to preventing any one of them from developing into an over-mighty subject, and also so that they might spy upon and delate each other to their morbidly suspicious master. In short, little progress had been made by 1611, and the Charter in this respect contained demands very similar to those which had been put forward in 1594.[3]

The first five or six years after 1611 seem to have been a period in which the provincial administration gradually assumed a firmer contour. Although no general enactment was issued by the government, it is clear that the division of the country into fixed and permanent *ståthållaredömen* proceeded apace, and may be said to have been completed by 1621.[4] Traces of the old confusion still survived in plenty: as late as 1618 Kalmar had two *ståthållare* at the same time, and two were appointed to Älvsborg upon its redemption in the following year; until as late as 1627 Lindorm Ribbing combined the offices of *ståthållare* and *lagman* in Östergötland; but on the whole there was a steady progress towards rationalization.[5] The need for reform of some sort had never, perhaps, been more obvious than in just these years, when the disorders in the administration, and the lawlessness of aristocratic ruffians, provoked a steady rain of complaints. Among the worst offenders were the Crown's own bailiffs. An Exchequer Instruction of 1613, which aimed at curbing their illegalities and bringing them under proper control, showed by its ineffectiveness the need for supervision less remote, and punishment more speedy and certain, than the Exchequer was able to provide.[6] The atrocities committed by the government's agents in Finland, the alarming disturbances in

---

[1] F. Wernstedt, *Ståthållaren Christoffer Wernstedt*, p. 40.

[2] Karl appointed no less than seven at one time to Kalmar castle in 1603: Hallenberg, I. 375. This was really a survival of the mediaeval institution of the *slottsloven*.

[3] For the above account of local government to 1611, see especially J. A. Almquist, *op. cit.*; Nilsson; Swedlund; Staf; O. Sörndal, *Den svenska länsstyrelsen*; N. Herlitz, *Ett och annat om självstyrelsens betydelse i svensk förvaltningshistoria*; *Självstyrelse i svenskt samhällsliv*; A. W. Boisman, *Om rättskontrollerna i den svensk-finska civila inre forvaltningen*; F. Lindberg, *Till landshövdingeämbetets äldsta historia (HT* 1939).

[4] Wernstedt, pp. 73, 80; B. Broomé, *Nils Stiernsköld*, pp. 138, 141, 174.

[5] Hallenberg, I. 374; H. Almquist, *Göteborg*, I. 6-7; F. Lindberg, *op. cit.*, p. 156; Broomé, pp. 137, 141-7.

[6] *SICF*, pp. 23-6.

Västbo *härad* in 1616 (which had been provoked by the behaviour of a bailiff), and the King's first-hand experience of the problem, acquired in the course of his visit of investigation to the disturbed areas, probably combined to push him into action.[1] At all events, from 1616 onwards there begins a series of Instructions to individual *ståthållare* which shows that Gustav Adolf had recognized the need for using them as a mediate term between his central government and his bailiffs. An Instruction to the *ståthållare* in Kalmar, of November 1616, lays upon him the duty to see to it that the bailiffs do not defraud the peasantry; another, of the same year, to the *ståthållare* in Kexholm, makes him responsible for ensuring that the bailiff takes proper care of the farming of the royal manors; while two more, of 1618, require their recipients to keep the bailiffs punctual in presenting their accounts.[2] The Exchequer Ordinance of 14 October 1618 made special regulations about the bringing of such accounts to the Exchequer: as yet, therefore, no attempt was made to subordinate them in this respect to the *ståthållare*. But in all other respects they were rapidly passing under his control. An Instruction of April 1618 to the two *ståthållare* of Kalmar laid it down that they were to be the sole channel for the transmission of the orders of the central government to the bailiffs[3]; and in a comparatively short time they seem to have been generally recognized as the bailiffs' official superiors.

The decisive phase in the remodelling of local government began in 1620. In April of that year a general Memorandum to all *ståthållare* inaugurated a new phase in their activities. They were now to provide themselves with a secretary apiece; to supervise the bailiffs in their collecting of revenue; to keep a book in which the bailiff's receipts should be entered; to exact reports from bailiffs twice a month; and to forward their own reports to the Exchequer once a month, for which purpose a special postal service would be provided.[4] Thus for the first time an attempt was made to subordinate the bailiff to the *ståthållare* in financial as in other matters; and the *ståthållare* was made responsible to the Exchequer for the bailiff's accounts. The question now was, whether the *ståthållare* had the financial

---

[1] Bratt, *Om svenska allmogen under Gustaf II Adolphs regering*, p. 18. As late as 1625 Nils Bielke wrote from Finland: 'the bailiffs are so hardened in their wickedness that it is impossible to bring them to righteousness': Melander, p. 108.
[2] *SILR*, pp. 107, 95, 115, 122.
[3] *SILR*, pp. 110-12.
[4] *SILR*, pp. 131-49; Broomé, pp. 151-2.

training requisite to these new duties; and whether in any case they could discharge them without additional skilled staff. The answer in each case turned out to be in the negative. At least two *ståthållare* were clamouring for more staff in the summer of 1620; and in 1624 there were still accounts of 1620 which had not yet been closed.[1] In 1622, therefore, it was decided to make special provision of financial experts. By an ordinance of that year the government made a real revolution in its financial procedure: henceforward, instead of every bailiff's personally submitting his accounts to the Exchequer for audit, he was to present them to the *ståthållare*, who would audit them on the spot, and draw up a general balance-sheet for his *ståthållaredöme*. In this financial work he would have the assistance of qualified book-keepers. On the basis of these provincial balance-sheets (*landsböcker*) the Exchequer would be able to prepare, with much less difficulty than in the past, a general national balance-sheet (*rikshuvudbok*).[2]

The majority of the *ståthållare* regarded these developments with consternation. That their superiority to bailiffs should be made clear, that the nature of their duties should be made more precise, the area of their jurisdiction less ambiguous—these things were not unacceptable to them; but that they should be expected to turn themselves overnight into auditors and accountants—this seemed to them an unreasonable hardship. They protested piteously that they were not good at figures, and Gabriel Gustafsson Oxenstierna was sadly confounded by the 'fractions' which bristled in these alarming calculations.[3] In November 1623 all the *ståthållare* met the King at Strängnäs; and there they seem to have been given the chance to examine in advance the government's plans for them in 1624. At all events they delivered a unanimous protest, affirming their willingness to try, but doubting their ability to succeed, and asking the King's indulgence for the first few years, until they became accustomed to the new methods, and had grown more adept at filling in the new forms which were now to be prescribed.[4]

The King refused to be deterred by this demonstration. In July 1624 he issued a definitive ordinance dealing with the fiscal

---

[1] Wernstedt, p. 80; *AOSB*, II. IX. 17; J. A. Almquist, *op. cit.*, I. 137 *note* 2.

[2] J. A. Almquist, *op. cit.*, I. 139-42. Abraham Cabeliau was appointed Auditor-General (*Generalbokhållare*) in 1624.

[3] *AOSB*, II. III. 67: 'there are not three *häradsskrivare* in the whole of Uppland capable of doing such a calculation, because of the many fractions in it'. Rather than endure this, he resigned office.

[4] *SILR*, p. 184 *seqq.*

side of the *ståthållare's* duties, and appended to it model instructions which covered the whole field of his activities.[1] These latter may be said to inaugurate a new period in the history of local government, and the change was marked by the alteration of the *ståthållare's* title to that of *landshövding*, and the denomination of his area of jurisdiction by the old name of *län*. The change of names did not become fully effective in Gustav Adolf's lifetime; but it was made final in the Form of Government of 1634. The model instructions of 1624 never obtained the King's final approval: their implementation involved a development of the local machinery and an expansion of the staff which necessitated the postponement of their adoption for at all events a few years. But they were considered to be valid in principle; and bit by bit they were applied in practice. The Form of Government, and the Instruction for *landshövdingar* of 1635, put the crown on these reforms. By the Form of Government the Swedish dominions were divided up into 23 *län* (11 for Sweden proper), each administered by a *landshövding*; plus one *län* for Stockholm, which obtained an *överståthållare*, and was treated as a sort of county borough.[2] The Instruction of 1635 re-enacts, in somewhat greater detail, the model instructions of 1624, and is to be considered as essentially Gustav Adolf's work. The *landshövding* is now defined as the King's representative within the *län*, discharging almost all the functions which the King performs for his kingdom. His business therefore falls naturally under the purview of the five Colleges; and henceforth his correspondence and files are to be managed on that basis. In his town of residence he is to maintain an office of a prescribed pattern, housing a small but competent staff, and from it he is to administer his *län* as the central government administers the kingdom from Stockholm. Socially and politically, he is the first man in his *län*: as Axel Oxenstierna truly said, he is *vice-rex*.[3] His duties touch every side of government, even the military and the judicial; though he himself remains a civilian, and is now expressly forbidden to act as a judge.

Such, then, was Gustav Adolf's reform of the local government. It did not, of course, spring at once in 1635 into general and efficient

---

[1] *SILR*, pp. 169-84. Supplementary instructions for book-keepers were issued in 1628 and 1631: *SILR*, pp. 392-7, 398-400; and see J. A. Almquist, *Frälsegodsen i Sverige under storhetstiden*, I. viii-ix.

[2] *Överståthållareämbetet*, pp. 32-8.

[3] Odhner, *Sveriges inre historia under Drottning Christinas förmyndare*, p. 175: text of the 1635 Instruction in *SILR*, p. 191 *seqq*.

activity: the old confusion and the old abuses were deeply rooted, and it took some years to eliminate them. But the decisive step forward had been taken. The new local government turned its back for ever on the Middle Ages—as also upon the personal monarchy of the earlier Vasas—and the *landshövding* and his *län* have remained from that day to this an essential part of the government of the country. It was certainly among the more important achievements of the period. Sweden could hardly have aspired to the position of a great power had she retained the primitive and chaotic provincial administration of the sixteenth century. Government was growing more complex at the periphery no less than at the centre: the national effort which the war demanded needed organization in Småland and Östergötland quite as much as in Stockholm; the new imposts of the 'twenties could hardly have been managed by the bailiffs without more stringent and proximate control; and without such control domestic discontent might well have numbed the avenging arm of Gideon. At a time when Richelieu was still hesitating between Intendants and *commissaires*, Sweden obtained a system of local government which is still flourishing a century and a half after the last Intendant was extruded from his office by the representatives of the sovereign people.[1]

The *ståthållare* and bailiffs, *landshövdingar* and book-keepers, were only one aspect of local government. They were the agents through which the Crown, or the central offices of government, dealt with the provinces: in no sense popular officials. But side by side with them were other forms of local government, older, equally viable, and still equally effective; but, unlike them, representative, popular and elective. For local government was then, as it still is, largely self-government; and the hundred moot had been functioning for many a generation before the first royal bailiff began to interfere in its affairs. The hundred moot was indeed the real centre of political activity for the average yeoman farmer in the provinces; and as late as King Sigismund's time it had shown that its political importance had not wholly been eclipsed by the new-fangled *riksdag*. The *häradsting* was a conservative body, strongly traditional in its procedures, and even in the seventeenth century uncouth with survivals of the primitive barbarism of a distant age. Meetings (which took place at least twice a year) might still occasionally be

---

[1] For these reforms, see especially O. Sörndal, *Den svenska länsstyrelsen*, and K. Edin, *Gustav Adolfs planer på landtregeringens organisation*, pp. 225-58.

held in the open air; the freemen still came armed; the right of every man to speak his mind was still sufficiently well established for meetings to be noisy and sometimes tumultuous, so that the *härads-hövding*, in the chair, had need of his gavel, and of more than his gavel, to keep the *ting* in order; and in general the proceedings were more than faintly reminiscent of the first Act of *Arnljot*. The memory of an earlier age, when the only valid social distinction had been between free and thrall, still lingered in the *häradsting*; and the nobles of the hundred not seldom sat beside the *häradshövding* on the bench, even though the meeting might be dominated by their own tenants. The *häradshövding* himself was supposed to be a noble resident in the hundred; but by Gustav Adolf's time he was often an absentee, and his functions were discharged by deputy. The Crown's interests—mainly fiscal—were safeguarded by the presence of the bailiff, but the proceedings were in no sense under his control. It was to this hundred moot that the King turned when for one reason or another he deemed it inexpedient to deal with the assembled Estates; and it was the hundred moot which assisted at the choice of the Peasantry's representatives to the *riksdag*—who were indeed usually selected from among the twelve [1] men of the hundred jury (*häradsnämnd*). The *häradsnämnd*, for its part, co-operated with the King's Commissioners in the selection of new recruits by *utskrivning*, and by its presence ensured that the rights of the individual were safeguarded against the hand of arbitrary power. Much use was made of the hundred moot to assist the government in matters of tax-assessments: the expert local knowledge of the countryman could be of considerable service to the bailiff in the granting of exemptions, or the determining of whether or not a farm stood within a seven-mile radius of a noble's seat, and so was free of fiscal burdens. But apart from these direct aids to the government's agents, the *häradsting* took in hand a multiplicity of tasks which the King was well content to leave to their management. They supervised the important matters of fencing, ditching and swine-ringing; they organized bear- and wolf-hunts; they adjusted disputes over mills and streams; they kept an eye on burn-beat cultivation, and advised the Crown whether to tolerate it or no. Upon the hundred moot fell the main administrative burden of maintaining roads and bridges, organizing *skjutsning*, and establishing inns. They dispensed charity to the victims of fires; and they had a

[1] Twelve in theory; but the number varied in practice.

hand in the maintenance of the poor. In order to be able to do these things, they had the power to levy a rate (usually in kind); and they had also the power to make bye-laws, and enforce them with fines. They provided a shoal of minor officials—some purely voluntary, some paid by way of small tax-exemptions—and they devoted themselves to the service of the community with admirable seriousness, punctuality and patience.[1]

The hundred moot was not the only popular organ of local government in the provinces; and sometimes it had difficulty in obtaining the personnel it needed for the discharge of all the tasks for which it was responsible. In this matter a competing body was the parish-meeting (*sockenstämma*), which was almost as ancient as the hundred moot itself, and often even more democratic; since in some cases nobles and cottars participated on a footing of equality, and since usually its decisions to be binding had to be unanimous. It concerned itself primarily with questions of religion and morality, but it was also largely responsible for the care of the parish poor; and it had other secular interests which varied widely according to the zeal and personality of the local incumbent, and the energy and conscientiousness of his coadjutors, the Vestrymen.[2]

About the same time as the appearance of the first reforming instructions for *ståthållare*, appeared also a draft for a comprehensive reform of the municipalities. The connection between the towns and the central government had always been unusually strong in Sweden. The towns had grown up comparatively late; they had always been few in number and inconsiderable in population; and the strong foreign element had been much dependent upon royal favour and protection. Their position therefore had always been relatively weak, and they never wholly succeeded in shaking off some measure of control by the King's bailiffs.[3] The Town-Law of the mid-fourteenth century had laid down a pattern of municipal government drawn after contemporary German models; but except for Stockholm, few towns were able to provide the lavish allowance of burgomasters and town-councillors which it prescribed. In

---

[1] On the hundred moot as an organ of self-government, see Herlitz, *Ett och annat* . . ., pp. 73-9, 138-41; Boisman, *Om rättskontrollen*, pp. 142-4, 149, 156, 160; K. G. Westman in *Minnesskrift ägnad 1734 års lag*, I. 26, 30, 37; Munktell, *Det svenska rättsarvet*, pp. 111-12; S. Hallberg, *Från Sveriges storhetstid: Charles Ogiers dagbok* (cited as Ogier), p. 72; *Självstyrelse*, pp. 46-56.

[2] On this, see R. Gullstrand, *Bidrag till den svenska sockensjälvstyrelsens historia under 1600-talet*; and below, pp. 398-9.

[3] F. Lindberg, *Fogde, råd och menighet*, pp. 12-14, 25, 27.

Gustav Adolf's time Stockholm had 4 burgomasters and some 12-16 councillors; for moderate-sized towns such as Uppsala or Jönköping the figures were 2-3 and 8-12; for small towns, 1-2 and 6-10.[1] Originally these corporations had been self-recruiting; but by the seventeenth century they had become elective. The electors were the burghers (*i.e.* all who had burgage rights) meeting in Common Hall (*allmänna rådstugan*), and to this extent town-government was popular; but the magistracy managed current affairs without much reference to the burghers, and the King's bailiff (or, latterly, the *ståthållare*) still presided over the town council from time to time, and even on occasion sat on the bench in the municipal courts. These courts were two: the court of the town council (*rådstuvurätt*) and a subordinate court for petty cases, known as *kämnärsrätt*. The town was thus to a great extent self-governing both administratively and judicially. There was a considerable number of minor municipal offices, most of which were unpaid and hence difficult to fill satisfactorily: the only fully-paid full-time municipal officer seems to have been the hangman or executioner—a social outcast with whom decent folk would not associate.[2]

Upon this venerable compromise between municipal liberties and royal control fell the impact of Oxenstierna's reforming zeal—in its turn provoked, no doubt, by the King's anxiety to foster the economic welfare of the towns and concentrate the trade of the country in them. In 1619 Oxenstierna elaborated a Statute for the Administration of the Towns; and at meetings of representatives of the towns in December 1619 and February 1620 he took soundings as to their attitude towards it, and simultaneously began what was no doubt intended to be a comprehensive reissue of their privileges in an amended and modernized form.[3] But in the event the Statute was never promulgated; and only six towns received new privileges. The attitude of the meeting in December 1619 had been so unfavourable to reform that the King, rather than risk a violent clash in the *riksdag* with the Estate of Burghers, evidently decided to introduce the new arrangements piecemeal by way of revision of privileges, each town being dealt with separately; but the resumption of the

---

[1] In the 1620's Sundsvall had one burgomaster who was also customs officer and bailiff: Ahnlund, *Sundsvalls Historia*, I. 71.

[2] On the hangman, see L. Levander, *Brottsling och bödel*. It was a gross insult to call a woman 'the Västerås hangman's daughter'.

[3] F. Lindberg, *1619 års stadga om städernas administration, passim*; Stiernman, *CPO*, I. 731-55; *AOSB*, I. 1. 294-324.

war and the pressure of other business in the end prevented even this course from being carried out. Nevertheless, though the Statute remained no more than a draft which had not been finally sanctioned by the King, and still less 'assented to by those concerned', it was gradually applied, at least in part; and in that curious haphazard way so characteristic of the reign it came presently to be considered as valid law.

The aims of the Statute are clear. While abiding as far as possible by the old Town Law, it seeks to give the municipalities a more modern administration. And because the towns are held to be of such vital importance to the national economy, the Crown takes measures to strengthen its own effective control. The *ståthållare* (or in his absence the bailiff) is to preside on all important occasions, both administrative and judicial, and in particular is to attend at the annual elections to municipal offices. On the other hand, the generality of the burghers is to be provided with a more effective organ for expressing its views than the old Common Hall: this is now to be abolished, and in its place is set up a representative organ of 48 'Elders', who are to have the right to negotiate with the magistracy, and whose duty it is to be to watch over the interests of their constituents. A new committee of seven is to manage town-finance; and there is a revolutionary scheme for levying rates and taxes by making an assessment upon a return of property made by the owner—a dim and distant foreshadowing of an income-tax form.[1]

Some of these items, though not all, are contained in the new privileges issued to Arboga, Jönköping, Kalmar, Norrköping, Västervik and Sala; and traces of them appear in the Instructions to *ståthållare* issued in April 1620[2]; but on the whole the Statute is important mainly as indicative of the Chancellor's passion for efficiency, the King's illusions about the importance of towns, and the desire of both of them to bring municipal affairs regularly under the cognizance of the central government. The 'Elders' were undoubtedly an improvement on the Common Hall, but for the present very few towns adopted the institution; and in Jönköping, which was one of them, they numbered no more than twelve.[3] The towns were inclined to resent the interference of the *ståthållare*

---

[1] This was not quite a novelty. It had been employed by Karl IX in 1601. See S. Hedar, *Karl IX:s förmögenhetsbeskattningar (HT* 1937), p. 369.

[2] And *cf. SILR*, p. 113.

[3] Björkman, *Jönköping*, II. 230.

in judicial affairs, and Göteborg succeeded in excluding him altogether.[1] The Form of Government of 1634 yielded to this feeling by expressly prohibiting the *ståthållare* or the bailiff from sitting on the bench, as hitherto; but his administrative field of action was not curtailed, and he remained an important link between the municipalities and the central government. The institution in the later 'thirties of Royal Burgomasters, as a kind of stipendiary magistrate paid by the Crown, strengthened the control of the central government still further. And in 1636 Stockholm introduced a system for departmentalizing its affairs, whereby the Town Council was divided into four Colleges for different classes of business: an idea later adopted by other towns also. Thus in local government too the administrative innovation for which the reign is best remembered obtained a foothold within a decade of the King's death.[2]

What then were the general effects of these reforms upon Swedish local government? It must in the first place be recalled that there were considerable areas of Swedish territory which they affected not at all. The Countships and Baronies were almost wholly withdrawn from the control of Stockholm. The Counts appointed their own officials, maintained their own councils, administered their own justice, and collected the revenues which the Crown assigned them. Per Brahe spoke habitually of 'reigning' in his County of Visingsö, and appointed a Council of Regency to provide against his premature demise. The dower-lands of widowed queens were also only partly supervised by the central government. The mining areas had special administrative divisions with a *bergmästare* at the head of each.[3] But on the whole, for most of Sweden proper, the advance was enormous, and had a permanent influence. The *landshövding*, a real viceroy now in his *län*, controlled an administration which had a plan, and standards, and routine, and which increasingly attracted to it trained and capable administrators. The last trace of the personal monarchy of the earlier Vasas was being obliterated; and if administration became more bureaucratic, it probably also became less arbitrary. But it did not therefore become

---

[1] H. Almquist, *Göteborg*, I. 106-7.
[2] For town government see, in addition to works already cited, Herdin, *Uppsala på 1600-talet*, I. 5-28, 31-44; III. 16-19; Odhner, *Sveriges inre historia under Drottning Christinas förmyndare*, pp. 67-8, 183-4, 186-7.
[3] Swederus, *Bidrag till kännedom om Sveriges bergshantering 1612-1654 (Jernkontorets Annaler* 1910), pp. 39-41.

more popular. The bureaucratization of local government brought with it a threat—as yet remote—to the fundamental democratic forms of self-government which were as old as Sweden herself. The hundred moot was slowly declining in political importance, and its administrative functions were beginning to be taken over by the royal administration. There was still, it is true, no disposition on the part of government flatly to reject the old democratic methods: the *ståthållare*-instructions of 1624 provided, on the contrary, for the creation of a new elective official in each parish—the parish-writer (*sockenskrivare*)—whose duty it was to be to safeguard the peasant from the danger of being mulcted twice over. But still, the cult of efficiency, above all in this century, imported danger to liberty. The *häradsting* and the *sockenstämma* were losing their traditional leaders, the local nobility: more and more the office of *häradshövding* was becoming a convenient sinecure whose duties were discharged by deputy. And these deputies—called law-readers (*lagläsare*), no doubt because they were sometimes illiterate and often knew no law [1]—could not provide the leadership which the local magnates had provided. More and more the hundred moot was thrown back on its own resources, in circumstances increasingly unfavourable. The nobles, if efficient and public-spirited, tended to enter the King's service; the office of *landshövding* became an object of noble ambition; and at a time when a serious clash of classes lay just ahead, the King's government in the provinces passed into the hands of men now become inimical both by birth and interest to the peasant democracy of the *härad*. It has therefore been contended that Gustav Adolf's reforms paved the way for the occlusion of provincial self-government which followed under the absolute kings of the Palatine House. But however that might be, one part of the hundred moot's activities remained as a bulwark of the nation's liberties: the *härad* might weaken on the administrative side; on the judicial it continued in its habitual rude health.

(v) *Justice*

Among the proposals submitted for inclusion in the Charter in December 1611 had been one which requested the correction of

---

[1] The *lagläsare* seem to have varied much in quality. Though there were many complaints against them, the best of them seem to have been men of good education, highly respected, and of a social standing not differing much from that of the *häradshövdingar*. Some of them went on to distinguished careers in the law or the civil service. Broomé, pp. 177-8.

certain abuses and imperfections in the administration of the law. It was complained that in certain parts of the country there was no *lagman* or *häradshövding*, and that litigants were unable to get the sentence of the court executed; that instances had occurred where the *lagman* was also functioning as *häradshövding* (and was thus sometimes in the position of hearing appeals from his own judgments); that other individuals duplicated the offices of *häradshövding* and bailiff, thus undesirably confusing the executive and judicial functions; and that the revenues raised for the payment of the salaries of *lagmän* and *häradshövdingar* were improperly diverted to other purposes.[1] In Clauses 8 and 9 of the Charter these abuses were in part attended to; and in the sequel the promises then made by the King were, on the whole, observed. But the reforms demanded, and the pledges extorted, were really quite inadequate to the situation. At the time of Gustav Adolf's accession four things were urgently wanted if the law were to function satisfactorily: a recodification; an effective organization of instances and a recognized court of appeal; greater uniformity in practice and proper supervision of the lower courts; and lastly, a modernizing of procedure.

The need for a recodification had been felt for some time. Two versions of the *landslag* were still used: the original *landslag* of Magnus Eriksson, and the revised *landslag* of King Kristoffer, dating from 1442. Each had equal validity, for neither was formally prescribed, though Kristoffer's *landslag* had perhaps the more general acceptance; and until 1608 neither was printed. Karl IX had been keenly aware of the need for a modernized, printed, and easily accessible code, and in 1603 had charged Peder Nilsson to prepare a revision of Kristoffer's *landslag*. This revision was laid before the Norrköping *riksdag* of 1604, and there referred to a scrutinizing commission—the so-called Rosengren Commission—which in due time produced a code of its own. Their proposals, however, were very unacceptable to the King, since they appeared to be strongly coloured by aristocratic class-interest. The result was a deadlock; and in 1608 Karl, despairing of further progress, determined at all events to obtain some printed text, and accordingly issued a correct version of Kristoffer's *landslag* which henceforth was accepted as the law of the land. At the same time Karl began the printing of the old provincial laws (*landskapslagar*), which still had some practical legal importance. But in 1611 the situation was still

---

[1] *SRDA*, I. 62-4.

obviously very unsatisfactory.[1] It cannot be said that Gustav Adolf
did a great deal to better it. He did indeed issue a printed version of
the Town Law in 1618 [2]; but erroneous copies of the *landslag*
continued in circulation; it was possible for a *lagläsare* to base a
judgment upon a citation from a supposed clause in the *landslag*
which had in reality no existence; and the position was not improved
by the importation into current practice of principles drawn from
the Roman or the Mosaic law, which were not accordant with
native legal tradition. No further attempt at a revision of the law
was in fact made until the appointment of the Commission of 1643;
no progress was constated until 1686; and the new code did not make
its tardy appearance until 1734. As a legal historian justly comments
on this more than Eldonian *tempo*, 'the acceptance of new laws and
legal principles has always been prepared in Sweden with great
care'.[3]

The reign did, however, witness one publication which, even
though it was an unofficial one, was of great importance to the
future of the legal system. This was the printing in 1616 of Olaus
Petri's *Rules for Judges*. The *Rules for Judges* were written probably
about 1544, and while showing signs of the influence of Roman law,
are really a crystallization of the spirit that lay behind the best
Swedish practice. They laid it down, for instance, that a judge
must look to the intention; that punishment must be reformatory;
that there must be the same law for the rich as for the poor. 'A
good judge is better than good laws', was one of Petri's maxims,
and others were 'it is always better to free a criminal than to afflict
the innocent'; 'the good of the common man is the highest law';
'that which is not right and reasonable cannot be law'. These and
similar apophthegms now gained a wider currency than ever before,
and soon obtained a sort of official endorsement; for in 1635 they
were prefixed to the printed text of the *landslag*, and they have been
prefixed to successive editions of the laws of Sweden ever since.[4]

The establishment of a regular court of appeal, and the fixing of
a definite hierarchy of courts, had also been given some attention
by Karl and his ministers. The *landslag* had provided for two types

---

[1] T. Berg, *Skytte*, pp. 134-6; J. Posse, *Bidrag till svenska lagstiftningens historia
från slutet af sextonde århundradet till stadfästelsen af 1734 års lag*, p. 30; Westman,
De svenska rättskällornas historia, pp. 56-7.

[2] Posse, p. 57.

[3] Munktell, *Det svenska rättsarvet*, p. 36.

[4] Holmbäck, *Våra domareregler* (in *Festskrift tillägnade Axel Hägerström*),
pp. 266-74; Munktell, *op. cit.*, pp. 164-71.

of royal court for the exercise of supreme jurisdiction (*räfsteting* and *rättareting*), either by the King in person or by a Commission on Eyre. But these courts had become obsolescent, if not extinct, and no fixed institution had grown up to take their place. In the popular mind the King was still the fount of justice, the natural corrector of abuses and the resort of the oppressed; and the peasant followed a deeply rooted instinct when, ignoring all lower instances, he 'went to the King's' (*gick till kungs*) for justice. And the King on his side held fast to his judicial functions, and never forgot that it was his duty to exercise a certain residual equity jurisdiction—in the obscure phrase of the *landslag*, '*att bryta offsocknir och skrocksocknir*'—and supply the deficiencies, or adjust the absurdities, of more formal jurisprudence. Nevertheless, unlimited direct access to the sovereign had serious inconveniences, and had indeed been prohibited as early as 1491; and from King Erik's time efforts had been made to interpose some sort of buffer, in the shape of a Supreme Court, between the majesty of the King and the swarms of petitioners. Karl, for instance, had attempted in 1598 and 1600 to constitute a Supreme Court, composed mainly of the *riksråd* and the *lagmän*, which was to have met in Uppsala and Linköping at the time of their great annual markets, and to which the old name of *rättareting* was to have been given; but the scheme was tried only once, and thereafter fell into oblivion. His plan of 1604, to set up a permanent court under the presidency of either the Chancellor or the Steward, was not tried at all. Throughout his reign the greatest confusion and irregularity prevailed; and the functions of a Supreme Court seem to have been discharged by the *råd*, sitting, curiously enough, in Stockholm Town Hall, and unsuitably afforced by indiscriminately chosen members of the nobility and the higher command.[1]

The Judicature Ordinance of 1614 was thus a most necessary measure. It established a permanently constituted *hovrätt*, and so provided an appellate court which should protect the King from molestation by pertinacious litigants. It laid down a clear hierarchy of instances (*häradsrätt—lagmansrätt—hovrätt*, or in the case of towns *kämnärsrätt—rådstuvurätt—hovrätt*), and it insisted that

---

[1] For Karl's plans for law reform, see Staf, pp. 231-3; Tham, *Oxenstierna*, p. 154; Munktell, *op. cit.*, pp. 93-107; N. Edling, *Den högsta rättsskipning under 1500-talet* (*HT* 1939), pp. 398-400; T. Berg, *Skytte*, pp. 134-6; B. Broomé, *Nils Stiernsköld*, p. 41; Bergendal, *Bidrag till de svenska rättsmedlens historia*, pp. 36-7; Melander, pp. 1-2. Appeal from Karl's *råd* seems to have lain to the King: *Abraham Brahes Tidebok*, p. 63.

there should be no appeal to the *hovrätt*, and still less to the King, until the case had been decided, or justice denied, in the lower court.[1] It was a principle not made good without opposition from conservative legists such as Chesnecopherus, who held that the concentration of appellate jurisdiction in Stockholm contravened the *landslag*; and it provoked spirited resistance from the Queen-Mother, who scented an infringement of the ducal privileges. Apart from its function as a court of appeal, the *hovrätt* was also made to serve another purpose: it became the privileged *forum* for the nobility in cases of felony. But even here the case had first to be opened in the appropriate local court. There were, however, a few classes of case for which the *hovrätt* was to serve as a court of first instance: *e.g.*, where an action was brought against a judge of a lower court for denial of justice (*querela neglectae justitiae*), and also in cases of *lèse-majesté*, blasphemy (*crimen laesae majestatis divinae*) and some others.[2]

The Procedure Ordinance of 1615 slightly modified these arrangements. On the suggestion of the Burghers the King now inserted a clause debarring appeals in civil suits to the value of less than 50 *daler* (or 100 *daler* for Stockholm). It was also laid down that the *hovrätt* was not to sanction the death penalty except when the King was 'far away'; when he was present, or reasonably accessible, capital sentences were always to be submitted for his approval. And one important provision made it clear that the King had never intended to divest himself entirely of his judicial prerogative; for it was now explained that on certain conditions a litigant might *petition* the King to act as revisor of the judgment of the *hovrätt*. There was still no right of *appeal* from a decision of the *hovrätt*; its position as a Supreme Court was in no way impugned; but unsuccessful suitors might implore the King of his grace to look into the matter.[3] There was no real inconsistency between the

---

[1] In practice the *lagmansrätt* ceased to concern itself with criminal cases, which went directly from the *häradsrätt* to the *hovrätt*: *Vendels sockens dombok 1615-1645*, p. 42. In the duchies the highest court was normally the duke's own *hovrätt*: only in cases 'concerning life, limb or honour', or involving an amount exceeding 4000 marks silver, did an appeal to the royal *hovrätt* lie: F. Lindberg, *Hertig Johan av Östergötland och hans furstendöme* (*HT* 1941), p. 122.

[2] *SRDA*, I. 392-425; Hallenberg, III. 301-4; Bergendal, pp. 37-8, 44; Melander, pp. 60, 68, 71.

[3] Haralds, *Konungsdom och konungsnämnd* pp. 28-45; Melander, pp. 63-7. But see Petrén, *Kring Svea Hovrätts tillblivelse*, pp. 180-4, for the suggestion that Gustav Adolf may have inserted the *beneficium revisionis* in order to protect Erik Göransson Tegel from unfavourable judgments in the *hovrätt*. Text of Procedure Ordinance in Schmedemann, I. 143-63.

Judicature Ordinance and the Procedure Ordinance; but there remained for some time considerable obscurity as to the relations between the King and the new court. In the early years of its existence, Gustav Adolf interfered far more with its working than might have been supposed likely from the letter of the Ordinance which had established it. This was partly the court's own fault, for they made a habit of approaching the King for guidance, and he did not hesitate to give it.[1] He made no scruple, either, of violating his own Ordinance by permitting cases to come before the *hovrätt* which had not previously been submitted to a lower court. And he scolded them on occasion in language whose violence recalled the more trenchant efforts of his father.[2] They had other difficulties too: with the vested interests of *lagmän* who felt that they were being deprived of their court, or with unrepentant brigands like Count Sten Leijonhufvud, who cared no more for a *hovrätt* than for any other instrument of the law.[3] The *landsting* of Norrland successfully maintained its right to contract out of the new arrangements, and conditions in Västergötland and Dalsland were exceptional too.[4] A famous case in Finland [5] raised in acute form the question of the court's relationship to the jurisdiction of the Church; and the King's absences overseas presently posed a delicate question as to the *hovrätt's* relationship to the *riksråd*. Gustav Adolf clung tenaciously to his right to judge petitions, and when he was at home personally conducted any investigation that might be required, even to the hearing of fresh evidence.[6] When he was abroad he tried for some years to retain the effective control of this judicial business, and it was not until 1630 that the Instructions for the interim government finally handed it over to them. Formally, of course, this did not make the *råd* a superior instance to the *hovrätt*: it was

---

[1] See *e.g.* Schmedemann, I. 185-6.

[2] The *hovrätt* minutes for 5 November 1618 read: 'H.M. has counselled and urged the royal court, that they show favour to no man. And should any one of the judges judge after the desire either of H.M. or of any other, then will H.M. make such an example of him that he will have him flayed alive and nail his hide to the Bench and his ears to the stocks.' Geijer, *Svenska Folkets Historia*, III. 69.

[3] Hallenberg, II. 863; V. 146-51. Hallenberg quotes a case (V. 152) of a woman who complained of the *ståthållare* in Åbo because he had had her 'whipped at the stocks and both her ears cut off, after she had been taken under the protection of the *hovrätt*, and that others who had letters of protection from the *hovrätt* had been pitifully imprisoned and beaten'.

[4] Broomé, pp. 185-9.

[5] Barthollus Stephanus *versus* The Bishop and Chapter of Åbo: for this, see below, pp. 407-8.

[6] J. E. Almquist, *Kungl. Maj:t som revisionsrätt*, pp. 63-4; Melander, pp. 7-8.

merely that this part of the royal functions was discharged by commission, the commissioners being—not the *råd*, but the members of the *råd* nominated as constituting the interim government. Yet whatever the formal position, in practice the *råd* did come to occupy something like the anomalous situation of being a superior instance to the Supreme Court. And lastly, the creation of other *hovrätter* involved thorny problems as to their relative status. Nevertheless, though the first decades were years of trial, the reforms of 1614 and 1615 amply justified themselves, and *Svea Hovrätt* and *Göta Hovrätt* remain essential parts of the Swedish legal system to this day.

The *hovrätt* had not been intended merely as a court of appeal, and the purpose of the Ordinances had not only been to relieve the burden of judicial business upon the King. The Ordinances had been intended to regularize the proceedings of the inferior courts, and the *hovrätt* had been designed from the beginning as a court of revision for their judgments. By the terms of the Ordinances the *lagmansrätt* had been ordered to be held at least once every three years, and the hundred court at least three times a year. Their records were to be forwarded to the *hovrätt* once a year for scrutiny and approval by the Advocate-Fiscal. The executive officers of the law were forbidden to carry out capital sentences until they had received the sanction of the *hovrätt*, except in a few heinous crimes, and even then only upon admission of guilt. It appears doubtful whether all of these provisions were immediately effective. In Vendel, for instance, the *häradsrätt* was most irregular in its meetings: instead of the prescribed three, there might be four in one year and none in the next.[1] Some *häradsrätter* are said to have been embarrassed by the order to send in their records once a year, since it might happen that they had no case before them for a whole year together; and others seem to have been lax in compliance, at least to begin with. But gradually the new arrangements came to be accepted; the rulings and decisions of the *hovrätt* began to have their effect on the practice of the inferior courts; the old abuses began to disappear; and the heavy slaughter which would have resulted if the death sentences of the lower courts had all been carried out was mercifully averted when they were reviewed at the higher level.

This improvement did not extend to a modernization of procedure. The only noticeable contribution of the *hovrätt* in this respect was

---

[1] *Vendels sockens dombok*, p. 36.

its admission of advocates to plead before it. The practice of using advocates was considered thoroughly un-Swedish, and the permission given by the Procedure Ordinance had been as grudging as possible. For the rest, procedure was extraordinarily antiquated. The Swedish contemporaries of Coke and Carpzovius lived in a legal world which seemed to have stood still for half a millennium; a world of wergilds and frankpledge, compurgators and outlawry. It was still possible for a man who had committed manslaughter to be reconciled with the relatives of the deceased upon payment of an appropriate sum of money; and even a murderer might on occasion escape with a fine, especially when the proceeds of justice had been assigned to an avaricious *häradshövding*. The idea of common responsibility of the family, of the kinship-group as a legal entity, still persisted: not long before Gustav Adolf's accession a family had been mulcted of a collective fine (*ättebot*), and it was still not unusual for a family to be accepted as bail for the appearance of one of its members who was charged with murder and had taken to the woods. There were still occasional instances of the court's handing over to an aggrieved person or his relations the task of catching, keeping and bringing to justice an evil-doer, and thus virtually legalizing private vengeance. In Gustav Adolf's time the 'bier-test' was still used (it was, however, a comparatively recent importation), whereby a men suspected of murder was forced to make oath of his innocence upon the corpse of his supposed victim, which (it was considered) would bleed afresh if he swore falsely. The woods had a constant floating population of fugitives from justice, who might condescend to appear before the court if provided with a safe-conduct; and if they duly appeared and were found guilty, the safe-conduct was always observed, and the criminal given time to return to his hiding-place. It might still happen that the *häradsting*, in indignation at some especially odious crime, might declare its perpetrator an outlaw, and with ancient pagan ceremony raise the 'wolf-yell' (*ulvsgäll*) over him, after which he could be killed at sight by any man.[1] The use of oath-helpers was among the most ordinary incidents in litigation, even at the highest level: in 1614 the *hovrätt* ordered a German sea-captain, suspected of murder, to purge himself, first by the oaths of six oath-helpers, and secondly

---

[1] For these examples, see *Vendels sockens dombok*, pp. *33, 42-3*, 13-14, 45; *AOSB*, II. XII. 150; Melander, pp. 199-203; Hallenberg, III. 296; Geijer, III. 71; Westman, *Minneskrift ägnad 1734 års lag*, I. 38-40.

by drinking the allegedly harmless cathartic which he had administered to his supposed victim.[1] There were signs, however, that compurgation was declining in importance: Olaus Petri's *Rules for Judges* had laid it down that oaths might be a means of rebuttal, but not of establishing a charge ('*med ed skall man svara och icke klaga*'); and further that the obligation to provide compurgators should be imposed on the defendant only if the plaintiff brought sufficient evidence to establish a *prima facie* case: failing such evidence, he was to be immediately acquitted. Compurgation in Gustav Adolf's time was in fact coming to be considered rather as a supplementary means of proof than as bearing the onus of the case; and at times it degenerated into a somewhat empty symbolism, as when the compurgators failed to appear, but sent their gloves instead. And at least one case is recorded where the court, relying on other evidence, rejected oaths spontaneously offered by twelve compurgators. In short, Swedish practice was just beginning to feel its way towards a grasp of the elements of the rules of evidence, and in this development it was probably hastened and aided by the new *hovrätt*. But compurgation died hard. Kristina's Criminal Code of 1653 enacted that only the party upon whom the obligation to provide compurgators was imposed could swear to the *truth* of a statement: the compurgators could swear only to his *credibility*. But the oaths of plaintiff and defendant continued to be accepted as evidence; as late as 1692 a defendant was ordered to produce twelve oath-helpers; and compurgation was not formally abolished until 1695.[2]

The sentences imposed on the guilty were often cruel: the wheel and stake, burning, riding the wooden horse with heavy weights attached to the feet, running the gauntlet; and a whole series of death penalties imposed under the Mosaic law, not only for sexual delinquencies, but also for such offences as striking an unruly stepmother. Fortunately the punishment inflicted by no means tallied with the sentences pronounced. Burning took place only when the culprit had already been executed; the wheel and stake meant only that the decapitated body was divided into four parts, each of which was laid on a wheel. Often a complainant (for instance the unruly stepmother) was horrified at hearing the death sentence pronounced, and pleaded for the defendant. But the great safeguard against undue

---

[1] Hallenberg, III. 290.
[2] On compurgation, see Holmbäck, p. 274; Herdin, I. 160; *Vendels sockens dombock*, pp. *39*, 6; Melander, p. 77.

savagery was provided by the clause in the Judicature Ordinance which insisted that all capital sentences should be confirmed by the *hovrätt*. The effect of this provision was startling. Almost all the death sentences imposed in accordance with Mosaic law were commuted; while of the 126 death sentences pronounced in Uppsala between 1630 and 1700, only 17 are known to have been carried out. The one crime for which the *häradsrätt* was anxious to see the death penalty enforced was theft; but even here the action of the *hovrätt* and of the King greatly diminished the mortality. Gustav Adolf's principle seems to have been that it was desirable that the inferior courts should impose the old savage sentences, *androm till warnagel* (as a warning to others), but that it was the business of the *hovrätt* to make the adjustments proper to a humaner age.[1]

This matter of the sentences imposed in inferior courts was really bound up with the much more important question as to whether native law was or was not to receive a large admixture of foreign elements. These foreign elements were two: one was the law of Moses; the other was the Roman law. With the vanishing of the church-courts at the Reformation, the punishment of a number of moral offences devolved upon the inexpert hands of the secular authorities, who in many cases had no rules or precedents to guide them. Throughout the sixteenth century the clergy pressed for the application of the Mosaic law to these offences; and the question was among the problems considered by Karl IX and his advisers at the time of their projected revision of the law. Skytte, indeed, on the King's orders did draw out a revised code based on the ecclesiastical chapters of the old *landslag*; but it met with a cold reception from the Estates, and was in consequence abandoned. Karl now, as a temporary measure, and in order to provide some authorized standard for the courts, appended to the printed version of Kristoffer's *landslag* an order that in certain grave cases—swearing, blasphemy and perjury; disobedience, manhandling and ill-treatment of parents; all sorts of sexual offences; usury; and false

---

[1] Herdin, I. 162-3, 168, 210-11; *Vendels sockens dombok*, pp. 26, 93, 183; Melander, pp. 195-8; Petrén, *Häradsnämnden vid storhetstidens början* (*Sv. Jur. Tidskr.* 1945), p. 854. Nevertheless, practice was by no means uniform. An active *ståthållare* such as Nils Stiernsköld was continuously interfering in judicial matters; he increased or decreased punishments freely on his own authority, even in cases which ought to have been submitted to the *hovrätt*, and on one occasion pronounced and carried out a death sentence and submitted it to the *hovrätt* afterwards—and the *hovrätt* endorsed his action! B. Broomé, *Stiernsköld*, pp. 183-4, 192-3.

witness—the courts were to follow God's law as laid down in the Scriptures. The result was to import into Swedish law a collection of foreign legal principles ill-adapted to Swedish conditions, and a list of penalties so bloodthirsty as to be almost impossible to carry out. Modification took place almost from the beginning: it had to be explained, for instance, that by usury was meant only interest at the rate of more than five per cent. But the inferior courts were allowed little discretion in applying the Mosaic principles; and as a result the *hovrätt* was burdened with much more work in revising judgments than was really necessary. The Mosaic law did not really make good its foothold in Sweden; but it was an element of confusion in the courts during most of the seventeenth century, and it had steady support from the clergy. It played its part, undoubtedly, in fostering the Old Testament fighting spirit which was so widely disseminated in Gustav Adolf's Sweden; and it may have had some importance for the outburst of witch-hunting which marked the reign of Karl XI.[1]

In the long run Moses was potentially less dangerous to liberty than Justinian. The Mosaic law looked askance on torture, for instance, while the Roman law tolerated it. Torture was certainly more freely used in Gustav Adolf's reign than at any other time in Sweden's history; but this may have meant no more than that her rulers felt themselves driven to every means to defend the state in exceptionally critical times. At all events it never became a regular practice, and it was always resorted to with a certain uneasiness, and mainly because of reluctance to condemn on incomplete evidence, and desire to obtain a confession from the accused.[2] A more serious matter was the concept of regalian rights, with the associated idea that ultimate ownership of land inhered in the King, while the subject possessed no more than a *dominium utile*. In Gustav Adolf's time this doctrine is to be seen operating in regard to the preservation of game and the conservation of certain forest trees. Those who shot elks or felled oaks were transported to Ingria, to colonize that desolate province. So too in regard to the settlement of waste- and forest-land at home: the Crown, assuming ultimate ownership, was beginning to grant licences to colonists irrespective of the existing

---

[1] For the Mosaic law, see J. E. Almquist, *Karl IX och den mosaiska rätten*, pp. 1-27, correcting Munktell, *Mose lag och svensk rättsutveckling*, pp. 132-44. For examples of it in operation, *Vendels sockens dombok*, pp. 66, 94, 98.

[2] For torture, see Munktell: *Tortyren i svensk rättshistoria* (*Lychnos* 1939, 1940), *passim*.

rights of villagers in the neighbourhood.[1] As the study of law developed at Uppsala, a new generation of legists came under the influence of Roman law concepts, and provided theoretical support for these claims. Yet in the end, no important Reception took place. Swedish law remained, like English law, predominantly case-law; and the Roman influence was confined to systematizing and supplementing. Two things helped to stem the tide: one was the creation by Gustav Adolf of a Chair of Swedish Law (a most unusual step for that age: England had to wait for a Chair of English Law till 1759); the other was the solid resistance of the traditional principles of Swedish liberty, as embodied in the hundred courts. It was these courts which, in defiance of the King's orders, imposed fines instead of transportation upon poachers, and which in spite of royal grants forced the settlers upon the waste to respect existing rights. The old days when the whole assembly of the free men of the hundred actively participated in deciding cases were indeed past: the transference of the meeting-place from the open air to the *tingstuga* had made that plain. But the result had been a strengthening of the position of the permanent jury of the hundred; and as the noble *häradshövding* gave way to the peasant-born *lagläsare*, the jury for a time seems to have dominated the proceedings, and probably even to have pronounced verdict and sentence. It is the hundred jury, then, that defends the traditional rights and liberties of the common man against the new dangers: against the Crown and its Roman law, against the retrograde ideas of Baltic or German feudalism which washed back to Sweden like scum from the whirl-pool of the Thirty Years' War, against the new bureaucracy's efficient impatience with forms that were antiquated and slow. 'The land shall be built upon law', said the *landslag*; and 'no man shall be destroyed in life or limb, nor his goods taken from him without due judgment of law.'[2] The Kings might promulgate their

---

[1] For Roman law and its influence, see B. Boëthius, *Rättsreception och folklig rättsvård* (*Sv. Tidskr.* 1927), pp. 272-6; B. Boëthius, *Skogen och Bygden*, pp. 178-193; Westman, *De svenska rättskällornas historia*, p. 40. For examples of the game laws in operation, and of transportation to Ingria, *Vendels sockens dombok*, pp. 64, 69; *RRP*, I. 89.

[2] And Messenius makes one of his characters say (*Signill*, VI. 5, in *Samlade Dramer*, p. 74):

> Lagh och Rätt är i Swealan.
> Här döör ingen Ogärningsman,
> För än Saken för Dom är stält,
> Och en rättwijs Sententz är fällt.

(Law and right are in Svealand. Here no criminal dies until the case has been brought to judgment, and a just sentence pronounced.)

Charters, they might make solemn oath at their coronations; but though their intentions be never so good, their eye could not be everywhere, nor their protecting hand always near to save the common man harmless from the evil-doer. The rights of the peasant depended upon the survival in his own breast of a vigorous attachment to the principles of law, and an unsleeping resolution to maintain them, whether against bailiff or bandit, Baltic noble, Dutch capitalist, or colonizing Finn. Even under the later absolute Kings, Sweden never lost her ideal of the rule of law; and one of the most potent agents in its preservation was the hundred court and its standing jury.

(vi) The 'Form of Government', 1634

Eight days after the battle of Lützen, Axel Oxenstierna wrote a despatch to the interim government in Stockholm, enclosing a draft of a Form of Government.[1] This draft was by no means the first of its kind. At some time in the mid-'twenties he had prepared the first version[2]; during the period between the truce of Altmark and the outbreak of the German war he made another, and this he took with him to Germany in the autumn of 1631, where (he asserted) the King saw it and approved it in all essentials. In the following summer this or another draft was discussed between them at Nuremberg; and the version which the Chancellor now sent home was further amended by him before its presentation to the Estates at the *riksdag* of 1634. But despite this long history, it does not appear that the text which then obtained their sanction differed much in its main features from the various concepts which had preceded it; and it might seem natural to discuss it as being essentially a product of Gustav Adolf's reign, and the logical fulfilment of the lines of development which had been inaugurated by him. It is, however, possible to hold various views about the origin and purpose of the Form of Government; and especially of recent years there has been a tendency to regard it rather as the negation of Gustav Adolf's policies than as their natural conclusion, and to deny that the King could ever have given such a document his blessing. The thought is not, indeed, very new: Queen Kristina remarked darkly in 1660 that her father 'possibly never saw a word of it', and even in 1634 the *råd* was alive to the possibility of being charged with making

---

[1] *AOSB*, I. vii. 648; *AOSB*, I. 1. 254-85.   [2] *AOSB*, I. 1. 251-3.

unwarranted use of the great King's name. Kristina refused to
accept it when she came of age; Karl X Gustav endeavoured to
circumvent it by his Will; and both plainly considered it to be anti-
monarchical in character. It is not very surprising, therefore, that
it should have been considered by some as in effect a constitution
foisted on the country by the ruling aristocracy, with the idea of
replacing the power of the King by that of the *råd*-families—the
final triumph of the constitutional ideas of Erik Sparre, which,
crushed in 1600, realized only imperfectly in the period after 1612,
now overpowered all opposition and established a real oligarchy.[1]
A still bolder interpretation seeks to show that even this was but a
secondary object: the prime motive behind the *Regeringsform*, it is
asserted, being in fact the lust for power and office of Axel Oxenstierna and his numerous relations.[2]

The Form of Government of 1634 is a long document of 65
clauses. It opens with a preamble which recites how Gustav Adolf
in his lifetime had intended to promulgate 'a proper government,
wherein to the King should be reserved his sovereignty, to the *råd*
their authority, and to the Estates their reasonable rights and
liberties', and which would in particular have made provision for a
Regency in the event of a minority, or the King's illness, or his
absence at a distance. At his command the Chancellor had drawn
up a plan which the King had approved; and it is now laid before
them. Thereupon follows the text of the statute, introduced by a
second preamble, this time in Gustav Adolf's name; and at the end,
after Clause 65, follows a brief statement of the assent of the Estates.
The great bulk of the document is thus represented to be in Gustav
Adolf's name, and approved by him; and the share of the Estates in
1634 is limited to providing a frame for it.[3]

The Form of Government falls into three main portions, clearly
marked off from one another. After Clause 1, which defines the
country's religion (and includes Luther's catechism for the first
time as one of the bases of the official creed),[4] and Clause 2, which

---

[1] *e.g.* C. A. Hessler, *Den svenska ståndsriksdagen*; and E. Hjärne, *Från Vasatiden
till Frihetstiden.*
[2] Sven Nilsson, *1634 års regeringsform* (*Scandia* 1937), and reply by Ahnlund
in *HT* 1937 at p. 179.
[3] The text of the Form of Government is most easily accessible in E. Hildebrand, *Sveriges Regeringsformer*, pp. 1-41.
[4] An account of the circumstances which led to the inclusion of Luther's
catechism is provided by H. Pleijel, *Vår kyrkas bekännelse*, pp. 68-93, who concludes
that Laurentius Paulinus Gothus was mainly responsible.

is a reaffirmation of the Succession Agreements of Västerås and Norr-köping, come a group of clauses (3 to 42) which are concerned with the organization of the country's administration. Clause 5 fixes the number of the *råd* at 25; Clause 6 establishes the five Colleges. Clauses 7 to 17 enter in some detail into the organization of these Colleges, upon lines which are familiar from earlier legislation. One novelty is the establishment of an extraordinary court to try exalted persons, by which is intended members of the Colleges or of the Regency, or persons of similar condition.[1] Clauses 18 to 22 deal with certain other high offices, such as that of the Master of the Buckhounds, or the Master-General of the Ordnance. Clauses 23 to 30 elaborate and make explicit the earlier reforms in local government; Clauses 31 to 34 fix the normal establishment of the Army, and its relations with the Civil Service; and Clauses 35 to 42 provide for the effective control of this new bureaucracy by the central government.

With Clause 43 begins a new group of clauses, which touch more upon constitutional theory than the preceding. Clause 43 enacts that the general annual meeting of senior civil servants (provided for in the clauses immediately preceding) may be invited to discuss and advise upon matters which do not call for the summoning of a *riksdag*; and the following clause legalizes and fixes the constitution of Committee Meetings. They are to be of a very restricted type: only two nobles from each *lagsaga*, the bishops and superintendents, and one representative each from Stockholm, Uppsala, Göteborg, Åbo and Viborg. The obvious tendency of this clause and its predecessor becomes explicit in Clause 45, where the summoning of a *riksdag* is contemplated only for coronations 'and other notable causes'. Moreover, the representation of the non-noble Estates is apparently seriously diminished: there is now to be one priest for every two *härader* (instead of every *härad*) and one peasant (instead of two) for every *härad*. But this was perhaps no more than habitually appeared in fact. Clauses 46 and 47 limit the right to sit in the *riksdag* to those who are resident in Sweden and Finland. On the other hand, the legislative authority of the *riksdag* is now formally and finally recognized.

There follow four clauses (48 to 51) of minor importance; and then comes the third of the main groups of clauses. These clauses (52 to

[1] For this, see Kjellen, *Rikrättsinstitutionens utbildning i Sveriges historia*, specially pp. 84-110.

65) deal with the arrangements to be observed if the King is absent at a great distance, incapacitated by illness from discharging the royal functions, or a minor. In such an event the Regency is to be entrusted to a Commission composed of the five great officers of state, who are now of course also the heads of the five Colleges. Their powers are most carefully defined (though, strangely enough, no provision is made for filling any vacancy among them); and a clear distinction is drawn between what they may do in the case of a minority and what they may do when the normal participation of the sovereign in the government is only temporarily suspended by illness or absence. In the latter event the Regents may enter into no treaties or negotiations with foreign powers, except in virtue of a special commission from the King; they may make no new law, nor grant any new privileges; and any minor alteration in existing arrangements is subject to the King's ratification. By a provision which recalls the preceding group of clauses they are discouraged in the strongest manner from holding any meeting of the *riksdag* in the absence of the King. As Regents during a minority, their powers are a good deal wider. The conduct of foreign policy is unrestricted; it is open to them to make new laws and grant new privileges, provided they are not to the prejudice of the Crown; and the calling of the *riksdag* is left entirely to their discretion.

It must probably remain an open question whether or not Gustav Adolf did in fact approve the Form of Government in the shape in which the Estates accepted it: the evidence seems insufficient for dogmatism. But this does not debar us from considering whether the enactment is or is not repugnant to the spirit in which government was conducted in his lifetime. In regard to one large section of the document there can be no hesitation about the answer. All those clauses which regulate the composition and functioning of the central and local administrations are entirely of a piece with the reforms which we have already examined. In this respect the Form of Government is indeed the coping-stone to an edifice which at the time of his death was all but complete. The institution of a special High Court for great offenders no doubt lacks any antecedent in Gustav Adolf's time, but it was an idea familiar to the Vasas since the days of Erik XIV. In general, the process of bureaucratization is carried a good deal further than in the King's lifetime; but there is no development which was not implied in what had gone before —no development, indeed, which was not necessary, if the policy already embarked upon were to be effective. The machine of government is now organized so that it may run of its own accord, without the King's personal supervision; but this had been precisely the object of Oxenstierna's reforms since the very early days of the reign, when King and Chancellor were both absent in the Russian theatre of war. To say that the Form of Government created a state of affairs in which the King could be dispensed with is true,[1] as far as the routine of administration is concerned (though not so as regards policy); but that does not therefore make it the expression of an oligarchical crypto-republicanism.

More dubious, perhaps, appears the second group of clauses, to which may be added Clause 58. The combined effect of these clauses is undoubtedly to curtail the share of the *riksdag* in public affairs, and to relegate it to the position of an extraordinary assembly, rather than a normal recourse of government. It would be going too far to attribute such a policy to Gustav Adolf on the evidence available from his lifetime; but it is undeniable that he had shown certain tendencies in this direction. The Secret Committee was his invention; the Committee Meeting was his favourite resource, at all events during the last decade of his life. He had on more than one occasion taken very important decisions with the consent of very small and unrepresentative gatherings. The provision in the Form of Government which imposed on the Regents the duty of avoiding by every means the calling of a *riksdag* in the King's absence was the mere echo of Gustav Adolf's own sentiments, and is to be regarded more as a safeguarding of the authority of the Crown than as the effort of a ruling oligarchy to escape the control of the Estates. Whether Gustav Adolf would have hit upon the idea of doing the business of the Estates at an annual meeting of senior civil servants is perhaps an open question; but there had at least been one occasion on which *landshövdingar* had formed part of a small Committee Meeting. As Gustav Adolf grew older, busier and more harassed, he seems a little to have lost the taste for *riksdagar*, to have become impatient of the quadrilateral negotiations they necessitated, and to have preferred the easier and more expeditious Committee Meeting. His father and grandfather had used the Estates as it suited their purpose, and Gustav Adolf himself had no especial superstitious reverence for the *riksdag* as an institution. He was disposed to reign with the consent and good-

---

[1] So, *e.g.*, C. Weibull, *Drottning Christina*, pp. 22-3.

will of his people, rather than without it; but the business of war and foreign policy (he probably considered) entitled him to a large discretion in the choice of the means for maintaining contact with the nation. The Estates, on their side, reformed and regularized by his care, and freed now from the embarrassment of feeling that they were a weapon in a party struggle, had grown conscious of their new position and authority, and tenacious of retaining them. At the end of the reign, as we have seen, they were more ready to complain of being ignored than of being harried with too many sessions. The Estates looked on Clauses 43 to 48 with concern, and even the *råd* felt misgivings. Had Gustav Adolf lived another fifteen years, it seems a probable supposition that he would have found himself embroiled in a constitutional conflict provoked by his growing habit of avoiding *riksdagar*.

We come, finally, to the group of clauses concerning the Regency. Of these it has been argued that they cannot have had the King's approval, since they put the monarchy in leading-strings to the heads of the Colleges, and since they pass over the Queen and John Casimir, both of whom were obvious candidates for the position of Regent. It is certainly true that the Regency government established in 1634 was in fact endowed, during a minority, with almost all the royal rights and prerogatives. Such a government did indeed make a King unnecessary, demonstrated the idea of the immortality of the state as against the transience of the monarch. At this, however, it is difficult to raise any astonishment, for that seems to be the natural object of any properly organized regency. If there was to be a regency at all, it had better be strong and efficient, above all in times of crisis: the country, after all, was at war. No one can seriously contend that the King would have preferred Maria Eleonora as Regent. But it is possible to contend that his natural choice was John Casimir, and that the very omission of John Casimir is an indication that the King never approved these clauses. On the other hand, there were objections to John Casimir, from every point of view: he was no doubt highly efficient, but he was a foreigner; he was a Calvinist; he was father of a prince who might possibly one day be Kristina's rival for the throne; and his choice would be most unwelcome to many, and not least to Axel Oxenstierna. After over twenty years of the closest collaboration, it is hardly to be supposed that Gustav Adolf would make a choice which might result in the virtual exclusion of Oxenstierna from affairs.[1] Abandoning, however, these unprofitable speculations, we can feel ourselves on firmer ground in suggesting that the elaborate provisions for the conduct of government in the King's absence 'far away' argue for their having been intended for Gustav Adolf's eye. And the care with which in every case the rights of the absent sovereign are safeguarded makes it probable that he may have seen and approved them. They are wholly in Gustav Adolf's manner. However far his campaigns may lead him, he holds fast to the ultimate responsibility and control. But indeed it is difficult to see, in any of the provisions for the Regency (whether during a minority or an absence), any serious diminution of the authority of the Crown, or any great transfer of weight to the *råd*: again and again the right of the sovereign to disallow the actions of the Regents is expressly secured. It is, indeed, not easy to discern in these arrangements much more than a natural development from the interim governments of the last decade of the reign.

Nevertheless, contemporaries felt that something of serious constitutional import was happening. Whatever Gustav Adolf may have intended, the aristocracy on the one hand, and the Estates on the other, did feel that the Form of Government implied a change in the balance of the constitution, and that the Crown and the *riksdag* were in some way diminished. The insistence of the *råd*, in the face of much hesitation by the Estates, on making the Form of Government 'eternally' valid—a 'fundamental law'—certainly lent colour to this view; and there is no doubt that men like Per Banér looked upon it as a useful weapon against the monarchy, in case of the accession of an 'evilly-disposed' sovereign; for, as Per Banér bluntly said, every future King must accept the Form of Government 'if he wants to wear the crown at all'. The aristocracy, in fact, were prepared to use the occasion to strengthen their position. There was still a hint of Erik Sparre republicanism in the air, blended with the now fashionable doctrine of a 'mixed' constitution. On the other side, the virtual continuance of the interim government, without the comforting safeguard of an adult (if distant) monarch, naturally suggested to the unprivileged classes, who were just beginning to feel the impact of the social and economic pressure of the acquisitive nobility, that the political balance had tilted dangerously towards oligarchy; and the court party had every interest in representing the new constitution as a fetter upon the

[1] See the King's letter to Oxenstierna, 4 Dec. 1630: *AOSB*, II. 1. 669.

ruler. If it was so, it was a fetter which Kristina shook off easily enough. In short, there appears to be little in the Form of Government to which Gustav Adolf could have taken exception (most conspicuously, perhaps, to 'eternally'); and there is no great reason to doubt his having seen and approved it in the main. It is a document which not unfairly reflects his latest constitutional practice, a document which may well represent his probable line of future constitutional development, a document above all which reveals his nightmare anxiety to ensure that if he fell in battle Sweden should have a government strong enough and popular enough and able enough to secure for her the recompense to which she was entitled. It belongs, therefore, essentially to the history of his reign, as well as to that of his successor.

CHAPTER VII

THE CHURCH

(i) *From the Reformation to 1611*

In Gustav Adolf's time, and for many years afterwards, the Lutheran Church held a central position in Swedish society.[1] Its clergy bridged the gap between nobles and peasantry: on the one hand its bishops were the confidants and occasionally the advisers of the sovereign; on the other its parish priests were the comforters and natural resort of the common people. The clergy were not, indeed, admitted to hold the great offices of state, and since the Reformation no man in Holy Orders had been a member of the *råd*; but they were, nevertheless, great public servants. Without their cooperation, many of the most important of Gustav Adolf's reforms could scarcely have been contemplated, still less carried through. In education, in the primitive social services of that age, they were the natural instruments of governmental policy. In every vicarage of Sweden dwelt a government agent, upon whose shoulders rested responsibilities which ranged from propaganda to hospitality, from public morals to fiscal accounting.

The Church was thus one of the main props of the monarchy, and the monarchs on their side recognized in the Church one of the most important of national interests. In a very real sense both were indissolubly linked in fortune. The highest duty of Kingship consisted in the encouragement of the Gospel and the protection of the Church: the sovereign must see to it that the pure milk of the Word could flow unchecked by temporal hindrances, and that no froward spirit prevailed against the godly regiment which was entrusted to him; just as the bishops and clergy, on their side, were bound to restrain any who might show inclination wantonly to set themselves against their lawful ruler. But this was not all; for, reinforc-

---

[1] The best outline history of the Swedish Church is the collective work *Svenska Kyrkans Historia*, of which vol. III. (*Reformationstidevarvet*) and vol. IV. 1. (*Svenska Kyrkan under Gustav II Adolf*) are by Hj. Holmquist. A short text-book by Holmquist is *Från Reformationen till Romantiken*. L. A. Anjou, *Svenska Kyrkans Historia ifrån Upsala möte år 1593 till slutet af sjuttonde århundradet*, is still useful. J. Wordsworth, *The National Church of Sweden*, is very good for its size and date. W. Schmitt, *Finlands Kyrka*, is a short outline.

ing these considerations of abstract duty, there was the plain fact that, as a matter of history, Sweden's Church and Sweden's independence had for a century stood in the closest connection. The Swedish Reformation had proceeded immediately from Gustav Vasa's need to liberate himself from the burden of his debt to Lübeck, and so to establish his throne upon a firmer foundation. Without the plunder of the Church, the war of emancipation might have been in vain. So too, three-quarters of a century later, the cause of the Reformation had been linked with that of the nation, in resistance to a Catholicizing, absolutist and polonized ruler. Lutheranism in Sweden, for all the apparent artificiality of its beginnings, had become before the end of the century a Church so firmly rooted that only revolution and systematic persecution could have shaken it. Thus patriotism and religion went hand in hand; and the most pressing considerations of practical politics bound throne and pulpit in alliance. But indeed, even in the earliest days of the Reformation, the Reformers had laid emphasis on this aspect of the question. The independence of the individual, who was henceforth to stand in no mediate relation to God, was to be matched by the independence of the State, whose native sovereign should own no earthly superior, and whose essential claim it was to be numbered among the nations. In 1530 Olaus Petri, defending the use of the vernacular in the services of the Church, wrote: 'We Swedes also belong to God, as well as doth any other nation; and the tongue we speak, that hath God given us. He contemneth not us above the nations of the earth, neither despiseth He our speech beyond the speech of others.' To the Swedes, indeed, as to the Germans, the Reformation brought the opportunity for the expression and realization of a patriotism and a national self-consciousness which had hitherto been denied full scope. The Lutheran Church, therefore, accepted the growing school of Swedish historical romanticism; it identified itself with Swedish national ambitions; and it gave to Sweden's foreign wars the blessings proper to Crusading expeditions. In the name of patriotism it steeled the nation to sacrifice; in the cause of religion it exhorted to zeal. The Swedish Lutheran believed that he was fighting, in Poland or Germany, for the preservation of his religion; but he was not insensible to the swelling pride of a lineage which could be traced back to the ancient Goths, nor immune to the ambition of emulating them.

The aims of Church and State were thus in the broadest sense coincidental, or at worst reconcilable, once Sigismund had retreated to Warsaw. There were, no doubt, many points upon which they might differ; but at bottom their interests were the same. Karl IX and his bishops might come into sharp conflict; but neither was prepared to push matters to extremes, since a common interest always reminded them of the undesirability of a breach. Yet though this was true, the differences between King and Church in Karl's time were serious enough, and the situation at the moment of Karl's death anything but satisfactory. In the ecclesiastical field, as in the political, the accession of Gustav Adolf was felt to be the occasion for settling many awkward questions; and churchmen, no less than laymen, looked forward to the new reign, and earnestly hoped for an improvement on the old.

The Swedish Reformation, unlike the German, had for long been comparatively indifferent to the subtleties of the theologians. The papal authority had been destroyed; the more obviously Romish elements in the Mass had been prohibited; the pulpit had replaced the altar as the focus of popular piety; and the monastic orders had more or less disappeared. But no steps had been taken to provide a clear definition of dogma. Gustav Vasa, like Henry VIII, pursued a course which was marked by occasional petulant reactions towards a Catholic orthodoxy: fortunately for Sweden, these vacillations were not accompanied by persecution. The leading Swedish reformers had come under Luther's influence in Germany, and it was therefore natural that the Reformation in Sweden should have a Lutheran complexion: the excesses of Anabaptism or iconoclasm were firmly repressed. Yet although the Reformation was Lutheran; although it was laid down that the creed of the Church was to be 'based upon God's Holy Word'; there was, for the first two generations, a broad tolerance for divergences. Even the adherents of the old faith escaped persecution; since, as Olaus Petri put it, 'No man can be compelled to God's word; it must be freely and voluntarily accepted, if it is to bear fruit.' Thus Swedish Lutheranism for some decades escaped being bound to any German 'Confession'; and was, perhaps, a good deal more certain of what it rejected than of what it accepted.

This comfortable latitudinarianism persisted for so long as Laurentius Petri remained Archbishop, and its last expression is in the Church Ordinance of 1571, which was Laurentius Petri's work;

but the course of events in the 'seventies and 'eighties made it increasingly difficult to maintain an attitude of parochial indifference to the theological controversies which raged on the Continent. In Germany, a new school of Lutheran theologians had arisen who followed Philip Melanchthon in believing that some form of comprehension, to include moderate Calvinists, ought to be possible. In opposition to this 'philippist' school there now emerged the so-called 'gnesio-orthodox' Lutheranism, which narrowed the basis of doctrine, decided all doubtful points in a sense hostile to Calvinism, and took its stand upon the letter of the *Liber Concordiae*. German Lutheranism was thus divided into two bitterly warring camps; and something of the same spirit began for the first time to appear in Sweden. The adherents of Gustav Vasa's vague and easy solution tended naturally to become philippists, and were frequently accused by the more rigorous of being tainted with Calvinism; while the gnesio-orthodox school made a strong appeal to those who wished for more precision in dogma and less tolerance of divagations. Equally obnoxious to both schools was the quasi-Anglicanism of Johan III, with its liturgical experiments and its hankering after a reunion with Rome. Thus by the end of the 'eighties gnesio-orthodox Lutheranism appeared in Sweden as a middle way (and a very narrow one) between the philippists and the liturgists; and as such it increasingly attracted the most vigorous elements in the Church. Its focus lay in Norrland, or rather in the school at Gävle where most Norrland boys were educated, and it found its most trenchant and truculent exponent in Abraham Angermannus. It was this school of theologians which emerged victors from the Uppsala meeting of 1593. At that meeting the old tolerant attitude was abandoned for ever. Not only was Johan III's *Nova Ordinantia* thrown overboard, but all popish, Zwinglian, Calvinist and Anabaptist errors were explicitly repudiated. For the first time Sweden pinned her faith to a foreign Confession: from henceforth the *Augustana* was to be the rock upon which the Swedish Church was built. 'Now,' exclaimed Nicolaus Olai Bothniensis triumphantly, 'now is Sweden become one man, and we have all one Lord and God!'[1]

There was, however, at least one person who was out of step with the onward march of the Norrland zealots, and that was Duke Karl.

---

[1] For a discussion of the authenticity of this remark, see H. Pleijel, *Svensk Lutherdom*, pp. 47-52.

For most of the 'nineties the depth of the differences between them was masked by the need for a common front against Sigismund; but once the battle of Stångebro was won, and Karl established as ruler of the country, it became only too plain. Karl himself appeared in the guise of one of those 'unruly and lopped-off members' against whom the Söderköping *riksdag* had breathed threatenings and slaughter. For Karl, in religion as in so much else, was the true son of his father. He was not prepared to pin his faith to man-made formularies, whether of Luther or of anybody else: his religion was based on 'the pure word of God', as Gustav Vasa's had been, and this he felt justifiably confident of being able to interpret for himself. He had all his father's dislike of hierarchical tendencies in the Church; and more reason, perhaps, to fear them. He was determined that the royal Supremacy should be a reality. The shifting of the lines of religious controversy in the preceding decades had made him, what Gustav Vasa could not have been, a philippist; but he was a philippist not only because he disliked the sectarian intolerance of the gnesio-orthodox school, but because he had a constant and overmastering sense of the menace of Rome and of the need for Protestants to close their ranks in the face of that menace. In matters of ceremony he was decidedly a Puritan. In foreign policy he looked for aid mainly to the Calvinist princes of Germany. It was natural, therefore, that he should be suspected by his clergy of crypto-Calvinist leanings; and that foreign statesmen should take him to be of the Reformed religion: much later Gustav Adolf could count on some Calvinist sympathies because it was imagined that he had inherited the religious views of his father. But though it was an error to suppose Karl a Calvinist, it was an error which derived a good deal of support from his religious proceedings. He took a Calvinist—Micronius—for one of his Court chaplains; he arranged a disputation between an exiled Scottish Presbyterian, John Forbes, and the flower of the Uppsala theologians, apparently in the hope of inducing the University to broaden its outlook. He attempted to alter the liturgy by the insertion of characteristically philippist or quasi-Calvinist elements, and condemned the existing version as smacking too much of popery. He evolved a service-book of his own for use at Court, and a catechism modelled on that of Heidelberg. He conducted a regular pamphlet-war against his archbishop, Olaus Martini. He long refused to accept the resolutions of the Uppsala meeting as binding; and when the Clergy pressed him to do so as part of his coronation Charter, he insisted on adding a saving proviso which ran: 'as far as they are founded on the prophetic and apostolic Scriptures, and are consonant with them'. It was only under strong pressure that he accepted the Confession of Augsburg; and he persisted in maintaining that the Church Ordinance of 1571—the other great pillar upon which the Swedish Church now reposed— was not in accordance with the word of God and had never been accepted by the monarchy. In short, Karl showed himself throughout his reign irreconcilably hostile to the very bases upon which Swedish Lutheranism was established: the doctrinal quarrel was constant and apparently insoluble.[1]

It was accompanied, moreover, by incessant friction upon matters of Church government. The struggle between the principles of royal Supremacy on the one hand, and ecclesiastical self-government on the other, had been going on ever since the Reformation. It now came to a climax. Karl showed plainly that he intended to function as *dominus religionis* within his kingdom, and to exercise a real control over the working of the Church. He had no scruples, for instance, about interfering in elections to vacant sees. The Church Ordinance of 1571 had laid it down that bishops were to be elected by persons appointed from among 'the clergy and others who may be somewhat experienced in these matters'—which came in practice to mean the Chapters; and thereafter the elected person was to seek letters of confirmation from the King. But Karl rode rough-shod over this arrangement: in 1607, for instance, he offered the see of Åbo to Laurentius Paulinus Gothus, and two years later translated him to Strängnäs, without in either case troubling to consult the Chapters concerned. The election of Kenicius to the primacy in 1609 was voted by such of the Clergy as were assembled at the meeting of the *riksdag*, upon Karl's simple intimation of his wish that Kenicius should be elected. This high-handed interference by the Crown was much resented.[2]

Another cause of difference concerned the Chapters. Both Gustav

---

[1] For Karl's religious position, see H. Block, *Karl IX som teolog och religiös personlighet*; O. S. Holmdahl, *Karl IX:s förmenta kalvinism*; S. Kjöllerström, *Kyrkolagsproblemet i Sverige*, pp. 58-66; Ahnlund, *Storhetstidens gryning*, p. 31; O. S. Holmdahl, *Studier öfver prästeståndets kyrkopolitik*, I. 111-34; H. Cnattingius, *Den centrala kyrkostyrelsen i Sverige 1611-1636*, pp. 52-9.

[2] For the episcopal office in the sixteenth century, see R. Askmark, *Svensk prästutbildning fram till år 1700*, pp. 116 seqq. For Karl's interference, H. Lundström, *Laurentius Paulinus Gothus*, I. 93, 109-16.

Vasa and Erik XIV had regarded the cathedral Chapters, and the cathedral functionaries who composed them, as useless survivals from the pre-Reformation epoch. In the 'forties they had been stripped of their corporate property and their membership reduced to a bare minimum: in some cases the only members remaining were the bishop, the vicar of the cathedral town, and the schoolmaster. The cathedral, which had hitherto been the normal centre for the training of priests, was consequently able to continue that work only with the greatest difficulty; and the training of vicars-choral and choirboys ceased altogether. Johan III, as might have been expected, reversed this tendency: in his reign the Chapters revived; they recovered, in the form of prebends, their corporate income; and their membership was increased to include a *lektor* in theology. The business of electing to vacant sees passed once again into their hands. But Karl was interested in Chapters only in so far as they provided educational services for their dioceses: he disliked the idea of their forming a corporation, and shared the opinion of Erik XIV and Gustav Vasa that no advantage was to be expected from an excess of clergy cumbering the purlieus of Sweden's modest cathedrals. Experience at Strängnäs[1] had persuaded him, moreover, that from a purely educational point of view it would be better to transfer the *lektor* in theology from the cathedral Chapter to the cathedral school. In the early years of his reign, therefore, Karl endeavoured to reduce the Chapters to the exiguous dimensions favoured by Erik XIV. This attempt was resisted by the Church. The clergy were not unmindful of the educational obligations of the cathedral; and they hoped to induce Karl to increase the size of the Chapters by afforcing them with mainly educational personnel. The struggle came to a head at the Norrköping *riksdag* of 1604; and after some debate they were successful in persuading Karl to modify his attitude. In addition to the bishop, vicar and schoolmaster, the Chapter was now to include a *lektor* in theology and a *conrector*, or vice-principal of the school; so that more than half of the members of the Chapter would be teachers. Thus the Chapter maintained itself as a body of importance, and so far Karl was defeated; but on the other hand a decisive step had been taken towards its transformation from a corporation of cathedral functionaries into a gathering whose backbone would be the masters of the

---

[1] The diocese of Strängnäs had lain within Karl's duchy of Södermanland.

local school. This, however, was a development which was not complete until the reign of Gustav Adolf.[1]

A more difficult problem was that of the right to appoint to benefices. By the Church Ordinance of 1571 it had been laid down that, when a benefice became vacant, the initiative in providing a priest should lie with the congregation, who were to present their candidate to the bishop or ordinary for his examination and approval. This represented a recurrence to the democratic traditions of the early mediaeval Swedish Church, which in the period immediately preceding the Reformation had been somewhat obscured. The provisions of the Church Ordinance were, however, exposed to attack from three sides—from the ecclesiastical Supremacy of the King, from the hierarchical pretensions of the bishops, and from the claims of the nobility to the right of patronage. Ever since the Reformation the King had freely exercised the right to deprive and condemn peccant priests; and Karl had without hesitation punished clerics whose loyalty appeared to him to be in any way suspect. But latterly he had also been asserting a claim to a preponderant influence in the choice of incumbents. By the time of Johan III it had become the accepted practice that the presentation to livings in the towns, and in the more important country parishes, should be in the hands of the King; and such livings were called 'regalian'. It was tacitly agreed also that the King had the presentation of livings in the more remote and desolate parts of the kingdom, and also to any new parishes which might be formed in such districts—a matter which was to be of some importance as the colonization of the forest areas proceeded and as the mines were developed. Johan III, however, had endeavoured to insist upon royal approval for candidates to *all* livings, and Karl in 1586 had made the same claim for his duchy. After his accession he seems to have interfered in the appointments to non-regalian benefices, and in 1606 he promulgated an ordinance which asserted his control over all preferments, and even forbade ordination without his approval. So extreme a pretension could not be maintained, and never seems to have been enforced; and it naturally provoked the liveliest indignation on the part of the bishops. But the bishops, on their side, had also shown an inclination of recent years to overstep the bounds laid down in 1571. It was one of Karl's charges against them that they forced ministers of their

[1] Askmark, pp. 51-88; Hj. Holmquist, *De svenska domkapitlens förvandling till lärarekapitel*, pp. 1-38.

choice upon congregations unwilling to receive them. Of recent years they had been consistently endeavouring to ensure that the Chapters should have a share in the approval of candidates for livings; and this was not calculated to mollify Karl. But King and Church were at one in resisting the claims of the nobility, which, if acceded to, would have injured the interests of both. The nobility were demanding not merely that their rights should be recognized for those parishes where the living was in their gift as patrons but that they should also be allowed to dictate the choice of parson for those parishes in which they actually resided—a most important extension.[1]

Thus King, Church and nobles were engaged in a triangular conflict, and each naturally sought support from the peasantry, who were, indeed, the class most concerned in the business. The Reformation had fallen heavily on the parish and its organization. Not content with the plunder of the monasteries, Gustav Vasa had attacked the property of the parish, and to such effect that nearly one-half of the 13,700 manors resumed by the Crown were manors which had previously been assigned to the support of the parochial clergy. At a stroke the parishes were reduced to penury; with the result that it 'was as sweet to walk in the desolate woods, as to go into a church'.[2] The blow seems, however, to have stimulated the congregations to fresh exertions; and the latter half of the sixteenth century was a period of vigorous parochial life. The parish developed its own elected representative organ, the vestrymen (sexmän), to whom the churchwardens made their annual report and by whom the business of the parish was transacted; it set about accumulating fresh financial resources; and it guarded most jealously its right to choose its own pastor. Where it had reason to fear opposition from a bishop, the parish would appeal direct to the King. It resisted vigorously the pretensions of the resident nobility. It represented, more truly than either King or nobles, the evangelical claim of the layman to choose his own minister. The King was able to trade on this, in order to play off the parish against the bishops; while the bishops on their side were willing to accept the parish's right of election in order to defeat the claims of the nobility. In the last

[1] For this question of presentment to benefices, see Holmquist, *Tillsättningar av gäll i Sverige under Reformationsårhundradet, passim.*
[2] R. Gullstrand, *Bidrag till den svenska sockensjälvstyrelsens historia under 1600-talet,* p. 25, for this quotation, and *passim* for the history of parochial self-government.

four years of Karl's reign, when the whole question was vehemently debated, these manœuvres produced a series of suggested settlements; but the conflict of interests was so plain that compromise was impossible; and when Karl died, a settlement was as far off as ever.

The same clash of apparently irreconcilable viewpoints wrecked the efforts which were made in 1608 to revise the Church Ordinance of 1571 and the attempt to incorporate a fundamental law for the Church into the proposed recodification of the *landslag*.[1] King and bishops were agreed upon the need for some such reform of the law; but whereas the bishops would have used it to strengthen the episcopal authority, the object of the King was undoubtedly to revive that absolute control of the Church by the Crown which Gustav Vasa had exercised in the 1540's. In short, Karl appeared to be aiming at what was known in Germany as a 'landesherrliche Kirchenregiment'; and, objectionable as that was to the bishops considered merely as a form of Church government, it became doubly alarming when the sovereign who put forward these claims was not doctrinally sound. The tension in the relations between Church and State had, in fact, become intolerable; and the accession of Gustav Adolf came at a crisis in the Church's history. It had become plain that the numerous controversies with the Crown must be resolved without delay: the 'pathological suspicion'[2] existing between Karl and the bishops could not be suffered to continue without serious prejudice to the religious settlement. Some compromise must be found between the Church's claim to independence and the Crown's assertion of the right to unlimited interference. The whole question of a central government for the Church must be faced, together with the problem of providing a supreme tribunal for the trial of ecclesiastical causes. The vexed questions of the revision of the Church Ordinance, the service-book, the catechism, and the translation of the Bible, must somehow be settled. The relations between the lay and spiritual authorities in regard to public morals and the maintenance of Church discipline were in need of definition. The utilization by the State of members of the clergy as an auxiliary and unpaid civil service was already provoking resentment. The development of the educational system presented numerous points of controversy. But essentially all these matters

---

[1] Kjöllerström, *Kyrkolagsproblemet*, pp. 58-66.
[2] The expression is Holmquist's: *Tillsättningar av gäll*, p. 123.

were reducible to a single question: was the King to be, as
Melanchthon had desired him to be, simply *minister et executor
ecclesiae*; or was he to be permitted to arrogate to himself a
supremacy over doctrine and discipline alike? Was the Church to
be subjected, as the State had been, to a 'rule of secretaries'? The
experience of Karl's reign had shown that it was no longer possible,
as it had been possible in the time of Gustav Vasa, for the King to
impose his will on the nation in matters of religion without serious
resistance. The complexion of affairs had changed with the Uppsala
meeting of 1593. The Church had become a truly national and
popular institution: religion had become the concern not only of
the Estate of the Clergy but of the lay Estates too. The constitutional resistance to absolutism, which in the political field had been
led by nobles such as Erik Sparre and the Bielkes, had as its counter-
part in the religious field the opposition to the Crown of a new
generation of able and resolute bishops. And as Oxenstierna in
1611 represented the demand for a check on the Crown's abuse of
political power, so men like Kenicius, Paulinus and Rudbeckius
emerged as the champions of the Church against the encroachments
of the lay authority. In the religious as in the political sphere the
feeling was general that the nation could not tolerate another such
reign as that of Karl IX. There must be an end to the unseemly
wrangles between the sovereign and the Church. The new King
must work in harmony with his bishops; a *modus vivendi* must be
sought on vexed questions; the frontiers of lay and spiritual authority
must be drawn with a proper clarity; above all, the King must
conform to the doctrinal standpoint of his subjects. If these conditions were not fulfilled, there could be little hope of national solidarity
in the face of the danger from without.

(ii) *The Charter and the Church Ordinance*

A settlement with the Church was therefore among the tasks
which Gustav Adolf on his accession could not avoid. And the
clergy had certainly no intention of neglecting their opportunity.
At the Nyköping *riksdag* of December 1611 they were present in
force, and it was a thoroughly representative body which collaborated
in extracting the Charter from the King. They could count on the
sympathy of the other Estates; for both Nobles and Burghers
included in their demands upon the Crown a request that the

country's religion be firmly based upon the Confession of Augsburg. Nevertheless, the Charter, as far as it concerned the Church, did not represent as complete a victory as might have been expected. On the contrary, it was in many important respects in the nature of a compromise.

This emerges very clearly, for instance, in the matter of the definition of doctrine. In the project for a Charter laid before the King by the *råd* and Estates, Gustav Adolf was required to assent not only to the Confession of Augsburg, and to the decisions of the Uppsala Meeting of 1593, but also to the *Liber Concordiae*, the sheet-anchor of gnesio-orthodox Lutheranism. It is true that it was suggested that acceptance of the *Liber Concordiae* might be deferred until the King's coronation, if it were 'not convenient' to press the matter at this stage. But in the Charter it was not mentioned at all. Gustav Adolf promised to maintain and protect 'God's pure and unambiguous Word, and the true and right practice of the Holy Sacraments, as founded upon sacred, prophetic and apostolic Scriptures, and on the unaltered Augsburg Confession ... and afterwards ... accepted and resolved in the Uppsala *concilio*, *anno* 93'. He refused, therefore, to commit himself to the gnesio-orthodox position. On the other hand, he went further than his father had ever done, in accepting the resolutions of 1593 without reservation. So too on the question of toleration. Oxenstierna's draft had been liberal enough: non-Lutherans were to be under the protection of the law, and not to be molested provided they behaved themselves, though they were not to be employed in any official post. The project of the *råd* and Estates is much more intolerant: heretics and sectaries are to be denied private as well as public worship, and they are not to be permitted to '*byggia och boo*' (build and dwell) within the kingdom. But the Charter, while fully accepting the demand that no heretic or sectary be employed in the public service, omits the clause forbidding them to 'build and dwell'; and instead inserts provisions for the toleration of foreigners who may be settled in Sweden for purposes of trade. These provisions are defended, partly on grounds of economic necessity, and partly because 'no sovereign has the power to rule and control a man's conscience'. The amendment was the work of Johan Skytte and Michil Olofsson, and reflects both the religious standpoint of Karl IX and the tradition of tolerance from the earlier years of the Swedish Reformation.

In the matter of Church government, the Charter on the whole recurred to the Church Ordinance of 1571, which was once again accepted as a fundamental basis of the Swedish Church. Thus it was provided that bishops should be elected as laid down in the Ordinance—a provision which in fact restored to the Chapters the power of choice. The Chapters themselves were now safeguarded against the Crown's hostility: after 1611 they were in no danger of being abolished. As to the control of presentation to livings, it was agreed that candidates were to be presented by congregations to the bishop for his approval, and that for non-regalian benefices no confirmation by the King should be required. For regalian benefices, on the other hand, the choice was recognized as being a matter for arrangement between King and congregation. Some attempt had been made by the clergy to limit the number of regalian benefices to three for each diocese; but the only trace of it in the text of the Charter is to be found in the provision that when the Church Ordinance should be revised the regalian benefices would be specified by name. As to the claims of the nobility, the Charter itself does no more than safeguard their *jus patronatus* (which indeed the Church had never seriously contested); but the position was a good deal compromised by the grant of privileges to the nobility which followed on 10 January 1612, for there the extreme claims of the nobility to interfere in appointments were in fact conceded, since it was laid down that they could exercise the right of patronage for any parish in which they effectively resided, the bishop being entitled to interfere only if two or more noblemen, resident in the same parish, were unable to agree upon a candidate.

For the rest, the Charter provided that no priest was to be tried and punished, and still less deprived of his cure, unless his case had been in the first instance investigated by the bishop and Chapter. In regard to the provision of a proper disciplinary instance for dealing with charges against bishops, the Charter was less definite, and merely referred to the unsatisfactory precedent of 1571; and in reality no adequate solution of this problem was offered. But it was sufficiently plain, from the clause about criminous clerks, that there was to be an end of the high-handed methods of the preceding reign.[1]

And this is true of all those clauses of the Charter which concern the Church. Karl IX and his methods are everywhere implicitly

[1] For the Charter, and the negotiations that preceded it, see *SRDA*, I. 48-77.

condemned; the Church everywhere reasserts its independence within the State. The Clergy, no doubt, would have liked a special grant of privileges such as was given to the Nobility[1]; they had still plenty of small grievances which required redress; but, on the whole, the Charter gave them the guarantees they desired. As to doctrine, Gustav Adolf had certainly balked at the *Liber Concordiae*, but on the other hand he had freely accepted the Uppsala resolutions of 1593; and there was no reason to fear that the small concession to the principle of toleration, as concerned foreigners, implied any real danger: the predominance of Axel Oxenstierna gave security enough for the present. Karl's attempt at ecclesiastical absolutism, at control of the Church through the Chancery,[2] had certainly been defeated; and the bishops might hope that the revision of the Church Ordinance, to which the King was now committed, might make their victory still more explicit. The influence and position of the Chapters had been safeguarded, and they had even been strengthened by the provision which permitted every cathedral to employ an *oeconomus (syssloman)* who should also be a priest and take duty in the cathedral. In the matter of presentation to livings, Church and nobles had vanquished the monarchy; though it is important to note that in all cases the rights of the congregations were safeguarded. In short, though the extreme Lutheran zealots might be disappointed, moderate churchmen could sleep more soundly than at any time since 1593. In the religious as in the political sphere a sharp rebuke had been administered to the monarch; and a basis had been provided, by the pruning away of dangerous extensions of the royal power, for a healthier collaboration between King and subjects.

And such collaboration did in fact take place. In the years after 1611 experience proved that in one or two small points the Charter required to be modified in practice: thus the bishops found it wise to seek royal confirmation for presentations to non-regalian benefices, so that at need the secular authority might reinforce the spiritual—a precaution especially necessary in turbulent Finland[3]; the method of electing bishops seems to have varied considerably[4]; Calvinist

---

[1] *SRDA*, I. 31. [2] *SRDA*, I. 67.

[3] H. Cnattingius, *Den centrala kyrkostyrelsen i Sverige 1611-1636*, pp. 99-102. The position, however, seems to have been somewhat confused: see Anjou, pp. 193-6. *SRDA*, II. 47, for an example of the dissatisfaction of the clergy with the system of presentation to benefices; J. E. Waaranen, *Samling af urkunder rörande Finlands historia*, IV. 33-4, for an example of the safeguarding of the rights of the congregation.

[4] Compare Hallenberg, I. 410, with IV. 640.

services were occasionally connived at; and the restriction of public offices to Lutherans was conspicuously ignored in the person of the King's brother-in-law, John Casimir. In some dioceses (*e.g.* Västerås) the bishop compelled his clergy to subscribe to the *Liber Concordiae*; in others, no such demand was made.[1] But, on the whole, the settlement of 1612 subsisted without undue friction. Church and State recovered confidence in one another, and worked together instead of in opposition.

There remained, however, two controversial matters from the previous reign which the Charter did not succeed in settling. One was the demand for an amended Service Book (*Handbok*); the other, the demand for a revision of the Church Ordinance of 1571. The question of the Service Book was soon disposed of. It had already been revised in 1608, at Karl's order; but the bishops had at that time had so little confidence that the new version would be acceptable to the King that they had not troubled to hand over their suggestions to him. At the opening of the new reign they had asked that Gustav Adolf should approve this draft of 1608; but the King not unnaturally refused to bind himself to the authorization of a version which he had not seen. Upon investigation, however, it was found to be unobjectionable; and in 1613 leave was given to print it. It appeared in the following year, and remained in force until 1693.

It was not to prove so easy to come to an agreement about the Church Ordinance. When Archbishop Laurentius Petri drew up the Church Ordinance in 1571, he had himself recognized the possibility that it might be found in the light of experience to be less than adequate in all points, and that subsequent additions might have to be made to it.[2] But no one seems to have felt that any *alteration* in the version of 1571 was required; all that was needed was that it should be *completed*: even Johan III's *Nova Ordinantia* was regarded by its authors in this light. The Church Ordinance, in fact, quickly came to be considered as one of the fundamental documents of the Swedish Church; and the Uppsala Meeting of 1593 confirmed it in that position. Throughout Karl IX's reign the question of revision came intermittently under discussion, until in 1608 the bishops, under pressure from the King, produced a Draft

---

[1] G. Westin, *Negotiations about Church Unity*, p. 57 *note 23*.
[2] For what follows, see Kjöllerström, *Kyrkolagsproblemet*, pp. 28-89; Holmquist, *Sv. Kyrkans Hist.*, IV. 1. 176-82; Cnattingius, *op. cit.*, p. 278 *seqq.*; O. Holmdahl, *Studier öfver prästeståndets kyrkopolitik*, I. 137 *seqq.*

Ordinance. This was in many respects a hierarchical counterblast to the ecclesiastical policy of Karl, and could never have been approved by him. In the event, it was not even submitted for his consideration, but lay dormant until the opening of the new reign. One of the points in the Charter to which the Church attached most importance was Gustav Adolf's promise that this Draft should now be printed. But in the sequel, the King neglected to implement that promise. The Clergy declined to submit their Draft to him before publication, fearing, perhaps, a renewal of the squabbles of the previous reign; and Gustav Adolf on his side was not prepared to sanction its publication until he had seen it. When at the *riksdag* of 1614 he was asked to have it printed without delay, he simply replied that he must first be provided with a copy; and a similar request at the coronation *riksdag* three years later elicited the same answer: at the same time a renewed attempt by the Clergy to obtain a grant of privileges was also rejected. It was not until 1619 that the bishops made up their minds to hand over the Draft to the King; in the hope, undoubtedly, that he would not merely acquiesce in its publication but also grant them the privileges which they had failed to obtain two years earlier. The Draft of 1619 represents an improved version of that of 1608[1]: the bishops had been polishing it assiduously in the interim. But to the consternation of the clergy, the King made no move to proceed to its publication. The Draft vanished into the royal pocket, and showed no signs of emerging; and despite the efforts of the bishops to pin him down, Gustav Adolf slipped off to Riga without having taken any action in the matter. Instead, he produced various plans of his own for educational and ecclesiastical reform, the most important being for the setting up of a *consistorium generale*—one of whose functions, it appeared, was to be the examination and possible modification of the Draft Ordinance.[2]

By 1625, however, it had become plain that the King had no hope of obtaining the assent of the clergy to his plan for a *consistorium generale*; and the bishops accordingly brought forward a third version of the Draft Ordinance, which they presented to Gustav Adolf in 1626. This time it seemed that something would be done; for the King promised that he would confirm and sanction

---

[1] It is an enormous document, running to over 200 pages, and may be found in *Kyrko-ordningar och förslag därtill före 1686*, I. 355-561.
[2] For his educational plans, see below, p. 449 *seqq*. For the *consistorium generale*, see below, p. 405 *seqq*.

the Draft without delay. But for some reason this promise, like that of 1612, was never carried out; and the reign closed with the position precisely as it had been in 1611. The Draft of 1626, however, though it was not legally valid, seems to have been regarded by the Church as more or less in force; and it remained the basis for further discussion of the problem.

The history of the failure to secure the acceptance of the Drafts of 1608, 1619 and 1626 sheds some light on the attitude of the King and his Chancellor to Church affairs. Oxenstierna was well fitted by interest and training to act as intermediary between King and bishops. His mother had destined him for the Church; he was accounted no mean theologian; he would have made a capital bishop, and once at least it was rumoured that a bishopric was to be conferred on him.[1] In short, as a contemporary is said to have remarked of him, he was 'sacerdos sed sine sacerdotio'. He had many friends among the clergy, and a whole volume of his correspondence comes from clerical or academic sources. He was, in fact, a man in whom the leaders of the Church could feel real confidence. But, friendly as he was to the cause of religion, and willing as he showed himself to serve the Church, he had his own ideas and policies, and they were not always such as the bishops could approve. He was, after all, the King's minister; and it was the government's policy, not the Church's, to which he was committed. He had opposed the encroachments of the royal power under Karl IX; but that was no reason in his view for countenancing episcopal aggression under Gustav Adolf—and still less under the Regency. Nor was he blind to the latent antagonism between Church and nobility, which, partially obscured in Gustav Adolf's time, became open and avowed under Kristina; and he shared too fully in the natural sympathies of his order not to oppose the bishops on this issue. For over-mighty bishops, indeed, he had as little liking as for over-mighty Kings; and in this, as in much else, he was the true successor of the generation of Erik Sparre.[2]

Gustav Adolf had inherited all his father's impatience of opposition and inability to suffer fools gladly; but he had his temper under better control. He was more regardful of his dignity, both as a man and as a sovereign. He had no wish to quarrel with his bishops,

[1] *Peder Galts Depescher*, p. 42.
[2] For Oxenstierna and the Church, see Ahnlund, *Oxenstierna*, pp. 370-8; *id.*, *Storhetstidens gryning*, pp. 38-76; Tham, *Axel Oxenstierna*, pp. 45-91.

and he perceived the wisdom of keeping on good terms with them. He had, moreover, more of the traditional Swedish respect for law than Karl had ever had; and he was better able to combine the idea of royal Supremacy with that of national consent. Upon the sincerity of his devotion to the cause of religion, upon the depth and genuineness of his personal piety, the Church could always rely; though indeed (to be just) this last had been equally true of Karl IX. But Gustav Adolf on one famous occasion suffered himself to be rebuked for immorality by his chaplain, Rudbeckius, and was magnanimous enough to give him quick preferment to the see of Västerås.[1] He had been educated, under Skytte's direction, in a broader churchmanship than was usual in Sweden at that time (his reading included even Thomas à Kempis); and doctrinally the distance that separated him from his father was not, perhaps, very great.[2] Throughout his adult life he showed a tolerance of religious dissent—provided it had no dangerous political implications—which was at that time unusual, and which, at the close of his career, expanded to include even the Roman Catholics of conquered Germany. His open, enlightened and candid spirit was singularly immune to the grosser superstitions; and in this he contrasted favourably with many of the more rigidly orthodox of his clergy. There was little or nothing in his religion of the rigour, the narrowness, the disputatiousness, the lack of charity, which were the besetting sins of the stricter Lutherans. He was, no doubt, a competent theologian, as his father had been before him; but he was the last man to sacrifice spiritual values to the fine-drawn ecstasies of theological polemic. Yet it never occurred to anyone to impugn the soundness of his Lutheran orthodoxy. Had it been otherwise, he could never have permitted himself to indulge his *penchant* for toleration, and still less to dabble in those oecumenical and eirenical projects which interested him towards the end of his life. The court-chaplains whom he chose for himself were of the severest orthodoxy; and he habitually showed them so much deference that at least one foreign observer was misled into concluding that the King was under the thumb of his clergy.[3]

[1] For Rudbeckius' sermon on this occasion, see B. R. Hall, *Till Johannis Rudbeckii karakteristik*, pp. 5-9.

[2] At his coronation in 1617 Gustav Adolf wished to insert into the oath the very generally phrased formula used by Karl; but the Estates insisted upon an explicit adherence to the Confession of Augsburg; and the King yielded to show that 'he means his religion in all seriousness': Holmquist, *Sv. Kyrkans Hist.*, IV. 1. 142.   [3] Westin, *Negotiations*, p. 134.

Gustav Adolf's views on the proper relations between the civil and the ecclesiastical powers were very much in the spirit of Luther. He did not conceive Church and State as coequal Orders set over against one another, nor yet as twin facets of a single body; he considered the Church rather as a body within the State, and resting upon its support: some of his bishops undoubtedly held the converse of this proposition. The sphere of the Church's activity was for him, as for Luther, the spiritual lives of the subjects, its duty the administration of the sacrament and the exhortation of the people: in so far as it concerned itself with matters temporal— for instance, matrimonial causes, divorce, the punishment of sinners —it did so in virtue of powers derived from the prince, whose duty it was to see to it that such matters were taken care of as might be most convenient and efficacious. With these things, as with the internal order and discipline of the Church, the State would not normally interfere; but it could by no means stand passively by, if it should appear that its aid had become necessary. Such matters (to employ the terminology of Pareus, then becoming current) were *external*, as contrasted with the strictly spiritual and dogmatic aspects, which were *internal*.[1] This distinction, and the practice which Gustav Adolf pursued, was to prove adequate in ordinary circumstances to secure a comfortable, empirical solution of most of the issues between Church and State; but it was obvious that between the two spheres lay a debatable ground over which dispute was more than possible. The question of a *consistorium generale*, for instance, provoked a conflict with the episcopate which, under a less trusted and popular ruler, might have resulted in a serious crisis.

Gustav Adolf, in fact, was as little disposed as ever his father had been to abridge what he considered to be his rights. He had no idea of diluting the royal Supremacy in order to conciliate his episcopate. Again and again he showed himself determined to follow his own line, irrespective of the susceptibilities of his bishops. And so, conspicuously, in this matter of the Church Ordinance. His failure to promulgate the Draft of 1626 may possibly have depended, as in so many other similar instances in the constituional field, upon lack of time and military preoccupations; but it is more likely to have proceeded from a constitutional preference for not

---

[1] H. Lundin, *Joannes Baazius' kyrkliga reformprogram*, pp. 96-102, etc. But see too H. Cnattingius, *Johannes Rudbeckius och hans europeiska bakgrund*, Chapter II, especially pp. 49-57.

tying his hands unnecessarily by precise written formulae, and above all from a dislike of the excessive pretensions of the bishops. The Drafts of 1619 and 1626 both show a distinct tendency to enhance the episcopal power at the expense of possible competitors, and that of 1619 included the acknowledgment of the *Liber Concordiae*, which the King had already refused in 1612.

But by 1626 Gustav Adolf had already won for himself, both in Europe and at home, a position of unassailable prestige as the most hopeful champion of the Protestant cause; and much of the strength of his position *vis-à-vis* the Church derived from this fact. Like Karl IX, he aspired to unite Protestant Christendom against the 'dark forces' of Rome; but unlike him he seems to have been animated by the consciousness of a Mission. He appears not to have doubted that the conduct of the fight against advancing Catholicism was the work which had been given him to do. This feeling, by a natural extension, was transferred from the King to his country; and Sweden became not merely a Fatherland to be served and defended but an instrument of Divine Providence. As the rough breakers of the popish flood spread over Germany, the rhetoric of the pulpit acquired an actuality which made it natural and proper to apply to Sweden the imagery and prophecies of the Old Testament. With far more justification than in Cromwellian England, men saw their political enemies as in very truth Midianites to be smitten with the sword of the Lord and of Gideon; and the Lion of the North assumed the lineaments of the Lion of Judah. And hence the Swedes, when they emerged upon the historic scene, appeared not only as a nation of resurgent Goths but as the godly heritors of Israel.[1]

(iii) *Lutheran Orthodoxy and its Adversaries*

The danger from Catholicism did nothing to affect the attitude of the Swedish Church to the Calvinist wing of the Evangelical army. For the abominable heresies of the Reformed brethren there could be no excuse, no palliation; and Swedes subscribed very

---

[1] Holmquist (*Sv. Kyrkans Hist.*, IV. 1. 273-4) quotes Isak Rothovius: 'The kingdom of Sweden is not less blessed of God than were the Jews aforetime; for God of His mere grace hath taken us out of darkness and the shadow of death, and given us the knowledge of blessedness to the remission of sins. . . . Is not our dear fatherland of Sweden rich in every blessing of God, on the earth, in the waters, and under the earth?' Compare Rudbeckius' views: Hall, *Den kyrkliga folkuppfostran i Joh. Rudbeckius' stift*, p. 118.

generally to the current Lutheran dictum 'better a Papist than a Calvinist'. They found it difficult, however, to maintain this attitude inflexibly. The exigencies of foreign politics drove Sweden into dealings with Calvinist princes in Germany; while the economic necessities of the country forced men to a grudging connivance at home. The Netherlanders who settled in Sweden for trade or manufacture were often of the Reformed persuasion; and it proved in practice impolitic to interfere with them if they chose to celebrate their services according to their own rite. Men like Abraham Cabeliau or Louis de Geer—the latter a man of great piety—were too useful to the kingdom, and stood too well with the King, for the law to be applied against them. There was a strong Walloon Church in Stockholm; while in Göteborg (a predominantly Dutch town) there was a congregation of Arminian exiles which it was found expedient to place to some extent under the official supervision of the Superintendent of Göteborg.[1] The King's attitude was that he was not prepared to tolerate any congregational worship, either in public or in private, by non-Lutheran religious bodies; but there was no active persecution, and—with Arminians, at all events—his hope was that they might be brought to an orthodox Lutheran position 'more by allurements and good persuasions than by cursing and railing'.[2] And when in 1627 the King invited by proclamation all persecuted German Protestants to seek refuge in Sweden, it was difficult to compromise his hospitality by religious persecution. From time to time the zealots complained[3]; but their complaints were rarely followed by effective action, and the Church had to confine the expression of its indignation to such matters as the relegating of Calvinists to the less honourable burying-places in the churchyards, and the refusal to permit Lutheran ministers to officiate at Calvinist funerals.[4]

---

[1] The Superintendent was imported by Gustav Vasa from Germany to supplement or replace the episcopate. Superintendents were essentially the local agents of the royal Supremacy. They derived their authority not from the ceremony of consecration but from appointment at the hands of the King. They exercised quasi-episcopal functions, and could by special permission even ordain priests; but they remained vicars to whom special rights of inspection and discipline had been entrusted. Many of the old dioceses were subdivided into superintendencies of more convenient dimensions; and bishops and superintendents continued to exist side by side: it was not until 1772 that the distinction between them was obliterated.

[2] H. Almquist, *Göteborgs Historia*, I. 290-9; Anjou, p. 181.

[3] *AOSB*, II. XII. 235; *RRP*, I. 115, 117; but contrast *AOSB*, II. IX. 693.

[4] At Strängnäs in 1623 the three Mälar bishops were asked to give a ruling on the question of burying Calvinists who might be permitted to live in the country

The enforced relaxation of the ban upon Calvinists did not, however, do anything to alter the essential attitude of the Church. This may be seen clearly from the determined resistance of the majority of its leaders to any attempt at reconciliation; and more particularly to the efforts of John Durie. Durie was a Scottish Presbyterian who became minister to the English colony at Elbing, and there came into contact with the Swedes through James Spens in 1627. Durie was an enthusiast for the reunion of the Protestant Churches. His mind had been influenced by David Pareus of Heidelberg, who in 1615 had published an *Irenicum* which had earned the sharp censure of the mild Archbishop Kenicius.[1] The aim of Pareus had been a general synod of the Lutheran and Reformed Churches, under the joint patronage of Kristian IV and James I—a project stigmatized by a leading German Lutheran as 'a product of hell and an abominable syncretism'. Durie revived Pareus' scheme, and tried to persuade the Lutheran Churches to distinguish between fundamental dogmas (on which all Protestants agreed) and non-fundamental dogmas (on which the Churches might surely agree to differ). He memorialized Gustav Adolf on the subject as early as 1628, and pursued him intermittently thereafter until the King's death, when he transferred his attention to Axel Oxenstierna. He found an ally in Sir Thomas Roe, and both of them succeeded in arousing a certain interest for the scheme in the English episcopate, and notably in Abbot, Laud and Williams. Roe was interested in the project because it chimed in with his desire for a more actively Protestant foreign policy on the part of Charles I; and Oxenstierna's interest was probably mainly political also. To Gustav Adolf, on the other hand, Durie's plan must have appealed on religious grounds. It was typically 'philippist', and very much in the spirit of Karl IX. It accorded well with Gustav Adolf's own position. And he could not but react favourably to Durie's suggestion that 'the Magistrates of both sides should inhibit railing disputes in the Pulpit, and put down names of partiality'. But the King was too busily engaged with the affairs of Germany to be able to give his undivided attention to Durie, who

---

for economic or military reasons. They answered that if such persons kept quiet the Church might stretch a point, and even officiate at the funeral on certain conditions; but they could do nothing in the case of 'Dogmatists', who despise our religion': such persons were worthy only 'sepultura Asini': P. E. Thyselius, *Bidrag till svenska kyrkans och läroverkens historia utur Archiver*, p. 88.

[1] *AOSB*, II. xii. 17-18.

was accordingly referred to the court-chaplains. In one of them—Johannes Matthiae Gothus—he soon recognized a kindred spirit; but the sympathy of Matthiae only threw into stronger relief the uncompromising hostility of the orthodox Lutherans, represented by the formidable Court-Chaplain Bothvidi. The negotiations thus opened dragged on until 1638, and Durie paid a prolonged visit to Sweden in order to argue the matter with the Uppsala theologians; but he made no real impression. The truth was that neither side was yet prepared to forgo the satisfaction of 'railing' at the other. And whatever might be the personal predilections of Gustav Adolf, or the political calculations of Oxenstierna, they were both unwilling to risk a quarrel with the Swedish Church by enforcing eirenical policies which were repugnant to the vast majority.[1]

As regards the Calvinists, therefore, religious conviction and political advantage were in sharp opposition. As regards the Roman Catholics, they were obviously in accord. Catholicism was indeed by this time almost exclusively a political danger: unless popery were re-established by violence from without, it had no hope of preserving even the simulacrum of life in Sweden. There was infinitely less Catholicism in the Sweden of Gustav Adolf than, for instance, in the England of James I.[2] Nevertheless, when this has been admitted, it remains true that survivals of custom and nomenclature from pre-Reformation days were not very uncommon, and an occasional Catholic fell sometimes into the net of authority. Habit or superstition preserved, here and there, the cult of local saints, just as the last shrines of paganism had persisted into the Christian era. Thus at Flistad in Östergötland the cult of St. Staffan maintained itself; while from all over Uppland, and far beyond it, men came to cast their wooden crosses into the holy water of Svinnegarn well; and neither Church nor State ventured to interfere.[3] Something very like the old fee to the priest for Masses for the souls of the dead persisted in Lappland until the nineteenth century.[4] No one apparently felt any incongruity when

---

[1] For Durie, see G. Westin, *Negotiations about Church Unity*, and *John Durie in Sweden, passim*: the same author's *Svenska kyrkan och de protestantiska enhetssträvandena under 1630-talet* is also useful; G. H. Turnbull, *Hartlib, Dury and Comenius*, p. 127 seqq.; J. M. Batten, *John Dury*, pp. 13-77. For Matthiae, see Holmquist, *Johannes Matthiae Gothus*, pp. 97-105, 161.

[2] See the illuminating comments of Gabriel Gustafsson Oxenstierna on his visit to England in 1625: *AOSB*, II. III. 87.

[3] Ahnlund, *Svensk Sägen och Hävd*, pp. 37, 78.

[4] *Journal av Petrus Laestadius*, I. 171-2.

in 1626 the master of a poor-house was casually referred to as the
'abbot'.[1] In Finland, priests toured their parishes, collecting the
population for confession; and on these occasions they not merely
took fees from their parishioners but participated in a kind of
'Church-ale' which was obnoxious not only on doctrinal but also
upon moral grounds.[2] As late as 1659 Samuel Enander, the then
Bishop of Linköping, found it necessary to forbid the worshipping
of images, whether of the Blessed Virgin or not, and to prohibit the
adorning of such images with clothes or crowns of straw.[3] On the
contemporary stage, one character could adjure another to make the
sign of the Cross without apparently exciting the disapproval of the
audience.[4] But, indeed, Swedish Lutheranism preserved far more
of the ceremonies and external trappings of the old Church than the
straiter sort of Protestant could approve. The Church Ordinance
of 1571 had adopted a very tolerant attitude towards paintings and
images in church, and even in the 'nineties there had been no great
destruction of such things. The *Handbok* of 1614 permitted the
sign of the Cross in baptism; and it was in fact used in the dioceses
of Västerås and Strängnäs throughout the reign. So too with
exorcism at baptism. The use of surplices and other vestments,
and of round wafers; the practice of choral funerals; the retention
of the ringing of bells for liturgical purposes; and even the observance of some of the old festivals of the Church (such as that of the
conversion of St. Paul) as public holidays—these were all features of
Swedish Lutheranism in Gustav Adolf's time, though not all of them
were universal.[5] A *Liber Cantus* for the Latin Mass appeared in
1620 and again in 1623; and there is no doubt that it was widely
used.[6] In view of all this, it is hardly to be wondered at that the
austere Puritanism of Whitelocke should have been scandalized by
what he saw at Skara in 1653:

In the choir [*sc.* of Skara Cathedral] are many pictures of saints and

[1] L. Levander, *Fattigt Folk och Tiggare*, p. 169.
[2] J. Cederlöf, *Det finländska prästerskapets ekonomiska ställning i ntill sjuttonde
seklet*, pp. 189-200.
[3] O. Hassler, *Linköpings stift under Biskop Samuel Enander*, p. 134.
[4] J. Rondeletius, *Judas Redivivus*, p. 11.
[5] *Svenska Synodalakter*, I. 28; Hall, *Kyrkliga och kulturella interiörer* (1916),
p. 256 (henceforward cited as Hall, *KKI*); E. Rodhe, *Svenskt Gudstjänstliv*,
p. 251 (for the cross in baptism); Anjou, pp. 209, 234, 300); Herdin, *Uppsala på
1600-talet*, III. 198 (for funerals); M. Åmark, *Kyrkklockor, Klockare och Klocksägner*, pp. 71-6 (for bells); *SRDA*, II. 38 (for observing the conversion of St.
Paul as a holiday). Other examples in Ahnlund, *Från Medeltid och Vasatid*,
pp. 67, 103.
[6] T. Norlind, *Från tyska kyrkans glansdagar*, II. 26.

other images; and at the east end of it a high altar, with a rich carpet of velvet embroidered with gold, and a stately crucifix upon it: there are also divers other and lesser crucifixes in several places of the church and choir. In the vestry he saw the chalices and pyxes, with pieces of the wafers in them; and none could see a difference betwixt this and the Papists' churches.[1]

Despite this state of affairs, Sweden had less to fear from crypto-Catholics than from crypto-Calvinists—provided she were left to herself. But it was unhappily inherent in the political situation that she should not be left to herself. The dynastic quarrel with Poland, and the religious war in Germany, had as a necessary consequence the endeavour by Sweden's enemies to subvert the established order by the introduction of Roman Catholic agents, who conceived it to be the highest patriotism to work for the recovery of their country for the old faith. The situation was thus strictly comparable with that of England in the latter part of the reign of Elizabeth. The danger from Catholicism came really from outside: from the exiled partisans of Sigismund, and from the young and impressionable students who, leaving Sweden to make the tour of the German universities, fell into their clutches, and returned home animated with the zeal of the convert. It was by these means that the tragedy of Messenius was prepared; it was by these means that the Lutheranism of Erik Niurenius was subverted; it was such agents that lay behind the conspiracy of Bähr and Anthelius in 1624. Such attempts, in the existing circumstances, fell plainly into the category of treason; and there could be but one opinion upon the need for drastic measures. The Ordinance of Örebro in 1617, therefore, was less a measure of religious persecution than an act of self-defence; and it is noteworthy that the death penalty was imposed only for the purely political offences: for lapsing to Roman Catholicism the culprit was to suffer only deprivation of all civil rights. And it should not be forgotten that the efforts of the Estate of the Clergy at the Örebro *riksdag* were all in the direction of moderation. The Lutheran Church might be narrow and intolerant, but no man suffered death merely for the sake of his religion.

This did not preclude considerable severity against those whose religious opinions were especially obnoxious, or seemed to threaten social upheaval. 'Enthusiasts' (*svärmare*), for instance, who

---

[1] B. Whitelocke, *Journal of the Swedish Embassy*, I. 187-8; and *cf. ibid.*, I. 161-2.

propagated quasi-Anabaptist doctrines subversive of the social order, would soon find themselves condemned to fine and penance, or deported to their native Germany.[1] Atheists, 'prophets', warlocks and other doubtful characters would do well to keep out of the way of an energetic prelate such as Rudbeckius. Yet it so happened that it was Rudbeckius' diocese of Västerås, more than any other part of Sweden, which was vexed by the odd aberrations of a kind of Judaistic heresy, whose professors observed Saturday as the Sabbath and denied the historicity of Christ. Religious movements of this sort had appeared in the time of Gustav Vasa, and in Gustav Adolf's reign they were not very uncommon in the provinces of central Sweden. In at least one instance the Judaizers stirred up dangerous agitations among the peasantry; and at this point it was felt that it was time for the secular arm to intervene. The ringleader, a certain Per på Hyttan, was arrested, tried and executed, and there was an end to Judaism in Västerås for that time.[2]

The Treaty of Stolbova brought into the Swedish state for the first time an appreciable number of subjects professing the Greek Orthodox religion, and thus made necessary a decision upon the question as to whether they should be compelled to conformity or no. The situation had been foreseen before the conclusion of peace; and Gustav Adolf seems to have made up his mind from the beginning that there was to be no attempt at constraint. In 1615, for instance, he was explaining to his prospective Orthodox subjects that 'faith and religion are things which cannot be enforced by violence'. A new Lutheran bishopric was indeed established at Viborg in 1618, and Lutheran colonists from Savolax soon settled in the new Karelian province; but the Russians were allowed to keep their religion undisturbed. Monks were permitted to leave the ceded area—a permission of which they availed themselves *en masse*; but it was stipulated that the Greek Orthodox parish priests must remain, lest the peasants decamp over the frontier in search of religious ministrations. None the less, the Swedish government found difficulty in ensuring a supply of priests who should be both politically reliable and (from the point of view of their flocks)

---

[1] *RRP*, II. 16. Or, in extreme cases, executed, as happened to Jon Olofsson in 1619: Anjou, pp. 352-3. The authorities looked with especial disfavour on Rosicrucians: see, *e.g.*, Hall, *KKI* (1915), p. 358; Ahnlund, *Vem var 'Duken'?*
[2] See H. Valentin, *Judarnes Historia i Sverige*, pp. 29-38, for this movement. Judaistic notions were still current among the Finnish settlers in Dalarna when Linnaeus visited the area in 1734: Linné, *Ungdomsresor*, II. 46.

regularly ordained; and by 1625 the number had so diminished
that there was even talk of obtaining in Constantinople the consecration of a special Orthodox Bishop for Ingria. Nothing came
of this, however; and the government was really more interested in
the possibility of conversions to Lutheranism. As long as Gustav
Adolf lived, very little progress in this direction could be constated,
largely owing to the deplorable quality of the Lutheran clergy who
were sent to the province, and to the great age and greater
inefficiency of the first three bishops of Viborg. Indeed, the
tendency seems rather the other way, if we may judge from the fact
that in February 1630 Johan Skytte, as Governor-General, was
empowered to punish conversion from Lutheranism to Orthodoxy
by death. It was not until the later 'thirties that the protestantizing
of the country made much headway. Nevertheless, the setting up
of a Russian printing-press in Stockholm, and the translation into
Russian of Luther's Lesser Catechism, were not without effect.
The Russian government took special precautions to prevent the
infiltration of Lutheran notions; but in spite of its efforts the Catechism penetrated to Moscow, and made a few converts. It was as a
result of this danger from heresy that the Muscovite government
began to seclude its foreign residents in special self-contained
suburbs.[1]

At first the Swedish theologians had been genuinely uncertain
whether the Russians were to be accounted Christians or no: in
1614 Kenicius was unable to decide whether a little Russian boy
might be baptized, since he could not say whether Russian baptism
(which had already been administered) was to be counted as valid.[2]
But in 1620 Bothvidi published an enquiry entitled *Utrum
Muschovitae sint Christiani?*—a question to which he was able to
give an affirmative answer. This was just as well; for in the last
year of his life Gustav Adolf was actually toying with the idea of a
Union with the Greek Church. It happened that Kyrillos Lukaris,
the Patriarch of Constantinople, had fallen under the influence of
the resident Dutch agent, Cornelis Haga, who expounded Calvinism
to him, and encouraged his fear of Roman Catholic influence among
the Greek clergy—a fear which was no doubt prompted by the growth

---

[1] For the religious problems of Ingria, see C. Öhlander, *Om den svenska kyrkoreformationen uti Ingermanland*, pp. 4-22; for the Russian reaction, P. Miliukov
Outlines of Russian Culture: Religion and the Church, pp. 12, 81-4; for the printing-
press, *Handlingar rörande finska kyrkan och prästerskapet*, I. 475.
[2] *Synodalakter*, I. 29.

of the Uniate Church in the Ukraine. Sir Thomas Roe, who was British agent with the Porte from 1621 to 1628, seconded Haga's efforts. And in due time Paul Strassburg, Gustav Adolf's ambassador to Transylvania, who was in touch with Haga in 1631, conceived the idea of the union of the two Churches. The notion was not quite so fantastic as it seemed; for Lukaris knew the Baltic, having in earlier years been Rector of a school at Vilna, and he had followed with sympathy and interest Gustav Adolf's victorious career. He had come to the conclusion that the King of Sweden was the divinely appointed saviour of Christianity, and he was very ready to listen to Strassburg's suggestions. In 1632, therefore, he and Strassburg opened conversations, which proved so promising that they were continued even after Gustav Adolf's death. The removal of the King, however, had destroyed the best hope for their success; in 1635 the Turkish government, growing suspicious, threw Lukaris into prison; and with that this curious episode comes to an end.[1]

It was not only with false doctrine, heresy and schism that the leaders of Gustav Adolf's Church were called upon to do battle. Behind and below the official Protestantism of the country there still survived considerable remnants of the paganism of an earlier age. In out-of-the-way districts Odin is said to have been worshipped as late as the close of the sixteenth century; and at the beginning of the eighteenth a young girl informed her accusers that the name of the devil who had welcomed her at a Witches' Sabbath was *Frö*—the fertility god of the old Nordic Pantheon. The housesnake could still rely on its daily portion of milk, and was encouraged to sleep in the cradles of infants; the midsummer rites at St. Ingemo's Well—despite the cross over the well-head—had an obviously pagan character; in conjurations and spells the names of Jesus and Thor might be heard in curious proximity: in short, paganism was not far below the surface, and the old gods lived on in the new demonology. Anything like a real pagan cult was of course as extinct as the Vikings, but as an accessory to or ingredient in the practice of superstition it could still vex the godly. Roman Catholicism had found it wise to compromise to some extent with the old folk-beliefs, or at need had repelled the Devil with exorcism

---

[1] For this see Ahnlund, *Kring Gustav Adolf*, pp. 79-96; C. Wibling, *Sveriges förhållande till Siebenbürgen*, Chapters I and II; and A. Boëthius, *Romanus Nicephori och Gustaf Adolf*. And *cf.* Batten, *John Dury*, p. 21.

and holy water; but Protestantism, appealing to reason and faith, found the struggle considerably more uphill. The wood-sprites and water-sprites and gnomes against whom in popish days the sign of the Cross had frequently availed, appeared now more formidable, because more uncompromisingly hellish. And the thunders of the Protestant preachers may possibly have helped to defeat their ends by keeping the supernatural too steadily before the attentions of their congregations. This was especially the case where—as Rothovius found in Finland—superstition was found to have a characteristically popish, as well as a pagan, flavour.

At all events, the Church was seriously concerned to stamp out superstition; and no responsible churchman at this time was entirely sceptical about the existence of witchcraft. The extermination of witches was enjoined by Scripture, and failure to obey the Divine command in this matter might entail the heavy responsibility of having provoked the wrath of God against the nation as a whole. Nevertheless, in Gustav Adolf's reign the majority of cases were of a comparatively innocent type: of women who used their medicine-magic in all good faith to effect cures (lövjeri), or practised spell-binding (signeri) and divination; or of the trivial superstitions of the private individual—as of that litigant (though this is a case from a later period) who sought to ensure success by appearing in court wearing two hats, both back to front. Sweden had, it seems, an unusually large supernatural population: trolls and gnomes, mermaids and wood-maids, and above all the formidable Näcken, or water-sprite, who was to be observed on occasion swimming about and playing its false fiddle under the very walls of the royal castle in Stockholm.[1] The Finns, in particular, were reputed powerful magicians, able to slay their enemies at a distance of hundreds of miles by a magic bullet (Finnskott) cast from the north; while in the Arctic the Lapps would sell winds to mariners—or the enemies of mariners—for 'dead drink and old doublets'. Worst of all, and most severely punished, were those

---

[1] King Karl IX on one occasion observed the Näcken from his castle window. Feeling its presence to be an impertinence, he characteristically seized a musket and took a shot at it, but (equally characteristically) missed. It was perhaps as well for him that he was out of reach; for in 1607 one Stockholm citizen, having occasion to visit the public conveniences located on the water's edge, was seized by the Näcken and severely mauled; the municipal authorities paying compensation. *Svenska folket genom tiderna*, IV. 190. In 1588 the inhabitants of Piteå and Luleå refused to migrate to Torneå, because of the trolls who abounded there: B. Steckzén, *Umeå stads historia*, p. 16.

who allowed themselves to be seduced to attend the orgies of the Witches' Sabbath, and fared with the Devil to Blåkulla.

But in Gustav Adolf's time the more obnoxious forms of witch-craft seem to have been less common than they became in the time of the great witch-hunts which disgraced the reign of Karl XI. The leading bishops met in 1619 and 1620 to consider the problem, and laid down standards of guilt and lines of treatment which were to have some importance in the future; but on the whole there was no systematic persecution, and the penalties imposed were usually quite mild. But in at least one famous case a witch was burnt. Duke Johan of Östergötland was towards the end of his life in a very enfeebled state of health, and his duchess was actually insane. It occurred to Johan's chaplain, Claudius Prytz, that these mis-fortunes must have been caused by witchcraft. He accordingly cast about for a culprit; and in due course unearthed a witch, fixed the responsibility upon her, and had her burnt alive near Söder-köping; after which both Johan and his wife took a decided turn for the better.[1]

If the Church's belief in witches was virtually unanimous, Gustav Adolf and Oxenstierna were (at least on occasion) more sceptical; and in regard to astrology the opinions even of leading churchmen were divided. Laurentius Paulinus Gothus was a waverer: he had owed his restoration to Karl IX's favour to his astrological expertness in interpreting the significance of Halley's comet, and for a time was certainly a believer in *astrologia judiciaria*—*i.e.* in the view that the heavenly bodies actually determine the course of events; but in later life he seems to have modified this opinion. Rudbeckius seems to have wavered too. Petrus Jonae was robustly sceptical. But the intellectual atmosphere was so choked with eschatological specula-

---

[1] For the above account, see E. G. Geijer, *Svenska folkets historia*, II. 319 (for Odin-worship); Ahnlund, *Storhetstidens gryning*, p. 27 (for house-snakes); R. Gothe, *Från trolldomstro till Kristendom*, p. 36 (for the two hats), and *passim*; F. Lindberg, *Hertig Johan av Östergötland*, p. 131; E. Seaton, *Literary Relations of England and Scandinavia*, pp. 252-3 (for Lapps) and 285, quoting Fletcher:

Sure, his devil
Comes out of Lapland, where they sell men winds
For dead drink and old doublets.

And, in general, E. Linderholm, *De stora häxprocesserna i Sverige*; E. Reuterskiöld, *Den folkliga vidskepelsen och den svenska katekismen*; G. Granberg, in *Svenska folket genom tiderna*, IV. Burning at the stake was disliked by the peasants, not so much because of its cruelty as because they feared that the smoke would have a bad effect on the growth of crops: C. Annerstedt, *Om samhällsklasser och lefnads-sätt under förra hälften af 1600-talet*, p. 54.

tion that it was difficult to dismiss astrological predictions which chimed in with and reinforced such theories. On the whole, however, the trend of informed opinion was already beginning to set against astrology: Paulinus' successor in the Chair of Astronomy at Uppsala, Martinus Olai Stenius, in 1611 presented a dissertation *'de incertitudine et vanitate praedictionum astrologicarum'* which marks the beginning of real scepticism about *astrologia judiciaria*; in 1619 Sigfrid Aron Forsius was reproved by the bishops for his astrological and chiromantic publications, and *astrologia judiciaria* was formally repudiated by the Church; and in 1645 the astrological annotations which had hitherto accompanied the Calendar which was usually bound up with the Psalmbook were for the first time omitted.[1]

(iv) *The Bishops and the Church*

If the Swedish Church was fortunate in its temporal sovereign, it was no less happy in its spiritual leaders. Gustav Adolf's reign was remarkable for the energy, piety and learning of the episcopate, which in his day attained a position of commanding authority within the Church and of considerable prestige in the body politic. Some of the bishops pitched the dignity of their office so high that on at least one occasion they came near to an open breach with the King; and when Gustav Adolf was dead, their pretensions were to excite the disapprobation of the Regency that ruled in the name of his successor.

The primate, Petrus Kenicius, Archbishop of Uppsala for the whole of the reign, was not likely in his own person to plunge into contention, or provoke resentment by his behaviour. Kenicius continued the Norrland tradition of Angermannus, but in a very different spirit. His temper was equable and conciliatory, and he had a natural dignity which was enhanced by the habitual moderation of his language; so that he was able to enforce his authority without undue effort upon colleagues who were not by nature tractable. He excelled rather as an administrator than as a theologian, and the primacy gave plenty of scope for his talents. His

[1] Holmquist, *Sv. Kyrkans Hist.*, IV. 1. 83; Anjou, pp. 341-2; *Svenska folket genom tiderna*, IV. 114; E. Linderholm, *Om kometernas och andra natur-företeelsers religiösa tolkning i äldre tider*; H. Sandblad, *De eskatalogiska föreställningarna i Sverige under Reformationen och Motreformationen*, pp. 247-52; *AOSB*, II. XII. 33.

successor, Laurentius Paulinus Gothus, was throughout Gustav Adolf's reign Bishop of Strängnäs.[1] John Durie, who met him in 1636, described him as 'a godly plaine dealinge old man',[2] but this was to do less than justice to his varied interests and accomplishments. He was the leading episcopal representative of the Ramist school in education[3]; he was an author of extraordinary copiousness and astonishing range; he was a notable mathematician and astronomer; and he was passionately fond of music. Though quick-tempered and authoritarian, he was an excellent bishop, untiring in labour and zealous for the improvement of standards.

But both Paulinus and Kenicius were somewhat overshadowed by the majestic figure of their colleague of Västerås.[4] Johannes Rudbeckius, after making a name for himself in battle with Messenius at Uppsala, and thereafter as the reprover of the King's youthful irregularities, was in 1618 consecrated Bishop of Västerås, in succession to the weak and aged Bellinus. For the rest of the reign he was undoubtedly the leading personage in the Church. He stands outside his cathedral, in Milles' noble statue, burly, dominant, minatory and formidable, the very pattern of the zealot who is not to be trifled with. His tempestuous enthusiasm seemed at times to have almost as little pity for the weakling as for the wrongdoer; his determined temper was only rarely moderated by an access of self-distrust. His private life was beyond reproach; his ardour was the despair of spirits less toughly constituted; as a preacher he declaimed with Mosaic majesty (in a voice likened by contemporaries to a trombone) against the external foes of his country and the domestic shortcomings of his backsliding congregations.[5] Of his courage, as of his obstinacy, it was impossible to entertain a doubt. The lower orders found in him a consistent and undaunted champion, a friend unwearied in well-doing, a benefactor

---

[1] The standard biography is H. Lundström, *Laurentius Paulinus Gothus*.
[2] Westin, *John Durie in Sweden*, p. 23.
[3] For this, see below, p. 446.
[4] For Rudbeckius, see his *Dagbok*; B. R. Hall, *Johannes Rudbeckius*, I.; *id.*, *Till Johannis Rudbeckii karakteristik*; *id.*, *KKI*; *id.*, *Kulturella interiörer från Storhetstidens uppryckningsarbete*; *id.*, *Den kyrkliga uppfostran i Joh. Rudbeckius' stift*; *id.*, *Rudbeckii kyrkodisciplin och vissa av dess förebilder*; H. Scheffer, *Johannes Rudbeckius*; S. J. Boëthius, *Johannes Rudbeckius*; H. Cnattingius, *Johannes Rudbeckius och hans europeiska bakgrund*.
[5] The voice seems to have run in the family. It is recorded of his son, Olof Rudbeck, that his voice was so powerful that it 'drowned the strongest brass instruments': T. Norlind, *Svensk Musikhistoria*, p. 126.

generous and discriminating in his charity.[1] Among his diocesan clergy he was popular, for he was kindly as well as imperious, and made it his business to care for underpaid sacristans and sextons, and to keep a watchful eye on the interests of clergy widows and orphans. He lacked, perhaps, the Christian virtue of humility. His pugnacious and domineering character, and a certain acerbity of style, provoked resentment, and not least among the nobility. 'A man of qualities', Oxenstierna called him; 'a driving-force, a *pertinax*, who would sooner go to the stake than give way'. It was not without reason that Durie wrote of the 'turbulent humour' and 'boisterous behaviour of him of Westerose'.[2] Nor was it altogether surprising that he should have been passed over in favour of Paulinus, when Uppsala became vacant in 1636. His pride made enemies; and in the next reign they were able to take their revenge upon him.

It was of Rudbeckius that Oxenstierna remarked that 'he had a good piece of St. Peter's kirtle'; but he was by no means the only bishop to whom that expression could have been applied. Isak Rothovius, Bishop of Åbo from 1627 to 1652, was not much behind Rudbeckius in force of character and zeal in the service of the Church. His brother, Jonas Rothovius,[3] the Superintendent of Kalmar, was a force of importance in the life of the south-east, and an especial friend of Oxenstierna; while Petrus Jonae of Växjö has been called 'the Småland Rudbeckius'.[4] Bishop Kylander of Linköping, too, would have been accounted remarkable in any age less distinguished for its churchmen. There were some, no doubt, who fell below the average standard, and who for one reason or another compromised the Church's welfare—Bellinus at Västerås, Eric Erici Sorolainen at Åbo, Nils Krok at Växjö—but it remains true that the Swedish episcopate in Gustav Adolf's time was of exceptional quality.

In the first three decades of the seventeenth century the power of the bishops was steadily on the increase. In the *riksdag* their voice weighed very heavily in the debates of the Estate of Clergy; and indeed that Estate was to some extent their creation. There was no established practice governing the election of clerical represen-

---

[1] See the description by his son, Olof Rudbeck, in Hall, *Till Joh. Rudbeckii karakteristik*, pp. 18-22.

[2] Westin, *John Durie in Sweden*, pp. 129, 79.

[3] The brothers spelled their names differently.

[4] C. Lindsten, *Biskop Petrus Jonae Angermannus, en småländsk Rudbeckius.*

tatives, and in effect they were often simply nominated by the bishops. There was a notable tendency to exclude the laymen and lower clergy from any appreciable share in the government of the Church. The bishops wielded an almost uncontested authority over their dioceses, and managed them very much according to their individual taste and fancy. The failure to obtain the King's approval for the Draft Ordinances of 1619 and 1626 meant that the Church was governed by the Ordinance of 1571, which left all sorts of contingencies unprovided for; and to supplement the gaps in that enactment the bishops were driven to diocesan legislation, promulgating 'constitutions' or 'ordinances' for their own sees, with the result that considerable divergence of practice might occur between one diocese and another.[1] Thus the bishops, as Oxenstierna later complained, usurped the legislative function. They had indeed the Chapters to advise them, and the Chapters seem to have met quite frequently; but though they were regularly consulted about appointments to non-regalian benefices, they had no powers in law, since neither the Church Ordinance of 1571, nor any of the supplementary Drafts, mentioned their rights or functions. In Västerås, and later in Strängnäs, the bishop so arranged matters by a system of weighted voting (with four votes to himself, and two to each of the senior clergy) as to give a preponderance to himself and his closest collaborators. Rudbeckius' ideal for the constitution of a Chapter was an *aristocratia mixta*, and his object was to obtain not a majority decision but unanimity, by the identification of the minority with the views of the majority. Despite current constitutional fashions, he had no intention of allowing the Chapter to become a *Collegium*. It may perhaps be true that the Rudbeckian system actually signified an increase in the acknowledged rights of the capitularies; and it was no doubt theoretically easy for a Chapter of 14 or 15 members to vote the bishop down; but in practice the unanimity which Rudbeckius desired seems to have been achieved by the mere force of his personality: it would have been a hardy Chapter indeed that

---

[1] Petrus Jonae of Växjö was particularly prominent in such diocesan legislation. One matter in which practice varied was in regard to oaths taken upon ordination: Rudbeckius was alone in demanding a pledge to accept the *Liber Concordiae*; while Paulinus demanded a declaration of adherence to his own theological works *Thesaurus Catecheticus* and *Exegesis Pauliniana*. Paulinus and Isak Rothovius both demanded a pledge that the ordinand would not get engaged to be married without the consent of bishop and chapter. At this point the State intervened: in 1636 Oxenstierna said, 'if you will make such regulations, no government or sovereign can maintain its *jus: ferre leges est magistratus*': Hassler, pp. 76-8.

ventured to thwart his purposes. The clergy of Västerås and
Strängnäs might rebut, with praiseworthy loyalty, the accusations of
despotic conduct brought against their bishops; but the fact seems
to have been that a strong bishop ruled his see almost as an autocrat,
and that such concessions as he might make to the idea of representation had in practice no inhibiting effect upon the free
exercise of his will. It was felt desirable, no doubt, that the rural
clergy should be interested in the affairs of the diocese: hence the
institution, in Västerås and Strängnäs, of *capitulares rurales*, to form
a *consistorium majus*. The government approved of this development; and Gustav Adolf made a special point of it in his instructions
to Bothvidi upon his appointment to Linköping in 1631. Again,
it was the custom (as enjoined by the Church Ordinance) to hold
synods of the diocesan clergy from time to time. Apart from
business of general diocesan interest, the main purpose of these
meetings was either to test the abilities and intellectual standards of
the younger clergy, or to act as a 'refresher course' in theology for
the more mature. But neither synod nor *consistorium majus* had any
real voice in determining the policy to be pursued by their bishop.
The bishops knew very well what needed to be done, and they had,
perhaps, too intimate an insight into the failings of the parochial
clergy to set much store by their advice.[1]

A great part of the time of a conscientious bishop was inevitably
spent in the conduct of episcopal visitations; and all the better
bishops seem to have performed prodigies of exertion in this respect.
It was a wearisome and somewhat monotonous task, entailing arduous
journeys over bad roads to remote parishes; and on arrival the same
dreary catalogue of drunkenness and lechery, deeds of violence and
outbursts of strong language, superstition and magic, black or white.
But though the power of Satan must often have seemed but too
operative among the laity, and the efforts of the Church unavailing
against the tide of evil, the bishop might hope by frequent visitations
to maintain some sort of standard among his clergy. And from the

---

[1] On this question of bishops, chapters and synods (a somewhat controversial
one), see S. Kjöllerström, *Consistorium majus, passim*; Cnattingius, *Johannes
Rudbeckius och hans europeiska bakgrund*, Ch. IV.; H. Lundström, *Skisser och
Kritiker*, pp. 124-57; *Synodalakter*, I. 26-34; S. Kjöllerström, *Kyrkolagsproblemet*, pp. 83-5; and (for Gustav Adolf's instruction for Bothvidi) Thyselius,
Bidrag, pp. 161-4. For Oxenstierna's censure of the excessive concentration of
power in the hands of the bishops, see *RRP*, X. 677 (4 Dec. 1644). For the contemporary attack on the bishops by Baazius, see below, pp. 389-90. For the repudia-
tion of his charges by the Strängnäs clergy, *Synodalakter*, II. 105, 109.

clergy, in fact, a higher standard was demanded; and punishment for any lapse from it was heavier than for the layman. Some priests, especially if they had served overseas as army chaplains, were notorious for the low level of their morality, and for the barbarism of their manners; and for such as these, measures of greater severity were necessary: most bishops maintained a special cell for peccant ministers. Apart from men of this sort, the general body of the parochial clergy was as a class inclined to practices which a conscientious bishop could not approve: they shared, for instance, the pugnacity of their parishioners, and were often to be found with a bloody nose on Sunday; they quarrelled with their sacristans; they intrigued for promotion. Many of them were lazy and did not serve their church as they ought. Some took it upon themselves to alter the appointed form and order of service. Many engaged in trading enterprises forbidden by law; and some had a financial interest in those ale-houses which were usually to be found in the immediate neighbourhood of the church, and to which the congregation was in the habit of resorting before the service began.[1] That the clergy themselves should get drunk now and then was something which no bishop could hope to prevent: drunkenness was so common as hardly to be accounted a vice; and an eminently respectable and trusted parson such as Elaus Terserus indulged upon occasion. Habitual drunkenness, however, entailed punishment and even deprivation.[2] But even if the sobriety of the incumbent were above suspicion, and the grosser malpractices were avoided, there was plenty for the bishop to take note of. The fabric of the church might have been neglected; or the duty of catechizing ignored; or there might be pigs in the churchyard. Some parsons were obscure in their preaching; others permitted dogs in church; others again would be fined because their church accounts were not ready for presentation; and we hear of one in the diocese of Västerås who positively did not know his catechism.[3] But all, whether defaulters or no, would make the bishop a present upon the occasion of his visitation; and since these presents tended to be bulky—for instance, a bear's head, a pair of cartwheels, or a copper

[1] L. Levander, *Landsväg, Krog och Marknad*, p. 84; C. T. Odhner, *Sveriges inre historia under Drottning Christinas förmyndare*, pp. 374-5.

[2] R. Holm, *Joannes Elai Terserus*, p. 13. Rudbeckius imposed upon one clerical toper the punishment of presenting the Chapter with a satisfactory Temperance Sermon: Hall, *KKI* (1916), p. 262.

[3] Hall, *KKI* (1915), p. 376.

cauldron—the bishop, when he went on visitation, took his largest waggon for as long as the road held, and usually returned heavily laden.[1]

The supervision of the diocesan clergy was a constant pre-occupation of the bishop, even after he had got safely back to his own fireside, and could for a space leave it to the rural deans to conduct visitations until such time as he should have an opportunity to return.[2] For the bishop was responsible, through the *gymnasia*, for the training of priests; and he was often only too conscious that some of the ordinands were men of 'feeble genius' (*swagha ingenia*). Rudbeckius drew up hints for his ordinands, enjoining decent clothes, frequent hair-cuts, and diligence in study.[3] But only too many of the clergy seem to have forgotten his injunctions. Some would run about in short trousers like farmers' boys, instead of in the sober habit proper to their office; others, inflamed by misplaced social ambitions, rioted in 'great wide French trousers, jackets, and other such things; and go about like Captains, so that no one knows them for clergymen. . . . Some cut themselves Hejduk's uniforms and wear coloured laces . . . some let their hair grow long all round, and clip away a piece to see through, so that their hair slops about hither and thither, and they must always be putting up their hand to their face to keep the hair out of their eyes'—not to mention the abomination of high hats and provocative shirt-collars.[4] And even if these evils could be stamped out, there remained the formidable prospect of combating the sartorial excesses of the parsons' wives. Paulinus, tackling the problem at its root, insisted on his clergy's taking an oath not to marry without the consent of bishop and Chapter; but it appears that this regulation was unpopular. So too, we may imagine, was his encouragement and reward of those that delated erring priests to their superiors.[5]

The bishop was concerned, of course, in all preferment, except

---

[1] Rudbeckius always distributed these presents to the deserving poor. They probably had a mediaeval origin: see Cederlöf, pp. 68-79.

[2] The rural deans (*prostar*) were a mediate instance between the bishop and the ordinary clergy, and had a general authority subordinate to that of the bishop within their deanery (*kontrakt*); but their main business was to hold intercalary visitations once a year, since several years might elapse between the visitations of the bishop. *Synodalakter*, II. 64; Hall, *Den kyrkliga folkuppfostran*, pp. 175-81; Anjou, pp. 246-7.

[3] Hall, *Kulturella interiörer*, p. 5.

[4] Hall, *Kulturella interiörer*, p. 2; *SRDA*, I. 135; *Synodalakter*, I. 31-2; Thyselius, *Bidrag*, II. 264. The effect was small: almost the same complaints occur half a century later: O. Quensel, *Strödda drag af svenskt kyrkolif*, p. 147.

[5] Lundström, *Paulinus*, I. 303, 323, 326.

perhaps to regalian benefices; and it fell to him to adjust the conflicting claims of rival candidates and to reconcile the often divergent views of congregations and resident nobility. Some of the difficulties here were of the bishops' own making; for they ordained more priests than were needed, and thus contributed to embitter the scramble for benefices. This was no new thing: as long ago as 1593 Nicolaus Bothniensis had remarked that 'one had only to beat a bush, and out popped ten priests'[1]; but there was now a new factor in the situation over which the bishops had little control. This was the intrusion of returned army chaplains into the domestic field, which resulted often in the normal order of promotions being upset in favour of some incomer who enjoyed the patronage of a noble with whom he had scraped acquaintance in the Polish or German wars. In such cases it needed great determination on the part of the bishop if the rights of church and congregation were to be safeguarded.[2]

Apart from those activities which had to do with matters strictly spiritual, the bishop discharged a multitude of functions of more generally social character. He bore a great burden of administrative work, of which not the least part was the management of the finances of the diocese. The predominance of a natural economy, and the confusion of weights and measures, must have made this at times a business of singular complexity. But the financial experience acquired in this way was sometimes placed at the service of the public; for at Västerås, at all events, the bishop seems to have established a sort of savings bank, and to have advanced diocesan moneys against good security.[3] A good deal of the bishop's financial transactions had to do with the care of the poor. This was a charge which fell to a considerable extent upon the Church, and in any event the church officers inevitably played the major part in the administration of relief.[4] They were equally prominent in the control and management of hospitals and houses of correction, for in the latter considerable importance was attached to religion as a means of reformation.

---

[1] H. Pleijel, *Svensk Lutherdom*, p. 50.
[2] There is a typical instance in Waaranen, *Samling*, IV. 47-8: a certain Georgius Matthiae, who had been an army chaplain in Russia, induced the government to write on his behalf to Sorolainen, instructing him to give Georgius the next vacant preferment 'before any other claimant'. And this was in 1612: the evil grew worse later on. The road to preferment was sometimes anything but clean: in 1619 Petrus Jonae forbade priests to espouse the mistresses of the nobility: Anjou, p. 346.
[3] Rudbeckius, *Dagbok*, pp. xiii, 9, 13, 40.
[4] For the care of the poor, see Vol. II, Chapter XI, below.

In the sparsely populated Sweden of the seventeenth century, where towns were few and travelling difficult, quite small centres of population had an importance as economic and cultural foci for very wide areas. The cathedral towns did not rank high in the scale of population, even by the standard of that day; but they were vital centres in the intellectual life of the country. There, as offshoots of the cathedral, were the cathedral-schools, and later the *gymnasia*, over which the bishops presided like Chancellors over so many tiny universities. The development of the educational system is discussed elsewhere[1]; here it must suffice to point out the additional burdens imposed upon the bishops by the vigorous progress in this field throughout the period. Associated with the development of the *gymnasia* as so many provincial academies was the establishment, in more than one cathedral town, of printing presses owned by the Chapters, which very often became the vehicles for that impressive flood of edifying or erudite literature poured out by the indefatigable churchmen who directed them. The cathedral town, in short, maintained the old civilizing tradition of Christianity. Here was a library; here a botanical garden, maybe; and here could be heard music less primitive than that discoursed by the ordinary town-pipers' gild. And to all these sides of life the bishop gave attention according to his capacities; dealing at one moment with the planting of cherry-trees, at the next with some chiliastic prophesyings; now enforcing sanitary regulations, now composing the differences of a shrewish wife and drunken husband; preaching three or four times a week; catechizing incessantly; lecturing the diocesan clergy; ordering trombones from Germany; mapping the diocese; tabulating statistics; and diligently practising authorship in his spare time. A man had need of Rudbeckius' physique and temper, if he were not to sink under it.

(v) *The Parochial Clergy*

The diocesan clergy, if the truth were told, viewed the bishops and their activities with mixed feelings. As good Christians they could not blame such zeal; but equally they could not help feeling that the episcopate was assuming too much to itself. Rudbeckius and Paulinus exercised a real despotism, however benevolent. To many of the clergy it appeared that a hierarchical tendency was

[1] See Chapter VIII, below.

creeping into the Church, that the bishops were claiming an authority hardly less extensive, and almost as odious, as that of Rome. The gulf between higher and lower clergy was growing wider rather than narrower: the rural dean, the parish priest, the local congregation, were increasingly excluded from any real say in the affairs of the Church. Rudbeckius, certainly, was to some extent vulnerable to such accusations. In 1636 he boldly claimed all the authority which had been enjoyed by the episcopate in pre-Reformation times—a claim of which Skytte remarked that 'a more dangerous document has not been seen here in Sweden these hundred years'.[1] In the next generation the social cleavages between higher and lower clergy became marked; the bishops grew to be great landowners; their sons were sometimes ennobled; and their sympathies, which had traditionally been on the side of the peasantry, began to incline to the aristocracy.[2] These developments lay as yet in the future, but already in Gustav Adolf's time the middling sort of clergy began to take alarm. There are hints of a rising presbyterian temper, as when a correspondent writes to Oxenstierna in 1625: 'humiliter suadeo cogitandum, archiepiscopatum esse traditionem papalem et forte gravibus de causis annihilandum'.[3] And even if most men were not prepared to go so far, there were certainly some who believed that a stop must be put to the encroachments of the episcopal power.

The most prominent, and the boldest, of these men was Joannes Baazius, who in the 1620's was Vicar of Jönköping, and was in the next reign to become Bishop of Växjö. Baazius was later to be known as the learned author of *Inventarium Ecclesiae Sveo-Gothorum*, the first history of the Swedish Church; but his literary reputation was made as a controversialist and pamphleteer, with a book entitled *Prosphonesis*. *Prosphonesis*, which appeared anonymously in 1629, was a frontal attack on the bishops. In it Baazius denounced the sovereignty ('*Dominium*') which they pretended to exercise over the Church, and their habit of treating other churchmen as their subjects ('*subditi*')—terms which gave the greatest offence, and which Baazius eventually (in 1636) was driven to retract. He complained that they hand-picked the members of the Estate of Clergy at the *riksdag*; that they made decisions affecting the whole

---

[1] Lundin, *Baazius*, pp. 73-5.
[2] C. Weibull, *Drottning Christina*, p. 60; E. Hildebrand, *Kristina*, p. 189.
[3] *AOSB*, II. xii. 538, Lars Vallius to Oxenstierna, 28 May 1625.

Church on their own responsibility; that they consented to the
levying of new taxes upon their own authority; that they interfered
with the free choice of ministers by congregations. He warned
them that even bishops might be abolished. For his own part, he
preferred to retain the episcopate, provided it were properly
integrated with the whole body of the Church. The Chapters must
become something more than the obedient echo for Rudbeckius or
Paulinus; the generality of the clergy must be allowed to take a real
share in the administration of the Church and the deciding of great
questions; and the laity might well be asked to collaborate. This
last was a favourite idea of Baazius, and it had considerable importance; for it was shared by Gustav Adolf and Oxenstierna, and played
a great part in the King's scheme for a *consistorium generale*. Baazius
was impatient of the stereotyped activities of the bishops—the
preaching, the catechizing, the visitations: too much emphasis, he
believed, had been laid upon the mechanical memorizing of the
articles of faith; too little upon inculcating the love of God. In
this, as in other respects, Baazius was more truly evangelical than
most of his contemporaries. He represented the demand for a
reformation within the Reformation, a demand which was beginning
to gain ground in Germany, and which in Sweden found its only other
champion at this time in Johannes Matthiae Gothus. Baazius and
Matthiae believed that faith should manifest itself in the Christian
life, and in a charity to which orthodox Lutheranism had become
increasingly indifferent. It was this fresh, reawakened piety, this
distaste for the bitter husks of theological controversy, which was
to attract Matthiae to John Durie.[1]

Prosphonesis made something of a sensation in Church circles
(though it was in fact never printed), and the anger of the bishops
was great. They did their best to compel Baazius to retract, or
failing retractation to punish him; and he would scarcely have
succeeded in defying the displeasure of the bench of bishops if he
had not happened to live in the diocese of Växjö, where Bishop

---

[1] For Baazius, see H. Lundin, *Joannes Baazius' kyrkliga reformprogram*;
Hj. Holmquist, *En kyrklig oppositionsman*; and R. Björkman, *Jönköpings Historia*,
II. 250-73. Baazius' accusations against the bishops did not go unanswered:
the clergy of Strängnäs and Västerås protested against them; and in the diocese
of Växjö a certain Martin Haquin Stalenus publicly compared Baazius with Nils
Dacke, who had rebelled against his lawful sovereign. This led to a libel action
before the Jönköping *rådstuvurätt*, in which Baazius had the better of it, especially
after Stalenus was unwary enough to quote Bellarmine in support of his contentions: Björkman, II. 263-4. For Johannes Matthiae Gothus' relations with
Baazius, see Holmquist, *J. Matthiae Gothus*, pp. 148-53.

Petrus Jonae was old, ailing, and when possible non-belligerent. A still more important advantage was that Baazius succeeded in persuading the government to take him under the King's protection. The fact that both Gustav Adolf and Oxenstierna should have lent themselves to the support of Baazius is to be explained, no doubt, by the services he had rendered in supporting the project for a *consistorium generale*; but also by the fact that both King and Chancellor agreed with him to some extent about the bishops. The *consistorium generale*, as we shall see, had been wrecked upon the intransigence of Rudbeckius; and though Gustav Adolf could not afford a breach with the bishops, and did not desire one, he was probably not averse from giving some encouragement to their severest critic.

Among the measures of reformation which were urged by Baazius was an increased share in Church government for parochial assemblies and their Elders. Baazius, in fact, was an advocate of decentralization in Church government; which was natural enough in a man who was vicar in an important parish and also rural dean. In Baazius, we hear the voice of the parochial clergy; and, bishops or no bishops, the parochial clergy were the backbone of the Church. They were, to some extent, men sprung from the people[1]; and to their congregations they could have said with truth, 'we are men of like passions with yourselves'. An education at the cathedral school, finished off at Uppsala or the diocesan *gymnasium*, had given them often enough a sufficiency of narrow learning; but it could not alter the provincial accent of their minds nor do away with early environmental influences. Once settled down in their parsonages, with only the occasional diocesan meeting, or the visitation of the rural dean, to keep a check upon them, the less gifted found it easy to forget their learning, and the more pliable early learned to abandon the struggle to impose their standards, and to take the easy road of conformity to local conditions. The better sort, dominating or leading their congregations, were among the great civilizing influences of the period, and (incidentally) among the most useful instruments of the civil government. There were many parishes

---

[1] Pleijel reckons (*Svensk Lutherdom*, p. 96) that in the seventeenth century half the clergy came from clerical homes; and one in five from peasant homes. Another estimate (for a rather later period) gives 40 per cent. of the clergy as having clerical fathers, and 30 per cent. as having fathers who were peasants. For their wives, however, the estimate is 65 per cent. and 5 per cent. respectively: S. Carlsson, *Svensk ståndscirkulation*, pp. 27-8.

where the pastorate descended from father to son in an unbroken
dynasty, as was the case for more than a century with the Laestadii
at Arjeplog[1]; and in such instances the possibilities for subduing
environment, or being subdued by it, were exceptionally great.
The clerical dynasty was no new thing: we hear of it already in
the middle of the sixteenth century, and by Gustav Adolf's time the
custom was well established. And if the male line of parsons failed,
it was not unusual for the incomer to marry the widow or daughter
of his predecessor, and so, as the phrase went, 'conserve the house'
(*konservera huset*): such a marriage gave him obvious and substantial advantages, while on the other hand it relieved the Church
of any obligation to provide for the support of widow and orphans.
Congregations often stipulated for this arrangement. The father
of Linnaeus obtained the vicarage of Stenbrohult by these means.[2]
The system was of course liable to abuse: we hear of widows
'conserved' three or four times running; there were occasions when
the diocesan administration, in its anxiety to provide 'conservation',
degenerated into something like a matrimonial agency; but it was
convenient and cheap, and its advantages probably outweighed its
defects.[3]

In such circumstances, the influence of the parson was potentially
enormous. There were large tracts of country, only beginning to
be exploited by colonists, where churches were as rare as coaches;
and in the wilder districts, even of the centre and south, there were
still many communities which lived in great isolation. For such
people the priest was not merely their spiritual pastor; he was
doctor, magistrate, schoolmaster, oracle and lawgiver.[4] The vicarage
was the natural resort of the unfortunate, as it was the obvious
hospice of the traveller. Not that the wayfarer was likely to find
entertainment on any very lavish scale: the standard of life was
decent, but it was of a Spartan simplicity. The food was often
coarse and monotonous: in bad years the parson, like his parishioners,

---

[1] *Journal av Petrus Laestadius*, I. 79.

[2] K. Hagberg, *Carl Linnaeus*, p. 21.

[3] The expression, and the system, occurred also in the Craft Gilds. For a
richly Pecksniffian petition from a sacristan in the diocese of Strängnäs for leave
to marry the widow of the late incumbent, see H. Lundström, *En drastisk supplik*,
pp. 123-7.

[4] Compare Laestadius, I. 50-1: 'For here [*sc.* Lappland] a priest must indeed
be, like another Moses, his people's prophet as well as priest, their doctor and
lawgiver and—(*sit venia verbo!*)—king. ... Everything, which elsewhere comes to
the officers of the crown or the lawcourts, of whatever kind it may be, is here usually
brought to him: he is often both first and last instance.'

might be reduced to bark-bread. Charles Ogier, visiting Sweden in the 'thirties, described the typical parsonage as a log-cabin, the roof of which was covered with turf as a protection against the snow. From the outside the low range of buildings looked like a collection of pigsties; but inside it was better, for the walls and roof were a blaze of paintings, crude enough, no doubt, but attractive from their bright colourings. Even among the higher clergy there was little that could be called luxury, or real comfort: the only ornament in the archbishop's house was the pewter cups and dishes ranged on shelves around the walls.[1] Conditions naturally varied with the wealth or poverty of the parish, the hardness or mildness of the season, the distance from Stockholm; but it would be a poor parsonage which could not boast one or two silver spoons, and everywhere there would be a sufficiency of pewter tankards. The tankard and the Bible were inseparable table-companions, and might indeed stand as symbols of the conflicting influences which made of every country cure, no matter how docile the flock, an unending struggle between light and darkness.

If the parson lived sparely, he was at any rate better off than the lower clergy—those chaplains and bell-ringers whose condition so often exercised the mind of their bishop. From the end of the sixteenth century there had emerged a class of chaplains, unbeneficed clergy, whose position was as yet undefined. Their duties were usually those of a curate, for they were supposed to assist in the spiritual care of the flock; but they were also very often something not far removed from the vicar's personal servant. Petrus Jonae found it necessary to prohibit parsons from treating their chaplains as servants; though he added that a chaplain ought not to esteem himself too good to 'look after the parson's interests with his hired labourers, go errands, and sometimes, where there are fishing waters, see to the fishing tackle, particularly when the fish are running'.[2]

The parish priest, if he were to maintain even the modest standard of life to which he was accustomed, must be a good farmer; his wife must be able to do the work of a farmer's wife; though both he and she would never forget that they were set apart from their neighbours by the dignity of their calling. But apart from the produce of the glebe, the parson had the important resource of tithe. The

---

[1] Ogier, pp. 22, 54, 76.
[2] Quoted by Pleijel, *Svensk Lutherdom*, p. 111. Their social position (and minimum wage) were still undetermined thirty years later: Hassler, pp. 147-51.

Reformation had diminished the Church's share of the tithe by one-half, since the Crown or the landlord now took two-thirds of the contributions, instead of one-third. Tithe was paid on grain, stock, game and fish; to which were added supernumerary contributions in malt, tar, butter, cloth and other commodities. Like most of the taxes, tithe was commonly paid in kind; and thus the priest had either to pickle or sell a great deal of his income. An ordinance promulgated by Gustav Adolf in 1617 did a good deal to remove ambiguities and anomalies, and thus to secure to the clergy a more regular and certain revenue. In addition, the pastor enjoyed certain other rights which helped him to eke out an existence: his congregation was bound to maintain the parsonage in good condition; his farm-servants were usually exempt from conscription; he had a right to the Easter offertory (which was now a compulsory contribution); he derived a certain revenue—often very considerable—from fees for baptisms, marriages and funerals; and he was entitled to certain contributions of food (*matskott*).[1] It is clear then that his earthly welfare was intimately bound up with that of his parishioners: late frosts or wet harvest-weather affected him as directly as them. It is no wonder that the Estates of Clergy and Peasantry should so often have taken the same line at the *riksdag*. Gustav Adolf called the clergy 'the tribunes of the people', and the phrase was hardly an exaggeration. Again and again we find the clerical Estate intervening to plead with the government for some abatement of taxation, or protesting against a new impost, or making representations upon the unwisdom of a new militia-levy (*utskrivning*) and these services were the more valuable since the Clergy or their leaders were summoned to the Committee Meetings (*utskottsmöte*); from which the Peasantry were excluded. As the most dignified of the *ofrälse* (taxpaying) Estates, the Clergy took the lead in withstanding the

---

[1] The economic position of the clergy after the Reformation is not easy to unravel. The best guide to it is provided by J. Cederlöf, *Det finländska prästerskapets ekonomiska ställning intill sjuttonde seklet*, though it deals primarily with Finland. The essential distinction between tithe and *matskott* was that tithe was a payment to the *church*, while *matskott* (which was older than tithe) was paid to the *incumbent*; also, *matskott* was not a graduated impost. The Crown had an obvious interest in seeing that tithe was fully and punctually paid. For Gustav Adolf's regulation of fees and Easter offertory in 1617, see Waaranen, *Samling*, V. 197-9; for the tithe ordinance, *ibid.*, V. 203-5. For current abuses, see K. G. Leinberg, *Finska prästerskapets besvär*, p. 4; F. Hedenius, *Anteckningar rörande svenska bondeståndet under Gustaf II Adolfs regering*, p. 16, and the authorities there cited. For income from fees, Herdin, III. 201 (an example from the 'fifties). The compulsory Easter offertory at the rates laid down in 1617 proved difficult to enforce in practice: see Hassler, *Enander*, p. 146.

increasing pretensions of the Nobility, and in endeavouring to set some limits to the ever-widening concept of *frälse*.[1] In the next reign their attitude involved them in a sharp struggle with the aristocracy: 'the Clergy', said Per Brahe, 'want all the Estates to stand on the same footing'[2]; and in 1650 they delivered a historic protest against the threat to reduce the peasantry to a condition of virtual serfage.

It is not easy for the present age to imagine what the village church meant to seventeenth-century Sweden. It was in a very real sense one of the fixed points around which all life revolved. The age might be rude and brutal, but it was deeply religious; and church-going was as natural and inevitable, as much the fulfilment of a normal need, as tippling or fighting. Attendance at church had, no doubt, to be enforced on certain reprobates; but for most men it was a social function as well as a religious duty. In the churchyard, or on the churchyard wall, one sat and gossiped between visits to the alehouse next door. The allotment of seats in church was a matter of intense interest, for it was a matter of social prestige, and fierce encounters might result from a usurpation of precedence. Rudbeckius, with characteristic thoroughness, worked out a detailed plan of the seating arrangements in Västerås Cathedral, and having allotted places in due order, tolerated no further argument.[3] Another problem, even more delicate, was presented by the apportionment of burying-places; for here again position varied according to circumstances. North of the church no decent man would lie: that was reserved for outlanders, suicides, Finns, heretics, or persons who could give no satisfactory account of themselves; for it was well known that when the Last Trump should sound, and the dead be raised, the church towers would fall towards the north, and thus make of resurrection an undertaking somewhat perilous for those who lay in that quarter.[4] But it was a matter of some consequence

---

[1] The Estate of Nobles was exempt from taxation, save by its own consent; all other Estates were liable. The Swedish word for this exemption is *frälse* (deliverance): *ofrälse* means literally not-exempt, unfree.

[2] Holmquist, *Svenska Kyrkans Historia*, IV. 1. 133.

[3] Rudbeckius, *Dagbok*, pp. 53-8. It was probably these contentions which led the nobility about this time to withdraw from the common benches into private pews: Anjou, p. 206.

[4] Ahnlund, *Svensk Sägen och Hävd*, pp. 113-34. Petrus Gyllenius is careful to point out that his father was buried south of the church: *Diarium Gyllenianum*, p. 10. The superstition was not unknown in England: compare the following passage: 'The churchyard [at Crosthwaite, near Keswick] is large and the people do not seem to have the same prejudice against burying on the north side of the church as they have in the South [of England]': *The Diary of Benjamin Newton, 1816-1818* (Cambridge 1933), p. 178.

whether a man's bones should moulder to east or west or south of the church; for though in these positions there was no danger from the steeple, there might be some risk of finding oneself in low company on the Day of Judgment.

There were many parishes in Sweden where a regular attendance every Sunday was a physical impossibility. Distances were too great, and roads too bad. In West Dalarna, for instance, it was so far to church that children often could not be baptized until they were old enough to go on foot to the ceremony; and there were serious difficulties about burials. When the rains of autumn or spring thaws made travelling impossible, there was nothing to be done with a man who might die thirty English miles from the nearest churchyard, except to bury him on the spot. Rudbeckius was much concerned about unauthorized burial-places up in the forests; but necessity was stronger even than the Bishop of Västerås.[1] Nor was a distance of thirty miles exceptional in the remoter parishes: on the borders of Hälsingland and Härjedalen there were Finnish settlers in the Orsa area who were as much as sixty miles from the nearest church.[2] It was impossible for dwellers in these outlying regions to do more than put in an appearance at the great festivals of the Church; and even this was an arduous undertaking for which special arrangements had to be made. The following description of churchgoing in Lappland, though dating from as recently as 1827, gives some idea of the difficulties with which the piety of the woodsman and the settler had to contend, in the somewhat similar conditions which prevailed over much of north and central Sweden in the time of Gustav Adolf.

In this place [Arjeplog], where many have several miles to go to church [a Swedish mile is ten kilometres], it is impossible to leave home only on Sunday morning, as in the southern part of the country: they have to start on Saturday or Friday, or even Thursday, if they have a very long and hard road to church. They arrive on Saturday, and naturally cannot sleep in the open. And so every peasant or pioneer has his own hut on the church-place to stay in, and if the festival lasts several days, as at Christmas, Easter or Whitsuntide, then of course they cannot go home in the middle of it, but must stay for the whole festival in the village. Stalls, too, are built for stabling the horses in winter.[3]

---

[1] Gothe, *Från trolldomstro till Kristendom*, p. 135.
[2] *ibid.*, p. 87.
[3] Laestadius, I. 91-2; *cf.* Linné, *Ungdomsresor*, I. 82. W. Tham, *Lindesberg och Nora genom tiderna*, I. 239, has a good picture of a 'church-town' such as

The religious festival thus merged in the social gathering, where a man might with reasonable certainty count on meeting a friend from the other side of the country. Business could be done, marriages arranged; or failing these, what better excuse and opportunity for conviviality?

If the road to church was a long one, the service upon arrival was usually a long one too; for a proper sermon must last a full hour. Preaching was an essential part of the equipment of the Lutheran pastor: as Olaus Petri put it, 'preaching God's word is a priest's job, as smithing is a smith's job; and just as you cannot really call a man a smith who does not do any smithing, so you cannot really call him a priest if he does not do any preaching'. The Draft Ordinance of 1619 put the matter on an even higher plane; for there it was laid down that the preaching office 'is the *only* means of salvation, whereby God calls, enlightens, sanctifies and justifies his Christian congregation in this world'.[1] The clergy was not unmindful of this; and if practice in preaching makes perfect, the standard of excellence must have been high. Three sermons on Sundays (or two in country districts) and two more during the week—such was the assignment of the parish priest, as laid down by Rudbeckius for his diocese; but these were possibly abnormally heavy demands, for the energetic Isak Rothovius estimated that in the course of his twenty-three years as Vicar of Norrköping his total of sermons was no more than 3183—which is considerably below the Rudbeckian average.[2]

Training in preaching was an essential part of education for the ministry, and no doubt ordinands were instructed (as Petrus Jonae instructed the clergy of Växjö) to 'use such words and similitudes as are understandable by the most unlearned and vulgar'. But it seems that they could not always resist the temptation to adorn their discourse with Latin, Greek or even Hebrew; and this may

Laestadius describes, at Lövånger; but in this case the huts are arranged in a straggling street, instead of being grouped round the church. Other excellent illustrations between pp. 336 and 337 of Hj. Furuskog, *Vårt Land* (Stockholm 1944).

[1] Quoted in Holmdahl, *Studier öfver prästeståndets kyrkopolitik*, I. 148.

[2] Ahnlund, *Oxenstierna*, p. 375, for Rothovius. Rudbeckius himself was comparatively concise in his sermons, and actually reproved two parsons for preaching too long: Hall, *KKI* (1916), p. 265. For the restiveness of congregations under longwinded preachers, see Anjou, pp. 311-12. For Rudbeckius' style of preaching, see G. Lindberg, *Johannes Rudbeckius som predikant*; and for clerical oratory in general, A. Wifstrand, *Andlig talekonst*.

account in part for the frequency with which the ecclesiastical authorities had to deal with cases of sleeping in church.[1]

The delivering of sermons and the administration of the sacraments occupied an important place in the parson's catalogue of duties; but (in the opinion of Rudbeckius, at all events) they did not stand first among them. The main task of the parish priest, as of the bishop, was rather to 'investigate, judge and command', to decide which of his parishioners were worthy to receive the Sacrament and be given absolution, and from which these privileges should be withheld. The parson, in fact, was to rule the parish as the bishop ruled the diocese. The parallel, however, was not quite exact; for whereas there was little or no effectual check upon the absolutism of the bishop within the limits of his see, there was some control upon the potential despotism of the vicar. Parochial organization was more popular and more democratic than was diocesan. By the side of the parson stood the two churchwardens, officials elected at a vestry meeting, usually for a three-year term of office. It was the duty of the churchwardens to collect the church's income, whether in rents, fines or fees; to receive and take charge of materials for building or repair of the fabric of the church; to buy the communion wine and take care of it. Associated with the wardens were the vestrymen (*sexmän, tolvmän, sockennämnd*), who were elected by the general body of parishioners. Usually they were six in number, though in some cases (notably in the diocese of Linköping) they numbered twelve. The Vestry was responsible, with the parson, for the care of the church and churchyard; and twice a year it reviewed the state of the parish and made its recommendations. Behind the Vestry, again, was the parochial meeting (*sockenstämma*) which all settled residents within the parish (including women) could, and should, attend once a year; and to which the Vestry, or the wardens, or the parson, or all three, would explain the decisions they had reached and the measures they had taken. Each parish was thus to a considerable degree a self-governing community; and in the intervals between the visitations it fell to the parish and its elected representatives to apply any general principles which the bishop might have laid down, and to supplement them if need be by local ordinances of their own. This parochial organization had no

---

[1] A special official (the '*spögubbe*') was entrusted with the duty of awakening slumbering worshippers with a flick of his long cane: see the tale of *Spögubbarnes Skrå*, in Strindberg's story, *Nya Vapen* (A. Strindberg, *Skrifter*, VI. 185 *seqq.*).

real legal sanction behind it—a Vestry Ordinance (*Sexmänsstadga*) of 1617 was never promulgated[1]—but it was rather encouraged than otherwise by the constituted authorities. Bishop Kylander of Linköping, in particular, seems to have prized the collaboration of the 'generality' in the government of the Church and the maintenance of the Church's principles. Hence no opposition was offered to the growing practice of promulgating bye-laws by Vestries and parochial meetings, in spite of the fact that this very often resulted in considerable differences in practice between one parish and another. Thus at a time when all the tendencies in the Church seemed to be in the direction of the aggrandizement of the episcopal power, and in a century when the currents of political thought were setting strongly towards absolutism, Sweden preserved in her parochial organization the principle of self-government. The parish was, and remained, the smallest administrative unit in the country; and it was also the field in which the average man's interests were most nearly engaged. The representative democracy of the parish looks back on the one hand to the free peasantry of the Middle Ages, and forward on the other to the modern administrative unit of the commune, which is its direct successor. Its foundations were laid so firmly in the earlier half of the seventeenth century that the absolutism of the Palatine Kings could not shake it. Long use, habit, tradition, have made this form of local government seem natural, inevitable and peculiarly Swedish: the problems, the methods, the personalities, and perhaps even the faces, did not alter greatly between the time of Bishop Kylander and the time of Albert Engström.[2]

(vi) *Church Discipline*

Among the most important duties of the Vestry was the obligation to constitute themselves as a sort of jury, to do justice under the parsons' presidency upon notorious sinners, and to exercise a general supervision over the morals of the parish—taking note, for instance, of those who were absent from church, of those who 'drank tobacco', and of all turbulent spirits and inciters to disorder. This

---

[1] Apparently because it would have bound vestrymen by an oath to be zealous and faithful, not merely in the service of the Church and parish, but also in the service of the Crown, and this obligation was disliked by the vestrymen. Text in Gullstrand, pp. 143-5.

[2] For all this, see Gullstrand, pp. 51, 59-65, 72-5, 107, etc.

obligation was of comparatively recent date. In 1596 Archbishop Abraham Angermannus had conducted a famous, if not a notorious, visitation, in the course of which he had caused sinners to be punished with a stringency unknown before that time. Offenders were not merely constrained to private or public penance, compelled to 'stand in the porch', excluded from participation in the Sacrament (lesser excommunication) or thrust out of the community of the faithful (greater excommunication); they were also subjected to physical punishments, to drenching with ice-cold water, to the stocks, and to public whipping. Angermannus may possibly have been a person of abnormal psychology, who took a morbid delight in the details of moral offences and in the administration of corporal correction [1]; at all events, his visitation seems to have shocked his contemporaries, and his successors took care not to imitate its extravagances. But in one thing Angermannus established a precedent which was followed by those that came after; for it was he who first called in the laity of each parish to assist in the business of discovering and punishing evil-livers and other undesirable persons. At the Nyköping *riksdag* of 1611, the Estate of Clergy resolved that excommunication should be pronounced only after judgment by priest *and congregation*; and though the laity showed little desire to sit in judgment on their neighbours, the practice gradually established itself. Such cooperation was desirable from two points of view. In the first place, it ensured that the priest should not be left to fight his battle in isolation: the assistance of the more responsible of his parishioners made the imposition of adequate punishment easier, and created a public opinion in favour of morality. In the second place the participation of the laity enabled the parson to preserve the spiritual character of his priestly office, which forbade him (according to the best Lutheran doctrine) to inflict temporal punishments: he might deal in admonition, penance and (in extreme cases) excommunication; but it did not pertain to the clerical Estate to impose fines, imprisonment or personal chastisement. And, unfortunately, the temporal penalties could not be entirely dispensed with. The excesses of Angermannus were not repeated; but the resolution of the Clergy at the *riksdag*

---

[1] This view has recently been challenged; and it has been contended that Angermannus' visitation was no more severe than was usual, or at least than was necessary, and that his reputation was subsequently blackened by Karl IX for political reasons: see R. Ohlsson, *Abraham Angermannus*, pp. 268-84. But contrast the review by Cnattingius in *Svenska Dagbladet*, 4. viii. 46.

of Örebro in 1617 expressly retained birching as an *ultima ratio* which it would be inadvisable to relinquish. As late as 1631 the Chapter of Västerås was enjoining whipping and the learning of the catechism as penalties for adultery; and on at least one occasion Rudbeckius ordered the birching of a man who had been sick in church.[1]

The most usual punishment, however, seems to have been the imposition of penance and the levying of a fine. Most of the offences with which the Church had to deal could apparently be compounded for money-payments; and bishops even went so far as to permit marriage within the prohibited degrees upon payment of a fine. It is easy to see how this system might be abused until it became indistinguishable from the dispensations and indulgences of the Romish Church, of abhorred memory. Yet the level of popular morality was so low, the rudeness of manners so urgently in need of amendment, that it is difficult to see how else the Church could have escaped from its dilemma. It was reluctant to inflict corporal punishment; it had a shrewd suspicion that mere penance might not bite very deep into the offender's conscience; a fine, therefore, seemed to offer the best hope of ensuring amendment, and at the same time provided a welcome supplement to diminished revenues. The scale upon which fines were imposed often appears arbitrary and capricious: offences which we should consider serious escape with a lighter penalty than others which we should dismiss as trivial; the same offence is cheaper in the one case, dearer in another. But, with all its apparent illogicality, the system worked; and no one can read the diary of Rudbeckius without coming to the conclusion that in the majority of cases the offenders came off lightly.

What then were the offences with which the vicar and his parish council, or the bishop on his visitations, had to deal? A majority of them was probably sexual, for morals seems to have been extraordinarily lax; but an almost equal number concerned drunkenness or its consequences. Crimes of violence were frequent, and manslaughter not rare. A particular category occurring with depressing regularity was that of overlaying children—which, it has been suggested, was one of the seventeenth-century's methods of family limitation.[2] Other frequent offences were swearing—which contem-

---

[1] Hall, *Kulturella interiörer*, p. 35; Waaranen, *Samling*, V. 189 *seqq.* (for the resolutions of 1617); Scheffer, p. 76.
[2] Though the Church authorities on one occasion attributed it to the heavy sleep produced by overwork: *Synodalakter*, I. 24.

porary euphemism was in the habit of describing as 'wielding an unprofitable mouth'; usury; marriage within the prohibited degrees, then much more extensively defined than now; working on a Sunday; absence from church; sleeping in church; brawling; libel; matrimonial discord; superstition and witchcraft; and offences against the *patria potestas*. It is difficult to select characteristic cases from the wealth of material; but the following may be considered as typical samples of Church discipline in action. A boy who had been plied with liquor at a funeral and had subsequently vomited in church was fined 6 *daler*. 'Lars Erichson of Flatenbergh in Norrebercke beat his mother black and blue. *Videtur furiosus*. Is punished.' 'Lars Nilson (Finne Lasse) a smelter, never goes to church, on account of his baldness. Excommunicated'— but later, as we learn from the margin, '*absolutus*'. A woman at Sala mine, having had seven illegitimate children, the two last by Erik Jonsson, did 'false penance' and subsequently died without receiving the Sacrament: Rudbeckius' comment, more remarkable for pith than Latinity, is '*sicut vixit, sic morixit*'. A disobedient son is sentenced to fall on his knees before his father and ask his forgiveness. A man who made a habit of giving people nicknames is excluded from the Sacrament. 'Anders Pålson of Bysaal in Malme hundred wielded an unprofitable mouth for some time in the bishop's courtyard ... *Sententia*: to give one *daler* to the Chapter; this *daler* to be given to a little child in the hospital for clothes.' More doubtful was the case of Erik Eriksson, who was alleged to have said 'The devil alone knows how a man can sow in all this rain. I wish the same devil who has taken away the sun would take the rain away': the Chapter of Västerås deemed it expedient to remit this case for further examination. But there could be no doubt about Herr Lars, who hit his mother-in-law in the eye, and threw horsedung down her well: Herr Lars was made to pay in cash for his amusements. A typical tragedy was that of Hemmethe Sara, who 'being drunk, on leaving the taproom fell flat on the road with her child, and there she lay till she was almost dead of cold; but the child was frozen to death entirely'. Sara was cited to appear before the Chapter, and a fortnight later was condemned to stand in the porch at service-time, until the bishop should have come back from the *riksdag* and could give the matter his attention. And finally, an example of how the spiritual authorities coped with the high spirits of the undergraduate. 'Daniel Achatii is accused of rushing boisterously into the school, where he tore down the board upon which the *Constitutiones* are inscribed, threw the scholars' caps about, and behaved in an unseemly fashion, and was therefore put in the school's prison. *Sententia.* He may lie there for a while until he comes to his senses.'[1]

Such cases as these, which are only typical of countless others, make it clear that the Church in Gustav Adolf's time kept a watch on the private lives of the people stricter than England ever knew, even under the rule of the Puritans. The encouragement of delation, the system of fines, offered opportunities for grave abuses; and in Finland, at all events in the time of Bishop Sorolainen, abuses seem in fact to have provoked justifiable complaint.[2] The punishments may sometimes appear inadequate; but on the other hand they were often inflicted for matters which a more liberal age would have left entirely to the arbitrament of private conscience. The infringement of the liberty of the individual must at times have been felt as an almost intolerable grievance. Yet, as far as can be judged, the system was not unpopular: if it had been, the cooperation of the laity could hardly have been obtained. And it is remarkable that the Church seems to have enforced its punishments even on the nobility.[3] From time to time some hardened sinner is reported to have sworn at the parson, or even to have manhandled him; but public sympathy was not with such persons. For indeed, onerous as this Church discipline may have been, it was needed, and was felt to be needed. When Laurentius Paulinus Gothus came first to the diocese of Strängnäs, he found there 'an almost incredible barbarism and *inscitiam*'. But though men might live like beasts and drink like swine, they were sincere Christians after their fashion. The rigours of the campaign against sinners were endured precisely because most men did admit the absolute standards of Christian conduct, and acquiesced in a retribution which acted as a deterrent to backsliding. Sin was sin, without equivocation or casuistry; and they were against it, even though they might fall into it themselves. They did their penance, stood in the porch, paid their fines, and promised amendment in all sincerity; and thought none the

---

[1] For these cases, see Rudbeckius, *Dagbok*, pp. 23, 211, 219, 243, 258; Hall, *Kulturella interiörer*, pp. 3, 7, 15, 22, 42-3, 47; and for further examples, Hall, *KKI* (1915), pp. 357-8, and Hall, *Den kyrkliga folkuppfostran*, pp. 80-5. Whitelocke had a poor opinion of Swedish Sabbath-observance, all the same: Whitelocke, I. 379, 402-3.

[2] Cederlöf, pp. 79-80.

[3] B. Broomé, *Nils Stiernsköld*, p. 29, for a good example.

worse of the parson because he did his duty in haling them before
the Vestry or the bishop.

The punishment of moral offences, though it was mainly undertaken by the ecclesiastical authorities, was not wholly their concern.
Certain of the more serious—for instance, rape—involved a breach
of the ordinary law, and some were debatable ground between the
secular and spiritual spheres. The tightening-up of Church discipline
which dates from the latter half of the reign of Johan III, and of
which Angermannus' visitation was one of the first examples, led
to increasing collaboration between Church and State in these
matters; and also to a certain confusion of competence which it
was desirable to remove. The Church, for its part, was anxious to
enlist the support of the State, whose arm alone could subdue the
more hardened or privileged of offenders. But the State was somewhat hesitant. Ever since the Reformation it had been the practice
for matrimonial cases, blasphemy and sexual offences to be dealt
with by the Church. It had been freely admitted, even by churchmen, that the State courts had a right to take cognizance of such cases;
but hitherto the lay authorities had tacitly left them to the Church.
The State, however, admitted an obligation to take an interest in
these matters, and Crown bailiffs and civil servants were repeatedly
instructed to give the ecclesiastical authorities every assistance.
Johan of Östergötland issued a special patent dealing with moral
offences within his duchy, and prescribed severe penalties for those
convicted of adultery. By the time of Gustav Adolf the opinion
seems to have been gaining ground, even among the clergy, that it
was time for the lay courts to revive their jurisdiction in these cases.[1]
For one thing, lay opinion disliked the sentence of excommunication,
and was anxious for safeguards against its abuse; and it is noteworthy
that Rudbeckius seems to have employed excommunication somewhat freely. By 1636 Oxenstierna had been stirred to protest against
Church fines. From about 1620 onwards it became usual to obtain
dispensations for marriage within the prohibited degrees from the
civil authorities, upon the understanding that the congregation to
which the contracting parties belonged was not offended thereby.
In difficult cases the *hovrätt* sought the expert advice of the bishops
and based its judgment on that. Charges of moral laxity, too, were
more frequently dealt with by the local courts, and sometimes even
by the *hovrätt*. Rudbeckius' diary shows that a fair proportion of

[1] See, *e.g.*, *SRDA*, II. 134, 150.

the cases of immorality which came before him had already been investigated and judged by the civil authorities. Under Gustav Adolf the practice grew increasingly common of permitting the civil courts to impose a sentence of penance, often as a substitute for a heavier penalty; the Chapter concerned was then asked to prescribe what form the penance should take. The *hovrätt* seems to have taken this line consistently from the start of its career. In fact, Gustav Adolf's reign saw the beginning of that development which culminated in the Church Law of 1686, which laid it down that penance was a punishment for civil offences, and could be imposed only by a civil court.[1]

(vii) *Gustav Adolf's project for a Consistorium Generale*

There were those—Baazius was one of them—who thought that the State ought to make up its mind to a much more systematic interference in ecclesiastical affairs. It should, for instance, assume responsibility for periodical inspections; it should take some positive steps for the creation of a court of highest instance for ecclesiastical causes; it should impose uniformity upon the differences existing, in ritual and discipline, between the various dioceses. Demands of this sort touched a number of difficult problems. Ever since 1571 the Church had been consistent in asserting its right to conduct the preliminary examination of priests accused of offences against the law. It had obtained assurances on this point in the Charter: it reiterated its claim at the Örebro *riksdag* of 1617. Formally the demand was not conceded until 1647; but throughout Gustav Adolf's reign it was in fact complied with. Except for one solitary instance, when two priests were deprived by the King for complicity in the Västbo disturbances of 1616,[2] the invariable procedure was that the accused was tried by the bishop and Chapter, suspended, and handed over to the local court for civil trial. This was an arrangement satisfactory to both parties. But let us suppose a priest condemned by bishop and Chapter for an offence against Church discipline; let us suppose him dissatisfied with the verdict: to whom was he to appeal? To the *hovrätt*? Or to some other ecclesiastical instance? Where could a

---

[1] For the preceding paragraphs, see Cnattingius, *Den centrala kyrkostyrelsen*, pp. 128-41, 149-50, 161, 220-8, 229-31; Lundin, pp. 256-74.
[2] The King's letter to Petrus Jonae is in S. Loenbom, *Historiska Märkwärdigheter*, III. 54-6; and see Björkman, *Jönköping*, II. 64-5.

priest find redress against a tyrannical bishop? Where was the ultimate instance in matrimonial causes? Questions of this sort revealed the fact that Sweden lacked any real central government for the Church. Both Johan III and Karl IX had meditated the establishment of a permanent consistory to discharge these responsibilities, and each had intended that it should include lay members; but for one reason or another nothing had come of these designs, and Sweden in fact failed to obtain any tribunal analogous to the Court of High Commission. The old authority of the archbishop no longer had any legal basis: he remained, indeed, the leader of the Estate of Clergy in the *riksdag*, but he lost disciplinary control over any other see than his own. As a matter of courtesy, or because of the force of tradition, the other bishops did sometimes refer difficult cases to the archbishop and the Uppsala Chapter; but Rudbeckius, for instance, made it quite clear that all the bishops were '*fratres et collegae*, of equal rank in their several offices, *jure Divino*', and that the primacy was a matter of honour only, '*velut Consul in Senatu*'.[1]

Since the Reformation, Church councils had met only with the approval of the King, in ordinary times; and they had not been frequent. The Vasas, when they wished to consult the Church, might summon a special 'Church Meeting' (*kyrkomöte*), just as they might call representatives of the towns together to discuss economic questions; but as a rule they preferred to use the meetings of the *riksdag* as the occasion for any negotiations. By the end of the sixteenth century, therefore, the Estate of Clergy, assembled for a *riksdag*, had drifted into the position of a central organ for Church affairs, and, considered in this aspect, came to be called *consistorium regni*. If, as sometimes happened in Gustav Adolf's time, a Committee Meeting (*utskottsmöte*) were summoned instead of the full *riksdag*, then the functions of *consistorium regni* were assumed by such of the bishops and other Church dignitaries as might have been bidden to attend. The *consistorium regni* fulfilled many, and perhaps most, of the duties of a central organ of government for the Church. Bishops laid before it doubtful or difficult cases from their own dioceses; it acted as a court of highest instance in matrimonial causes; as a court of appeal in cases between clergy, or in cases where a priest who had been deprived unjustly sought redress. Sometimes the King referred civil cases to it, and on such occasions

---

[1] Cnattingius, *Den centrala kyrkostyrelsen*, p. 236.

it was usual for a few members of the *råd* to be present as assessors. It suffered, however, from serious defects. It had no legal standing. Its sittings were short, and separated by long intervals; since it met, by definition, only when there was a meeting of the *riksdag*. If the King should summon an *utskottsmöte* instead of an ordinary *riksdag*, the priest appealing against his bishop would find his cause committed to a tribunal which could hardly fail to be prejudiced against him. And, lastly, no provision was made for the representation of lay interests.

To whom, then, could the ecclesiastical litigant turn, if the *consistorium regni* were not in session, or if its composition foreshadowed an unfavourable verdict? He could turn, of course, to the King; though if he did so it was likely enough that the King in his turn would consult the bishops. And in any case appeals to the King were discouraged after the Judicature Ordinance and the institution of *Svea Hovrätt*. Could he then turn to the *hovrätt*? It is clear that he could, and often did so. This was especially the case in matrimonial causes. But essentially the situation was not greatly altered, since the *hovrätt* was in the habit of referring the case to the *consistorium regni* for its opinion; and it was upon this opinion that the decision of the court was usually based. There remained the *riksråd*. It was supposed that, with the creation of the *hovrätt*, the concern of the *råd* with justice would come to an end. But in ecclesiastical affairs, at all events, it certainly continued; and as late as 1632 the *råd* was complaining of the burden of essentially consistorial work which was being laid upon it. When such appeals were made, the main concern of the *råd* seems to have been to transfer them elsewhere. It preferred, if possible, to refer them to a mixed tribunal, composed equally of *råd*-members and of bishops; but the bishops contended that the proper procedure was to send the matter to the *consistorium regni*. In a famous case of 1632, when a priest was involved in litigation with Paulinus, they referred the case to the *hovrätt*.[1]

From all this it is plain that there was a real need for a clarification of the position. Matters were brought to a head by the notorious case of Barthollus Stephani *versus* Eric Erici Sorolainen and the Chapter of Åbo, which revealed how little redress a priest could obtain from a hostile bishop and Chapter—and also, incidentally, revealed the deplorable laxity of the Finnish Church. The

[1] Cnattingius, *op. cit.*, pp. 213-19.

case dragged on from 1620 to 1628, and in the course of it Barthollus appealed successively to the *consistorium regni*, the *råd*, and *Svea Hovrätt*. The evidence it provided of the lawlessness of life in Finland was probably one of the causes which led to the establishment of the Åbo *hovrätt* in 1623; and the whole case may well have given the final impetus to Gustav Adolf and Oxenstierna to launch their scheme for an entirely new supreme court for ecclesiastical affairs.[1]

It is clear, however, that the King had been contemplating the setting up of such a court for some years: as early as 1620 he was adducing, as a reason for refusal to promulgate the revised Church Ordinance, his intention to refer it for consideration to a *consistorium generale* which he was planning to institute; and there seems some reason to believe that it was the problems connected with the Church Ordinance which convinced Oxenstierna that something of the sort must be provided. At all events, whether the stimulus came from the revised Church Ordinance of 1619, or whether it was provided by the anfractuosities of the case of Barthollus Stephani, Gustav Adolf and Oxenstierna in 1623 elaborated a plan for a *consistorium generale*, and in November laid it before an *utskottsmöte* at Strängnäs.[2] The occasion of the meeting was the funeral of the King's brother, Karl Filip; and the only clergy present were the three bishops of the Mälar region—Kenicius of Uppsala, Paulinus of Strängnäs, and Rudbeckius of Västerås. Gustav Adolf proposed to set up a consistory of twelve members, half spiritual, half lay. He suggested, as suitable clerics, the three Mälar bishops, the Vicar of Stockholm, the senior Court-Chaplain, and the first theology professor at Uppsala; as suitable laymen, the High Steward, two members of the *riksråd*, and three members of the *hovrätt*. The archbishop and the High Steward would preside alternately. The sphere of action of this tribunal was to be extremely wide. It was to revise the Church Ordinance; to exercise a general supervision and inspection over the Church; to advise the *hovrätt* in border-line cases; to act as an

---

[1] For the case of Barthollus Stephani, see *Handlingar rörande finska kyrkans historia*, I. 441, 446, 453, 455, 465; II. 11.

[2] For the whole question of the *consistorium generale*, see the collection of documents in Thyselius, *Bidrag*, I. 59-163, and II. 199-255; Cnattingius, *Den centrala kyrkostyrelsen*, Chapters VII and VIII; Lundin, *Baazius*, especially Chapters III-V; Kjöllerström, *Kyrkolagsproblemet*, p. 109 seqq.; Cnattingius, *Johannes Rudbeckius och hans europeiska bakgrund*, Chapters II and III (replying in effect to Kjöllerström); Holmdahl, *Studier öfver prästeståndets kyrkopolitik*, I. 149-65; Edén, *Den svenska centralregeringens utveckling*, pp. 298-307.

ecclesiastical forum for cases between priests and their bishops, and in general as a court of appeal in ecclesiastical causes; it was to have a large control over schools and students, poorhouses, hospitals and foundlings; to act as a censor; and it was to keep an especially watchful eye upon the Baltic Provinces and Finland.

This proposal must be considered in the context of the administrative reforms which at this time were taking place in the central government. There can be little doubt that Oxenstierna intended the *consistorium generale* to function as a *Collegium*, on the pattern of the Chancery or the Exchequer, with a permanent staff, permanent quarters, and prolonged sessions. It would act as a spiritual supreme court; but it would in addition deal with all the mass of Church business which at that time normally passed through the Chancery. It would, he hoped, ensure uniformity of practice in all dioceses. And it would give to the lay authorities a share in the government of the Church, and (a matter which the Chancellor had much at heart) a share in the control of education.

The three bishops immediately showed their dislike of lay participation. They were prepared to consider the scheme at a forthcoming *riksdag*, for they were willing to admit that some more permanent form of central government for the Church was desirable; but they earnestly hoped that the King would not persist in his intention of making the consistory a 'mixed' body. When the *riksdag* met at Stockholm in March 1624, the Clergy, led by Rudbeckius, were ready with a counter-proposal. They suggested the recognition of the *consistorium regni* as the central authority for all Church affairs—a proposal which ignored the disadvantages entailed by the necessarily rare and brief meetings of that body. Gustav Adolf replied immediately, *extempore*, to this proposal; adhered to his own scheme; and ended with the threat that if the Clergy would not take '*politicos* for their *collegas* and *assessores*, then they might be quite certain (and let them think this over!) that they would be forced to take them as *censores*'. The Clergy, however, stood their ground, and no agreement was reached at this *riksdag*. Gustav Adolf informed them that he intended to promulgate his scheme; and the only concession they could obtain was a promise that he would 'look over it'. The real temper of the Clergy was revealed by the counter-proposal which they handed to the King after the close of the session. This had been drawn by Rudbeckius, and suggested that the proposed consistory should be in effect a committee of thirteen of the Clergy (including all the bishops and superintendents, the Vicar of Stockholm, and the first Court-Chaplain) with two or three lay jurists as assessor members when 'mixed' cases were dealt with, and one or two of the *råd* or nobility as the King's permanent representatives. A proposal of this sort, which gave overwhelming weight to the bishops, was exactly what the King had wished to avoid; and it was naturally rejected by him in favour of his own plan—the more so because it had already become apparent that he could count on the support of a small minority among the Clergy, led by Jonas Rhotovius, the Superintendent of Kalmar, and Baazius, who was deputizing for Petrus Jonae of Växjö.

The *riksdag* met again at Stockholm in March 1625. Gustav Adolf had not carried out his threat: the project for the *consistorium generale* had not in fact been promulgated; but he was still determined on having his way, and the bishops were equally determined to oppose him. Among other reasons, they adduced the impossibility of a bishop's absenting himself from his diocese for long periods in order to serve on the consistory. The King seized on this objection, and produced an alternative proposal, which would have staffed the new *Collegium* with thirteen ordinary parsons living in the neighbourhood of Stockholm, and would have turned the lay members into mere assessors without vote. Since the bishops were too busy to govern the Church, they should be ruled by their own clergy! It seems likely that the King was here deliberately playing upon the growing feeling of hostility to the bishops among the ordinary clergy, a hostility of which Baazius was to make himself the spokesman. Naturally the proposal was at once rejected by the indignant episcopate, and for the time being the negotiations came to an end. Gustav Adolf seems to have persisted in his idea for a little while longer; there were renewed discussions in 1626 and 1627; and Baazius, pursuing his campaign against the bishops, several times urged the King to renew the attempt; but no serious effort to revive the project was made during the remainder of the reign. Under the Regency and in Kristina's reign the question came up again on a number of occasions; but it still proved impossible to arrive at any reconciliation of the divergent viewpoints of Church and State.[1]

The outcome of the controversy about the *consistorium generale*

---

[1] When Durie was in Sweden in 1636 he suggested to Oxenstierna the setting up of a Court of High Commission, and at his request obtained particulars from England. Oxenstierna professed to be attracted by the scheme, but nothing came of it; Batten, *Dury*, p. 71; Turnbull, *Hartlib, Dury, and Comenius*, p. 179.

was thus a clear defeat for the Crown—perhaps the most serious that Gustav Adolf suffered in the whole course of his reign. His purpose had been to integrate the administration of the Church into the general administrative system of the country, as it was being reshaped in the new *Collegia*. The idea was entirely accordant with his policy of improving the efficiency of government, eliminating defective instruments and replacing them by better. It was a move in the direction of the modern, centralized, bureaucratic state at which the King was aiming; and it was directed, as those other more successful moves had been directed, against the undue independence of a particular Estate. The Clergy must be assimilated, partly, if not wholly, to the general body of subjects. The royal Supremacy must be made more effective than in the past. Gustav Adolf was probably influenced in a general way by contemporary examples of similar consistories in the Lutheran states of Germany; and the bishops certainly thought that he was aiming at the introduction of something resembling the *landesherrliche Kirchenregiment* of the typical German Lutheran prince. Yet on this cardinal point of policy the King had given way to interests which were, perhaps, less the interests of the Church as a whole than the interests of the leaders of the Church. The explanation of this surprising meekness must be sought first in the distractions of foreign policy. The Polish war and the preoccupations of diplomacy did not leave time enough for a prolonged wrangle in the *riksdag*. Secondly, the King probably reflected that a victory in this matter would be dearly bought at the price of the ill-will of the episcopate. The loyalty of the Church was above suspicion, but a bench of sulky bishops could be embarrassing to the government, for much depended upon their cooperative zeal. They and their clergy and Chapters did a great deal of work which the State itself ought to have undertaken, and it would have been highly inconvenient to be deprived of their services, or to have had them slackly performed, at this particular moment. And lastly, Gustav Adolf was too well aware of the influence of the clergy upon public opinion, and of their power to lead or mislead the common man, to risk giving serious offence to the Church.

The bishops, for their part, genuinely disliked the prospect of mixed tribunals. They felt that the argument by analogy from Germany had no force; for the German Lutheran Churches seemed to them to be rather a warning than a useful precedent. There was probably not much disagreement between Rudbeckius and Gustav

Adolf upon the necessity for a clear line of demarcation between the
secular and the spiritual spheres: the disagreement was rather on
where the line was to be drawn. It was not so much that there was
a clash of principles as a dispute as to how those principles were
to be applied. How far did the King's rights as '*minister et executor
ecclesiae*' extend? To Rudbeckius, at all events, it appeared intolerable that 'the same person should sit one day in the *hovrätt* . . . and
the next day in the Chapter': such a thing smacked of the Papists,
who 'appropriate to themselves both swords, and have one foot in
the pulpit and the other in the town-hall'. All the bishops were
disquieted by the prospect of interference by politicians in Church
affairs. 'Once we let the politicians in,' said Rudbeckius, 'they will
have it all their own way.' But it was probably not so much the
politicians that they feared as the nobles. They dreaded any
increase in the influence of the privileged classes. The Church was
still the bulwark of the *ofrälse* Estates: once admit noble participation
in its highest forum, and that bulwark might be sensibly weakened.
This motive certainly told against the *consistorium generale* when the
project was renewed under the Regency. There was, too, another
reason for their opposition, and it was perhaps the most powerful
of all: the bishops' intense jealousy of anything that seemed to
threaten their control of the Church. Had it been merely lay- or
noble-participation that they disliked, they might have acquiesced
in Gustav Adolf's alternative scheme of 1625, from which lay
influence was virtually eliminated. But that scheme would have
placed the central organ of the Church in the hands of thirteen of
the lower clergy: it would have withdrawn control from the bishops.
Hence their opposition. Baazius, in fact, was right. The bishops
resisted the plan for a general consistory very largely because they
were animated by hierarchical notions; because, having long ruled
their dioceses with an undisputed sway, they were unwilling to share
their authority over the whole Church with anybody else, whether
priest or layman, noble or civil servant. As to the necessary contacts
with the civil government, they were content that these should be
made by each individual bishop. They would deal with the
Chancery, as before—indeed, more than ever before, since the
Chancery Ordinance of 1626 had given so many matters that concerned the Church into the Chancery's care; and, as before, they
would if necessary lubricate the sluggish machine of government by
acceptable presents to the Chancery staff at nicely calculated intervals.

(viii) *The Clergy as Civil Servants*

The failure of the plan for a *consistorium generale* thus left relations between Church and State unchanged. Neither party could afford to quarrel seriously with the other, for each counted upon the other's assistance and support. The Church, as we have seen, looked to the State for aid in the enforcement of its discipline, and relied with justified confidence on the King's practical sympathy for all good works. The State, on its side, saw in the Church an indispensable instrument of government. In an age of bad communications and a primitive civil service, the clergy provided the government with the easiest means of access to the great mass of the population. If a new tax were to be levied, or a proclamation against Polish spies were to be brought to the general notice, it was of no use to print placards and post them up: illiteracy was too widespread, and the influence of cold print less potent than that of the spoken word. It fell, therefore, to the parish priest to act as the mouthpiece of the civil authorities; and it was his duty to make announcements in the course of the Service, and to add to them his personal exhortations to compliance.[1] For it was through the pulpit that legislation was brought to the notice of the nation. The government, moreover, relied upon the priest's influence with his flock to secure obedience to its decrees; and when those decrees were unpopular or controversial, it took steps at the *riksdag* to convince the assembled Clergy of their necessity; for the King was only too well aware that the spiritual Estate 'had the heart of the common man in their hands, to twist and turn it as they pleased'.[2] Gustav Adolf, therefore, deliberately sought to make use of the clergy to reconcile the nation to his policies, or to prevent discontent from flaring into rebellion. So in 1613 and 1614, when there was serious unrest in Dalarna, it was to the local parson, Elaus Terserus, that Oxenstierna turned for assistance in the task of restoring order.[3] The clergy were expected to act as police-agents, keeping an eye open for danger, and reporting upon suspicious characters. Their assistance was invoked upon the occasion of those Days of Intercession, which the King ordered at regular intervals throughout his reign. On such

---

[1] cf. Ogier, p. 45; Holmquist, *Sv. Kyrkans Hist.*, IV. 1. 324.
[2] *SRARP*, I. 141; *RRP*, II. 90.
[3] *SRDA*, I. 495, 499, 507-11; *AOSB*, I. II. 153-4.

days the priest would read from the pulpit manifestos issued by the central government, which usually contained a review of foreign politics couched in terms calculated to nerve the nation to further sacrifices or to arouse its fighting spirit. As a method of propaganda they were extremely effective; for the day of prayer was a day of rest also: no journey could be undertaken or proceeded with; and all over Sweden the common man was forced to reflect upon the danger overhanging his country and upon his duty to help to avert it.[1] But even at ordinary Services the parson was expected to mix patriotism with religion. And, to do them justice, the Swedish clergy needed no urging. They felt their responsibilities to the country; they saw eye to eye with their sovereign upon the great issues of the day; and their adjurations were the more effective, because they sprang from honest conviction.

But there were other duties laid upon the Church which were less congenial, less proper to the cloth, and less willingly undertaken. Since the time of Gustav Vasa it had been the practice of the central government to use the clergy as its local agents in various administrative and financial matters. They were required for instance to prepare tax-assessments, and to return lists of tithe-payments. They were more or less heavily burdened with the obligation to contribute to the provision of accommodation for travellers (gästning).[2] As early as 1593 there were complaints on these heads. But as the work of government increased more rapidly than its technical resources, and as one extraordinary levy after another established itself as a permanency, it became less and less possible to dispense with the voluntary—or rather, involuntary—assistance of the Church. In Gustav Adolf's time one task after another was piled on their unwilling shoulders. The clergy were made responsible for preparing the lists of contributions for Älvsborg's ransom. With the sexmän they were enjoined to assess and assist in the collection of the Stock Tax in 1620.[3] They were forced to keep a record of derelict farms. They were made responsible for the poll-tax lists (mantalslängder). They were forced to cooperate in utskrivning.[4] In 1625 the vicar of each parish, with one responsible parishioner, was entrusted with the receipt of moneys paid towards the mill-tax—a duty which

---

[1] On this subject, see S. Arnoldsson, Krigspropagandan i Sverige före trettioåriga kriget, pp. 7-13.
[2] For this, see the convenient account in Cederlöf, pp. 49, 61-3, 79, etc.
[3] SILR, pp. 132-3.
[4] AOSB, II. XII. 588.

entailed considerable clerical work; while in 1628 the clergy were set to collect the 'three-marks' aid'. The country parson, especially if he belonged to an older generation which had not learnt arithmetic at school, groaned under the calculations which were required of him, and grew indignant when an over-zealous Exchequer, not content with getting its information in triplicate, demanded more and more additional copies.[1] There were repeated complaints from the Estate of Clergy, and no one was more vehement upon the iniquity of forcing the cleric to undertake layman's work than Baazius; but it was not until 1647 that they obtained any real relief. The plain fact of the matter was, that the central government could not, in Gustav Adolf's time, have provided lay officials to take the clergy's place. Administration was still in process of organization, and reached a fairly solid ground only with the Form of Government of 1634; and in any case it took some little time for the educational reforms of Gustav Adolf's reign to produce a new generation of men who had been trained, at school and at the university, expressly for the public service, rather than for the Church. In the country districts only the clergy had an education adequate to the discharge of such tasks; and only the clergy had the information which the government required. They were the natural repositories of local statistics, and the natural judges of the validity of pleas for special consideration or exemption; and, since they were somewhat aloof from their parishioners in virtue of their office, they were the natural resort of a government in search of an impartial opinion. It is none the less understandable that they should have resented the burden. It withdrew them from their spiritual duties; it hampered them in their uphill fight to wring a bare livelihood from their farms; and above all it placed them in an invidious position in regard to their parishioners, and thus diminished that moral influence which was so necessary to them if they were to control their turbulent flocks.

---

[1] The clergy of Borgå rural deanery (in Finland) complain that they 'are most vexatiously forced by everybody, *ståthållare*, bailiffs, clerks, tax-farmers, and under-clerks, to write and copy so many fair copies of the Poll-Tax and Stock-Tax lists as *they* desire, apart from the fact that we usually hand over at least three. He who shall mind his book and get some fruit from his congregation, must not be burdened overmuch with such things, and become every man's clerk anew, while paper (moreover) is not so easy to come by. And they are very untimely with their clerkings and their summings, and anticipate or prevent us often from serving the congregation on festal days, as happened now most lately on the three usual days of intercession before Whitsuntide, when the church was almost empty, but the town-hall full, where the *ståthållare* preached after his fashion.' Leinberg, *Finska prästerskapets besvär*, p. 4.

But in Gustav Adolf's time, at all events, their objections went un-heeded. The work of the state must go on; the pay of the army must be forthcoming; the recruits must be provided, if the Protestant cause were to be saved. And to that supreme end all lesser considera-tions must be subordinate.[1]

(ix) Gustav Adolf's Bible

It would be unjust, however, to represent Gustav Adolf as sacrificing the welfare of the Church to the requirements of the State. Few Kings, engaged as he was in a great European struggle, would have found time to devote to the Church's interests as much attention as he did. The sympathy and active support of the government were almost always at the disposal of churchmen who stood in need of it; and the improvement in the condition of the Church throughout the period would hardly have been so marked, if the bishops had not been able to rely upon the aid and encourage-ment of the King and the Chancellor.

This was conspicuously the case in two of the most notable religious enterprises of the reign—the printing of the Bible in 1618, and the reformation of the Church in the Baltic Provinces. The need for a new edition of the Bible had long been felt. The edition of 1541 was now difficult to procure, and it was in many respects unsatisfactory. Its accuracy as a translation was more than suspect; it lacked glosses, notes and critical apparatus; and, as with all Bibles before that of Pagnino, the text was not divided up into verses. A committee had been working on revision during the reign of Karl IX, and in 1605 had published a version of the New Testa-ment, together with notes on the Bible as a whole (the so-called *Observationes Strengnenses*). Gustav Adolf on his accession was confronted with a request from the clergy for the publication of a new translation which should incorporate these notes. He at once agreed in principle, and ordered the levying of a contribution to defray expenses of printing. Very soon, however, a serious difference of opinion between the King and the bishops revealed itself. The bishops desired the new version to be published under their control and supervision, and were prepared if necessary to finance it by

---

[1] For the preceding paragraphs, see, in general, Lundin, pp. 215-48; Cnat-tingius, *Den centrala kyrkostyrelsen*, p. 49; S. Nilsson, reviewing A. Sandberg, *Linköpings stifts kyrkoarkivalier*, in *Hist. Tidskr.* (1949), pp. 91-3.

voluntary subscription; they wished Luther's last revision to be taken as a basis, and the *Observationes Strengnenses* to be incorporated, and they took the view that the translation should reflect the sense rather than aim at literalness. The King, on the contrary, was most emphatic that the undertaking should be under royal control, financed by public funds, and was inclined to resent the implication that he might be neglecting his duty as a Christian King. He preferred the Hebrew or the Greek originals, and declined to commit himself to the version of Luther, or indeed to any other. And, influenced probably by the Kabbalistic notions of Johannes Bureus, he pronounced for a literal translation. The committee he appointed in 1615 to carry out the work, though it included Rudbeckius, was dominated by Bureus, and excluded Kenicius and Paulinus; though the primate was indeed given the somewhat humiliating task of compiling an index. Kenicius protested to Oxenstierna at this slight; but the departure of the King for Russia prevented the question's being pursued. In the following year, 1616, the matter of the translation suddenly became urgent, for the printers who had agreed to undertake the work arrived from Germany, and the government felt that it could not afford to support them in idleness for an indefinite period. The committee seems to have done but little preparatory work. In this emergency the King and the bishops reached the somewhat unsatisfactory decision simply to reprint the text of 1541 with some necessary corrections; to add notes and glosses; to divide the chapters into verses; to insert summaries for each chapter; to give some indication of parallel passages; and to add an atlas of maps. Kenicius made the summaries for Genesis, and the Index for the whole; the King's chaplain, Bothvidi, did a good deal of work on the Pentateuch; but the main burden fell on Rudbeckius, with some assistance in the later stages from Lenaeus. Essentially, the Bible of 1618 was Rudbeckius' achievement—a remarkable monument to his learning and to his phenomenal energy. And if in the end the new Bible was not quite all that the bishops had hoped that it might be, it was at least a noble volume, by far the most splendid example of typography and book-production that had hitherto come from a Swedish press.[1]

The Bible, however, was still too expensive and too unwieldy for the average man. In part his needs were catered for by the

---

[1] Cnattingius, *Tillkomsten av Gustav II Adolfs Bibel 1618*; *Observationes Strengnenses* (ed. J. Lindblom and H. Pleijel); H. Pleijel, *Bibeln i svenskt fromhetsliv*; *ÅOSB*, II. xii. 18-19, 47; Thyselius, pp. 155-9.

separate issue of the Psalms and the New Testament; and in part, it seems, by special 'household Bibles' printed at Västerås by the diocesan press on the initiative of the indefatigable Rudbeckius.[1] But the staple of religious reading, for all except the well-educated and the affluent, was not so much the Bible as the Shorter Catechism of Luther. This was to be found, for instance, in the Old Uppsala Psalmbook (*sc.* metrical psalm-book, or hymn-book) of 1622, which was only one, though the most celebrated, of many such Psalmbooks published in the course of the reign. The hymns it contained became the fundamental songs of faith of Swedish Lutheranism; but the Shorter Catechism became in a very real sense the 'layman's Bible'. Here, in convenient and easily memorized form, the ordinary man found the concentrated essence of his faith, and the rule of his conscience to which he could turn in the day of temptation. It was no wonder that the Church concentrated so much of its effort upon the inculcation of the catechism; that it imposed penalties upon those who neglected to come and be catechized; that catechizing was among the first duties of bishops and clergy. A synod of the diocese of Strängnäs laid it down uncompromisingly that 'no one shall be permitted to enter into the state of matrimony without knowing the catechism'. The learning of the words of the catechism represented the first step to education; the learning of its meaning, the first step to a godly life. Its educative influence, its part in shaping the characteristic Lutheran piety of the later seventeenth century, would be difficult to over-estimate; and it is hardly surprising that in the Form of Government of 1634 it was included among the confessional writings to which the Swedish Church and State gave their adherence.[2]

---

[1] Rudbeckius, *Dagbok*, p. 10. A grant of privilege to print simply the text of the Bible in a portable format was given to Johannes Matthiae Gothus in 1630, but nothing seems to have come of it: Thyselius, *Bidrag*, p. 160.

[2] For the catechism, see H. Pleijel, *Katekesen som svensk folkbok*; *id.*, *Svensk Lutherdom*, pp. 60-1; *Synodalakter*, II. 85. As Hall points out (*Den kyrkliga folkuppfostran*, pp. 127-8), the mere learning of the catechism was considered to have almost magical powers, and to be an unfailing means of grace. But Sweden had still far to go before attaining the position of the Reformation dramatist who inserted a scene representing God the Father examining the souls of the dead in Luther's Lesser Catechism: F. Böök [etc.], *Svenska Litteraturens Historia*, I. 167. For Swedish 'psalms', see E. Liedgren, *Svensk psalm och andlig visa, passim.*

(x) Church Reform in the Baltic Provinces; and elsewhere

The initiative in the publication of the new edition of the Bible had come from the leaders of the Church: the State had merely seconded their efforts. The reformation of the Church in the Baltic Provinces, on the other hand, was due directly to the action of the government. It was certainly a very necessary measure. In Livonia, from about the time of Gustav Adolf's accession, Roman Catholicism had been making great progress; and the Lutheran Church of the country was in no state to offer effective resistance. The devastation of war had ruined most of the churches, and in 1622 there were no more than seven Lutheran parsons in the country, and of these two shortly died. The Church lacked not only buildings and priests; it lacked any sort of efficient organization. It was in an attempt to remedy this state of affairs that Gustav Adolf in 1622 appointed Herman Samsonius as Superintendent for Livonia, with instructions to supervise all presentations to benefices, to carry out inspections every six months, to remove bad priests and appoint better ones.[1] Samsonius, however, though well-meaning, was kept busy by his duties as Ober-pastor at Riga; and it was in any case difficult for him to persuade the Livonian towns to admit his authority over their clergy. In 1625 he was given further instructions and wider powers, and was ordered to hold annual synods; but the pace of reform remained very slow. De la Gardie, as Governor-General, was carefully ordered by Gustav Adolf to assist in the work of reformation[2]; and no doubt the danger from Roman Catholicism diminished as Sweden's grip on the country grew tighter; but in effect it was not until the arrival of Johan Skytte as Governor-General in 1630 that real progress was made. Samsonius had done his best; but he had not succeeded in overcoming the shortage of parish priests who could speak to their congregations in their own language.

Skytte's instructions as Governor-General devoted considerable space to Church affairs. He was to reform the Church, in collaboration with Samsonius; he was to impose payment of tithe (which had latterly been neglected); he was to see to it that the nobility did not

[1] For the Reformation in Livonia and Estonia, see R. Liljedahl, *Svensk förvaltning i Livland*; Fr. Westling, *Bidrag till Livlands kyrkohistoria*; *id.*, *Estlands kyrka 1571-1644*; J. Blees, *Gustaf II Adolf och Estland*.
[2] Styffe, p. 273.

abuse their patronal rights; and he was to found a *gymnasium*. Skytte found it impossible to carry out the whole of this programme, but he certainly imported vigour into Livonia's ecclesiastical administration. He found the province with still no more than seventeen churches standing; he found 'appalling idolatry' among the people; he found the clergy 'indescribably monstrous'[1]; and he did not get on very well with Samsonius. Nevertheless, he pressed on with the work of reform. In 1630 he ordered a sort of Domesday inquest of Church affairs; he repressed idolatry; he tried to secure regular attendance at church by the peasantry; he purged the clergy of unsatisfactory elements. And in February 1633 he promulgated a great Church Ordinance for Livonia. It was a pity that Gustav Adolf did not live to see this Ordinance, for the Supreme Consistory which it set up came near to realizing his plan for a *consistorium generale*: it was a 'mixed' tribunal (three laymen, three priests and a lay president); it had regular yearly sessions; and its sphere of competence corresponded closely with that which Gustav Adolf had marked out for his consistory. A year later Skytte gave the Livonian Church a standard of ritual by issuing the ordinance which Bothvidi had drawn up for the dioceses of Magdeburg and Halberstadt. He was very active, too, in the cause of education, both elementary and advanced. The foundation of the University of Dorpat in September 1632 did more, perhaps, than any other measure to amend the condition of the Baltic lands; for at Dorpat special attention was given to the local languages— Estonian, Lettish, Ingrian—and the preconditions were thus provided for the production of a priesthood which should be in a position to exercise a real influence on the peasantry.[2]

If in Livonia the condition of the Church was bad, in Estonia it was appalling. The country was sunk in misery under the harryings of prolonged war; the peasants were the wretched serfs of an alien aristocracy, which openly avowed its intention of preventing any improvement in their condition; the churches were ruinous; the clergy scanty in number and scandalous in their lives. Paganism flourished, for it was identified in the mind of the peasantry with resistance to the German landowning class that had once Christianized, and now oppressed them. The nobles themselves were degraded in morals, indifferent to religion, and brutalized by

---

[1] *AOSB*, II. x. 341.
[2] For further consideration of education in Livonia, see below, pp. 478-9.

war. Had the Church been stronger and healthier than it was, it could have done little by its own exertions to raise the level of civilization; for the nobles worked their serfs so hard that on Sundays they had no energy to come to church. The whole economic basis of the Church in Estonia had been subverted by the exemption, purchased by the nobles in the thirteenth century, from the obligation to pay tithe; and by the fact that in recent years the lands which had been assigned to the Church instead of tithe had either proved inadequate to the provision of a decent revenue, or had (since the Swedish conquest) been donated to private persons. The clergy were in consequence impoverished, except in the handful of towns; education was almost non-existent; and there were no resources available to keep in repair such churches as had escaped damage from military operations. The Estonian Church had no sort of organization: ministers used the Church Ordinances of Kurland, Mecklenburg or Pomerania, according to their taste; no visitations had taken place since 1595; the clergy were not only poor and ignorant, but for the most part grossly immoral, and usually they were imported Germans who did not trouble to learn Estonian. The management of Church affairs had passed almost entirely into the hands of the nobility, who appointed, dismissed and even ordained priests exactly as they chose. In the fourteenth century it had been said that Estonia was 'heaven for the nobles, paradise for the priests, a gold mine for the foreigner, and hell for the peasants': in Gustav Adolf's time the position had not greatly altered, except that the average priest probably found the country more of a purgatory than a paradise.

In 1626 Gustav Adolf paid a visit to Reval after his victory at Wallhof. His object was partly to induce the town to contribute to the Little Toll, and to reform the civil administration of the province; and partly to effect a reformation in the Estonian Church, if that were possible. He met with the most pertinacious resistance on both heads. The affairs of the Church were debated in a meeting of the local Diet in February, and here the King encountered strong opposition from the nobility. They denied that the condition of the Church was as bad as the King supposed; or alternatively they pleaded that the fault was not theirs. They refused to consent to the reintroduction of tithe; and they would listen to Gustav Adolf's plans for education only on condition that his projected school should be reserved for their own children. In short, they showed themselves quite unwilling to cooperate; and in spite of very sharp language from the King, they did not give way one inch. For the moment, Gustav Adolf accepted defeat; but he intimated that he intended to send a commission to Estonia to continue the negotiations on both the political and the ecclesiastical issues.

In July 1627 this commission duly arrived at Reval. It consisted of four members; but as far as Church affairs were concerned the only member who carried any weight was Johannes Rudbeckius. The inclusion of Rudbeckius is the best possible witness to Gustav Adolf's determination to carry through a drastic reform of the Estonian Church. If the great Bishop of Västerås, clothed with the fullest powers and backed by the royal authority, could not effect some sensible improvement, then there was probably no man in Sweden who could. Rudbeckius had the advantage of some prior knowledge of the country, acquired during his service as chaplain during the Russian war; he had the experience of a decade of vigorous administration in his own diocese; and he had, as Gustav Adolf probably knew, a sympathy with the lower orders which would make him the more zealous in resisting the outrageous pretensions of the Estonian serf-owners.

Rudbeckius began at once by calling a synod to Reval, to which were summoned not only all the clergy but four peasants from each parish. The clergy turned up in force; but only a handful of peasants put in an appearance: their masters would not allow them to attend. The town of Reval, too, which had a superintendent of its own, declined to send representatives, holding that Rudbeckius had no authority over its clergy. Despite these unfavourable auspices, Rudbeckius proceeded to force reforms through. The entire body of clergy from the superintendent downwards were made to preach test sermons, and their fate was determined on the basis of their performance; vestrymen were introduced on the Swedish model; stipends were regulated, the size of glebes prescribed; the country was divided into six deaneries; annual inspection was arranged for; regulations for the conduct of services were laid down; and, finally, the synod resolved on the reintroduction of tithes.

The last item was a challenge to the lords; but it was by no means the only one. Rudbeckius bluntly blamed the deplorable condition of the peasantry upon the greed and brutality of their masters. All his inherent Swedish respect for law and personal

liberty was revolted by the institution of serfdom; and he proposed
that peasants should be free to seek new masters if they would, and
that they should have the right to send their children to school.
On these and similar issues he fought a great battle with the
Estonian nobility. His behaviour was not conciliatory; indeed, it
was at times grossly provocative, as when he refused to speak
German (the language of the nobles) and insisted on speaking
Swedish, which they did not understand. His enemies accused him
of wrecking any chance of a compromise by his intolerable arrogance.
Yet it was no bad thing that Rudbeckius should have called evil by
its proper name, and demonstrated to the barbarous Balts that they
cut a poor figure in the eyes of civilized humanity. '*Esthiae bestiae*',
as one of the Commissioners remarked. Gustav Adolf's own
experience had not suggested that the nobles would respond to
tender handling; and Rudbeckius was not the man to shrink from a
fight, especially a fight in the Lord's service. In the end, it came to
a complete rupture. The threat of a Polish invasion finally
terminated the negotiations. The commission went home; and
Rudbeckius sent in a report to the King which did not spare his
adversaries. The upshot of the affair was less satisfactory than
might have been expected. The question of tithe was not pressed,
and the matter of popular education remained undecided. The
tyranny of the nobles was scarcely checked; the lot of the serfs
remained virtually unaltered: Rudbeckius himself wrote (quoting
Jeremiah) '*Curavimus Babylonem, et non sanata est*'.[1] Yet his efforts
had not been wholly vain. Estonia did obtain a bishop (not a very
good one, it is true) and a consistory; the level of the clergy was
raised; the Swedish Church Ordinance was introduced; and provision was made for the holding of regular visitations and synods.
Had Gustav Adolf been able to devote his entire attention to the
Estonian Church, the story might have ended differently. Even as
it was, the gains were considerable. The modern State and the
Church militant, united, had driven back the forces of darkness—a
little way in Estonia, rather further in Livonia; and in the religious,
as in the political sphere, a beginning had been made with the work
of civilization in one of the darker corners of the Swedish realm.

In Sweden herself, and in Finland, there was nothing to compare
with the abuses that ran riot in the Baltic Provinces. Yet even here
there were areas neglected or intractable, areas which the ecclesias-

[1] Westling, *Estlands kyrka*, p. 203.

tical authorities acknowledged to be in need of attention. Norrland, for example, was such an area, and so were the wilder parts of Finland. In both these cases the authority of the Church was dangerously diluted by distance; and in both the population was thinly scattered and sometimes primitive. The Church in Finland had throughout the Reformation period remained even more isolated from Continental controversy than the Church in Sweden. Lutheranism had triumphed in the 1540's, and in 1543 Michael Agricola, the 'father of the Finnish language', had published his translation of the New Testament. But Finnish Lutheranism remained extremely conservative; and memories of heathen times still not too distant mingled with a liking for the ceremonial of the old Church to produce a type of Protestantism which Luther and Melanchthon might have found difficulty in recognizing. As late as 1595 the Bishop of Åbo could recommend caution and tact in proceeding against popish rites; and nowhere, perhaps, was the liturgical experiment of Johan III better received than in Finland. The Bishop of Åbo for most of Gustav Adolf's reign, Eric Erici Sorolainen, had conformed without difficulty to Johan III's requirements; and his relations to Karl during the crisis of the 'nineties had been such that he was lucky to retain his see. He seems in any case to have been lacking in the energy and administrative talents which the state of the Finnish Church demanded of its bishop. The country was extremely poor; in remoter parts manners were rude almost to barbarism; and the clergy were in need of a strong hand to control them. Sorolainen was unequal to the task. He devoted the closing years of his long episcopate (he was consecrated to Åbo in 1583 and died in 1625) rather to the writing and publication of religious manuals in Finnish and to prosecuting his interminable lawsuit with Barthollus Stephani, while the abuses of the Church were allowed to proceed almost unchecked. The institution of a new see at Viborg in 1618 did something to repair the negligence of the Bishop of Åbo and to relieve him of work; but the beginnings of better times in Finland really date only from the appointment of Isak Rothovius as Sorolainen's successor in 1627. Rothovius accepted the call with the gloomiest forebodings, and was wont to complain bitterly of the barbarism of his charges[1]; but he was the right man for the position. Under his rule the Church recovered much lost ground; the translation of the Bible was more actively

[1] *AOSB*, II. XII. 243-4.

proceeded with; and Åbo Academy was founded.   In the last five years of the reign a fresh breeze was blowing for the Finnish Church.[1]

The Church in Norrland had somewhat similar problems.   The province fell within the diocese of Uppsala, but it was really too big, and at its extremities too distant from the seat of the bishopric to be properly controlled.   Its clergy, however, were self-reliant and usually of high quality; but their ministrations affected mainly the string of towns stretching up the coast to Luleå and Torneå: the Lapps of the interior were as a rule neglected, and were in consequence half-heathen.   Karl IX had shown a certain interest in their religious needs, as an element in his Arctic policy; but it was not until Gustav Adolf's reign that much was done for them.   In 1614, when the King was travelling to Finland round the head of the Gulf of Bothnia, a deputation of Lapps met him in Torneå and complained of the neglect of the priests who were supposed to care for them. Some, it appeared, had not heard a sermon for three or four years; and the majority of the deputation alleged that they had never seen their parson.[2]   Gustav Adolf therefore ordered Oxenstierna to see to it that Kenicius ordained additional priests for this service. Stimulated, perhaps, by the King's intervention, Kenicius in 1616 undertook an important visitation to Lappland and reorganized the appointments to inland pastorates.   In doing so, he took the advice of one of the greatest friends and champions of the Lapps, Olof Niurenius, later Vicar of Umeå, who with his brother Erik did invaluable missionary work among the Lapps and was greatly beloved by them.[3]   Niurenius was especially anxious to train Lapps as priests, so that they might have religious instruction in their own tongue; and in this he was warmly supported by Gustav Adolf, who urged the setting up of a Lapp school, and encouraged the printing of religious books in Lappish.   In 1619 Nicholas Andreae Rhén did in fact institute the first primary school for Lapps; but it was not until 1631 that a real start was made with Lapp education: in that year there was founded at Piteå, on the initiative of Skytte and

---

[1] For the Finnish Church, see Handlingar rörande finska kyrkans och prästerskapet (ed. K. G. Leinberg); K. G. Leinberg, Finska prästerskapets besvär; the letters of Sorolainen and Rothovius in AOSB, II. xii.; Cederlöf; Schmitt; and E. Anthoni's review of R. Holmström, Eerikki Eerikkinpoika Sorolainen: piispa ja teologi kansanopettaja ja saarnaaja, in Hist. Tidskr. för Finland (1937).

[2] AOSB, II. i. 31-2.

[3] AOSB, II. xii. 28.   For the brothers Niurenius and the Lapp Church, see Ahnlund, Kring Gustav Adolf, pp. 59-74; Hallenberg, IV. 640; J. Nordlander, Om birkarlarne (1906), p. 249.

Olof Niurenius, the famous Skytteanska Lappskolan, with Niurenius as its first rector. A generation later, in Piteå Lappmark at all events, services in Lappish had become the general rule.[1]

The same care for the religious needs of minorities was shown in the case of the Finnish colonists in central Sweden. Churches were built for them; and by a resolution of the Chapter of Västerås in 1629, a beginning was made with the provision of bilingual clergy.

It was not only for the isolated Finns of the high forests that churches were constructed. The reign was a great period for church-repairing. In the Reformation period the fabrics had been neglected; and when Gustav Adolf came to the throne, some cathedrals were so dilapidated as to be almost ruinous: this was the case, for instance, at Västerås. In these respects the reign saw a great alteration. Thatched roofs were replaced by copper; windows were reglazed; new seating was installed; spires or towers were often added; the plunder of Germany began to flow in, to the enrichment of buildings which had hitherto been somewhat austere; ecclesiastical vestments were standardized; and church music improved. The lead in these developments, as in so much else, was taken by Rudbeckius and Paulinus. Paulinus was especially interested in church music and congregational singing; and Rudbeckius, in his regulation of internal arrangements of his cathedral, is in many respects reminiscent of Laud: he placed the altar, for instance, against the east wall, and installed a choir screen to exclude the laity from the chancel.

(xi) Conclusion

It is in Gustav Adolf's time that Swedish Lutheranism first stands securely established, rid of external menace, purged of internal discord, free to develop according to the nature of its being. Until 1600 the danger from Catholicism or quasi-Catholicism was not wholly overcome, and the Church lived in an atmosphere of crisis. Until 1611 it was handicapped by the crippling suspicion between bishops and King. Gustav Adolf gave it rest and ease,

---

[1] Laestadius, I. 166. The observations of Burton in *The Anatomy of Melancholy* (as quoted in Seaton, *op. cit.*, pp. 252-3) seem to lack other confirmation: Burton remarked of the Lapps that they were 'the Devil's possession to this day . . . which is to be admired and pitied; if any of them be baptised, which the Kings of Sweden much labour, they die within seven or nine days after, and for that cause they will hardly be brought to Christianity. . . .'

confidence and solidarity. As the Protestant Hero, he made it conscious of a European mission. The relations between King and Church were in the nature of a cooperation for all godly ends: the Church was not, as in the Lutheran States of Germany, made to feel from day to day its subordination to the prince. The political quietism which was too often the reproach of Continental Lutheranism could not be charged against a Church which was led by Rudbeckius and Paulinus and which imposed an absolute veto upon the sovereign's most cherished plan for the reform of its governance. It was indeed a Church popular, temperate and strong; a Church zealous and hardworking; a Church at once self-confident and self-sacrificing. By its care for the under-privileged, by its exhortation and its example, by its unremitting assiduity in catechizing, it was to make an indispensable contribution to the cultural development of the Swedish nation.

CHAPTER VIII

EDUCATION

(i) *Swedish Education at Gustav Adolf's accession*

THE reign of Gustav Adolf inaugurates the modern history of Swedish education. By his reforms in the schools, by his encouragement of experiment, and, above all, by his virtual refoundation of the University of Uppsala, Gustav Adolf has won a deserved reputation as one of the great educators of his country.[1]

At the date of his accession, Swedish education was ripe—indeed overripe—for reform. The organization of instruction, the curriculum of the schools, the teaching methods by which that curriculum was imparted, had all long since ceased to answer to the real needs of society. Education was still, as in the Middle Ages, mainly shaped by the requirements of the Church: its aim was to produce satisfactory material for the priesthood. With the rising demands of secular society it was hardly concerned at all. And thus it would have been possible, without any great violence, to treat education in the preceding Chapter; for though Gustav Adolf was more successful than any of his predecessors in giving a secular aspect to education, the control of schools and university remained, to the end of his reign, very largely in the hands of men in Holy Orders; the great reforming bishops (as we shall see) were educational reformers too: the teachers at the new *gymnasia* sat in the cathedral Chapters; and the teaching profession was virtually monopolized by the Church.[2] The School Ordinance of 1571, which determined the nature of Swedish education at the moment when Gustav Adolf came to the throne, was itself no more than a section of the Church Ordinance of the same year.

[1] General histories of Swedish education are: *Svenska folkskolans historia* (ed. E. Rodhe and A. Warne), I.; G. Brandell, *Svenska undervisningsväsendets och uppfostrans historia*, I.-II.

[2] As Holmquist puts it (*De svenska domkapitlens förvandling* . . ., p. 142), 'The intimate collaboration between Church and school, between Lutheran Christendom and national education, which distinguishes Sweden in her Age of Greatness, found its strongest and most logical expression in this: that just as the Church, through the bishops, led the development of the school and of popular education, so also the leading men in the school were the principal collaborators of the bishop in the diocese.'

The Reformation, in Sweden as elsewhere, had had a depressing effect upon the country's educational system. The number of schools had fallen sharply; and even more alarming had been the diminution in the number of scholars.[1] Gustav Vasa had shown little of Luther's interest in education; and though there had been some improvement under Erik XIV and Johan III, the position was admittedly unsatisfactory even in the time of Karl IX. In such schools as survived or were refounded, the education was of that characteristically Lutheran type which compared so unfavourably with the methods followed by the Calvinists on the one hand and the Jesuits on the other. All that was new and inspiring in Luther's educational theory seemed forgotten; and under the distortion of Melanchthonian methods which obtained almost universal currency, education fell into a deep rut of scholasticism—scholasticism which had indeed been saved from the corruptions of mediaeval education by the assimilation of a good dose of humanism, but which had none the less contrived to make of Ciceronian Latin a study scarcely less arid and vain than the dronings of its unregenerate predecessors. There was little trace of the broader humanism, nor any attempt to produce that Universal Man so dear to the Italian Renaissance. The aim of education had indeed been defined by Sturm as *eloquentia*, *sapientia* and *pietas*; but in practice it was the first person of this pedagogic trinity that received most of the adoration of the average Lutheran schoolmaster. And *eloquentia* was to be achieved, it appeared, by the soulless cramming of grammar, by the collection of Ciceronian tropes got by heart, by the culling of the syntactical flowers of Terence for use in light conversation. Melanchthon had never intended, when he separated the study of grammar from that of literature, that the one should be cultivated to the virtual exclusion of the other. Yet that is what occurred. The few classical authors upon whom the aspirant to a pure Latin style was forced to concentrate became degraded into so many quarries from which he might at need hack his own examples of lapidary Latin. Content, intellectual or aesthetic, was a secondary consideration, if indeed it was a consideration at all. There was an unhealthy concentration on the blind learning by heart, not merely of grammatical rules, but of whole passages of recommended text. These defects of method were not wholly accidental, nor were they to be attributed entirely to perversions of Melanchthon's teaching; for Lutheran pedagogues

[1] Brandell, I. 304-7. But contrast Hall, *Rudbeckius*, pp. 6-18.

were conscious of what they were doing, and believed themselves justified. Thought and judgment, they held, do not come easily or naturally to the immature; but the learning of language, being more mechanical, presents less difficulties. And hence in their schools they deliberately confined themselves to *verba*, deferring *res* until the pupil should be better fitted to receive them—*i.e.* until he became an undergraduate. Most young men, therefore, went up to their university with little or no knowledge of any academic subject other than Latin, and possibly Greek; and though their knowledge of the Latin language fitted them to understand the words of the lectures which they attended, their lamentable deficiency in the elements of all other subjects precluded them from obtaining much clue as to the sense.

Sweden followed Continental Lutheranism in her educational system; though, as she was more backward than Germany, her schools were proportionately less satisfactory. The School Ordinance of 1571 prescribed a Melanchthonian system, with a division into two-year classes reminiscent of Sturm. Nowhere was there any sign that the wider demands of the new age were appreciated. No *trivial*-school taught Swedish, or allowed its pupils to speak anything but Latin; and this is the less surprising when we find that more than a century later a learned bishop could confess that while everybody knew the Latin word for a thing, a man must think twice to hit upon the Swedish.[1] Yet at this time Calvin was teaching French at Geneva, and Richard Mulcaster in England was maintaining the superiority of his native tongue.[2] The new movement in courtly education, which takes its rise in Castiglione's *The Courtier*, seemed not to have penetrated to Sweden at all. The Swedish nobility could indeed show its cultured men of the world, who moved easily in polite cosmopolitan society: Erik Sparre was such a one; some of the Bielke family made a habit of using Italian for their private correspondence[3]; and Per Brahe, in his *Oeconomia* (1581), provided a guide-book to gentility and *savoir-faire* for his brother aristocrats[4]; but in so far as such men succeeded in con-

---

[1] Lundström, I. 15.
[2] Mulcaster wrote (in 1581): 'I love Rome, but London better; I favour Italy, but England more. I know the Latin, but worship the English.' And again: 'English, a tongue of itself both deep in conceit and frank in delivery.' (Quoted in W. Boyd, *History of Western Education*, pp. 244, 247.)
[3] T. Kleberg, *Italienska språkets ställning i 1600-talets Sverige* (*Lychnos* 1939), p. 2.
[4] Per Brahe, *Oeconomia eller Huuszholdz-Book för ungt Adels-Folck*. He recommends *Il Cortegiano*; Erasmus, *De Vita Aulica*; and *Reynard the Fox* (p. 30).

forming to the current Italianate type, they usually did so as the result of education received, and experience acquired, abroad.

The lack of any sort of education for public life (apart from the life of the Church) was felt with especial severity in Sweden. The earlier Vasas had experienced the utmost difficulty in finding native Swedes with the educational qualifications required for the discharge of public business: Gustav Vasa was driven to import men like Konrad von Pyhy and George Norman to manage his affairs; and it is doubtful whether Göran Persson would have proved so useful a servant to Erik XIV if he had not received his training in Germany. The problem was an international one, as a passage in Bacon's *Advancement of Learning* reminds us[1]; but nowhere was it more acute than in Sweden, where the techniques of administration had to be hammered out afresh on the morrow of independence. At the close of his reign Gustav Vasa expressed his exasperation at this state of affairs in a famous letter[2]; but, after all, it was a state of affairs which he had done singularly little to remedy. Half a century later Karl IX was ordering his nobility to fit themselves for the public service by the acquisition of foreign tongues and the study of 'modern subjects'; but, like his father, he did little enough to provide facilities for such training at home.[3] It was not until the reign of Gustav Adolf that any real effort was made by the lay authorities to provide anything in the nature of an education for the layman, the statesman and the citizen.

[1] 'This dedication of colleges and societies to the use only of professory learning has not only been inimical to the growth of the sciences, but has also been prejudicial to states and governments. For hence it proceeds that princes when they have to choose men for business of state find a wonderful dearth of able men around them; because there is no collegiate education designed for these purposes, where men naturally so disposed and affected might (besides other arts) give themselves especially to histories, modern languages, books of policy and civil discourse, whereby they might come better prepared and instructed to offices of state.'

[2] Gustav Vasa to Nils Bengtsson, 16 August 1559: 'But we find that those persons who are for the most part sent to us by the schools to give us aid in the aforesaid high offices, are much less apt for such great matters than one who might serve as embroiderer or goldsmith, so that you, and the schoolmaster who should assist and promote our cause in this, choose out the worst of the whole pack, to wit none other than ale-hounds and tosspots, dissolute arrant rascals, who would be better to walk behind the plough with a stick than be used in the realm's high and careful concerns. But how it is possible or tolerable for us to bear rule and take upon us the necessities of the state with such inefficient and contemptible persons, who have neither honour, nor aptitude, nor capacity to think, that we remit to you and to every honest and intelligent man for your considerations.' *Brev av Gustav Vasa: ett urval* (ed. N. Edén), pp. 133-4.

[3] Karl IX did indeed start a school for young nobles at his court, which about a dozen attended; but mostly they went overseas. Brandell, I. 381.

What then were the educational facilities available in Sweden in 1611? Deferring for the moment any discussion of university education, which will receive separate consideration presently, let us enquire what schools there were, what subjects they taught, how they were staffed, housed and financed, and what it was like to be a schoolboy in the early years of the seventeenth century. The answers to these questions will not only provide a picture of education as it was in 1611 but will also yield much information relevant to the whole of Gustav Adolf's reign. For though Gustav Adolf made many changes, he did not wipe the slate clean; and living conditions for a scholar at Strängnäs *gymnasium* in the late 'twenties did not differ greatly from those experienced by Skytte as a schoolboy at Nyköping, or by that formidable constellation of talent which had endured the hardships of the *trivial*-school at Gävle in the 'eighties.

Popular education in the broadest sense was still at the lowest level. The goal aimed at was not even a general literacy: it was rather the inculcation of the bare minimum of religious knowledge. For this the art of reading, though certainly desirable, was by no means essential. As we have seen,[1] the Bible was too bulky and too expensive for the average man. Religious instruction concentrated therefore on Luther's Smaller Catechism, which, with the Creed, the Lord's Prayer and the Ten Commandments, provided all that the unlearned could reasonably be expected to assimilate. The Vadstena Articles of 1559 had prescribed knowledge of these as an indispensable prerequisite for admission to the Sacrament.[2] It was not until the Church Ordinance of 1571, however, that any systematic attempt was made to organize the necessary instruction. The institution of Confession, which had survived the Reformation in a modified, corporate form, gave an opportunity to the priest to teach his flock; and in the last quarter of the century catechizing grew in importance: we have seen what weight was attached to it by the great bishops of Gustav Adolf's time. The Church Ordinance of 1571 prescribed special 'catechism sermons' twice a year, and in general preachers were exhorted to shape their discourses 'so that they land upon some point in the catechism'—which thus became almost a fifth Gospel, to be preached like the rest. But here, as in the higher branches of learning, the teaching was of the most mechanical kind. The congregation was examined not so much upon

---

[1] Chapter VII, *supra*.   [2] *Svenska folksk. hist.*, I. 96.

the content of the catechism as upon their knowledge of the words. Thus in 1607 the Chapter of Uppsala laid it down that no one was to be admitted to Communion 'unless they can read [*sc.* recite by heart: in Swedish *läsa utantill*] the catechism, and, *as far as possible*, understand it.'[1] Such a system may have provided some of the preconditions for education, but it can hardly be said to have made a start with education proper.[2]

The infants' schools went a little further. Here at least the child was taught to read, though the range of his reading might probably be restricted to the same religious texts as his less fortunate fellow-parishioners were painfully learning by rote. More advanced were the 'writing-schools'. Here was taught reading, writing, elementary arithmetic, and, of course, religious knowledge; and with these the boy who aimed at a career in trade might consider himself adequately equipped. For such a boy Latin was hardly necessary, unless his business should lead him into dealings with merchants overseas. Many of the larger towns had schools of this sort, which were usually kept by private schoolmasters for profit. Johan Skytte's brother went to such a school.[3]

Skytte himself, more able or more fortunate, was sent to a 'Latin school', which in his youth represented the highest level of education available in Sweden, short of the university. This type of school went under various names: it was also called the 'learned' school, and (in reference to its curriculum, which was modelled on the mediaeval *trivium*) the '*trivial*-school'. Some of these schools had a considerable local reputation in their day, as those at Gävle, Örebro, Nyköping and Norrköping; but all of them were handicapped by a narrow curriculum, an unsound teaching method, inadequate staff, and lack of equipment. All towns which were the seat of a bishopric or a superintendency had schools of this sort; and by the end of the century they seem to have numbered about 28 in Sweden and 7 in Finland, though of these only 20 gave the full four-class course.[4]

The type of education they provided had been prescribed by the Ordinance of 1571. As the name *trivial*-school implied, they taught grammar, rhetoric and dialectic, to which under Melanchthon's influence had been added religious instruction and music.

[1] *ibid.*, I. 114. My italics.
[2] For this aspect, see *Sv. folksk. hist.*, I. 82-117; H. Pleijel, *Katekesen som svensk folkbok*, pp. 19-31; Brandell, I. 397-413, etc.
[3] T. Berg, *Skytte*, p. 13; Brandell, I. 352-3.
[4] Brandell, I. 306.

In practice, the boys learnt Latin grammar and very little else. They were indeed taught to read from a Swedish ABC-book which contained the Lord's Prayer and the Ten Commandments, but thereafter they put Swedish behind them; and among the older boys at all events it was a grave offence to speak anything but Latin. By 1611 many of these schools also provided teaching in Greek and Hebrew,[1] though in some of them these subjects, if they were desired, had to be got by private tutoring at the pupil's expense.[2] School hours were long—from 5 a.m. to 5 p.m., with a three-hour break in the middle of the day. They thus managed to work a 51-hour week, allotting 31 hours to Latin, 13 to music, and 7 to religious instruction.[3] When one considers the unremitting insistence upon learning by rote, the lack of any attempt to interest the pupils in anything beyond the linguistic side of Latin, this programme must appear formidable indeed.[4]

Each *trivial*-school was conducted by a master who was entirely responsible for it, though he might make no alteration in the curriculum without the consent of his bishop. No provision was made for any staff to assist him. He might indeed appoint, from day to day, pupil-teachers (*informatores*) to help with the drudgery in the lower forms; or he might if he pleased employ one or more ushers (*hörare*); but if he chose the latter alternative he had to pay the ushers out of his own pocket.[5] And since schoolmastering, even in the sixteenth century, was badly paid, it often happened that he was unable to afford the cost of such assistance.[6] A teaching post was too often looked upon as a sort of purgatory which must be endured as a stage on the road to clerical preferment. And this in

---

[1] In 1595 a Church Council recommended the teaching of Greek in all schools attached to a cathedral.

[2] Sweden was behind Denmark in this respect. Greek became a normal subject in all Danish *trivial*-schools from 1543, and in all German learned schools from about 1580. Askmark, pp. 271-3; Holmquist, *J. Matthiae Gothus*, 59-60; Brandell, I. 320-30; T. Berg, *Skytte*, pp. 15-23.

[3] Brandell, I. 324.

[4] These rigours were, however, to some extent mitigated by a certain generosity in the matter of granting holidays: thus at Karlstad in the 'thirties the school was given leave for eight days, that the scholars might collect nuts; and a little later they were let off for a whole week in order that they might go dancing: *Diarium Gyllenianum*, pp. 28, 30. This diary, of Petrus Gyllenius, gives a vivid picture of the typical peasant lad who by industry and sheer persistence (he was twelve years at Karlstad school, and was 26 when he left) rises out of his class into that of the clergy.

[5] Brandell, I. 324, 350.

[6] Vadstena school, however, when Messenius attended it in the 'eighties, had two ushers: Schück, *Messenius*, p. 9.

its turn reacted unfavourably on the standard of teaching, since the less qualified found it more difficult than the able to remove from the schoolhouse to a country vicarage. The standard of schoolmasters tended therefore to be low, and there were many complaints on this head. In the 'nineties Duke Karl ordered that all masters were to be examined and approved by the university, and then by the bishop and Chapter; but this seems to have been applied only in the archiepiscopal diocese of Uppsala. The university was also supposed to secure some sort of uniformity of standards; and masters were bidden to send in a written report to it every year on the work they had done; but this was an obligation generally neglected. The schoolmaster would in practice be approved by the bishop of the diocese in which the school lay, and was supposed to have been examined by him before appointment; but there seems no doubt that some unsatisfactory characters secured posts. There were complaints of masters who to conceal their ignorance wasted time with useless dictating, and did not make the pupils do any exercises (*imitatio*); while others, though learned, were bad teachers because they talked above the heads of their pupils.[1] But these were evils not peculiar to the sixteenth and seventeenth centuries. Karl IX in 1604 lamented the badness of Swedish schools compared with those of the Continent, and characteristically imputed it to lack of zeal in the masters. The bishops retorted that the remedy was not more zeal but more staff. The upshot was an improvement in the staffing of schools situated in cathedral towns; for as a result of the resolution of the Norrköping *riksdag* of 1604 the Chapters were afforced with a *Lektor* in theology and a *Conrector* (or vice-principal of the school).[2] These improvements, however, had as their real object the better teaching of theology, and the number of schools affected by them was small.[3] Nevertheless, it now became possible to form higher classes at such schools, for the benefit of ordinands; and thus was initiated that demarcation of cathedral schools from provincial schools which was to be one of the leading features of the School Ordinance of 1611.

Any possibility of good teaching which may have remained, when the pernicious effect of the methods then in vogue has been deducted, and the inadequacy of the staff discounted, was as a rule effectively disposed of by the unsuitability of the school buildings

---

[1] Brandell, II. 33-4.   [2] Askmark, pp. 82-3.
[3] Holmquist, *De svenska domkapitlens förvandling* . . ., pp. 35-8.

for teaching purposes. Usually, they consisted of two rooms, at worst of one. The School Ordinance of 1571 contemplated as normal the taking of the three upper classes simultaneously in the same room. When each class was doing different work, and all were learning by the method of repetition aloud of rules and selected passages for imitation, only the highest powers of concentration could have prevailed against the din. Örebro school, when Wivallius attended it in the early years of the seventeenth century, was accounted one of the best in Sweden; yet it consisted of a ruinous old two-storey house, the ground floor being of stone, the upper of wood, with a roof of turf and birch-bark, which at this time was half fallen-in. There were four rooms, a hall and a 'chamber' on each floor, though the upper hall was used only on solemn occasions. All the hundred boys worked as a rule in the lower hall.[1] Rudbeckius in 1610 complained that in winter pupils could not attend to their lessons because of the cold: often the schoolrooms were unheated; and if there happened to be a stove, it was the duty of one of the senior boys to see to its stoking. Often there was no artificial light, so that the pupils had to work in half-darkness.[2] In 1615, when Örebro school had 102 pupils, its total inventoried equipment comprised one Bible, six songbooks, and a copper horn.[3]

Discipline was strict, and sometimes savage; and in the upper classes prefects (*notarii, custodes, corycaei*) were expected to assist in its maintenance by delation of their fellows. The birch and the ferule (a wooden instrument resembling a broad, flat circular shovel) were the schoolmaster's indispensable allies, and indeed often figured upon the school's seal, or even, as honourable insignia, upon the schoolmaster's tombstone.[4] Instead of the dunce's cap, the ass's ears were placed upon the peccant grammarian; while for less academic offences the master had at his command the stocks and the black hole, or school prison, in which the offender could meditate his unwisdom upon a spare diet.[5] There were even instances of forcible ducking, as for witches. Altogether, considering the type

---

[1] Schück, *En äventyrare* (in *Svenska bilder*, III. 63); Hall, *Rudbeckius*, pp. 19-21. As late as the early eighteenth century five classes were taught in one room at Skara *gymnasium*: Brandell, II. 411; and conditions at Västerås *trivial*-school when Böttiger attended it in 1814 seem to have been identical with those described above: C. W. Böttiger, *Självbiografiska anteckningar*, pp. 52, 111-12.

[2] Brandell, II. 205.

[3] Hall, *op. cit.*, p. 27.

[4] Holm, *J. Elias Terserus*, p. 15.

[5] Hall, *Rudbeckius*, pp. 296-304: these conditions applied equally to the later *gymnasia*.

and level of instruction, the availability of texts, the standard of accommodation, and the provision of amenities, a school such as Örebro must appear to us to have borne a dismal resemblance to Dotheboys Hall.

The responsibility for the provision of suitable quarters lay as a rule upon the town authorities. Apart from this, the cost of the *trivial*-schools was borne by the Crown, which allotted its share of the tithes of certain parishes to the support of each school, and gave further assistance in the way of some remission of taxation for schoolmasters. But it can hardly be said that this provision bore any reasonable relation to the ecclesiastical revenues annexed to the Crown at the Reformation. Some of the Reformers had, to their credit, urged the application of the resources of the Church to educational purposes on a generous scale; but Gustav Vasa was unsympathetic, and hence it fell out that the financial position of most schools was weak, the schoolmasters ill-paid, and the scholars ill-provided with emoluments.[1]

Most schoolboys at *trivial*-schools came from the middle or lower classes: the nobility as a rule employed private tutors; and it was only at schools of exceptional prestige (such as Nyköping was in Skytte's time) that the children of the first Estate consented to sit on the same bench with their social inferiors.[2] The school roll was therefore made up of the sons of the clergy, of burghers, and of peasants, and such boys could scarcely hope to complete the eight years or more of their schooling without assistance. The cost of a year's attendance at Västerås *gymnasium* in the 1620's came to about 32 *daler*, which was roughly three-quarters of the income of the average parson.[3] Assistance was forthcoming from various sources: town-councils would often give generous aid to deserving boys[4]; Gustav Adolf was later to provide royal *stipendia*[5]; and towards the end of Karl IX's reign a much-prized *stipendium* for scholars of Växjö was founded upon the bequest of Anna Trolle.[6] But the main resource of needy scholars was the charity of the general public. Since at least as early as the fourteenth century it had been customary

---

[1] T. Berg, *Skytte*, p. 138; Brandell, I. 293, 314.
[2] T. Berg, *Skytte*, p. 33.
[3] Hall, *Rudbeckius*, pp. 312-13.
[4] Thus Johannes Matthiae Gothus was indebted for much of his education to the town of Norrköping: Holmquist, *J. Matt. Gothus*, p. 68.
[5] See, *e.g.*, *AOSB*, II. XII. 7, and *infra*, p. 450.
[6] *AOSB*, II. XII. 663, 353; C. Lindsten, *P. Jonae Angermannus*, p. 202; Holmquist, *Sv. kyrkans hist.*, IV. I. 83.

for schools to organize collections, in money or in kind, from the inhabitants of a specific group of parishes, and this practice had been legalized—somewhat reluctantly—by the School Ordinance of 1571. Twice a year, at harvest-time and Christmas, the scholars set off on a tour of their allotted area to collect '*eleemosynam ecclesiasticam*' either '*in primis*' or '*in secundis*', according to the season. The collecting-tour was known as *sockengång* (*lit.* the parish walk) and the proceeds termed *sockenhjälp* (the parish aid). Each school had its well-defined collecting area, comprising mainly those parishes from whose tithes the Crown had made allotment for the school's support; but disputes between schools over the right to collect were not unusual. Upon the size and open-handedness of the collecting area depended the welfare of the scholars; and this perhaps was one reason why the school at Gävle (which had nearly all Norrland to draw upon) attained such prosperity in the second half of the sixteenth century.[1] The creation of new schools had therefore the disadvantage that it necessarily involved curtailment of the *sockengång* area of some older foundation.[2]

At the end of the school year the Rector of each school proceeded to arrange for *sockengång* for the forthcoming year. Usually only two or three pupils were assigned to each parish; and, as *sockengång* was a most material privilege, it was reserved as a rule to those in the highest class, with the possible addition of some pupils of exceptional merit lower down in the school; for the parishes were not numerous enough to go round. Anciently it had been understood that the privilege was to be reserved for poor scholars; but since most scholars were poor, the stipulation had lost any restrictive effect. Parishes might be rich or poor, populous or the reverse; and thus the Rector's allotment became a matter of very great interest to his pupils. Parishes, in fact, had a well-defined monetary value; and it was perhaps not surprising that when a pupil was too lazy to tramp the countryside, or too much in need of ready money to be able to await the harvest of his tour, he should have sold his parish to a comrade who had not been allotted one. And in fact parishes were bought, sold and exchanged freely among the boys. Those who eventually departed, two by two, in almost apostolic simplicity, were straitly enjoined by their Rector so to comport themselves as

---

[1] Askmark, p. 137.

[2] For instance, when a new school was started at Göteborg in 1629, sixteen parishes were lopped off from the area hitherto reserved for Skara: H. Almquist, *Göteborg*, I. 313.

to bring credit upon the school. They were told to speak of the learning they had acquired, to recite their catechism constantly, and to attend punctually to their religious duties. On arrival in their parish, they would present a letter of credence from the Rector, and normally would be entertained by the vicar in his parsonage, which they made their headquarters; and in return for hospitality they were expected to help with the services and give the parish clerk assistance with the singing. During the week, they made excursions to outlying farms, returning to the parsonage for the week-ends. They were expected, moreover, as men of learning, to make themselves generally useful to the unlettered. They taught the children to read, wrote letters for those who had occasion for that unusual expedient, interpreted troublesome passages in Holy Writ for such as were assailed by untimely doubts, and even played the quack by mumbling a Latin prayer over ailing men or sick beasts. And, above all, they sang: for this at least they were sure to have learned at school. Singing from door to door (*ostiatim*) was an important source of revenue to scholars in town parishes, and in Stockholm, at least, it produced a considerable annual income—supplemented, as it often was, by singing at funerals, or even (as at Åbo) by keeping an eye on the cathedral washing. But even in the country the *djäkne*[1] sang, quite literally, for his supper. For the contributions he received were not as a rule in hard money. On his back he carried a leathern bag, and into it the hand of charity emptied bread and salt fish, butter and candles and pieces of Christmas ham; and, if the parish were distant or extensive, and the ways arduous by reason of a late winter, these perishable viands may have experienced some deterioration before they reached the school larder or were sold in the local market-place. The profits from the sale of these miscellaneous provisions did not all go to the pupils who had collected them: the school took its share, and used the money to assist its poorer pupils; and the unfortunate ushers (and even, in some cases, lektors) claimed a portion, as a supplement to their meagre salaries. But the greater part did eventually find its way to the schoolboy's own pocket.

The *djäknar* had a strong corporate pride. However harsh the realities of school life, the scholar was prepared to idealize the pursuit of learning to himself, and to proclaim to the outside world its superiority over all other avocations. At school, his music-

---

[1] *Djäkne*; a scholar, a *gymnasist*.

teacher taught him songs of which this pride was the simple burden,
as in the following example:

> *O scholares discite,*
> *auribus percipite,*
> *oculis videte,*
> *quam beatam ducitis*
> *vitam, quam diligitis*
> *studium quiete.*
>
> *Mane scholas petite,*
> *vesperi recedite*
> *domum repetentes;*
> *quis status felicior?*
> *Quae vita securior*
> *inter nunc viventes?*
>
> .   .   .   .   .
>
> *Rustici sunt asini,*
> *quibus terrae domini*
> *dominantur mire.*
> *Quicquid habent rapiunt;*
> *si non habent, adigunt*
> *pauperes abire.*   etc.[1]

The *rustici*, however, were not so asinine as to admit these pretensions
as an excuse for bad manners or downright criminality. To them,
the roving scholars must often have appeared little better than high-
class beggars; and it was precisely as such that the town of Luleå
regarded them when it ordered that scholars on *sockengång* were to
be given a free bath whenever the public baths were heated, and a
can of fresh ale whenever there was a brewing. When school life
was so hard, it was only to be expected that many should seize upon
sockengång as an opportunity for working off high spirits, and the
perpetration of adolescent pranks which, if they had indulged them

---

[1] C. von Bonsdorff, *Djäknelif och djäknegång*, p. 4. For *sockengång*, see also
L. Levander, *Fattigt folk och tiggare*; Hall, *Rudbeckius*, pp. 307-11; H. Schück,
En äventyrare; *Diarium Gyllenianum*, p. 35 (for the sale of a parish); T. Norlind,
Svensk musikhistoria, pp. 60-1. There is a vivid description of the system as it
existed in the 1760's in S. Ödmann, *Hågkomster från hembygden och skolan*,
especially pp. 37-8, 42-5. Singing at funerals long remained a resource of the
impecunious student: *cf.* August Strindberg, *Den romantiske klockaren på Rånö*,
Ch. IV. Between 1631 and 1638 the number of funerals attended by the scholars
of Stockholm school averaged 227 per year: E. Källquist, *Jacob Rudbeckius'*
Latinstad, p. 155.

at school, would soon have landed them in the Rector's *carcer*. Complaints of the ill-conduct of *djäknar* were frequent; fierce fights with the local youth not rare. In Finland the scholars extort alms 'with evil words'; at Strängnäs one plays a stupid practical joke on the bishop's wife which causes her death.[1] Some seize the occasion to play truant for months at a time. *Sockengång*, indeed, could be a severe test of character; and it is clear that for many it was the start of the road to the everlasting bonfire. Continual begging was relaxing to the moral fibre. It was easy to get into bad company, and to drift into an existence which was at first irresponsible, then irregular, and finally criminal—the sort of existence of which the earlier half of the career of the poet Wivallius is the classic example. The hopeful ordinand degenerated all too readily into the typical scamp of a picaresque novel. Such a one was the luckless Erik Petri, whose path crossed that of Wivallius for a moment in 1631, and who may be taken as representative of many another.[2] Erik invited the attention of the authorities in 1631 by drinking three flagons of communion wine in a church at Ornö, and leaving upon the altar (by way of payment) a poem to the Devil, and another of unmistakably popish sentiment. On investigation it was found that he had attended school at Uppsala from the age of eight, and there studied (as we should expect) grammar, rhetoric and dialectic. Thence he transferred to Gävle, where he spent twelve years under the brothers Niurenius. He then 'divagated to various places'—or more plainly, took to begging; made an excursion to Norway; returned and put in three months' study at the school at Enköping; divagated again; and finally (at the age of thirty) went to school at Jönköping for a year, by way of completing his education. His popish poem proved his undoing, for he was tortured and executed. He died a good Lutheran; but it is difficult to resist the impression that Erik fell a victim to an unsatisfactory system acting upon a character of less than ordinary robustness.

Sockengång was indeed a bad solution of a difficult social problem, and the age (to do it justice) was well aware of this. Most educationalists disliked it [3]; but none could think of anything to put in its place. Gustav Adolf, as we shall see, tried to tackle the problem; but even he was in the end forced to admit defeat.

[1] Lundström, I. 328.
[2] Schück, *Svenska bilder*, III. 148-51.
[3] *e.g.* Rudbeckius: Brandell, II. 205.

(ii) *The School Ordinance of 1611: Ramism*

Such, then, was the condition of Swedish schools in 1611. Gustav Adolf's accession coincided with the appearance of a new School Ordinance, which represented a deliberate attempt to remedy some of the defects which had been revealed by the experience of the preceding forty years. Work on the new Ordinance had begun at the Örebro *riksdag* of 1610-11, while Karl IX was still alive; and obviously Gustav Adolf was too young, and too preoccupied with military affairs, to have had much hand in shaping it. Yet the Ordinance of 1611 has a place in a history of Gustav Adolf's reign, since it was not sanctioned by the Church till 1612, nor published till 1613, and since it determined the country's educational policy until it was supplemented by Gustav Adolf's own reforms in the early 'twenties.

The School Ordinance of 1611[1] for the first time drew a clear distinction between an education for ordinands and an education for laymen. The old Latin school was now subdivided into two distinct types: the cathedral school, which provided a training for the priesthood; and the provincial school, which did not. The difference was seen principally in the length of the respective courses: the cathedral school had six two-year classes, while the provincial school had only four. There was a corresponding difference in the curricula. While both types were now to teach Greek, the provincial school's syllabus appeared elementary in comparison with the Hesiod, Demosthenes, and Greek Testament which fell to be studied in the cathedral school. The cathedral school had, naturally, a more intensive course in theology, culminating in the sixth class (called *classis theologica*) where only theology and Hebrew were taken. Both schools, of course, taught rhetoric and logic, and also music. The emphasis on Latin remained overwhelming; but the range of authors was extended to include Horace and Ovid. One important innovation was implied in the assumption that henceforth there would be one teacher to each class. Schools were to provide playgrounds, and games were to be compulsory; and schoolmasters were enjoined to see that there was no swearing while at play. Provision was made for annual examinations, with external examiners; and school holidays were fixed at sixteen weeks

[1] For the S.O. 1611, see Brandell, II. 83-101, and p. 447 *note* 1, below.

a year: the length of the school week was curtailed by the insertion of an extra half-holiday on Wednesdays.

The School Ordinance of 1611 was never formally confirmed by the King: it never became, as that of 1571 had been, the binding law of the land. And this is the less surprising when we consider how small was the advance it represented towards a useful training for the public service. The only concessions to the lay point of view that it made, were the provision that arithmetic might be taught —if time permitted—in class IV of the provincial schools, and (with astronomy and the elements of natural science) in class V of the cathedral schools. Swedish was to be taught in the two lowest forms in either branch; but this meant little more than reading and writing, for boys could enter school at the age of six. No provision was made for history, geography, law or modern languages. The reform, valuable as it undoubtedly was in some respects, was largely a matter of ecclesiastical policy. Its shapers were most concerned with improving the facilities for the teaching of theology and the training of priests; as appears from the provision that hence-forward no one is to be admitted to Orders unless he has spent at least two years at an Academy *or a cathedral school*. The provincial schools were made to conform, as far as their teaching went, to the policy designed for the cathedral schools. The transference of theology lektors from the cathedral to the cathedral school, consequent upon the decision of the Norrköping *riksdag* of 1604, meant that the ordinands would now seek their advanced training not at the hands of the cathedral Chapter but in the school; and the school curriculum was remodelled to fit this new state of affairs.[1]

In many ways, no doubt, the new arrangements were an improvement on the old. Modern subjects were optional, but at least their existence was acknowledged. Latin was still predominant, but something had been done to make it a more humane study: the rigid insistence on mere grammar was now tempered by some slight interest in the content of the text. It is partly upon this last particular that the School Ordinance of 1611 has been pronounced to represent the triumph of Ramism in Swedish educational policy. This view has recently been shown to be erroneous[2]; but since the controversy over Ramism will recur when the de-velopment of university education is considered, it may be

[1] Askmark, pp. 81-93.
[2] W. Sjöstrand, *Till ramismens historia i Sverige* (*Lychnos* 1940), *passim*.

well at this point to explain what Ramism was, and why it provoked controversy.

Peter Ramus (Pierre de la Ramée) first attracted attention in 1536, when he presented to the University of Paris the audacious thesis 'That all that Aristotle has said, is false'; and confounded the orthodox by successfully defending it.[1] His subsequent career did not belie this promising start: he became professor at the Collège Royale, acquired a European reputation for his educational theories, and perished at last in the Massacre of Saint Bartholomew. In the meantime he had gathered around him a band of disciples, who spread the doctrines of 'Ramism' to Germany, Switzerland, England, Scotland and Scandinavia. Ramism was, essentially, an attack upon the outworn teaching techniques of the Middle Ages, which, in conservative strongholds such as the University of Paris, had persisted into a world that got no benefit from them. And it was also (though this was ultimately less important) an attack upon the supreme authority of Aristotle—an authority which had in some sort received the sanction of the Church, and which therefore it was next-door to heresy to impugn. Ramus challenged Aristotle's verdicts in most of the fields covered by that philosopher; especially, perhaps, in that of logic (where Ramus made a contribution of his own) and that of natural science. His real importance in the history of education, however, seems to lie not so much in the attack upon Aristotle (though that had its value as a contribution to the emancipation of the human spirit) as in his reforms in method. These were based upon his personal experiences. He had found that the dreary routine of formalized logic, the prolonged concentration upon the finesses of grammar, had really taught him little: he had left the schools with the husks of learning only, while the kernel had been systematically withheld. He had none of the humanism of Italy; the educational ideals of Castiglione made no appeal to him; education for him, as for the Middle Ages, was still an education for the religious life: but granting all this, it appeared plain to Ramus that current methods did not efficiently subserve the ends at which they aimed. Education was not, in fact, a satisfactory preparation for life—even for the religious life. The rules of the grammarian, the fine distinctions of dialectic, had never

---

[1] For Ramus and Ramism, see F. P. Graves, *Peter Ramus*; Boyd, *A History of Western Education*; T. Berg, *Skytte*, pp. 24-31; Sjöstrand; Brandell, I. 354-60; B. Boëthius, *Rudbeckius*, pp. 152-3; E. Billing, *Johannes Rudbeckius' aristotelism* (in *Från Johannes Rudbeckius' stift*), pp. 92, 96-7, 100-3, 108, 129, 138, etc.

been brought into relation with reality. A greater appeal to the student's intelligence was needed; less reliance on his memory. Accordingly, he enlivened his lectures in logic with examples taken from classical authors; he showed the relevance of dialectic to rhetoric; he was not content merely to enumerate rules, but strove to find interesting examples of their operation, from literature and from life: in a word, he condescended to explain, to illuminate; he appealed from the dictum of the master to the judgment of the student, and by appealing aided the ripening of that judgment. His great aims were simplicity, perspicuity and brevity; his methods included the tutorial system; his text-books (which were very numerous) were full of original 'short-cuts'. His enemies called him a 'Utilitarian'. His curriculum was notable for the attention paid to mathematics and the natural sciences, and for the wider range of classical authors which he encouraged his students to read. He was not an original thinker: Vives had preceded him in attacking Aristotle, as had Erasmus in pleading for the reform of grammar-teaching. Nor was he, perhaps, very profound; and it seems that his inflexible hostility to Aristotle may have developed into something of a pose, since in his later writings he did not scruple to borrow freely from that philosopher. Yet when all deductions have been made, he was a real pioneer in the field of educational method, and his influence on his contemporaries was great.

In middle life Ramus turned Calvinist, and this caused the stricter Lutherans of Germany to look on his theories with suspicion. But the attack on Aristotle was in any case bound to be considered as an oblique blow at Melanchthon, who was an orthodox Aristotelian, and whose methods enjoyed unchallenged prestige among Lutherans. Melanchthon's followers naturally rallied for a counter-attack. By the end of the century the reaction against Ramism had taken shape as 'neo-Aristotelianism'. This was based on a new and deeper study of Aristotle, and upon a realization that much of the dialectical apparatus which Ramus had thrown overboard as worthless lumber was useful, indeed indispensable, in the polemical theology which was becoming increasingly the only intellectual exercise of German Protestantism. The neo-Aristotelians, moreover, were more willing to admit the ethical teachings of pagan antiquity than Ramus, or at least than the Ramists, who found the classical philosophers hardly consonant with Christian principles. They objected, besides, to Ramus' methods, which, they contended, might serve for those who did not wish to proceed to higher studies, but were too slap-dash and too superficial to content accurate scholarship: their sphere might perhaps be the school; certainly not the university.

The two schools of thought were not necessarily mutually exclusive. And in fact, in Germany and elsewhere, there grew up a body of 'Philippo-Ramists', who, while accepting some of Ramus' improvements, followed Melanchthon in refusing to abandon Aristotle altogether. Among the most influential of the Philippo-Ramists was David Chytraeus, of the University of Rostock. This was a circumstance of importance for Sweden; for Rostock was the favourite German university for Swedish students at that time, and many of the most influential churchmen around the turn of the century were Chytraeus' pupils. Most of them came back to Sweden more convinced Ramists than their master; and thus from Rostock the Ramist doctrine came to Sweden. By the last decade of the sixteenth century it had obtained considerable authority in high places. Nicolaus Bothniensis, Kenicius the future archbishop, and Laurentius Paulinus Gothus—all three pupils of Chytraeus—were among the foremost Swedish Ramists. Johan Skytte, soon to be selected as Gustav Adolf's tutor, was an ardent Ramist too. The Church Council of 1595, which considered educational problems, recommended the adoption by all schools of certain Ramist textbooks. On the other hand, the reign of Karl IX saw the arrival of neo-Aristotelianism in Sweden, in the person of Johannes Rudbeckius, the future Bishop of Västerås; and at Uppsala a neo-Aristotelian group of professors centred round Rudbeckius and Lenaeus, in opposition to the Ramists led by Paulinus and Kenicius.

The School Ordinance of 1611 was the work of Kenicius, Paulinus and Rudbeckius working in collaboration; and, as might have been expected, it represents in fact a compromise between the two viewpoints, or rather, a broad-minded eclecticism and a refusal to enlist in either camp. If the Ordinance must be labelled at all, then it was Philippo-Ramist, in the tradition of Chytraeus. It was certainly not the full-blooded embodiment of Ramist theories which some have thought it. The extension of the range of classical authors was in conformity with Ramus' practice, and the strong emphasis on the need for students to do exercises, instead of merely copying from dictation or blindly memorizing rules, is Ramist too. But the authors go out of their way to point out that it is not vitally important either to be for Ramus or against him, and they earnestly urge tolerance upon both sides:

They who present Ramus' philosophy shall not decry Aristotle in order to frighten their pupils from the study of this author. On the contrary, they shall refer to him as to a richer source, so that he who may chance to proceed to the Academy, may not from a preconceived hatred of Aristotle turn aside from the study of him, to their own loss. They again who lecture on Aristotle . . . ought not to condemn Ramus' logic as useless, but only show what further can be collected from Aristotle with profit. They, finally, who dispute either of Ramus' or Aristotle's point of view, should without bitterness or insult honourably and courteously defend what seems to them to be true.[1]

In the years after 1611 we hear both of Ramist and anti-Ramist schoolmasters.[2] In certain subjects even anti-Ramists like Rudbeckius used Ramist text-books. Paulinus, indeed, who was the fiercest Ramist of them all (he pushed Ramism to a point at which Ramus would have drawn back), published in 1615 a weighty pamphlet denouncing the Aristotelian corruption which was poisoning Swedish schools[3]; but no one seems to have been seriously perturbed. As far as the schools were concerned, the clash between the two parties was probably never of great importance; and it seems likely that the undue significance which has sometimes been attached to it is to be ascribed to the effect of the spectacular quarrels which during the first decade of the reign convulsed the University of Uppsala.

(iii) The coming of the gymnasia

The fact that the School Ordinance of 1611 never obtained royal confirmation meant that its execution depended mainly upon the zeal of each individual bishop; and though most cathedral schools appear to have applied it at least in part, and some provincial schools undoubtedly adopted the new curriculum,[4] it is very un-

---

[1] The text of S.O. 1611 is in P. E. Thyselius, *Handlingar rörande den svenska kyrkans och läroverkens historia*, pp. 54-69: the quoted passage is at p. 67. See too Hall, *Rudbeckius*, pp. 135-9.

[2] *e.g.* Erik Niurenius at Gävle 'propounded *Ramum* and *Caspari Bartholini logicam*' (Schück, *Sv. bilder*, III. 149); while on the other hand a master was appointed to Växjö school in 1622 to teach Hebrew 'by the Giessen method' (*i.e* on neo-Aristotelian principles): *AOSB*, II. XII. 397, 401.

[3] Sjöstrand, p. 218.

[4] *e.g.*, Örebro under Jakob Rudbeckius: Holm, *J. Elai Terserus*, p. 21.

certain whether it can be considered to have established itself as a norm. The sixth (theology) class at cathedral schools was still so unusual that in 1620 neither Gustav Adolf nor the bishops were proposing more than five teachers to a school; and even at the close of the reign there seem to have been many priests who had never proceeded beyond the provincial-school level. A stronger urge and a fresher outlook were needed if educational reform were to make real progress in the country. Gustav Adolf provided both. In the relatively peaceful years after Stolbova, he turned his attention, among other domestic concerns, to education; and though he did not succeed in reorientating the whole system, as he had hoped to do, he did effect changes which have left their trace on Sweden to this day.

Gustav Adolf was no more an expert on education that his father or his grandfather. Like them, he judged the system by results; like them, he found the results unsatisfactory. Just as Gustav Vasa had complained of the lack of skilled men to fill the offices of state, so his grandson was moved to protest at the difficulty of staffing that expanded, reorganized and modernized civil service which was one of the most characteristic achievements of his reign. At the Stockholm *riksdag* of 1620 he presented to the Clergy a general indictment of the whole educational system, from the university downwards. There was not a single good town-clerk or bailiff in the country; civil servants in country districts were often so ignorant that they could not even write their names. The real scholar was too often hampered by poverty, and compelled to waste his time and run into temptation by going on *sockengång*. School holidays were too long. Education was altogether too religious and theological in tone: it might serve well enough (he conceded) as training for the priesthood, but it had little relevance to the service of the state in peace or war. 'The land is become barren and unfruitful of useful folk, so that despite the hardness of the times we are in greater straits for men than for money.' [1] In short, education had ceased to be practical: it might indeed equip men to pursue the endless course of theological controversy, but it did not teach mathematics to aspiring artillerists, nor ground the budding diplomat in foreign tongues. The King's own ideal for the average citizen he expounded in 1631: he would have boys taught to fear God; to read, write and reckon; to know herbs and their properties; to be familiar with the

---

[1] Thyselius, *Handlingar*, I. I, *seqq.*

configuration of the heavens and the disposition of the earth; and to know their Bible, catechism, law and history. Such an education, he felt, might prove a sound basis for a career either spiritual or temporal.[1]

Since the energies of schools and university had been so mis-applied, what was now to be done? What remedies could be proposed? The aims of Gustav Adolf's policy, as it affected the schools, are clear enough, though his measures at times may appear tentative and uncertain. He desired, first, to widen the school curriculum so as to include 'modern' subjects—and hence to diminish the traditional predominance of Latin. He hoped to secure the proper teaching of these subjects by extending the control of the lay authorities over the educational field. And he was concerned to apply the financial support of the state in such a way as to eliminate waste, and to obtain the most satisfactory return for the resources which the schools received.

All these objects are revealed in his proposals to the Clergy in 1620. He then suggested the setting-up, at Åbo and Linköping, of two full *gymnasia*, of the type which had been popular in Germany since the reforms of Sturm at Strassburg. These would be new foundations, and would provide, at the upper level, an education not much below the university standard. Five 'half-*gymnasia*' or *trivial*-schools (he revived the old name for a new thing) were to be established at suitably well-distributed centres (Västerås, Växjö, Skara, Viborg, and either Härnösand or Uleåborg). These were to be an improvement on the old provincial schools. Thus the cathedral schools would vanish; or rather, two of them would be transformed into *gymnasia*, and most of the rest would be degraded into the new *trivial*-schools. State aid for education would thus be concentrated on a much smaller number of institutions. This, however, need not inevitably involve an absolute diminution of the available facilities; for the King intimated that he expected the towns to maintain *trivial*-schools of their own, independently of state assistance; and the whole responsibility for the starting and maintenance of infant schools and primary schools was now to be taken from the central government and transferred to the local authorities. Nevertheless, the new system would undoubtedly mean a curtailment of the 'scholastic' type of education in favour of

---

[1] Thyselius, *Bidrag till svenska kyrkans och läroverkens historia utur archiver* (cited as Thyselius, *Bidrag*), p. 163.

the more 'practical' grounding in the elements which it was to be the function of the *trivial*-schools to provide.

The new schools were to teach a standardized and improved curriculum. In the *gymnasia* this was to include ethics, politics and Swedish law, with some provision for mathematics, astronomy, and natural science; in the *trivial*-schools mathematics and science were for the first time to be compulsory. The comparison with the School Ordinance of 1611 was striking: whereas the cathedral and provincial schools had taught six subjects, the new *gymnasia* were to teach thirteen, and the new *trivial*-schools nine. The tyranny of Latin was thus sensibly abated; and by the introduction of Swedish law the possibility of a lay career after schooldays was for the first time openly entertained. Further, the ardour of students was to be encouraged by scholarships, and by the expulsion of those who did not make reasonable progress: hitherto a pupil had been allowed to remain stationary in the same class for so long as his resources should hold out. And lastly, Gustav Adolf proposed the institution of an Inspector-General, who should be a layman; and the commutation of parochial contributions for a cash payment to the school.

The King's programme was not much to the taste of the Clergy, to whom it was submitted. Their plan was for the conversion of *all* the cathedral schools into *gymnasia*, and for the setting-up of *trivial*-schools in twelve other towns: they were thus opposed to the concentration of state aid proposed by the King. They offered no concessions in the matter of broadening the curriculum. They passed over in silence the proposal for lay inspection, and recommended instead annual examinations by a board consisting of the bishop of the diocese and two other learned men. And, while admitting the disadvantages of *sockengång*, they protested that no substitute for it was likely to prove equally satisfactory. In short, the Church, as might have been expected, showed itself unsympathetic to any laicizing of education, and anxious rather to extend than to curtail its control of the nation's schools.[1]

Nevertheless, the King persisted; and in the next two or three years his policy, in so far as it was actually enforced (a matter of some doubt), was in the spirit of his proposals of 1620. In 1620, for instance, he limited the area within which parochial contributions

---

[1] Holmquist, *Sv. K.Hist.*, IV. 185; Brandell, II. 111-18; Thyselius, *Handlingar*, I. 3-4, 7-18, 28 *seqq.*; C. A. Brolén, *Bidrag till Västerås läroverks historia*, I. 32.

might be taken to a radius of six Swedish miles—*i.e.* a day's journey from the school; and thus, as he hoped, prevented some of the waste of time which *sockengång* usually entailed.[1] In 1624 he went further, and ordered the commutation of these contributions for money.[2] But this proved impossible to enforce: the custom was too deep-rooted to be destroyed by proclamation.[3] A century and a half later Gustav III made another attempt, and was no more successful; for though parochial collections were thereafter deprived of any legal status, they continued on a voluntary basis; and for many years afterwards *djäknar* took the road to beg their bread from door to door. As late as the beginning of the nineteenth century the practice persisted, under the name of *viatikering*, in the diocese of Härnösand.[4]

But if national resistance defeated the King over the question of *sockengång*, he was more successful in his attempt to assert the principle of lay control. Although he never appointed an Inspector-General of schools, as he had threatened to do, the desire for lay supervision of education was one of the motives that led him to launch the plan for a *consistorium generale*[5]; and when the opposition of the bishops made success on these lines impossible he did not abandon the schools to the bishops as easily as he abandoned the Church: the Chancery Ordinance of 1626 *e silentio* left the Chancellor in the position of virtual Minister for Education.[6]

At the same time Gustav Adolf was encouraging the local authorities to take the initiative in providing themselves with elementary education. Some of the charters he granted to new towns, or reissued to old ones, contain the condition that the town council shall set up a school.[7] The most remarkable example, and the most characteristic for Gustav Adolf's standpoint, is that of Jönköping. It was the King's desire that Jönköping should become the great trading and manufacturing centre for the southern border districts and the Småland highlands. He therefore insisted that the town should support a special technical school, whose duty it was to be to provide the citizens with a 'sound commercial education'. The

---

[1] von Bonsdorff, p. 18; Brandell, II. 114.
[2] von Bonsdorff, pp. 19-20; Brandell, II. 127.
[3] When Gustav Adolf founded Åbo *gymnasium* in 1630 he expressly permitted *sockengång*: von Bonsdorff, p. 21.
[4] Laestadius, I. 105; von Bonsdorff, pp. 35-9.
[5] See Chapter VII, above.
[6] Ahnlund, *Oxenstierna*, pp. 351-2.
[7] *Sv. folksk. hist.*, I. 149; Brandell, II. 371, 390.

burghers of Jönköping seem to have been less appreciative of this advantage than they ought to have been. It became necessary to send a special royal instruction to Jönköping, containing what must have been one of the earliest recorded orders for compulsory universal education. Every inhabitant of Jönköping having a son of the age of seven years was bound to send him to school. Either the boy must go to a *trivial*-school, or to Jönköping's technical school, or he must be set to learn a craft. Fathers who neglected to send their sons to school were to be fined. Boys who idled, or were stupid, in their work at the *trivial*-school, were to be removed to the technical school to learn book-keeping. And if, in defiance of this care for his future welfare, a boy should at the age of 16 have no noticeable progress in any direction to his credit, the resources of civilization were even then not exhausted; for the town was to confiscate one-third of his inheritance, and retain it until such time as he might amend his ways and resign himself to becoming a useful citizen.[1]

By 1623 Gustav Adolf was probably beginning to entertain doubts as to the effectiveness of the policy of 1620. That policy, if it had been fully carried out, would certainly have entailed some disadvantages. It appeared to give the financial blessing of the state to the *trivial*-school at the expense of the *gymnasium*; to the lower levels at the expense of the upper. In any case, if the cathedral schools were thus to disappear, the contemplated provision of only two *gymnasia* (one of them in Finland) as a supplement to or substitute for the university, was quite inadequate. Gustav Adolf may or may not have realized this from the beginning. At all events, when he did at last proceed to the setting-up of a *gymnasium*, he chose neither Åbo nor Linköping for the experiment: he chose Västerås, and thus tacitly admitted that the provisions of 1620 had been too narrow. The choice of Västerås may to some extent have been accidental. In 1623 there was a severe outbreak of plague in Stockholm, and the King and government moved for safety to Västerås. Rudbeckius, the Bishop of Västerås, perceived the opportunity, seized it, plied the King with arguments; and before Gustav Adolf returned to the capital he had agreed in principle to the institution of a *gymnasium* at Västerås, and promised handsome financial assistance.

[1] Stiernman, *CPO*, I. 926-8; Thyselius, *Handlingar*, I. 84-5; Björkman, *Jönköping*, II. 280; Holmquist, *Sv. k. hist.*, IV. 1. 298; Brandell, II. 123-4; *Sv. folksk. hist.*, I. 152-4.

The foundation of the *gymnasium* of Västerås in 1623 was followed by the establishment, in quick succession, of *gymnasia* at Strängnäs (1626), Linköping (1627), Åbo and Dorpat (1630), Reval and Riga (1631); and, in the years immediately after Gustav Adolf's death, at Stockholm, Skara and Viborg (1640), and Växjö (1643); so that by the close of Kristina's reign the *gymnasium* had made good its position, never afterwards to be shaken, as the type of Swedish high-school education. Each *gymnasium* from its foundation had features peculiar to itself—features which, as a rule, reflected the personal interests of the bishop in whose cathedral-town it was located; but there was much that was common to all of them, and their foundation within the space of a generation was an event of major importance in Swedish cultural history.

It had been one of the most serious defects of Swedish education, in the years before the *gymnasia*, that it provided no real preparation in the schools for continued studies at a university. Even in the matter of Latin, where, if anywhere, one would have expected the schools to achieve a satisfactory result, the record was disappointing. The university complained of the ignorance of its freshmen. It was partly to cover the gap between school and university that men like Rudbeckius and Messenius established their private coaching-colleges at Uppsala.[1] What was really needed, however, was some sort of propaedeutical instruction in the schools themselves. The academic level at the top of the provincial schools, and even of the cathedral schools, fell so far short of university standards that it was difficult to solve the problem without remodelling the schools. The grant to Västerås in 1623 provided the answer for which men were looking. Into the gap between school and university was thrust the *gymnasium*, as a superstructure upon the old *trivial*-school. The cathedral school had provided one more class than the provincial school (or two, if the *classis theologica* existed): the new *gymnasia* usually provided three extra classes after the *trivial*-school education was completed, and superadded to these a special theological school of its own. The transition from school to university could thus be made smoothly, and the freshman might expect to benefit from his university studies from the moment of his matriculation.

---

[1] See below, pp. 464-5. In October 1623 the negotiations with Poland were embarrassed because in Axel Oxenstierna's absence no diplomat could be found whose Latin was pure enough to escape the contempt of the classically languaged Poles: *AOSB*, II. v. 238. Even thirty years later Whitelocke had a poor opinion of the standard of Latin among the boys at Skara *gymnasium*: Whitelocke, I. 189-90.

Besides this fundamental improvement, the institution of the
gymnasia brought other changes of great importance. The improvement in the finances of the schools, which was the result of the new
royal grants, meant better staffing and better pay for the staff. The
basic equipment of a *gymnasium* was recognized to be at least two
theological lektors, and at least four philosophical lektors. The old
system of class-masters was now abandoned: the lektor no longer
taught all subjects to his own especial class; he taught all classes his
own especial subjects. With better revenues came better buildings,
and hence the possibility of some sort of separation of the advanced
pupils from the beginners. Rudbeckius and Paulinus were particularly distinguished by their zeal as builders. The system of one-year,
instead of two-year courses, which had been initiated at Västerås
by Rudbeckius in the years before 1623, now became general in the
gymnasia, and this resulted in a great saving of time, since it
eliminated the dreary revision-work which had filled the second
year of each course under the old régime. It also made more time
for new subjects in the curriculum. This, undoubtedly, was one of
the objects Gustav Adolf had at heart in his endowment of the
gymnasia, and it seems very likely that he stipulated with Rudbeckius
for concessions on this point, as the price of his sanction.

In point of curriculum the *gymnasia* showed considerable
variation. Strängnäs concentrated (once Latin, Greek, Hebrew and
theology had been given their share) upon mathematics, astronomy
and music. It was at Strängnäs, too, that Paulinus developed a
rigid perversion of Ramism which had a narrowing effect on the
study of the classics; for he rejected all classical authors who were
not consonant with Christian doctrines, so that in practice Virgil
and Cicero were the only profane authors to be read, and they
simply as the indispensable exemplars of style. Strängnäs, indeed,
if it had not been for the mathematics (a study in which Paulinus
enjoyed a deserved reputation) would have been little better than a
seminary for ordinands, and thus by no means what Gustav Adolf
had hoped from the *gymnasia*. Västerås under Rudbeckius was both
more humane in its treatment of classical authors and more catholic
in the range of its subjects. Besides mathematics and astronomy,
which now generally made good their footing in the schools as
regular subjects, Västerås taught geography, history, science, ethics,
politics and Swedish law, in addition to the biblical languages,
theology and music. A period was even set aside for modern

languages, though admittedly only a period which might alternatively be devoted to private reading. The number of subjects was considerably in excess of the number of lektors (though the lektorships rose steadily from the original figure), and hence it followed that each lektor taught several subjects: thus at Strängnäs *philosophus primus* taught eloquence and logic; *secundus*, arithmetic, algebra and geometry; *tertius*, physics, medicine and botany. When in 1632 Joannes Elai Terserus was appointed lektor in Greek at Västerås, he was compelled to take over the instruction in music, though this was really the duty of the lektor in rhetoric. This system was not so inconvenient as it is to-day, for in the seventeenth century the goal of omniscience seemed often almost within reach, and no self-respecting lektor need feel many qualms about undertaking tuition in any of these subjects. The majority of such of them as were not purely linguistic were based essentially on a knowledge of the classics: 'physics', for instance, was derived mainly from Aristotle; astronomy from Ptolemy; history from Livy, Tacitus, and the Bible.[1]

From the King's point of view the new curricula must have been something of a disappointment. There were now 'modern subjects' in the syllabus, certainly; but for the most part they were still taught on mediaeval lines. Nevertheless, it was of great importance that they had made good a footing, on terms, if not of equality, at least of poor-relationship to the others. The empire of *verba* was crumbling: the school, no less than the university, was henceforth to concern itself with *res*. It was not the least of Gustav Adolf's achievements.

A school which aimed at providing a complete education, from the rudiments to the university level, and whose pupils might easily vary in age from 5 to 30,[2] was bound to be somewhat unwieldy. It was soon found necessary to differentiate between the various levels. The development at Västerås under Rudbeckius provides a

---

[1] Rudbeckius at Västerås taught Swedish and Scandinavian history, bringing the story down to Gustav Adolf's victories in Germany. Hall, *Rudbeckius*, p. 271.

[2] *ibid.*, p. 313. It was considered a scandal to have married pupils, however; but not, apparently, to have bearded ones: Whitelocke writes: 'From the church Whitelocke went to the free-school hard by, which is a large room, and in it between three and four hundred scholars, and some of them at the upper end with great beards, of thirty years of age, yet as subject to the rod's correction if they offend as the young boys among whom they sit. It caused smiling to see the disproportion and gravity of these scholars in respect of the others. Many of them are choristers and did in the school make the same vocal music as in the church, louder than ordinary, but not sweeter or more skilful.' Whitelocke, I. 188.

good example of the process. Until 1628 the *trivial*-school and the *gymnasium* had a single Rector and a staff partly common to both. In 1628, however, Rudbeckius promulgated the *Leges et Constitutiones* of the school. Henceforth the *trivial*-school became a separate institution with a Rector of its own. It had seven classes, all of which were one-year classes except the lowest, which took two. The *gymnasium* had three one-year classes. No student might remain longer than three years in any class. But now came a new development, with the appearance of the so-called *Collegium Candidatorum*. This was designed exclusively for ordinands, and corresponded (on a higher level) to the old *classis theologica*. It provided a two-years' course, mainly in theology, and was thus superimposed on the *gymnasium* as the *gymnasium* had been superimposed on the *trivial*-school. In the following year, 1629, another change was made. The lowest (two-year) class in the *trivial*-school was split off to form a new institution called the *pedagogium*, which became a reading-and-writing school of two (later three) one-year classes, with its own Rector. Thus in the final stage Västerås had four distinct institutions, housed in three separate buildings: the three-year *pedagogium*, the five-year *trivial*-school, the three-year *gymnasium*, and the two-year *Collegium Candidatorum*.[1]

The *gymnasium* and the *Collegium Candidatorum*, between them, offered an education for ordinands which did not fall much below the level of that available at Uppsala. It was an advantage to have such facilities in every diocese, especially since each diocese had its own well-marked style in religious observances and Church music, and would thus be anxious to train its own clergy. Thus there was

---

[1] The royal letter founding Västerås *gymnasium* is printed in full in a Swedish translation in *Valda aktstycken*, pp. 53-6; the first curriculum in *ibid.*, pp. 58-9; the statute of 1628, including rules, curriculum, salary-rates, in *ibid.*, pp. 60-100; and a schematic time-table in *ibid.*, pp. 102-3. Much information about early days at Västerås is in Brolén, I. The annual number of entrants rose from 37 in 1621 to 75 in 1626; and the total number of scholars for the *gymnasium* and school combined was, in 1630, 190: Brolén, I. 7. The chapter-headings of the rules shed some light on the social habits of the boys: *e.g.*

Cap. VI: De pugnis et grassationibus.
Cap. VII: De ebrietate et nocturnis clamoribus.
Cap. VIII: De luxu, libidine et immodestia.
Cap. IX: De furto et negligentia.   (etc.)—Brolén, I. 19-21.

Rudbeckius also founded in 1632 a girls' school at Västerås, where the pupils were taught the three R's and craftwork. This was probably the first regular girls' school in Sweden. On this, and women's education in general, see B. R. Hall, *Rudbeckii flickskola och dess föregångare* (in *Från skilda tider: studier tillägnade Hj. Holmquist*), *passim*.

from the beginning a clear tendency for the *gymnasia* to aspire to the position of so many diocesan universities. This tendency was reflected in their teaching techniques, which were frankly modelled on university practice—for instance, as regards disputations. It was apparent in the staffing arrangements: as at Uppsala the Rectorship was a short-term office which went to the lektors in rotation. The lektors formed a hierarchy with a strictly determined order of precedence which corresponded to the order in the university. As one lektor died or left the school, all others moved a step upwards on the ladder of promotion: *philosophus quartus* became *philosophus tertius*, and henceforward lectured on a different set of topics, since subjects were annexed to the office rather than to the man who filled it. Paulinus tried hard to persuade the King to allow Strängnäs to confer the fil. mag. degree; but Gustav Adolf refused thus to obliterate the distinction between *gymnasium* and university. The most that he would concede was permission for candidates who completed their course at the *gymnasium* with distinction to be given the degree of fil. kand., which really meant no more than that they had been adjudged fit to pursue a course of higher studies at a university. The *gymnasia* therefore reconciled themselves to their proper function—to providing an adjunct to, and preparation for, a university education, rather than attempting to compete with it. For the less distinguished pupils they had all that was required; but no schoolmaster would be likely to get a post, and no parson a benefice, unless he had also been to a university.[1] Rudbeckius, indeed, encouraged his students to go to Uppsala, giving them scholarships on condition that they returned after taking their degree to teach or preach in the diocese of Västerås; and it was not unusual for the successful university student to come down to his old *gymnasium* and give proof of his newly won learning in a lecture to his former school-fellows.

The quality of the lektors at the new *gymnasia* was extremely high: Georg Stiernhielm was for a time lektor at Västerås,[2] and many of his colleagues would have adorned a university. A lektorship in theology was often the highroad to Church preferment. In this, too, Gustav Adolf's reign inaugurated a tradition which continues to our own day; for there can be few countries where the

[1] The training of priests tended gradually to be transferred to the university and away from the *gymnasia*, especially after the School Ordinance of 1649. Askmark, pp. 145-53.

[2] B. Swartling, *Stiernhielm*, p. 21.

standard of learning in secondary-school masters can compare with that usual in Sweden.[1]

Gustav Adolf's final decision to concentrate the state's aid to education upon the *gymnasia* had inevitably disastrous effects upon some of the old *trivial*-schools, from which that aid was now withdrawn. Thus Strängnäs was allotted revenues which had hitherto supported schools at Nyköping, Örebro, and Södertälje—the two former of which, at least, had been famous schools in their day and done good work according to their lights; while the foundation of Linköping *gymnasium* meant the end of state aid for the schools of Norrköping, Söderköping and Vadstena. Not all *trivial*-schools were thus deprived in favour of *gymnasia*; but for the most part they were now bidden to look for support from the towns in which they were situated.

This was, no doubt, unfortunate; but Gustav Adolf seems to have made up his mind that the state's resources would not suffice for all. He chose at last to devote them to higher education, and there can be no doubt that he was right. Municipal authorities might conceivably endow a *trivial*-school; but it was scarcely to be expected that they should finance a *gymnasium*. The King's decision was of the greatest importance for the future of his country. It meant that a secondary education of high quality, on a democratic basis, would henceforth be available to all. The great *gymnasia* of Sweden have played a part in her history comparable to that of the public schools in the history of England; and though it would be untrue to say that the battle of Lützen was won on the playing-fields of Västerås, it would be strictly accurate to attribute to the *gymnasia* those enduring triumphs in the more civilized fields of human endeavour upon which Sweden's reputation rests so securely to-day. The *gymnasia* at the time of Gustav Adolf's death certainly fell far short of his ideal for education. A new scholasticism informed their studies, hardly less rigid and artificial than the old. The School Ordinance of 1649 showed how little progress had really been made in modernizing the curriculum. Yet to Gustav Adolf belongs the credit of making the first breach in the wall. A genera-

---

[1] For the above section on the *gymnasia*, see Brandell, II. 118, 151-75, 200-222, 359, 399; Askmark, pp. 95-116, 140, 330-2; Rudbeckius, *Dagbok*, p. 49 (for *ordo lectionum*, etc., at Västerås); Risberg, p. 234; Lundström, I. 223, 227-9; Hall, *Rudbeckius*, pp. 145-87, 194, 267-71, 313; Boëthius, *Rudbeckius*, p. 154; Holm, pp. 45-51; Sjöstrand, pp. 216-17; Bergman, p. 22; Blees, pp. 100-3; Schmitt, p. 141; *AOSB*, II. XII. 621.

tion after his death Olof Rudbeck was rising to eminence; and from him it was not a far cry to Linnaeus.[1]

These reforms in secondary education were matched by important progress at the very lowest level. It was in this reign that the first real assault upon illiteracy was made. Hitherto, as we have seen, it had been considered sufficient if the mass of the population had a good knowledge of at least the text of the more important portions of the catechism. In Gustav Adolf's time catechetical instruction was systematized and extended from the church to the home (the so-called *husförhör*); and more attention was paid to instilling a real grasp of religious principle, as against the mere memorizing of words. In this Paulinus was especially prominent, though the other bishops did not lag much behind. Special intervention by the Crown was felt to be necessary in the case of backward Norrland: a succession of royal Instructions to the Rural Deaneries of Upper Norrland reinforced the efforts of the clergy with the weight of the secular arm. And having gone so far, Gustav Adolf went further. His Norrland Instructions contain, for the first time, provisions for the compelling of parents to see that their children were taught, not merely to know their catechism, but to read. It was a most important advance. Paulinus, for all his enthusiasm, had not dared to hope for so much in his own see. The effects were not immediately felt; but there is general agreement that the number of literates rose decidedly between the beginning and end of the reign.[2]

The movement towards literacy was no doubt aided by Gustav Adolf's Ordinance for Parish Clerks (*klockarestadga*). This Ordinance defined the duties of the clerk; and among others it laid upon him the obligation to teach and catechize the parish children. For this work most of the existing parish clerks were quite unsuited; and hence there arose a movement, inaugurated by Paulinus in 1618, and followed soon after by Rudbeckius, to require that parish clerks

---

[1] The old type of cathedral school survived here and there, as the result of special local circumstances: thus at Uppsala, where the presence of the university made a *gymnasium* superfluous; or Kalmar, where Jonas Rhotovius, disappointed in the early 'twenties of seeing the school erected into a 'half-*gymnasium*', himself remodelled the school as an essentially priest-training institution. Herdin, III. 203 (for Uppsala); F. Petersson, *Olaus Svebilius intill ärkebiskopstiden*, pp. 16-20 (for Kalmar). For a notable educational experiment, linking Ramist teaching techniques with anticipations of Comenius, see E. Källquist, *Jacob Rudbeckius' Latinstad, passim*. A useful survey of the process of transition from *trivial*-school to *gymnasium* is N. Beckman, *Vår skolas historia*, I. (Skara). Skara was a very large school: in 1624 they had not less than 480 boys divided into five classes, with one teacher to each class: Beckman, *op. cit.*, I. 25-6, 39.

[2] *Sv. folksk. hist.*, I. 118-33; Lundström, I. 189-90.

should in future be educated (*boklärda*) men, preferably (though this was a counsel of perfection) in priest's Orders. The new generation of 'learned' clerks was not received with much enthusiasm by rustic congregations, but it undoubtedly had some effect in raising the standard of popular education.[1]

(iv) *The University*

The accession of Gustav Adolf found the University of Uppsala —at that time the only university in the Swedish dominions—in a somewhat critical situation.[2] Its foundation dated from 1477, and for a few decades thereafter it had dragged on an uncertain existence, hampered by inadequate resources, by shortage of books, and by the general backwardness of the society it had been intended to serve. The troubles of Kristian II's time had overwhelmed it, and when Sweden won her freedom at last, the university had ceased to exist. Gustav Vasa had lacked the resources, and perhaps the interest, to revive it, in spite of a personal appeal from Melanchthon in 1539; and had confined himself to facilitating, to a modest extent, the exodus of Swedish students to universities overseas, and above all to the Protestant universities of Germany.

Throughout the sixteenth century, then, the Swedish youth was forced to seek higher education outside his own country. Per Brahe, in his *Oeconomia*, was emphatic upon the need for the noble-man to acquire polish and knowledge of the world by foreign travel[3]; and the great nobles of the second half of the century, as well as the leading figures in the Church, went to Germany to complete their training. The arrangements for such study-tours were not easy, for the incomes of private individuals, like the revenue of the state itself, were mainly in kind; and to finance his son's studies a father might often have to negotiate complicated business transactions involving the disposal of kegs of butter in one place, or the shipping

---

[1] *Sv. folksk. hist.*, I. 138-45; Lundström, I. 188-90; Brandell, II. 489-499. For educational work among the Lapps, see *supra*, p. 425; Waaranen, *Samling*, V. 246-7. Good work for popular education was also done by Skytte in Livonia: Liljedahl, p. 388.

[2] For what follows, see Annerstedt, *Upsala Universitets Historia*, I. 1-267; Schück, *Messenius*, p. 51 *seqq.*; T. Berg, *Skytte*, pp. 35-42, 117-33; Brandell, I. 373-8; II. 32-76.

[3] *cf.* the extraordinary panegyric on foreign travel by J. Matthiae Gothus (Holmquist, *J. Matt. Gothus*, p. 89).

of consignments of copper to another[1]; while an additional difficulty was presented by the custom of studying, not at one university only, but at several in succession. The favourite resort for Swedish students was Rostock. Ever since the foundation of the university there in 1419 it had been much frequented by undergraduates from Scandinavia; and since the town turned Lutheran at the Reformation, the tradition persisted all through the sixteenth century, and beyond it. For a time its claims were seriously challenged by Wittenberg; but the too eirenical temper of Melanchthon after Luther's death made it suspect to the straiter sort of Lutherans. Moreover, from 1551 Rostock had a powerful attraction in the person of David Chytraeus. His brilliant synthesis of the teaching techniques and educational theories of Ramus and Melanchthon made a great appeal, and he enjoyed great authority in the Lutheran world as one of the authors of the rigid Formula of Concord. Rostock really moulded two generations of Swedish statesmen and divines: Kenicius, Paulinus, Axel Oxenstierna and his brothers, were all Chytraeus' pupils. Wittenberg, however, continued to attract students from Sweden—among them Johannes Rudbeckius, Raumannus, and Isak Rothovius; Greifswald was increasingly frequented; Leipzig had its quota; and Giessen, Helmstädt and Frankfurt on the Oder (which was Skytte's first university) all drew contingents to sit at the feet of this or that now-forgotten celebrity. By Gustav Adolf's time the Dutch universities, too, were beginning to come into favour. The students, though often assisted by the state, had on occasion to contend with extreme penury when by some accident supplies from home failed; they were exposed to strong moral temptations; and also to the more insidious lure of pursuing theological speculation along paths which led to the poisoned wells of Jesuit or Calvinistic learning. Defection from Lutheran orthodoxy was a danger from which every anxious father prayed that his son might be delivered; and not seldom his prayers were vain. Hence the decision of the Örebro *riksdag* in 1617 that students going abroad to study must obtain from their bishop an attestation of their doctrinal orthodoxy.[2]

---

[1] See, *e.g.*, *AOSB*, II. xii. 250, 568; W. Tham, *Oxenstierna*, pp. 58-9. Cash in bulk, however, was sent occasionally: *Abraham Brahes tidebok*, p. 131.

[2] For Swedish students abroad, see Tham, pp. 56-82; T. Berg, *Skytte*, pp. 43-75; *Valda aktstycken till svenska undervisningsväsendets historia*, pp. 48-50; Wrangel, pp. 46-9, 57, 91; *SRDA*, II. 151; Schück, *Sv. bilder*, III. 25-34; Ahnlund, *Storhetstidens Gryning*, p. 52; Rudbeckius, *Dagbok*, where (at p. 134) a list for 1621 is given. Most of the names are noted as 'ordinatus'; but one as 'ribaldus'. Boys from Västerås could usually get a scholarship for overseas study from the diocese: C. A. Brolén, *Bidrag till Västerås läroverks historia*, I. 18.

At the end of his life Johan III is said to have expressed regret that he had not seriously set about the revival of the university. Duke Karl atoned for his brother's neglect. The great national demonstration of Protestant solidarity at the Uppsala Meeting of 1593 was made the occasion for the refounding of the university, which thus became the symbol of Sweden's invincible Lutheranism. Seven Chairs were instituted, three in the theological, four in the philosophical faculty, and definite revenues assigned for their support. An eighth, in medicine, was shortly added; but it was never filled in Karl's lifetime. A grant of privileges followed in 1595, whereby the university was empowered to try, punish and imprison its members for all except serious offences; was given authority to make its own appointments; was exempted from all taxes and impositions; and was bidden to set up a 'Community'.[1] And lastly, two students from every diocese, after examination, were to be maintained abroad at a Protestant university—a clause indicative of no very great faith in the academic standards of the revived foundation.[2]

The most remarkable of the new professors was undoubtedly Laurentius Paulinus Gothus, professor successively of logic, astronomy and theology. Under his guidance Uppsala became strongly Ramist. As a whole, however, the staff was not very distinguished; and the troubled history of the university in the years after 1593 was such as to deter, rather than to attract, fresh talent. The university authorities were coerced, much against their will, to give some ambiguous support to the campaign of Angermannus in favour of Sigismund; with the inevitable result that they drew upon themselves the resentment and suspicion of Karl IX. In 1602 and 1603 Karl was meditating the foundation of a new university at Strängnäs, with Johannes Bureus as Professor of Hebrew and Runic.[3] The idea was abandoned in 1604 in favour of a reform of Uppsala; but the only tangible result of that reform was the appointment to Chairs of Rudbeckius and Lenaeus. Their arrival added much-needed academic weight to a very indifferent professoriate; but unfortunately it also precipitated a severe internal struggle. For Rudbeckius and Lenaeus were vehement neo-Aristotelians, and against Paulinus and his Ramists they opened a violent assault.

---

[1] A 'Community' was a student hostel, in this instance for 40 scholars: they lived and ate together; 24 of them had all their expenses paid, while the remaining 16 were charged at the modest rate of 8 öre per week.

[2] Text in Thyselius, *Handlingar*, II. 6-13.

[3] *Anteckningar af J. T. A. Bureus*, pp. 24, 27.

Karl grew increasingly annoyed at the university's independent attitude towards himself, and his doubts of their loyalty strengthened as he grew older. He refused to sanction the Statutes drawn up by Rudbeckius in 1606. He suspended the university's privileges in 1607. The retirement of Rudbeckius and Lenaeus to Germany in the same year, for a period of further study, deprived Uppsala of two of its strongest men. The Chairs changed hands incessantly, and few of their holders were equal to their duties. In 1609 Karl seems actually to have put into effect a proposal to abolish professorships in theology and entrust instruction in this subject to the Archbishop and Chapter of Uppsala.

The university was indeed in a state of chaos. There was no proper division into faculties. The power of the Rector, and the period of his tenure of office, were alike uncertain. No Chancellor had been appointed. There was no entrance examination of any sort. There was no library or bookshop in Uppsala, and no printing-press; and the straggling hovels that made up the town provided little accommodation for students or staff. With the retirement of Paulinus to a bishopric, the last outstanding member of the staff was removed. And half the Chairs were vacant.

This, however, marked the nadir of the university's fortunes. For in 1609 Karl appointed, as professor in the new subjects of law and politics, one of the most remarkable Swedes of his generation— Johannes Messenius.[1] Messenius was far superior to any of his colleagues in learning, in enthusiasm, and in capacity for work; and he had in addition an ability to attract and fascinate under-graduates which alarmed his fellow-professors, and which made him a dangerous force in university politics. He was a Ramist, rather than an Aristotelian—or, at least, he took the Ramist side in the great debate; but in reality he was the first practising exponent in Sweden of 'courtly' education, and he aimed at engrafting upon the university curriculum a training which would be useful to the statesman as well as to the priest. His brilliance, his personal charm, his genius for self-advertisement, and the real need for the sort of education he provided, proved an irresistible magnet. The under-graduates flocked round him; and for the first time in its history Uppsala came to be popular among the sons of the nobility—a circumstance which gave great satisfaction to Messenius, who was an inveterate and unrepentant snob.

[1] For the earlier career of Messenius, see Chapter IV, *supra*.

Messenius' plan was to collect his pupils into a *Collegium Privatum* under his own supervision. It had, of course, no buildings, though a number of students boarded with Messenius; it was simply an organized study-group, bound together by Messenius' personality and the instruction which he offered. Besides lecturing on law, politics and most of the regular subjects of the curriculum, he encouraged his pupils to exercise themselves in riding, fencing and dancing. He wrote plays for them to act—plays based on popular historical legends, strongly nationalist in tone, and written, not in imitation of Terence's Latin, but in Swedish verse. The undergraduates acted with enthusiasm; the outside public was delighted; and Messenius' reputation grew inside and outside the University. He worked hard, and he made his pupils work; and all might have been well enough but for the appearance on the scene of a most formidable rival.[1]

This was Rudbeckius, who at the beginning of 1610 returned to Uppsala fortified by his refresher-course at Wittenberg. Almost immediately he came into sharp conflict with Messenius. In Messenius he saw a Ramist, a rival, and a crypto-Jesuit. He suspected his learning to be unsound, and he disliked his obvious efforts to curry favour in all possible quarters. But he was not above taking a leaf out of his book. Rudbeckius' new course in history soon became almost as popular as Messenius' new course in politics; the student body divided into two camps; and Rudbeckius found it expedient to form his followers into a *Collegium Privatum* on the Messenian model. Here he gave instruction more varied than Uppsala had ever known. With easy mastery he took in his stride everything from botany to bibliography. If Messenius had set Uppsala a new standard of industry and conscientious devotion to duty, Rudbeckius far exceeded it. His labours were prodigious. In 1610 he corrected over 8000 Greek and Latin proses, arranged 14 declamations, conducted 32 disputations, and held 6 examinations. In 1611 the pace was even hotter, for the number of proses soared to 200 per week.[2] Whereas Messenius smiled upon the gentlemanly arts, Rudbeckius was austerely academic. Messenius' College was

[1] Schück, *Messenius*, pp. 74-123. Messenius charged fairly high fees: Tegel, who sent his three stepsons, paid for 29 weeks' stay 130 *daler*, 2 rosenobles, a tun of Rostock ale, a sugar-loaf, and some flasks of wine. Ljung, *Tegel*, p. 86.

[2] A full account of the work of the *Collegium*, with its annual reports for 1610 and 1611, is in B. R. Hall, *Till Johannes Rudbeckii karakteristik*, pp. 42-93. The figures for Latin proses are on pp. 62, 72.

JOHANNES MESSENIUS

JOHANNES BUREUS

designed to produce men of the world; Rudbeckius' was avowedly a propaedeutical establishment which aimed at fitting freshmen to make the best of the course provided by the university, and may perhaps without unfairness be described as a 'crammer's'. There was another difference, too, and an important one: Rudbeckius' pupils were all registered and matriculated students of the university; they acknowledged themselves subject to its discipline; and they were never allowed to let their work in the College interfere with their attendance at university lectures. Messenius' pupils, on the other hand, had very often not matriculated at all; and if they had, were disposed (with Messenius' active encouragement) to defy the university authorities. Whereas Rudbeckius' *Collegium Privatum* might easily have developed into something like an Oxford College, that of Messenius was disruptive of the university, and seemed indeed to aim at setting itself up as a university on its own account.

Here, if anywhere, lay the real justification for the attitude which Rudbeckius took up. In 1610 he secured the first round in the struggle by raking up an old pamphlet against Karl IX, written by Messenius in his Jesuit days; and Messenius was forced to make public recantation of the Roman Catholic faith. But Messenius had ample revenge when Karl appointed Raumannus as Rector at the close of the same year. Messenius had hitherto justified the resistance of his pupils to the authority of previous Rectors by pointing out that the constitution of the university was still suspended, and that, by old mediaeval tradition, the Rector was the representative of the students, and ought therefore to have been elected by them.[1] But with the appointment of Raumannus he abandoned this line; for Raumannus was his strong supporter, and could be relied upon to back him in his fight with Rudbeckius.[2] The tables were now turned, and for the time being Messenius had the whip-hand.

The years 1611 and 1612 passed without any major outbreak; but it was clear that sooner or later there must be an explosion. In 1613 it came; and Gustav Adolf was called upon for the first time to intervene in the affairs of his distressful university.

The new King had upon his accession appointed a professor of logic, who by the terms of his appointment was to lecture upon the

---

[1] *cf.* the rectorial election at the Scottish universities.

[2] Raumannus' conceit was almost equal to Messenius': he described himself, with more truth than modesty, as 'solus, unicus et primus doctor theologicae inter limites regni Suetici natus post reformatum religionem': *AOSB*, II. XII. 507.

logic of Ramus.[1] Gustav Adolf was much under Skytte's influence, and Skytte, as we have seen, was an ardent Ramist. It seems therefore likely that the King approached university questions with some predisposition to Messenius' side.[2] If so, the conduct of Messenius must soon have alienated his sympathies. In accordance with a promise given in the Charter of 1612 Gustav Adolf had confirmed the privileges which Karl IX had suspended in 1607. But he had made one alteration: he insisted that the Rectorship should be an annual appointment. Raumannus therefore would retire at the end of 1612, and it would be necessary to elect a new Rector for 1613. Messenius and Rudbeckius both put themselves forward as candidates; but Messenius was unpopular among his colleagues, and in the result obtained but one vote to Rudbeckius' five and Lenaeus' two. Rudbeckius was therefore declared elected. Messenius refused to accept the decision, boycotted the new Rector's Installation, incited his own students (who, perhaps, needed little encouragement) to defy the Rector's authority, and succeeded in plunging the whole university into a most unedifying turmoil.[3]

At this point Gustav Adolf intervened, in a letter to the University couched in terms of proper severity[4]; but matters had reached such a pitch that royal admonitions had little or no effect. Messenius' students went about with drawn swords; Messenius himself heaped insults and objurgations, in the grossest language, upon all who did not actively take his part; his termagant wife, Lucia Grothusen, entered the fray to beard the *Consistorium Academicum*; 53 windows were broken by Messenius' enthusiastic and aristocratic supporters; and Messenius went so far as to challenge Rudbeckius to a duel, which Rudbeckius prudently declined. Messenius took the line that he stood *in loco parentis* to his pupils, who were therefore responsible to him, and amenable to no other control than such as he might think fit to exercise; and in the case of Åke Tott (the same Tott who was to distinguish himself by his incapacity in Germany twenty years later) he defied the university to do its worst. The

---

[1] Hallenberg, *Svea Rikes Historia under . . . Gustaf Adolf*, II. 764 *note* (c).

[2] Oxenstierna's sympathies, on the other hand, were Aristotelian; but he tried his best to preserve official impartiality. Ahnlund, *Oxenstierna*, pp. 379-81.

[3] For what follows, see Schück, *Messenius*, pp. 107-17; Annerstedt, I. 136-163; Hallenberg, II. 764-8; *AOSB*, II. XII. 3-6, 7-10, 119, 510-11.

[4] Hallenberg, II. 766-7: 'Had We not Ourself experienced and known what gain and advantage are inherent in bookish arts, We should have had but little reason to exert Ourself on behalf of the said Academy, or to shew any especial grace or favour toward such as are employed there, and who pay less heed to their duty and service than to their own ambition, private hates, and jealousies. . . .'

archbishop, Kenicius, though Ramist in sympathy, was driven by these excesses to take action against Messenius, and struck at the root of the trouble by forbidding private lectures and private colleges in future. Messenius replied by consigning 'the archbishop and the whole lot of them to seven thousand devils'.[1]

The King now intervened once more. The rectorial election was cancelled; Lenaeus was appointed temporary pro-Rector; and Rudbeckius and Messenius were summoned to Stockholm to argue their cause before a special committee of investigation, presided over by Oxenstierna.[2] Even here they could not behave themselves; and Rudbeckius produced an unpointed Hebrew Bible and scornfully challenged Messenius to read it. There was but one thing to be done: Gustav Adolf removed both these *esprits forts* from Uppsala. Rudbeckius was made a Court Chaplain, and shortly accompanied the King to Russia; Messenius was given the post of Chief Archivist, and soon after made a member of the new Supreme Court (*hovrätt*). His students had already deserted Uppsala and followed him to Stockholm.

It seems to be generally agreed that the major share of the blame for these incidents must lie with Messenius, whose vanity, unscrupulousness and jealousy are as undoubted as his ability. On the other hand, there is something to suggest that Rudbeckius' supporters formed a narrow academic clique, bound together by family connections and concerned to defend a monopoly of academic appointments against intruders; and no doubt the starchy piety of Rudbeckius provoked Messenius' sceptical and mischievous temper. But the whole episode was deplorable; and it was a great misfortune for Uppsala that she was not able to retain the services of two men so far above the average level of contemporary Swedish professors. It would be an error, however, to suppose that Uppsala was exceptionally cursed with the spirit of contention: academic feuds were then conducted with a violence both of word and deed which would pain a twentieth-century common room. The history of Ramus at Paris, half a century earlier, or the vitriolic outpourings of Anthony à Wood, in the Oxford of Charles II, remind us that broils of this sort long remained part of the normal stuff of academic life.

In the calm that succeeded the departure of Messenius and Rud-

---

[1] Hallenberg, II. 766 *note* (a). It should perhaps be explained that in Swedish 'seventeen', 'a thousand', 'seven thousand' are expletives of increasing degrees of violence, and 'devil' is much stronger than in English.

[2] Thyselius, *Handlingar*, II. 28-30.

beckius, Oxenstierna drew up a plan for the development of the
university which foreshadows, and indeed in some respects surpasses,
the reforms of the following decade.[1] But the desperate state of the
country's finances made it impossible to take any action at this time.
Gustav Adolf for the moment could do no more than apply palliatives.
He presented the university with the royal printing-press, which it
certainly had great need of: hitherto Swedish text-books had been
printed abroad; and this, besides being humiliating, resulted in
many printer's errors.[2] At the same time he made better provision
for the payment of the professors' salaries, allocated funds for
scholarships, and revived the 'Community'. These were much-
needed improvements, but they fell considerably short of what was
required: as early as 1614 the clergy were complaining of the
inadequacy and irregularity of the university revenues.[3]

The retirement of Raumannus to a country parsonage, early in
1614, and his death later in the same year, removed the last strong
partisan of Messenius[4]; but the Ramist controversy remained to
occupy the academic mind, and with the appointment of Johannes
Magni as professor of politics it grew more acute than ever, for
Magni was an Aristotelian and was soon involved in a furious
pamphleteering warfare with Bishop Paulinus, which dragged on
for some years. It ended with the triumph of Magni; and from
that moment Ramism in Uppsala was definitely on the defensive.[5]
The King's coronation in 1617 gave some relief from these petty
squabbles, in the form of a great degree-day, when Uppsala registered
a stage in her advance by conferring her first doctorates in theology,
and Axel Oxenstierna, who during these years acted as virtual—
though not official—Chancellor of the University, himself appeared
as Promoter. The four recipients, it is true, were given their degrees
honoris causa; but at least Sweden could now boast of Doctors of
her own.[6]

Despite these bright appearances, the university was still in no
very flourishing condition. Some improvements were indeed made
in 1617[7]; but the professors grumbled at the inadequacy of their
pay; between 1616 and 1621 only six Chairs were permanently filled;

---

[1] Ahnlund, *Oxenstierna*, p. 382.   [2] Hallenberg, II. 769-70.
[3] *AOSB*, II. xii. 122, 125, 127.   [4] *AOSB*, II. xii. 508.
[5] Annerstedt, I. 171-8; Sjöstrand, pp. 218-21; Holmquist, *J. Matt. Gothus*,
p. 74.
[6] Annerstedt, I. 182-3; Ahnlund, *Oxenstierna*, pp. 382-4. The graduands
were Kenicius, Paulinus, Rudbeckius, and Johannes Bothvidi.
[7] *SRDA*, II. 50, 151-2, 176-7.

above all, the King was gravely dissatisfied with the standard and nature of the instruction given. His sweeping condemnation of Swedish education, in his speech to the Clergy in 1620, included the university no less than the schools. The only solution that seemed to offer was the wholesale importation of talent from abroad. But the Clergy, to whom he turned for advice, deprecated this. The difficulties could be met, they considered, by increasing the number of Chairs, by raising the level of salaries, and by the appointment of a Bursar to manage the university's finances. 'And' (they added), 'since in Uppsala it is hard to buy meat and fish fresh, each professor ought to have a bit of ground and some meadow land near the town.'[1]

The King seems to have been impressed by their arguments: at all events he said no more for the present about foreign scholars, and in some important respects he followed the Clergy's advice. In 1620 he raised the number of professorships to thirteen—three in the theological faculty, two in law (one for Roman, one for Swedish law), two in medicine, and six in the philosophical faculty (history, Hebrew-and-Greek, astronomy, mathematics, logic and eloquence). To these he added in the following year a further Chair in theology, a now separate Chair of Greek, a Chair of poetry, and a curiously composite professorship in optics, music and mechanics. At the same time he ordered that the salaries of professors should be paid for the future in cash, and not, as hitherto, in grain, and thus withdrew them from the effects of the vagaries of the weather; he provided endowment for 20 (later 30) scholars; and he made provision for a 'Community' of 60 poor students. Further, he acceded to the Clergy's request, and allowed the university to employ a Bursar. And lastly, he presented them with a considerable collection of books, which formed the nucleus of the university library: he was subsequently to enrich it by successive donations of the treasures of Riga, Braunsberg, Würzburg and Mainz—the plunder of his victorious campaigns.[2] In 1622 he gave Uppsala her first Chancellor, by the appointment of Johan Skytte. Skytte was an ideal person for the office, and had already commended himself to the university by endowing the Skyttean Professorship in Eloquence and Politics.[3]

---

[1] Annerstedt, I. 187.

[2] Thyselius, *Handlingar*, I. 33-7, 38-42. Even so, Whitelocke formed a poor opinion of their library in 1654: Whitelocke, II. 148-9.

[3] *ibid.*, 196-7; The Skyttean Professor was bound to deliver every month an oration in praise of God's goodness, and to write and publish the history of the Kings of Sweden, especially those of the Vasa dynasty: Anjou, p. 264.

Uppsala was now respectably equipped with eighteen professorships, and though for the remainder of the reign there were usually
several that were vacant—and though in the end it did prove necessary to fetch professors from abroad—yet the problem of providing
a satisfactory staff might be considered almost solved. The
financial position of the university, however, was still very weak;
and in 1624 Gustav Adolf proceeded, by a magnificent act of
generosity, to remedy this defect, and to place Uppsala for centuries
beyond the reach of monetary cares. The death of Johan of Östergötland and of Karl Filip had been followed by the falling-in to the
King, as the only male representative of the reigning line of Vasas,
of all their private estates. His personal property now totalled upwards of 3500 manors (*hemman*).[1] By his great donation of 1624
Gustav Adolf presented to Uppsala in perpetuity 271 whole *hemman*,
one three-quarter *hemman*, 74 half *hemman*, 32 quarter *hemman* and
one one-sixth *hemman*, together with the royal share of tithe from
these manors.[2] All this property was exempt from all ordinary taxes,
aids and corvées, though it was to be liable for *skjutsning* and *gästning*
for the King's personal journeys; and, what was also of great importance, any future donations to the university from private individuals,
and any noble land (*frälsegods*) which the university might purchase
at any future time, were to be exempt too.

The effect of this splendid munificence—which remained un-
equalled in Swedish history until the days of Alfred Nobel [3]—can
be seen by a comparison of the university's income in 1613 with
the corresponding figure for 1625. In 1613 the university's income
consisted of 1560 *tunnor* of grain, whose value was about 2400 *daler*.
In 1625 the figure was 15,212 *daler*, to which must be added a further
donation of tithes from parishes in Hälsingland and Västmanland,
which brought in an annual income of 3831 *daler*. To-day, when
the university still owns about 200 of the original manors (the
balance having been sold or exchanged), the value of the land, as
assessed for taxation, is nearly eight and a quarter million *kronor*
(about £577,000).[4]

At the same time Gustav Adolf increased the number of royal

---

[1] The *hemman* was a fiscal unit of account: it was possible therefore to have
multiples or fractions of a *hemman*.
[2] S. E. Bring and O. Kollberg, *Gustav II Adolf donation till Uppsala Universitet*, p. 14, correcting Annerstedt, I. 204-5.
[3] Bergman, p. 17.
[4] For Gustav Adolf's donation, see Bring and Kollberg, pp. 7-42; Annerstedt,
I. 201-6.

scholars to 64; authorized the appointment of a university book-seller; and established the 'Community' at a figure of 100 students.[1]

All that now remained for the King to do, in order to smooth the path of the university, was to revise its privileges, sanction its statutes, and thus launch it fairly as a self-governing, independent academic corporation; and these last steps followed, with the minimum of delay, in 1625 and 1626.[2] The university henceforward had a regular constitution and definite examination regulations. The powers and functions of the Chancellor, pro-Chancellor, Rector Illustris, and Rector were defined; the duties of the Bursar laid down. A division into faculties was made at last, and Deans appointed for each. The 'time and exercises' required for each degree were prescribed, and the subject-matter of each course indicated. Members of the university were freed from civic burdens.[3] And it was ordered that no one should presume to study in Uppsala who was not a matriculated member of the university.[4]

For the remainder of the reign the university made quiet and steady progress. A sharp dispute between Lenaeus and Wallius necessitated Skytte's intervention in 1627; there were some complaints that the income of the university was being diverted to war funds; and once at least the råd debated a matter which, it might have been thought, was wholly the university's concern[5]; but on the whole the new arrangements worked well. In 1632, 16 of the 18 professorships were filled, and only 5 of these were held by foreigners. The number of students increased, until at the end of the reign it stood at about 1000, with an average yearly enrolment of about 160. The habit of visiting foreign universities had by no

---

[1] The students paid 8 öre per week, the state contributing 20 öre. Admission was by examination. The food was distinctly good; but three students had to share a room. Two professors were appointed as Inspectors. Schück, Sv. bilder, III. 70. Schück suggests that the Community might have formed the embryo of an English College-system. The Community founded by Karl Karlsson Gyllenhielm in 1629 was certainly tending in this direction: the students were to be governed by the Skyttean Professor, who was to be responsible for them morally and academically, and was to eat with them in Hall. But the organization fell to pieces as early as 1637, and the model was not imitated. Schück, Sv. bilder, IV. 8-11.

[2] The revised privileges were the work of Oxenstierna; the statutes (in the version of 1625) of Skytte. The 1625 statutes proved unsatisfactory, and were revised by Oxenstierna and Skytte in the definitive version of 1626. Ahnlund, Oxenstierna, pp. 387-8; Thyselius, Handlingar, II. 32-40.

[3] The råd decided, however, that stock on the glebe of professors, where it lay outside Uppsala, should not be exempt from the stock-tax. RRP, II. 170.

[4] Annerstedt, I. 212-14.

[5] RRP, I. 115; AOSB, II. XII. 535; Annerstedt, I. 231; Hall, Rudbeckius, p. 184.

means ceased: to the German universities formerly in favour were now added Leiden and Paris; and the King, anxious as he was to increase the prestige of Uppsala, was always willing to facilitate further studies abroad for a promising student. But more and more Swedes came to Uppsala for higher education.[1]

Nevertheless, Uppsala in 1632 was still in many respects a university in the making, and halted awkwardly half-way along the road that led from mediaeval to modern conditions. The Constitutions of 1626 laid great weight on the religious duties and moral standards of the undergraduate: he was expected to read his Bible every morning and evening, to refrain from swearing, to go to church regularly, and to attend often at Communion. Failure to appear at the public lectures meant relegation. Every student, moreover, had the right to complain if his professor were negligent, or lived an immoral life; and in such cases the anonymity of the complainant was to be preserved. Students were not to make a noise at night, nor to break windows, nor to fight; and any undergraduate who might discharge a firearm loaded with ball would be sent down. The Chapter of Västerås cautioned young men of the diocese who proceeded to the University against irregular living, and exhorted them to take care that they did not become puffed-up with much learning. Scholars or holders of bursaries were liable to be deprived of their emoluments *propter Luxum in Vestitu*.[2]

Such regulations had little effect. The student body was notorious for pugnacity and rowdiness. Drunkenness was not in itself an offence; and riotous living, especially by wealthy or noble undergraduates, was common. 'Town and Gown' rows were frequent, for it was the habit of the students to go '*grassatim*' through the streets; and as the university had a proctorial system, while the Town had no police force, each outbreak tended to exacerbate relations.[3] It was very difficult to control a student body which lived almost entirely in lodgings; and the disciplinary measures of the authorities were singularly ineffective: it was notoriously easy to escape from the university's gaol.[4] The students were still largely unorganized, though already undergraduates from the same province tended to associate; but these loose associations existed

---

[1] Wrangel, pp. 53, 71-82; Holmquist, *Sv. K. Hist.*, IV. 428; Annerstedt, I. 260-2.
[2] Hall, *Kulterella Interiörer*, pp. 27, 30.
[3] Schück, *Sv. bilder*, III. 241-62, 291.
[4] *ibid.*, 241-3.

mainly for the purpose of 'ragging' freshmen, and for consuming the liquor which the freshman was forced to supply as part of his initiation. The Constitutions of 1626 had expressly forbidden these initiatory drinking-bouts (called 'cornute-ales', since the freshman's brow was adorned with horns); but they continued in spite of prohibitions, and in the 1640's they developed on a specifically regional basis, to form the nucleus of those 'Nations' which are still a unique feature of Swedish universities, and which first obtained legal standing in 1663.[1]

One of the problems of university administration was the great variation in the ages of undergraduates. Most of them came now from the *gymnasia*, but many still came straight from the *trivial-school*; and some—sons of noblemen or wealthy parents—went up to the university at the age of 10 or 12, accompanied by a tutor. Such boys could not get any benefit from the lectures, and indeed nobody seems to have expected that they should: they lived in Uppsala, not for their own instruction, but so that their mentor might have the advantage of attending courses. At the other end of the scale of age were those dullards who made slow progress, and those who registered themselves as students, though they might be middle-aged men with families, in order to escape conscription for the militia.[2]

The younger members of the student body required special coaching; and thus there arose a class of private tutors who eked out a living by teaching Latin—and often very elementary Latin indeed. The more fortunate undergraduates who had the luck to board with one of the professors could expect some private instruction from their host. Much of the work had necessarily to be done in the professor's houses, since the university had hardly any buildings of its own: the Gustavianum, begun in 1624, was still a building of only a single storey, for the upper floor and the graceful cupola were not added till Karl XI's time. Professors tended, therefore, to collect their own classes around them, to act as moral tutors to their members, and to give tutorials in a manner not greatly differing from that of Rudbeckius in the days of his *Collegium*

---

[1] *ibid.*, 66-7; IV. 13-19. On the subject of the 'ragging' of freshmen, see especially G. Berg, *Studentdeposition i Uppsala på 1600-talet*, pp. 96-114, where he points out the resemblance to similar initiation ceremonies for journeymen. See D. Mathew, *Social Structure in Caroline England*, p. 59 *note* 1, for similar practices at Cambridge.

[2] *ibid.*, III. 251; Anjou, p. 275.

Privatum. The institution of the private college, despite the ban of 1613, had never really died; and until this kind of coaching was taken over by the Nations in the 1660's it remained a feature of Uppsala life. Its working was facilitated, of course, by the fact that, no matter what Chair a man held, his teaching work would in practice resolve itself into tuition in theology, philosophy and Latin.[1]

The new Chairs, and the new subjects, which had been introduced to the university by Gustav Adolf's reforms of the 'twenties, had by the end of his reign done little to change the nature of the studies of most of the undergraduates. History, law and politics are said to have been rising in importance; but in 1627 Loccenius, the very distinguished professor of history, had only four students attending his lectures.[2] History remained a moral science, a repository of examples from which ethical lessons might be deduced, framed in a dreary and largely fictitious chronology imbibed from the text-books of Melanchthon and Sleidan: it was not so many years, after all, since Laurentius Paulinus Gothus had defined it as a branch of astronomy very useful to theologians.[3] Law and medicine were as yet in their infancy as serious disciplines: of the 62 freshmen who came up in the autumn of 1629 only 5 read law, and only 2 medicine; the rest were all entered in the faculties of theology and philosophy.[4] Mathematics and natural science, though they shared three Chairs to philosophy's one, were in equally bad case; for the mathematical training provided by the schools did not fit the student to cope with the subject at the university level. When Skytte visited Uppsala in 1627 he found that the university had no mathematical instruments of any sort.[5] The influence of Aristotle was still paramount in the field of science, as may be seen from the case of astronomy. The Copernican system was by this time beginning to be known in Sweden (it was familiar, for instance, to Paulinus), and a few Swedes outside the university had accepted the Tychonian variant of it; but all these speculations were rejected, not because they were held to be astronomically impossible, nor even as being impious, but because they conflicted with the *dicta* of Aristotle. It was not until the 1670's that the heliocentric theory of the universe

---

[1] Schück, *Svenska bilder*, IV. 11-12.
[2] Annerstedt, I. 231.
[3] Askmark, p. 288; Annerstedt, I. 223, 246.
[4] Askmark, p. 198.
[5] Annerstedt, I. 245.

began to prevail in Uppsala.[1] Thus, though the curriculum had in appearance been enlarged, the reality remained much the same: it was the old wine in new bottles.

The kernel of the university remained the theological and philosophical studies; and these had altered little in the course of the previous century. Latin, which continued to be the invariable language of instruction for another half-century,[2] had three professors—those of eloquence, poetry, and the Skyttean Professor. Theology had four: it was a subject which even the layman and the statesman could not afford to omit. It was compulsory on all students to pass a test and attend a course in theology; while on the other hand ordinands were compelled to obtain a certificate of competence in philosophy.[3] 'Philosophy', in the main, meant Ramus' logic; but in the 'thirties Ramus was increasingly felt to be too superficial for university students, and by the 'forties his long predominance came entirely to an end. Hebrew and Greek derived their chief importance from the fact that they were Biblical languages and indispensable to the theologian.

This unsatisfactory state of affairs was not mended by the examination system. The Constitutions of 1626 had carefully prescribed the requirements for the various degrees; but as very few candidates entered for any degree but that of fil. kand., the regulations remained largely inoperative.[4] During the whole of the seventeenth century only a handful of students took the theol. lic.; and all attempts to make a theol. kand. a prerequisite for ordination broke down. Most ordinands were content with a fil. kand.; a few, more ambitious, achieved a fil. mag., which was reckoned a sure avenue to preferment.[5] The majority of theologians left the university with but a scrappy knowledge of theology, reinforced by so much of the fil. mag. course as they had time or inclination to take. Their university career was, indeed, punctuated by frequent *tentamina*,

---

[1] H. Sandblad, *Det copernikanska världsystemet i Sverige* (*Lychnos* 1943), pp. 150-81. Sigfrid Aron Forsius was a Tychonian; but Johannes Bureus was a real Copernican, denied that the universe had a centre or a circumference, and held that all heavenly bodies are in motion; and Stiernhielm, his pupil, accepted the doctrine of the infinite universe, and held that the earth is a planet, while the sun is a star. But all this had no influence on Uppsala.

[2] Brandell, II. 74-5.

[3] Theology, it should be pointed out, at this time comprised only exegesis and dogmatic. Askmark, p. 290.

[4] For all this, see D. Almqvist, *Fackutbildning och humanistisk tradition* (*HT* 1934), *passim*; Askmark, pp. 188-97.

[5] Askmark, p. 213.

and the ordination examination (which was conducted by the bishop of the diocese, and was thus not a university examination at all) seems to have been a testing one; but in each case theology took second place to subjects in the philosophical faculty; and parsons with an Uppsala degree in theology were about as rare as Jesuits.[1] In the other higher faculties it was the same story: only very rarely did an Uppsala student obtain a licentiate in medicine or law.

From all this it will be plain that the university had still little to offer to the aspiring youth in search of a 'courtly' education, or the training necessary for the public service. No instruction in modern languages, for instance, was available—a state of affairs which contrasted unfavourably with foreign universities: Wittenberg had appointed a lektor in French as long ago as 1573, and a lektor in Italian twenty years later.[2] Wivallius, who was up at Uppsala in the 'twenties, and who wished to learn modern languages, had to go abroad for his instruction. Yet the demand for some regular provision of this type of education was insistent: it had been heard under Karl IX, and it continued throughout the reign of his son. The *Collegium Privatum* of Messenius, indeed, would probably have developed into the type of institution required; but Messenius was languishing in an Arctic prison, and no one came forward to take up his work.

The establishment of the *Riddarhus* in 1626 provided the opportunity for which the aristocracy had been looking; and they took advantage of it. It was decided to establish a school for the sons of the nobility, to be attached to the *Riddarhus*, and to be called the *Collegium Illustre*. The King endowed it handsomely with an annual revenue of 2000 *daler*, and gave it a Charter. The initiative came from Skytte and Oxenstierna, both of whom had seen similar institutions abroad, either at Tübingen or Cassel; and possibly they were influenced also by the similar establishment founded in 1621 by Kristian IV at Sorø.[3] As professor of theology they appointed Johannes Matthiae Gothus, and it was he who was ordered to draw up the College's curriculum. Matthiae was in many ways an

---

[1] Askmark (pp. 217-18) gives a list of the *tentamina* taken by one ordinand between 1630 and 1638: he took 18 tests in philosophical subjects, and 14 in theology. The ordination examination at Strängnäs lasted seven days, and the candidate was examined in Latin, rhetoric, dialectic, Greek, Hebrew, mathematics, astronomy, geodesy and 'physics', as well as in theology. Askmark, pp. 284-5.

[2] Kleberg, pp. 22-6.

[3] Holmquist, *J. Matt. Gothus*, pp. 110-11. For a good description of this kind of 'courtly' education, see *Per Brahes Tänkebok*, pp. 3-9.

admirable choice.[1] He was a most excellent linguist, speaking faultless English, German and French; he was a resolute enemy of barren theological controversy; and he was an unusually enlightened educational thinker. In later years the education of young Queen Kristina was not the least remarkable of his achievements. He had been influenced when in Germany by Wolfgang Ratke, and also by J. H. Alsted, who influenced Comenius. At Uppsala he had been a pupil of Messenius, playing female parts in his plays with some success; and though on Messenius' retirement he had tacked about and followed the Aristotelian Johannes Magni, he had really retained, both as an educator and as a theologian, a strong imprint of Messenius' personality. The *Ratio Studiorum* which he proposed for the *Collegium Illustre* certainly bore a strongly Ramist character. The boys were to enter the College at the age of 7, and to continue for seven years in the Lower School. They would be taught Latin, and rather less Greek; but there was to be no dreary learning of rules in the early stages: the boys would be taught first to read and enjoy Latin, and the rules would be explained and learnt as they arose in the course of reading. Texts would be selected in order to interest as well as instruct: even at this stage they would deal in *res* as well as *verba*. And hence he had no compunction about expurgating and bowdlerizing, when required. Theology was not allowed to take up much time, and was taught only on Sundays, lest the boys, by hearing it on a week day, might forget that it had a real connection with religion. Modern languages were to be taught by special tutors. The boys were not to be overworked: school hours were to be 7-10 and 2-5. The rod was to be used as sparingly as possible, and the spirit of honest emulation excited by prizes. All sorts of sports, from bowls to chess, were to be encouraged, and the gentlemanly accomplishments—dancing, fencing, riding—were to receive due attention. At 15 the boys would move up to the *Auditorium Publicum*, or Upper School, where the chief emphasis would be upon science, history and philosophy.

This was a curriculum very much to Gustav Adolf's taste. It offered precisely the sort of training that his budding civil servants required; and if the pill of learning was a little gilded, so too was the youth for whom it was designed. From a modern point of view it was far in advance of anything the *gymnasia* could offer. Un-

[1] Holmquist, *op. cit.*, pp. 112-27; *Sv. folksk. hist.*, I. 170-2; Brandell, II. 134-43, 235-42.

fortunately it remains quite uncertain how far this admirable scheme was put into practice. We know that a tutor in French was appointed; that Georg Stiernhielm came from Västerås to join the staff; and that in 1627 there were some 30 pupils. But the support from the nobility was always rather disappointing; and in 1629 the College had to be closed down, owing to an outbreak of plague in Stockholm. It never effectively reopened; and in 1632 its career came to an end. It has considerable importance in the history of Swedish educational thought; but its practical effect was small.

With its disappearance, attention was naturally turned once more to the possibility of providing what was required in Uppsala. A beginning was made by the appointment of a lektor in French in 1637, followed by that of a lektor in Italian in 1640[1]; but the facilities for dancing, fencing and riding were still lacking. It was not until 1663 that those deficiencies were made good by the munificence of the university's Chancellor, Magnus Gabriel de la Gardie.[2]

The last great achievement of Gustav Adolf's reign in the field of education was the foundation of the University of Dorpat.[3] This really set the crown upon the humanizing and civilizing work attempted by Sweden in her Baltic provinces at this period. The reform of the Church, the establishment of something resembling the rule of law, were now rounded off by the provision of proper educational services. A *gymnasium* had been founded at Dorpat in 1630, and another in 1631 at Reval; but from the start the school at Dorpat had clearly been designed to become an 'academy'—its teachers, for instance, bore the title of professor. By its statutes the Dorpat *gymnasium* was bound to give the Estonian and Lettish peasants equal privileges with the sons of the German nobility; and the foundation also provided for a Community of 50 poor scholars. The *gymnasium* was entirely the creation of the civil power, for the Church was weak and discredited, and had little influence in the matter. Johan Skytte, the Governor-General, was therefore able to enforce Gustav Adolf's educational policy to an extent which had not been possible in Sweden. The curriculum concentrated on producing civil servants able to govern the Baltic

[1] Kleberg, p. 26.

[2] R. Fåhraeus, *Magnus Gabriel de la Gardie*, p. 167.

[3] For this, see J. Bergman, *Universitetet i Dorpat*, pp. 11-15, 22-40; R. Liljedahl, *Svensk förvaltning i Livland*, pp. 396-403; Anjou, p. 269; Fr. Westling, *Bidrag till Livlands kyrkohistoria, 1621-56* (*K.H.Å.* 1900), p. 129; Broomé, *Stiernsköld*, p. 268.

provinces and familiar with their languages. Hence, besides Latin, Greek, Hebrew (and perhaps Chaldean), this remarkable school taught French, Lettish, Estonian and Ingrian: a knowledge of German and Swedish was, of course, assumed. The academy was so successful that Skytte pressed the King to establish it as a university; and at length, in June 1632, Gustav Adolf signed its Charter in his camp at Nuremberg. The new university continued the educational policy of the *gymnasium* from which it had sprung; and Skytte in his inaugural address took pains to emphasize the fact that it was to be a university, not only for nobles and burghers, but for peasants.[1]

The subsequent history of Dorpat somewhat disappointed these high hopes. The development of the Baltic tongues as literary languages was no doubt stimulated (religious literature in Estonian dates from 1632; in Lettish from 1631); but the university suffered from inadequate endowment at the start, and its progress was fatally affected by Kristina's mortgaging of the estates from which it derived its revenues.

(v) *Conclusion*

The reign of Gustav Adolf saw a decisive advance in Swedish education. For the first time the university was placed on a secure footing, beyond the reach of the hazards of war or the caprice of the ruler. For the first time Sweden acquired, in the *gymnasia*, a system of high-schools which might bear comparison with that obtaining in any other European nation. And for the first time, in the Norrland Instructions, an organized attempt was made to secure a literate population.

The King's views upon education were the views of the layman and the practical statesman. He had no theoretical knowledge of the subject. But he had a certain empirical knowledge which was a useful corrective to the conservatism of the schools. He judged educational methods by their products; and that was not the worst criterion he could have applied. From his observation he reached the conclusion that the education available at the time of his accession was not practical. He tried by his reforms to widen the curriculum,

---

[1] And he added: 'Wollte Gott, dass die Ritterschaft solches erkennten und recht sich drin schickten, alsdann würde nach der grossen Verwüstung eine neue Wiederaufbauung, nach der barbarischen Grobheit ein neues liebliches Licht aller Tugenden, und nach dem Fluche Gottes Segen in dieser Prowinz häufig wieder angehen und darin verspüret werden.'

to relax the predominance of narrow dogmatic theology and the drudgery of Latin grammar. As a pupil of Skytte, and therefore a Ramist at second-hand, he was predisposed to favour a revolt against outworn teaching techniques and a breach with the Aristotelian tradition. He had little patience with the tedious refinements of the theologians: the Uppsala Constitutions of 1626 laid it down that pupils should 'eschew the tangles of the scholastics, and all metaphysical speculations, conceits, and hair-splittings'.[1] The goal at which he aimed is sufficiently indicated by that remarkable provision, in these same Constitutions, that at least half of the royal scholarships are to be reserved for men intending to enter the civil service.[2] In trying to shape his educational system along these lines Gustav Adolf anticipates the Benevolent Despots of the next century. But whereas in that enlightened age the methods of a ruler like Maria Theresa could only hamper the development of a broader education, the policy of Gustav Adolf, in the educational darkness of the early seventeenth century, certainly promoted it.

If then the first element in his educational policy was secular, the second was undoubtedly nationalist. The King felt it as a humiliation that his country's university should be of no account in the community of the learned; he was sensitive to gibes about the barbarism of the Swedes; he was ashamed that, only too often, a foreigner had to be imported to fill a post for which there ought to have been an adequately qualified native. Educational reform was a matter of national prestige. Sweden must show that she was independent of Continental aid in this matter. And hence Gustav Adolf dissuaded Johannes Matthiae Gothus from accepting a Doctorate in Theology from Marburg, promising him an Uppsala Doctorate instead.[3] But this was not all; for education, he hoped, could be made to stimulate and fortify that spirit of national pride and national self-consciousness without which his military exertions would have been impossible. The Uppsala Constitutions, once again, make this very clear:

But above all the youths shall learn not to entertain low and mean-spirited thoughts of themselves and the present condition of the country, whereby is usually produced wailing and lamentation, admiration for everything that is foreign, and mistrust of one's own ability to achieve greatness—which is the worst hindrance to the governance of a state.

[1] Annerstedt, I. 223.
[2] D. Almqvist, p. 19.
[3] Holmquist, *J. Matt. Gothus*, p. 163.

This ought to be corrected by training and education, so that the spirits of the youths may early gain that impetus which is furnished by the certain hope of great deeds.[1]

It was this that lay behind Gustav Adolf's interest in the teaching of Swedish history; his institution of a Chair of Swedish Law; his desire that learned works should be translated into Swedish, so that the richness and flexibility of the language might be demonstrated[2]; his toying with the idea of instituting a Chair of Swedish, and of putting in Johannes Bureus as Professor of National Antiquities.[3] It was this that caused him to have the duties of the professor of poetry thus defined:

The poetry professor he shall both read the poets to his hearers and train them in composition, so that they may become skilled in holding declamations *as well upon the deeds of the old Gothic men* as upon other things.[4]

Education, in fact, was not merely to be equal in quality to any that was offered abroad; it was to be deliberately given a Gothic flavour.

Gustav Adolf was not wholly successful in achieving his aim. The solid mass of academic conservatism easily withstood his spirited assault: the more easily since the assault was necessarily intermittent. The changes in the curriculum turned out to be more concerned with names than with realities. When in 1632 he asked for secretaries to be sent out from Sweden to his generals, no suitable persons could be found at Uppsala, since all studied theology and none studied politics. Yet he had shown the way; he had provided something of the nominal framework to which, one day, the reality would conform. Whitelocke in the 'fifties might look down his nose at Swedish scholarship; but twenty years after that an Italian traveller could write: 'What has much contributed to raise the Swedes from their natural condition of cloddishness, is that they have so generally applied themselves to studies.'[5] For this, Gustav Adolf's *gymnasia*, and the new Uppsala which he raised from penury, had afforded the facilities. It is not easy to think of a seventeenth-century monarch whose services to education are fit to be drawn into comparison with his.

[1] Annerstedt, I. 224.
[2] And also because it was a 'popish trick' to bury learning in foreign languages: K. Leinberg, *Handlingar rörande finska kyrkan och prästerskapet*, I. 481-2.
[3] *ibid.*, 249; H. Hildebrand, *Bureus*, p. 127.
[4] Holmquist, *J. Matt. Gothus*, p. 95: italics mine.
[5] L. Magalotti, *Sverige under år 1674*, pp. 64-5.

CHAPTER IX

THE ARTS AND LITERATURE

(i) *Architecture and Painting*

THE Renaissance, as reflected in art and architecture, reached Sweden very late—a full generation later than it reached England—but it brought with it a break with the traditions of the past which was unusually sharp and abrupt.[1] While it is possible in England to trace the spirit of the Renaissance encroaching upon the Gothic by infinitesimal gradations—a detail of ornament here, a hint of classical symmetry there—in Sweden the change comes all in a moment. Gripsholm (begun in 1537) is—outwardly at least—a mainly Gothic building; Vadstena (begun in 1545) is decidedly Renaissance. The swift victory of foreign ideas was made possible because there was in Sweden no such strong native tradition as there was in England. The Renaissance in England came upon a numerous and well-organized body of architects and masons trained in the peculiarly English Perpendicular style; and if by the close of the fifteenth century that style was showing signs of having outlived its first freshness and vigour, it was none the less deeply ingrained in the artistic habits of the nation. No such circumstances existed in Sweden to offer opposition to the invasion of Italian ideas. Swedish Gothic was not so much a style as a sparer and more austere version of other styles; there was no strong body of native workmen to offer a conservative resistance to the new ways; most of the new work seems to have been carried out by imported craftsmen; and since the King long remained the only patron of art, there was less scope for the variety and the compromise which mark contemporary architecture in England. In short, the Renaissance style was in Sweden a fashion imposed from above—imposed, moreover, not by King and aristocracy combined, but by the King (or at least the royal family) almost alone. The contrast is great, not only with Tudor and Elizabethan England, but also with the adjacent Danish

---

[1] There are a number of good general guides to the history of Swedish art: see, for instance, A. L. Romdahl and J. Roosval, *Svensk konsthistoria*; H. Cornell, *Den svenska konstens historia från hedenhös till omkring 1800*; and most recently A. Lindblom, *Sveriges konsthistoria från förtid till nutid*, II.

province of Skåne, where the sixteenth century was an age of splendid castle-building by the local nobility—the massive Torup, the Dutch-Jacobean Svenstorp, the fairy-castle Vittskövle, the exquisite quasi-Tudor Rosendal, to name only a few examples.

Outside the scope of royal patronage, the Gothic lived on—in church architecture, for instance, and in the mural decorations of country churches. Domestic building was still mainly in wood, and seems to have remained impervious to Renaissance ideas. But it was of the essence of the situation that outside the scope of royal patronage very little art or architecture was stirring. Since the Reformation there had been no great demand for new churches; and the great age of aristocratic building had not yet arrived. Hence the main artistic achievements of sixteenth-century Sweden were the royal castles—Gripsholm, Vadstena, Kalmar, Örebro, Borgholm, Svartsjö, Stockholm, Uppsala, and some others long since vanished. It was here that the artistic experiments were made, often under the personal supervision of interested and well-informed monarchs.[1] Erik and Johan were well versed in the new architectural fashions: Erik had a Vitruvius in his library, and Johan read the works of Serlio.[2] Both were keen builders.[3] And Karl IX, though he may have had less natural taste, and certainly cultivated it less, was not much behind them. Under these sovereigns there emerged a distinct 'Vasa style', which is still employed, not always very appropriately, in modern Swedish buildings. The irregularities of the Gothic were tamed, and the desired vivacity of silhouette was now provided by cupolas, lanterns and weather-vanes; the new stepped gables came in from Flanders in the 'eighties, with their volutes, pediments, pilasters and niches[4]; but the material was still stone, though Dutch brick was working its way north from the Danish frontier. Yet despite foreign details, despite the friezes and entablatures, the arcadings and the cartouches, these Vasa castles remained curiously individual and national. The heavy round towers of Gripsholm, the waved cupola and lantern of Vadstena (though this was a later addition), the massive bulk of Örebro and Uppsala, and in general the union of great plainness and simplicity of outline with

---

[1] See, for these Vasa castles, A. Hahr, *Vasatidens borgar*; and G. Upmark, *Svensk byggnadskonst 1530-1700*.

[2] Upmark, *op. cit.*, pp. 10-11; Cornell, p. 191.

[3] With Johan, building was almost a passion: 'building is our chiefest delight', he is said to have confessed.

[4] Upmark, *op. cit.*, p. 13.

spontaneous little outbreaks of quite rich decoration, produced an effect peculiarly Swedish[1] and obstinately (if obscurely) Gothic; and the irregular jumble of buildings of all sorts of styles and ages in the old castle of Stockholm must have presented, notwithstanding Johan III's arcading, a general appearance the reverse of classical.

As with architecture, so with the other arts: the Court was the main purchaser, and was responsible for the importation of foreign masters. It was so, for instance, in regard to painting, which was virtually restricted to court portraiture in the Dutch and Flemish manner. A Dutchman, Johan Baptista van Uther, was dominant here: he worked in Sweden for no less than thirty-five years (1562-1597), and ended by founding something like a Swedish school of portraiture.[2] It was at this period that the first known Swedish painters made their appearance. Hans Erichsson was sent to Antwerp to improve himself, in King Erik's time; and van Uther himself trained the most important Swedish-born painter of the next generation, Holger Hansson. Discussion of the merits of the work of native Swedes has been hampered by the impossibility of attributing any picture to any one of them with absolute certainty; but it is fairly clear that now and for a long time to come Swedish art was dominated by the imported master, and native talent occupied a modest place. Van Uther's school seems to have been old fashioned and unprogressive, as we should expect from the relative isolation of Sweden at that time, and it clung to the stiff, formal portrait, usually full-face, without any attempt to relate the subject to an environment.

Decorative painting, of which there was a good deal, on exterior as well as interior walls, shows how the old quasi-peasant style, with its fresh colouring and naïve charm, was being supplanted by the strapwork, *amorini*, fruit-swags, grotesques and arabesques of the new mode. Stucco and intarsia-work came into fashion also, and at Kalmar achieved spectacular results in 'King Erik's Chamber' and the 'Chequer Room' (*rutsalen*). But these were exceptional examples: the appointments of ordinary houses were of a very modest nature. Nothing could be more striking than the contrast between the English and Swedish great house of the sixteenth century. In Sweden, even in the houses of the aristocracy, furniture

---

[1] 'Precious stones on a duffle coat', as Lindblom puts it: Lindblom, II. 333.
[2] K. E. Steneberg, *Den äldsta traditionen inom svenskt porträttmåleri*, pp. 94, 118; Lindblom, II. 370-1.

was still rude and massive, and often permanently attached to the walls, and tapestry was a rarity; and for richness, or even for comfort, there was nothing to compare with the Great Hall and Parlour of an English mansion.

The reign of Gustav Adolf is in many respects a transitional period. On the one hand it sees the fulfilment of tendencies which had been gaining ground since the closing decades of the previous century; on the other it may be regarded as the opening phase of new developments which were to lead to quite different styles under Kristina and her two successors. The tinge of Italian influence which had occasionally been perceptible under Johan now vanishes, and the Dutch style comes fully into its own; brick and sandstone arrive at last; and Vibyholm presents perhaps the richest example of this type of building that Sweden was to know. But side by side with the Dutch come new influences from Germany, the result, it is said, of Gustav Adolf's marriage with a Brandenburg princess[1]; and this north German influence was to have a considerable effect on the domestic architecture of the capital. The heavy swags and fleshy figures, and that ear-shaped ornament (*broskverk*) with which the Germans loved to support their pilasters and pediments, look forward to the Baroque. But Baroque when it came would be Roman Baroque; and before its definitive victory the middle years of the century would see the temporary triumph of French classicism.

Gustav Adolf had the hereditary passion for building; but in his case the press of other preoccupations prevented his giving it free play. Nevertheless, his reign was full of activity: the King continued, as before, to be a great employer of artists.[2] The most continuous and perhaps the most important effort was devoted to Stockholm Castle. Rebuilding had begun under Johan, and had continued almost without intermission ever since. Johan's aim had been to convert the old Gothic fortress into a palace fit for a monarch of taste to live in; but at his death much still remained to do. It was in Gustav Adolf's reign that the process was really completed; for the reconstruction of the fortifications at Vaxholm now safeguarded the capital from attack by sea, and the military importance of the Castle in consequence declined. Gustav Adolf, however, did not merely wish to obtain a more comfortable residence: he aimed also at adapting the Castle to serve as headquarters of the

[1] Lindblom, II. 359.
[2] For the following, see T. O. Nordberg, *Gustav II Adolf som byggherre, passim.*

central government; and the most considerable work he did was the building of a 'Chancery Wing' parallel to the modern Skeppsbron. Thus the central government, concentrated for the first time in Stockholm as the result of Gustav Adolf's and Axel Oxenstierna's administrative reforms, was provided with appropriate offices—which were, indeed, an almost essential precondition for its efficient functioning.

For these building operations in Stockholm Gustav Adolf relied, as his predecessors had relied, mainly upon Dutch workmen. The first of them of any note in this reign was Hubert de Besche, one of a numerous and gifted family of which several members emigrated to Sweden at this time[1]: he was appointed to take charge of the works in 1616. His second-in-command (who seems in fact to have been the better man of the two) was a Swede, Hans Fleming, distinguished also as a sculptor and an engineer. Most of the work on the Chancery Wing was done under their supervision. In 1622, however, de Besche was replaced by another Dutchman, Kasper Panten, who was undoubtedly the best architect of his day in Sweden. In 1623 Panten was sent back to Holland to buy ebony, ivory, marble and special woods for use in the interior decoration of the palace, and was instructed to enlist workmen in his native country. He succeeded in recruiting over forty of them; and though some stayed in Sweden only a short while, and some deserted, this compact contingent of highly trained craftsmen and artisans was probably not without influence on Swedish practice. Panten was the first person to be given a permanent appointment as architect to the King—hitherto appointments had been for the execution of specific pieces of work—and though he seems to have borne no special title, he is the real forerunner of Simon de la Vallée and Nicodemus Tessin, who were to hold the position of *riksarkitekt* in the next reign. His tenure of office was short, for he died in 1630, to the King's great regret; but his production was very considerable. In addition to his work on Stockholm Castle, he built the Gustavianum in Uppsala, was employed on building or rebuilding operations at Uppsala and Svartsjö Castles,[2] and was responsible for the Queen-Mother's splendid country-house, Vibyholm. Vibyholm was apparently his masterpiece. The building has been altered

---

[1] For the de Besche family, see E. W. Dahlgren, *Louis de Geer*, I. 26-8.

[2] For earlier work at Uppsala, see F. Wernstedt, *Ståthållaren Christoffer Wernstedt*, pp. 42-3, 66.

out of all recognition, but Erik Dahlberg's drawing in *Svecia Antiqua et Hodierna* gives some idea of its appearance.[1] Panten seems to have been the first architect in Sweden to build houses on the H- or E-shaped plan which afterwards became so popular for the palaces of the nobility; and Vibyholm was such a house. With its high twin turrets, its ornate obelisked gables, its fantastic, over-large and decidedly clumsy pediment in the centre, its rich portal surmounted by a rather bloated oriel window, it produces a somewhat fatiguing effect which is not lessened by the long-and-short sandstone quoins (the building was of red brick), the numerous sandstone pilasters which break up the surface, and the sandstone surrounds of the windows. If Vibyholm is a fair sample, Panten's architecture must be pronouced a trifle highly spiced. But very little of Panten's work survives, and this may possibly be a rash conclusion.

Gustav Adolf did not merely do a great deal of building himself; he was also responsible, directly or indirectly, for a great deal of building by his subjects. He was, for instance, much concerned about town-planning; and at Jönköping, and above all at Kalmar, he took the opportunity afforded by the destruction of the war of 1611-13 to replan these towns on more modern and regular lines. But his most notable effort in this field was in Stockholm.[2] In September 1625 a great fire broke out in the south-west corner of the city, and caused widespread destruction before it could be checked. The King seized on this chance. He drove a new straight street (the present Stora Nygatan) through the ruins, and continued it northwards beyond them; he pulled down the old town wall on the east side, and built what is now Skeppsbron outside it; he eliminated a number of the dark alleys which were a menace to public health and to public order; and he forbade for the future the building of timber or half-timbered houses within the city limits. The result was that the burnt-out areas were rebuilt in brick or stone; and for this foreign workmen were commonly employed. In place of the quadrilateral clusters of one-storied wooden shacks which had been usual before, Stockholm now obtained rows of high houses of three to five stories, with narrow façades to the street and

---

[1] E. Dahlberg, *Svecia Antiqua et Hodierna*, p. 156. Dahlberg's drawing is said to exaggerate the height of the building at the expense of its breadth.

[2] G. Hellström, *Gustav II Adolf's nyreglering av staden inom broarna, passim*; K. Hildebrand, *Stockholms historia*, p. 99. For the work at Kalmar, L. W. Munthe, *Fortifikations historia*, I. 243-52. N. Ahnlund, *Från medeltid och Vasatid*, pp. 176, 186, 189; *Stockholms stads privilegiebref*, pp. 201-2.

an interior courtyard; with imposing portals and highly decorated gables; with ornamental iron ties, and often with diamond rustic round the windows. The effect is partly Dutch, but mainly German, and it lends the Old Town of Stockholm much of its peculiar charm. In Gustav Adolf's time the portals and gables were still relatively unpretentious; but within a generation after his death they would reach a climax of richness in the thoroughly German *Petersenska Huset*.

Thus Stockholm began to be transformed from a mediaeval town of low wooden buildings clustering under the shadow of the castle, and protected by walls, into a comparatively modern city of a type common enough along the southern shores of the Baltic. But the transformation was not completed all in a moment: though White-locke in 1654 thought that most of the houses were stone or brick, Magalotti twenty years later reported that so many were still roofed with turf that the town had the appearance of a meadow, most delightful to the eye.[1] And the reform did not extend to the suburbs (*malmarna*): here building in wood remained usual; and in the disastrous fire of 1652 it was said that of the three or four hundred houses destroyed on Norrmalm, only five or six were of stone.[2] But the number of stone or brick houses in the suburbs was increasing, for as the city 'between bridges' grew more and more crowded, the nobility were forced to move out to Norrmalm, if they were to find sites big enough for their palaces: thus the Torstensson palace lies on Norrmalm, and so too did Jakob de la Gardie's *Makalös*; with the result that the social standing of these areas was greatly improved. Most of the palaces of the nobility, however, were still squeezed into the narrow compass of the Old Town—as, for instance, Axel Oxen-stierna's was. This growing habit—it developed very strongly in the twenty years after 1632—of building great town houses, was something altogether new. The Swedish nobility had hitherto been a rural nobility; and though they did not now lose that character, they acquired a tolerance of town life, if not a taste for it; and, whether they liked the town or not, they were compelled to maintain houses there.[3] Stockholm was now a real capital; the days when administration had been concentrated upon the peripatetic person of the monarch were nearly over; the civil service chained more and

[1] Whitelocke, II. 294; Magalotti, p. 10.
[2] *Johan Ekeblads brev*, I. 167-8.
[3] *cf.* D. Mathew, *Social Structure in Caroline England*, p. 39, for parallel developments in England.

more of the upper ranks of society to the new government offices in the Castle; the growing class feeling of the nobility (of which the building of *Riddarhuset* was one expression) demanded that their lodgings in Stockholm should have a certain distinction. And consequently they built their palaces in the Old Town or in the suburbs, and employed foreign artists to design and decorate them.

This emergence of the aristocracy as patrons of art on a large scale is really the most important artistic development of the time. It extended far beyond the construction of comparatively utilitarian residences in Stockholm. It covered the country with that wonderful galaxy of great houses which the tactful and patriotic pencil of Erik Dahlberg depicted in *Svecia Antiqua et Hodierna*; it transformed Sweden from a country of barbaric simplicity to a land where Magnus Gabriel de la Gardie could deploy a luxury and magnificence which would not have seemed out of place at Versailles.[1] This development is said to have been encouraged by Gustav Adolf, who, it is alleged, wished to see his nobility living according to the standards of their equals abroad[2]; but the main impetus came from men who returned from the wars of Germany with their pockets bursting with plunder and their heads filled with a notion of emulating the hitherto undreamed-of splendours which they had observed abroad. There was a conscious feeling, too, that Sweden's international position was now such that she could not afford, for reasons of prestige, to maintain the old austerity of living: Swedish pride was wounded by the covert smiles of visiting diplomats. At a time when Axel Oxenstierna was treated as the equal of an Elector, it was not fitting that he should be housed in anything less than a palace. From all this came a period of feverish building activity: it is said that some fifty castles or country houses were built in the first half of the century. Most of them date from the years between 1630 and 1650; but Gabriel Gustafsson Oxenstierna built Tyresö in Gustav Adolf's reign; and Axel Oxenstierna's Tidö and Johan Skytte's Grönsöö fall within the same period. And it was in 1630 that Jakob de la Gardie began the construction of his great Stockholm palace which he (rightly) named *Makalös* (Nonsuch). It was the work of a Strassburg architect, Hans Jakob Kristler, and fortunately it was, as its name implied, unique; for it was a very gorgeous, very expensive, and very vulgar building indeed—real *parvenu* architec-

---

[1] For M. G. de la Gardie, see R. Fåhraeus, *Magnus Gabriel de la Gardie*.
[2] *Handlingar rörande Skandinaviens Historia*, VIII. 42.

ture.[1] Many of the houses built at this time have now vanished, and upon most of the remainder discretion, or pricks of artistic conscience, have imposed a more sober and classical appearance; but as they appear in Erik Dahlberg's pages they present an extraordinarily lively and festive exterior: gaily gabled, high-lanterned, picturesquely weather-vaned; their gardens sweeping down to the water, with ornamental landing-stages and boathouses; their orangeries and garden houses and parterres bidding defiance to meteorological reality. No one could call them chaste art, but Sweden is the poorer for their disappearance.[2]

Compared with this outburst of secular architecture, ecclesiastical buildings at this period make but a meagre showing. St. Jakob's Church in Stockholm, upon which work was proceeding all through the reign, and Kristina Church in Falun, begun soon after the end of it, are the most important surviving examples, and both are predominantly Gothic in character, though the details of ornament are North German Renaissance. Neither of these could compare with the work that was being done in Denmark at the same period. The 'Kristian IV Style', of which Holy Trinity, Kristianstad, is a glorious example, reached Sweden only a little later; and the real Swedish pendant to Kristianstad Church is the little church at Jäder, which did not assume its present form until the 1640's. A good deal of work was done on Uppsala Cathedral, which was, as usual, in need of repair[3]; but it has mostly vanished. More important was the improvement in the interior fittings of churches, a matter

---

[1] The pictures in *Svecia Antiqua et Hodierna* (pp. 38-9) do not do justice to its original appearance: its more garish effects have already been toned down. An idea of what it looked like towards the end of the 1630's can be obtained from the picture in *Svenska folket genom tiderna*, IV. 346. Kristler's Jakobsdal (also built for Jakob de la Gardie), on the other hand, was a delightful building in the Dutch-North German style.

[2] This applies only to the houses of the wealthier nobility. The ordinary noble of moderate means still lived in a one-storied timber grange, with outhouses arranged round a courtyard. See the pictures of Espelunda and Ekeberg in Dahlberg, p. 174; and *cf.* Whitelocke's description (I. 193-4): 'some of these seats Whitelocke viewed, and found their building to be only fir timber, the bodies of great trees squared and laid one upon another, keyed together by other great pieces of timber, all set upon huge stones about a foot from the ground. Between the bodies of the trees which make the wall of the house, is great store of moss forced in, like the caulking of a ship, which keeps out the sun, and makes the rooms cool in summer, and, keeping out the frost and cold air, makes them more warm in winter. The roof is of deal boards jointed close together, and laid a little sloping, upon which they put pieces of the bark of birch-trees to cover it, and the bark they cover with turf, and lay them as flat as a roof is made with lead.'

[3] Wernstedt, p. 67.

in which Rudbeckius took the lead.[1] Little had been done since the Reformation to make the furnishings of churches more apt to the Lutheran rite, and in particular there was a lack of pulpits. That lack was now generally supplied. Large pulpits in wood or stone, often intricately carved or brightly gilded and painted, began to be installed; and one of the acknowledged masters in this specialized branch of art was a Swede, Lars Strångeson.[2]

The most notable work in ecclesiastical art, however, was done in the carving of tombs and the building of private burial chapels. The employment of foreign artists to design and execute tombs and monuments of the royal family had been usual in the past; and the best known chapel of the period—that which was built on to the Riddarholm Church in Stockholm to receive the body of Gustav Adolf—was a royal commission also. But in Gustav Adolf's reign the habit spread to the nobility, and even beyond. The age's characteristic itch for reputation, the desire to perpetuate one's name after death in a fashion that should be permanent, found congenial outlet in epitaphs, monuments and tombs—executed now, not in perishable wood, but in stone or marble. The men who carved and designed these monuments were foreigners, as their great predecessor Willem Boy had been in the previous century, and mostly they were Dutchmen: when the gild of sculptors was founded in 1638 not one of the seven masters was a Swede. The most celebrated of them were probably Aris Claeszoon, Jost Henne and Heinrich Wilhelm. Such men were now often employed on a full-time basis by noble families, to carve tombs or design chapels for them: thus the Oxenstiernas employed Wilhelm, and the Banérs Aris Claeszoon. The result was an epidemic of large and expensive mural monuments and isolated tombs, executed with great realism and a lavish deployment of appropriate allegorical figures, and frequently highly coloured and gilded. To avoid encroaching unduly upon the floor-space of the church, or for greater glory and privacy, the aristocracy now took to adding private chapels to their parish churches, often with the most incongruous results. All the arrogance and pomp which was the darker side of Sweden's Age of Greatness is reflected in these chapels; and this is especially true with the coming of the Baroque, when they appear as bulbous excrescences,

---

[1] G. Boëthius, *Konsthistoriska riktlinjer inom Västerås stift under 1600-talet*, *passim*.
[2] Lindblom, II. 393.

puffed up with the vainglory of their tenants, quite eclipsing the in-
offensive little churches upon whose fabric they have battened.[1]

As the nobility now deemed it only consistent with their dignity
to retain the services of sculptors and architects, so too they found
it expedient to take painters into their pay. A man like Per Brahe,
ruling his county from Visingsö almost as a sovereign prince, took
care to secure the proper establishment of court-painters; and other
great men such as Torstensson and the de la Gardies imitated his
example. The increase in the volume of patronage and commissions
attracted numbers of foreign painters to Sweden: some of them
became almost naturalized Swedes; but the majority were mere
birds of passage. The older generation of painters, pupils of van
Uther, or pupils of his pupils, was represented still by Holger Hansson, and also by Arendt Lamprechtz; but Lamprechtz's son Cornelis
belonged to the new school which had learnt from van Dyck, and so
too did the Strassburger Jakob Elbfass, who did much work in this
period. The birds of passage—Hoefnagel, van der Plas, van Dort—
were painters of some quality (Hoefnagel had worked for Rudolf II);
but the great majority of those domiciled in Sweden were mediocre,
and Ogier, when he toured the country in the 'thirties, formed but
a poor opinion of them.[2] Their pictures were portraits, without
exception: the beginnings of Swedish landscape had to wait for
another decade or more.

As the booty of Germany poured in, as one fortune after another
was founded in Bohemia or on the Rhine, the Swedish nobility
became more cosmopolitan in taste, habits and dress. It learnt to
speak in foreign tongues—in French or German, or Dutch; and by
the 'fifties a young courtier like Ekeblad would be proficient in
modern languages, but confess himself shaky in his Latin. This
transformation of the upper classes, and the deliberate cultivation
of luxury which went with it, brought increased activity to all the
lesser arts—to the glass-blower [3] and the bookbinder, and above all
to the gold- and silversmith. In the last of these arts, native work of
high quality was being turned out—even, it seems, in provincial
towns; but though the name of one outstanding Swedish goldsmith

---

[1] Two particularly formidable examples were Lars Kagg's chapel at Floda,
and Erik Dahlberg's monstrous effort at Turinge: see Dahlberg, pp. 143, 155.
A recent dissertation on this topic is M. Liljegren, *Stormaktstidens gravkor* (Lund,
1947).
[2] Ogier, p. 52.
[3] H. Seitz, *Äldre svenskt glas med graverad dekor*, pp. 201-2.

—Peter Kiämpe—has been preserved (and the glorious gold horn he made also), the majority of the active goldsmiths seem, to judge from their surnames, to have been foreigners. Nevertheless, in an age when Swedish national styles were obscured or abandoned, the goldsmiths appear to have been successful in retaining their national individuality in the face of the Renaissance, even though they were not ashamed to import ready-made ornaments from Germany for use on less important work.[1]

But the goldsmiths were very much the exception. In all other forms of art, the coming of the Age of Greatness meant, in the first place at all events, a more eager embracing of the teaching and fashion of the foreigner than ever before; and it was to be a generation or two before Swedish-born artists arose who should be capable of pronouncing the international commonplaces with an unmistakably Swedish accent.[2]

(ii) *Music*

The general history of music in the sixteenth century showed no such revolution in style as the supersession of the Gothic in architecture. The polyphonic tradition moved smoothly to its climax of perfection in the music of Palestrina; and if strange new doctrines were adumbrated towards the end of the century in Venice, they had little effect on general practice for a decade or so. In Sweden, development had conformed closely to the pattern elsewhere.[3] There was no Swedish school of composers, and the cultivation of serious music was necessarily much restricted in a country where the urban population was so small, but from the music that has been preserved in Swedish libraries it would appear that most of the great contemporary composers were known and performed, from Josquin des Prés, Willaert and Morales to Lassus and Vittoria. The Vasa Kings were as enlightened in their patronage of music as their resources permitted, and Erik XIV appears to have been a composer of real distinction—the first Swedish composer,

---

[1] G. Upmark, *Guld- och silversmeder i Sverige 1520-1850*; O. Källström, *Guldsmedsyrket i äldre tid*; Lindblom, II. 409, for Peter Kiämpe.

[2] *cf.* Magalotti, p. 9: 'The Swedes, although they desire to follow their own taste, nevertheless content themselves with imitating, not indeed in everything, but yet more than other nations.'

[3] There are two good books about music under Gustav Adolf: C.-A. Moberg, *Från kyrko- och hovmusik till offentlig konsert*; and T. Norlind, *Från tyska kyrkans glansdagar*, I.-II. An outline history of Swedish music is T. Norlind, *Svensk musikhistoria*.

moreover, of whom any music is preserved. Like his brother Johan, he strove to build up a Chapel Royal (*hovkapell*), and he was for a time sufficiently successful to arouse the envy of Fredrik II of Denmark. But though musicians were hired from time to time, the century closed without the establishment of any permanent *hovkapell*; and for the performance of large-scale music the Court was still in the habit of relying upon the assistance of the Stockholm schoolboys, and above all upon the aid of the German Church in Stockholm, which made a special point of maintaining a good standard of music and performance. Considerable resources could be collected by these means; and the coronation of Karl IX in 1607 showed that Sweden could rise to the double choirs and divided orchestras required by the new Venetian manner.

Church music had undergone some vicissitudes since the Reformation, as Puritan feeling strengthened or relaxed its hold upon the Church; but though much of the old ritual of the Mass had disappeared, with the music proper to it, and though Vicars-Choral were now a thing of the past, the general character of church music had remained substantially unchanged. The notion that the Reformation entailed the supplanting of polyphonic music by congregational singing of Lutheran chorales is certainly not true of Sweden. It is not until Johan III's *Nova Ordinantia* of 1575 that an official document gives any hint that congregational singing is contemplated or even tolerated, and it was certainly not usual before Gustav Adolf's time. The *musica figurativa* remained the basis of church music; the new chorales were sung, when they were sung at all, by the scholars; and the organ was not employed to accompany the voices. The Reformers fortunately shared Luther's views upon the ethical value of the practice of music; and music remained one of the staples of the ordinary school curriculum, to the great benefit of the country at large.[1]

Among the upper classes, music was recognized as a social obligation, to be acquired by a gentleman 'so that asses' ears be not set upon him, as befel Midas, who deemed the donkey to have sung better than the nightingale'.[2] The lute was popular; but the virginals, clavichord and other keyboard instruments do not seem to have had anything like the same vogue as in England. And, in general, the

---

[1] It was always allotted the hour from 12 to 1, since music was considered to be good for the digestion, as well as for the character.

[2] Per Brahe, *Oeconomia*, p. 13.

practice of good music, outside the schools, the churches and the Court, seems to have been much less common. In this century, moreover, almost no music appears to have been printed in Sweden.

Gustav Adolf was a warm friend to music; and his reign is of considerable importance in Swedish musical history. For, as a eulogist wrote of him soon after his death, he 'not only embraced music with great affection, and himself practised it (and in especial performed excellently well upon the lute) but likewise manifested his love for the art by calling hither the most distinguished musicians, the most famous singers, and the cunningest instrumentalists'. It is to him that the credit must be given for the establishment of a *hovkapell* upon a permanent basis. He began to interest himself in the matter shortly before his marriage, and by the end of 1620 had imported an entire new *kapell* from Germany, which is especially noted to have included string-players. It was not, perhaps, very large—at the close of the reign it numbered 14 players, together with 3 Swedish fiddlers and 10 trumpeters and drummers—but it was probably as much as he could afford.[1] Compared with the lavish expenditure of Kristian IV, the patron of Dowland, it was modest enough; but it was at least a firm nucleus upon which his successors could build.

Among the German musicians who came into Sweden at this time was a certain Anders Düben, one of a dynasty of musicians which was to play a great part in Swedish musical history. Düben's father had been organist at the Thomaskirche in Leipzig, and Düben himself had studied under Sweelinck, through whom he may possibly have been brought under the influence of the new Venetian school.[2] Düben soon became a member of the *hovkapell*; and since he was a fine organist he was appointed to the German Church in 1625, and so preserved the close connection between the two which had been traditional since the time of Johan. He was also a composer of moderate abilities, in the massive antiphonal style which was fashionable at the time.[3]

The King also showed his interest in music by personally

---

[1] Their annual wages in 1629 totalled no less than 12,000 *daler*.

[2] Norlind's statement (*Svensk musikhistoria*, p. 86) that Sweelinck was the pupil of Andrea Gabrieli is contradicted by the article on Sweelinck in *Grove*: *Grove's Dictionary of Music and Musicians*, V. 196-7.

[3] He is best remembered for his funeral cantata for Gustav Adolf, *Pugna Triumphalis* (1634). I was fortunate enough to hear a broadcast performance of this work and its companion piece by Thomas Boltz, *Threnodia* (1632). Neither made a very strong impression at a single hearing.

intervening to improve the teaching of the subject at the university. In 1627 he sent Jonas Columbus to Uppsala to combine (for the first and only time) the Chairs of Music and Poetry; and the effect upon musical life is said to have been good. This may well have been so, for Columbus (himself a minor composer) had taught music from 1619 to 1625 at Västerås School, and there seems no doubt that the standard there was remarkably high. The boys were rigorously trained not only in the theory and practice of the old polyphonic style, but in the newer, more homophonic and dramatic methods of such north German composers as Hieronymus and Michael Pretorius of Hamburg, and their repertory was extensive. They had also a school orchestra of imposing dimensions: in 1630 the inventory of instruments listed 1 bass-viol, 2 tenor viols, 2 alto viols, 1 discant viol, 3 'common' (gemena) discant viols, 1 common bass-viol, one large bass-viol, 1 cornett,[1] 3 bass trombones, 2 tenor trombones bought in Germany, and 1 double-bass trombone.[2] The boys were sufficiently good performers to obtain employment as members of a dance-orchestra, for the regulations of 1622 lay it down that 'he who uses his instrument at any party or in any tavern without the permission of the bishop and the rector shall lose it, and also pay a fine'.[3] But Västerås, though outstanding, was not unique: to judge from the library of music which belonged to the school at Kalmar, the art must have been flourishing there also,[4] and Örebro under Jakob Rudbeckius was probably not much behindhand.

The days were now past, however, when the schoolboys were wholly responsible for singing in church, and here Gustav Adolf's reign forms a watershed. The weakening of the polyphonic school, the more Puritan tone of the Swedish Church in the years after the Uppsala Meeting of 1593, combined to consummate a breach with the past, and the new Church *Handbok* of 1614 prescribes congregational singing for the first time. The standard of performance is said to have been low at first, but it had risen sufficiently in twenty years to make the most favourable impression on Charles Ogier.[5]

---

[1] '*Tuba cornea* or *sinka*.' This must be a cornett: see art. 'Cornett', *Grove*, I. 728.
[2] Presumably for the use of the more elderly and bearded scholars to whom Whitelocke alludes: a schoolboy would have had difficulty with it.
[3] Brolén, I. 14-15; Norlind, *Från tyska kyrkans glansdagar*, II. 56-7.
[4] Petersson, *Olaus Svebilius intill ärkebiskopstiden*, p. 20.
[5] Ogier, pp. 43-4. But this was the German Church, where the standard was perhaps exceptionally high.

The organ was still used antiphonally with the voices, but congregations were increasingly anxious to have a good instrument and a good performer, and Gustav Adolf's reign is a time when many new organs were installed. The repertory for the instrument, it is interesting to note, included works by Byrd, Bull and Peter Phillips.

Lastly, this was a period when considerable advances were made in secular music. The old habit of setting secular verses to psalm tunes persisted; but the secular song-melody was beginning to appear. The lute was very fashionable, and the standard of execution appears to have been high. The music collection of the university library at Uppsala testifies to the popularity of Dowland. The new mania for dancing penetrated to Sweden, and here—as also in all forms of instrumental music—there was considerable English influence. As with painting and sculpture, the habit of patronage began to spread from the royal family to the great aristocracy; and the day was not far distant when a Magnus de la Gardie or a Per Brahe would have his private Chapel of Musicians. Ogier in the 'thirties took a much more favourable view of Swedish music than of Swedish painting; and Whitelocke twenty years later permitted himself an enthusiastic commendation of the standard of performance at Kristina's Court.[1]

(iii) *Literature*

In the history of Swedish literature the sixteenth century is one of the dark ages.[2] The work produced by native authors was small in bulk and poor in quality; and in the whole period of the earlier Vasas there was but one writer—Olaus Petri—of real merit. The Reformation blighted the humanism which had been one of the redeeming features of the old Church, and theology became the intellectual preoccupation of those classes from which the production of literature might have been expected. Virtually the only poetry was the crude rhyming of the hymnographers; virtually the only prose was devoted to the unprofitable pursuit of religious controversy. The ardour of national liberation from the foreign yoke brought forth no such literary fruits as were to mark the emancipation of the Netherlands from the thraldom of Spain. The period

[1] Ogier, pp. 38, 68, 82; Whitelocke, I. 239, 293.
[2] For a general history of Swedish literature, see H. Schück and K. Warburg, *Illustrerad svensk litteraturhistoria* (3rd ed.) II.; or its abridgment, *Huvuddragen av Sveriges litteratur*; F. Böök [etc.], *Svenska litteraturens historia*, I.; and, most recently, E. N. Tigerstedt, *Svensk litteraturhistoria* (excellent bibliography).

did not see any such emergence of a truly national school of literature as was occurring in Elizabethan England, or the France of Ronsard and the *Pléiade* ; and in this respect Germany and even Denmark were ahead of Sweden. One great gift the men of the sixteenth century did indeed bequeath to posterity, in the form of Gustav Vasa's Bible of 1541, which by the purity and vigour of its language, and its rejection of foreign expressions and constructions, may be said to have created modern Swedish, as Luther's Bible created modern German; but for the rest there was little upon which to build. It must be admitted that conditions in Sweden had not been very propitious for authorship: as late as 1600 there was but one printing-press in the country, managed by a total staff of one master-printer and one journeyman; paper was still wholly imported from Germany, for there was no Swedish paper-mill; the book-making and bookselling trades were largely in German hands; and the first Swedish bookshop had been opened as late as the 1590's.[1]

These unfavourable circumstances no doubt do something to explain why it was that Gustav Adolf's reign did not give birth to an Elizabethan age of literature. The foundations were lacking; the handicaps were too great. 'Swedish poverty', which imposed a certain chaste austerity upon the other arts, and gave a beneficent wiriness and toughness to the national character, was not an asset in the literary sphere, where too often it implied simply crudity, harshness and dreariness. Neither Gustav Adolf's reign nor Kristina's succeeded in wholly liberating Swedish literature from these trammels: Gustav Adolf's time is a time of beginnings; Kristina's produced the first really great Swedish poet; but it was not until the age of Karl XI that Sweden began to accumulate a *corpus* of literature comparable in quantity and quality to that of other countries.

Nevertheless, the beginnings have some interest; and even if Breitenfeld was not followed by a great literary outburst, it must be admitted that the situation had greatly changed for the better in the years since 1611. The political and military triumphs did have a stimulating effect; Sweden's international position as a great power was felt as a challenge to her writers to produce a literature worthy of her new position. The great questions of the day struck a few sparks from flinty Swedish pens—especially in the way of oratory and sermons—that still shine brightly through the mirk. The

[1] Schück and Warburg, *Illustrerad sv. litteraturhistoria*, II. 55-6, 89.

definitive triumph of orthodox Lutheranism with the accession of
Gustav Adolf had the salutary effect of freeing men's minds from
an exclusive attention to theological polemic; literature became more
secular than it had been for a century; creative energies began to be
directed to other than religious channels: *Fjäriln vingad syns på Haga*.[1]

On the purely material plane, moreover, conditions became
easier. Gustav Adolf started a paper-mill at Uppsala in 1612;
Stockholm, which had obtained an additional printing-press in Karl
IX's time, now acquired three more (though it lost one to Uppsala);
and with provincial presses established at Västerås, Strängnäs and
Kalmar, Sweden in 1632 could show eight printers, as against two
in 1611. The university now had a bookseller of its own; in 1630
the gild of bookbinders obtained its charter; and in 1619 the King
did his best to encourage the publication of books in Sweden by
prohibiting the importation of Swedish books printed overseas.
To these developments, and to the gradual formation of a book-
buying public, the settlement of numerous foreigners in the country
and the closer contacts with Europe which were one of the consequences of Gustav Adolf's campaigns probably contributed, as
they certainly did to the widening of the intellectual horizon of very
many. One symptom of this was the Chancery's concern for the
dissemination of news, which was to lead, soon after the King's
death, to the publication of the first Swedish newspaper.[2] Sweden's
exiguous libraries were reinforced until they became almost un-
recognizable by the princely plunder of Riga, Braunsberg, Würzburg
and Mainz.[3] It is true that they still compared ill with libraries
abroad: Whitelocke was scornful of what he saw at Uppsala; and
it is a remarkable fact that as late as 1649 the university library had
only *five* Swedish books on its shelves.[4] Even in 1672 Schefferus
had to send his *Lapponia* to be printed in Germany because the
technical facilities in Sweden were not adequate.[5] But the change
within twenty years had none the less been striking. In part it was
the result of the King's own encouragement of literature. Gustav
Adolf believed that the Swedish language was as capable as any other

[1] 'The winged butterfly is seen at Haga': the first line of Bellman's most
celebrated lyric.
[2] The first regular newspaper was the *Ordinarie Post Tidender* of 1645; but
there had been newspapers of a sort since 1633.
[3] For an account of the booty, see O. Walde, *Storhetstidens litterära krigsbyten*, I.
[4] Schück and Warburg, II. 106-8, 61; Whitelocke, II. 148; and *cf*. Seaton,
p. 196, for an unfavourable English opinion of Uppsala's library in 1688.
[5] Seaton, p. 214.

of expressing ideas; he was anxious to encourage the writing and
publication of serious works in Swedish, rather than in Latin; he
contemplated the establishment of a Chair of Swedish at Uppsala.
In 1622 he took practical steps to forward some of these objects.
A special levy had been imposed to cover the cost of the new edition
of the Bible (the so-called *Bibeltunnan*), and it continued to be collected even though publication had taken place. It was now set aside
as a fund for the encouragement of Swedish literature, and assigned in
the first instance to Erik Schroderus (Johan Skytte's brother), who
was commissioned to produce a series of translations into Swedish.
Schroderus was no Florio, but he was diligent—among his translations were Sleidan, Livy and Commines—and in the existing condition of Swedish literature the money was probably not ill-bestowed.

Throughout the later Middle Ages, and indeed down to Gustav
Adolf's time, such Swedish literature as there was had been much
under foreign influence, especially German; and verse, for instance,
in so far as it aimed consciously at art, followed German fashions at
a distance. It is strongly indicative of the isolation of Sweden from
the general currents of literary development that the first Swedish
sonnet (by Stiernhielm) was not written until 1644. For most of the
sixteenth-century Swedish verse had been a barbarous *knittel*[1];
but about the end of the century this tended increasingly to give
way to an equally barbarous syllabic verse, though for didactic
poetry the old *knittel* persisted for some time longer. Most of the
verse-writers of the earlier part of the reign wrote syllabic verse—
for instance, Messenius in his plays, and the amateurs of occasional
poetry. Such verse, in the hands of inexpert writers, produced
painful contradictions of the normal stress of words in a sentence,
and of syllables in a word. When, as in the case of Messenius, the
verse was designed to be declaimed, the effect must have been
distressing; for it was read, apparently, as though it had been
accented verse. And since the rhymes were frequently highly
approximate, or valid only if the ordinary syllable stress were
violated, the result was very curious. By the middle of the reign
some appreciation of these improprieties was beginning to dawn,
and in Sigfrid Aron Forsius' metrical version of *Reynard the Fox*[2]

---

[1] *Knittel* was rhyming verse with four (rarely three or five) accented, and an
arbitrary number of unaccented syllables. For this, and all other metrical matters,
see O. Sylwan, *Den svenska versen*, I.

[2] For Forsius' authorship of *Reyncke Fosz*, see S. Belfrage, *Översättningen av
Reyncke Fosz*, and C. A. Dymling, *Reyncke Fosz och Forsius*.

an attempt was made to write rhymed syllabic verse which should not offend the ordinary rules of pronunciation. Popular taste in verse was low enough, even among the educated classes,[1] and the impetus to reform came, as usual, from Germany. There in 1624 Opitz laid down canons for the writing of syllabic verse; and in due time they came to be accepted in Sweden, first by Anders Sparrman, later and above all by Georg Stiernhielm, the great poet of the next generation, and the first Swedish verse-writer with a sovereign command of the technical resources of his art.[2]

In the meantime, however, there had once again been an abandonment of syllabic verse and a return to accented verse; and the two most notable literary figures at the close of the reign, Lars Wivallius and Schering Rosenhane (if he be indeed identical with 'Skogekär Bergbo') were using accented verse with some assurance. The interest of Skogekär Bergbo—or at least of the only poem he can possibly have written in this reign—is not primarily poetic, and consideration of his importance may for the moment be deferred; but something must be said of Wivallius, partly because he is the only Swedish poet before Stiernhielm whose work can be read with real pleasure, and partly because he was a typical product of his age. Lars Wivallius came of peasant stock; but his parents were in moderately comfortable circumstances, and he was educated—in part, at all events—at Örebro School under Jakob Rudbeckius, and subsequently for a short time at Uppsala. After leaving the university under something of a cloud, he began a roving life which took him to the Continent. He was a clever, vain, ambitious and plausible scamp, without principles, morality or bowels of compassion, born to get into scrapes and able to talk himself out of most of them. He took advantage of the fact that some members of the Gyllenstierna family were still in exile in Poland to pass himself off to them as a member of the Swedish branch, and in this guise he succeeded in persuading a foolish old Danish nobleman to give him the hand of his daughter in marriage. This escapade, when the

---

[1] If it had not been low C. I. Ulfsparre would hardly have printed the extraordinary rubbish contained in his *Några Bordrim* (1620). Ulfsparre was a man of culture: in the same year in which he published this wretched farrago, he published also *En kort Regementzbok*, which was a treatise on the art of politics, culled from thirty-three authors, ranging from Aristotle to Justus Lipsius.

[2] It is possible that Stiernhielm was the author of the poem *Bröllopsbesvärs ihugkommelse*, and, if so, that it was written in 1629; but the date and authorship of this piece being alike a matter of controversy, it seemed better to omit any consideration of it here. P. Wieselgren, *Georg Stiernhielm*, pp. 88-90.

deception was discovered, landed him in litigation (and no poet was ever more litigious) and eventually in prison, and his suspected connection with Roman Catholic emissaries of Sigismund reinforced the bad impression produced on the Swedish government by his irrepressible impudence.   After a variety of adventures and a spell in prison in Stockholm he was at last sent to Kajaneborg, from which Messenius had but recently been released.   He remained there until 1641.   After his liberation he set up as a shady advocate, settled down, abandoned poetry, and became an approximately respectable citizen.   Although it has been said of him that his best poem was his own life-story, his verse has a strong individuality (and he is the first Swedish poet of whom this is true) and mirrors faithfully the strong and weak sides of his nature.[1] Almost all of it was provoked by external circumstances, and much of it was written to aid him in achieving some end he had in view—to curry favour with a patron, to display his erudition, to enlist sympathy as a patriot, to commend himself to the common people, or to soften the hearts of his judges. Much of it is trivial, pompous and unreadable.   He was a consummate actor, and he could identify himself with any part he chose to play: in turn prophet, imperialist, contrite sinner, man of the people, he could face death with jesting, bitterness or grovelling supplication—and most of these attitudes he contrived to convey successfully in his verse.   But almost always he was thinking of himself; only rarely did he achieve absolute sincerity.   Technically, he was decidedly superior to any Swedish poet before Stiernhielm; but his art was not as a rule serious art, and when it could serve him no more he dropped it without regret.   Yet despite all this he left behind him a handful of verses which have a place in any anthology of Swedish poetry.   Such, for instance, is *Som en sjöman uti stor far* (*As a sailor in the hour of danger*) (1632), which foreshadows, with characteristic garrulity, the thought of Geijer's lapidary *På nyårsdagen 1838* (*New Year's Day 1838*).   Such is the fine outburst of bitterness in *Warer nu glad min fiende all* (*Rejoice now, mine enemies*), with its melancholy refrain,

> Jag föres nu bort
> nordost i fjällen i bojor.[2]

---

[1] For Wivallius' life, see H. Schück, *Svenska bilder*, III.; N. Ahnlund, *Kring Gustav Adolf*, pp. 37-56; for his poetry, see S. Ek, *Lars Wivallius' visdiktning*.
[2]   They bear me away,
           North-east to the fells in my fetters.

But above all the rest stand *Ack Libertas, du ädla ting!* (*Ah! Liberty, thou noble thing!*), with the prose-poem addressed to his judges which is its companion-piece [1]; and the delicious *Klagevisa över denna torra och kalla vår* (*Lament over this dry and cold spring*), written after his liberation in 1641. In these poems Wivallius is moved by a genuine emotion: in the one case a love of freedom, in the other a love of nature. The liberty for which he thirsts is not, perhaps, the liberty which Bishop Thomas had extolled: it is a personal rather than a political liberty, freedom from physical restraint, freedom with the freedom of wild nature. Wivallius, like other predatory animals, felt his heart grow sick in captivity; and this, perhaps, was one reason for his idealization of nature. For he had—and it was unusual at his time—an intermittent longing to withdraw from intercourse with mankind and seek consolation for the injustices of the world amid the impartial indifference of natural objects. Yet he felt too (and it was characteristic) almost a grievance against the very bird on the bough, since it sang untrammelled, while he was a prisoner. But his love of nature was real, none the less; and he had a discriminating eye for natural beauty, and a knowledge of bird and beast and fish which must have stayed with him since his boyhood. Here at least he was not striking an attitude. He is the first Swedish poet of nature,[2] and few can have written of it with more immediate freshness and charm. In his *Klagevisa* a Swedish national characteristic finds its earliest and not its least attractive expression: that extraordinary emotion at the coming of spring which is the result of winter's over-long tarrying, and which even when clad in the stereotyped forms of the twentieth century and the stiff shirt-front of academic oratory, at first astonishes, and then moves, the sympathetic foreigner.[3]

If Wivallius was the first real Swedish poet, his predecessor in Kajaneborg, Johannes Messenius, may fairly claim the title of the first Swedish playwright. In the Middle Ages Sweden, like the rest of Europe, seems to have had its miracle- and morality-plays; but no examples of them have survived. The sixteenth century was as barren in this, as in other forms of literature; though the versatile Olaus Petri in 1550 wrote a Biblical drama entitled *Tobie comedia*.

---

[1] Quoted in Schück and Warburg, II. 127.
[2] Sigfrid Aron Forsius had some feeling for nature too, or at least for zoology: see the verses quoted in S. Lindroth, *Paracelsismen i Sverige intill 1600-talets mitt*, p. 405.
[3] *cf.* the admirable comment of Bertil Boëthius: *Skogen och Bygden*, p. 25.

And, indeed, such plays as there were seem to have been mainly or wholly based on Bible stories, and bore a general resemblance to the Biblical drama in other countries. The personages of the drama were mere puppets reciting their parts; the story was known beforehand; the characters of the actors fixed and changeless; the dramatic interest *nil*. By 1611, however, the Biblical drama was in a decline, and its final demise not far distant; and in its later manifestations it was increasingly blended with purely secular elements, some of them of a sufficiently gross nature. The purely profane drama is usually reckoned to begin with Magnus Olai Asteropherus' *Tisbe* (1610)—a version of the story of Pyramus and Thisbe which a modern Swedish authority compares unfavourably with that of Bottom the Weaver.[1] The decay of the Biblical drama was in part the result of the growing habit of producing classical plays at schools and universities, which was no doubt brought home from Germany by Swedish students. Here Terence was for long the favourite author, until towards the end of the century Ramist influences raised objections to his paganism, and demanded more specifically Christian sentiments.

All this while Sweden—like Germany—had no regular theatres or actors; the standard of production was primitive; and a cultivated taste non-existent. The touring companies of English players who visited Germany and Denmark about the turn of the century revealed new techniques, new standards, a new world of art; and on those countries their visits had a stimulating effect. Little enough of all this filtered through to Sweden[2]; yet from the point of view of the theatre Gustav Adolf's reign marks the boundary of the absolute dark and the beginnings of better times. Plays were performed with increasing frequency; by the end of the reign Sweden had acquired her first theatre manager; and in 1637 the first permanent theatre was built, in a style resembling that of the *Globe*. School drama flourished: Rudbeckius at Uppsala produced Terence in Latin and Swedish, and even Euripides in Greek; the plays of Frischlinus (a German author of the sixteenth century) had a considerable popularity: we even hear of one of them being put on in 1627 for the diversion of the diocesan synod of Strängnäs.[3]

[1] Tigerstedt, p. 98. For a more favourable view, see Böök [etc.], I. 175.
[2] There seem to have been isolated English players and musicians at the ducal court of Karl IX in the 'nineties, but they remained without influence. See K. M. Lea, *English Players at the Swedish Court*, pp. 78-80.
[3] *Synodalakter*, II, 109; but *cf.* H. Lundström, *Skisser och Kritiker*, pp. 134-5.

Unluckily, these developments came too late. Before a popular native drama could establish itself securely enough to produce work of good quality, it was threatened by competition from other and less serious forms of entertainment. It was not only the revived passion for tournaments (an obscure consequence, perhaps, of the current craze for all things 'Gothic'), and the pageants (*upptåg*) that increasingly accompanied them[1]; it was also the coming, under Kristina's lavish patronage, of masques and ballets and operas. Such diversion required less intellectual effort, and offered an opportunity for that new luxury which the soldiers had brought back from Germany to deploy itself in competitive splendour; but its value as art (as the more intelligent of those who took part in it realized)[2] was small. Thus the Swedish drama had the misfortune to pass from the barbarism of Messenius to the decadence of Kristina's court without enjoying a period of efflorescence in between.

Of the dramatic authors active during the reign (apart from Asteropherus), the most important were Rondeletius, Prytz and Messenius. Rondeletius' play *Judas Redivivus* (published 1614) is a curious mixture. Essentially it is a moral tale, illustrative of the evil effects of sparing the rod (it was performed by schoolboys before an audience of appreciative parents); but this intelligible explanation of Judas' misdeeds and ultimate perdition is contradicted by the author's hanging the action simultaneously upon a quite different peg: the determination of the comic Devil (Karrick) to create a child so evil that he may be assured of his soul for Hell, and Karrick's interventions by supernatural means to defeat every attempt to thwart this *dénouement*. Mixed up with all this is the Oedipus motive, for Judas, after killing his father, compels his mother to marry him. But though the motivation is thus a muddle, and the dramatic interest minimal, the play is readable. The characters in many cases *have* character; the dialogue is quite crisp; Karrick and his partner, the witch Glorela, indulge in vigorous low-comedy scenes which must have set the groundlings roaring, though they can hardly have edified Rondeletius' pupils. The verse is extremely crude, but

---

[1] For tournaments, see Å. Meyersson, *Adligt nöje*; F. J. Fielden, *Court Masquerades in Sweden in the Seventeenth Century*, passim. For the *upptåg* (which Fielden considers to bear 'some resemblance to the English "Barriers,"') see Fielden, *op. cit.*, pp. 162-3; *Johan Ekeblads brev*, I. 59, 61, for the barbaric diversions of Kristina's court; *ibid.*, p. 102, for tilting.

[2] *Johan Ekeblads brev*, I. 42, 66, 73, 74. Cf. Whitelocke, II. 111.

no more so than in the plays of Prytz and Messenius. And certainly it must have been an entertaining enough play to act.

The works of Messenius and Prytz, on the other hand, are barely readable, and it is difficult to imagine anyone's deriving much satisfaction from taking part in them. In 1611 and the following years, until Messenius was removed from Uppsala, he wrote four plays for performance by members of his private college: *Disa*, *Signill*, *Swanhuita*, and *Blankamäreta*. Two more, *Christmannus* and *Gustavus*, were written in prison.[1] The purpose of the author was not merely to train his pupils in elocution, or to divert the public, or even to go one better than his rival Rudbeckius. The plays were essentially didactic pieces, and the intention was to disseminate a knowledge of Swedish history, in what Messenius conceived to be an easily assimilable form. All the subjects were historical, or were at least believed by Messenius and his audience to be so; and if Thor and Odin and Frigga appeared on Messenius' stage (to say nothing of Penthesilea, Queen of the Amazons), they were accepted as being no less authentic than ordinary mortals such as King Sigtrud and Queen Blanka. Messenius, with his weakness for the colossal, projected a series of fifty plays, to cover the whole of Swedish history; and the fact that his imprisonment in Kajaneborg deterred him from proceeding with this project is perhaps the only consideration which can be adduced in favour of that harsh measure. The plays were intended to be popular—Messenius contemplated their production in public squares on market-days— and there is no doubt that they were well received. *Disa* ran to seven editions, *Signill* to eight, *Swanhuita* to four, *Blankamäreta* also to four, in the course of the seventeenth and eighteenth centuries. They hit the taste of the time exactly, for they appealed to national pride, historical romanticism, and a primitive sense of humour; and they imposed virtually no strain upon the intelligence. *Disa*, which is perhaps the best of them, was repeatedly performed in this century and even in the next, and was revived by pious undergraduates as late as 1926. They have their interest still, these plays, but it is not a literary or dramatic interest. For they are indeed, one and all, of an appalling tedium. Essentially, they are chronicles, inexpertly adapted to the stage; arbitrarily cut up into acts and scenes in obedience to no dramatic principle; distributed among

---

[1] An excellent study of Messenius as a dramatist is H. Lidell, *Studier i Johannes Messenius dramer.*

huge, and superfluously huge, casts; narrated in verse which a literary historian has rightly called 'excruciating'. No motivation, no characterization, no tension, with knockabout comedy scenes for muddy oases on the formidable progress. Literary historians have argued as to whether Messenius was influenced by the Jesuit drama of Braunsberg, by Hans Sachs, or by the English touring companies, and the balance of opinion seems now to favour Hans Sachs; but the question is merely of academic interest. From a literary point of view, the one good thing about these plays is the introduced songs, which have at times something of the authentic note of folk-song; but there seems to be some doubt as to whether these are to be considered as Messenius' work.

Andreas Prytz was Messenius' pupil at Uppsala, and followed faithfully in his footsteps as a dramatist. His *Olof Skottkonung*, a historical play dealing with the conversion of Sweden by St. Sigfrid, is said by some to be inferior to Messenius. It does not seem to merit such extreme condemnation; and on the whole the distinction between the two seems a very fine one. *Olof Skottkonung* has the advantage that its low-comedy scenes are written in prose and in dialect. On the other hand it is more diffuse in form (some of the scenes have no conceivable connection with anything else in the play), and it harks back to the old morality-plays by making the Virtues and Vices appear in person.[1]

If we turn now from poetry and drama to pure prose, the land appears barren still—at all events as concerns prose written in Swedish, rather than in Latin. The glories of the reign lay in the spoken rather than in the written word. And above all in the King's own speeches, which rank with the best political oratory of that, or perhaps of any, age. Their effect when read is strong; their effect upon listeners, in the peculiar circumstances in which they were delivered, must have been overwhelming. They were undoubtedly calculated and conscious art, but they make their impression by the sense of spontaneity and urgency which they convey, and by a simplicity and naturalness of diction which never degenerates into the vulgar. Gustav Vasa and Karl IX were no mean orators, and both wrote prose without knowing it; but Gustav Adolf as a rule avoids the coarseness and violence which disfigured the style of his predecessors. The speeches from the two *riksdagar* of 1617 show

---

[1] Prytz wrote another play—*En lustig comoedia . . . om Gustav then Första*—but this I have not read. Possibly it is better. Possibly not.

him at the height of his powers as an orator, and his farewell to the Estates in 1630 is the only prose classic of the reign.[1]

For the rest there were sermons, and yet more sermons; sermons learned and sermons popular, funeral orations and allocutions comminatory, with the stately orchestral brass of Rudbeckius audible above the rest of them. They were, perhaps, much like other sermons of their day, piling up allusions to the Old Testament into massive oratorical tumuli, grouping into fresh patterns those verbal counters of Scriptural parlance which were the stock-in-trade of the divine. The group of funeral sermons for Gustav II Adolf produced things which have been admired, and that by Rudbeckius has been compared with Bossuet[2]; but they were after all but the most notable examples of exercises in a stereotyped form, and originality was not their strong point.

There remain the works of the learned; written in Latin, usually of gigantic proportions, and forgotten to-day save by the historians of learning and the writers of dissertations. Such were Forsius' *Physica*, the first work of its kind by a Swede, which Gustav Adolf asked Uppsala to report upon with a view to publication[3]; such was Laurentius Paulinus Gothus' *Ethica*, which began as a text-book and ended by running to some 4000 pages and including most branches of knowledge; such was Messenius' *Scondia Illustrata*, to be discussed presently. And with that the view of Swedish literature in Gustav Adolf's time is almost complete. Almost, but not quite: for the writings of the period are in the main less interesting for their literary quality (only Wivallius and Gustav Adolf can really be said to be alive) than for the fact that so many of them are permeated or coloured by a species of historical romanticism which, though it converts them into learned oddities for a modern reader, was the essence of their appeal to contemporaries. Messenius may have been a wretched dramatist, but both as a

---

[1] They are conveniently collected into a single volume in C. Hallendorff, *Gustav Adolf: Tal och Skrifter*, pp. 34-65, 114-18.

[2] Tigerstedt, p. 90. A collection of funeral orations for Gustav Adolf is B. R. Hall, *Vid Gustaf Adolf's bår*, I.-II. On Rudbeckius as a preacher, see G. Lindberg, *Johannes Rudbeckius som predikant*. On clerical oratory in general, A. Wifstrand, *Andlig talekonst*. The specimen which Lindberg holds up for admiration on p. 77 seems really to be the type of routine sermon which any self-respecting parson could have turned out in his sleep; and about which, indeed, the irreverent might detect a faint flavour of Mr. Chadband.

[3] See *Handlingar rörande Skandinaviens Historia*, XIV. 216-18, for his letter. Uppsala reported unfavourably; and a similar recommendation from Kristina twenty years later brought a similar reply.

dramatist and as a historian he was a great intellectual force. Skogekär Bergbo is far more important for what he had to say than for how he said it. The same is true, perhaps, of Forsius; and it is pre-eminently true of Johannes Bureus.

The theory, or myth, or religion (for it was almost that) which in greater or lesser degree affected all these men, and most other writers of the time, is called in Swedish *storgöticism*, which perhaps may be Englished, for want of a better term, as 'megalogothicism'. *Storgöticism* was first popularized by the *Historia de omnibus gothorum sveonumque regibus* of Johannes Magnus, the last Catholic Archbishop of Uppsala, which was published in Rome in 1554; but Johannes Magnus was not its inventor: he merely gave canonical form to a theory which had been in the air for some time. It is possible, indeed, that it arose out of genuine folk-memories of the Viking ages, for the first traces of it are to be discerned as early as the second half of the thirteenth century. It first received coherent literary expression in Spain, where the strength of the Gothic tradition appeared in the works of Jordanes, Isidore of Seville and Jimenez de Rada[1]; and it was this Spanish *storgöticism* which provoked the first classic exposition of the creed from the Swedish side. For at the Council of Basel in 1434 a contest for precedence arose between the representatives of England and Castile, in the course of which the Castilians made the point that they were an older nation than the English, since they were identical with the ancient Goths. This brought up the Archbishop of Uppsala, Nicholas Ragvaldi, who claimed precedence for the Swedes, as being the genuine and original main stem of the Gothic people, whereas the Castilians were no more than a side-branch. For the moment, the arguments of Castile prevailed; but Ragvaldi's speech was not forgotten, and in Gustav Adolf's time it was sold freely in translation as a popular broadsheet.

Ragvaldi may have been influenced in his outburst at Basel by a desire to score a point off the Danes, for Erik of Pomerania was at that time unpopular with his Swedish subjects: it is at all events certain that notions of this sort struck root in the period of political enthusiasm which began with Engelbrekt, and that they set their mark on the semi-official historiography of Karl Knutsson's time.[2]

---

[1] J. Nordström, *Goter och Spanjorer*, passim.
[2] G. Carlsson, *Senare medeltiden: tidsskedet 1389-1448*, p. 509; S. Kraft, *Senare medeltiden: tidsskedet 1448-1520*, p. 45.

The struggle of the Stures against the Union, Gustav Vasa's liberation of the country from the tyrant Kristian, strengthened an already existing disposition to accept an account of Sweden's early history which glorified her past at the expense of that of Denmark. It happened, therefore, that Johannes Magnus came forward with his book at a moment when his countrymen were ripe to receive it.

What, then, was the *storgöticist* theory as enounced by Johannes Magnus? and what was its importance for the reign of Gustav Adolf? [1] The gist of it is the contention that the Swedes are identical with the ancient Goths, are descended from Japhet, and are the begetters of some thirty nations. They are the oldest nation in the world, since the Flood; for Sweden and Finland were the first portions of the earth's surface to be settled after that catastrophe—108 years earlier than Italy, which was itself occupied much earlier than (for instance) Babylonia. Their first King was Japhet's son Magog, and his sons were Sven, Gothar (whence Svealand and Götaland), Thor, German and Ubbe. Sven was succeeded by Ubbe 1903 years after the Creation; and Ubbe, a century later, by Sigge: it was Ubbe that built Uppsala, as it was Sigge that founded Sigtuna. Magog's grandson, who acceded in the year 2012 after the Creation, was Erik I; and in the year 2493 came Berik, who united the Svear and Götar, and was the first 'external' King—that is, the first to fare abroad and conquer foreign lands. Berik, after sailing to Pomerania, Poland and Mecklenburg, went finally to Spain, which he conquered. He had an army made up both of men and of women, for the Amazons were Goths also. Besides Spain the Goths conquered Germany, France, Britain, Italy, Asia, Africa, Constantinople 'and several other powerful lands'; fought Darius, King of Persia, and Xerxes, and Cyrus; overran Rome in the time of Sulla; and provided the Emperor Augustus with a wife, Julia. The Gothic Kings also fought at Troy, and so, of course, did their Amazons. It was in the time of the sixteenth King from Magog (one Humle) that they subdued Denmark and England—countries which took their modern names from Humle's sons Dan and Angul. In all, the list of Swedish Kings, from Magog to Gustav Vasa, numbered well over a hundred, and of nearly all of them Johannes Magnus had something of interest to relate. In the earliest times the country

---

[1] For what follows, see J. Nordström, *De yverbornes ö*, and H. Hildebrand, *Minne af Riksantikvarien Johannes Bureus*, p. 184 *seqq.*

had been remarkable for its unity, respect for law, and true religious feeling; but on the death of Erik I (which occurred some 400 years after the Flood) the inhabitants turned to the worship of idols, and it was then that the cult of Odin and Thor established itself. Even so, the level of culture was very high, and the land abounded in riches. Great poets were produced, greater than Homer; though, as a result of theft, Danish ravages, the coming of Christendom, and other misadventures, their works had all unfortunately perished. The Goths derived their laws from Zamolxis (or Salmoxes), who had been slave to Pythagoras; but most of the learning and arts of the ancient Greeks had been taught to them by the Goths, and the Runic alphabet was the oldest alphabet of all, with the possible exception of the Hebrew.

Such, in summary, was the wondrous story which Johannes Magnus unfolded to his astonished and delighted fellow-countrymen. It was an immediate and enormous success. In the sixty years after its first publication the book was translated into Swedish no less than four times. One of the translators was Erik XIV, who firmly believed in it, as the 'XIV' after his name clearly testified; and the last version was commissioned from Erik Schroderus by Gustav Adolf in 1620. There was also an abridgment made in Karl IX's reign, and a German translation, specially arranged for by Johan Skytte. It would be difficult to exaggerate the influence of this book upon the men of Gustav Adolf's time. *Storgöticism* permeated the minds of all educated men; it coloured the sermons of the clergy; it was used as an argument in government propaganda.[1] It gave to the whole nation a stimulus which does something to explain the extraordinary outburst of national energy in the seventeenth century. The astonishing success of Swedish arms, the conquest of fresh provinces, the appearance of Swedish armies on the Rhine, the Alps and the Danube, did not appear so very extraordinary to men who

---

[1] In 1625 Peder Eriksson, secretary in the Exchequer, made a tour of Uppland, Bergslagen and Norrland to raise a loan for the Crown. The arguments he used to encourage contributions were taken straight from Johannes Magnus, which he had studied in Schroderus' translation; and either they, or the promise of 12 to 14 per cent. interest, seem to have been effective: J. Nordström, *Historieromantik och politik under Gustav Adolfs tid*, pp. 378-91. There is a choice example of the general dissemination of these ideas in F. Lindberg, *1619 års stadga om städernas administration*, p. 10: the citizens of Kalmar, disliking the idea of a municipal brewery, claim that they should be allowed to brew at home 'according to the liberty of the ancient Goths'. For other examples, see (*e.g.*) Whitelocke, I. 188; II. 149-50; T. Berg, *Skytte*, p. 64; *Johan Skyttes kommentar till stadslagen*, p. xv.

viewed them as a *restoration* of Sweden to her historic position of ascendancy—of overlordship—in Europe, and as the tardy redress of a long-standing distortion of the proper order of things. Gustav Adolf himself was affected by these notions: Skytte and Bureus—both fervent believers—were his tutors; at his coronation tournaments he assumed the pseudonyms of Berik and Alarik; and he was apt to boast to foreigners of the immense wealth and historic lustre of his country.[1] The extraordinary prickliness of Swedish diplomacy on points of predecence was another manifestation of the same thing: it was not for the successor of Magog to make concessions to *parvenus* such as the Kings of France and Poland, and still less to the Tsar of Muscovy. It was the same pride in a past more illustrious than that of any other nation that led Gustav Adolf to create the office of Antiquary-Royal, in order that the evidence for it might be collected and presented to the learned world, and the jealous slanders of foreigners confuted.[2]

One aspect of the *storgöticist* movement was linguistic, and of this Skogekär Bergbo is the pre-eminent example.[3] It appears now to be all but certain that Skogekär was really Schering Rosenhane, and that his poem *Thet swenska språketz klagemål* (*The Complaint of the Swedish Language*) was written about the year 1632, some time between Breitenfeld and Lützen. The poem, which is a long one, is supposed to be a monologue by the Swedish Language, who laments her neglect by the Swedish people, and the consequent contempt of foreign nations. Swedish, for instance, was not one of the eleven languages included in Calepinus' famous polyglot dictionary (neither was Danish, for that matter); and this is to be attributed to the low esteem in which it appears to be held by the Swedes themselves. They make all haste to learn foreign tongues, and consider it a mark of gentility to speak German or French; and if they do speak their native language, they debase it with foreign words and un-Swedish constructions, so that the language is becoming bastardized. It was thus that Latin degenerated into

---

[1] Nordström, *De yverbornes ö*, pp. 69-75. Gustav Adolf had a naïve pride in Sweden's natural curiosities. In 1615, by way of improving relations with John George of Saxony, he sent him a Lapp boy and girl and some reindeer: B. Boëthius, *Skogen och Bygden*, p. 209; and *cf.* Whitelocke, I. 412. When Gustav Adolf went to Finland in 1614, he took care that the 'tapestries about the histories of the Goths' should go with him in his baggage: Cronholm, III. 233.

[2] For further discussion of this, see below, p. 520.

[3] The following paragraphs are based on E. Källquist, *Thet swenska språketz klagemål, passim.*

Italian; and the Roman people lost their best qualities when they ceased to care for the purity of their speech. One consequence of this unnatural attitude was the discouragement of native authors, who could find neither publisher nor public for their works. Yet Swedish was a language as old as Latin, or older, and at least the equal of it in richness and ability to express thought: the blame for the existing situation lay not with the language but with the men that used it. If it were a question of literary merit, Sweden had produced Gothic poets in the old days as great as Homer, or greater, and might well do so again; if it were a matter of policy, Sweden had as good a claim to be a language of diplomacy as German or French.[1] It was the duty of Swedish writers to praise and defend their country and their speech against the malignity of the foreigner, and especially of the Dane. There was no need, and it would indeed be inexpedient, to seek to revive archaic or obsolescent words and expressions, for the language was sufficiently copious already. Swedish had once been the first language in Europe, and already the day was dawning when it would be so again.

In so far as Skogekär was pleading for a purer Swedish, and censuring the adulteration of the language by foreign importations, he had a good deal of right on his side. A glance at any volume of Axel Oxenstierna's letters will reveal the extent to which Swedish was becoming Germanized and Latinized. Soldiers of fortune were beginning to settle in Sweden on their retirement from the wars, foreign capitalists like De Geer were fixing their residence in the country; by the early 1640's the debates in the Estate of Nobles might be conducted in three or four languages; and in 1635 the government found itself obliged to resolve, out of consideration for the common man, that no foreign words should be used in the Propositions to the *riksdag*.[2] But though from this point of view there was something to be said for Skogekär, he was in the main simply voicing a Swedish, *storgöticist*, variant of a species of linguistic nationalism which had been very prevalent in the previous century,

---

[1] On the language of diplomacy, see N. Ahnlund, *Svenskt och nordiskt från skilda tider*, pp. 114-23; and Whitelocke, I. 300: 'He [Axel Oxenstierna] spake Latin, plain and fluent and significant; and though he could, yet would not speak French, saying he knew no reason why that nation should be so much honoured more than others as to have their language used by strangers; but he thought Latin more honourable and more copious, and fitter to be used, because the Romans had been masters of so great a part of the world, and yet at present that language was not peculiar to any people.' And *cf.* the words of Olaus Petri, p. 351, above.

[2] F. Lindberg, *Axel Oxenstierna som riksdagstaktiker*, p. 254.

2 K

and which had now at last reached the far North. Some eighty years earlier Du Bellay, in his *Deffense et illustration de la langue françoyse* (1549), which was the manifesto of the group to be known as the *Pléiade*, had said many of the things that Skogekär was to say. Earlier still, the writers of the Italian Renaissance (and Dante before that) had championed the use of the vernacular and rebutted the suggestion that it was a barbarous *patois*, unapt for literary uses. More recently, in Holland, Johannes Goropius Becanus had contended, in his *Origines Antwerpianae* (1569) that Dutch (the 'Cimbrian' tongue, as he called it) was the oldest language in the world, and had been spoken by Adam: it had remained unaffected by the confusion of tongues at the tower of Babel, since the Cimbrians had dwelt too far off to assist in the construction of that building.   Linguistic nationalism was strong in Holland, under the influence of the Eighty Years' War; and it received its Bible in Hendrik Laurensz Spieghel's *Tweespraack vande Nederduitsche Letterkunst*.   Scientific literature began to appear in Dutch; and in 1617 Samuel Coster founded his 'Duytsche Academie'.   In Germany, Opitz, with his *Aristarchus* (1618) did for his countrymen what Du Bellay had done for France; and at the same time the claim was advanced that the Germans were descended from Tuitschen, son of Noah.   It is plain, then, that Skogekär was not an isolated phenomenon, and it is not impossible that he may have read, and been influenced by, Spieghel.   In some respects he was more moderate than his foreign colleagues, for he did not expressly claim for Swedish that it was the language of Adam.   This, however, was a development of the *storgöticist* theory which was not long delayed.   Johannes Bureus indignantly refuted Goropius Becanus' absurd claims for Dutch, and showed that Swedish was the next oldest language after Hebrew (which was the language in which God spoke to men)[1]; and Bureus' pupil, the great Stiernhielm, asserted that Swedish was older even than Hebrew, and was in fact the primaeval language (*urspråk*) for which the philologists of that age were seeking, the language from which all other languages took their rise.   Stiernhielm boldly rejected the story of the tower of Babel: the speech of Noah, he contended, was preserved most purely in the language of the Scythians, who were identical with the Goths (and consequently the descendants of Japhet), and modern Swedish was the nearest extant language to it; and since Scythians

---

[1] S. Lindroth, *Paracelsismen i Sverige*, p. 216.

were the first inhabitants of Greece, Greek poetry and religion are of Scythian origin.[1]

The *storgöticist* theory, thus strikingly evident in the field of philology, naturally made a deep impression on contemporary historiography. Indeed, since the time of Johannes Magnus only one Swedish historian had succeeded in emancipating himself from those exhilarating visions of a glorious pre-history which Johannes Magnus had conjured up. This was Olaus Petri, whose unpublished Chronicle (*En swensk crönika*) was the first attempt at critical use of the sources by a Swedish historian. Olaus Petri rejected Johannes Magnus *in toto*, suggested that the Goths were not nearly so ancient as was commonly supposed, expressed the view that they originated 'where Hungary now is, or even further off', and flatly stated that no information was available about them before the Christian era.[2] This sober and refreshing scepticism, however, long remained unique, and Olaus Petri failed to find a publisher. His successors, for a long time to come, all more or less follow in the wake of Johannes Magnus. Gustav Adolf's historiographer-royal, Johann Narssius of Dordrecht, need not detain us: he was a learned hack, employed to recount the military achievements of his patron in Latin verse at the handsome annual stipend of 800 *daler*, with leave to continue his original profession of medicine between onsets of the poetic afflatus.[3] Nor were the three chronicles of Aegidius Laurentii Girs, covering the period 1523-92, of any great importance. But the *Short and Useful Chronicle* of Petrus Petrejus, published in 1614, is of more consequence. He is a wholehearted *storgöticist*, and succeeds in considerably lengthening Johannes Magnus' fabulously long list of early Swedish Kings. Also, this is the first history of Sweden in Swedish to achieve publication.[4]

The two most considerable historians of Gustav Adolf's time are, however, those inveterate enemies Tegel and Messenius. Tegel treated of comparatively modern history: apart from some genealogical researches, his main works are his histories of Gustav Vasa

---

[1] Nordström, *De yverbornes ö*, p. 122. For Stiernhielm, see B. Swartling, *Georg Stiernhielm, hans lif och verksamhet*. The comparatively moderate claims of Skogekär, as against those of Stiernhielm, may perhaps be considered an additional argument for an early date for *Thet swenska språketz klagemål*.

[2] For a short appreciation of Olaus Petri as a historian, see H. Schück, *Riksantikvarieämbetet genom 300 år*, pp. 4-5.

[3] *RRP*, I. 104 *note* 3; and for further details about him, E. Wrangel, *De Betrekkinge tusschen Zweden en de Nederland op het Gebied van Letteren en Wetenschap*, p. 66.

[4] S. Clason, *Historiska betraktelser af Karl IX*, p. 152 note 1.

and of Erik XIV. The former of these was written to refute the Danish historian Arild Huitfeldt; and in the latter Tegel, as the son of Erik's hated minister Göran Persson, had a strong personal interest. Nevertheless, both are said to have considerable merit, for Tegel had apparently clearly grasped the superiority of an original document to a mere statement in a chronicle, and his text is liberally studded with extracts which here appeared in print for the first time.[1] But as a historian Tegel cannot stand comparison with Messenius. Messenius impresses first of all by the mere bulk of his publications. From the time when he went as professor to Uppsala, to the moment of his fall in 1616, works of learning poured from him in astonishing profusion—the more astonishing when it is remembered that this was the period when most of his plays were being written, and that he was for part of it conducting his private College in Uppsala, with a very heavy programme of teaching, correcting and lecturing.[2] Messenius was a real scholar, who pursued his researches without much looking to the rewards that might be expected, and upon his transference to the Archives he devoted himself with enthusiasm to his new employment. By his publication of sources,[3] by his comprehensive knowledge of his subject, he paved the way for a proper care of the country's documents; and it was a cruel stroke of fate that his fall should have been caused by his own incautious zeal for the recovery of material which had somehow drifted over to Poland. At Kajaneborg, in spite of every obstacle and the harshest treatment by his gaolers, he indomitably pursued his researches. Excerpts, transcripts and books were sent to him in his remote Arctic prison, and with their aid he set himself to the composition of a gigantic history—not of Sweden only, but of Scandinavia (in itself an original idea)—which should

[1] For Tegel as a historian, see S. Ljung, *Tegel*, pp. 126-57.
[2] His publications at this time were:
  1610. *Amphitheatrum* [a list of Swedish Kings from Magog, each provided with a rhymed distich].
  1611. *Sveapentaprotopolis* [a history of Sweden's five capitals].
  1611. *Tumbae veterum ac nuperorum apud Sveones Gothosque regum.*
  1611. *Chronicon Episcoporum per Sveciam Gothiam et Finlandiam.*
  1612. *Specula* [a historical-ethnographic description of Sweden].
  1612. *Retorsio Imposturarum* [a reply to an attack upon Johannes Magnus by a Dane named Hans Svaning].
  For these, see H. Schück, *Messenius*, pp. 124-68.

[3] He published in 1614 an edition of Ragvald Ingemundi's translation into Latin of Magnus Eriksson's *Landslag*; in 1615 editions of Ericus Olai: *Historia Svecorum Gothorumque*, and of *Twå små gamble Rijm Krönikas första deel*; and an original work of his own, *Theatrum Nobilitatis Svecanae.*

confound foreign critics and vindicate Johannes Magnus and his theories. The result was the enormous *Scondia Illustrata*, fourteen volumes of which were eventually published under Peringskiöld's auspices between 1700 and 1705. Messenius was perhaps as good a historian as a *storgöticist* could be.[1] With all Tegel's preference for original rather than secondary sources, he had some realization of the difference in value between one primary source and another, and he was not afraid to reject an authority altogether. He was the first Swedish historian to make use of Icelandic material for the history of Scandinavia. As a result, he found himself as he progressed less inclined to swallow Johannes Magnus whole, and he ended by modifying and criticizing him in many respects. But if he was thus willing to apply textual criticism to the *storgöticist* Bible, he did not remain any the less faithful to the true creed; and *Scondia* was in its way just as much a patriotic exaltation of the part played by the Swedes in history as Johannes Magnus' *Historia* had been. It was for this reason that the government gave facilities to Messenius for carrying on the writing of it; and it was for this reason that Messenius' widow (who had laid hold of Messenius' literary remains, and took them with her to safety in Poland) was able to bring pressure to bear to obtain the liberation from prison of her son, as the price of handing the manuscript over to the Swedish government.[2] It is only when we take into account Messenius' passion for history that we are able to forgive him his plays. For essentially they were products of the same creative enthusiasm; and both were intended as proclamations of the *storgöticist* faith—the one to the learned world that read Latin, the other to the man-in-the-street who craved (or at least required) enlightenment about his own heroic ancestors.[3]

Messenius was a man of many parts and much learning; but he was not the most learned Swede of his time. That distinction must probably be reserved for Johannes Bureus, who throughout his long life (1568-1652) busied himself insatiably with the more obscure and esoteric types of knowledge. Bureus was a person of extraordinarily various gifts. He was an etcher, a maker of wood-cuts, a diamond-cutter, a seal-engraver; he may fairly be called the father

---

[1] For *Scondia*, and a general view of Messenius as a historian, see H. Olsson, *Johannes Messenius Scondia Illustrata, passim*; H. Schück, *Messenius*, pp. 282-318; N. Ahnlund, *Kring Gustav Adolf*, pp. 195-204.

[2] For this episode, see H. Olsson, *op. cit.*, pp. 20-4.

[3] Lidell, pp. 33-4, 41-5, 62, 75, 80-2, 88, 101.

of Swedish grammar; he was a versifier more venturesome than
Messenius (he was one of the first Swedes to attempt hexameters)
and certainly no worse in quality; he was one of the earliest Swedish
Copernicans, at a time when the Copernican theory was frowned
on in orthodox Uppsala circles; he was interested in music, and
apparently played some keyboard instrument [1]; and he had a knack
of picking up languages: he taught himself Hebrew at school, and
later acquired Finnish, Arabic (which he began at the age of sixty,
at 8 o'clock in the evening, as he carefully informs us),[2] Russian,
'Abyssinian', and a smattering of Chinese. He published a grammar
of old Norse, and began the first Swedish dictionary. He invented
a system of stenography, and had an odd passion for impracticable
ciphers—one of the most curious being the *alphabetum vegetabile*,
whereby each word was represented as a tree, distinguished from
other trees by the arrangement of leaves and branches: this he
thought of in bed, on 1 May 1609, at 8.30 in the morning.[3] He was
a notable rescuer of early MSS., and produced an important edition
of the Västgöta Laws. And he left behind him a diary in which
his thoughts and fancies, superstitions, dreams and domestic misfortunes ('*rixosa dies mulieribus*')[4] are recorded with an intimacy and
simplicity which is very disarming. But it is not for any of these
things, nor even for having produced two such pupils as Gustav
Adolf and Stiernhielm, that Bureus is celebrated. His fame rests on
his pioneer work for Runic studies, and upon the extraordinary
superstructure of Kabbalistic, Paracelsian, and Rosicrucian speculation which he built upon that foundation.[5] He was, of course, a
storgöticist, and in the development of that theory he holds a particular place. Since Johannes Magnus, the theory had remained
virtually static: Messenius' criticisms long remained in manuscript
and unknown, and when the time came for them to be printed,
storgöticism had passed beyond the point reached by Messenius, and
the new High Priest of the movement could no longer approve what
Messenius had written.[6] The first real advance on Johannes Magnus

[1] H. Hildebrand, *Bureus*, p. 70, quoting an entry in Bureus' journal: 'bought
the symphony for 8 *daler*': for 'symphony' in the sense of a keyboard instrument,
see T. Norlind, *Från tyska kyrkans glansdagar*, I. 56 *note* 1.
[2] *Anteckningar af J. T. A. Bureus* (1883), p. 109.
[3] *ibid.*, p. 39.
[4] *ibid.*, p. 80.
[5] For Bureus, see *Anteckningar af J. T. A. Bureus, passim*; H. Hildebrand,
Bureus; S. Lindroth, *Paracelsismen i Sverige*, pp. 82-251; Nordström, *De yverbornes ö*, pp. 100-3.
[6] H. Olsson, *op. cit.*, p. 24.

came with Bureus, for it was Bureus who first identified Sweden with the Hyperborean Land of the Greeks, and so paved the way for those elaborations which were to lead, through Stiernhielm and Verelius, to the fantastic, grandiose finale, in which Olof Rudbeck would identify Sweden also with Atlantis.

The study of Runes was still in its infancy when Bureus began upon it. Olaus Petri had indeed published a short book on the subject,[1] but hitherto it had had no successor. Bureus is said to have learned the Runic script from peasants in Dalarna, and though the story may be apocryphal, it does at least reflect the undoubted fact that in Bureus' time the use of Runes still survived in remote districts[2]: indeed, as a measure of time rune-staves have survived almost to our own day. It was in 1599 that he published his first work on Runes—an engraving of Runic inscriptions with commentary attached—and thenceforward he was busy with Runes for the rest of his life. *Runaräfst* followed in 1602, a Runic A B C-book in 1611. He had already been commissioned by Karl IX to tour the country in order to draw rune-stones and transcribe their inscriptions; and for a moment, as we have seen, Karl thought of making him Professor of Runic in a projected new university at Strängnäs. It was Bureus' ambition to publish a drawing of every rune-stone in Sweden, with a translation of its inscription; and the magnitude of the task he set himself may be judged from the fact that even to-day it has hardly been completed. Nevertheless, his industry and energy were prodigious, and by the end of his active life he had probably transcribed as many as one-quarter of all the rune-stones in Sweden.[3] And he had transcribed them well, for he was a careful and intelligent copyist. The importance of the work he was doing was fully appreciated by Gustav Adolf, who saw in the Runes (as Bureus did also) one more piece of evidence for the ancient culture of the Goths: it was laid down in the regulation for the Chair of History in 1620 that its holder should be bound to learn Runic.[4] In view of the national importance of Runic studies, it is therefore intelligible that the strongest emotions should have been aroused by the publication in 1626 of a book by the Danish savant Ole Worm, in which Danish Runic inscriptions were deciphered, Bureus' work

[1] H. Schück, *Riksantikvarieämbetet genom 300 år*, p. 5.
[2] H. Schück, *Messenius*, p. 140; *cf.* Linné, *Ungdomsresor*, II. 55.
[3] For an account of Bureus' work for runology, see E. Svärdström, *Johannes Bureus' arbeten om svenska runinskrifter*.
[4] Schück, *Riksantikvarieämbetet*, p. 6.

upon runology passed over almost in silence, and the monstrous theory propounded that Runes were really of Danish origin, since culture had spread gradually northwards, and hence had reached Sweden from Denmark. And the crowning insult came when it was contended that the ancient Goths (or Cimbri, or Dacians, or Scythians—there was a fine catholicity about Ole Worm) were really Danes. Worm's book undoubtedly stole Bureus' thunder: the learned antiquaries of the West accepted Worm at his own valuation, and the priority of Bureus' Runic studies (and their importance) was not realized, at all events in England, until some decades after Bureus was dead.[1] In confutation of Worm Bureus published *Runa Redux*; but it did not appear until 1643, and it was in any case a slight performance, apart from the fact that it was in verse. The real reply to Worm came with the creation of the office of Antiquary-Royal for Bureus in 1630, and the issuing of the Instruction of 20 May 1630, which Gustav Adolf (and it was symptomatic of the importance attached to the question) found time to sign on the eve of his departure for Germany. The Instruction was extraordinarily comprehensive.[2] The Antiquary-Royal and his assistants were not merely to take drawings of old monuments and Runic inscriptions; they were also to hunt for old manuscripts, statutes, privileges and other legal antiquities; to note down old sagas, anecdotes of famous men, and folk-songs; to collect popular remedies; to record tidemarks and water levels; they were to make ethnographical collections, and to concern themselves with place-name research; and finally they were to be responsible for many of the duties of a Surveyor-General.

If Bureus' work had stopped now, he would have been remembered only as a distinguished antiquary in an age of distinguished antiquaries. But Runes were more to Bureus than a hobby or a profession; they were a passion and almost a religion. He would have liked to revive Runic script for ordinary use (the Latin letters, he held, had been introduced by the Catholic Church to enchain men's souls); and he had even experimented with a cursive form of Runic, devised by himself. Already before Gustav Adolf's accession he had come round to the view that though Hebrew was no doubt the oldest language, Runic was the oldest alphabet; and even earlier

---

[1] Seaton, pp. 225-31.
[2] O. Almgren, *Om tillkomsten av 1630-års antikvarieinstruktion, passim*; H. Schück, *Riksantikvarieämbetet, passim.*

—probably soon after 1600—he had begun to evolve his theory of
'Adulrunes'. As the Hebrews and the Egyptians had used their
alphabets in esoteric and secret ways for mystical and divinatory
purposes, so the Goths had used Runes; and behind the ordinary
Runes were the magical Adulrunes, which (if one could only discover
the art of using them) would show the way to eternal truths and
divine knowledge. In thus attributing to Runic writing a magical
and necromantic purpose, Bureus was, oddly enough, perfectly
right[1]; but he arrived at his conclusion by the wrong road. The
theory of Adulrunes came to him by analogy from the Hebrew
Kabbala, and what he was attempting to create was in fact a Kabbala
of Runes.[2] His interest in Kabbalism dated back to the early
'nineties; and since he could read Hebrew he was able to go to the
original sources: we know, for instance, that he read the *Liber
Jezira*, one of the books of secret lore of the Hebrews; and he was of
course familiar with the modern Christian Kabbalists such as Pico
della Mirandola, Reuchlin, and Agrippa of Nettesheim. And as he
was a person of strong religious feeling, he shared the view, which
had been common to most of these authors, that the operative force
in the white magic which he desired to master must be prayer, and
the precondition for success in the pursuit of these mysteries was the
adoration of God. By the turn of the century he was already deep
in the *temura*—the art of the mutation of letters in accordance with
certain occult and complex rules in order to extract from words the
precious intimations of divine mysteries which lay concealed in them.
Thus Bureus came to believe that, since all knowledge had once
been *one*, all knowledge might well lie hidden behind the Runes,
in the Adulrunes; and the pansophists' dream of a *scientia
scientiarum* would be within the grasp of the man who could read
the Adulrunes aright.

In all this there was no authority to whom Bureus looked more
often, or with more reverence, than to Paracelsus—or at least to
certain of the many pseudo-Paracelsian writings, such as the *Liber
Azoth* and *Arbatel*. And since these writings had a highly
'spiritual', mystical side, occult, theosophical and 'divinely wise',
Bureus was led on by them to religious mystics such as Khunrath
and Johan Arndt, to the '*religio paracelsica*', to Rosicrucianism, and

---

[1] This emerges clearly from the general argument in S. Agrell, *Runornas
talmystik och dess antika förebilder*.

[2] A succinct account of what Kabbalism was is given by H. Odeberg, *Till
Kabbalas väsen* (in *Från skilda tider: studier tillägnade Hj. Holmquist*, pp. 444-52).

so to chiliasm and apocalypticism.   A decisive moment occurred in
1613, when Bureus seems to have experienced some kind of religious
revelation, or mystical communion; and thereafter he grew more
obscure and fantastic than ever.   The outward and visible sign of
this development was the publication of his *Buccina iubilei ultimi*, a
work so learned and so dark that even a leading Continental occultist
had to have it carefully explained to him by the author.   By the
beginning of the 1620's, Bureus' fantasies were beginning to attract
the unfavourable notice of the leaders of the Church, and it was
probably only the personal intervention and protection of the King
that saved him from unpleasant consequences.[1] But Bureus was not
to be turned from his speculations.   As he grew older they took on
more and more an eschatological and apocalyptic form, and in a
series of writings, of which *Nordlandalejonsens rytande* (*The roaring
of the Lion of the North*) may stand as an example, he plunged ever
deeper into mysterious chronological calculations, wherein the
Emperor Constantine figured as one of the Beasts of the Apocalypse,
John Huss as Jeremiah's swallow, Martin Luther (more plausibly)
as the Cherubic Ox, and the Jesuits as the Tails of the Locusts
(Revelation ix. 10), with the end of the world fixed (as with so many
other such calculations) for the year 1666—though in actual fact
the event would occur in 1647, since God had shortened the days
(Mark xiii. 20) by nineteen years.   And it is said that in 1647 Bureus
did indeed divide his property among the poor and prepare for the
Day of Judgment; and was forced afterwards to apply to Kristina
for financial support. He lived for five years longer, active and
ingenious to the last. In spite of his passion for the more tenebrous
by-paths of knowledge, and a certain oddity which struck even his
contemporaries, he was a very learned and very good man; and it
was not the least of Gustav Adolf's merits to have protected him
against the jealous zeal of the orthodox.

   The eschatological speculations of Bureus, fantastic as they may
appear, were far from being peculiar to him. They were shared in
greater or lesser degree by many of the scholars of that age, and had
an influence which extended, through the pulpit, to the semi-
literate masses. In the sixteenth century the idea of the approaching
end of the world was common enough, especially among Protestants:
Luther, Zwingli and Calvin were all convinced that the Pope was
that Antichrist which had been foretold; that his power would

---

[1] *Anteckningar af J. T. A. Bureus* (1883), p. 74.

shortly be overthrown; and that his downfall would herald the coming of the Latter Days. In Melanchthon's view the Papacy and Islam were identical with the Gog and Magog mentioned both in the Old and New Testaments [1]; and he believed that they would reveal themselves in that character in 1600 or 1607. The Kabbalists had long speculated on the idea that the history of the world was divided into seven epochs, the last of which was at hand (Revelation viii. *seqq.*); and the sensational appearance of a brilliant new star in Cassiopeia in 1572 provoked what was almost a united chorus of prediction pointing to 1588 as the year for the end of the world. For after all, the predestined age of the earth was only 6000 years, and by the best chronologers this period was held to have practically expired. And the astronomical conjunctions for 1588 were of the most portentous and ill-omened description.[2]

This type of theory had found adherents in Sweden before the time of Bureus, and most notably among the Lutheran zealots of the gnesio-orthodox school, many of whom seem to have absorbed it from Chytraeus; and through them some flavour of it must have reached a wide public, in whose minds it speedily got mixed up with older folk-legend. And though events proved that God had allowed Himself to be persuaded in 1588 to stay His hand for a little, the wave of popular superstition and religious emotion rose again about the time of the battle of Stångebro, and once more with the appearance of Halley's Comet in 1607—an event which Karl IX took as portending his own early death. Thereafter the excitement subsided for nearly two decades, only to rise to a fresh peak of intensity immediately prior to Gustav Adolf's landing in Germany in 1630. The bishops of the generation of Rudbeckius were perhaps less affected by it than the contemporaries of Angermannus and Bothniensis; but it is curious to find Rudbeckius arguing against Gustav Adolf's plans for a *consistorium generale* on the ground that the old arrangements might well stand 'for the little time of the world's life that remains'.[3] Nevertheless, Rudbeckius and his colleagues deprecated attempts to calculate the date of the Day of Judgment, and they feared the antinomian and mystic tendencies in Paracelsism and Rosicrucianism: hence the disfavour with which

[1] Ezekiel xxxviii. and xxxix.; Revelation xx. 8.
[2] For eschatological speculations, see H. Sandblad, *De eskatologiska föreställningarna i Sverige under Reformationen och Motreformationen*, and *id.*, *Politiska prognostika om Johan III och Karl IX.*
[3] H. Cnattingius, *Johannes Rudbeckius och hans europeiska bakgrund*, p. 129.

they looked upon Bureus. They were unable, however, to do much to curb the rising tide of hysteria which throughout the late 'twenties and early 'thirties was powerfully influenced by the dramatic course of politico-religious events in Germany: at no time was there more widespread and impassioned interest in such high and hard matters as the number of the Beast, the dimensions of the Temple, the hour of Ahasuerus' Feast, and the number of the Cherubims' wings. Wivallius, for instance, made a characteristic attempt to exploit these interests in *Svea Rikes Ringmur* (*The Rampart of the Swedish Realm*), and other pieces more curious than intelligible, which blended flamboyant *storgöticist* patriotism with current Paracelsist jargon.[1] And one of the most pertinacious dabblers in these dark waters was Sigfrid Aron Forsius.

Forsius was a Finn by birth, and possibly this gave him a natural disposition to mysticism and the occult. He began life as an army chaplain, and seems to have picked up in the army a certain easiness in standards of behaviour which was to get him into trouble later on; but he soon passed to other employments, for he was an excellent mathematician, surveyor and astronomer, and Karl IX found work for him to do in all these capacities. He especially commended himself to the King's favour by his interpretation of Halley's Comet, and in 1609 and 1610 he was installed as temporary professor of astronomy at Uppsala. He was also, as we have seen, a poet. In 1613 he was given a privilege to issue almanacs; and at the same time he took to himself the title of Astronomer-Royal. But his private life continued riotous, and in 1618 he committed the indiscretion of commending the writings of a certain Jon Olofsson, an unlearned peasant who had been causing some concern to the government by his semi-Judaistical prophesyings. The consequence was that Forsius was arrested and imprisoned, and a commission of divines was appointed to investigate his opinions. The commission condemned some of them, and in particular repudiated *astrologia judiciaria*[2] and chiromancy; and it extorted a retractation of errors from Forsius, after which he was set at liberty. He retired to a country vicarage at Ekenäs, where he ended his life not long afterwards.[3]

---

[1] For Wivallius' prophetic poems, see Ek, pp. 123-7; and B. Lövgren, *Wivallius som patriotisk siare samt Wivallii gravskrift, passim.*

[2] *Astrologia judiciaria*: the type of astrology which held that the stars absolutely determine the actions and fate of men.

[3] For Forsius, see Lindroth, *Paracelsismen*, pp. 393-418; Sandblad, *De eskatologiska föreställningarna*, pp. 260-71; Waaranen, *Samling*, IV. 173-4; Holm-

Forsius was a typical representative of the Paracelsist-Rosicrucian school. Like Paracelsus, he looked forward to—and in his *Prognosticon* for 1609 predicted—the coming of an Elias Artista, who should be the supreme Alchemist, and lay bare the hidden mysteries of the Universe. He translated into Swedish the Books of Esdras, so highly prized by occultists for their dark sayings and mystical significance. He was perhaps the most distinguished Swedish representative of the extreme deterministic view of astrology. His *Physica* has considerable Paracelsist colouring; his psalms (of which he wrote a considerable number) are typical of the 'spiritual' tendencies which were frequently associated with Paracelsism at this time.[1] In short, Forsius would have been memorable as a representative of one of the strongest intellectual currents of the day if he had not been overshadowed by the more impressive figure of Bureus.

It was from this world of fantastic speculation and Biblical brooding that there emerged the belief in the coming of the Lion of the North.[2] It was based in the first instance upon the authority of the Old Testament; for it was possible to interpret passages in Isaiah, Jeremiah, Daniel, Ezekiel and Esdras in such a way as to make it appear that they foretold the coming of a victorious hero who should arise in the North to carry out God's judgment upon Babylon. These passages had long attracted the attention of commentators, and had been applied at various times to the Emperor Fredrick II and to Charles VIII of France. In the late sixteenth century, however, they were reinforced by the famous prophecy of Paracelsus,[3] which had foretold that after the nations of the earth had suffered all sorts of afflictions, a golden Lion should one day descend from the North, and should conquer the Eagle; he should overrun Asia and Africa, and should discover a great hidden treasure; and thereafter peace should reign on earth, and the Second Coming

quist, *Sv. kyrkans hist.*, IV. 1. 66-74, 166-8; *Handlingar rörande finska kyrkans historia*, I. 422-3; Hallenberg, IV. 851-2; N. Ahnlund, *Svensk sägen och häved*, pp. 203-38.

[1] For Forsius as a writer of religious poetry, see E. Liedgren, *Svensk psalm och andlig visa*, p. 198 *seqq.*

[2] For the Lion of the North, see J. Nordström, *De yverbornes ö*, pp. 9-51; G. Rein, *Populära föreställningar om Gustaf II Adolf i trettioåriga krigets flygskriftslitteratur, passim*; B. V. Lundqvist, *Gustaf II Adolf och folkfantasien, passim*; N. Ahnlund, *Gustaf Adolf, lejonprofetian och astrologien, passim*; Sandblad, *Politiska prognostiker*, pp. 86, 87; N. Ahnlund, *Storhetstidens Gryning*, p. 168 *seqq.*; Isaiah xli. 25; Jeremiah l. 9, 41; Daniel xi.; Ezekiel xxxviii. and xxxix.

[3] Paracelsus' authorship seems more than doubtful, for the prophecy is dated either 1546 or 1549, and Paracelsus died in 1541.

should be at hand. Tycho Brahe had made a similar prophecy in 1572 with reference to the new star in Cassiopeia, and had indicated 1632 as a probable date for its fulfilment.

From about the second decade of the seventeenth century the mystic Lion began to appear in pamphlets and broadsheets with increasing frequency, particularly in writings of a Rosicrucian complexion; the astrologers increasingly lent their authority to the support of the idea; and visionaries, epileptics, charlatans and *exaltés* of all sorts duly observed portents and saw visions of a conformable character, especially in Germany. For some time the Lion remained unidentified: some said it was Karl IX; some, Frederick V; others, Kristian IV; but by the end of the 'twenties the general opinion in Germany was virtually unanimous for Gustav Adolf. How far these notions had any effect in Sweden seems uncertain; and their influence on Gustav Adolf himself has recently been denied.[1] But they served the Swedish cause in Germany well, both by producing a state of rapt ecstatic expectation, in which Gustav Adolf was awaited as a divine deliverer; and by giving to his progress in Germany a nimbus of predestined fate. His landing was preceded by the most extraordinary deluge of meteorological and biological phenomena; his victory at Breitenfeld hailed as the fulfilment of the appointed overthrow of Babylon, which Luther had begun, but had been forced to leave unfinished.[2] Twelve editions of Paracelsus' prophecy were exhausted in Germany in 1631, and nine more in 1632. The disaster at Lützen made little difference; for it was now contended that the Lion was not the Swedish King but the Swedish nation; and Oxenstierna adroitly traded on this belief by striking *riksdaler* upon which appeared a crowned lion, with the legend ROBORE DIVINO CORONATUS VINCET LEO. Even after the Peace of Westphalia, men clung to the theory: William Lilly's prediction for 1659 makes Karl X Gustav the Lion; and there was a great revival of belief in the time of Karl XII. As late as the opening of the nineteenth century Gustav IV Adolf held that Napoleon was the Beast, since the letters of his name could be juggled to make 666[3]; and positively the last edition of Paracelsus' prophecy was struck off by the Swedish Field Printing Unit in 1814—Napoleon

---

[1] By Ahnlund: *Gustav Adolf, lejonprofetian och astrolgien*; and see Ahnlund, *Kring Gustaf Adolf*, p. 9.

[2] Revelation xiv. 8 and xviii. 2; and see B. V. Lundqvist, *Gustaf II Adolf och folkfantasien* in *Ny Militär Tidskrift*, V. (1932), pp. 300-5.

[3] B. von Beskow, *Levnadsminnen*, pp. 304-8.

this time being cast for the rôle of the Eagle, and Bernadotte for that of the Lion. Whether this deliberate revival of the old belief as a weapon of war propaganda had much effect upon the Germans may perhaps be doubted; it was at all events hardly taken seriously in Sweden. The chilly breezes of the eighteenth century had effectively cooled the ardours of apocalyptic speculation; the fabric of Olof Rudbeck's *Atlantica* lay in ruins, blasted by the historiography of the Age of Freedom; and if the last Rudbeckian still survived—he was not to die till 1820—he had become an eccentric out of tune with his times.[1] *Storgöticism* as Forsius and Bureus had known it was dead; but by a Paracelsian alchemy which they would have appreciated there had arisen from its ashes the new literary romanticism of the Gothic League; and in Geijer history and poesy would go hand in hand, linked in a partnership more equal than Messenius had ever been able to compass.

But in the Sweden of Gustav Adolf *storgöticism* was a living faith; and it played a part second only to Protestant fervour in producing that extraordinary exuberance of the national energies, that highmettled, adventurous temper, that youthful ardour of spirit, which enabled Sweden to sustain exertions and achieve triumphs no less remarkable than those of the Elizabethan seamen half a century earlier. *Storgöticism* was the creed of a nation in the springtime of its vigour, in the first intoxicating unfolding of its glory; and in Gustav Adolf Sweden had a sovereign whose victories and personal character made him, in the eyes of his subjects, the proper instrument of destiny, the agent of the historic process, the fulfiller of the prophecies, and the inspired architect of a long-overdue Gothic revival.

[1] See H. Schiller: *En originell herre. Pehr Tham till Dagsnäs, den sista Rudbeckianen.* Thorild might perhaps be counted as a *storgöticist* of a sort; but hardly of Olof Rudbeck's sort: see F. Lagerroth, *Konung och adel*, pp. 64, 116.

BIBLIOGRAPHY

PART I

THIS bibliography is not exhaustive. It includes only works which have in one way or another proved useful in the writing of this book. Books to which reference has been made in this volume are included in it, even if they are to appear in the special chapter-bibliographies for Volume II.

Separate bibliographies for Social and Economic History; The Army; The Navy; and Political History 1626-1632, will be appended to Volume II.

A. BIBLIOGRAPHICAL AIDS

The standard bibliographies of Swedish history are:

Ågren, S., and *Setterwall, K.*: Svensk historisk bibliografi (1771-1874), Uppsala 1937.

Setterwall, K.: Svensk historisk bibliografi (1875-1900). Stockholm 1907.

Setterwall, K.: Svensk historisk bibliografi (1901-1920). Uppsala 1923.
　　This series is continued as an annual supplement to *Historisk Tidskrift* (Stockholm), until 1929 under the editorship of *K. Setterwall*, thereafter under that of *P. Elfstrand*. A more modern bibliography, though less full than the foregoing, is:

Bring, S. E.: Bibliografisk handbok till Sveriges historia. Stockholm 1934.

Useful short-cuts to academic dissertations are:

Nelson, A.: Akademiska afhandlingar vid Sveriges universitet och högskolor 1890/1-1909/10. Uppsala 1911.

Tuneld, J.: Akademiska afhandlingar vid Sveriges universitet och högskolor 1910/11-1939/40. Lund 1945.

Useful for Polish and Estonian literature are:

Blumfeldt, E.: Den svenska tiden i estnisk historieforskning. (*Svio-Estonica*, vol. I.) Tartu 1934.

Liske, X.: Öfversigt af den polska litteraturen med särskilt afseende på den svenska historien, V. (in *Silfverstolpe, C.*: Historisk Bibliotek, N.F. vol. III). Stockholm 1878-9.

Koczy, L.: Scandinavian things in Polish literature. (*Baltic and Scandinavian Countries*, vol. III. 1937.)

Loone, L.: Den svenska tiden i estnisk historieforskning 1934-1938. (*Svio-Estonica*, vol. V.) Tartu 1938.

Wędkiewicz, S.: La Suède et la Pologne. Essai d'une bibliographie des publications suèdoises concernant la Pologne. Stockholm 1918.

Guides to pictorial material are:

Snoilsky, C.: Svenska historiska planscher. Stockholm 1893-5.

Malmborg, B. von: Samtida porträtt av Gustav II Adolf. Stockholm 1944.

For the historiography of Gustav Adolf, see:

Ahnlund, N.: Gustaf II Adolf i 1600-talets svenska historieskrivning. Helsingfors 1944.

Paul, J.: Gustaf Adolf in der deutsche Geschichtsschreibung. (*Historische Vierteljahrschrift*, vol. 25 [33].) Dresden 1931.

Milch, W.: Gustaf Adolf in der deutschen und schwedischen Literatur. Breslau 1928.

and more generally:

Jacobson, G.: Från Geijer till Hjärne. Stockholm 1945.

B. PRINTED PRIMARY MATERIAL

Adlersparre, C.: Historiska samlingar, vol. III. Stockholm 1797. [Pp. 64-272 have the official reports of Johan Fegraeus.]

Avenel, L.: Lettres, instructions diplomatiques et papiers d'état du cardinal de Richelieu. Vols. II-IV. Paris 1856- .

Borgareståndets Riksdagsprotokoll före frihetstiden, I. (ed. *N. Ahnlund*). Uppsala 1933.

Brahe, A.: Abraham Brahes tidebok (ed. *C. M.* and *R. Stenbock*). Stockholm 1920.

Brahe, P. (the elder): Oeconomia eller Huuszholdz-Book för ungt Adels-Folck. Stockholm 1920.

Brahe, P. (the younger): Svea Rikes Drotset Grefve Per Brahes Tänkebok (ed. *D. Krutmeyer*). Stockholm 1806.

[*Breyer, C. W. F.*, ed.]: Beyträge zur Geschichte des dreyssigjährigen Krieges. Munich 1812.

Bureus, J. T. A.: Anteckningar af Johannes Thomae Agrivillensis Buraeus (ed. *G. E. Klemming*). (*Samlaren*, vols. IV-V.) Stockholm 1883-4.

Calendar of State Papers (Domestic):

James I, 1623-25. London 1859.
Charles I, 1625-26. London 1858.
Charles I, 1627-28. London 1858.
Charles I, 1628-29. London 1859.
Charles I, 1629-31. London 1860.
Charles I, 1631-33. London 1862.

Calendar of State Papers (Venetian):

vol. XVIII, 1623-25. London 1912.
vol. XIX, 1625-26. London 1913.
vol. XXII, 1629-32. London 1919.

Christian IV.: Kong Christian den fjerdes egenhændige Breve, vols. I-III. (ed. *C. F. Bricka* and *J. A. Fridericia*). Copenhagen 1887- .

Crosfield, T.: The Diary of Thomas Crosfield (ed. *F. S. Boas*). London 1935.

Dagbok förd i det svenska fältkansliet, 26 maj 1630—6 november 1632 (ed. *E. Zeeh* and *N. Belfrage*). Stockholm 1940.

De Geer, L.: Louis de Geers brev och affärshandlingar 1614-1653 (ed. *E. W. Dahlgren*). Stockholm 1934.

Diarium Gyllenianum eller Petrus Magni Gyllenii dagbok (ed. *R. Hansen*). Helsingfors 1880.

[*Droysen, G.*, ed.]: Schriftstücke von Gustaf Adolf, zumeist an evangelische Fürsten Deutschlands. Stockholm 1877.

[*Edén, N.*, ed.]: Brev av Gustav Vasa. Ett urval. Stockholm 1917.

Edling, N.: Lagläsaren Per Larssons dombok 1638. Uppsala 1937.

Ekeblad, J.: Johan Ekeblads bref (ed. *N. Sjöberg*), vols. I-II. Stockholm 1911.

Ett par bref om slaget vid Lützen 1632. (*Historisk Tidskrift*, vol. XII.) Stockholm 1892.

[*Feith, H. O.*, ed.]: Lettres de Gustave Adolphe . . . à son général Dodo von In- und Kniphausen. Groningen 1860.

Fleetwood, G.: Letter from George Fleetwood to his father, giving an account of the battle of Lützen. (Camden Society Miscellany, vol. I.) London 1847.

Fryxell, A.: Handlingar rörande Sverges historia, vol. IV. Stockholm 1843. [Pp. 13-65 have 'Sånger och skrifter om Gustaf II Adolfs deltagande i tyska kriget.']

Förster, F.: Albrechts von Wallenstein . . . ungedruckte, eigenhändige vertrauliche Briefe und amtliche Schreiben aus den Jahren 1627 bis 1634. Vols. I-III. Berlin 1828-9.

Galt, P.: Peder Galts depescher, 1622-1624 (ed. *N. Ahnlund*). Stockholm 1920.

Gustav II Adolf: Tal och skrifter (ed. *C. Hallendorff*). Stockholm 1915.

Hahr, A.: Ur en schlesisk adelmans dagbok i Sverige på 1590-talet. (*Ord och Bild*, vol. XVII.) Stockholm 1908. [Diary of Erich Lassota von Steblau.]

[*Hall, B. R.*, ed.]: Vid Gustaf Adolfs bår. Ur samtida minnestal. Vols. I-II. Uppsala 1910-11.

Handlingar rörande finska kyrkan och prästerskapet, vols. I-II (ed. *K. G. Leinberg*). Jyväskylä 1892-3.

Handlingar rörande Skandinaviens historia, vols. I-XL. Stockholm 1816-60. [The following volumes contain relevant matter: II; IV; V; VIII (interesting collection of first-hand anecdotes of Gustav Adolf and the leading men of his time): IX; XIV; XVI; XXIV; XXV; XXVI (three poems by Gustav Adolf): XXVII (Gustav Adolf's 'Character of Karl Filip'): XXXV; XXXIX (documents relating to the Finnmark controversy).]

Handlingar rörande Sveriges äldre, nyare och nyaste historia, samt historiska personer. Utgifna af ett sällskap. Vol. vi. Stockholm 1831.

Handlingar ur von Brinkman'ska archivet på Trolle-Ljungby, vol. i (ed. G. Andersson). Örebro 1859. [Pp. 75-121 have a collection of letters to Gustav Horn.]

Handlingar till Konung Gustaf II Adolfs historia (ed. J. Hallenberg). Stockholm 1784.

Hand, J.: Johan Hands dagbok under K. Gustaf II Adolfs resa till Tyskland 1620. (Historiska Handlingar, viii, 3.) Stockholm 1879.

[Hildebrand, S., ed.]: En holländsk beskicknings resor i Ryssland, Finland och Sverige 1615-1616. Stockholm 1917.

Historical Manuscripts Commission Reports:
The Duke of Buccleuch and Queensberry MSS., vol. i. London 1899.
The Duke of Hamilton MSS. London 1887.
The Duke of Hamilton MSS. Supplementary Report. London 1932.
The Duke of Rutland MSS., vol. i. London 1911.
Various MSS., vols. v and vii. London 1909.

Hjärne, H.: Utdrag ur ryska krönikor, hufvudsakligen angående Jakob de la Gardies fälttåg (in Historisk Bibliotek, vols. vi-vii). Stockholm 1879-1880.

Kammarkollegiets Protokoll, vol. i. Stockholm 1934.

Kiechel, S.: Samuel Kiechels resa i Sverige 1586 (in Historisk Tidskrift, vol. xii). Stockholm 1892.

Klemming, G. E.: Skrå-Ordningar. (Samlingar utgifna af svenska fornskriftsällskapet.) Stockholm 1856.

[Klinckowström, R. M., and Mankell, J, ed.]: Arkiv till upplysning om svenska krigens och krigsinrättningarnes historia, 1630-1632, vols. i-iii. Stockholm 1854-1861.

Kyrko-ordningar och förslag dertill före 1686, vol. i. (Handlingar rörande Sveriges historia, II. Series, vol. ii.) Stockholm 1872.

[Leinberg, K. G., ed.]: Finska prästerskapets besvär och Kongl. Majestäts därpå gifna resolutioner. Från slutet af 1620-talet intill stora ofredens slut. Helsingfors 1892.

Letters and Documents illustrating the relations between England and Germany at the commencement of the Thirty Years' War, vols. I-II (ed. *S. R. Gardiner*). (Camden Society, vols. 90 and 98.) London 1865, 1868.

Letters relating to the mission of Sir Thomas Roe to Gustavus Adolphus 1629-1630 (ed. *S. R. Gardiner*). (Camden Society.) London 1875.

Loenbom, S.: Anecdoter om namnkunniga och märkwärdiga Swenska Män, vol. II. Stockholm 1773. [Contains notes on Bengt Oxenstierna.]

Loenbom, S.: Berättelse om Swea Rikes Arf-Furstes samt Hertigens til Södermanland, Carl Philips Lefwerne och Utländska Resor. Stockholm 1772.

Loenbom, S.: Historiska Märkwärdigheter til Uplysning af Swenska Häfder, vols. I-IV. Stockholm 1768.

Loenbom, S.: Historiskt Archivum, innehållande Märkwärdigheter, Uplysningar och Anecdoter i Swenska Historien, vols. I-II. Stockholm 1774.

Loenbom, S.: Svenska Archivum, vols. I-III. Stockholm 1766-1772. [I. 159-253 has documents concerning Duke Johan of Östergötland; II. 51-122 has documents concerning Gabriel Gustafsson Oxenstierna's embassy to Denmark, 1625.]

Loenbom, S.: Uplysningar i Swenska Historien, vols. I-IV. Stockholm 1768-71.

Loenbom, S.: Upplysningar i Svenska Historien, vols. I-IV. Stockholm 1771-4.

Magalotti, L.: Sverige under år 1674 (ed. *C. M. Stenbock*). Stockholm 1912.

Moser, F. C. von: Neues Patriotisches Archiv für Deutschland, vol. I. Mannheim and Leipzig 1792.

Moser, F. C. von: Patriotisches Archiv für Deutschland, vol. V. Frankfurt and Leipzig, 1786.

Observationes Strengnenses (ed. *J. Lindblom* and *H. Pleijel*). Stockholm 1943.

Ogier, C.: Från Sveriges storhetstid: Charles Ogiers dagbok under ambassaden i Sverige, 1634-5 (ed. and trans. *S. Hallberg*). Stockholm 1914.

Oxenstierna, A.: Rikskansleren Axel Oxenstiernas skrifter och brefväxling. I. Series, vols. I-VIII; II. Series, vols. I-XII. Stockholm 1888- . [The first series contains Oxenstierna's own letters and papers, arranged chronologically; the second series has letters to Oxenstierna, grouped under correspondents.] [Cited as: *AOSB*.]

Oxenstierna, G. G.: Riksrådet Gabriel Gustafsson Oxenstiernas berättelse om mötet mellan k. Gustaf II Adolf och k. Kristian IV i prestgården Ulfsbäck i Markaryds socken i Småland februari 1629. (Historiska Handlingar, VIII, 4.) Stockholm 1881.

[*Posse, G. K.*]: Hertigh Carls Slaktarebenck (ed. *T. Berg*). Stockholm 1915.

Register öfver rådslag i Konung Gustaf II Adolfs tid (ed. *E. W. Bergman*, in Meddelanden från Svenska Riks-Archivet, IX). Stockholm 1885.

Richelieu: Mémoires du cardinal de Richelieu, vols. I-II (in *Michaud* and *Poujoulat*, Nouvelle Collection des mémoires pour servir à l'histoire de la France, II. Series, vols. VII-VIII). Paris 1838.

Rudbeckius, J.: Dagbok (ed. *B. R. Hall*). Lund 1938.

Rusdorf: Mémoires et négotiations secrètes de Mr de Rvsdorf . . . pour servir à l'histoire de la Guerre de trente ans (ed. *E. G. Cuhn*). Vols. I-II. Leipzig 1789.

Samling af instructioner för högre och lägre tjenstemän vid landtregeringen i Sverige och Finland (ed. *C. G. Styffe*). Stockholm 1852. [Cited as: *SILR*.]

Samling af instructioner rörande den civila förvaltningen i Sverige och Finland (ed. *C. G. Styffe*). Stockholm 1856. [Cited as: *SICF*.]

[*Schmedemann, J.*, ed.]: Kongl. stadgar, förordningar, brev och resolutioner ifrån år 1528 in til 1701 angående justitiae och executions-ährende, vol. I. Stockholm 1706.

Schybergson, M. G.: Sveriges och Hollands diplomatiska förbindelser 1621-1630. Helsingfors 1881.

Skytte, J.: Riksrådet Johan Skyttes kommentar till stadslagen (ed. *E. Wolff*). Göteborg 1905.

Sparre, E.: Pro lege rege et grege. (Historiska Handlingar, XXVII.) Stockholm 1924.

[*Stiernman, A. A. von,* ed.]: Alla riksdagars och mötens besluth, vol. I. Stockholm 1728. [Cited as: Stiernman.]

[*Stiernman, A. A. von,* ed.]: Samling utaf kongl. bref, stadgar och förordningar etc., angående Sweriges Rikes commerce, politie och oeconomie uti gemen, ifrån åhr 1523 in til närwarande tid. Vol. I. Stockholm 1747. [Cited as: Stiernman, *CPO.*]

Stockholms stads privilegiebref, 1423-1700 (ed. *K. Hildebrand*). Stockholm 1900.

[*Styffe, C. G.,* ed.]: Konung Gustaf II Adolfs skrifter. Stockholm 1861. [Cited as: Styffe.]

Svenska riksdagsakter jämte andra handlingar som höra till statsförfattningens historia. I. Series, 2. section, vol. I, 1611-6, vol. II, 1616-7 (ed. *N. Ahnlund*). Stockholm 1932-1943. [Cited as: *SRDA.*]

Svenska riksrådets protokoll, vols. I-II (ed. *N. A. Kullberg*). Stockholm 1878-1880. [Cited as: *RRP.*]

Svenska synodalakter efter 1500-talets ingång, vols. I-II (ed. *H. Lundström*). Uppsala 1903, 1911. [Vol. I, Uppsala; vol. II, Strängnäs.]

Sverges traktater med främmande magter, vol. V, parts 1-6. Stockholm 1890-1909.

Sveriges historiska och politiska visor, vol. I (ed. *G. O. Hyltén-Cavallius* and *G. Stephens*). Örebro 1853.

Sveriges regeringsformer 1634-1809 samt konungaförsäkringar 1611-1800 (ed. *E. Hildebrand*). Stockholm 1891.

Sveriges ridderskaps och adels riksdags-protokoll, I. Series, vol. I. Stockholm 1904. [Cited as: *SRARP.*]

Testament politique du cardinal de Richelieu (ed. *L. André*). Paris 1947.

Thyselius, P. E.: Bidrag till svenska kyrkans och läroverkens historia utur archiver. Stockholm 1848.

[*Thyselius, P. E.,* ed.]: Handlingar rörande svenska kyrkans och läroverkens historia, vols. I-II. Örebro 1839, 1841.

Tigerstedt, K. K.: Bref från generalguvernörer och landshövdingar i Finland, förnämligast under drottning Kristinas tid, vol. I. Åbo 1869.

Tungel, L. N.: Lars Nilsson Tungels efterlämnade papper (ed. *P. Sondén*). (Historiska Handlingar, XXII.) Stockholm 1907.

Valda aktstycken till svenska undervisningsväsendets historia (ed. *B. R. Hall*). Stockholm 1912.

Vendel Sockens dombok 1615-1645 (ed. *N. Edling*). Uppsala 1925.

Vosbergen, G. van: Verbaal van de Ambassade van Gaspar van Vosbergen bij den Koning van Denemarken, den Neder-Saxischen kreits en den Koning van Zweden, 1625. Utrecht 1867.

[Waaranen, J. E.]: Samling af urkunder rörande Finlands historia, vols. IV-V. Helsingfors 1874-1878.

Wagner, J.: Die Chronik des Jakob Wagner über die schwedischen Okkupation in Augsburg (ed. *W. Roos*). Augsburg 1902.

Whitelocke, B.: A Journal of the Swedish Embassy in the years 1653 and 1654, vols. I-II (ed. *C. Morton*). London 1855.

C. GENERAL HISTORIES OF THE REIGN

Ahnlund, N.: Gustav Adolf den store. Stockholm 1932.

Almquist, H.: Svenska folkets historia, vol. II: reformationstidens och stormaktstidens förra skede. Lund 1922.

Andersson, I.: Sveriges historia. Stockholm 1944.

Cronholm, A.: Sveriges historia under Gustaf II Adolphs regering, vols. I-VI. Stockholm 1857-72.

Droysen, G.: Gustaf Adolf, vols. I-II. Leipzig 1869-70.

Geijer, E. G.: Svenska folkets historia, vol. III. Malmö 1929.

[Generalstaben]: Gustaf II Adolf: minneskrift på 300-årsdagen av slaget vid Lützen. Utarbetad inom Generalstabens Krigshistoriska Avdelning. Stockholm 1932.

Hallenberg, J.: Svea Rikes Historia under konung Gustaf Adolf den stores regering, vols. I-V. Stockholm 1790-6.

Hjärne, H.: Gustaf Adolf, protestantismens förkämpe (in Samlade Skrifter, vol. II). Stockholm 1932.

Hornborg, E.: Konung Gustav II Adolf. Stockholm 1932.

Kotzde, W.: Von Riga bis Lützen. Der Weg Gustav Adolfs. Stuttgart [1932].

Paul, J.: Gustaf Adolf: I. Schwedens Aufsteig zur Grossmacht-stellung. Leipzig 1927. II. Schwedens Eintritt in den dreissigjährigen Krieg. Leipzig 1930. III. Von Breitenfeld bis Lützen. Leipzig 1932.

Westphal, O.: Gustav Adolf und die Grundlagen der schwedischen Macht. Hamburg 1932. [Not recommended.]

Wittrock, G.: Gustav II Adolf. (Sveriges historia till våra dagar, vol. VI.) Stockholm 1927.

The following is the only Marxist history:

Mehring, F.: Gustav II Adolf. Stockholm 1924. [Original German edition, 1894.]

with which may perhaps be associated:

Höglund, Z.: Den patriotiska Lögnen. Gustav Adolf-legenden i sanningens ljus. Stockholm 1915.

Strindberg, Axel: Bondenöd och Stormaktsdröm. Studier över skedet 1630-1718. Stockholm 1937.

D.   GENERAL POLITICAL HISTORY TO 1626

(Chapters I-V)

Ahlqvist, A. G.: Konung Erik XIV : s sista lefnadsår. Stockholm 1878.

Ahnlund, N.: Axel Oxenstierna intill Gustav Adolfs död. Stockholm 1940.

Ahnlund, N.: En stor mans vanor. (*Ord och Bild*, vol. LIV.) Stockholm 1944.

Ahnlund, N.: Gustaf II Adolf och tyska kriget 1620-5. (*Historisk Tidskrift*, I. Series, vol. 37.) Stockholm 1917. [Cited as: Ahnlund, *HT* 1917.]

Ahnlund, N.: Gustaf II Adolfs första preussiska fälttåg och den europeiska krisen 1626. (*Historisk Tidskrift*, I. Series, vol. 38.) Stockholm 1918. [Cited as: Ahnlund, *HT* 1918.]

Ahnlund, N.: Kring Gustav Adolf. Stockholm 1930.

Ahnlund, N.: Storhetstidens gryning. Stockholm 1918.

Ahnlund, N.: Svensk östersjöpolitik under det tidigare 1600-talet. (*Forum Navale*, 1946.) Uppsala 1946.

Ahnlund, N.: Weichselmynningen i svensk historia. (*Svio-Polonica*, No. II.) Stockholm 1940.

Almquist, H.: Die Carenwahl des Jahres 1613. (*Zeitschrift für osteuropäische Geschichte*, vol. III.) Berlin 1913.

Almquist, H.: Henrik IV i sitt förhållande till Polen och Sverige. (*Historisk Tidskrift*, I. Series, vol. 31.) Stockholm 1911. [Reviewing *W. Sobieski, Henryk IV wobec Polski i Szwecyi*. Kraków 1907.]

Almquist, H.: Sverge och Ryssland 1595-1611. Uppsala 1907.

Almquist, H.: Tsarvalet år 1613. Karl Filip och Michael Romanov (in Historiska studier tillägnade Harald Hjärne). Stockholm 1908.

Anderson, J.: Historia om svenska kronprinsen Gustaf, konung Erik den fjortondes och Catarina Månsdotters olycklige son. Jönköping 1832.

Andersson, I.: Erik XIV. Ett biografi. Stockholm 1948.

Andersson, I.: Erik XIV:s engelska underhandlingar. Lund 1935.

Andersson, I.: Källstudier till Kalmarkrigets historia. (*Scandia*, vol. IX.) Lund 1935.

Andersson, I.: Svenskt och europeiskt femtonhundratal. Lund 1943.

Angyal, D.: Gabriel Bethlen. (*Révue Historique*, vol. 158.) Paris 1928.

Annell, G.: Erik XIV:s etiska föreställningar och deras inflytande på hans politik. Uppsala 1945.

Anthoni, E.: En förteckning över flyktingar i Polen i början av 1620-talet. (*Historisk Tidskrift för Finland*, vol. 27.) Helsingfors 1942.

Anthoni, E.: Kring en förteckning över politiska flyktingar i polsk tjänst. (*Historisk Tidskrift för Finland*, vol. 18.) Helsingfors 1933.

Anthoni, E.: review of *R. Holmström*, Eerikki Eerikkinpoika Sorolainen. Piispa ja teologi, kansanopettaja ja saarnaaja. (*Historisk Tidskrift för Finland*, vol. 22.) Helsingfors 1937.

Arnell, S.: Die Auflösung des Livländischen Ordenstaates. Lund 1937.

Arnoldsson, S.: Krigspropagandan i Sverige före trettioåriga kriget. Göteborg 1941.

Arup, E.: Danmarks Historie, vol. II (1282-1624). Copenhagen 1932.

Attman, A.: Den ryska marknaden i 1500-talets baltiska politik. Lund 1944.

Attman, A.: Freden i Stolbova 1617. En aspekt. (*Scandia*, vol. 19.) Lund 1949.

Attman, A.: Till det svenska östersjöväldets problematik (in Studier tillägnade Curt Weibull). Göteborg 1946.

Baehrendtz, F.: Striden om Kalmar 1611. (Meddelanden från Kalmar läns fornminnesförening.) Kalmar 1903.

Ballesteros y Beretta, A.: Historia de España y su influencia en la historia universal, vol. IV, part 1. Barcelona 1926.

Barkman, G. B. C:son: Gustaf II Adolfs regementsorganisation vid det inhemska infanteriet. (Meddelanden från Generalstabens Krigshistoriska Avdelning, vol. I.) Stockholm 1931.

Barkman, B. C:son: Kungl. Svea Livgardes historia, vol. II (1560-1611). Stockholm 1938-9.

[Batory, S.]: Etienne Batory, roi de Pologne, prince de Transylvanie. [Joint publication by Académie Polonaise des Sciences et des Lettres and Académie des Sciences Hongroise.] Kraków 1935.

Belfrage, N.: Erik Soop och Västgöta ryttare. Stockholm 1934.

Bennedich, C.: Ur det gamla Gardets öden. Stockholm 1926.

Berg, T.: Johan Skytte. Hans ungdom och verksamhet under Karl IX:s regering. Stockholm 1920.

Björlin, G.: Johan Banér, vols. I-III. Stockholm 1908.

Björkman, R.: Jönköpings historia, vol. II. Jönköping 1918.

Blok, P. J.: Geschiedenis van het Nederlandsche Volk, vol. IV. Groningen 1899.

Boëthius, B.: article 'Karl Bonde', in *Svenskt Biografiskt Lexicon*, vol. V.

Boëthius, S. J.: Om den svenska högadeln under konung Sigismunds regering. Stockholm 1877.

Bonsdorff, C. von: Huru Gustaf II Adolf hyllades i Finland. (Strödda uppsatser, vol. 1.) Helsingfors 1898.

Brandenburg, E.: Gustav Adolf. Leipzig 1932.

Broomé, B.: Nils Stiernsköld. Stockholm 1950.

Bowman, F. J.: Gustavus II Adolphus and the Protestant Reformation. (*Baltic and Scandinavian Countries*, vol. III.) 1937.

[Cambridge.] The Cambridge History of Poland, vol. 1. Cambridge 1950.

Carlsson, G.: Senare medeltiden, I: tidsskedet 1389-1448. (Sveriges historia till våra dagar, vol. III, part 1.) Stockholm 1941.

Carlsson, W.: Gustaf II Adolf och Stralsund. Uppsala 1912.

Celsius, O.: Geschichte König Erichs des vierzehnten. Flensburg 1777.

Cichocki, M.: Medjacja Francji w rozejmie altmarskim. Kraków 1928.

Clark, G. N.: The Seventeenth Century. Oxford 1929.

Clason, S.: Förhållandet till Polen och Petrus Petrejus' sändning till Danzig 1615. (*Historisk Tidskrift*, I. Series, vol. 21.) Stockholm 1900.

Clason, S.: Historiska betraktelser af Karl IX. (*Historisk Tidskrift*, I. Series, vol. 26.) Stockholm 1906.

Clason, S.: Till reduktionens förhistoria. Stockholm 1895.

Dahlgren, E. W.: Louis de Geer, 1587-1652. Hans lif och verk, vols. I-II. Uppsala 1923.

Dedouvres, L.: Le Père Joseph de Paris, Capucin. L'Éminence grise, vols. I-II. Paris 1932.

Edmundson, G.: Anglo-Dutch rivalry during the first half of the seventeenth century. Oxford 1911.

Elander, R.: Sturemordens gåta. Stockholm 1928.

Enewald, N.: Sverige och Finnmarken. Svensk Finnmarkspolitiken under äldre tid och den svensk-norska gränsläggningen 1751. Lund 1920.

Engelstoft, P.: Christian IVs Tidsalder. (Det Danske Folks Historie, vol. IV.) Copenhagen 1928.

Ericsson, G. J. V.: Gustav II Adolf och Sigismund 1621-1623. Uppsala 1928.

Essen, A. van der: Le Cardinal-Infant et la politique européenne de l'Espagne 1609-1641, vol. I. Brussels 1944.

Fleischhacker, H.: Russland zwischen zwei Dynastien (1598-1613). Vienna 1933.

Forssell, H.: Gustaf II Adolf. En minnesteckning. Stockholm 1894.

Forssell, N.: Svenska postverkets historia. Stockholm 1936.

Fridericia, J. A.: Danmarks Riges Historie, vol. IV, 1588-1699. Copenhagen, n.d. [Cited as: *Fridericia, DRH.*]

Fridericia, J. A.: Danmarks ydre politiske Historie i Tiden fra Freden i Lybek til Freden i Prag, vol. I. Copenhagen 1876. [Cited as: *Fridericia, YPH.*]

Gade, J. A.: Christian IV. London 1927.

Gardiner, S. R.: History of England from the accession of James I to the outbreak of the Civil War. London 1904.

Geyl, P.: The Netherlands Divided (1609-1648). London 1936.

Gibb, M. A.: Buckingham, 1592-1628. London 1935.

Gindely, A.: Beiträge zur Geschichte des dreissigjährigen Krieges. (*Archiv fur österreichischen Geschichte*, vol. 98.) Vienna 1901.

Gitermann, V.: Geschichte Russlands, vol. I. Zürich 1944.

Goll, J.: Der Convent von Segeberg (1621). Prague 1875.

Granstedt, E.: Carl Carlsson Gyllenhielm och Vasahuset. (*Person-historiska Tidskrift*, vol. 42.) Stockholm 1943.

Granstedt, E.: Karl Karlsson Gyllenhielms fångenskap i Polen 1601-1613. (*Svio-Polonica*, No. 6-7.) Stockholm 1944-5.

Green, M. A. E.: Elizabeth Electress Palatine and Queen of Bohemia. London 1909.

Grill, E.: Jakob de la Gardie, affärsmannen och politikern 1608-1636. Göteborg 1949.

Hagberg, K.: Av Vasarnas ätt. Stockholm 1929.

Hammarstrand, S. F.: Bidrag till det trettioåriga krigets historia. Uppsala 1859.

542   BIBLIOGRAPHY

Hammarstrand, S. F.: Försök till en historisk framställning af förhandlingarne om Sveriges deltagande i trettioåriga kriget. Uppsala 1855. [Cited as: *Hammarstrand, HF*.]

Hammarstrand, S. F.: Historisk öfversigt af förhandlingarne mellan konung Gustaf II Adolf af Sverige och kurfursten Fredrik V af Pfalz, åren 1618-1620. Uppsala 1855.

Hanotaux, G. and *La Force, Duc de*: Histoire du Cardinal de Richelieu, vols. II-IV. Paris 1893- .

Hassø, A. G.: Den danske regering og Kofferdifarten Nord om Norge i det 16. aarhundrede. (*Historisk Tidskrift*, X. Series, vol. II.) Copenhagen 1932-4.

Heckscher, E. F.: Ett svenskt krigsskadestånd för 300 år sedan. (*Ekonomisk Tidskrift*, vol. 35.) Stockholm 1933.

Heckscher, E. F.: Ekonomi och historia. Stockholm 1922.

Heckscher, E. F.: Det äldre Vasakonungadömets ekonomiska politik och ideer (in Studier tillägnade Ludvig Stavenow). Stockholm 1924.

Hermerén, H.: Uppsala möte. Stockholm 1944.

Hildebrand, E.: Gustav Vasa. (Sveriges historia till våra dagar, vol. IV.) Stockholm 1920.

Hildebrand, E.: Gustav Vasas söner. (Sveriges historia till våra dagar, vol. V.) Stockholm 1923.

Hildebrand, E.: Kristina och Karl X Gustav. (Sveriges historia till våra dagar, vol. VII.) [Revised by *G. Jacobsson*.] Stockholm 1926.

Hill, C. E.: The Danish Sound Dues and the command of the Baltic. Durham, N.C. 1926.

Hjärne, H.: Moskovitiska rikets uppväxt. (Samlade skrifter, vol. III.) Stockholm 1933.

Hoppe, I.: Israel Hoppe's Burggrafen zu Elbing Geschichte des ersten schwedisch-polnischen Krieges in Preussen, nebst Anhang (ed. *M. Toeppen*). Leipzig 1887.

Hornborg, E.: Kampen om Östersjön. Stockholm 1945.

Hornborg, E.: Finlands hävder, vol. II: Stormakten Sverige-Finland. Helsingfors 1930.

Irmer, G.: Hans Georg von Arnim. Leipzig 1894.

Jacobsson, P.: Gästgifveri- och skjutsningsbesvärens uppkomst och äldsta utveckling. (*Ekonomisk Tidskrift*, vol. 21.) Stockholm 1919.

Janssen, J.: A History of the German People, vols. IX and X. London 1906.

Jenš, G.: Rivalry between Riga and Tartu for the trade with Pskov in the XVI and XVII centuries. (*Baltic and Scandinavian Countries*, vol. IV.) 1938.

Johnsen, O. A.: Finmarkens politiske historie, aktmaessig fremstillet. Kristiania 1923.

Kampen om Østersjøen, sett fra norsk, dansk, svensk og finsk synspunkt. [Symposium issued by Oslo Militaere Samfund.] Oslo 1935.

Kerner, R. J.: The Urge to the Sea. The Course of Russian History. The Role of Rivers, Portages, Ostrogs, Monasteries, and Furs. Berkeley and Los Angeles 1946.

Kernkamp, G. W.: De Sleutels van de Sont. 's Hage 1890.

Kidd, B. J.; The Counter-Reformation. London 1937.

Kluchevsky, V. O.: A History of Russia, vol. III (trans. C. J. Hogarth). London 1913.

Konopczyński, Wł.: Dzieje Polski Nowożytnej, vol. I. Warsaw 1936.

Korzon, T.: Dzieje wojen i wojskowości w Polsce, vol. II. Kraków 1912.

Koser, R.: Geschichte der brandenburgischen Politik bis zum westfälischen Frieden von 1648. Stuttgart and Berlin 1913.

Kraft, S.: Senare medeltiden, II: tidsskedet 1448-1520. (Sveriges historia till våra dagar, vol. III, part 2.) Stockholm 1944.

Krüner, F.: Johan von Rusdorf, kurpfälzischer Gesandter und Staatsman während des dreissigjährigen Krieges. Halle 1876.

Kutrzeba, S.: Danzig and Poland in History. (*Baltic and Scandinavian Countries*, vol. IV.) 1938.

Lenz, M.: Landgraf Moritz von Hessen (in Kleine historische Schrifter, vol. II). Munich and Berlin 1920.

Lindberg, F.: Hertig Johan av Östergötland och hans furstendöme. (*Historisk Tidskrift*, II. Series, vol. IV.) Stockholm 1941.

Lindsten, G.: När Elfsborgs lösen betalades (in Historiska studier tillägnade Ludvig Stavenow). Stockholm 1924.

Ljung, S.: Erik Jöransson Tegel. Lund 1939.

Lubimenko, I.: Les Relations commerciales et politiques de l'Angleterre avec la Russie avant Pierre le Grand. Paris 1933.

Lubimenko, I.: A Project for the Acquisition of Russia by James I. (*English Historical Review*, vol. xxix.) London 1914.

Lubimenko, I. : The Struggle of the Dutch with the English for the Russian Market in the Seventeenth Century. (*Transactions of the Royal Historical Society*, 4th Series, vol. vii [1924].)

Lybeck, O.: Öresund i nordens historia. Malmö 1943.

Małowist, M.: Baltic affairs in the sixteenth and seventeenth centuries in the light of historical literature. (*Baltic and Scandinavian Countries*, vol. iii.) 1937.

Mankell, J.: Om Gustaf II Adolfs politik. Stockholm 1881.

Mankell, J.: Om orsakerna till Gustaf II Adolfs deltagande i trettioåriga kriget. Stockholm 1878.

Mariéjol, J.-H.: Henri IV et Louis XIII. (Histoire de la France depuis les origines jusqu'à la révolution, ed. *E. Lavisse*, vol. vi, 1.) Paris 1911.

Massa, I.: Histoire des guerres de la Moscovie (1601-1610), vols. i-ii (trans. and ed. *M. Obolensky* and *A. van der Linde*). Brussels 1866.

Mitchell, T.: History of the Scottish expedition to Norway in 1612. London and Christiania 1886.

Mommsen, W.: Kardinal Richelieu. Seine Politik im Elsass und in Lothringen. Berlin 1922.

Nordlander, J.: Om birkarlarne. (*Historisk Tidskrift*, I. Series, vols. 26 and 27.) Stockholm 1906, 1907.

Odhner, C. T.: Om orsakerna till Gustaf II Adolfs deltagande i trettioåriga kriget. Kritisk belysning. Stockholm 1874.

Ohlsson, N. G.: Hertig Sigismunds tukto- och läremästare. Stockholm 1941.

Pagès, G.: La Guerre de trente ans. Paris 1939.

Palme, S. U.: Karl IX—bondekonung? (*Svensk Tidskrift*, vol. 30.) Stockholm 1943.

Palme, S. U.: Sverige och Danmark, 1596-1611. Uppsala 1942.

Palme, S. U.: Till kännedomen om Karl IX:s muntliga framställ-ningssätt. Några lybska bidrag. (*Historisk Tidskrift*, II. Series, vol. 1.) Stockholm 1938.

Pastor, L.: The History of the Popes from the close of the Middle Ages (trans. *Dom E. Graf*) vol. xxviii. London 1938.

Paul, J.: Die nordische Politik der Habsburger vor dem dreissig-jährigen Kriege. (*Historische Zeitschrift*, vol. 133.) Berlin 1925/6.

Petri, G.: Kungl. Första Livgrenadjärregementets historia, vols. I-II. Stockholm 1926.

Petrini, H.: Källstudier till Erik XIV:s och nordiska sjuårskrigets historia. Lund 1942.

Pihlström, A.: Kungl. Dalregementets historia, vols. I-II. Stock-holm 1902-4.

Platzhoff, W.: Europäisches Staatensystem 1559-1660. Munich and Berlin 1928.

Quazza, R.: Preponderanze straniere. (Storia politica d'Italia, vol. viii.) Milan 1938.

Reiter, P. J.: Kristian Tyrann. Stockholm 1943.

Ritter, M.: Deutsche Geschichte im Zeitalter der Gegenreformation und des dreissigjährigen Krieges. Stuttgart and Berlin 1908.

Rydfors, A.: De diplomatiska förbindelserna mellan Sverige och England 1624—maj 1630. Uppsala 1890.

Schäfer, D.: Der Kampf um die Ostsee im 16. und 17. Jahrhundert. (*Sybels Historische Zeitschrift*, vol. 83 [N.F. vol. 47].) Munich and Leipzig 1899.

Schweitzer, V.: Christian IV. von Dänemark und die niederdeutschen Städte i. d. J. 1618-25. (*Historisches Jahrbuch*, vol. xxv.) Munich 1904.

Schybergson, M. G.: Underhandlingarna om en evangelisk allians åren 1624-5. Helsingfors 1880.

Schybergson, M. G.: Historiska studier. Stockholm 1904.

Sepp, H.: Stephan Báthorys och Gustaf II Adolfs krigståg mot Pskov. (*Svio-Estonica*, 1937.) Tartu 1937.

2 M

Siccama, J. H. Hora: Schets van de diplomatieke Betrekkinge tusschen Nederland en Brandenburg 1596-1678. Utrecht 1867.

Simonsson, I.: Älvsborgs lösen 1613. (Meddelanden från svenska riksarkivet, N.S. 1.) Stockholm 1927.

Sobieski, W.: Der Kampf um die Ostsee von den ältesten Zeiten bis zur Gegenwart. Leipzig 1933.

Sobieski, W.: Historja Polski. Kraków n.d.

Sobieski, W.: Żółkiewski na Kremlu. Warsaw 1920.

Sondén, P.: Axel Oxenstierna och hans broder. Stockholm 1903.

Sondén, P.: Johan Skytte och Oxenstiernorna. (*Historisk Tidskrift*, I. Series, vol. 21.) Stockholm 1901.

Soom, A.: De ingermanländska städerna och freden i Stolbova 1617. (*Svio-Estonica*, vol. III.) Tartu 1936.

Sprinchorn, C.: Om Sveriges politiska förbindelser med Frankrike före Gustaf II Adolfs tid. (*Historiskt Bibliotek*, vol. VII.) Stockholm 1880.

Stählin, C.: La Russie des origines à la naissance de Pierre le Grand. Paris 1946.

Stavenow, L.: Det svenska stormaktsväldets uppkomst. Uppsala 1918.

Stavenow, L.: Freden i Knäred år 1613. Göteborg 1913.

Steckzén, B.: Johan Banér. Stockholm 1939.

Svedelius, W. E.: Om konung Gustaf II Adolfs karaktersutveckling, serdeles under den tidigare delen af hans lefnad. Uppsala 1863.

Svenska Flottans Historia, vol. I. Malmö 1942.

Sveriges Krig 1611-1632, vol. I, Danska och ryska krigen; vol. II, Polska kriget. Appendix vol. I, Sveriges sjökrig 1611-1632. [Published by the Military History Section of the Swedish General Staff.] Stockholm 1936-8.

Szelągowski, A.: Der Kampf um die Ostsee 1544-1621. Munich 1916.

Szelągowski, A.: Sprawa północna w wiekach XVI i XVII. I. Walka o Bałtyk. II. Śląsk i Polska wobec powstania czeskiego. III. O ujście Wisły. Wielka wojna pruska. Lwów and Warsaw 1904-5.

Söderberg, T.: Sveriges ekonomiska struktur och utveckling under Gustav Adolf. [Typescript in Krigsarkivet.] 1935.

Söderberg, V.: Högförräderimålet emot Arnold Johan Messenius 1624. (*Historisk Tidskrift*, I. Series, vol. 21.) Stockholm 1901.

Tapié, V.-L.: La Politique étrangère de la France et le début de la Guerre de trente ans (1616-1621). Paris 1934.

Tham, W.: Axel Oxenstierna, hans ungdom och verksamhet intill år 1612. Stockholm 1935.

Thyresson, B.: Sverige och det protestantiska Europa från Knäredfreden till Rigas erövring. Uppsala 1928.

Toijer, D.: Sverige och Sigismund 1598-1600. Stockholm 1930.

Tongas, A.: L'ambassadeur Louis Deshayes de Cormenin. Paris 1937.

Trypucko, J.: Svenskarna i Polen under Sigismund III:s tid. (*Svio-Polonica*, vol. IV.) Stockholm 1942.

Tunberg, S.; *Palmstierna, C.-F.*; *Munthe, A.*; *Forssell, A.* [etc.]: Den svenska utrikesförvaltningens historia. Uppsala 1935.

Vagts, A.: A History of Militarism. London 1938.

Vreede, G. W.: Inleiding tot eene geschiedenis der Nederlandsche Diplomatie, vols. I-III. Utrecht 1856-61.

Vreede, G. W.: Nederland en Zweden in staatkundige Betrekking, vols. I-II. Utrecht 1841-1844.

Waaranen, J. E.: Landtdagen i Helsingfors 1616 och Finlands dåvarande tillstånd. Helsingfors 1862.

Waaranen, J. E.: Öfversigt af Finlands tillstånd i början af sjuttonde seklet. Helsingfors 1860.

Wadén, I.: Ett kanslidiarium från Carl IX:s sista och Gustaf II Adolfs första regeringsår. (*Scandia*, 1938.)

Wadén, I.: Samtida bilder över belägringen av Kalmar stad och slott år 1611. (*Rig*, vol. 19.) Stockholm 1936.

Wadén, I.: Berättande källor till Calmarkrigets historia. Lund 1936.

Waliszewski, K.: La Crise révolutionnaire 1584-1614. Paris 1906.

Waliszewski, K.: Le Berceau d'une dynastie. Paris 1909.

Wedgwood, C. V.: The Thirty Years' War. London 1938.

Weibull, C.: Drottning Christina. Studier och forskningar. Stockholm 1934.

Weibull, M.: Gustaf II Adolf och Christian IV, 1624-1625. Lund 1894.

Wertheim, H.: Der toller Halberstädter. Herzog Christian von Braunschweig im pfälzischen Kriege, vols. I-II. Berlin 1929.

Wibling, C.: Sveriges förhållande till Siebenbürgen 1623-1648. Lund 1890.

Wiese, E.: Die Politik der Niederländer während des Kalmarkrieges (1611-1613) und ihr Bündnis mit Schweden (1614) und den Hansestädten (1616). Heidelberg 1903.

Wigert, V.: Erik XIV. Stockholm 1920.

Wikberg, S.: Gustav Vasa, vols. I-II. Stockholm 1944-5.

Wittrock, G.: Svenska Handelskompaniet och kopparhandeln under Gustaf II Adolf. Uppsala 1919.

Zeeh, E.: Ett och annat om 'Älvsborgs lösen'. (*Göteborgs försvar* 1935.) Göteborg 1935.

Zettersten, A.: Svenska flottans historia, vol. I. Stockholm 1890.

Öhlander, C.: Bidrag till de adliga privilegiernas historia. Uppsala 1903.

E. CONSTITUTIONAL HISTORY. (Chapters II (i) and VI)

Ahnlund, N.: Die Ostseeprovinzen und der Reichstag Schwedens (in Pirmā Baltijas Vēstūrnieku Konference, Riga 1937). Riga 1938.

Ahnlund, N.: Landskap och län i Norrland (in Norrland: natur, befolkning och näringar). Stockholm 1942.

Ahnlund, N.: Ståndsriksdagens utdaning 1592-1672. (Sveriges Riksdag, I. Series, vol. III.) Stockholm 1933.

Ahnlund, N.: Sundsvalls historia, vol. I. 1621-1721. Sundsvall 1921.

Ahnlund, N.: criticism of *S. A. Nilsson*, Axel Oxenstierna och regeringsform 1634 (*Scandia* 1937), in *Historisk Tidskrift*, I. Series, vol. 57. Stockholm 1937; and reply to Nilsson's answer in *Historisk Tidskrift*, II. Series, vol. I. Stockholm 1938.

Almquist, H.: Göteborgs historia, vol. I. Göteborg 1929.

Almquist, H.: Polskt författningslif under Sigismund III. (*Historisk Tidskrift*, I. Series, vol. 32.) Stockholm 1912.

Almquist, J. A.: Den civila lokalförvaltningen i Sverige 1523-1630, vols. I-III. Stockholm 1917-1922.

Almquist, J. A.: Frälsegodsen i Sverige under storhetstiden. Stockholm 1931- .

Almquist, J. E.: Karl IX och den mosaiska rätten. (*Lychnos*, 1942.) Uppsala 1942.

Almquist, J. E.: Kungl. Maj:t som revisionsrätt 1614-1632. (*Svensk Jurist-Tidningen*, vol. 27.) Stockholm 1941.

Almquist, J. E.: Mannen, som offentligt förklarade sig hellre vilja mista huvudet än bliva assessor i Svea Hovrätt. (*Person-historiska Tidskrift*, vol. 42.) Stockholm 1943.

Berg, T.: De särskilda fögderierna för förbrutna gods under Karl IX:s och Gustav II Adolfs regeringar. Stockholm 1927.

Berg, T.: Riksdagens utveckling under den äldre Vasatiden 1521-1592. (Sveriges Riksdag, I. Series, vol. II.) Stockholm 1935.

Bergendal, S.: Bidrag till de svenska rättsmedlens historia. Uppsala 1916.

Bergfalk, P. E.: Om utomordentliga penningehjälpen till kronan under sekstonde århundradet och början af det sjuttonde. Uppsala 1893.

Boëthius, B.: Rättsreception och folklig rättsvård. (*Svensk Tid-skrift*, vol. XVII.) Stockholm 1927.

Boëthius, B.: Skogen och Bygden. Stockholm 1939.

Boëthius, B.: Ur de stora skogarnas historia. Stockholm 1917.

Boisman, A. W.: Om rättskontrollerna i den svensk-finska civila inre förvaltningen. Helsingfors 1908.

Bratt, A. W.: Om svenska allmogen under Gustav II Adolphs regering. Stockholm 1863.

Carlgren, W.: Riksdagsutskottet före 1680 med särskild hänsyn till sekreta utskottet. Uppsala 1909.

Carlsson, A. B.: Den svenska centralförvaltningen 1521-1809. En historisk öfversikt. Stockholm 1913.

Carlsson, A. B.: Riksrådsutnämningarna i januari 1617. (*Historisk Tidskrift*, I. Series, vol. 37.) Stockholm 1917.

Clason, S.: Om uppkomsten af bestämda perioder för den svenska riksdagens sammanträde. (*Historisk Tidskrift*, I. Series, vol. 12.) Stockholm 1892.

Edén, N.: Den svenska centralregeringens utveckling till kollegial organisation, i början af sjuttonde århundradet (1602-1634). Uppsala 1902.

Edén, N.: Den svenska riksdagen under femhundra år. Stockholm 1935.

Edén, N.: Gustav Adolfs Riksdagsordning. Uppsala 1902.

Edén, N. [and others]: Kammarkollegiets historia. Stockholm 1941.

Edén, N.: Om centralregeringens organisation under den äldre Vasatiden. Uppsala 1894.

Edin, K. A.: Gustaf Adolfs planer på landtregeringens organisation 1623-1624 (in Historiska studier tillägnade Harald Hjärne). Stockholm 1908.

Edling, N.: Den högsta rättsskipningen under 1500-talet. (*Historisk Tidskrift*, II. Series, vol. 1.) Stockholm 1938.

Haralds, H.: Kansliet—anima regni. (*Statsvetenskaplig Tidskrift*, N.S. vol. 10.) Lund 1928.

Haralds, H.: Konungsdom och konungsnämnd. (*Historisk Tidskrift*, I. Series, vol. 47.) Stockholm 1927.

Hartman, J. L.: Sveriges riksdag under fem århundraden. Stockholm 1935.

Hedar, S.: Karl IX:s förmögenhetsbeskattningar. En undangömd källa till vår inre historia. (*Historisk Tidskrift*, I. Series, vol. 57.) Stockholm 1937.

Hedenius, F.: Anteckningar rörande svenska bondeståndet under Gustaf II Adolfs regering. Uppsala 1863.

Herdin, K. W.: Uppsala på 1600-talet, vols. I-III. Uppsala 1926-9.

Herlitz, N.: Ett och annat om självstyrelsens betydelse i svensk förvaltningshistoria. (*Statsvetenskaplig Tidskrift*, vol. 24.) Lund 1921.

Herlitz, N.: Grunddragen av det svenska statsskickets historia. Stockholm 1928.

Herlitz, N.: Om lagstiftning genom samfällda beslut av konung och riksdag. Studier i svensk statsrätt. Stockholm 1930.

Herlitz, N.: Sveriges Riksdag. Stockholm 1932.

Hessler, C. A.: Den svenska ståndsriksdagen. (*Scandia*, vol. VIII.) Lund 1935.

Hessler, C. A.: Gustaf II Adolfs konungaförsäkran. (*Scandia*, vol. V.) Lund 1932.

Hildebrand, E.: Svenska statsförfattningens historiska utveckling. Stockholm 1896.

Hildebrand, K.-G.: Gustav Vasas arvförening. Dess medeltida bakgrund och förutsättningar. (*Historisk Tidskrift*, I. Series, vol. 54.) Stockholm 1934.

Hjärne, E.: Från Vasatiden till frihetstiden. Stockholm 1929.

Holmbäck, Å.: Våra domareregler (in Festskrift tillägnade Axel Hägerström). Uppsala and Stockholm 1928.

Kammarkollegiets historia. Stockholm 1941.

Kjellén, R.: Riksrättsinstitutets utbildning i Sveriges historia. Uppsala 1895.

Konopczyński, Wł.: Liberum Veto. Paris 1930.

Kuylenstierna, C. W. U.: Om rekognitionsskogar och under bruk skatteköpta hemman, med särskild hänsyn till å desamma förbehållna enskilda rättigheter. Lund 1916.

Lagerroth, F.: Frihetstidens författning. Stockholm 1915.

Lagerroth, F.: Konung och adel. Ett bidrag till Sveriges författningshistoria under Gustav III. Stockholm 1917.

Lagerroth, F.: Nordens frihetsarv. Stockholm 1945.

Lagerroth, F.; Statsreglering och finansförvaltning i Sverige till och med frihetstidens ingång. Lund 1928.

Lagerroth, F.; *Nilsson, J. E.*; *Olsson, R.*: Frihetstidens maktägande ständer, I. Stockholm, 1934.

Levander, L.: Brottsling och bödel. Stockholm 1933.

Levander, L.: Fattigt folk och tiggare. Stockholm 1934.

Levander, L.: Landsväg, krog och marknad. Stockholm 1935.

552 BIBLIOGRAPHY

Lilliestråle, N. F.: Riksdagarna 1609 och 1610. Nyköping 1888.

Lindberg, F.: Axel Oxenstierna som riksdagstaktiker. Ett bidrag till belysningen av riksdagsdoktrin och riksdagspraxis under förmyndartiden. (*Statsvetenskaplig Tidskrift*, vol. 34 [N.S. vol. 13].) Lund 1931.

Lindberg, F.: Fogde, råd och menighet. Några drag i den svenska stadsförfattningens utveckling under medeltiden och 1500-talet. Stockholm 1941.

Lindberg, F.: Till landshövdingeämbetets äldsta historia. Östergötlands län före 1635. (*Historisk Tidskrift*, II. Series, vol. 11.) Stockholm 1939.

Lindberg, F.: 1619 års stadga om städernas administration. (*Svenska stadsförbundets tidskrift*, vol. 1.) Stockholm 1937.

Lundqvist, K. G.: Om hertigdömenas statsrättsliga ställning till kronan i Sverige 1556-1622. Norrköping 1895.

Lövgren, B.: Ståndsstridens uppkomst. Uppsala 1915.

Melander, K. R.: Drag ur Åbo Hovrätts äldre historia och ur rättslivet i Finland under förra hälften av 1600-talet. Helsingfors 1936.

Munktell, H.: Brott och straff i svensk rättsutveckling. Stockholm 1943.

Munktell, H.: Det svenska rättsarvet. Stockholm 1944.

Munktell, H.: Mose lag och svensk rättsutveckling. (*Lychnos*, 1936.) Uppsala 1936.

Munktell, H.: Tortyren i svensk rättshistoria. Ett bidrag till straffprocessrättens historia. (*Lychnos*, 1939, 1940.) Uppsala 1939-1940.

Nilsson, S. A.: Krona och frälse i Sverige 1523-1594. Rusttjänst, länsväsendet, godspolitik. Lund 1947.

Nilsson, S. A.: 1634 års regeringsform. (*Scandia*, vol. x.) Lund 1937.

Nilsson, S. A.: Axel Oxenstierna och regeringsform 1634. [Reply to Ahnlund]. (*Scandia*, vol. x.) Lund 1937.

Nordwall, J. E.: Om svenska riksrådets utveckling mot centralisation under Gustaf II Adolf. Uppsala 1891.

Odhner, C. T.: Bidrag till svenska städernas och borgareståndets historia före 1633. Uppsala 1860.

Odhner, C. T.: Sveriges inre historia under drottning Christinas förmyndare. Stockholm 1865.

Palme, S. U.: Stånd och klasser i forna dagars Sverige. Stockholm 1947.

Petrén, S.: Häradsnämnden vid storhetstidens början. (*Svensk Jurist-Tidningen*, vol. 30.) Stockholm 1945.

Petrén, S.: Kring Svea Hovrätts tillblivelse. (*Svensk Jurist-Tidningen*, vol. 30.) Stockholm 1945.

Posse, J. A.: Bidrag till svenska lagstiftningens historia från slutet af sextonde århundradet till stadfästelsen af 1734 års lag. Stockholm 1850.

Rosén, J.: Statsledning och provinspolitik under Sveriges stormaktstid. (*Scandia*, vol. XVII.) Lund 1946.

Rydin, H. L.: P.M. angående det svenska skatteväsendets utveckling. Stockholm 1882.

Självstyrelse i svenskt samhällsliv. [A radio symposium.] Stockholm 1934.

Staf, N.: Marknad och möte. Stockholm 1935.

Stavenow, L.: Sveriges riksdag. (*Historisk Tidskrift*, I. Series, vol. 55.) Stockholm 1935.

Steckzén, B.: Krigskollegii historia, vol. 1. Stockholm 1930.

Steckzén, B.: Till frågan om krigskollegii uppkomst. (*Historisk Tidskrift*, I. Series, vol. 51.) Stockholm 1931.

Steyern, N. von.: Bidrag till svenska riksdagens historia 1600-1650. Uppsala 1863.

Sundquist, S.: Finlands folkmängd och bebyggelse i början av 1600-talet. (Meddelanden från Generalstabens Krigshistoriska Avdelning, vol. II.) Stockholm 1931.

Sundquist, S.: Sveriges folkmängd på Gustaf II Adolfs tid. Lund 1938.

Sveriges Riddarhus [ed. *C. Hallendorff*]. Stockholm 1926.

Swedlund, R.: Grev- och friherreskapen i Sverige och Finland. Donationerna och reduktionerna före 1680. Uppsala 1936.

Swenne, H.: Svenska adelns ekonomiska privilegier 1612-1651, med särskild hänsyn till Älvsborgs län. Göteborg 1933.

Sörndal, O.: Den svenska länsstyrelsen. Lund 1937.

Tham, W.: Bidrag till svenska riksdagarnes historia 1626-1629. Stockholm 1855.

Thomson, A.: Grundskatterna i den politiska diskussionen 1809-1866. Lund 1923.

Toijer, D.: Sveriges riksdag från Engelbrekt till våra dagar. Stockholm 1935.

Tunberg, S.: Riksdagen under medeltiden. (Sveriges riksdag, I. Series, vol. I.) Stockholm 1931.

Vasar, J.: Utvecklingen av böndernas rättsläge i Estland till Karl XI. (*Svio-Estonica*, vol. III.) Tartu 1936.

Wernstedt, F.: Ståthållaren Christoffer Wernstedt 1542-1627. Stockholm 1929.

Westman, K. G.: Från landskapslagar och folkting till rikslag och ämbetsmannamässig rättstillämpning (in Minneskrift ägnad 1734 års Lag). Stockholm 1934.

Westman, K. G.: De svenska rättskällornas historia. Uppsala 1912.

Wieselgren, O.; *Forssell, N.*; *Munthe, A.* [etc.]: Kungl. Maj:ts Kanslis Historia, vol. I. Uppsala 1935.

Wingqvist, O.: Om svenska representationen i äldre tider, till och med riksdagen år 1617. Stockholm 1863.

Wittrock, G.: Krigskollegiets tillkomst. Ett genmäle. (*Historisk Tidskrift*, I. Series, vol. 51.) Stockholm 1931.

Wittrock, G.: Regering och allmoge under Kristinas förmyndare. Uppsala 1948.

Östman, N.: Stockholms magistrat och rådhusrätt (in Stockholms rådhus och råd, vol. I). Stockholm 1915.

Överståthållareämbetet 1634-¹⁶/₁₀-1934. Stockholm 1934.

F. THE CHURCH. (Chapter VII)

Ahnlund, N.: Oljoberget och Ladugårdsgärde. Svensk sägen och hävd. Stockholm 1924.

Ahnlund, N.: Svensk sägen och hävd. Stockholm 1928.

Ahnlund, N.: Vem var 'Duken'? (*Historisk Tidskrift*, II. Series, vol. I.) Stockholm 1938.

Anjou, L. A.: Svenska kyrkans historia ifrån Upsala möte år 1593 till slutet af sjuttonde århundradet. Stockholm 1866.

Askmark, R.: Svensk pråstutbildning fram till år 1700. Stockholm 1943.

Batten, J. M.: John Dury, Advocate of Christian Reunion. Chicago 1944.

Billing, E.: Johannes Rudbeckius' aristotelism (in Från Johannes Rudbeckius' stift). Stockholm 1923.

Blees, J.: Gustav II Adolf och Estland. Norrköping 1932.

Block, H.: Karl IX som teolog och religiös personlighet. Studier öfver utvecklingen af hans åskådning. Lund 1918.

Boëthius, A.: Romanus Nicephori och Gustaf Adolf. (*Historisk Tidskrift*, I. Series, vol. 32.) Stockholm 1912.

Boëthius, S. J.: Johannes Rudbeckius. (*Svensk Tidskrift*, vol. XI.) Stockholm 1921.

Carlsson, S.: Svensk ståndscirkulation 1680-1950. Uppsala 1950.

Cederlöf, J.: Det finländska prästerskapets ekonomiska ställning intill sjuttonde seklet. Helsingfors 1934.

Cnattingius, H.: Den centrala kyrkostyrelsen i Sverige 1611-1636. Stockholm 1939.

Cnattingius, H.: Johannes Rudbeckius och hans europeiska bakgrund. En kyrkorättshistoriska studie. Uppsala 1946.

Cnattingius, H.: Tillkomsten av Gustav II Adolfs Bibel 1618. Uppsala 1941.

Gierow, A.: Bidrag till det svenska militärkyrkoväsendets historia. Vols. I-II, 1. Uppsala 1918.

Gothe, R.: Från trolldomstro till Kristendom: studier rörande det kulturella tillståndet bland skogsfinnarna i Sverige under 16—1700-talen. Stockholm 1943.

Gothe, R.: Medelpads finnmarker. Kulturhistoriska undersökningar om finsk bosättning i mellersta Norrland under 15-, 16- och 1700-talen. Stockholm 1945.

Gullstrand, R.: Bidrag till den svenska sockensjälvstyrelsens historia under 1600-talet. Stockholm 1923.

Hall, B. R.: Den kyrkliga folkuppfostran i Joh. Rudbeckius' stift. (*Kyrkohistorisk Årsskrift*, vol. 21.) Uppsala 1919.

Hall, B. R.: Johannes Rudbeckius, vol. 1. Stockholm 1911.

Hall, B. R.: Kulturella interiörer från storhetstidens uppryckningsarbete. Stockholm 1915.

Hall, B. R.: Kyrkliga och kulturella interiörer från storhetstidens uppryckningsarbete. (*Kyrkohistorisk Årsskrift*, vols. 16-17.) Uppsala 1915-6.

[*Hall, B. R.*, ed.]: Rudbeckii kyrkodisciplin och vissa av dess förebilder. (*Årsböcker i svensk undervisningshistoria*, 1928, 1930.) Lund 1928, 1930.

Hall, B. R.: Till Johannis Rudbeckii karakteristik. Hittills otryckta urkunder. (*Årsböcker i svensk undervisningshistoria*, vol. III [1923].) Lund 1924.

Hassler, O.: Linköpings stift under Biskop Samuel Enander, vol. 1. Lund 1935.

Holm, R.: Joannes Elai Terserus. Lund 1906.

Holmdahl, O. S.: Karl IX:s förmenta kalvinism. (*Kyrkohistorisk Årsskrift*, vol. 20.) Uppsala 1919.

Holmdahl, O. S.: Studier öfver prästeståndets kyrkopolitik under den tidigare frihetstiden, vol. 1. Lund 1912.

Holmquist, H.: De svenska domkapitlens förvandling till lärarekapitel. Uppsala 1908.

Holmquist, H.: D. Johannes Matthiae Gothus och hans plats i Sveriges kyrkliga utveckling. Uppsala 1903.

Holmquist, H.: En kyrklig oppositionsman. En kulturbild från Gustav II Adolfs Sverige. Lund 1937.

Holmquist, H.: Tillsättningar av gäll i Sverige under reformationsårhundradet. (*Historisk Tidskrift*, I. Series, vol. 53.) Stockholm 1933.

Holmquist, H.: Svenska kyrkan under Gustav II Adolf. (Svenska kyrkans historia, vol. IV, 1.) Uppsala 1938.

Holmquist, H.: Reformationstidevarvet. 1521-1611. (Svenska kyrkans historia, vol. III.) Uppsala 1933.

Holmquist, H.: Från reformationen till romantiken. (Handbok i svensk kyrkohistoria, vol. II.) Stockholm 1940.

Kohlmeyer, E.: Gustav Adolf und die Staatsanschauung des Altluthertums. Halle 1933.

Kjöllerström, S.: Consistorium majus i Linköpings stift (in Från skilda tider; studier tillägnade Hj. Holmquist). Stockholm 1938.

Kjöllerström, S.: Kyrkolagsproblemet i Sverige 1571-1682. Stockholm 1944.

Kjöllerström, S.: Striden kring kalvinismen i Sverige under Erik XIV. En kyrkohistorisk studie. Lund 1935.

Laestadius, P.: Journal av Petrus Laestadius för första året av hans tjänstgöring såsom missionär i Lappmarken (ed. *G. Hasselberg*). Vols. I-II. Stockholm 1928.

Liljedahl, R.: Svensk förvaltning i Livland 1617-1634. Uppsala 1933.

Lindberg, G.: Johannes Rudbeckius som predikant. Stockholm 1927.

Linderholm, E.: De stora häxprocesserna i Sverige. Uppsala 1918.

Linderholm, E.: Om kometernas och andra naturföreteelsers religiösa tolkning i äldre tider. (*Bibelforskaren*, vol. 27.) Uppsala and Stockholm 1910.

Lindsten, C.: Biskop Petrus Jonae Angermannus, en småländsk Rudbeckius. (*Hyllén Cavallius-Föreningens Årsbok*, 1941.)

Linné, C. von: Ungdomsresor, vols. I-II (ed. *K. Hagberg*). Stockholm 1929.

Lundin, H.: Joannes Baazius' kyrkliga reformprogram. Lund 1944.

Lundström, H.: En drastisk supplik från år af en sacellan från Strängnäs stift till änkedrottning Kristina d. ä. (*Kyrkohistorisk Årsskrift*, vol. x.) Uppsala 1909.

Lundstrom, H.: Laurentius Paulinus Gothus: hans lif och verksamhet, vol. I. Uppsala 1893.

Lundström, H.: Skisser och kritiker. Stockholm 1903.

Miliukov, P.: Outlines of Russian Culture. I. Religion and the Church. Philadelphia 1942.

Nilsson, S. A.: review of *A. Sandberg*: Linköpings stifts kyrkoarkivalier till och med år 1800, in *Historisk Tidskrift*, II. Series, vol. 12. Stockholm 1949.

Ohlsson, R.: Abraham Angermannus. Stockholm 1946.

Petersson, F.: Olaus Svebilius intill ärkebiskopstiden. Stockholm 1940.

Pleijel, H.: Bibeln i svenskt fromhetsliv. Lund 1941.

Pleijel, H.: Katekesen som svensk folkbok. Lund 1942.

Pleijel, H.: Svensk Lutherdom. Stockholm 1944.

Pleijel, H.: Vår kyrkas bekännelse. Lund 1941.

Quensel, O.: En inblick i svenskt församlingslif från år 1600. (*Kyrklig Tidskrift*, vol. XI.) Uppsala 1905.

Quensel, O.: Strödda drag af svenskt kyrkolif under gångna tider. Uppsala 1912.

Reuterskiöld, E.: Den folkliga vidskepelsen och den svenska katekesen. Uppsala 1921.

Rodhe, E.: Svenskt gudstjänstliv. Uppsala 1923.

Scheffer, H.: Johannes Rudbeckius. Stockholm 1914.

Schmitt, W.: Finlands kyrka genom tiderna. Stockholm 1940.

Sepp, H.: Bidrag till Ingermanlands historia under 1600-talet. (*Svio-Estonica*, vol. I.) Tartu 1934.

Tham, W.: Lindesberg och Nora genom tiderna, vol. I. Lindesberg 1943.

Thyselius, P.: Det af Gustaf II Adolf tillämnade Consistorium Ecclesiasticum Generale (in Smärre bidrag till svenska kyrkans historia, vol. I). Uppsala 1851.

Turnbull, G. H.: Hartlib, Dury and Comenius. Liverpool 1947.

Valentin, H.: Judarnas historia i Sverige. Stockholm 1924.

Westin, G.: Negotiations about Church Unity 1628-1634. Uppsala 1932.

Westin, G.: John Durie in Sweden 1636-1638. Uppsala 1936.

Westin, G.: Svenska kyrkan och de protestantiska enhetssträvandena under 1630-talet. Uppsala 1934.

Westling, F.: Estlands kyrka 1571-1644. (*Kyrkohistorisk Årsskrift*, vol. 21.) Uppsala 1921.

Westling, F.: Bidrag till Livlands kyrkohistoria 1621-1656. (*Kyrkohistorisk Årsskrift*, vol. I.) Uppsala 1900.

Wifstrand, A.: Andlig talekonst. Stockholm 1942.

Wordsworth, J.: The National Church of Sweden. London 1911.

Åmark, M.: Kyrkklockor, klockare och klocksägner i Dalarne. Stockholm 1928.

Öhlander, C.: Om den svenska kyrkoreformationen uti Ingermanland. Ett bidrag till svenska kyrkans historia åren 1617-1704. Uppsala 1900.

G. EDUCATION. (Chapter VIII)

Almqvist, D.: Fackutbildning och humanistisk tradition vid stormaktstidens svenska universitet. (*Historisk Tidskrift*, I. Series, vol. 54.) Stockholm 1934.

Annerstedt, C.: Upsala Universitets Historia, vol. I. Uppsala 1877.

Beckman, N.: Vår skolas historia, vol. I. Göteborg 1926. [A history of Skara School.]

Berg, G.: Studentdeposition i Uppsala på 1600-talet (in Svenska Kulturbilder, vol. III). Stockholm 1930.

Bergman, J.: Universitetet i Dorpat under den svenska tiden. Uppsala 1932.

Bonsdorff, C. von: Djäknelif och djäknegång. (Strödda uppsatser, vol. I.) Helsingfors 1898.

Boyd, W.: The History of Western Education. London 1932.

Brandell, G.: Svenska undervisningsväsendets och uppfostrans historia, vols. I-II. Lund 1931.

Bring, S. E., and *Kollberg, O.*: Gustaf II Adolfs donation av arvegods och kronotionde till Uppsala Universitet 1624. Uppsala 1924.

Brolén, C. A.: Bidrag till Västerås läroverks historia, vols. I-II. Västerås 1892-6.

Böttiger, C. W.: Självbiografiska anteckningar. Stockholm 1929.

Fåhraeus, R.: Magnus Gabriel de la Gardie. Stockholm 1936.

Graves, F. P.: Peter Ramus and the educational reformation of the sixteenth century. New York 1912.

Hall, B. R.: Rudbeckii flickskola och dess föregångare (in Från skilda tider: studier tillägnade Hj. Holmquist). Stockholm 1938.

Källquist, E.: Jacob Rudbeckius latinstad, ett pedagogiskt dokument från Gustav II Adolfs tid. (*Lychnos*, 1936.) Uppsala 1936.

Kleberg, T.: Italienska språkets ställning i 1600-talets Sverige. (*Lychnos*, 1939.) Uppsala 1939.

Lindberg, S.: Till Uppsala Universitets äldre historia. (*Lychnos*, 1936.) Uppsala 1936.

Lundström, H.: Handlingar angående Karl IX:s räfst med professorerna i Uppsala med anledning af deras bref till konung Sigismund år 1598 m.m. (*Kyrkohistorisk Årsskrift*, vol. x.) Uppsala 1909.

Mathew, D.: Social Structure in Caroline England. Oxford 1948.

Risberg, B.: Linköpings gymnasiums historia och Gustaf II Adolfs fundationsbrev. (*Historisk Tidskrift*, I. Series, vol. 49.) Stockholm 1929.

Rodhe, E., and *Warne, A.*: Svenska folkskolans historia, vol. 1. Stockholm 1940.

Sandblad, H.: Det copernikanska världssystemet i Sverige. (*Lychnos*, 1943.) Uppsala 1943.

Schück, H.: review of *C. Annerstedt*: Upsala Universitets Historia, in *Historisk Tidskrift*, I. Series, vol. 29. Stockholm 1909.

Schück, H.: Messenius. Några blad ur Vasatidens kulturhistoria. Stockholm 1920.

Schück, H.: Svenska Bilder. Valda smärre skrifter i svensk kulturhistoria. Vols. I-VII. Stockholm 1939-41.

Sjöstrand, W.: Till ramismens historia i Sverige. (*Lychnos*, 1940.) Uppsala 1940.

Ödmann, S.: Hågkomster från hembygden och skolan. (Samuel Ödmanns skrifter och brev, ed. *H. Wijkmark*, vol. 1.) Uppsala 1925.

H. THE ARTS AND LITERATURE. (Chapter IX)

Agrell, S.: Runornas talmystik och dess antika förebild. Lund 1927.

Ahnlund, N.: Från medeltid och Vasatid. Uppsala 1933.

Ahnlund, N.: Gustav Adolf, lejonprofetian, och astrologien. (*Historisk Tidskrift*, II. Series, vol. 11.) Stockholm 1939.

Ahnlund, N.: Svenskt och nordiskt från skilda tider. Stockholm 1943.

Almgren, O.: Om tillkomsten av 1630 års antikvarie-instruktion, (*Fornvännen*, vol. 26). Stockholm 1931.

Annerstedt, C.: Om samhällsklasser och lefnadssätt under förra hälften af 1600-talet. Stockholm 1896.

Belfrage, S.: Översättningen av Reyncke Fosz 1621. (*Nysvenska studier*, vol. IV.) Uppsala 1924.

Berg, G.: Boskapsskötsel och Jordbruk i det gamla Stockholm. (*Samfundet St. Eriks Årsbok* 1932.) Stockholm 1932.

Beskow, B. von: Levnadsminnen. Stockholm 1928.

Boëthius, G.: Konsthistoriska riktlinjer inom Västerås stift under 1600-talet (in Från Johannes Rudbeckius' stift). Stockholm 1923.

Böök, F.; Castrén, G.; Steffen, R.; Sylwan, O.: Svenska litteraturens historia, vol. I. Stockholm 1929.

Cornell, H.: Den svenska konstens historia från hedenhös till omkring 1800. Stockholm 1944.

Dahlberg, E.: Svecia Antiqua et Hodierna. [New edn. edited by A. Rydfors.] Stockholm 1924.

Dymling, C. A.: Reyncke Fosz och Forsius. (*Nysvenska Studier*, vol. IV.) Uppsala 1924.

Ek, S.: Lars Wivallius' visdiktning. Stockholm 1930.

Fielden, F. J.: Court Masquerades in Sweden in the Seventeenth Century. (*Modern Language Review*, vol. XVI.) Cambridge 1921.

Hahr, A.: Architecture in Sweden. Stockholm 1938.

Hahr, A.: Studier i Vasatidens konst, och andra nordiska Renässansstudier. Stockholm 1920.

Hahr, A.: Vasatidens borgar. Studier i nordisk konsthistoria. Stockholm 1917.

Hellström, G.: Gustav II Adolfs nyreglering av Staden inom Broarna. (*Samfundet St. Eriks Årsbok*, 1943.) Stockholm 1943.

Hildebrand, H.: Minne af riksantikvarien Johannes Bureus. (Svenska Akademiens Handlingar, vol. 33.) Stockholm 1908.

Hildebrand, K.: Stockholms historia. Stockholm 1897.

Karlson, W.: Ebba Brahes hem. Lund 1943.

Källquist, E.: Thet swenska språketz klagemål. Litteraturhistorisk undersökning jämte text och tolkning. Uppsala 1934.

Källström, O.: Guldsmedsyrket i äldre tid. Stockholm 1943.

Lea, K. M.: English Players at the Swedish Court. (*Modern Language Review*, vol. xxvi.) Cambridge 1931.

Lidell, H.: Studier i Johannes Messenius dramer. Uppsala 1935.

Liedgren, E.: Svensk psalm och andlig visa. Uppsala 1926.

Liljegren, M.: Stormaktstidens gravkor. Lund 1947.

Lindblom, A.: Sveriges konsthistoria från förtid till nutid. Vol. ii. Stockholm 1944.

Lindroth, S.: Paracelsismen i Sverige till 1600-talets mitt. Uppsala 1943.

Lundqvist, B. V.: Gustaf II Adolf och folkfantasien. (*Ny Militär Tidskrift*, vol. v.) Stockholm 1932.

Lövgren, B.: Wivallius som patriotisk siare samt Wivallii gravskrift. (*Samlaren*, vol. 33.) Stockholm 1912.

Magalotti, L.: Sverige under år 1674 (ed. and trans. C. M. Stenbock). Stockholm 1912.

Messenius, J.: Samlade dramer. Stockholm 1886.

Messenius, J.: Christmannus, efter författarens egen handskrift för första gängen utgifven. Stockholm 1888.

Meyerson, Å.: Adligt nöje. Tornering och ringränning under äldre vasatid. (*Fataburen*, 1939.) Stockholm 1939.

Moberg, C.-A.: Från kyrko- och hovmusik till offentlig konsert. Uppsala 1942.

Nordberg, T. O.: Gustav II Adolf som byggherre. (*Fornvännen*, vol. 26.) Stockholm 1931.

Nordstrom, J.: De yverbornes ö. Stockholm 1934.

Nordström, J.: Goter och Spanjorer. Till den spanska goticismens historia. (*Lychnos*, 1944-5.) Uppsala 1945.

Nordström, J.: Historieromantik och politik under Gustav Adolfs tid. (*Lychnos*, 1937.) Uppsala 1937.

Norlind, T.: Från tyska kyrkans glansdagar. Bilder ur svenska musikens historia från Vasaregenterna till Karolinska tidens slut, vols. I-II. Stockholm 1944.

Norlind, T.: Svensk musikhistoria. Stockholm 1918.

Odeberg, H.: Till Kabbalas väsen (in Från skilda tider: studier tillägnade Hj. Holmquist). Stockholm 1938.

Olsson, H.: Johannes Messenius Scondia Illustrata. Studier i verkets tillkomsthistoria och medeltidspartiets källförhållanden. Lund 1944.

Prytz, A.: Olof Skottkonung. Stockholm 1620.

Rein, G.: Populära föreställningar om Gustaf II Adolf i trettioåriga krigets flygskriftslitteratur (in Historiska uppsatser tillägnade M. G. Schybergson). Helsingfors 1911.

Romdahl, A. L., and *Roosval, J.*: Svensk konsthistoria. Stockholm 1913.

Rondeletius, J.: Judas Redivivus, Thet är: En christeligh Tragicomoedia. Stockholm 1871.

Sandblad, H.: De eskatologiska föreställningarna i Sverige under reformationen och motreformationen. Uppsala 1942.

Sandblad, H.: Politiska prognostika om Johan III, Sigismund och Karl IX. (*Lychnos*, 1942.) Uppsala 1942.

Schück, H.: Riksantikvarieämbetet genom 300 år. (*Fornvännen*, vol. 26.) Stockholm 1931.

Schück, H., and *Warburg, K.*: Illustrerad svensk litteraturhistoria (3rd edition), vol. II. Stockholm 1927.

Schück, H., and *Warburg, K.*: Huvuddragen av Sveriges litteratur. Stockholm 1917.

Seaton, E.: Literary Relations of England and Scandinavia in the Seventeenth Century. Oxford 1935.

Seitz, H.: Äldre svenska glas med graverad dekor. (Nordiska Museets Handlingar, vol. v.) Stockholm 1936.

Sjöstrand, M.: Bonden i svensk litteratur. Stockholm 1948.

Steneberg, K. E.: Den äldsta traditionen inom svenskt porträttmåleri. (*Vetenskaps-Societeten i Lund Årsbok*, 1934.) Lund 1934.

Svenska folket genom tiderna (ed. *E. Wrangel*), vols. III-IV. Malmö, n.d.

Svenska Turistföreningens Årsskrift 1941. 1500-talet. Stockholm 1941.

Svärdström, E.: Johannes Bureus' arbeten om svenska runinskrifter. Stockholm 1936.

Swartling, B.: Georg Stiernhielm, hans lif och verksamhet. Uppsala 1909.

Sylwan, O.: Den svenska versen från 1600-talets början, vol. I. Göteborg 1926.

Tigerstedt, E. N.: Svensk litteraturhistoria. Stockholm 1948.

Ulfsparre, C. I.: Några Bordrim, höfligit och lustigt så wäl Andeligen som wärdsligen. Lefren. Some brukeligit är: at berimma, hwilka een til dygd vpwäkia och reeta kuna. Stockholm 1620.

Ulfsparre, C. I.: En kort Regementz bok, aff åtskillige Politiske Skribenters böken sammandragen och på thet kortests summawijs författat. Stockholm 1620.

Upmark, G. (the elder): Svensk byggnadskonst 1530-1700. Stockholm 1904.

Upmark, G. (the younger): Guld- och silversmeder i Sverige 1520-1850. Stockholm 1925.

Walde, O.: Storhetstidens litterära krigsbyten. En kulturhistorisk-bibliografisk studie, vol. I. Uppsala 1916.

Wieselgren, P.: Georg Stiernhielm. Stockholm 1948.

[*Wivallius, L.*]: Samlade vitterhetsarbeten af svenska författare från Stjerhjelm till Dalin, vol. IX (ed. *P. Hanselli*). Uppsala 1869. [Contains Wivallius' collected verse.]

Wrangel, E.: De Betrekkingen tusschen Zweden en de Nederlanden op het Gebied van Letteren en Wetenschap, voornamelijk gedurende de zeventiende eeuw. Leiden 1901.

INDEX

565

2 O

Printed in Great Britain
at Hopetoun Street, Edinburgh,
by T. and A. Constable Ltd.
Printers to the University of Edinburgh